GLOBALISATION OF INDUSTRY

Overview and Sector Reports

ORGANISATION FOR ECONOMIC CO-OPERATION AND DEVELOPMENT

ORGANISATION FOR ECONOMIC CO-OPERATION AND DEVELOPMENT

Pursuant to Article 1 of the Convention signed in Paris on 14th December 1960, and which came into force on 30th September 1961, the Organisation for Economic Co-operation and Development (OECD) shall promote policies designed:

- to achieve the highest sustainable economic growth and employment and a rising standard of living in Member countries, while maintaining financial stability, and thus to contribute to the development of the world economy;
- to contribute to sound economic expansion in Member as well as non-member countries in the process of economic development; and
- to contribute to the expansion of world trade on a multilateral, non-discriminatory basis in accordance with international obligations.

The original Member countries of the OECD are Austria, Belgium, Canada, Denmark, France, Germany, Greece, Iceland, Ireland, Italy, Luxembourg, the Netherlands, Norway, Portugal, Spain, Sweden, Switzerland, Turkey, the United Kingdom and the United States. The following countries became Members subsequently through accession at the dates indicated hereafter: Japan (28th April 1964), Finland (28th January 1969), Australia (7th June 1971), New Zealand (29th May 1973), Mexico (18th May 1994), the Czech Republic (21st December 1995) and Hungary (7th May 1996). The Commission of the European Communities takes part in the work of the OECD (Article 13 of the OECD Convention).

Publié en français sous le titre :
LA MONDIALISATION DE L'INDUSTRIE
Vue d'ensemble et rapports sectoriels

FOREWORD

This publication draws on work undertaken within the general framework of the activities of the OECD Industry Committee on industrial policy problems and issues and of the Trade Committee on trade issues for the 1990s. The overall project was carried out by the Secretariat of the Industry Division, Directorate for Science, Technology and Industry, and of the Policy Inter-relations Division, Trade Directorate, with inputs from the Directorate for Financial, Fiscal and Enterprise Affairs.

The publication draws on a set of case studies of manufacturing sectors, and extensive analytical work carried out in OECD. As part of this work, a Joint Report on Globalisation of Industrial Activities by the Industry Committee and the Trade Committee was submitted to the OECD Council meeting at Ministerial Level in 1994 and is published at the beginning of this publication.

The overall management and direction of the work was assured by Graham Vickery (Industry Division) and Anthony Kleitz (Policy Inter-relations Division). The report is published on the responsibility of the Secretary-General of the OECD.

TABLE OF CONTENTS

Part I
Globalisation of industry

Part II
Sectoral reports

Part I

GLOBALISATION OF INDUSTRY

JOINT REPORT BY THE INDUSTRY COMMITTEE AND THE TRADE COMMITTEE REPORT TO MINISTERS

The OECD has carried out considerable work aimed at a better understanding of the globalisation of industry and its implications for national and international policies. This report summarises the main findings and identifies policy areas where changes and greater international co-operation are needed.

SUMMARY

Globalisation of industry refers to an evolving pattern of cross-border activities of firms involving international investment, trade and collaboration for purposes of product development, production and sourcing, and marketing. These international activities enable firms to enter new markets, exploit their technological and organisational advantages, and reduce business costs and risks. Underlying the international expansion of firms, and in part driven by it, are technological advances, the liberalisation of markets and increased mobility of production factors.

These complex patterns of cross-border activities increasingly characterise the international economic system and distinguish it from the earlier predominance of arms-length trade in finished goods. National economies are becoming more closely integrated as firms spread their operations and assets across countries. This brings greater economic efficiencies and welfare, as well as more intense competition, greater need for adjustment and more demands on national and international policy. The current challenge for many countries – in a situation of low economic growth and high unemployment – is to ensure effective adjustment while minimising related international frictions, so that the potential welfare and efficiency gains from globalisation are attained.

Government policies influence in various ways the development of globalisation and the ways in which domestic economies react to the more competitive international environment. They include policies which facilitate globalisation, policy areas which need to be re-oriented, and areas where closer international co-operation may be required.

Globalisation is a powerful motor of world-wide economic growth. Policies which promote trade and investment liberalisation and non-discrimination are particularly important in facilitating globalisation. Trade and investment policies and related domestic policies must continue to strive for open and contestable markets which stimulate competition among firms. However, policies in many areas need to be better focused on strengthening the capacity of economies to deal with rapid change and growing competition. They include improving the business environment and infrastructure, upgrading the skills and adaptability of the workforce, and enhancing conditions for small firms. However, policy instruments which target "domestic" beneficiaries are less effective because globalisation has blurred the origin of goods and nationality of firms.

Globalisation heightens the need for closer co-operation among governments at the international level and increases the interlinkages between different policy domains. This applies particularly to areas such as R&D and technology policies, intellectual property protection, foreign investment policies and competition law and policies. In addition, differences among national systems, such as business practices and regulatory regimes, have increased potential to become sources of international frictions as a result of globalisation. Improved transparency and understanding of these differences, including their impacts on access to markets, is needed.

CHARACTERISTICS AND DRIVING FORCES OF GLOBALISATION

New trends and combinations of investment, trade and inter-firm collaboration are changing the patterns and scope of world business and expanding the presence and influence of foreign companies in national economies.

International direct investment. Direct investment flows grew dramatically in the 1980s, doubling as compared with GDP and trade, fuelled by liberalisation and international firm strategies. This has increased the role of transnational firms in the world economy, where the sales of goods and services by foreign affiliates are now one and a half times the value of world exports. Foreign affiliate activities remain low in Japan, are moderate in the United States, and highest in Europe, Canada and Australia. Foreign manufacturing affiliates tend to have higher labour productivity and greater investment and trade intensity than purely domestic firms. They also tend to be characterised by large firms employing advanced business methods in high-technology industries, with their R&D and other strategic management functions often centralised in the home country.

International trade. Certain forms of trade have become especially significant in the context of globalisation. International sourcing (the purchase of intermediate inputs from foreign sources) has grown faster than domestic sourcing and now accounts for at least one-half of all imports by major countries. Intra-firm trade appears to have kept pace with total trade and to be growing rapidly for countries most recently engaged in foreign investment, while intra-industry trade has risen significantly in almost all OECD countries.

International inter-firm collaboration. Collaboration (joint ventures, non-equity agreements, minority participations) enables firms to undertake projects that exceed individual technical and financial resources, gain market access and overcome investment and regulatory impediments. The annual number of new collaboration agreements doubled during the 1980s and has been maintained at a high rate subsequently. Collaboration tends to involve large firms from Europe, the United States and Japan, and is concentrated in sectors such as electronics, aerospace, telecommunications, computers and automobiles.

The characteristics of globalisation are crucially shaped by firm, industry, and country differences. Large multinational enterprises are the main actors, although a growing number of smaller firms are engaged in cross-border activities. In manufacturing, globalisation involves mainly R&D-intensive and assembly industries while labour-intensive industries are less globalised. Finally, this phenomenon is still largely concentrated in the OECD area although the Dynamic Asian Economies and China are rapidly becoming involved, as are some countries in Latin America and Eastern Europe.

Globalisation is the result of firm strategies to exploit their competitive advantages at international level, locate in final markets, and take advantage of favourable production factors and infrastructures. Global strategies are shaped by three sets of factors:

- *Technology.* Communication and transport costs have fallen, reducing geographical constraints. Innovation time and product life cycles have shortened, and R&D and knowledge intensity have increased, necessitating rapid and world-wide exploitation of new products and technologies.

- *Economic factors.* These include the availability and cost of key production factors, growth in foreign economies, productivity differentials and fluctuations in exchange rates.

- *Government policies.* Many governments have liberalised foreign trade, capital movements and investment, and some have been promoting different types of formal regional integration arrangements.

There are public perceptions that globalisation has impacts on employment in certain sectors. The Employment/Unemployment Study suggested that the net employment effects of international trade on OECD countries have been relatively small and that international investment in non-OECD countries has also had minor impacts on employment. Overall, the study suggested that technical progress had been more important than globalisation in reducing demand for low-skilled labour.

POLICY IMPLICATIONS

Changes in international business create the need to examine and, possibly, re-orient government policy at national and international levels, to obtain the gains and address problems arising from globalisation. These include policies that facilitate globalisation, policy areas which may need to be re-oriented or which have reduced impacts, and areas for greater policy co-ordination.

Policies facilitating globalisation

International trade and investment liberalisation and non-discrimination are of foremost importance in facilitating the globalisation of industry. The parallel liberalisation of capital movements has further aided this process. Despite the continuing shift towards liberalisation by most countries, further efforts are crucial to reduce trade and non-trade barriers to the international flow of goods and services. Such efforts should include consideration of ways to:

- further liberalise international trade and investment in information, technology and related services;
- reduce constraints on the participation of foreign affiliates in R&D and technology programmes sponsored by governments, taking into account the need to ensure that the right to non-discriminatory access does not lead to free-rider behaviour;
- reduce remaining restrictions on inward investment and strengthen the application of national treatment principles.

Policy impacts of globalisation

Greater interdependence of economies suggests that some areas of domestic policy may need re-orienting to take into account the competitive challenges of globalisation and improve their efficacy.

Domestic policies requiring improved focus

Some policies which traditionally have a largely domestic orientation may require improved focus. They include:

Business environment. Globalisation points to the need for a business environment which promotes the competitiveness of firms. This includes business infrastructures (technology and business services), access to investment capital at reasonable cost, the efficient operations of financial markets, and support-ing physical and services infrastructure.

Labour markets and skill formation. Greater availability of skilled labour, and expanded investment in education and training and in the local knowledge base are all crucial for strengthening the capacity of firms to confront competition and changing demand and to create new areas of growth.

Small firms. Globalisation produces both opportunities and challenges for small firms. Better infor-mation on foreign business opportunities and improved financing conditions may be needed to enable small firms to internationalise their operations. More general measures to encourage diffusion of best practice in management and technology, simplified regulations and other measures to lower financing costs also become important to enhance competitiveness.

Policy effectiveness reduced by globalisation

There are other policy areas whose relevance and effectiveness are reduced by globalisation. These include:

Industrial support policies. Support targeted to domestic firms or domestic production is even more difficult to devise and even less effective due to greater cross-border operations.

Trade policies. Underlying concepts on which certain trade policy instruments had traditionally rested, such as the origin of goods and the nationality of firms, are now more difficult to apply. This raises complex issues regarding the nationality of products and definition of local content.

Areas for greater international co-operation

There are a number of areas where greater international co-operation would be useful, without necessarily requiring close harmonisation of policies.

Structural differences between countries influence international business behaviour and performance, and access to national markets. Such differences in national systems and regulatory regimes arise, for example, with respect to taxation, financing, distribution, labour and the environment. Improved transparency and greater co-operation could help reduce international frictions stemming from these differences. Building on recent and ongoing work in OECD and elsewhere, consideration should be given to fostering greater co-operation in the following areas in particular:

R&D and technology development. Greater international co-operation in R&D and technology development programmes can help avoid unnecessary duplication and reduce costs, and ensure that benefits from R&D are more effectively captured. Intellectual property requires consistent approaches to coverage and protection, and better policy enforcement to encourage creation and wider diffusion of new technologies, products and services.

International direct investment. It is essential to continue work already being undertaken on investment liberalisation, freedom of capital movements and national treatment. At the same time greater transparency and discipline are needed to reduce the distortions and costs arising from competitive use of incentives at national and sub-national levels to attract foreign investment.

Competition law and policies. Despite the general pro-competitive implications of globalisation, competition policy enforcement is needed to prevent the creation of anti-competitive monopolies or dominant firms and to prevent collusive practices at global level. This suggests an increasing need for international co-operation in the enforcement of sound competition policies. Furthermore, concern has been expressed that there are private barriers to market access (with or without government involvement) that may be outside the scope of competition laws. Thus it may be useful to address market access concerns with concepts from different policy areas (industry, trade, investment as well as competition) and to explore the feasibility and desirability of integrating competition rules into a multilateral framework.

Chapter 1

OVERVIEW

Table of contents

LIST OF TABLES

LIST OF FIGURES

MAIN FINDINGS

Globalisation of industry refers to the transborder operations of firms undertaken to organise their development, production, sourcing, marketing and financing activities. A distinctive feature of globalisation is the division of firm operations into separate segments carried out in different countries. The most prominent features of globalisation are foreign direct investment, various aspects of international trade, and international inter-firm collaboration. What changed through the 1980s and 1990s, is that firms have used new combinations of international investment, trade and international collaboration to expand internationally and achieve greater efficiencies.

Growth in flows of international direct investment outstripped the growth of international trade and GDP over the 1980s, although trade grew rapidly, and the same pattern has been resumed after the international investment slow-down of the early 1990s. International collaboration agreements became much more common at the same time, despite difficulties in measuring them. Cross-border operations are still largely concentrated in the OECD area, but have involved an increasing number of firms from more OECD source and destination countries. A new pattern of cross-border inter-firm and intra-firm operations is developing, involving all functional areas of firms: technology development and co-operation, different phases of production, and sourcing and intra-firm trade in intermediate inputs. Outside the OECD area, the Dynamic Asian Economies and China have increasingly been involved in the process of globalisation. Furthermore, since the mid-1960s, there has been a trend towards a greater share of intra-regional trade in total regional trade, with intra-European trade and intra-Asian trade increasing, and only intra-North American trade decreasing.

International trade. An increasing share of international trade is taken up by R&D-intensive, high-wage products and industries for most OECD countries. In these industries, import penetration and export coverage tend to be highest, trade increased faster than total trade during the last twenty years, and they tend to be more trade intensive than almost all low-tech, low-wage industries with the exception of textiles, clothing and footwear. This parallels the relatively high and increasing level of foreign firm activity in R&D-intensive industries in most countries.

International trade in manufactured intermediate inputs has grown rapidly. Not only do manufactured intermediate inputs constitute at least one-half of all manufactured imports by major countries, but they have grown considerably faster than domestically sourced inputs. Imported intermediates are particularly important and have grown rapidly in technology-intensive assembly industries (computers, electronics, aerospace, motor vehicles) as well as textiles and clothing. Finally, intra-industry trade has grown as OECD economies come to specialise in the same product categories. Although data are limited, intra-firm trade has at least maintained its share of total trade, is growing most rapidly for new investing countries, and is particularly important in R&D-intensive industries.

International direct investment. International direct investment is a well-documented measure of the international expansion of firms. The flow of investment slowed in the early 1990s with the business recession but has subsequently increased again, and the world stock of international investment has grown continuously as investment liberalisation continues. Overall the OECD area has attracted around three-quarters of this investment. At the same time there has been diversification within the OECD area, with investment coming from a wider range of OECD countries, and going to the United States and European countries (Sweden, Spain, Portugal) which were not previously significant hosts for inward investment. Intra-European investment has grown, while US and Japanese investment shifted more towards inter-regional investment. OECD investment has risen dramatically in East Asia while other developing countries have seen their share fall.

Impacts of foreign affiliates. The result of increased inward investment has been an expansion of the importance of foreign-controlled firms in manufacturing in OECD countries. Levels were already high in some European countries (Ireland, France, the United Kingdom), and in Australia and Canada, but the relative importance of foreign firms has expanded in many OECD countries, and declined in a few which already had high levels. Investment has tended to concentrate in a few industries, particularly computers, chemicals, electronics and motor vehicles, but there are considerable cross-country differences in the relative importance of foreign affiliates, ranging from very low in Japan, growing in the United States, and high in Europe, Canada and Australia.

Overall, annual sales of goods and services by foreign affiliates are one and a half times the value of world exports, and a rising share of private sector GNP is accounted for by the combined value added of foreign-based firms and the foreign output of home-based firms: over 50 per cent for Belgium, Canada, the Netherlands, Switzerland and the United Kingdom, more than 30 per cent for Australia, France, Germany and Italy, and over 20 per cent for Japan and the United States.

R&D often remains centralised in the home countries of investing firms. The major exception is in the United States, where in a few high-technology industries (pharmaceuticals, chemicals, communications equipment), foreign firms are significantly more R&D intensive than the average. In countries with less developed R&D capabilities, foreign firms may also be significant performers of R&D compared with domestic firms, but R&D levels are low.

Successful firms operating internationally usually have technological and organisational advantages over purely domestic ones. Foreign affiliates tend to have higher labour productivity, are more investment-intensive and trade-oriented than the average for domestic firms, due to the high-technology, high-wage and capital-intensive industries in which international firms operate, their larger size, and their use of advanced production and management methods and a more skilled workforce. The share of employment in foreign manufacturing affiliates has also increased, or declined less sharply, than in domestic firms, but this has in part been due to merger and acquisition activity by foreign firms which transfers existing employment into the foreign-controlled sector, rather than generating new employment in completely new operations.

International inter-firm collaboration. International collaboration arrangements have become a much more important feature of firm operations. They enable firms to gain access to resources to improve competitiveness. They most commonly have technology motives, but many are also oriented towards production and marketing. They have tended to concentrate in a few technologies (information technology, biotechnology, new materials) and sectors (electronics, aerospace, telecommunications, computers and automobiles), and involve large firms. There is also significant small firm-large firm collaboration in assembly industries between suppliers and assemblers, and in R&D-intensive sectors where small firms can be very dynamic.

Globalisation at sector level. The sector studies show a wide range of strategies for international expansion. There are nevertheless common features among distinct groups of sectors. In science-based industries (pharmaceuticals, computers, and to a lesser extent semiconductors), the predominant mode of expansion is based on the internalisation of firm-specific advantages. Foreign investment is high and foreign affiliates have a large share of sales in host markets. International trade in these industries is largely intra-firm, because of the specialised characteristics of inputs into final products. International collaboration agreements focus on technology, because of the prime importance of product innovation. Pharmaceuticals is somewhat more market-oriented in international collaboration and is more intensive in international investment.

Motor vehicles and consumer electronics are scale-intensive industries based on assembly of components into complex final consumer products. The pattern of expansion has been more trade-oriented, with high levels of trade in components, and high and increasing intra-regional trade in components and/or finished products as "lean" production methods are more widely applied. Foreign direct investment has been less important in the past, except for US producers, but has increased rapidly, and intra-firm trade is relatively important for vertically integrated producers. Both industries are highly concentrated, so there have been few mergers and acquisitions, compared with pharmaceuticals, and international agreements are focused on production.

The third set of industries comprises steel and non-ferrous metals. They are resource-intensive and have high intensity in intermediate inputs. Their intra-firm trade is low, and although for example energy costs determine location of aluminium smelting operations, firms in these industries are increasingly oriented downstream towards final markets and away from their intermediate inputs. Their patterns of international investment have been somewhat different, with non-ferrous metals (aluminium) having higher levels of investment and sales by foreign affiliates, and the steel industry active in mergers and acquisitions as it rationalises operations and begins to invest in foreign markets. Finally the labour-intensive clothing industry is characterised by high levels of trade in finished clothing and high levels of international sourcing of textiles as inputs, although trade in clothing parts is not significant. It has little international investment, little intra-firm trade and few international collaboration agreements outside sourcing arrangements.

Localisation. Globalisation often intensifies local specialisation. Geographical concentration occurs particularly because of localisation economies. There are advantages in being in the same location as similar firms, specialised suppliers and contractors, knowledgeable customers, a good technological infrastructure, specialised training institutes, and a highly skilled labour force. Specialisation within firms enables extensive outsourcing, and encourages similar firms to set up in the location. Foreign firms invest in such locations to take advantage of favourable externalities stemming from local clusters of similar firms, reinforcing specialisation.

Small and medium-sized firms. Small firms globalise essentially through exports. More extensive international operations are being adopted by a low but increasing number of small firms competing on the basis of non-price factors such as innovation, quality, flexibility and specialisation. As large firms increase their outsourcing, small firms have opportunities for contracting and supply linkages with them, although there is increasing international competition in supply from small firms in other countries and from larger specialised international suppliers. The main impediments to expansion of international operations appear to be lack of information, marketing problems, shortages of management skills and financing.

Policy implications. Industrial globalisation is changing the scope and distribution of world business and expanding the presence and influence of foreign companies in national economies. Firms and industries are being restructured and rationalised at transnational level as production factors become increasingly mobile and communication costs decline. New patterns of industrial specialisation and new competitors emerge rapidly, changing the competitive position of firms and countries. At the same time, economies are being increasingly linked and integrated through the global strategies of firms.

While globalisation changes the context for policy, it simultaneously emphasizes the need to give high priority to pursuing trade and investment liberalisation and non-discrimination between domestic and foreign goods, services and firms, to encourage free flows of resources, and minimise restrictions and inefficiencies. Liberalisation of investment and trade in information, technology and related services is particularly crucial under globalisation. Globalisation also points to the importance of the local business environment which develops and sustains the competitiveness of firms.

Industrial policy implications are linked with improving the competitive environment for firms across a broad range of sectors, although inevitably the impacts of different policy measures will depend on distinct sectoral characteristics.

First, the environment for firm growth and competitiveness may require attention. This includes the services and communications infrastructure and physical and transport infrastructure. Second, the increasing importance of R&D, technology, knowledge and skills in firm strategies suggests that policy must take greater account of the national knowledge base and how globalised firms contribute to the development of this base. There are also continuing issues and international frictions related to differences among countries in the extent and structure of R&D subsidies, whether foreign firms can participate in government-backed R&D programmes, and differences in intellectual property right protection and enforcement.

Third, inter-firm linkages and policies for local development are being re-shaped by the diffusion of "lean" production methods and new forms of work organisation, the importance of local clustering of firms and the development of networking and contracting relations with international firms. Finally, in industries where small and medium-sized enterprises are particularly important, globalisation has tended to take place through international trade. Measures may be needed to strengthen the small-firm base to improve their international competitiveness and expand international operations.

The evolution of globalisation at sector level raises issues of how to increase national benefits without impeding global trajectories of industrial development. National and sub-national policies become more important and more complex as they aim at improving the general environment broadly across industries with different characteristics and different modes of globalisation.

Trade policy. The new realities of global business are challenging some of the key concepts on which trade policy has traditionally rested. The origin of goods and the nationality of firms are increasingly difficult to ascertain. This renders the operation of trade policy instruments considerably more complicated, while making attempts to use them in a protectionist fashion more arbitrary in their effects, and potentially counterproductive. Similarly, policies targeted towards "domestic" beneficiaries have become more difficult to devise in view of the cross-border interlinkages along value-adding chains. Open and contestable markets for goods, services and investment remain the essential tool to ensure the global competitiveness of firms and to promote the efficient allocation of resources. Hence, as globalisation becomes more marked in the world economy, policies to ensure open and non-discriminatory conditions for trade and investment continue to be the best practice at national and multilateral levels. By exposing the interlinkages between different policy areas, globalisation challenges policy makers to take a more integrated approach in adapting existing rules and devising new ones to better respond to the environment of global competition.

International direct investment. OECD countries have adopted an increasingly liberal approach to both inward and outward investment. However some general and/or sector-specific restrictions remain in a number of countries (*e.g.* in communications, broadcasting, news media, transport). Further issues relate to the development of common approaches to investment incentives. Incentive-based competition to attract foreign investment is widespread and costly. Improved transparency and greater multilateral discipline are of major importance for securing open, less costly, non-discriminatory outcomes.

Competition policy recognises the global nature of competition and the positive impacts of imports and the entry of foreign firms. In industries where there are significant economies of scale or scope, collaboration or mergers can develop more efficient firms that are more competitive in an increasingly international market place. However, technological and other advantages may give rise to single firm market dominance. While deregulation, trade liberalisation and further technology-based competition are likely to weaken such positions, competition policy needs to be enforced adequately both on mergers and on collaboration to prevent the creation of dominant firms or non-competitive markets.

Greater efficiency and improved resource allocation are gained from liberalisation and non-discrimination combined with policies which broadly facilitate business competitiveness. But there are asymmetries and mismatches in the distribution of costs and benefits of globalisation among countries and between governments and firms. International co-operation and co-ordination in many areas will help to tackle these problems, particularly where there are continuing or potentially new frictions among countries. Potential areas for further work include:

- *Competitiveness.* To reduce potentially distorting effects of measures targeting domestic firms, particularly if they lead to instances or perceptions of unfair competition between different "national" systems. OECD work on subsidies is a step towards improving transparency.

- *Research and development.* To ensure non-discriminatory participation in government-funded R&D, reduce subsidisation and improve transparency in government support to "strategic" technologies and industries.

- *Small business*. To improve the access of small and medium-sized firms to international technology collaboration networks and other international operations where there may be barriers to entry. The OECD is carrying out extensive work on SME-related issues.

- *Trade*. To consider how the operations of globalised firms and the complexity of current trade and production networks have affected the relevance of current rules, and to widen and deepen liberalisation on all fronts. Work on the trade issues of the 1990s includes investigating the inter-relationships between trade, investment and competition policies, and developing an integrated approach to achieving globally contestable markets.

- *International investment*. To ensure non-discriminatory treatment of foreign investors, and reduce the cost and distortions implicit in competition to attract investment. Stronger international disciplines, including through development of the OECD Multilateral Investment Agreement will help improve non-discrimination and reduce these costs.

- *Competition*. To consider ways of further integrating competition considerations in public policies, while exploring the feasibility and desirability of an integrated international framework for global competition.

- *Intellectual property*. To encourage better protection and increase the creation and diffusion of new technologies and services.

- *Employment*. To deepen study of the relations between globalisation and employment, particularly regarding shifts in location and restructuring of firms and associated impacts on employment and human resources.

I. GLOBALISATION OF INDUSTRY

A. Introduction

OECD work on globalisation of industrial activities has been undertaken to deepen understanding of the effects of developments in the international organisation of firms and industries and the implications which this has for both national and international policies. Businesses are operating in new ways as international investment becomes more important, inter-firm agreements more pervasive, and related-party trade and international sourcing more widespread. Because of these new ways of operating, the interaction between firm behaviour and government policies needs to be reviewed. This overview summarises recent trends in the globalisation of industry, discusses policy implications, and suggests areas for future work.

Globalisation of industry refers to the transborder operations of firms undertaken to organise their development, production, sourcing, marketing and financing activities. A distinctive feature of the globalisation phenomenon is the division of firm operations into separate segments carried out in different countries. The most prominent measures of globalisation are foreign direct investment, various aspects of international trade, and international inter-firm co-operation.

Historically, international expansion was mainly through trade, followed in the 1980s by a major increase in international direct investment and inter-firm collaboration. What has changed recently is that firms have used new combinations of international investment, trade and international collaboration to expand internationally and achieve greater efficiencies. International strategies of the past, based on exports, and multi-domestic strategies based on sales in separate foreign markets, are giving way to new strategies based on a mixture of cross-border operations – foreign investment, exports and sourcing, and international alliances. Firms adopting these strategies can reap the benefits from high co-ordination, diversified operations, and local presence.

At macroeconomic level, the term "globalisation" refers to the emergence of new patterns in the international transfer of products and knowledge. Globalisation is characterised by three main routes, none of which is really new: international trade, international direct investment, and international collaboration agreements. The differences lie in the development of these routes through the 1980s and the 1990s:

- *Composition.* The growth in international trade has been outstripped by the growth in flows of international direct investment (despite the downturn in the early 1990s) and in numbers of international collaboration agreements – although the magnitude of agreements is difficult to measure accurately.

- *Geographical diversification.* Cross-border operations are still largely concentrated in the OECD area, but have involved an increasing number of firms from more OECD source and destination countries. Outside the OECD area, the Dynamic Asian Economies (DAEs) and China have increasingly been involved in the process of globalisation.

- *Functional pattern.* The previous pattern of cross-border transactions linking firms to raw materials and final markets has been re-shaped by international inter-firm and intra-firm operations focused on specific intermediate functional areas of operations: technology development and co-operation, different phases of production, and external sourcing and intra-firm trade in intermediate inputs.

Although these patterns have partly emerged independently, for the most part they are the result of the same underpinning driving force – the international strategies of firms and associated microeconomic phenomena.

What is shaping globalisation?

Globalisation is the result of the innovative response of firms as they exploit opportunities and adapt to changes in their technological and institutional environment, and partly steer these changes. The factors shaping globalisation can be grouped into four general categories, many of which are inter-linked:

- Firm behaviour:
  - strategic: pre-emptive and imitative behaviour;
  - exploitation of competitive advantages: use of superior technology, organisation, production or marketing;
  - consolidation of competitive advantages: gain access to highly trained and skilled people, advanced technological and commercial infrastructure, lower labour costs, and to raw materials;
  - organisational changes: adoption of "lean" production methods and more horizontal internal and external organisational structures, including greater local and international outsourcing.

- Technology-related factors:
  - declining computing, communication, co-ordination and transport costs;
  - increasing importance of R&D, coupled with rising R&D costs;
  - shortening product lives;
  - shortening of imitation time-lags;
  - rapid growth of knowledge-intensive industries;
  - increasing customisation of both intermediate and finished goods;
  - increasing importance of customer-oriented services.

- Macroeconomic factors:
  - availability of key production factors;
  - productivity differentials;
  - fluctuations in exchange rates;
  - differences in the business cycle;
  - "catching-up" by lagging economies.

- Government policies:
    - liberalisation of international trade and capital movements;
    - promotion of regional integration;
    - inward investment incentives;
    - R&D, technology, small firms and related industry policies;
    - intellectual property rights and effective patent life;
    - competition policies.

In individual industries and countries these factors will have different levels of importance and will interact in different ways on the supply and demand sides. For example in science-based industries, R&D costs, availability of skills, communications costs, the national knowledge base and intellectual property protection are key supply-side factors, whereas on the demand side, market size, and, more importantly, good links with knowledgeable customers and dynamic markets will be of overwhelming importance. In labour-intensive industries on the other hand, labour costs combined with market size and distribution efficiency are the most important supply and demand factors.

The extent of globalisation of industrial firms can be stylised from purely domestic to advanced globalised operations:

- *Purely domestic.* Domestic operations only, but with supply to foreign firms in the home market increasingly common. *Example:* small-scale parts manufacturing firms.

- *Little globalised.* Some exports through foreign intermediaries or marketing affiliates, some international licensing, few foreign employees. *Example:* most small and medium-sized firms.

- *Moderately globalised.* Final assembly in foreign final markets. Design, development, key component manufacture are retained in home country. Domestic and foreign production increasingly integrated into international supply networks and goods and services sourcing. *Example:* firms in the clothing industry.

- *Substantially globalised.* Integrated foreign production, including key components. Design and development, finance and other core corporate functions begin to be distributed among affiliates. Intermediate inputs sourced globally, significant intra-firm trade. Significant foreign employment. *Example:* large firms in the motor vehicle industry.

- *Highly globalised.* Integrated international operations in all major regions including management, financial control, product and process R&D, production, marketing. Extensive intra-firm trade in intermediates and final products, high sales by affiliates in foreign markets, and high flows of international investment. *Example:* firms in the computer industry.

This descriptive "model" of how firms globalise their operations underlies the following discussion of aggregate measures of globalisation through international trade, international direct investment and collaboration agreements. Shifts in these aggregate measures, and changes in their structure, are a reflection of increasing globalisation at firm level, and changes in the ways that firms are organising their operations.

Globalisation of industry results in more optimal location of firm activities and greater efficiencies, particularly in production of intermediate inputs and components. Furthermore, firms operating internationally are usually competitive in both home and foreign markets, although there are exceptions. Overall, competition between firms is heightened, due to greater investment and trade in their domestic markets, and more competitors in foreign markets. Competition is based increasingly on skilled, trained and well-organised labour, and higher levels of R&D and technology applications to complement foreign technology in domestic and foreign operations. New competitors from outside the OECD area are often closely linked into OECD markets through international investment, and contracting and supply networks in both high-technology industries and traditional industries. These new competitors provide opportunities for OECD firms' exports and foreign investment – and wider economic benefits, as their firms and national economies are integrated into the world economy.

B.   Characteristics of globalisation

The following section examines the characteristics of globalisation: traditional international expansion through foreign trade; the rapid growth of international investment and some of its impacts on trade; R&D and technology development and how they are affected by increasing international investment; and trends in international inter-firm collaboration. This is followed by a summary of sectoral patterns of globalisation, as the environment in which firms operate and their channels of globalisation heavily depend on sectoral characteristics; the importance of local factors in building global competitiveness; and the impacts of globalisation on small firms.

a)   International trade

The overall pattern of trade has been changed in the past two decades by the spread of high technology and high wage industries across OECD countries, and their increasing international investment and sourcing. As firms and industries have spread across national borders, the structure of trade for most countries has become increasingly similar. International sourcing (the international purchase of intermediate inputs) has grown rapidly, and the limited data available on intra-firm trade shows that it has at least kept pace with the expansion of international trade through the 1970s and 1980s, and in the case of Japan and possibly other Asian economies, it has been more dynamic. Finally, measures of intra-industry trade confirm the growing similarity of national trade and production structures for almost all OECD countries as firms and industries globalise their operations.

Recent trends. Total OECD trade expanded during the 1970s at an annual average of nearly 20 per cent in nominal terms, bringing trade flows to 20 per cent of total OECD GDP (Table 1.1). During the 1980s, the expansion of OECD trade was much slower, in part due to the deceleration of GDP growth in that period. After slowing further in 1991 through 1993, trade picked up again in 1994 and resumed its role as an engine of growth.

Table 1.1.   **Trade and investment in the OECD area**

| | Annual growth rates of: | | | | | Percentages of OECD GDP | | |
	International direct investment flows [1]	Trade [2]	GDP	GFCF		International direct investment flows	Trade	GFCF
1970-80	15.9	18.9	13.8	14.1	1970	0.5	13.0	22.1
1980-89	16.3	6.2	7.2	6.8	1980	0.6	20.0	22.8
1989-90	−2.6	16.6	11.9	10.6	1990	1.2	18.9	21.8
1990-91	−21.7	1.9	5.3	1.8	1991	0.9	18.3	21.1
1991-92	−8.3	7.2	6.8	4.0	1992	0.8	18.4	20.5
1992-93	7.2	−3.6	0.7	−0.5	1993	0.8	17.6	20.3

1.   Average of OECD inflows and outflows.
2.   Average of imports and exports.
Source: OECD (1995), *National Accounts* and *International Direct Investment Statistics*, nominal values converted in current US$ at period average exchange rates.

Composition by country and regional groups. The long-term shifts that have occurred in the geographical distribution of world imports between major countries and regions from the 1960s to the 1980s are shown in Table 1.2. Care in interpreting these data has to be exercised, however, especially due to exchange rate fluctuations. Overall, the largest increases in world shares of total imports and manufactured imports have been in the EC and the newly industrialised economies (NIEs, Chinese Taipei, Hong Kong, Korea, Singapore), with some growth in Japan's share. Increases in export shares have been most important for the EC, Japan and the NIEs.

Table 1.2. **Trade among regional groups and countries**

Percentages of world imports, 1966-68 and 1987-89[1]

		Imported from:							
		Can-US	Japan	EC	EFTA	Aus-NZ	NIEs	Other	Total
CAN-US									
Total imports	1966-68	7.4	1.9	4.4	0.6	0.3	0.5	4.0	19.1
Total imports	1987-89	6.4	4.2	4.2	0.7	0.2	2.2	2.2	20.1
Manufactured	1966-68	8.6	3.1	6.0	0.9	0.1	0.7	0.6	20.0
Manufactured	1987-89	5.8	5.4	4.7	0.8	0.1	2.8	2.0	21.5
JAPAN									
Total imports	1966-68	1.6	..	0.4	0.1	0.4	0.1	0.8	4.4
Total imports	1987-89	1.8	..	0.9	0.2	0.4	0.7	1.5	5.5
Manufactured	1966-68	0.9	..	0.6	0.1	0.0	0.0	0.1	1.8
Manufactured	1987-89	1.1	..	0.9	0.2	0.0	0.1	0.5	3.7
EC									
Total imports	1966-68	5.3	0.6	20.2	3.6	0.8	0.2	8.0	38.7
Total imports	1987-89	3.4	2.0	27.3	4.3	0.3	0.8	6.7	44.9
Manufactured	1966-68	4.6	0.8	24.0	4.0	0.1	0.3	2.5	34.9
Manufactured	1987-89	3.3	2.5	27.5	4.2	0.0	1.1	2.0	40.5
EFTA									
Total imports	1966-68	0.6	0.2	4.8	1.1	0.0	0.0	0.6	7.4
Total imports	1987-89	0.4	0.4	4.9	1.1	0.0	0.1	0.2	7.1
Manufactured	1966-68	0.7	0.3	6.4	1.5	0.0	0.1	1.7	9.1
Manufactured	1987-89	0.4	0.5	5.5	1.2	0.0	0.2	0.5	7.8
AUS-NZ									
Total imports	1966-68	0.5	0.2	0.8	0.1	0.1	0.0	0.2	2.0
Total imports	1987-89	0.4	0.3	0.4	0.1	0.1	0.1	0.1	1.5
Manufactured	1966-68	0.8	0.4	1.2	0.1	0.1	0.1	0.1	2.7
Manufactured	1987-89	0.4	0.5	0.5	0.1	0.1	0.2	0.0	1.8
NIEs									
Total imports	1966-68	0.5	0.6	0.2	0.1	0.0	0.1	0.3	1.8
Total imports	1987-89	1.2	1.7	0.7	0.1	0.2	0.4	0.8	5.1
Manufactured	1966-68	0.4	1.0	0.4	0.1	0.0	0.1	0.5	2.0
Manufactured	1987-89	0.9	2.1	0.8	0.2	0.0	0.5	0.6	5.2
Other									
Total imports	1966-68	6.2	2.2	9.0	1.2	0.5	0.2	7.4	26.7
Total imports	1987-89	4.2	2.7	7.2	1.2	0.5	1.0	2.4	19.2
Manufactured	1966-68	..	..	..	..	..	..	..	..
Manufactured	1987-89	..	..	..	..	..	..	..	..
Total									
Total imports	1966-68	22.0	5.7	39.2	6.8	2.2	1.1	22.9	100.0
Total imports	1987-89	17.8	11.3	45.6	3.1	1.2	5.5	15.4	100.0
Manufactured	1966-68	..	..	..	..	..	..	..	..
Manufactured	1987-89	..	..	..	..	..	..	..	..

1. Numbers may not add because of rounding.
Source: UN Comtrade Database.

Both EC imports and exports increased as a share of world trade, with an increasing share between EC member States. North American imports increased marginally from 19 per cent in 1966-68 to 20 per cent in 1987-89, while the share of total world imports originating in North America (*i.e.* North American exports) declined from 22 per cent to 18 per cent. Japanese imports increased slightly to 5.5 per cent of total world imports, while exports doubled during the period to account for over 11 per cent of the total. Outside the OECD area, imports of the newly industrialised economies (NIEs) increased to 5.1 per cent of world imports. More importantly, the share of world imports originating in the NIEs (*i.e.* NIE exports) jumped from 1 to 5.5 per cent over the period and this has continued.

Intra-regional trade. In terms of total world imports, since the mid-1960s the share of OECD Europe (EC plus EFTA) has remained remarkably constant at 40-45 per cent of world imports, North America (Canada-United States) roughly constant at around 18-20 per cent, while there was a doubling of the share of Asian countries (Japan, Hong Kong, Korea, Chinese Taipei, plus ASEAN) to 15 per cent of the total. Intra-regional trade in Europe (the share of intra-European imports in total European imports) climbed from around 55 per cent in the mid-1960s to 70 per cent in 1989. Asian intra-regional trade doubled its share of Asian trade, to over 40 per cent at the end of the 1980s, while in North America (Canada and the United States), intra-regional imports fell from around 40 to 30 per cent (Lloyd, 1992). Similar patterns are shown in Table 1.2.

Manufactured trade compared with domestic demand and production. The international orientation of economies and their exposure to foreign competition is reflected in the importance of trade compared with production and consumption at aggregate and at sector level. The share of imported manufactured goods in total domestic demand (import penetration) varies significantly from country to country across the OECD. Import penetration grew in all countries since 1970, but fastest in the United States (almost tripling by 1991) and relatively slowly in Japan. The highest import penetrations are found for smaller European countries, the lowest are in Japan and the United States, with Canada, large European countries and Australia in between (Table 1.3).

Table 1.3. **Import penetration and export coverage in manufacturing**

	1970	1980	1991	Average annual growth	
				1970-80	1980-91
	Imports as a percentage of total domestic demand				
United States [1]	5.1	8.7	14.0	5.5	4.5
Canada [1]	25.3	30.7	35.9	2.0	1.4
Japan	4.0	5.5	6.1	3.2	1.0
Denmark	41.1	43.8	52.5	0.6	1.7
France	15.8	21.3	30.9	3.1	3.4
Germany	13.3	19.6	27.3	3.9	3.0
Italy [1]	15.7	19.9	20.9	2.4	0.4
Netherlands	42.0	53.0	66.4	2.3	2.1
United Kingdom	14.7	22.9	30.2	4.5	2.6
Finland	27.9	27.8	30.3	0.0	0.8
Norway	39.8	38.7	43.2	0.3	1.0
Sweden	29.5	35.9	40.6	2.0	1.1
Australia [1]	16.2	21.6	25.4	2.9	1.5
	Exports as a percentage of production				
United States [1]	5.3	9.2	11.0	5.6	1.6
Canada [1]	26.7	30.2	34.5	1.3	1.2
Japan	8.5	11.9	11.4	3.4	−0.4
Denmark	34.6	41.9	54.4	1.9	2.4
France	16.9	22.6	30.2	2.9	2.7
Germany	18.4	25.0	30.0	3.1	1.7
Italy [1]	18.3	22.1	22.5	1.9	0.2
Netherlands	40.9	55.3	68.3	3.1	1.9
United Kingdom	16.3	23.4	28.0	3.7	1.7
Finland	27.5	32.4	35.4	1.6	0.8
Norway	31.1	30.0	36.0	−0.3	1.7
Sweden	29.6	38.0	45.0	2.5	1.6
Australia [1]	11.4	16.1	13.5	3.5	−1.6

1. 1990 data used instead of 1991.
Source: OECD STAN database (DSTI, EAS division).

Levels of exports as a share of production (export coverage) are similar to those of import penetration. Export coverage was highest in smaller European countries, the lowest export coverage is in Australia, Japan and the United States, where exports accounted for only one-tenth of production, with Canada and the large European countries in between. The relatively low share of manufactured exports to production for Japan reflects the concentration of Japanese exports on a few competitive sectors (computers, electronic equipment, transport equipment), and low exports in other sectors. The importance of exports compared with domestic markets has increased over time, but the relative growth of exports slowed for most countries during the 1980s along with the general slowdown in trade, and declined for Japan and Australia (Table 1.3).

Trade composition by product group. The most significant overall shift in the composition of world exports by product category is seen in the machinery and transport equipment categories, which increased from one-quarter of total merchandise exports in 1980 to well over a third in 1991 (Table 1.4). Developing economies tripled their share of world exports in machinery and transport equipment during the 1980s, with Asian countries in particular increasing their share from 4 per cent to over 12 per cent. Japan also made significant gains in this product category, while the shares of the United States, Canada and the EC declined. Such shifts across regional groupings are underlined by the shift of exports within each country grouping (top panel of Table 1.4). Over 70 per cent of Japanese exports in 1991 were due to machinery exports (up from 58 per cent in 1980), while the corresponding share for Asian countries is 30 per cent (up from 13 per cent in 1980).

Table 1.4. **Structure of world trade by commodity classes and regions**

		Commodity composition of total exports of selected regions						
		World	United States	Japan	EU	EFTA	Aus-NZ	Asia
Total commodities	1980	100.0	100.0	100.0	100.0	100.0	100.0	100.0
SITC 0-9	1991	100.0	100.0	100.0	100.0	100.0	100.00	100.0
Food, bev., tobacco	1980	10.0	14.0	1.2	10.5	4.0	36.3	12.0
SITC 1 and 2	1991	8.9	9.1	0.6	10.3	3.9	22.2	7.4
Oils and fats	1980	6.9	11.9	1.2	3.5	8.6	28.9	13.1
SITC 2 and 4	1991	4.7	6.6	0.7	2.9	4.7	18.1	4.7
Minerals	1980	24.0	3.7	0.4	8.0	10.1	9.1	20.5
SITC 3	1991	9.5	3.1	0.5	3.7	9.1	15.3	7.4
Chemicals	1980	7.0	9.6	5.1	11.4	9.7	2.5	2.7
SITC 5	1991	8.7	10.5	5.4	11.8	11.6	3.0	4.7
Mach./transport	1980	25.6	39.0	58.4	32.7	28.1	5.0	12.9
SITC 7	1991	36.5	46.8	70.8	38.6	32.4	6.4	29.6
Other man. goods	1980	24.0	17.9	32.4	32.0	38.8	13.9	37.0
SITC 6 and 8	1991	28.9	19.2	20.5	30.9	37.7	14.4	44.8

		Origin of exports						
		World	United States	Japan	EU	EFTA	Aus-NZ	Asia
Total commodities	1980	100.0	10.8	6.5	34.5	5.6	1.3	8.1
SITC 0-9	1991	100.0	11.7	9.1	39.8	6.3	1.4	15.0
Food, bev., tobacco	1980	100.0	15.1	0.8	36.1	2.2	4.8	9.7
SITC 1 and 2	1991	100.0	11.9	0.6	46.1	2.8	3.6	12.6
Oils and fats	1980	100.0	18.6	1.1	17.6	6.9	5.6	15.3
SITC 2 and 4	1991	100.0	16.3	1.3	23.9	6.3	5.5	14.8
Minerals	1980	100.0	1.7	0.1	11.5	2.3	0.5	6.9
SITC 3	1991	100.0	3.8	0.4	15.5	6.0	2.3	11.7
Chemicals	1980	100.0	14.7	4.7	55.8	7.7	0.5	3.1
SITC 5	1991	100.0	14.0	5.6	53.6	8.4	0.5	8.0
Mach./transport	1980	100.0	16.5	14.8	43.9	6.1	0.3	4.1
SITC 7	1991	100.0	15.0	17.7	42.0	5.6	0.3	12.2
Other man. goods	1980	100.0	8.1	8.7	45.8	9.0	0.8	12.5
SITC 6 and 8	1991	100.0	7.7	6.5	42.4	8.2	0.7	23.2

Source: UN Comtrade Database.

Technology, wages and trade. There are major differences in trade performance (import penetration and export performance) by industry groupings with different technology and wage characteristics (Tables 5 and 6). Overall, in G7 countries and in other OECD countries for which disaggregated data are available, high-technology industries are characterised by higher import penetration, followed by medium-technology industries. Domestic demand in low-technology industries tends to be mostly satisfied by domestic production, but textiles and footwear are the exception and are relatively import-intensive, compared with the manufacturing average. Medium-technology industries in Italy are more import inten-sive than high-technology ones, and Japan imports most in low-technology industries, although Japanese imports in all groups are low compared with other countries. Definitions of technology intensity and wage cost groups of industries are given in OECD (1993*a*).

In terms of wages, the high-wage group is most import-intensive, followed by the medium-wage and the low-wage groups. These results run counter to the common perception that OECD trade is more import-intensive in low-wage, low-technology goods. It is explained by the fact that OECD trade reflects the specialisation of OECD countries in high-wage, high-technology industries which, with globalisation, have become increasingly dispersed across OECD countries. In Germany, for example, one-third of all domestic demand in high-wage industries in 1991 was met by imports, whereas imports accounted for only a quarter of all domestic demand in low-wage industries. In Canada, the corresponding figures were over half and one-fifth. Of the G7 countries, only in Japan was import penetration relatively high in the low-wage and low-technology groups of industries (see Table 1.5).

Export performance shows a similar pattern, with OECD countries concentrating exports on high-wage, high-technology products and industries (Table 1.6). In every G7 country, exports represented a larger share of production in high-wage industries than in medium-wage or low-wage industries. In addition, the export orientation of high-wage industries has increased, whereas that of the medium-wage and low-wage groups has in some cases declined. In the high-technology group of industries export coverage is highest for Canada and Europe, as is the case also for import penetration. Overall, exports of high-technology products accounted for 25 per cent of total manufacturing exports in 1991, up from 16 per cent in 1970, whereas low technology shrank to 32 per cent from 41 per cent in 1970. Medium technology, which includes motor vehicles, has remained stable (44 per cent in 1992).

b) International sourcing of intermediate inputs

International sourcing of parts and materials is a major feature of global production systems and sourcing accounts for a large part of total trade. There is some evidence that international sourcing is linked with international investment. Industries which have high levels of international inward investment are also more likely to source internationally.

OECD work which examined international sourcing in the manufacturing industries of six large OECD countries (Canada, France, Germany, Japan, the United Kingdom, and the United States) points to the interdependence of their economies (see Wyckoff, 1993). The study concluded that direct imports of manufactured intermediate inputs from abroad (which range from 50-70 per cent of manufactured imports for the six countries) rose more rapidly than domestic sourcing in all countries, with the highest growth rates more recently. The absolute growth was largest for Canada, France, and Germany followed by the United States and the United Kingdom. The smallest increase was in Japan. As a result of this growth, the ratio of imported to domestic sourcing in the latest period reached 50 per cent for Canada and 35-40 per cent for France, Germany and the United Kingdom. By comparison, the ratio was 13 per cent for the United States and 7 per cent for Japan.

The set of manufacturing products in which foreign sourcing was highest, relative to domestic sourcing, is similar across countries. This set includes R&D-intensive products such as computer parts, electronic components and aerospace inputs, as well as mass-produced goods such as ferrous metals and textiles. There are large differences between countries, however, in the magnitudes of the foreign to domestic sourcing ratios for particular inputs. For example, Canada acquires nearly five times as many motor vehicle parts from foreign than domestic sources (reflecting the organisation of the North American automobile industry), and more than three times as many computer components. In contrast, the highest

Table 1.5. **Import penetration by industry in the G7 group of countries**

Imports as a percentage of total domestic demand

ISIC		United States 1980	United States 1991	Japan 1980	Japan 1991	France 1980	France 1991	Germany 1980	Germany 1991	United Kingdom 1980	United Kingdom 1991	Italy 1980	Italy 1991	Canada 1980	Canada 1990
3	Total Manufacturing	8.9	14.6	5.3	5.9	21.3	30.4	19.6	27.1	23.4	32.8	20.0	21.9	30.7	37.3
31	Food, Beverages and Tobacco	5.0	4.9	7.3	8.0	12.6	16.8	11.9	15.2	15.8	17.9	14.9	17.7	10.4	11.6
32	Textiles, Apparel and Leather	11.9	26.1	9.3	14.3	25.5	42.8	39.4	58.6	28.6	45.6	11.3	14.4	22.9	33.0
33	Wood Products and Furniture	6.8	8.0	7.1	10.9	17.8	21.3	15.2	20.2	20.8	22.9	10.6	9.2	9.4	14.5
34	Paper, Paper Products and Printing	4.3	4.3	2.8	2.1	15.1	16.9	18.5	22.0	15.1	17.7	10.9	10.6	12.3	15.5
35	Chemical Products	6.8	10.3	7.7	7.7	22.1	31.8	19.7	24.8	18.7	30.1	35.0	27.7	20.4	27.8
	Chemicals excl. Drugs	7.2	12.1	7.0	9.7	40.2	53.1	25.3	36.4	26.5	41.6	39.7	n.a.	37.7	43.1
	Drugs and Medicines	4.5	5.0	6.9	6.1	11.5	20.7	16.1	24.4	11.2	20.2	15.1	n.a.	20.8	20.3
	Petroleum Refineries and Products	6.5	9.1	11.4	13.5	11.6	16.8	17.3	15.2	14.4	19.3	41.1	21.0	5.0	10.9
	Rubber and Plastic Products	7.8	11.2	1.1	2.1	17.4	21.7	14.1	17.6	12.2	19.1	18.6	12.2	23.0	30.2
36	Non-Metallic Mineral Products	5.0	8.5	1.0	2.6	13.3	18.1	10.3	14.4	6.9	12.7	6.2	6.5	18.3	23.2
37	Basic Metal Industries	11.9	12.8	3.6	5.4	25.6	31.0	21.4	24.0	31.2	34.8	26.0	21.1	18.6	27.0
	Iron and Steel	9.1	11.2	0.7	2.5	22.1	27.6	16.7	21.0	17.4	26.0	17.6	16.3	19.7	26.0
	Non-Ferrous Metals	16.2	15.0	12.3	15.6	31.7	36.4	29.5	29.3	52.8	49.8	64.0	34.7	17.5	28.0
38	Fabricated Metal Products	11.7	21.6	3.9	4.5	25.3	37.5	19.3	29.5	28.0	43.1	24.0	30.0	56.2	62.4
	Metal Products	4.4	7.1	2.0	2.3	15.5	20.7	10.7	14.7	12.3	19.3	10.9	14.5	18.8	27.9
	Non-Electrical Machinery	9.1	16.8	3.0	3.6	28.0	39.2	15.8	23.2	23.3	34.6	26.6	22.0	58.5	58.6
	Office and Computing Machinery	9.2	45.3	8.4	7.3	42.6	50.9	72.0	65.7	73.4	78.3	89.4	60.6	92.5	87.5
	Electrical Machinery excl. Comm. Equip.	8.9	24.1	2.2	2.7	23.6	38.5	12.4	21.0	18.9	34.8	12.9	15.5	32.0	53.7
	Radio, TV and Communication Equipment	15.0	33.8	3.6	4.5	20.7	31.5	21.1	30.5	22.0	48.4	29.7	47.6	55.0	65.1
	Shipbuilding and Repairing	2.6	3.8	8.0	4.6	14.7	15.1	12.3	24.6	15.5	14.9	9.9	26.9	16.4	21.0
	Motor Vehicles	23.7	29.6	0.9	2.7	28.0	38.5	17.5	27.2	32.7	48.2	29.9	38.8	74.5	72.2
	Aircraft	6.8	12.1	46.9	44.4	14.6	45.3	63.7	98.3	52.0	47.1	22.4	58.5	59.4	59.4
	Other Transport Equipment	20.6	29.9	-57.5	11.8	16.1	38.4	36.0	54.5	20.8	32.2	3.7	20.9	30.6	32.4
	Professional Goods	11.0	12.7	15.9	22.8	64.1	78.0	51.3	83.1	79.8	117.6	29.8	34.7	n.a.	n.a.
39	Other Manufacturing, nec	20.4	33.1	4.2	5.0	34.5	37.3	59.0	63.6	130.9	111.9	20.7	34.0	38.4	24.6
	High wage industries	10.4	18.6	7.3	7.3	24.3	38.0	22.3	32.3	28.0	43.4	35.2	50.1	45.3	51.7
	Medium wage industries	8.9	14.0	3.6	4.8	22.4	29.5	17.0	22.9	21.8	31.0	18.9	19.1	32.6	37.4
	Low wage industries	7.4	11.6	5.7	6.3	17.7	24.7	19.8	26.9	21.8	26.9	12.9	15.7	17.3	21.6
	High technology industries	10.3	22.0	6.0	6.1	25.4	40.4	24.9	39.0	34.0	50.9	23.4	36.0	57.1	59.6
	Medium technology industries	13.4	19.6	4.5	5.2	30.5	39.8	21.3	28.1	31.9	41.1	31.2	36.1	50.1	52.8
	Low technology industries	6.3	8.7	5.4	6.4	15.8	21.5	17.2	21.9	16.6	21.8	14.1	14.3	13.4	18.2

Source: OECD, STAN database (DSTI, EAS Division).

Table 1.6. **Export coverage by industry for the G7 countries**

Exports as a percentage of production

ISIC		United States		Germany		Japan		France		United Kingdom		Italy		Canada	
		1980	1991	1980	1991	1980	1991	1980	1991	1980	1991	1980	1991	1980	1990
3	Total Manufacturing	9.4	12.3	24.9	29.8	11.5	11.0	22.6	29.8	24.0	30.5	22.2	23.5	30.2	35.7
31	Food, Beverages and Tobacco	5.1	6.1	9.0	11.7	1.4	0.6	15.2	20.4	10.0	12.6	7.4	10.7	11.3	12.7
32	Textiles, Apparel and Leather	7.8	8.4	24.9	41.8	9.3	5.7	22.4	33.7	22.8	29.6	24.3	28.8	6.9	7.3
33	Wood Products and Furniture	3.5	4.6	10.0	14.0	0.7	0.7	8.7	12.9	5.5	6.0	12.7	15.8	39.3	40.4
34	Paper, Paper Products and Printing	4.2	4.5	15.6	21.2	1.7	1.6	9.7	12.3	7.8	10.3	7.7	8.4	44.0	41.0
35	Chemical Products	7.5	10.8	22.6	28.7	5.8	7.5	22.7	31.9	24.4	33.0	32.0	20.6	23.2	25.9
	Chemicals excl. Drugs	17.1	18.4	37.6	46.6	11.9	14.7	40.5	55.4	34.9	43.7	30.6	n.a.	39.1	40.1
	Drugs and Medicines	9.8	7.1	24.9	32.0	1.9	2.4	21.6	25.7	27.8	31.8	16.5	n.a.	8.2	5.9
	Petroleum Refineries and Products	1.2	4.5	7.6	6.3	0.7	1.9	10.1	8.9	16.0	23.6	39.0	14.6	13.4	18.0
	Rubber and Plastic Products	4.2	5.0	16.4	18.0	5.3	3.7	20.9	22.7	14.3	15.2	33.5	19.9	10.3	20.3
36	Non-Metallic Mineral Products	3.8	5.1	12.1	14.7	5.4	4.5	14.2	18.3	11.0	12.3	17.9	15.5	8.1	11.6
37	Basic Metal Industries	6.5	7.5	25.0	23.9	9.4	5.5	26.5	30.7	23.6	32.6	18.2	15.5	36.3	39.6
	Iron and Steel	3.8	5.5	25.6	24.3	10.5	5.8	27.9	32.5	12.3	28.5	16.4	15.0	25.2	23.6
	Non-Ferrous Metals	10.8	10.2	23.8	23.2	5.0	4.1	23.6	27.3	43.6	41.1	33.0	17.3	44.7	50.7
38	Fabricated Metal Products	15.2	20.0	35.3	37.4	23.0	19.1	29.9	37.9	33.8	43.4	28.5	32.6	43.9	55.2
	Metal Products	5.0	5.4	20.4	19.9	14.4	5.7	19.0	19.5	18.8	17.8	27.1	31.5	11.9	18.9
	Non-Electrical Machinery	19.8	21.8	38.4	40.9	15.6	16.5	30.0	35.5	36.6	38.5	44.6	39.1	37.7	34.3
	Office and Computing Machinery	25.1	42.3	71.7	52.8	16.9	23.9	35.8	39.9	70.6	76.0	90.4	53.7	85.5	76.5
	Electrical Machinery excl. Comm. Equip.	12.1	21.0	23.5	28.4	14.1	10.7	30.6	42.1	24.4	31.1	18.1	21.8	13.1	26.5
	Radio, TV and Communication Equipment	9.7	24.8	23.8	27.6	28.3	22.2	17.5	25.3	19.9	44.9	19.1	29.9	38.2	51.3
	Shipbuilding and Repairing	8.7	10.2	34.6	45.4	42.3	42.4	25.7	20.5	23.1	15.6	8.8	23.1	31.4	9.5
	Motor Vehicles	15.6	16.1	42.3	37.6	26.9	22.8	40.7	44.5	34.0	45.6	26.0	31.2	70.2	74.5
	Aircraft	24.4	31.4	59.5	97.9	6.0	12.5	18.5	56.1	56.3	58.8	16.7	55.3	45.6	64.5
	Other Transport Equipment	6.6	18.9	40.4	57.8	106.8	61.5	26.0	32.7	19.2	19.9	14.6	28.5	36.7	45.1
	Professional Goods	16.3	14.4	60.4	86.6	44.5	47.0	58.9	73.2	82.0	115.5	18.8	22.2	n.a.	n.a.
39	Other Manufacturing, nec	11.7	10.5	47.7	57.2	5.7	3.8	25.1	28.6	138.9	114.0	45.2	58.9	14.2	7.4
	High wage industries	12.3	18.1	31.6	37.1	13.7	17.4	27.6	40.3	32.4	45.6	30.5	30.3	41.8	52.3
	Medium wage industries	9.4	11.8	25.6	28.4	13.4	12.1	22.8	26.7	24.0	29.5	24.7	24.6	30.4	34.1
	Low wage industries	6.3	7.4	16.4	22.6	6.6	4.6	17.9	23.4	16.9	19.2	16.3	20.2	20.9	22.5
	High technology industries	16.2	23.4	31.4	39.3	21.3	18.7	26.6	40.0	37.5	52.4	21.6	28.7	36.7	48.8
	Medium technology industries	15.4	16.0	36.3	38.1	15.5	14.6	33.4	40.5	36.5	40.7	34.0	33.3	44.8	51.0
	Low technology industries	4.2	5.6	14.7	18.0	6.3	3.8	16.0	19.8	13.1	15.9	17.3	18.3	21.1	23.3

Source: OECD, STAN database (DSTI, EAS Division).

Table 1.7. **International sourcing compared with domestic sourcing**

International Linkage Index[1], mid-1980s

	Canada	France	Germany[2]	United Kingdom	Japan	United States
Motor vehicles	0.92	0.34	0.23	0.39	0.06	0.17
Aerospace	0.40	0.28	0.24	0.5	0.57	0.09
Communications/semiconductors	0.46	0.2	0.22	0.37	0.08	0.13
Computers	0.68	0.43	0.28	0.42	0.1	0.13
Textiles	0.33	0.36	0.35	0.51	0.16	0.11
Petroleum refining	0.22	1.1	0.72	0.35	0.75	0.13

1. Calculated taking into account both direct and indirect (upstream) inputs. For methodology, see OECD (1993).
2. Electrical machinery includes communications and semiconductors.
Source: OECD, STI/EAS.

ratios for Japan and the United States rarely exceed 30-40 per cent, while those of the European countries lie between these extremes.

To account for all imported inputs used directly and indirectly by firms, the OECD study developed an indicator of international linkage for each country's industries using input-output techniques, to take into account imports that enter the various stages of production. The international linkage indicator is the ratio of an industry's foreign inter-industry links to its domestic links, and it provides an estimate of an industry's relative reliance on international or domestic suppliers. If the ratio is over one, one unit of demand for that industry's product requires more interaction with foreign firms than with domestic firms, generating more economic activity in foreign countries than in the domestic economy. A ratio of less than one means that industry's links are with domestic rather than foreign industries.

The direct and indirect use of imported intermediate manufactured goods is most prevalent in six industries: petroleum refining, textiles, apparel and footwear, motor vehicles, computers, aerospace, and communication equipment and semiconductors. The computer industry was the second most commonly listed industry (after petroleum refining) with a high international linkage index, with Canada, France, Germany and the United Kingdom having foreign links from one-quarter to over two-thirds as large as domestic links. For Japan and the United States, the ratio was closer to one-tenth although the United States had a large increase from the mid-1970s. The motor vehicle industry followed in having high international linkages (see Table 1.7).

Geographical proximity plays an important part in determining the source of intermediates in many industries, particularly in assembly industries such as motor vehicles. The United States largely sources from Japan and Canada in many industries, and the European countries acquire many of their inputs from each other. Sourcing by Japan is primarily from the United States and, unlike other OECD countries, from Asian nations due to proximity and Japanese investment in Asia.

c) *Intra-firm and intra-industry trade*

With increasing globalisation of firms and industries, intra-firm trade may be expected to grow, as firms move components and parts to the location of final assembly and finished products to final markets within their organisational structure. Intra-industry trade may also be expected to increase, in part due to increasing international investment within the same sector (also giving rise to intra-firm trade) and partly due to increased world-wide competition and product differentiation within the same industries.

Intra-firm trade. Intra-firm trade (IFT) refers to international trade in products which stay within a multinational enterprise (MNE). It represents a significant portion of foreign trade for OECD countries with high levels of inward and outward international direct investment. OECD work (OECD, 1993b) for the United States and Japan shows that over a third of US trade is intra-firm but that, contrary to expectations, the overall share of intra-firm trade in total US trade did not show a significant increase between 1977 and 1989. The one component of US IFT which showed a significant increase between 1977 and 1989 was imports by affiliates in the US from their foreign parents. This increase is mostly due to increased activity by firms from Japan and the Republic of Korea and is largely concentrated in the wholesale trade of motor vehicles and other equipment. Unfortunately, only the United States and Japan consistently collect data on this kind of trade, and US data is the most comprehensive. Recent US work has confirmed the importance of IFT. Between 1983 and 1992 it made up on average 43 per cent of all US-European merchandise trade, with MNEs from the United States and Europe contributing approximately equally, whereas IFT made up 71 per cent of all US-Japan merchandise trade on average and over 90 per cent of that was conducted by Japanese MNEs reflecting asymmetries in US-Japan international investment structures (Congress, 1994).

Overall, US IFT is concentrated in industries with relatively high R&D and human capital intensity, including transportation equipment and other machinery. In Japan, intra-firm trade is also relatively more important for the machinery industries, including transportation equipment. Moreover, wholesale and retail trade account for a significant share of total Japanese IFT, both on the import and the export side. This is due to the trade significance of foreign subsidiaries established by Japanese trading firms.

Intra-firm trade is the replacement of market transactions by internal transactions within firms operating internationally. Market imperfections and high transaction costs provide an incentive for firms to internalise international transactions of goods which embody firm-specific knowledge and expertise. Results for the United States and Japan support the "internalisation" theory of IFT by showing that this type of international trade is more prevalent in manufacturing industries characterised by higher R&D and/or human capital intensity. Furthermore, an unknown part of trade, while not strictly intra-firm, may be due to collaboration and quasi-integration between independent firms through alliances and networking. For instance, there has been increasing use of contractual arrangements such as franchising operations, between unrelated parties. These are particularly prevalent in consumer goods and services with strong brand identity. (See also section on international inter-firm collaboration, below.)

Intra-industry trade. Intra-industry trade (IIT) is trade between countries within the same broad industry or product group. This trade pattern is often related to international investment and overseas production, intra-firm trade, and international sourcing of inputs by global firms. It also reflects growing

Table 1.8. **Intra-industry trade indices, all products**[1]

	1970	1980	1990
United Kingdom	53.2	74.4	84.6
France	67.3	70.1	77.2
Austria	60.4	73.2	75.2
Spain	41.7	48.9	74.2
Belgium/Luxembourg	61.4	67.5	72.8
Germany	55.8	56.6	72.2
United States	44.4	46.5	71.8
Netherlands	63.4	60.5	69.8
Sweden	52.3	58.2	64.2
Denmark	55.0	54.8	62.2
Switzerland	52.5	59.8	60.2
Canada	52.1	51.5	60.0
Italy	48.7	54.8	57.4
Ireland	48.2	55.1	56.9
Greece	32.4	28.3	50.5
Portugal	39.8	39.5	49.2
Finland	29.4	37.8	45.7
Norway	52.3	42.5	41.9
Turkey	6.7	12.5	34.6
Japan	21.4	17.1	32.4
Australia	20.7	21.6	30.5
New Zealand	10.6	16.3	25.9

1. Grubel-Lloyd indices calculated on SITC Rev.2 3-digit level; adjusted for overall trade imbalances.
Source: OECD, STI/EAS Division.

product differentiation with increased international competition between firms in the same industries, and the relative similarity of industrial structures in different countries.

Table 1.8 shows the broad evolution of intra-industry trade since 1970 in the OECD area. For all countries (except Norway), the proportion of total trade accounted for by intra-industry transactions increased significantly in the period 1970-90. At the same time, important inter-country differences remain. The highest IIT indices in 1990 can be found in the United Kingdom, France and Austria where over three-quarters of total trade is accounted for by intra-industry transactions. In general, high indices can be expected for smaller countries which have a highly integrated (i.e. trade-intensive) industrial structure, and for countries belonging to regional trading zones. Low IIT indices should in contrast be expected for larger countries, isolated countries subject to high transportation costs, and countries that have a very high specialisation in one group of products (for example natural resources, or a few manufactured products) or a high import dependence on certain products.

Intra-industry trade is more important in manufactured products than in primary commodities, and tends to be highest in chemicals and machinery and transport in most G7 countries. In these industries products tend to be most differentiated, and there are high levels of foreign direct investment in the industries producing them. Of the countries in the G7 group, Japan is unique in having a comparatively low level of intra-industry trade, due to its high raw materials imports and low manufactured imports, while being highly specialised in a few manufacturing exports.

Outlook. The volume and pattern of trade have been influenced by firm strategies and use of international sourcing and intra-firm transactions. In the future trade will be structured particularly by strategies in high-technology, knowledge-intensive industries that reflect the importance of local supply relationships, the necessity for firms to be close to markets for final products and to tightly control trade in intermediate inputs.

Overall, international trade is being reshaped by international investment and international collaboration between firms as they expand and organise operations abroad, particularly in the OECD area and in East Asia. Intra-regional trade, which is already very high in Europe and increasing in Asia, is likely to revive in North America as the North American Free Trade Agreement (NAFTA) encourages trade and investment flows and firms organise more of their operations on a regional basis. The diffusion of organisational changes – like those associated with "lean" production – is also likely to increase the importance of intra-regional sourcing and intra-firm trade. Finally, as the recent experience of the DAEs shows, developing countries that are building high-technology and high-skill industries will increasingly participate in world trade and investment.

d) International direct investment

The growth and structure of international direct investment provides a well-documented measure of globalisation, although new no- or low-equity forms of global expansion are probably increasingly important. International direct investment grew rapidly during the 1980s and after a slow-down in the early 1990s showed renewed growth from 1993. The rapid expansion of international investment has been driven by the changing economic environment in which firms operate, and to which they reacted by reshaping their international strategies. Main driving forces have been:

Technology-related factors. Technological change has worked both as a pull and push factor underlying international expansion. On the one hand, falling communication and transport costs have favoured international expansion of firms exploiting and consolidating their competitive advantages. On the other hand, rising R&D costs coupled with a shortening of product lives and imitation time-lags have forced firms to expand their local presence in major markets, so that R&D expenditures will be more quickly recouped, and new products will be more responsive to local consumer requirements.

Macroeconomic factors. Differences among countries in their resources, growth and performance have provided opportunities to exploit through investment and local presence. On the supply side, availability of key production factors (skilled labour, resources, capital) and productivity differentials are important, and differences in business cycle and exchange rate movements encourage expansion to spread risks and balance global revenues. On the demand side, higher growth, "catching-up", and closeness to markets are important factors.

Government policies. Liberalisation of international capital movements and investment, coupled with inward investment incentives and other incentives have favoured the spread of direct investment. Other policies have indirectly encouraged firms to set up affiliates abroad. First, the promotion of regional integration in Europe and North America provided opportunities for expansion, and prompted firms to circumvent real or expected trade barriers. Second, inter-country differences in intellectual property right regimes, testing, accreditation, safety and environmental standards make local presence and procedural knowledge a necessity to have new products and processes approved and accepted. Third, competition policies have limited domestic growth of dominant firms due to monopoly considerations, forcing them to expand internationally.

Recent trends. Flows of direct investment grew more rapidly than either domestic product or foreign trade (the traditional international "engine" of growth) over most of the 1970s and 1980s. Between 1970 and 1990, OECD direct investment flows doubled as a share of OECD GDP (from 0.5 to 1.2 per cent), while exports increased from 13 to 19 per cent and the share of domestic investment remained steady (Table 1.1). Direct investment showed particularly rapid growth over 1985-89. Flows of investment declined in 1990, 1991 and 1992 with the economic downturns, before growing rapidly again in 1993-94 with the economic upturn. Between 1985 and 1990, the world stock of direct investment measured in current US dollars grew by close to 20 per cent annually, but growth in the stock slowed in the early 1990s with the recession (US Department of Commerce, 1993b) before growing more recently.

Composition by country and region. New patterns of direct investment developed from the mid-1980s as firms took advantage of regional integration in Europe, new trading arrangements in North America and high growth in the DAEs. Around 80 per cent of all direct investment went to OECD countries in the 1985-93 period and most of this went first to the United States and subsequently to the European Community before swinging back to the United States with economic growth there from 1992. There has been an investment boom in the rapidly growing economies in Asia (South-East Asia and China). Recently there has been a revival of investment in Latin America as prospects in some countries have improved, and investment has begun to flow into Central and Eastern Europe.

Recent investment flows have been "global", although many poor developing regions did not benefit. There is substantial new outward investment from many more countries. This came notably from Japan, France, Italy and Sweden, as well as from the traditional large investing countries, and there were new outflows from smaller European countries such as Austria, Belgium, Denmark, Finland, the Netherlands, Portugal and Spain, as well as Australia and the DAEs. Japan became the largest source of direct investment from 1988 through 1990, although it was considerably less important than the EC countries combined. The United States and the United Kingdom increased outward investment from 1992 to become the largest investors as their economies strengthened and as the home economies of Japanese and European investors slowed.

The European Community replaced the United States as the main destination for direct investment from 1989 (the EC previously held this position in the 1970s). There were substantial inflows into Europe in 1991 and 1992 prior to the completion of the Single Market, while inward investment was very low in the United States in 1992 due to the slow-down in economic activity there.

Around one-half of EC investment goes to other EC countries, including over one-half of these flows and stocks from France, Germany and Italy, and estimates suggest that over 50 per cent of total European inward investment stock is intra-European (Thomsen and Woolcock, 1993). The exception is the United Kingdom, where both inward and outward investment has been with North America and much less concentrated on Europe. A little less than one-half of US outward investment goes to the EC, particularly the United Kingdom and the Netherlands. Although Japanese investment in Europe has risen since the late 1980s to over one-quarter of annual flows, the Japanese investment stock was still only 30 per cent of the US stock in Europe in 1993.

Over the 1980s the share of total inward investment held by OECD countries went up from less than two-thirds of the world total to over three-quarters, with two-thirds in the United States and Europe.

Despite recent policies to encourage inward investment into Japan, it continues to have a very low share of the total inward investment stock. This is attributed to a range of historical and current reasons, including market access, tightly-knit links between Japanese firms, and the high costs of doing business in Japan.

Apart from rapid growth in East Asia (Table 1.9) the share of developing countries and regions in the stock of direct investment fell through 1991, due to instability, poor market prospects, and debt servicing difficulties and debt overhangs in Latin America, Africa and the Middle East. There has been a dramatic increase in South-East and East Asia where market-oriented development policies and very high rates of economic growth have fed a direct investment boom which doubled the share of inward investment stock from 1980 to 1991. A similar path has been followed in Mexico, Chile and Argentina since 1990-91. In 1991, investment stocks in East Asian developing countries were greater than in the United Kingdom, and two-thirds of that in the United States according to US data (see Table 1.9). Investment in non-OECD countries is heavily concentrated in a few countries in Asia and Latin America, and Central and Eastern Europe. Firms investing in non-OECD countries concentrate particularly on countries within their own region, or with large and growing markets. Ten non-OECD countries attract around four-fifths of investment inflows. China, Singapore and Argentina have been leading destinations recently, along with Brazil, Malaysia, Indonesia, Thailand and a few countries in Central and Eastern Europe: Hungary, the Czech Republic and Poland.

Intra-regional investment. The pattern of international investment illustrates the extent to which three major production and trading regions are forming in Europe, North America and Asia. The direction

Table 1.9. **World stocks of inward direct investment, 1967-91**

	Amount (billion US$)			Distribution (per cent)		
	1967	1980	1991	1967	1980	1991
United States	9.9	83.0	414.4	9.4	16.4	22.0
Canada	19.2	51.6	113.9	18.2	10.2	6.0
Japan	0.6	3.3	12.3	0.6	0.7	0.7
European Community *of which:*	24.8	186.9	714.2	23.5	37.0	37.9
Belgium	1.4	7.5	39.3	1.3	1.5	2.1
France	3.0	21.1	89.0	2.8	4.2	4.7
Germany	3.6	47.9	122.2	3.4	9.5	6.5
Italy	2.6	8.9	61.6	2.5	1.8	3.3
Netherlands	4.9	19.2	78.3	4.6	3.8	4.2
Spain	0.4	9.1	55.8	0.4	1.8	3.0
United Kingdom	7.9	63.0	235.5	7.5	12.5	12.5
Other Europe *of which:*	6.6	24.7	93.2	6.3	4.9	5.0
Sweden	0.5	1.7	15.8	0.5	0.3	0.8
Switzerland	2.1	14.3	44.2	2.0	2.8	2.3
Australia	4.9	28.1	83.7	4.6	5.6	4.4
South Africa	7.2	16.5	11.1	6.8	3.3	0.6
Developing countries: *of which:*	32.3	111.2	440.0	30.6	22.0	23.4
Latin America	18.5	62.3	132.1	17.5	12.3	7.0
Africa	5.6	13.1	38.8	5.3	2.6	2.1
Middle East	3.2	4.3	12.3	3.0	0.9	0.7
East Asia	5.1	31.5	256.7	4.8	6.2	13.6
All countries	105.5	505.3	1 882.7	100.0	100.0	100.0

Source: Adapted from US Department of Commerce, *Recent Trends in International Direct Investment*, August 1993, Appendix Table 6.

Table 1.10. **Intra-regional international investment: 5 largest home and host countries**

Percentages of total investment stock at year-end

	1982		1991	1993	
Outward investment to region					
as share of total outward investment stock					
United States to North America	20.9		15.1	12.8	
Japan to Asia	26.7		15.0	15.5	
United Kingdom[1] to Europe	19.5	(EC 15.8)	30.0	35.0	(EC 32.0)
France[2] to Europe	58.4	(EC 46.4)	65.0	61.3	(EC 55.0)
Germany[1] to Europe	40.7	(EC 32.4)	60.6	57.1	(EC 48.0)
Inward investment from region					
as share of total inward investment stock					
United States from North America	9.4		8.7	8.9	
United Kingdom[1] from Europe	37.3	(EC 29.7)	40.5	39.6	(EC 31.1)
France[3] from Europe	n.a.		72.3	72.93	(EC 58.8)
Canada from North America	74.8		64.1	64.7	
Germany[1] from Europe	48.8	(EC 30.5)	58.7	61.1	(EC 41.7)

Note: Regions are: North America = United States + Canada; Europe = OECD Europe; EC = EC (12); Asia = DAEs + Indonesia, Philippines, China.
1. 1984 data.
2. 1987.
3. 1992.
Source: Calculated from OECD (1995), *International Direct Investment Statistics Yearbook.*

of investment in the 1980s and 1990s is very similar to patterns of trade. For the main investing and host countries in the European Community, intra-regional investment became more important over the 1980s and early 1990s (see Table 1.10). For North America, intra-regional investment became less important, matching the decreasing importance of intra-regional trade. Japan's outward investment stock shifted away from Asia to Europe and the United States, despite recent renewed investment in the Asian economies, and despite the long-term trend for intra-Asian trade to increase. The same trends have been observed in other work (Jungnickel, 1993).

Sectoral composition of investment. A large share of investment goes to manufacturing compared with the weight of manufacturing in OECD economies. In most countries the international investment stock in manufacturing was 30-45 per cent of the total, and for some countries over 50 per cent. This compares with less than 30 per cent of manufacturing in GDP. The major exception is Japan, where the stock of outward investment in manufacturing is a little lower than the share of manufacturing in Japan's GDP. A large share of investment continues to go to the primary sector, particularly into petroleum and extractive industries, although this share declined rapidly during the 1980s with declining commodity prices (see Table 1.11).

There are several reasons for the high share of investment in manufacturing compared to services. Manufacturing is capital intensive, and many manufacturing firms can reap advantages from dispersing operations to favourable locations to increase production and distribution efficiencies, hence their tendency to invest internationally. On the other hand, services are less capital intensive, service networks may take longer to establish due to their labour intensity and the time needed to build their customer base, and many areas of services (financial, communications and transport services) have been closed to foreign investment.

Acquisitions, mergers and green-field investments. Foreign investment can be through acquisitions of existing firms to strengthen market positions or expand commercial activities or through construction of new plants and facilities ("green-field" investment). Acquisitions are most common in countries where stock markets are extensively used as sources of finance (for example in Canada, the United Kingdom and the United States). Acquisitions as a mode of entry into new markets are less common in countries where the banking system has built long-term financing arrangements with industrial firms (for example in Germany and Japan).

Table 1.11. **Shares of international investment stock by broad sector**

Percentage shares

		Outward			Inward			GDP shares (1992)		
		Primary	Secondary	Tertiary	Primary	Secondary	Tertiary	Primary	Secondary	Tertiary
United States	1982-84	30.5	40.3	29.3	17.0	33.7	49.4			
	1991-93	13.0	37.3	49.7	10.2	37.9	51.9	4.0[7]	20.6[7]	75.4[7]
Canada[1]	1982-84	22.4	45.2	28.6	31.4	40.1	24.3			
	1991-93	7.6	43.1	49.3	15.1	51.5	33.4	6.7[7]	20.7[7]	72.6[7]
Japan[2]	1982-84	20.5	30.8	46.3	n.a.	74.7	25.3			
	1991-93	5.5	26.9	65.8	n.a.	57.5	42.5	2.6	29.5	67.9
France	1991-92	6.2	40.7	53.2	5.3	37.4	53.1	4.1	25.6	70.3
Germany[2]	1984	3.8	59.7	30.1	0.2	53.1	46.1			
	1991-93	1.3	50.6	44.8	0.1	48.6	51.1	1.9	33.9	64.2
Italy	1982-84	20.7	39.4	39.8	7.5	55.0	37.5			
	1991-93	6.4	31.1	62.5	3.3	39.9	56.8	3.7	24.0	72.3
Netherlands	1984	0.1[3]	68.6	31.3	0.3[3]	54.0	45.7			
	1991-92	0.1	54.7	45.2	0.1	52.1	47.8	7.8	21.6	70.6
United Kingdom	1984	33.3	31.8	34.8	33.9	40.8	25.3			
	1991-93	17.9	37.2	45.0	25.1	34.0	40.9	4.3	25.5	70.2
Finland[4]	1982-84	n.a.[3]	60.0	41.7	n.a.	n.a.	n.a.			
	1991-93	n.a.	73.2	19.0	n.a.[3]	51.4	36.2	7.0	28.6	64.5
Norway[1]	1991-93	15.1	57.8	25.4	34.8	11.6	53.1	20.9[7]	17.4[7]	61.7[7]
Sweden[5]	1991-93	n.a.	60.9	35.3	n.a.	46.5	48.2	3.4	25.8	70.8
Australia	1982-84	18.2	30.9	51.5	21.2[6]	30.1	48.6			
	1991-93[4]	16.1	28.6	50.9	17.1	25.2	51.4	7.6	15.0	77.5

1. Unallocated is 2% of outward investment.
2. Unallocated is 3-6% of outward investment, < ½% of inward investment.
3. Mining, oil, petroleum included in chemicals.
4. Unallocated fluctuates widely.
5. Unallocated is 2-6% outward investment, fluctuates for inward investment.
6. 1983-84.
7. 1991.
Source: OECD, calculated from *International Direct Investment Statistics*, and *National Accounts*.

Acquisitions accounted for around 85 per cent of foreign investment outlays in the United States in the 1980s through to 1994. Around 60 per cent of cross-border investment in the European Community in the late-1980s was acquisitions, and acquisitions have shown a rising trend in Canada to make up over one-half of foreign investment. Home-country influences play a part in the choice between acquisition or green-field investment. Firms from the United States, France and the United Kingdom have been much more active in foreign acquisitions in the EC than German and Japanese firms, coming from countries where acquisitions are generally less common. The overall effect of merger and acquisition (M&A) activity has been a re-shuffling and re-organisation of assets and production structures globally, leading to greater overall efficiency without necessarily significantly greater capacity or employment in OECD countries.

e) The impacts of foreign affiliates on domestic economies

International investment brings greater efficiency, enhanced structural adjustment and greater opportunities to participate in growth. International firms have organisational and technological advantages, and tend to be more efficient. They also tend to operate in more advanced industries and are leaders within their industries, hastening technological and structural change within countries, and, through international linkages, widening growth opportunities. Not all activities can be globalised, however, and not all countries participate equally. Until now, some services have not been subject to international investment due to government restrictions (communications, transport), or the difficulties in organising highly dispersed consumer and personal services. Similarly, resource-based industries have a more

Table 1.12. **Industrial deals of the 1 000 largest firms in the European Community**

Number of operations and geographic breakdown[1]

	1982/83	1983/84	1984/85	1985/86	1986/87	1987/88	1988/89	1989/90	1990/91	1991/92	1991/92[2]	1992/93[2]
	Mergers and acquisitions of majority holdings											
No. of operations	117	155	208	227	303	383	496	622	455	343	5 085	4 294
National share[3]	50.4	65.2	70.2	63.9	69.6	55.9	47.4	38.7	40.9	51.0	73.2	70.0
Community share[4]	32.5	18.7	21.2	22.9	24.8	29.2	40.0	41.3	37.4	34.7	15.0	14.8
Non-community share[5]	17.1	16.1	8.7	13.2	5.6	14.9	12.6	19.9	21.2	14.3	11.9	15.3
	Acquisitions of minority holdings											
No. of operations	33	54	67	130	117	181	159	180	146	121	290	296
National share[3]	60.6	68.5	67.2	71.8	71.8	63.5	64.2	40.6	41.1	49.6	56.2	66.2
Community share[4]	27.3	14.8	14.9	17.9	17.9	20.4	23.3	34.4	37.7	28.1	28.3	19.6
Non-community share[5]	12.1	16.7	17.9	10.3	10.3	16.0	12.6	25.0	21.2	22.3	15.5	14.2
	Joint ventures											
No. of operations	46	69	82	81	90	111	129	156	127	103	621	512
National share[3]	50.0	46.4	48.8	42.0	32.2	40.5	43.4	26.2	30.0	28.2	n.a.	n.a.
Community share[4]	17.4	15.9	18.3	24.7	17.8	27.9	27.9	35.3	38.6	32.0	24.3	29.1
Non-community share[5]	32.6	37.7	32.9	33.3	50.0	31.5	28.7	38.5	35.4	39.8	75.7	70.9

1. Data collected from the specialist press regarding operations involving at least one of the 1 000 largest firms of the Community, ranked according to their financial data.
2. Note break in series from 1992-93 due to wider coverage for all Community transactions. 1991-92 repeated for comparison.
3. Operations of firms from the same Community member State.
4. Operations of firms from different Community member States.
5. Operations of firms from Community member States and third countries which affect the Community market.
Source: Commission of the European Communities, Report on Competition Policy, various issues.

Table 1.13. **Share of foreign enterprises in manufacturing production and employment[1]**

Percentages

	Production		Employment	
	1980	1991	1980	1991
United States[2]	3.9	14.8 (1992)	5.1	12.3 (1992)
Canada	50.6	49.0 (1989)	37.8	38.0 (1989)
Japan	4.6	2.8 (1990)	1.6	1.2 (1990)
Denmark	–	14.2 (1986)	–	12.4 (1986)
France[2]	26.6	26.9	18.5	22.1
Germany	15.7	13.8 (1992)	9.0	7.2 (1992)
Ireland	46.1 (1983)	55.1 (1988)	37.9 (1983)	44.2 (1988)
Italy	19.2	22.3 (1988)	15.8	17.2 (1988)
Portugal	23.6 (1984)	–	17.7 (1984)	–
United Kingdom	19.3 (1981)	25.5	14.9 (1981)	17.2
Finland	2.5	6.7 (1992)	3.1	6.2 (1992)
Austria		25.7		15.6
Norway[2]	11.5	10.5 (1990)	6.5	7.7 (1990)
Sweden	7.9	18.0 (1992)	6.1	16.9 (1992)
Australia[2]	33.5 (1982)	32.0 (1986)	26.3 (1982)	23.8 (1986)
Turkey	6.2 (1986)	5.9 (1991)	2.3 (1986)	4.4

1. Includes minority holdings (equity holdings >10 or >20 per cent up to 50 per cent) for countries indicated. Percentages are calculated as a share of production from the annual census of production in most cases. This may overstate the share of foreign firms, if small firms (<20 employees) are excluded from the annual census, as small firms are predominantly domestic.
2. Includes joint ventures and minority participation (<50%). Values for France are unweighted by share of minority ownership.
Source: OECD, DSTI, EAS Division.

limited globalisation due to geographical location of primary inputs, although firms in these industries were the first to have high international dispersion of activities. Finally, location economies and "clustering" effects encourage regional integration and regional organisation of firms and industries, thereby excluding some peripheral countries and areas.

The international expansion of firms has increased the relative importance of foreign ownership in OECD countries. Overall, annual sales of goods and services by foreign affiliates are one and a half times the value of world exports, and a rising share of private sector GNP is accounted for by the combined value added of foreign-based firms and the foreign output of home-based firms: over 50 per cent for Belgium, Canada, the Netherlands, Switzerland and the United Kingdom, more than 30 per cent for Australia, France, Germany and Italy, and over 20 per cent for Japan and the United States (United Nations, 1993).

Wide differences remain, however, in the share of output and employment in foreign-controlled firms. The share of foreign-owned subsidiaries in manufacturing output, sales or turnover around 1991 was: over 30 per cent in Australia, Belgium, Canada and Ireland; 20-30 per cent in Austria, France, Portugal and the United Kingdom; 10-20 per cent in Denmark, Germany, Italy, Norway, Sweden and the United States; and less than 10 per cent in Finland, Japan and Turkey (Table 1.13 and Figures 1.1 and 1.2).

Penetration of foreign firms increased particularly rapidly from a low base in the United States, reflecting strong inflows of foreign investment in the 1980s, and in Sweden. In the European Community, it increased rapidly in Portugal and Spain following large inflows of foreign investment and continued to grow significantly in Ireland. With the boom in foreign investment from the second part of the 1980s, the relative importance of foreign ownership increased again in larger European countries (France, Italy, the United Kingdom) which already had 15-25 per cent of manufacturing output in foreign-owned subsidiaries in the 1970s. The share of foreign-controlled output has declined marginally from high levels in Australia and Canada. These trends show that, while foreign-controlled firms are increasingly important, their impacts are spread unevenly.

Sectoral distribution of foreign ownership. Foreign ownership has a particular sectoral incidence, and is most evident in high-technology industries. In most countries the computer, chemical, pharmaceutical, automobile, and electronics industries have the highest shares of foreign ownership. Table 1.14 shows that foreign enterprises account for a very large share of production in most of these industries in five of the G7 countries – the exceptions are the United States and Japan. Differences between countries remain however in the industries with the highest levels of foreign ownership. In the United States resource-intensive process industries which need to be located near to markets (cement, glass, chemicals, metal refining) are prominent amongst industries with extensive foreign ownership. In Japan, foreign ownership is low in all industries. The exception is chemicals and petroleum refining, but it is still only one-tenth of total production.

f) Differences in performance between foreign affiliates and domestic firms

Foreign affiliates usually have a higher share of output and value added than their share of employment, higher average labour productivity, and higher average wages as well as being more capital intensive than average. This is due to the technological and organisational advantages of firms which have the resources to operate internationally, the advanced industries in which they operate, and their larger average size. These competitive advantages of foreign affiliates of firms which operate internationally hold across most countries and most industries. Foreign affiliates are also more trade oriented than domestic firms. They tend to import more than average, particularly from their parent firms, and export more than average. Overall, foreign affiliates are usually large net importers (OECD, 1994b).

Foreign affiliate production and the direction of trade. Detailed data for the United States and Japan show that manufacturing affiliates mainly produce for the markets in which they have invested or for regional markets, Asian affiliates being the exception. In the case of US affiliates, there is considerable intra-regional exporting. Inter-regional exports from Asian affiliates back to the United States were the major exception, as US firms have taken advantage of low labour costs to supply the US home market. Japanese affiliates had high levels of domestic sales in the United States and intra-regional exports in Europe. The exceptions were Asian affiliates of Japanese firms, which exported much more globally

◆ Figure 1.1. **Share of foreign subsidiaries in gross manufacturing output and turnover**
In percentage

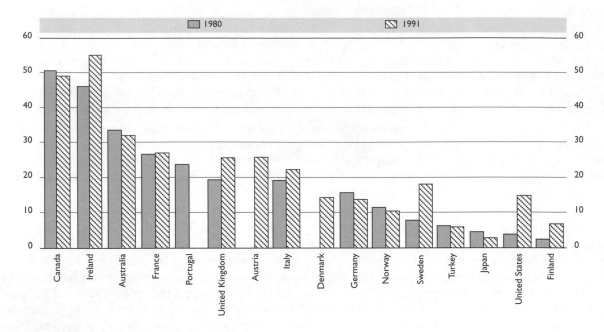

Note: Figures for 1980 and 1991, or nearest year.
Source: OECD, Industrial Activity of Foreign Affiliates data bank.

◆ Figure 1.2. **Share of foreign subsidiaries in manufacturing employment**
In percentage

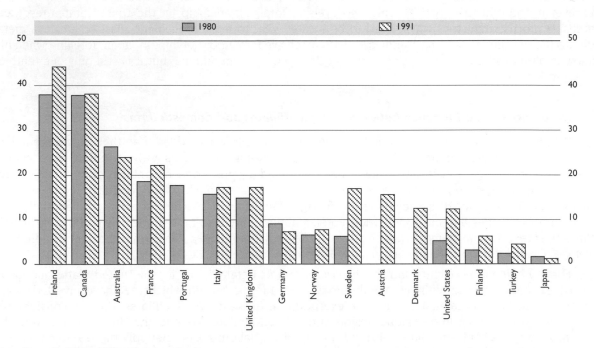

Note: Figures for 1980 and 1991, or nearest year.
Source: OECD, Industrial Activity of Foreign Affiliates data bank.

Table 1.14. **Industrial sectors with the highest share of production by foreign enterprises**[1]

Percentages

Canada 1987	France 1990	Germany 1990	Italy 1989	United Kingdom 1990	United States 1989	Japan 1989
Motor vehicles	Computers	Computers	Computers	Computers	Other manufacturing	Chemicals
85	74	82	78	78	30	11
Chemicals	Chemicals	Chemicals	Electronics	Motor vehicles	Non-metallic products	Machinery/ equipment
76	45	43	55	60	29	2
Non-metallic products	Electronics	Food/beverages	Chemicals	Chemicals	Chemicals	Basic metals
55	31	23	30	36	27	1
Machinery/ equipment	Non-metallic products	Motor vehicles	Food/beverages	Electronics	Basic metals	Other manufacturing
44	26	24	15	26	22	0.6
Other manufacturing	Machinery	Basic metals	Machines	Basic metals	Electronics	Paper/printing
35	28	21	12	21	19	0.5

1. Production from foreign-owned enterprises and enterprises with foreign participation as a share of production in industry in each country. Values may be overestimated if small firms (<20 employees) are excluded from the census on which figures are based, as small firms are predominantly domestic. Production refers to turnover, output or sales, depending on the source. For Japan, only 2-digit ISIC data available.

Source: OECD, DSTI, Industry Division.

– to Japan, the rest of Asia, North America and Europe, due to the heavy weighting of electronics in Japanese manufacturing production in Asia and export strategies of Japanese electronics firms (see Tables 1.15 and 1.16).

There are strong similarities between patterns of sourcing and foreign investment, illustrating the reliance of foreign investors on imported components for foreign production. Overall, the higher the level of international investment in a country or industry, the more intensive is international sourcing. This relation is particularly strong for Canada, France and the United Kingdom amongst the G7 countries, all of which have relatively high levels of foreign investment in industry. Exceptions are in textiles and clothing which have high levels of international sourcing and low levels of international investment, and non-metallic mineral products (building materials) which have high investment and low levels of international sourcing.

Foreign affiliates, employment, wages and productivity. Direct impacts on employment and wages associated with inward direct investment are analysed in an OECD study (OECD, 1994b). The study concluded that during the 1980s to the early 1990s jobs increased in foreign manufacturing affiliates compared with slower increase or declines in domestically owned companies. Increases in the number of jobs in foreign affiliates, against a fall for domestic firms, were recorded in the United States, Austria, the United Kingdom, Sweden, Portugal, Ireland and Finland, while Turkey recorded rises in both. In Australia, Japan, France, Canada, Germany and Norway the number of jobs in foreign-owned subsidiaries declined. In France, Australia and Norway they declined less than employment losses in domestic firms, in Canada they declined faster than job losses in domestic firms, while in Japan and Germany employment expanded in domestic manufacturing firms and declined in foreign affiliates. The study did not quantitatively examine the impact of international merger and acquisition (M&A) activity, which has transferred jobs into the foreign-owned sector, or attempt to compare the employment impacts of green-field additions to capacity with restructuring usually associated with M&As.

On average, value added per employee in foreign subsidiaries appears to be as high or higher than that of domestic firms, wages are also higher, and foreign subsidiaries tend to be more capital intensive

Table 1.15.   **Sales structure of US manufacturing affiliates abroad,
1989 and 1982**

Percentages

Host country	Total 1990 Bn US$	Sales of affiliates[1]									
		In host country		United States		Europe		Latin America		Asia/Pacific[2]	
		1989	(1982)	1989	(1982)	1989	(1982)	1989	(1982)	1989	(1982)
						Exports to					
World	509	62	(66)	14	(10)	19	(19)	1	–	3	–
Canada	99	61	(65)	**35**	**(29)**	2	–	0	–	1	–
Europe	292	59	(59)	6	(2)	**32**	**(33)**	0	–	2	–
United Kingdom	79	71	(70)	7	(3)	**18**	–	0	–	1	–
Other EC-countries	204	54	(54)	5	(2)	**37**	**(45)**	0	–	2	–
EFTA	9	63	(58)	10	(4)	19	(54)	0	–	1	–
Latin America/Western Hemisphere	48	78	(88)	14	(5)	2	(2)	**4**	**(4)**	1	–
Japan	22	83	(92)	9	(0)	3	(1)	n.a.		**4**	–
Other Asia-Pacific	45	56	(49)	23	(28)	5	(5)	n.a.		**14**	**(14)**
Other DCs	25	36	(33)	39	(46)	n.a.	(4)	n.a.		**n.a.**	**(12)**

1.   Intra-regional sales **in bold**.
2.   Underestimated due to incomplete statistics.
Source: US Department of Commerce (1985, 1992), *U.S. Investment Abroad, 1982* and *1989 Benchmark Survey*, Washington, DC.

Table 1.16.   **Sales structure of Japanese manufacturing affiliates abroad, 1983 and 1990**

Percentages

Host region/sector	Total 1990 Bn yen	Sales of affiliates[1]						
		In host country		Exports to				
				Japan		North America	Asia	Europe
		1990	1983	1990	1983	1990	1990	1990
Manufacturing	26 200	74	74	6	10	4	3	9
North America	12 080	90	85	3	6	**3**	1	1
Europe	4 910	58	72	1	2	1	0	**38**
Asia[2]	7 190	60	66	**12**	**10**	6	**10**	5
NIEs	4 240	57		**12**		5	**11**	5
ASEAN	2 540	62		**12**		7	**9**	5
Electronics	7 960	70	78	7	5	4	4	9
North America	3 330	95	96	3	0	**1**	1	1
Europe	1 880	61	72	2	1	1	0	**32**
Asia[2]	2 440	36	51	**17**	**12**	10	**13**	8
NIEs	1 680	38		**16**		8	**11**	8
ASEAN	640	27		**20**		16	**18**	11
Vehicles	6 980	84	87	2	7	7	1	5
North America	3 280	86	96	2	1	**11**	1	1
Europe	990	46	89	1	0	0	0	**53**
Asia[2]	1 770	87	79	**2**	**15**	5	**2**	3
NIEs	550	82		**2**		6	**4**	4
ASEAN	980	90		**1**		5	**1**	2

1.   Intraregional sales **in bold**.
2.   Excluding Middle East
Source: MITI (1992).

and have higher labour productivity due to plant size capital intensity and higher skill levels. Studies in the United Kingdom indicate that foreign-owned firms consistently generate higher value added per employee than UK-owned counterparts (Davies and Lyons, 1991). Even greater differences between foreign and domestic firms are recorded in Ireland, where the net output per employee in foreign affiliates is two to three times greater than in Irish enterprises, partly due to different sectoral distributions (Central Statistics Office of Ireland, 1991). In contrast, a study of foreign affiliates and domestic companies in the United States concluded that when account was taken of the tendency of foreign-owned companies to invest in capital-intensive and high-wage sectors, there are fewer differences in worker compensation between foreign and domestically owned firms (US Department of Commerce, 1993a).

Outlook. Foreign investment picked up in 1993-95, following the recession which discouraged new investment in weakening markets, reduced profits of potential investors, and led to over-capacity in numerous sectors. Liquidity problems in European and Japanese firms cut their foreign investment sharply. Many Japanese and European firms have yet to achieve the extensive networks of international investment outside their own region already achieved by US multinational enterprises (MNEs), which have around one-third of their production and employment outside of North America. There is considerable potential for re-organising production internationally for many enterprises. The shifts towards regional integration, growth prospects in some regions, and further liberalisation and privatisation suggest continuing growth in international investment as investment opportunities expand. The outlook is for continued growth, but with the business cycle having a strong influence on the timing of international investment.

g) Globalisation of R&D and technology

Technological advantages are a major component of the international strategies of firms, and there are differences between the international distribution of their R&D capabilities, and the commercialisation, application and use of the results of technological advance. Four intersecting factors determine the international location of R&D:

- *Centralisation.* Economies of scale in R&D and its strategic importance favours centralisation of R&D as a "headquarters" function.

- *Diversification.* The development of distinct Asian, European and North American regions encourages globalised firms to set up R&D activities in each, to gain access to complementary high-quality research resources, R&D staff and institutions, develop new products and processes and adapt products and technology to local conditions in large markets, spread risks and diversify technology sources.

- *Entry strategy.* International acquisitions of high-technology firms are often aimed at capturing R&D resources (for example acquisition of biotechnology firms in the United States).

- *Country-specific factors.* Firms from smaller countries (particularly European ones, such as the Netherlands, Sweden and Switzerland) perform more of their R&D in foreign countries because of limited domestic resources, and need to draw on developments in major R&D-performing countries. On the other hand, new investors (Japan, Korea) may perform less R&D away from home.

Overall, foreign investment has had the following effects on the distribution of R&D and technology:

- R&D has tended to remain concentrated in the home country of the foreign investor relative to the spread of production capacity and employment, although R&D functions are becoming more diversified.

- The share of R&D carried out in foreign subsidiaries is rising in many countries, particularly in countries where the share of manufacturing output in foreign firms is increasing. Firms are setting up R&D and technology operations in Asia, North America and Europe to spread risks and gain access to research resources, R&D staff and institutions. Acquisitions often aim at capturing R&D capabilities, and international firms from smaller countries have to perform more of their R&D in foreign countries due to limits on home-country resources.

- Diffusion and applications of new technology, particularly process technology, are rapid in subsidiaries of international firms, resulting in higher labour productivity and greater efficiency in foreign subsidiaries than domestic firms. These effects are in part due to affiliates' larger-scale and more capital-intensive operations, and the R&D-intensive, skill-intensive, high-wage industries in which foreign subsidiaries operate.

Inward investment in R&D. R&D intensities (R&D expenditures as a share of production or turnover) are generally lower in foreign subsidiaries than in domestic firms, and R&D activities of foreign firms are rarely much higher than in indigenous firms in the same industry. Reasons include centralisation of R&D functions at home where the research networks and infrastructure are most dense, the preference for government research contracts to be allocated to national rather than foreign firms, and poorly developed globalisation of small research-intensive firms (Figure 1.3).

There are two exceptions where foreign affiliates perform more than average R&D:

- In countries where R&D intensities of domestic firms are considerably lower than the international average, the R&D intensity of foreign subsidiaries may be higher than for domestic firms. This is in part due to the R&D-intensive industries in which foreign investment is concentrated. This is the case for Australia and Ireland, and probably for Spain and Portugal. R&D-intensities in Canada are only a little lower in foreign subsidiaries than in all enterprises.

- In the United States, the inward investment boom resulted in the concentration of R&D by foreign firms in a few high-technology sectors: pharmaceuticals, industrial chemicals and audio, video and communications equipment. This is often due to acquisitions of R&D-intensive US firms by foreign firms (usually European) which were already strong exporters or had comparative advantages in these sectors. The result has been a rapid rise in affiliate shares of all business R&D in the United States to over 16 per cent of the total in 1992. There is now higher R&D intensity of foreign-owned affiliates in drugs and audio, video and communications equipment, and higher R&D intensity of

◆ Figure 1.3. **R&D intensities[1] of foreign subsidiaries and of all firms in manufacturing industry, in 1989**
In percentage

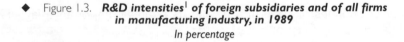
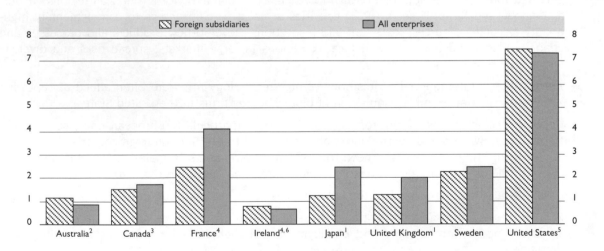

Note: R&D expenditures on production or turnover.
1. R&D expenditure on production.
2. 1986/87 including minority foreign-owned affiliates.
3. 1990.
4. Based on total national enterprises.
5. R&D intensity is based on value-added in 1987.
6. R&D expenditure on 1991 turnover; including minority foreign-owned affiliates.
Source: OECD, Industrial Activity of Foreign Affiliates data bank.

foreign-owned affiliates compared with US-owned firms in high-technology manufacturing overall (US Department of Commerce, 1993*a*).

Outward investment in R&D. Looking at the other side of the phenomenon, investing firms transfer R&D outwards to a more limited extent than production. US manufacturing affiliates abroad have the equivalent of one-third of parent firm employment and sales, but R&D expenditures are only 10-12 per cent and R&D employment 15 per cent of parents. These shares have remained stable over time and over industry groups, suggesting that US corporations had developed long-term globally optimum patterns of R&D and production activities, with a large share of R&D remaining at home. There were however significant US R&D activities in Germany and Japan compared with the general pattern of overseas activities of US firms, suggesting that US firms have a "Triadic" approach to global R&D operations building on strong technology bases. On the other hand, although Japanese firms have been rapidly building up their R&D activities in the United States and in some selected other countries, particularly in electronics, surveys have shown that the extent of these activities still remain limited compared with their domestic R&D activities and amounted to only 2.5 per cent of group R&D expenditures in 1992-93 (Kumar, 1995). Overall, despite the contribution of foreign-owned firms to R&D in some countries and international diversification of R&D activities, international transfer of R&D lags employment and production (OECD, 1992*d*).

On average the share of business R&D financed directly from foreign sources (excluding domestic financing) is still below 3 per cent. It has grown considerably however and is highest in Canada, the United Kingdom and France (OECD, 1995*a*).

The recent round of inter-firm alliances and joint ventures in R&D and technology, the acquisitions and minority holdings by foreign firms of small high-technology companies, and the development of networks of technology alliances may however globalise R&D efficiently without shifts in the location of R&D activities which run counter to the achievement of economic scale in R&D. There is also extensive international scientific collaboration outside strategic alliances and direct investment, which provides numerous connections between firms and research institutions.

h) International inter-firm collaboration

Increasingly dense and complex international inter-firm collaboration networks are being formed, not necessarily leading to re-location of technological and industrial activities. They range from non-equity contractual agreements (the most common) in development, production and marketing, minority equity participations to jointly-owned subsidiaries. Majority investments are excluded. A large proportion of them are in development of new products or processes in R&D-intensive industries (computers, electronics, communications, aerospace, automobiles) that are major international investors and that are trade-intensive.

These agreements are difficult to trace in any comprehensive way because of the wide variety of forms that they take. The following discussion of trends is illustrative rather than quantitative, and is based on compilations of announcements of arrangements between firms.

International collaborative arrangements have been driven by the following factors:

Technology-related factors. A large share of international co-operation is focused on technology development, a key factor in firm strategies. As there are more technology sources and potential partners than in the past, firms co-operate to mutually complement their own resources to develop "knowledge-intensive" goods and services, and reduce the time for innovations to reach the market. Co-operation has been further stimulated by increasing R&D costs, making co-operation necessary, and declining communication costs, making co-operation easy.

Macroeconomic factors. Collaboration is also promoted for production and market reasons. The increasing recourse of firms in assembly industries to out-source crucial parts and components requires a higher degree of co-ordination than in market transactions. Access to new markets is facilitated by using the complementary resources of local firms (distribution channels, product-range extension), in order to explore the new environment in a flexible way. International inter-firm co-operation is sometimes a second-best option to direct investment, particularly for resource-poor SMEs, to explore opportunities which may be exploited later through more elaborate global strategies.

Government policies. Apart from direct promotion of international collaboration, for example in EC programmes, government policies may indirectly favour co-operation, in the same way that they stimulate direct investment. First, areas where there are limits on local participation of foreign companies are often characterised by joint ventures and minority equity investments. Second, where there are inter-country differences in intellectual property, environmental standards and other regulations, inter-firm agreements may be used to help products be accepted by local regulatory authorities. Third, competition policies limiting collaboration on the home market may encourage firms to seek foreign partners and expand internationally.

Composition by region. A very large share of reported agreements are between firms from OECD countries and a very small share (of the order of 5-10 per cent) do not involve firms from Europe, North America or Japan. Agreements are most common between firms within the EC, between EC and North American firms and then between EC and Japanese firms, with high levels of agreements within larger countries, notably the United States, and high levels of intra-regional agreements.

Recent trends. Growth in the reported formation of collaboration arrangements between firms was very high in the 1980s. Numbers reported in various databases grew by over 10 per cent annually from the start of the 1980s when they were first widely commented on. They subsequently appear to have flattened out since the peak years of 1988-90, but numbers of new agreements were maintained at a reasonably high level through 1991 to 1993. There are some differences between different technologies and industries, so the detailed descriptions vary somewhat (see Hagedoorn, 1995). The general trend in activity runs in parallel with the growth in flows in direct investment (see Tables 1.1 and 1.17).

Composition by industry and activity. A large share of these agreements have been set up to develop new technologies and tend to be clustered in R&D-intensive industries. One major database which focused on technology-related agreements for the 1980-89 period, showed that over 70 per cent of agreements involved the three generic technologies of information technology, biotechnology and new materials, because of the rapid pace of developments in these areas (Table 1.18; Hagedoorn and Schakenraad, 1991). A different survey of co-operation arrangements between firms, covering production and marketing as well as technology development, also shows that an overwhelming share of them are in a few high-technology sectors, and that technology development is the most important purpose of agreements. Sectors which were most commonly involved include the high-technology group of electronics, aerospace, telecommunications and computers, as well as automobiles (Table 1.17).

Table 1.17. **Collaboration agreements, 1980-92**

Percentages

Number per year (average)	Main regions [1]		Main industries [1]		Main purpose	
1980-84 120	Europe/Europe Europe/North America	30 23	Automotive Electronics	21 17	Development Production	31 25
1985-89 240	Europe/Japan North America/Japan	15 11	Aerospace Telecommunications	15 14	Marketing Mixed	13 30
1990-92 220	North America/North America Other	10 10	Computers Other	13 20		
	Total	100	Total	100	Total	100

1. Including agreements before 1980.
Source: OECD Secretariat, from data provided by INSEAD. See Sector Reports.

Table 1.18. **Motives for technology-based strategic alliances, sectors and fields of technology, 1980-89**

Percentages

	Number of alliances	High cost/risks	Lack of financial resources	Technology complementarity	Reduction innovation time span	Basic R&D	Market access/ structure	Monitoring technology/market entry
Biotechnology	847	1	13	35	31	10	13	15
New materials technology	430	1	3	38	32	11	31	16
Information technology	1 660	4	2	33	31	3	38	11
Computers	198	1	2	28	22	2	51	10
Industrial automation	278	0	3	41	32	4	31	7
Microelectronics	383	3	3	33	33	5	52	6
Software	344	1	4	38	36	2	24	11
Telecommunications	366	11	2	28	28	1	35	16
Other	91	1	0	29	28	2	35	24
Total database	4 182	6	4	31	28	5	32	11

Source: MERIT/CATI, Hagedoorn and Schakenraad (1991).

Firm size. Large firms appear to be the major participants in these arrangements. This is true of both technology agreements and more general agreements, with the world's leading firms playing a major role. There are several reasons, including the focus on technology and R&D arrangements where formal R&D by large firms is concentrated, and also due to the concentration of these arrangements in electronics, aerospace, computers, automobiles and chemicals, all of which are R&D-intensive and have scale economies which favour large-firm dominance. The exception is in biotechnology and pharmaceuticals, where small technology-based companies led early technological developments, and large firms set up many arrangements with them.

Motivations. The main motives for setting up technology-related agreements have focused on (Hagedoorn and Schakenraad, 1991):

- the search for technological complementarities to extend R&D capabilities;
- reductions in the innovation time-span and increases in efficiency to get new products and processes to markets; and
- market access and restructuring in mature technologies and slow growth industries (see Table 1.18).

Technology-related motives appeared to be gaining in importance over the 1980s, whereas market access and market restructuring appeared to be declining. The pattern of motivations varies somewhat across sectors and technology areas, with biotechnology focused particularly on achieving technological complementarities. There is little analysis of the inter-relation between these new arrangements and foreign investment, industrial structure and concentration.

Outlook. The short- to medium-term outlook is for an increase in international collaboration due to the increasing importance of "knowledge-intensive" industries and products, along with diversification and out-sourcing which make use of collaboration agreements. Offsetting forces include the establishment of clear technological trajectories which require less exploration and search for external complementarities by firms (information technology is well-developed, biotechnology and advanced materials less so). Widespread diffusion of the lean production system and very tight user-producer relations may also favour national and/or sub-national sourcing networks over inter-country and inter-regional networks, reducing international collaboration.

i) Globalisation at sector level

Globalisation is analysed for eight industries: pharmaceuticals, computers, semiconductors, motor vehicles, consumer electronics, non-ferrous metals, steel, and clothing. Table 1.19 provides a matrix showing the surveyed industries along two basic dimensions: the technological trajectory characterising the industry, and the nature of its output (finished or intermediate products). On the extreme right is a list of those emerging sectors that provide opportunities and threats to these industries.

Table 1.19. **Stylised technology and product relationships among the surveyed industries**

Technological features			Industry positioning		Complementary emerging sectors
Major trajectory	Period of appearance	Actual impact	Intermediate products	Finished products	
Biotechnology	Mid-1970s	Low		Pharmaceuticals	Health care Environment
Information technology	Early-1960s	High	Semiconductors	Computers Consumer electronics	Entertainment Multimedia
Advanced materials	Late-1970s	Medium	Non-ferrous metals Steel	Motor vehicles Clothing	Environment

Source: OECD, DSTI, Industry Division.

In Table 1.20 the eight industries have been separated into four groups. Pharmaceuticals, computers and semiconductors are found in the *science-based* group, since their commitment to R&D activities is far above the manufacturing average. Motor vehicles and consumer electronics are part of the *scale-intensive* group, for they are characterised by increasing returns to scale. Non-ferrous metals and steel are included in the *resource-intensive* group, being raw materials processing industries. Clothing stands alone in the *labour-intensive* group, where the share of labour costs in total costs is well above the manufacturing average.

Common competitive challenges, reshaping forces, patterns of globalisation, policy issues, and the role of SMEs, can each be stylised by industry group: firms belonging to the same group operate in very similar industrial environments. The remaining intra-group discrepancies can be described in the light of the technology and product relationships presented in Table 1.19.

Differences and similarities in the patterns of globalisation of the eight industries can be derived from Table 1.21 (elaborated from the sector reports and supplementary data). All values included in the table are expressed in percentage of industry aggregates (total industry sales, total industry investment, etc.). On the left, four measures of international trade are given: trade in finished products and trade in intermediate products – both as shares of total sales; the share of foreign sourcing in total foreign and domestic sourcing; and the share of intra-firm trade (IFT) in total trade. These are followed by four direct investment-related measures: direct investment flows on gross fixed capital formation; sales of foreign affiliates on total sales; mergers and acquisitions; and equity participations (minorities and joint ventures) – the last two as shares of the total number of equity operations. On the right, the total number of international collaboration agreements is broken up by main purpose: development; production; marketing. Two values are given for each purpose: the first value refers to single-purpose agreements; the second to multi-purpose agreements.

The first column can be interpreted unambiguously: the share of finished trade in total sales is strikingly similar across the surveyed industries, and ranges from 20 to 30 per cent. Outlier values are for pharmaceuticals and consumer electronics. However, the value for the pharmaceutical industry may not be a true outlier, since most trade in intermediates is made of quasi-finished products, which only need to go through packaging and labelling operations before reaching the market. These intermediates are closer to final products than for example components in industries which assemble extensively (motor vehicles and consumer electronics). If the two are combined, pharmaceutical trade in finished and intermediate products amounts to around 18 per cent of total sales, which brings it almost in line with other industries. As regards consumer electronics, the high value of finished product trade can be explained by the undisputed leadership of Japanese companies, which together hold around 55 per cent of total world production and which ship finished products globally.

Intensity in intermediates trade is more varied. If consumer electronics is left aside for the reason just mentioned, a line can be drawn between the science-based plus scale-intensive industries and the resource- plus labour-intensive ones. Values for the former group range from 8 to 14 per cent of global sales, and for the latter from 21 to 45 per cent. This means that, although substantial *growth* in the ratio of international to domestic sourcing has characterised most manufactured goods in the last two decades, the *intensity* of intermediates trade is still higher in resource- and labour-intensive industries than in the science-based and scale-intensive ones.

The share of international in total sourcing is presented in the third column as a central range of shares calculated for major countries. Industry ranges are of the order of 10 to 40 per cent in most cases, except for computers and non-ferrous metals, which have higher values. Overall, it appears that the degree of openness on the input side is more country-specific than industry-specific. The intensity in the use of inputs is primarily industry-specific; the extent of dependence on foreign inputs is more country-specific.

The fourth column shows the level of intra-firm trade (IFT), that is to say, the share of total trade which takes place within a multinational enterprise, calculated for the United States (the only country for which comprehensive data are available). Also in this case two sub-groups can be identified, which correspond again to the science-based plus scale-intensive industries, and the resource- plus labour-intensive industries. The former has an IFT share ranging from 50 to 80 per cent, and the latter from 5 to

Table 1.20. **Stylised aspects of the surveyed industries**

Industry aggregation	Industries in the survey	Major competitive challenge	Major reshaping force	Features of globalisation	Common policy issues	SMEs presence
Science-based	Pharmaceuticals Computers Semiconductors	Capability to bring results of R&D and product development to the market	Steep rise in the R&D threshold	Limited to the Triad-area, with little trade regionalisation	Technology base, IPRs	Few and very technology-focused
Scale-intensive	Motor vehicles Consumer electronics	Capability to co-ordinate complex production processes	Diffusion of the "lean" production system	Mainly in the Triad-area, with high and increasing trade regionalisation	Local content, Standards	Numerous as sub-contractors
Resource-intensive	Non-ferrous metals Steel	Capability to reduce costs, optimise production-location and market-location	Substitution of materials by users	World-wide, with high trade regionalisation	Competition, Environment	Increasing in upstream-end operations and recycling
Labour-intensive	Clothing	Capability to provide quality and/or price competitive products	Decrease in the importance of labour-costs	World-wide, with increasing trade regionalisation	Tariffs and quotas	Dominant

Source: OECD, DSTI, Industry Division.

Table 1.21. **Pattern of globalisation of the surveyed industries**

	Trade				Direct investment				Co-operative agreements		
	Finished products (% sales)	Intermediate products (% sales)	International sourcing (% tot. src.)	Intra firm (% trade)	Flows (% gtcf)	Affiliate sales (% sales)	M&As (% ops)	Equity participation (% ops)	Development purpose (% agrs)	Production purpose (% agrs)	Market purpose (% agrs)
Pharmaceuticals	10	8	10-30	70	50-70	40-50	52	48	38-68	13-29	19-41
Computers	26	14	20-60	50-80	30-40	50-60	43	57	50-70	15-28	17-32
Semiconductors	20	n.a.	10-40	70	15-25	20-25	39	61	n.a.	n.a.	n.a.
Motor vehicles	21	13	25-35	50-80	15-25	10-20	33	67	24-48	39-66	9-20
Consumer electronics	55	30	10-40	30-50	20-35	20-30	39	61	24-40	36-62	12-33
Non-ferrous metals	21	21[1]	30-50	30	20-35	15-25	45	55	n.a.	n.a.	n.a.
Steel	27	35-45[2]	15-25	5-10	5-10	15-25	72	28	n.a.	n.a.	n.a.
Clothing	25-30	25-30[3]	10-40	5-10	15-20	5-15	n.a.	n.a.	(limited)		

1. Unwrought aluminium.
2. Iron ore, coking coal, scrap.
3. Textiles.
Source: OECD, DSTI, Industry Division compilation. Elaborated from data sources used for the Sector Reports.

30 per cent. These values compare with the IFT share of total US trade of somewhat over one-third. It is interesting to interpret the IFT column in connection with the one showing the intensity in intermediates trade. The groups identified in both columns are the same, but the situation appears reversed: low values for intermediates trade correspond to high value of IFT, and *vice versa*.

This last finding can be explained as follows. Firms in the resource- and labour-intensive industries are largely dependent on foreign intermediate commodity supply; their strategic interest is focused elsewhere, on activities such as product diversification and marketing. Lack of strategic interest means little necessity to directly control through internal trade within the firm, especially if commodity inputs can be acquired on competitive world markets. On the other hand, firms in the science-based and scale-intensive industries are less dependent on intermediate commodity inputs. Inputs in science-based and scale-intensive industries are usually high-tech, high-quality, high-skill and highly specific parts and components. Their acquisition has a high strategic value to firms, and firms prefer to maintain direct control over these inputs through direct investment and internal transactions with in the firm.

The fifth and sixth columns show the importance of international direct investment in the eight industries. The former contains the share of direct investment flows on gross fixed capital formation; the latter provides the share of foreign affiliate sales in total sales (shares are given as ranges as they are partly estimated). Direct investment flows measure the *current* intensity of direct investment activity, while affiliate sales is a function of *past* investment. It is worth noting that the latter, being a measure of impacts at the local market level, underestimates the real impact of foreign presence. Direct investment is undertaken not only to gain market access, but also to gain access to other resources: cheap production factors, technological skills, advanced infrastructure, and other local advantages. These enhance the overall operations of the firm and raise performance without directly appearing as affiliate sales.

For both columns a line can be drawn below the first two industries, pharmaceuticals and computers. They are characterised by above-average intensity in direct investment activity, and a share of affiliate sales which amounts to as much as 40 to 60 per cent of total sales in many markets. The lowest values are for steel (5 to 10 per cent direct investment flows in total investment) and clothing (5 to 15 per cent of affiliates sales in total sales). The industry aggregations of Table 1.20 are useful explanatory tools when applied to FDI, although the picture is less clear than from analysis of international trade. Useful explanatory support can be found in the relationships stylised in Table 1.19.

Pharmaceuticals and computers are science-based industries with products sold to final consumers. Closeness to consumers through significant local presence is of vital importance to pharmaceutical and computer companies, to allow them to turn high and increasing R&D expenditures into revenues with short delays. Semiconductor companies, although science-based, produce inputs for other industries, deal mainly with assembly companies, and do not have a comparable push to expand their presence abroad. Their direct investment activities are less intensive than in the other science-based industries.

At the bottom of direct investment activity, are the resource- and labour-intensive industries, with the exception of non-ferrous metals, which shows a somewhat higher foreign investment intensity. Companies operating in this industry are also involved in advanced materials research, and they undertake direct investment operations in order to diversify horizontally into related activities, such as ceramics and plastics production. Steel and clothing are currently less susceptible to developments in emerging technologies. The extremely low value of foreign affiliate sales for clothing derives from the dominance of SMEs, whose cross-border activity is almost exclusively focused on exports.

The conclusions that can be drawn on mergers and acquisitions and minority equity participations are more tentative, and do not easily allow industries to be placed in groups as before. Two industries (pharmaceuticals and steel) are relatively more active in mergers and acquisitions than their other international operations, but for somewhat different strategic reasons. Pharmaceutical firms are re-organising their activities internationally to capture the R&D resources developed in new biotechnology firms, and lowering costs by amalgamating and moving downstream into more efficient marketing systems. Steel firms on the other hand are rationalising their operations extensively in the face of declining demand and trade competition. In both industries, concentration is not particularly high, and there is more scope for international mergers and acquisitions than in the other industries studied.

The right-hand part of Table 1.21 provides a picture of the purposes for international collaboration agreements. (Values for only four industries were available.) The validity of the industry aggregations applied so far is further corroborated. Firms in science-based industries show a clear propensity towards technology-oriented co-operation. Development alone accounts for 40 to 50 per cent of the total, and together with other purposes for as much as 70 per cent. The market motive ranks second for these industries due to their orientation towards final consumers. Less than 20 per cent as a single purpose, from 30 to 40 per cent together with other purposes. Last ranks production: around 15 per cent as single purpose, less than 30 per cent together with other purposes.

Firms in scale-intensive industries are more inclined towards production agreements, although technology-oriented co-operation is also a primary concern. Production accounts for close to 40 per cent as a single purpose, and around 65 per cent together with other purposes. Development accounts for 24 per cent as a single purpose, and 40 to 50 per cent together with other purposes. Marketing is the least important motive for co-operation among companies in this group: around 10 per cent as a single purpose, and 20 to 35 per cent together with other purposes.

This review of sector case studies suggests that the pattern of globalisation corresponds to broad industry groups which were initially suggested to differentiate the knowledge bases on which these groups of industries draw. Industries in the science-based group are characterised by affiliate sales higher than exports, low intensity of intermediates trade, very high levels of IFT, high flows of direct investment (except semiconductors), and a large portion of collaboration agreements for development purposes, with production being the least important purpose. Industries in the scale-intensive group are characterised by lower affiliate sales, high levels of IFT, and a propensity towards co-operating in production activities, with technology development closely following. Industries in the resource- and labour-intensive group are characterised by lower affiliate sales (especially clothing), a high intensity of intermediates trade, and low levels of IFT.

There are variations within these groups, however. Within the science-based group, semiconductors is an intermediate input industry, and less oriented towards final markets than pharmaceuticals and computers. Within the scale-intensive group, consumer electronics, being largely dominated by Japanese companies, shows a far above average trade intensity. Within the resource- and labour-intensive group, non-ferrous metals often shows values similar to those of the scale-intensive and science-based groups, in particular as regards direct investment. This is in part because non-ferrous metals is the industry in its group most involved in the development of an emerging technology, advanced materials.

Overall, the sector case studies provide the microeconomic basis for policy considerations below. Due to the wide differences between groups of industries, they provide the contrasts and similarities which illuminate these considerations.

j)   Localisation and globalisation

Much recent analytical work has stressed the importance of the local dimension in development, particularly stressing the way that local economies are built on inter-linked networks of relations among firms and between firms, other institutions and their surrounding environment (de Vet 1993, Storper and Scott 1993). The basic argument is that early specialisation is reinforced by growth of similar firms and institutions to create highly competitive industrial and service clusters. Apart from local natural resource-based industries, there are many examples of these clusters, and they are certainly not new. Three broad groups of industrial and service activities are likely to be geographically concentrated:

- High-technology industries are a much-studied group where there has been a long period of clustering of new activities. Well-known examples include biotechnology in San Francisco, semiconductors in Silicon Valley, scientific instruments in Cambridge (United Kingdom), musical instruments in Hamamatsu (Japan).
- Highly competitive, traditional, labour-intensive industries, are highly concentrated, including textiles and clothing in some areas of Italy and the United States, furniture production, etc.
- Services, notably financial and business services, are concentrated in a few big cities, advertising, motion pictures, fashion design are highly concentrated, and so are R&D activities.

Geographical concentration occurs particularly because of localisation economies in production. There are advantages of being: in the same location as similar firms, specialised suppliers and contractors, knowledgeable customers, a good technological infrastructure, and specialised institutions; where a highly skilled labour force is available; and where specialisation within firms enables extensive out-sourcing (vertical dis-integration) and encourages similar new firms to be set up in the location (horizontal dis-integration).

Globalisation increases dynamic competition and competitiveness in these local economies in two ways. First, international firms entering local markets or setting up new production are likely to have an extensive range of firm-specific and industry-specific competitive advantages, which further benefit from being in a favourable geographical location. Second, established sourcing and supply relations are likely to be further enhanced by globalisation and entry of foreign firms. Local firm-level responses to heightened competition involve:

- Improving innovative performance of individual firms, and extending the local and national innovation "system" through greater local interactions between firms, their suppliers and users, production support facilities, and local institutions.

- Adopting "lean production" methods, more efficient management techniques, greater local outsourcing and increasing use of local production networks. This increases efficiency and flexibility, spreads risks and costs, and takes advantage of local specialisation. International sourcing has increased dramatically in high-technology industries, automobiles, textiles and clothing, and this provides greater international opportunities for efficient local suppliers to join sourcing networks. It is notable that international sourcing is low in Japan, where efficient local sourcing networks have built up over a long period.

- Improving production and service links with international firms investing locally. Local firms, particularly if they are highly specialised, will co-operate with international firms seeking complementary resources in the specialised assets of small firms.

To what extent has inward international investment increased or decreased the pattern of specialisation and concentration of economic activities? A major OECD study showed that foreign direct investment has been directed to prosperous regions in the United States, France, Germany, the Netherlands, and more urbanised and core regions in Canada and Spain (de Vet 1993). Only in the United Kingdom in manufacturing have peripheral regions attracted above-average investment. By industry, globalisation measured by incoming foreign investment reinforces regional specialisation in two-thirds of cases in the United States, France, Canada and Spain.

Overall, globalisation has accentuated the development of specialised local economies and enhanced the clustering of similar activities. Clustering and specialisation are driven by firms seeking to optimise their global activities by making maximum use of favourable local externalities and location economies.

k) Small and medium-sized enterprises

Does globalisation affect small firms, or is it a large firm phenomenon? In most countries the share of total employment in small and medium-sized enterprises (SMEs) has been increasing since the early to mid-1980s. Employment held up better in small firms than in large ones during the early 1990s recession and smaller SMEs have been important in generating employment. In most countries SMEs are particularly important in services (construction, transport), and in traditional manufacturing industries (footwear, clothing, textiles, wood industries, metal-working, miscellaneous manufacturing). Most SMEs carry out little formal R&D, but those that do are likely to be very R&D-intensive, and many SMEs carry out considerable informal incremental innovation (OECD 1996a).

SMEs are usually not highly globalised: the majority only operate in their home markets. Even in small European countries where international operations are most likely due to proximity effects, only about one-quarter of SMEs have foreign operations, compared with one-half to two-thirds of larger firms. Larger countries and countries more distant from other markets tend to have lower shares of SMEs with some kind of foreign operations.

Exports are by far the most common route for SMEs to spread their activities abroad. Foreign subsidiaries are only one-third as common as exporting for European SMEs for example. Extensive subsidiary operations are less than one-tenth as common as exporting, and foreign production is even less common. There is some evidence that small firms are more likely to be importers than exporters – in Sweden about 40 per cent of imports are attributed to independent small firms in services such as distribution, compared with only about 20 per cent of exports attributed to independent small firms.

Indirect exporting appears to have grown rapidly, although quantitative data on its magnitude is scanty. Subcontracting to large exporting firms is a feature of assembly industries typified by automobiles and electronics, and subcontracting and out-sourcing to SMEs have grown as large firms have shifted towards "lean" production methods, involving greater use of external suppliers and more highly co-ordinated operations.

Paradoxically, SME globalisation is more evident in less globalised industries. Highly globalised industries exhibit economies of scale and scope, and are dominated by large firms. In contrast, SME globalisation tends to be more extensive in industries where SMEs are more important (traditional industries such as wood products, clothing and textiles, some machinery, food processing, plus a few SMEs in new industries and niche markets). These industries are increasingly trade-oriented and SMEs face greater import competition in their home markets and export competition as they extend their operations to foreign markets.

Outlook. The outlook is for increasing globalisation of SMEs with strong internal capabilities, competing on non-price factors such as R&D, innovation, quality, flexibility, specialisation and a strong customer base in new areas of goods and services. There is some evidence that foreign operations grow faster than domestic operations for these firms once their domestic base is established. The main impediments to expansion are lack of information, marketing, regulatory and access problems, shortages of management skills and experience, and finance.

The global expansion of industry has more general implications for small and medium-sized firms operating in internationally trading industries even if they have no international operations themselves. They are major suppliers to large firms, and there are rising competitive pressures on large firms to increase efficiency and purchase more goods, intermediates and services inputs externally. This provides opportunities for small firms to form subcontracting and supply linkages into large ones. But these linkages are increasingly driven by international strategies, and local small firms face competition in supply from small firms in other countries, and from larger specialised international suppliers with internal R&D capabilities which smaller firms lack.

Globalisation is a firm-driven phenomenon to increase the efficiency of firm operations. It is re-shaping international, national and local economies, beginning with liberalised, open industries and economies and becoming increasingly widespread. Globalisation has important implications for all levels of policy. These are discussed in the next section.

2. POLICY IMPLICATIONS

Firms are globally re-organising their development, production and sales activities by using new combinations of international investment, trade and collaboration. This is creating efficient, highly co-ordinated industrial systems, extending international expansion which was first based on trade, and subsequently on the multi-domestic organisation of multinational enterprises. A contributing element in this process has been the emergence of global firms in science-based and scale-intensive industries. Through vertical integration or external networks, these firms are dispersing key parts of development, production and marketing internationally, but concentrating them within regionally integrated markets.

International expansion has been driven by firm strategies based on their technological and organisational advantages shaped by a number of factors and government policies. Technological factors driving expansion include the rapid growth of knowledge-intensive industries which are foreign investment intensive, use intra-firm trade intensively and collaborate extensively in development, the need to recoup growing R&D costs, find highly trained and skilled workers, and organise production more efficiently, underpinned by declining communications and transport costs. Macroeconomic factors include

Table 1.22. **Selected globalisation characteristics and policy implications**

Globalisation characteristic	Policy issue	Domestic policy actions	International issues
Increased competition	Competitiveness	Improve firm functions (strategy, R&D, production, marketing, skills, organisation), improve some kinds of firms (e.g. small or high-tech firms)	Subsidies
– Domestic markets	Import penetration	Trade restrictions/anti-dumping	Managed trade
	Link inward investment with domestic supply	Subsidies vs. (informal) local content requirements	Subsidy competition. Foreign firm conformance with local requirements.
	Attract high value added investment	Improve external environment (training, supporting institutions and infrastructure)	Differences between "national systems".
– Foreign markets	International competitiveness	Export information, trade finance/guarantees International investment, JV information, finance	Subsidies. Harmonisation of product and service standards.
Increased importance of R&D, technology in firm strategies	Strengthen leading firms, improve SME capabilities, maintain technology base	Support R&D, technology procurement, improve institutional efficiency (university/government laboratory-industry collaboration), promote technology diffusion.	Subsidies. Differences between "national systems". Foreign access to technology procurement. IPR protection and enforcement.
	Rising R&D cost/international collaboration	Promote R&D collaboration	Competition issues. Equal access to R&D consortia for foreign firms (national treatment).
Regional clustering, "lean" production	Local development, sub-contracting networks	Location incentives, network promotion	Subsidy competition
Increased international sourcing	Participation in supply chains	Improve firm functions	Product "nationality" blurs
SMEs low globalisation	Strengthen small firm base	Improve firm functions, special SME incentives	Subsidies
	Sub-contracting/linkages with large firms	Improve quality, standards, infrastructure, network promotion	Competition issues
Increased international investment	Increase national benefits	Liberalise investment regime, inward investment incentives, outward investment promotion	Subsidy competition between locations
Collaboration agreements more common	Increase national benefits	Promote R&D collaboration, relax competition laws	Competition issues

Source: OECD, DSTI, Industry Division, derived from country responses to questionnaire.

availability of production resources, and differences in growth potential and market development in different countries and regions.

Government policies significantly influence firm strategies by liberalising capital, investment and trade flows, promoting regional integration and promoting competitiveness. Trade policy and the liberalisation of trade and investment are enabling factors which have driven global expansion and increased the integration of production and markets.

All firms are confronted with new opportunities and challenges with increasing globalisation. Competition between firms is heightened, due to more optimal location of production and greater firm efficiencies, particularly in production of intermediate inputs and components, more foreign investment and trade in domestic markets and increased competition in foreign markets. Overall there are more operations of all kinds by foreign firms in all national markets. Competition is based increasingly on a skilled, trained and well-organised workforce, the performance of R&D and the domestic generation of technology to complement inputs of foreign technology. Firms from outside the OECD area are increasingly competing on the basis of the same high-quality inputs, and are closely linked into OECD markets through international investment, contracting and supply networks in high-technology industries, as well as in traditional industries.

To meet these challenges, businesses need to improve their competitive performance by:

- increasing global efficiency, using communications and computing capabilities to co-ordinate development, production and marketing;

- expanding internal R&D and external R&D collaboration and contracting;

- adopting new organisational methods such as "lean production", out-sourcing of production and services, workforce re-organisation and training;

- co-ordinating production with marketing and with R&D and design to more flexibly respond to changes and fluctuations in demand.

The following discussion of policy issues first examines policies and programmes to increase benefits from globalisation, by improving the business environment underlying firm competitiveness. It then discusses trade, international investment and competition policy, areas for international co-operation, and future work. Selected policy implications of globalisation are presented in simplified form in Table 1.22.

A. Competitiveness, technology and industry policies

Greater international integration of markets intensifies competition and places a premium on successful competitive businesses. Increased import competition, and greater international investment in domestic and foreign markets increases the need for firms to raise efficiency within a competitive business environment. Broad facilitating policies can promote technological development and improve firm performance and structural change, and enhance the business services infrastructure and communications and transport infrastructure. At the same time better co-ordination of policies can reduce direct subsidies to firms.

Changing the focus of industry policies. By the end of the 1980s, there had been a broad shift in expenditures on industrial support by OECD governments, away from general investment, short-term crisis aid and subsidies for sectors facing over-capacity and structural problems. Industry support expenditures became more strategic and shifted towards R&D, trade and support for foreign expansion. There was increasing focus on improving the operating conditions for firms and supporting intermediaries which deliver services to them. Furthermore, operational "decentralisation" of government support shifted in some countries to regional policy and small-firm policy, to improve out-reach to potential recipients of government assistance. Despite these promising trends, the major part of funding still went to conventional subsidies rather than to R&D, innovation and small firms. The distribution of government industry policy expenditures in the 1990s is shown in Figure 1.4.

◆ Figure 1.4. **Government support to industry: policy objectives of reported expenditures**
Net cost to government in billion US$

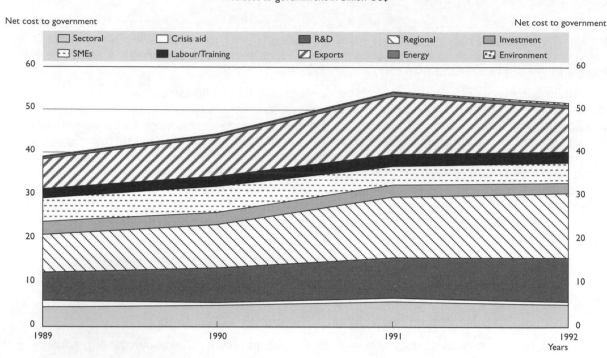

Source: OECD, DSTI, Industrial Support Database, April 1996.

To continue the shift to broad horizontal measures to improve business competitiveness, policies should focus on relatively neutral and non-targeted measures to:

- improve business operations and supply conditions by lowering production costs and prices, including removing market imperfections in the supply of production factors, liberalisation of product and factor markets, and removing barriers to entry of new competitors;

- expand markets by removing technical impediments which segment markets, and improving access to international markets through trade and investment liberalisation, trade and investment information and promotion;

- improve the general environment and infrastructure for business operations by improving quality and coverage of services infrastructure, communications and transport, commercial and technological infrastructure.

Narrowly focused actions to improve firm performance are most efficiently addressed by firms themselves, but some governments have attempted to overcome market failures in the supply of, and demand for, selected business inputs to upgrade R&D and technology, management methods and information, and worker skills. These measures often focus on particular categories of firms (small and medium-sized firms or start-up firms) and on increasing effective use of new technologies (most frequently IT) crucial to improving competitiveness.

Intangible investments in technology, human resources, software and market development are major determinants of firm competitiveness. Despite budget constraints, many countries have been examining investment incentives, to boost aggregate investment, improve the mix of investment between intangible and tangible investments, shift their distribution towards new activities and areas of market failure and underinvestment, and increase the efficiency of incentives.

There may be shortfalls in financing some kinds of investment, particularly in human capital and in complementary intangible assets (firm organisation, technology, markets). In view of the increasing importance of continuous human resource development and investments in intangibles, better financial accounting and reporting conventions are needed so that training is more clearly recognised as an investment, and qualifications acquired in training can be treated as assets, and similar procedures applied to other intangibles. Benefits for firms and investors include more realistic valuation of firm investments and assets, and improved information to facilitate lending and financial flows to enterprises with high intangible investments in human capital, organisation, markets, and technology, and low tangible investments. Accounting and financial reporting conventions and related institutional arrangements require overhaul to reflect the new realities of competition, and government leadership can promote change in this area.

Policy interactions at sector level. The sectoral analysis clearly shows that as firms re-organise their cross-border operations there will be increasing overlap and tensions among policies which originally had clear single targets. For example, policies to promote competitiveness will affect trade, foreign investment and international collaboration, as well as improving firm performance and accelerating structural change which are their primary aim. Furthermore, global expansion varies across sectors. Firms in science-based and scale-intensive industries have developed flexible forms of globalisation by using different channels for different activities: collaboration arrangements for development; direct investment and intra-firm trade to organise production; exports and affiliate sales to enter markets. On the other hand, firms in resource- and labour-intensive industries have a more traditional form of globalisation based on trade in both finished and intermediate products. These distinctions call for more subtle policy management and improved policy co-ordination.

Localisation and building on local resources. Two developments are reinforcing the clustering of firms. There is a general shift, particularly in assembly industries, to increase out-sourcing of supply of goods and services. Suppliers cluster together, close to their purchasers, where they benefit from favourable common externalities (infrastructure, institutions, business environment). Inward investment tends to go to regions where similar firms are already established, reinforcing existing specialisation. Regional clustering of component and parts suppliers is reflected in increasing intra-regional trade in assembly industries; international sourcing is increasing mainly among countries that are in close geographical proximity. Policy may focus on building or strengthening clusters of inter-connected firms but should avoid distorting competition and engaging in competitive subsidisation.

Potential areas of friction. Policies to promote competitiveness must take into account potentially distorting impacts on competition. This is particularly the case where support goes to expand the supply side (subsidising new production capacity for example), reduce firm costs, or encourage greater scale. Supply-side subsidies can have large effects on international competition and lead to perceptions of unfair competition between different "national" systems. These measures may also lead to zero-sum subsidy races between countries and/or sub-national regions to attract or expand investment. On the other hand, competitiveness and competition can both be promoted by encouraging the entry of new competitors, and/or lowering barriers to entry (*e.g.* by addressing financial market failures, or reducing bureaucratic and administrative burdens).

a) R&D and technology

The development and application of new and improved goods and services underlie firm competitiveness. Much government policy has focused on increasing R&D, but recently policy has shifted towards diffusing new technologies to improve competitiveness in traditional industries and small firms. This policy shift has become more necessary as competition pushes firms to adopt best practice in production and services.

Basic research and international collaboration. The following are important areas for attention:

• Maintain and, where necessary, strengthen the research base.

• Promote international co-operation in long-term and generic R&D in the business sector.

Innovation. Government policy has tended to focus on business R&D rather than innovation, but R&D is only a small fraction of the costs and effort of developing and commercialising new goods and services. There may be a need to improve the flow of financial, technological and service resources into innovative firms to overcome market failures in the supply of these resources, and to upgrade the broad infrastructure that provides design and quality support, diffuses new product technologies (*e.g.* new materials), and new production methods (*e.g.* advanced manufacturing technologies) which are intrinsic components of innovation.

Technology diffusion. Diffusion of new technologies may be facilitated by:

- general incentives (*e.g.* improving the flow of finance to small firms) and using public procurement and contracts to upgrade the performance of suppliers and procured products;

- ensuring that there is a strong technological infrastructure of market-driven institutions to diffuse and help the effective applications of new technologies (research associations, technology extension services, industry/university networks);

- promoting investments in the services infrastructure (*e.g.* communications, computing), and liberalisation of service markets to improve the quality of business services and enhance business efficiency.

Foreign firms and domestic R&D. Foreign firms are increasing their contributions to domestic R&D although this is often from a low level. They are important in R&D-intensive sectors, and may be significant performers of R&D in countries with a less developed research base, participating extensively in government-supported R&D projects. Eligibility for government R&D support usually requires that R&D is performed in the financing country, and that results are exploited to the maximum extent in the financing country to ensure domestic spill-overs from supported R&D, and to reduce free-rider behaviour.

Potential areas of friction. There are four areas where international frictions may arise. In all of these areas non-discrimination and greater transparency would improve R&D performance and lower its total cost:

- Subsidisation and/or lack of transparency in government support to "strategic" technologies. R&D support has been extensive in a few R&D-intensive and defence-related industries (aerospace and computers are examples), although the importance of government R&D funding has declined. Support for domestic R&D activities, coupled with institutional differences between different national systems of R&D and innovation can be seen to favour domestic firms in R&D development.

- The orientation of government R&D programmes and R&D procurement towards domestic firms in some science-based industries may pose long-term problems for foreign firms which do not participate. A major step to reduce international frictions is to extend national treatment to more fully embrace R&D and development of new technologies.

- The concentration of technological resources in international firms in a few major countries, coupled with extensive international technology collaboration among these firms, may pose entry barriers to firms which do not participate in collaborative networks.

- Intellectual property protection continues to present problems. There is insufficient protection and enforcement in some countries. The Uruguay Round strengthened the level and enforcement of intellectual property protection, but further multilateral agreement on intellectual property may be warranted to reduce uncertainties and distortions which impair the creation and diffusion of new technologies, particularly in science-based industries.

b) Small and medium-sized enterprises

Small firms are receiving increasing attention in government policy. They play an important role in production and employment, some are highly innovative and a few are extensively globalised. But for the majority of small firms, the challenge of globalisation is to develop new ways of dealing with heightened domestic competition and export competition. In domestic markets, small manufacturing firms must improve their performance along the value chain from design and product and process adaptation through to production, distribution and sales. Similar efficiency is required in service firms exposed to foreign competition (transport, communications and distribution, for example). Where small firms are suppliers to larger firms, they must improve their linkages with these firms for domestic and international supply.

Policies for SME globalisation and competitiveness. Few countries have introduced specific policies for small-firm globalisation. Given that small firms mainly globalise through exports and are facing increased international competition in home markets, policies have in the main focused on improving domestic performance and on trade promotion. Governments at all levels have policies to improve competitiveness, and correct market failures on the supply side (in information, technology, management, other intangible assets, finance, etc.). Support focuses on:

- Modernisation and adoption of international best practice. Programmes include supporting market-led diffusion of technological and related capabilities to improve general performance. In some cases they support group solutions to common problems.

- Improving management performance and adoption of organisational innovations by, *e.g.* improving information flow to small businesses, providing time-limited, market-directed consultancy and strategic advisory services if there are market failures in supply and/or demand for information and advice, and expanding decentralised partly self-financed training services.

- In traditional industries dominated by SMEs, measures may concentrate on industrial modernisation (restructuring, applied research, intangible investments) and targeted programmes for problem areas (*e.g.* lack of skills, poor technology diffusion, financing barriers).

- Developing supply links and achieving high standards in contracts with international firms (quality, flexibility, reliability).

Expansion of trade and foreign operations. General policies have impacts on SMEs and there may be special consideration of SMEs in general policies (*e.g.* trade information/advisory services, export promotion, trade insurance for SMEs, trade expansion guarantees). There are also general measures in some countries to assist foreign operations by domestic firms and enhance foreign production and market development. These measures can have significant impacts on SMEs in overcoming market failures linked with size of operations. They include: improving the market-driven supply of information, consulting, advisory services, and operations assistance; removing imperfections in the supply of outward investment finance (investment risk guarantees, financing guarantees for production joint ventures); improving the supply of venture capital, promoting or removing restrictions on equity participation and other mechanisms in support of international projects.

B. Trade policy

The new realities of international business suggest that trade policy makers must reassess procedures and instrument they use, as well as underlying concepts in order to respond to the new challenges posed by global competition. Through their international networks, global firms move inputs and outputs among geographically dispersed facilities. In the process, the national origin of end-products has become increasingly blurred. Production of and trade in technology- and investment-intensive components and sub-assemblies have become extremely important, raising backward and forward linkages among firms along the production chain. In many cases an "imported" product contains a higher proportion of local content (tangible and intangible) than a competing "domestic" product. For this reason attempts to tilt playing fields in favour of "domestic" firms through discriminatory trade measures, such as antidumping duties, voluntary export restraints, bilateral safeguard actions or preferential treatment, aside from being more complicated to carry out, may well become arbitrary and, sometimes, even harmful to the economic interests of the country imposing the measure.

In addition to the origin of products, the nationality of corporations has also become more difficult to ascertain in the wake of investment and capital market liberalisation. The administration of trade remedy laws and other forms of contingent protection has become more troublesome when petitioners may be affiliates of foreign firms and respondents affiliates of national firms or when there are complex contractual or equity relations linking the litigating firms. The relative economic importance of national versus foreign firms for the host country – the "who is us?" issue – is also much less clear-cut than in the past.

Compounding these difficulties, globalisation also appears to have brought about an erosion of the effectiveness of certain trade policy instruments. Global firms, through their flexible networks, are better equipped to circumvent and to absorb the costs that trade-restricting policies impose upon them. In many instances they may even be able to take advantage of them. Quite often programmes which seek to promote, subsidise or protect domestic businesses have become more difficult to devise and implement because of the web of cross-investment and corporate alliances. In particular, proactive innovation or technology policies aimed at assisting firms to develop new technologies for commercial use may seem particularly attractive in most of the high-technology sectors dominated by global firms. Given the oligopolistic market structures in which global firms often operate, governments have been tempted to adopt "strategic" trade policies aimed at targeting national champions in high-externality industries. Aside from the well-recognised difficulties of implementing these policies, the new reality of the network firms spreading across borders makes it more difficult to lock the external economies inside the interventionist country or to target them towards "domestic" beneficiaries. The above trends have prompted a number of observers to argue that the concept of national economic interest, and its security implications, need to be reassessed in light of the globalisation phenomenon.

Restrictive trade-policy and trade-related measures are not only more difficult to operate and often less effective in an increasingly borderless world economy, but they also have implications for corporate strategies which go well beyond firms' cross-border trade decisions. In a context of considerably heightened capital mobility, trade measures exert increasingly direct impacts on the volume and direction of investment flows. All trade restraints, including tariffs, quotas, non-tariff barriers, gray-area or other regulatory measures, may induce foreign investment to service protected markets, making restrictive objectives of the measures (to promote purely domestic firms for example) more difficult to achieve in a globalised highly interconnected world. In addition, trade measures have at times been designed or used as a surrogate for industrial policy. Local content rules or discriminatory procurement practices, for instance, in addition to favouring domestic producers, may force the setting-up of local production facilities. Export processing zones and export financing may also act as powerful incentives for attracting inward investment. Finally, regional trade and investment liberalisation through integration agreements have had a strong influence on global corporate strategies, both inducing foreign investment and facilitating it.

In a global market-place, international trade and investment in goods and services are linked in a complex but clearly complementary fashion. Local presence is an increasingly necessary ingredient to service a market effectively so that any trade policy concerned only with the cross-border dimension of trade may prove largely incomplete. Moreover, in sectors characterised by oligopolistic competition, access for both goods and services to the main world markets is essential to realise the necessary economies of scale, scope and learning. Conversely, the possibility for a firm to enjoy a sanctuary at home thanks, *inter alia*, to protectionist trade policy measures may confer substantial advantages to support an aggressive, if not predatory, global strategy. The fundamental importance of services as inputs in production processes makes the possibility of accessing international service networks a prime factor in firms' global competitiveness. This issue, combined with the increasing mobility of service providers, has become of great significance for trade policy. Similarly, growing trade in both technology and know-how as inputs and in technology-intensive products has heightened the importance of access to technology and protection of intellectual property, turning them into trade policy issues.

Various domestic policies, including in the areas of investment, competition, environment, taxation and labour, also have an important impact on the effectiveness of firms' market access and presence, and hence their overall performance. What appears increasingly clear is that globalisation renders it more difficult to pursue domestic policies in isolation, given the impact they have on corporate strategies and the spill-over effects they produce on trade and investment flows. In particular, all competition tends to become international competition as factors of production become more mobile.

Although globalisation is challenging many traditional trade-policy concepts, it still reinforces the general policy prescriptions of trade liberalisation and non-discriminatory trade and investment regimes. Restrictive policy stances shelter uncompetitive domestic firms from an inevitable confrontation with global competitors and delay necessary structural adjustments. In order to become successful global competitors, firms need to benchmark themselves against the best of their international rivals. Moreover, the complexities of global production networks make it much more difficult for any individual country to take advantage of protectionist policies. It is instead fundamental that trade policy, together with investment and other domestic policies, contribute to ensuring open, contestable and more competitive national markets which represent the best environment for global firms. Globalisation thus unequivocally strengthens the role of trade and investment liberalisation as competitiveness tools. But it also underscores the costly and ineffective character of discriminatory policies at a time when "domestic" firms and products are more difficult to recognise and interlinkages and policy leakages are the order of the day.

Trade policy makers have not remained insensitive to the needs of global firms. A great deal of the trade and investment liberalisation which has recently taken place at the national, regional and multilateral levels has been carried out in response to such needs. Such a trend was particularly evident in the inclusion of new issues – services, investment and intellectual property protection – in the Uruguay Round, and the generally more detailed treatment afforded these issues in the EU's Single Market programme and in the NAFTA. As is often the case, national and international policy- and rule-making lag behind the realities of business, so that much remains to be done to further the liberalisation frontier in these areas, particularly at the multilateral level.

By exposing the interlinkages and the interdependence between different policy domains, both within and across markets, globalisation also challenges policy makers to take a more integrated approach in trying to adapt existing rules and devising appropriate new ones to better respond to the environment of global competition. The evolution in the way of doing business internationally and the ensuing changes in the world economy require new approaches. These could address in a coherent way not only traditional trade issues, in light of the new realities, but also other domestic and structural policy issues which have become relevant, as well as the practices and behaviour of firms which clearly have a crucial impact in the unfolding of global competition as traditional barriers to trade continue to fall.

C. International direct investment

An increasingly liberal approach. OECD countries have adopted an increasingly liberal approach towards outward and inward investment. In many cases there are now few or no special approval procedures. Foreign-firm investment is treated in the same way as that of domestic firms, with equal access to general incentives (*e.g.* R&D, regional support). However, general and/or sector-specific restrictions remain in a number of countries (*e.g.* broadcasting, news media, communications, transport, and in public procurement). There is the continuing risk also of new measures designed to limit foreign penetration, especially in high-technology activities. In some countries there have been calls to use reciprocity measures to deny access to foreign investors from countries without equally open markets.

Investment quality. There are continuing issues concerning the quality of investment, ensuring that it contributes effectively to the local economy while remaining an efficient part of global strategies of investing firms. This means that the local business infrastructure and environment (human resources, institutions, supply and service firms) must be conducive to inward investment, and provide local advantages for international firms. On the other hand, firms face increasing pressures to decentralise and disperse their core activities and high-value-added, knowledge-intensive activities to host countries, and build more substantial links with local economies. Although the objectives of maximising local benefits while maintaining firm competitive advantages are not necessarily in opposition, they may diverge, particularly when location-specific specialisation is an important part of firm strategies.

Active inward location policies are more important for many countries, regions and localities, to capture high-value-added, high-technology investment in internationally competitive industries. These policies now focus on the contribution of international investment to production structures, research and innovation, jobs and job quality, local suppliers and the business infrastructure. A growing aim is to increase linkages between local and international firms, maximise local content, and assist in the diffusion of new technology and management practices. A wide range of measures are used to attract investment including: tax incentives (accelerated depreciation, extended loss carry-over, tax exemptions), loan guarantees, low interest loans, preferential treatment for some categories of business costs, training programmes and provision of business support services. There are extensive inward investment information services. These measures may be costly, and result in competition between countries and sub-national regions to subsidise investment.

International disciplines for incentives. There is extensive competition (investment subsidies and special treatment) to attract investment. This can increase public cost of investment, through direct subsidies, and reduce the net benefits to the local economy through relaxation of requirements for local inputs to be used by investing firms. Stronger international discipline could help reduce the costs of international competition to attract investment and increase the benefits from this investment.

D. Competition policy

The impacts of international competition. The main objective of competition policy is to preserve or protect competitive markets, whether these are local, domestic or international in nature. While competition laws do not specifically address the issue of globalisation, competition policy increasingly recognises the global nature of competition, and the actual or potential impacts of import penetration and foreign competition on markets. In industries in which there are economies of scale and scope in R&D, production or marketing, collaboration, restructuring and mergers between potential competitors, may develop more efficient and competitive firms and industries in an increasingly international context. Competition policy may thus be a dynamic instrument to promote competitiveness, by allowing R&D collaboration and the achievement of economies of scale in operations. On the other hand, competition rules must be enforced vigilantly against anti-competitive agreements and behaviour which distort resource allocation and reduce consumer welfare.

No discrimination between national and foreign firms. There is no competition legislation specifically aimed at globalisation nor is there discrimination in competition law between national and foreign firms. However there are many areas of interaction between competition law and international operations of firms. Greater transparency in application of competition law could aid international expansion in some cases, by easing entry into regulated foreign markets. Similarly, there is potential conflict between the aims and application of some government subsidies and promotion of market competition. The less rigorous application of competition law can allow firms in some countries to develop or maintain anti-competitive behaviour to the detriment of firms and consumers in other countries. Adoption and application of more similar competition rules and wider co-operation in enforcement could be a useful advance.

Technological and other advantages may give rise to single-firm market dominance. While deregulation, trade liberalisation and further technology-based competition are likely to lead to the weakening or erosion of these positions, competition policy needs to be alert to potential abuses by dominant firms and to include an adequate merger policy to prevent their creation. Most countries already address these issues in their competition laws.

E. Work of the OECD

There is a general need to examine the role of OECD in dealing with the issues raised by the globalisation of industry. The question is whether these issues can be handled through existing guidelines and recommendations (for example, the *1988 OECD Recommendation of the Council Concerning a General Framework of Principles for International Co-operation in Science and Technology,* the *OECD Declaration and Decisions on International Investment and Multinational Enterprises, Code of Liberalisation of Capital Movements, Code of Liberalisation of Current Invisible Operations, 1986 Revised Council Recommendation on Co-operation between Member Countries on Restrictive Business Practices Affecting International Trade),* and the extent to which they will be covered in additional new approaches, for example the work on the OECD Multilateral Agreement on Investment (MAI) (OECD, 1996*b*), particularly where they cross disciplinary boundaries.

The preceding analysis suggests areas where the need for international co-operation and co-ordination is growing, where there may be continuing or potentially new frictions among countries, and where the OECD could begin or continue pursuing further work. They include:

- Competitiveness policy, to reduce potentially distorting effects of measures targeting domestic firms, particularly if they lead to instances or perceptions of unfair competition between different "national" systems. OECD work on subsidies is a step towards improving transparency.

- International co-operation in S&T and R&D. Promotion of ways of extending bilateral and multi-lateral S&T and R&D collaboration in areas of fundamental science where costs are outstripping national financing capabilities.

- Research and development policy, to ensure non-discriminatory participation in government-funded R&D, reduce subsidisation and improve transparency in government support to "strategic" technologies and industries.

- Intellectual property policy, to encourage better protection, and increase the creation and diffusion of new technologies and services.

- Small business policy, to improve the access of small and medium-sized firms to international technology collaboration networks and other areas of international operations where there may be barriers to entry. OECD is carrying out extensive work on SME-related issues.

- Trade policy, to consider how the operations of globalised firms and the complexity of current trade and production networks have affected the relevance of current rules, and to widen and deepen liberalisation on all fronts. In this context, work on the trade issues of the 1990s is being pursued, which includes investigating the inter-relationships between trade, investment and competition policies and developing an integrated approach to achieving globally contested markets.

- International investment policy, to ensure non-discriminatory treatment of foreign investors, and reduce the cost and distortions implicit in competition to attract investment. Stronger international disciplines, including through development of the OECD Multilateral Investment Agreement, will help improve non-discrimination and reduce these costs.

- Competition policy, to consider ways of further integrating competition considerations in public policies, while exploring the feasibility and desirability of an integrated international framework for global competition.

- Employment policy, to deepen study of the relations between globalisation and employment, particularly regarding restructuring of firms and shifts in their location and associated impacts on employment and human resources.

BIBLIOGRAPHY

COMMISSION OF THE EUROPEAN COMMUNITY (1993), *International Economic Interdependence*, Discussion Paper, May.

CONGRESS OF THE UNITED STATES, Office of Technology Assessment (1994), *Multinationals and the US Technology Base*, Washington, DC.

DAVIES, W. and B. LYONS. (1991), "Characterising Relative Performance: The Productivity Advantage of Foreign-owned Firms in the UK", *Oxford Economic Papers*, Vol. 43.

DE VET, J. (1993), "Globalisation and Local and Regional Competitiveness", *STI Review*, No. 13, OECD, Paris.

DUNNING, J.H. (1993), *Multinational Enterprises and the Global Economy*, Addison-Wesley, Wokingham, England.

FEKETEKUTY, G. (1992), *The New Trade Agenda*, Occasional Paper No. 40, Group of Thirty, Washington, DC.

FISHLOW, A. and S. HAGGARD (1992), *The United States and the Regionalisation of the World Economy*, Research Programme on Globalisation and Regionalisation, Development Centre Document for Sale, OECD, Paris.

FREEMAN, C. (1993), *Technical Change and Unemployment: The Links between Macroeconomic Policy and Innovation Policy*, paper presented at the Conference on Technology, Innovation and Employment, Helsinki, Finland, 5-8 October.

GENERAL STATISTICS OFFICE OF IRELAND (1991), *Census of Industrial Production*, Dublin.

HAGEDOORN, J. (1995), "The Economics of Co-operation among High-tech Firms – Trends and Patterns in Strategic Technology Partnering since the Early Seventies", mimeo.

HAGEDOORN, J. and J. SCHAKENRAAD (1991), *The Role of Inter-firm Cooperation Agreements in the Globalisation of the Economy and Technology*, FAST Dossier, November, and various other papers by these authors.

JUNGNICKEL, R. (1993), *Globalization and the International Division of Labour – The Role of Technology and Wage Costs*, paper prepared for International Institute of Labour Studies, September.

KUMAR, N. (1995), "Intellectual Property Protection, Market Orientation and Location of Overseas R&D Activities by Multinational Enterprises", UNU/INTECH Discussion Papers, March.

LAWRENCE, R. (1991), *Scenarios for the World Trading System and their Implications for Developing Countries*, Research Programme on Globalisation and Regionalisation, Development Centre Technical Paper No. 47, OECD, Paris.

LEUENBERGER, T. and M.E. WEINSTEIN (1992), *Europe, Japan and America in the 1990s*, Springer-Verlag.

LLOYD, P.J. (1992), "Regionalisation and World Trade", *OECD Economic Studies*, No. 18, Spring.

OECD (1992*a*), *Technology and the Economy: The Key Relationships*, Paris.

OECD (1992*b*), *Globalisation of Industrial Activities. Four Case Studies. Auto Parts, Chemicals, Construction, and Semiconductors*, Paris.

OECD (1992*c*), "Globalisation, Corporate Citizenship, and Industrial Policy", OCDE/GD(92)171, Paris.

OECD (1992*d*), "Globalisation – Developments and Policy Issues", in *Industrial Policy in OECD Countries. 1992: Annual Review*, Paris

OECD (1992*e*), *International Direct Investment – Policies and Trends in the 1980s*, Paris.

OECD (1993, 1995), *International Direct Investment Statistics Yearbook*, 1993 and 1995 editions, Paris.

OECD (1993*a*), *Industrial Policy in OECD Countries. 1993: Annual Review*, Paris.

OECD (1993*b*), *Intra Firm Trade*, Trade Policy Issues Series No. 1, Paris.

OECD (1993*c*), *Obstacles to Trade and Competition*, Paris.

OECD (1993*d*), "Recent Developments in Foreign Direct Investment: A Sectoral Analysis", *Financial Market Trends, 54*, Paris.

OECD (1993*e*), "Direct Investment Flows in 1992: Overall Decline Continues", *Financial Market Trends, 55*, Paris.

OECD (1994, 1995), *Main Developments in Trade. Annual Report: 1993*, and *1994*, Paris.

OECD (1994a), "Globalisation of Industrial Activities. Joint Report by the Industry Committee and the Trade Committee", OCDE/GD(94)60, Paris.

OECD (1994b), *The Performance of Foreign Affiliates in OECD Countries*, Paris.

OECD (1994c), "Symposium on the Globalisation of Industry: Government and Corporate Issues", in *Industrial Policy in OECD Countries. 1994: Annual Review*, Paris.

OECD (1994d), *Trade and Competition Policies: Comparing Objectives and Methods*, Paris.

OECD (1994e), *Trade and Investment: Transplants*, Paris

OECD (1995a), *Industry and Technology: Scoreboard of Indicators 1995*, Paris.

OECD (1995b), "Recent Trends in Foreign Direct Investment", *Financial Market Trends*, 61, Paris.

OECD (1995c), *Linkages – OECD and Major Developing Economies*, Paris.

OECD (1996a), *SMEs and the Impact of Globalisation*, Paris (forthcoming).

OECD (1996b), *Towards Multilateral Investment Rules*, OECD Documents, Paris.

OMAN, C. (1994), *Globalisation and Regionalisation: The Challenge for Developing Countries*, Development Centre Studies, OECD, Paris.

PAPACONSTANTINOU, G. (1993), "Globalisation, Technology and Employment: Characteristics and Trends", *STI Review*, No. 15, Paris.

PORTER, M. (1990), *The Competitive Advantage of Nations*, MacMillan, London.

SHARP, M. and K. PAVITT (1993), "Technology Policy in the 1990s: Old Trends and New Realities", *Journal of Common Market Studies*, Vol. 31, No. 1, June.

STORPER, M. and A.J. SCOTT (1993), *The Wealth of Regions: Market Forces and Policy Imperatives in Local and Global Context*, Lewis Centre for Regional Policy Studies, UCLA, Working Paper No. 7.

THOMSEN, S. and S. WOOLCOCK (1993), *Direct Investment and European Integration: Competition among Firms and Governments*, Royal Institute of International Affairs, London.

TYSON, L.D. (1992), *Who's Bashing Whom? Trade Conflict in High-Technology Industries*, Institute for International Economics, Washington, DC.

UNITED NATIONS (1993), *World Investment Report, Transnational Corporations and Integrated International Production*, New York.

UNITED NATIONS (1994), *World Investment Report, Transnational Corporations, Employment and the Workplace*, New York.

US DEPARTMENT OF COMMERCE (1993a), *Foreign Direct Investment in the United States: An Update*, Economics and Statistics Administration, Washington, DC.

US DEPARTMENT OF COMMERCE (1993b), *Recent Trends in International Direct Investment*, report prepared by J. Rutter, Washington, DC.

WELLS, L.T., Jr. (1992), *Conflict or Indifference: US Multinationals in a World of Regional Trading Blocs*, Research Programme on Globalisation and Regionalisation, Development Centre Technical Paper No. 57, Paris.

WOMACK, J.P., D.T. JONES and D. ROOS (1990), *The Machine that Changed the World*, Rawson, New York.

WYCKOFF, A. (1993), "Extension of Networks of Production Across Borders", *STI Review*, No. 13, Paris.

Part II

SECTORAL REPORTS

Chapter 2

GLOBALISATION IN THE PHARMACEUTICAL INDUSTRY

by

Claudio Casadio Tarabusi and Graham Vickery,
Directorate for Science, Technology and Industry, OECD

Table of contents

LIST OF TABLES

LIST OF FIGURES

SUMMARY AND CONCLUSIONS

Globalisation in the pharmaceutical industry is seen in the broad geographical distribution of final production and marketing, high levels of foreign penetration of national markets and intra-firm trade. However, international trade including the sourcing of intermediate inputs is appreciably lower than in many other industries. The extent of globalisation has increased considerably as a result of cross-border acquisitions and mergers and collaborative alliances in R&D and marketing. Pharmaceutical products are essentially "universal" in their composition and use, but markets are highly segmented because of national health and price regulations and the incidence of particular diseases and traditions of medical practice which leads to decentralised final production, certification and marketing functions. There is a distinctive multi-country form of globalisation characterised by extensive production, finishing, packaging and marketing in countries of final sale, but with R&D still largely centralised in the home country.

The large European and US research-based firms which lead the industry and operate in all major world markets sharply increased their foreign investment activities in the late 1980s and mid-1990s. A large share of this investment in the United States and Europe has been mergers and acquisitions. Between 20 and 60 per cent of sales in major OECD countries come from foreign-controlled firms, and the share is even higher in some smaller OECD countries and developing countries. Sales of foreign-controlled firms in major markets are now two to five times greater than imports. In Japan compared with other industries, the level of foreign investment is exceptionally high (20 per cent of sales comes from foreign-controlled firms), whereas Japanese firms have small shares of other OECD markets.

Pharmaceuticals R&D still remains highly centralised in the home country, but growing cross-border consolidation and collaboration (mergers, acquisitions, joint ventures, strategic alliances) are helping firms to share risks and costs in product development, joining large firms with small biotechnology firms, and expanding markets to recoup R&D costs. New international collaboration agreements, directed mainly to product development and marketing, increased in the late 1980s at the same time as foreign investment. The United States is the overwhelming focus of international agreements between large pharmaceutical and small biotechnology firms.

International trade is not as important as in many other industries, reflecting the multi-country pattern of globalisation, high penetration of foreign firms, and the necessity to produce finished products in final markets. Intermediates make up a fairly high share of pharmaceutical trade (40 per cent), as international firms ship active ingredients for formulation in final markets, but overall the ratio of imported to domestic sourcing is still lower than for many other industries, reflecting strategies and requirements to produce locally. Detailed data for US trade in pharmaceuticals between affiliates and parent firms (intra-firm trade) shows that US trade between affiliates and parents in pharmaceuticals is considerably higher than the average of this trade for all manufacturing industries, as firms have adopted strategies to internalise their global operations as much as possible. The share of intra-firm trade does not seem to have increased.

World production and trade are concentrated geographically in OECD countries. In 1993-94, the five largest countries accounted for over 65 per cent of world markets, close to 60 per cent of exports and 40 per cent of imports. Developing countries took a declining share of around one-fifth of imports and smaller shares of production and, particularly, exports. In contrast, the industry is not highly concentrated at firm level. In 1995, only the three largest firms had more than 4 per cent of the world market; none had 20 per cent of any major national market. However, the leading positions of the largest firms are clearly established. The top ten firms in 1995 were all in the top 20 fifteen years earlier, global concentration has climbed recently and the 20 largest firms now take one-half of world sales.

Regulations specific to the pharmaceutical industry are the most important policy area affecting the industry and acting as barriers to trade. For health and safety reasons national administrations control admission of new drugs to domestic markets through complex regulations relating to standards, certification, packaging and labelling. However considerable progress has been made on international harmonization of regulations and standards to ease and simplify certification and acceptance which may help foster efficiency in drug discovery and development.

Industry policy and research policy play primarily a promotional role in the industry. This ranges from substantial government funding of general institutional biomedical research and development of therapeutics, to promotion of consortia for biotechnology R&D, and incentives to assist "start-ups" of new firms. For foreign investment, the industry is subject to the general regulatory framework of OECD countries with few if any impediments specific to pharmaceuticals. In some countries there have been specific inward-investment promotion programmes for foreign firms to establish or expand operations.

Patent protection plays a key role in the industry, and much attention has been paid to optimising the balance between providing adequate protection for new products and encouraging their widespread use. Competition policy has focused on the impacts of patents and licenses, attempting to provide incentives for inventors while ensuring reasonable prices for consumers. An area of change in competition policy has been in the growing acceptance of inter-firm collaboration in R&D and gradual expansion of these agreements to allow joint exploitation of results.

Three current trends are having major impacts on the industry. First, government cost-containment programmes in health care have become increasingly important with greater attention focused on generic products, monopoly-pricing, and price formation. Cost containment has encouraged firms to set up international joint ventures to share R&D and marketing costs, and to enter generic and over-the-counter markets through acquisitions and alliances.

Second, with the rising costs of developing new products, R&D will become more internationalised as firms draw on external resources in several countries (e.g. in biotechnology and the research infrastructure) to strengthen their product portfolios.

Finally, growing liberalisation and improving prospects for foreign investment in East Asia and Latin America is expected to significantly enlarge the market for pharmaceuticals. This could expand the scope of globalisation in the industry and reduce its present concentration in the OECD area.

I. INTRODUCTION: CHARACTERISTICS OF THE INDUSTRY

Pharmaceuticals can conveniently be divided into three categories, although there are further sub-categories which could be adopted (OECD, 1985):

- in-patent drugs;
- out-of-patent drugs, generic or multi-source drugs;
- over-the-counter (OTC) or proprietary drugs.

In-patent drugs, only sold on prescription, are the most important category and are responsible for the rapid growth of the pharmaceutical industry. Profit margins are high, but so are expenditures on R&D and marketing. These drugs are the basis for activities in the generic sector. Generic or multi-source drugs are out-of-patent products sold on prescription under their original patented brand name, other brand names or generic names. Price competition is often fierce and profit margins low. Over-the-counter drugs may be sold directly to consumers without prescription. OTC drugs generally have high advertising and low research expenditures, and competition turns on marketing established brands.

The first two categories are "ethical drugs". They are chosen by doctors, and mostly paid for by governments or by patients indirectly through health insurance. However, it is not always possible to separate generic and OTC drugs, due to differences in national regulations and to the considerable share of OTC drugs prescribed by doctors and, because of increasing competition and reduced profit margins in the industry, there are some trends towards selling in-patent drugs over-the-counter to attain higher sales volumes.

The share of each category in the world market is difficult to estimate as little consistent data is available. In the 1985-87 period the breakdown by value was approximately (Secretariat estimates for the six largest OECD markets):

- in-patent: 70 per cent of the total market;
- generics: 14 per cent;
- OTC drugs: 16 per cent.

European data for 1992 show a similar breakdown between prescription and OTC pharmaceuticals (Panorama of EU Industry 94). There are however large differences among countries in market share of each category. Generics made up about 20 per cent of the total market in the United States, about 17 per cent in Japan, and 6 per cent in Europe, and in Canada in-patent drugs are only around 40 per cent of the market due to government policy to encourage use of alternatives. Generics are generally less important in developing countries due to a combination of consumer behaviour and little marketing of generics in relatively small markets. OTC drugs also show large differences among countries in market share, with large shares in developing countries.

The main focus of this study is on ethical therapeutic drugs. These are by far the most important in terms of R&D, production, marketing and sales.

The pharmaceutical industry is based on global products sold into nationally segmented markets differentiated by health and safety regulations. Three inter-linked forces are driving rapid growth of the industry:

- *Widening the market* for health-care products, with better coverage of poorer people in OECD countries, and expanding markets in some non-OECD countries, particularly in dynamic economies of East and South-East Asia and in some Latin American countries. Potential markets in developing countries are large.

- *New products:* Ageing populations are expanding demand for new products to combat degenerative diseases (arthritis, cardiovascular, cancer, Alzheimer's disease, etc.). New viruses (AIDS) require new therapies, and the causes and cures of genetic diseases need greater attention.

- *Rapid technological progress* in the science base, particularly biotechnology, has spurred development of new generations of more specific drugs for the treatment of what were intractable illnesses.

The production of drugs is in two basic stages, the preparation of physiologically active ingredients, and conversion into final marketed products. Active ingredients may be extracted from animal or vegetable sources, prepared by fermentation, or chemically synthesised. Production runs are usually small, requiring manufacturing flexibility. Active ingredients are then converted into final form and packed for distribution.

Decentralisation of later processes is common. Volumes are small and transport costs of active ingredients are low. There are few technical barriers to decentralisation, and capital costs are relatively low, even though there are economies of scale in mixing, packaging and presentation. Multi-country forms of organisation are fostered by government regulation and supervision of new products to meet health and safety requirements, and by competition between large firms to build customer preferences. However, intensification of competition and slower growth and cost containment in health budgets is fostering cross-country rationalisation of production of both new and older products.

Data for ten major pharmaceutical firms show the importance of foreign markets and the extent of decentralisation. Foreign sales compared with total sales are high, and have tended to increase over time. (Table 2.1. Foreign sales were generally higher in 1993 than in 1990 for those enterprises which provide a breakdown). European firms have the highest share of foreign sales. American companies concentrate more on the domestic market, given its larger relative size. Japanese firms and Korean firms tend to focus to an even greater extent on their domestic market, due to particular features of their own markets, and fewer major new drugs in their product ranges.

Table 2.1. **Foreign sales as a percentage of total sales[1]**

	Rank	Home country	1981	1990
Ciba-Geigy[2]	7	Switzerland	97.9	98.2
Sandoz[2]	9	Switzerland	95.0	95.9
Glaxo[4]	2	United Kingdom	76.2	88.2
Bayer[2]	4	Germany	76.2	79.1
Hoechst[2]	5	Germany	72.4	79.0
Merck[2]	1	United States	48.7	46.8
Eastman Kodak (Sterling)[2]	6	United States	n.a.	44.0
SmithKline Beecham[2]	8	United Kingdom-United States	n.a.	43.8
American Home Products[2]	10	United States	33.6	30.9
Bristol-Myers Squibb[2]	3	United States	n.a.	29.5

1. The ten largest companies are listed, with 1-10 giving pharmaceuticals sales rankings in 1989/90.
2. Sales data refer to total company activities including pharmaceuticals.
3. Pharmaceutical activities only.
4. Pharmaceuticals and other activities.
Source: Based on SCRIP.

◆ Figure 2.1. **Pharmaceuticals**
Evolution of company cost structure, 1973-89

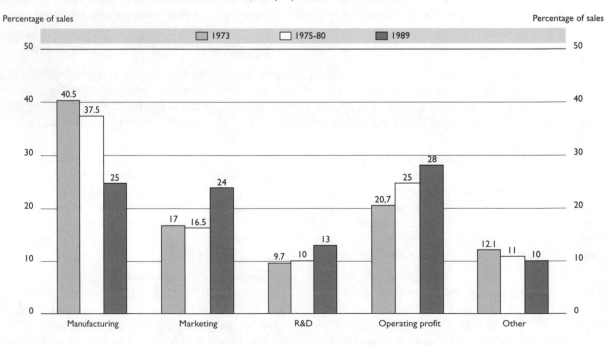

Note: Figures are based on data for research-based firms only.
Source: UNIDO estimates.

The multi-country structure of the industry has led to high levels of marketing costs as a share of total sales. They are approximately 25 per cent of sales revenues for a sample of research-based companies, larger than R&D expenses (Figure 2.1). Because of the way that ethical pharmaceuticals are chosen by doctors, large sales forces have been built up to quickly exploit new products during their patent lives. Patents generally expire about ten years after a new product is commercialised, and average effective patent lifetimes have become shorter thus encouraging larger marketing efforts. In generic and OTC markets advertising and mass promotion are major expenditures.

There is however a large degree of centralisation in the country of origin of essential functions of research-based companies. R&D is a "headquarters function", and is highly centralised, despite the wave of foreign acquisitions and collaboration agreements to develop new products. A large proportion of staff are also drawn from the home country.

2. TRENDS IN GROWTH AND STRUCTURE

A. Production and consumption [1]

Estimates of total market size of the pharmaceuticals industry depend on whether only ethical drugs are covered or OTC products are also included. In 1992 the world market for ethical pharmaceutical products was estimated to be US$188 billion (adapted from SCRIP[2]), and around US$225 billion in 1995 (Secretariat estimates), with rapid growth in 1995 despite government attempts to contain health-care costs.

Over 70 per cent of world production and consumption of pharmaceuticals is in OECD countries, with OECD countries producing more than they consume (Table 2.2). In 1993, world market shares of ethical pharmaceuticals were around 28 per cent in the United States, 30 per cent in Europe (Germany, France, Italy, the United Kingdom and Spain having the largest European markets), 17 per cent in Japan (estimated from SCRIP). These broad market-share rankings were maintained through the 1980s and 1990s (see Figure 2.2). The largest pharmaceutical firms are based in the United States (6 of the top 15 in the 1995 with some re-ranking taking place, see below) and Europe (6 of the top 15), or are European/US (3 firms), reflecting national and regional market size and relative strengths of research-based firms.

The industry has enjoyed considerably higher growth rates than manufacturing as a whole. From 1970 to 1992 the pharmaceutical industry increased its share of total manufacturing value added from around 1.5 per cent to almost 3 per cent (15 major OECD producing countries, not including Switzerland, see Figure 2.3). In general the pharmaceutical industry shows counter-cyclical growth. It grew steadily and increased its share of manufacturing value added during the general cyclical downturns in both the early 1980s and the early 1990s, and this was despite cost containment and downward pressure on prices in the 1990s. Value-added growth has been consistently greater than for manufacturing as a whole in all OECD countries except Portugal and Mexico. The industry was relatively most important in terms of its share of manufacturing value added in the United States, the United Kingdom, Sweden, Spain and Denmark.

Table 2.2. **World distribution of production and consumption – Pharmaceuticals**[1]

	Production		Consumption	
	1975	1990	1975	1990
OECD countries	67.2	72.9	65.2	71.6
Eastern European countries and USSR	10.2	8.6	10.6	9.3
Developing countries	22.1	18.0	23.4	18.4
Others	0.5	0.5	0.8	0.7
World	100.0	100.0	100.0	100.0

1. Derived from data on gross output at constant 1980 prices.
Source: Ballance *et al.* (1992).

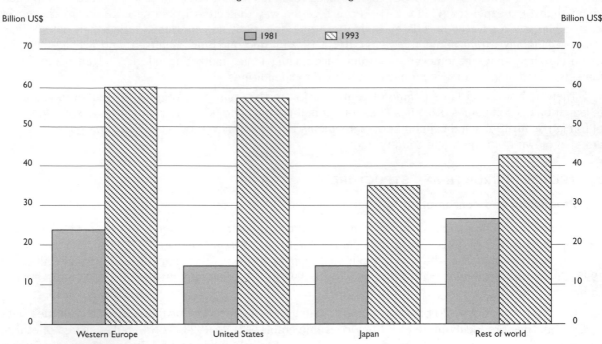

◆ Figure 2.2. **Pharmaceuticals**
Regional markets and their growth

Source: OECD estimations from SCRIP data.

A few OECD countries produce considerably more pharmaceuticals than they consume. European countries are consistent surplus producers. They comprise the large European producers – Germany, France and the United Kingdom – and smaller European countries with strong pharmaceuticals operations, notably Switzerland, Denmark, Sweden and the Netherlands. The United States and Japan are approximately self-sufficient, but because of the relative size of their production and markets, the United States is a consistently large net exporter whereas Japan is a large net importer. Most other OECD countries are net consumers, producing less than they consume (see Table 2.3 and Section 3).

B. Employment

Employment in pharmaceuticals has grown steadily (Figure 2.4). Total pharmaceuticals manufacturing employment in OECD countries in 1991 was 940 000 (Secretariat estimate derived from Figure 2.4). The share of pharmaceuticals in manufacturing employment increased from less than 1 per cent in the mid-1970s to 1.2 per cent in 1992. This share further increased in the mid-1990s as pharmaceuticals employment grew slowly or declined less than manufacturing employment. France and Italy had above-average employment shares, and in Denmark and the United Kingdom the share grew over the period, reaching around 1.5 per cent of manufacturing employment.

Growth in pharmaceuticals employment contrasts with declines in manufacturing employment in OECD countries. Pharmaceuticals employment grew from 1977 to 1991 on average by over 1.2 per cent annually. Fastest employment growth was in the Nordic countries and Austria (3.3 per cent, unweighted average), Canada (2.7 per cent), and the United Kingdom (1.5 per cent). Growing employment in pharmaceuticals was reported in all OECD countries where data is available.

C. Research and development

Research expenditures go to basic exploratory research followed by extensive development testing. There is a great deal of emulation of successful drugs by rival companies. After discovery, development

◆ Figure 2.3. **Value-added shares – Pharmaceuticals**
Share of pharmaceuticals in total manufacturing value added

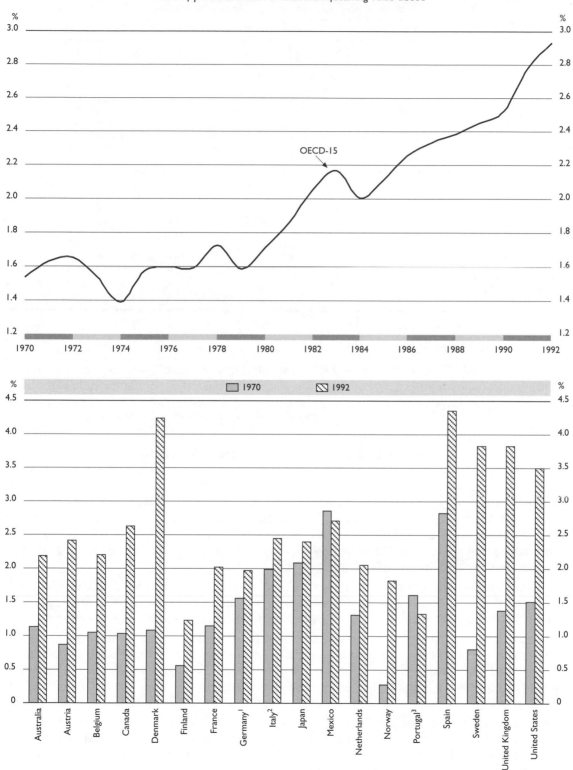

1. 1975-92;   2. 1970-87;   3. 1971-89.
Source: OECD, DSTI, STAN Database.

77

Table 2.3. **Indicators for production and consumption – Pharmaceuticals**

	Production/Consumption				Imports/Consumption				Exports/Production			
	1970	1980	1990	1993	1970	1980	1990	1993	1970	1980	1990	1993
Australia	0.82	0.90	0.75	0.74	0.26	0.18	0.34	0.40	0.11	0.09	0.11	0.19
Austria	0.72	0.81	0.89	0.88	0.38	0.46	0.45	0.53	0.14	0.34	0.36	0.43
Canada	0.93	0.86	0.85	0.78	0.17	0.21	0.20	0.30	0.08	0.08	0.06	0.09
Denmark	1.45	1.31	1.94	1.74	0.92	0.56	0.62	0.59	0.94	0.66	0.80	0.76
Finland	0.46	0.73	0.68	0.57	0.57	0.45	0.48	0.61	0.07	0.24	0.24	0.31
France	1.06	1.13	1.07	1.15	0.11	0.12	0.19	0.23	0.16	0.22	0.24	0.28
Germany	1.16	1.12	1.15	1.18	0.09	0.16	0.20	0.26	0.22	0.25	0.29	0.37
Italy	1.01	1.01	0.91	1.01	0.08	0.15	0.17	0.25	0.09	0.17	0.10	0.20
Japan	0.96	0.95	0.96	0.97	0.06	0.07	0.06	0.06	0.02	0.02	0.02	0.02
Netherlands	1.13	1.07	1.00	1.05	0.44	0.47	0.56	0.70	0.50	0.51	0.56	0.60
New Zealand	0.31	0.56	0.43	0.38	0.73	0.50	0.66	0.70	0.13	0.11	0.21	0.25
Norway	0.47	0.52	0.63	0.64	0.65	0.57	0.48	0.48	0.26	0.18	0.18	0.19
Portugal	0.71	0.65	0.70	0.61	0.45	0.45	0.43	0.47	0.23	0.17	0.18	0.14
Spain	0.92	0.98	0.96	0.92	0.09	0.09	0.14	0.19	0.02	0.07	0.10	0.12
Sweden	0.80	1.01	1.41	1.93	0.42	0.48	0.51	0.50	0.28	0.49	0.65	0.66
Switzerland [1,2]	2.38	..	2.77	..	0.36	..	0.51	..	0.73	..	0.82	..
United Kingdom	1.23	1.23	1.19	1.18	0.08	0.11	0.19	0.25	0.25	0.28	0.31	0.36
United States	1.05	1.06	1.03	1.02	0.01	0.05	0.05	0.06	0.06	0.10	0.07	0.08

1. 1975 instead of 1970.
2. 1989 instead of 1990.
Source: OECD STAN database (DSTI/EAS Division) and Ballance, R. *et al.* (1992).

involves synthesis and establishment of biological effects. This is followed by testing in animals (pre-clinical) and human beings (clinical), generally under supervision of regulatory authorities to determine activity and detect adverse effects. This process is lengthy, costly and uncertain. Only a handful of genuinely new drugs (new chemical entities) are commercialised each year, and their numbers have been declining.

The industry is R&D-intensive. Business enterprise R&D expenditures doubled from 7 to 12 per cent of production in the period 1973-92 (Secretariat calculations, average for 12 OECD countries). R&D-intensity increased consistently over the period (Figure 2.5). Pharmaceuticals is always one of the top-4 most R&D-intensive industries. It is currently ranked second, behind aerospace and ahead of computers and electronics (Secretariat calculations, all OECD countries combined). R&D expenditures are very high in the United Kingdom and the Nordic countries (Sweden, Denmark, Finland, Norway), averaging close to or over 15 per cent of production. The United States was around 12 per cent, with Japan rising rapidly from a low base, Germany and France following (Figure 2.5).

The large international firms are even more R&D-intensive. In 1992-93 the ten largest R&D spenders spent a total of US$9.1 billion on R&D, an average of almost 16 per cent of sales, and estimates for 1995 show that large firms consistently increased R&D effort despite pressures on prices and profits.

Research is among the most centralised activities in large pharmaceutical companies (see Table 2.4). Even the very largest carry out research and basic clinical evaluation in only a few locations, with the main centre of research in the home country. For example in 1992 the very large Swiss pharmaceutical/chemical industry had almost one-half of R&D expenditures in Switzerland, down only marginally from the mid-1980s, despite the limited size of the national scientific and technical pool which to draw from.

When they are set up, foreign R&D facilities are in nations with a proven record of success in innovation. US companies took the lead in setting up second and third research centres abroad. The specific requirements of different markets, including government regulations, necessitated establishment of local development and market-testing facilities.

Despite centralisation, most European firms have large R&D investments in the United States. In 1986, it was estimated that 26 foreign pharmaceutical firms, primarily European-owned, had R&D facilities in the United States. A different survey showed that by 1992 there were 74 large foreign-owned

◆ Figure 2.4. **Employment growth – Pharmaceuticals**

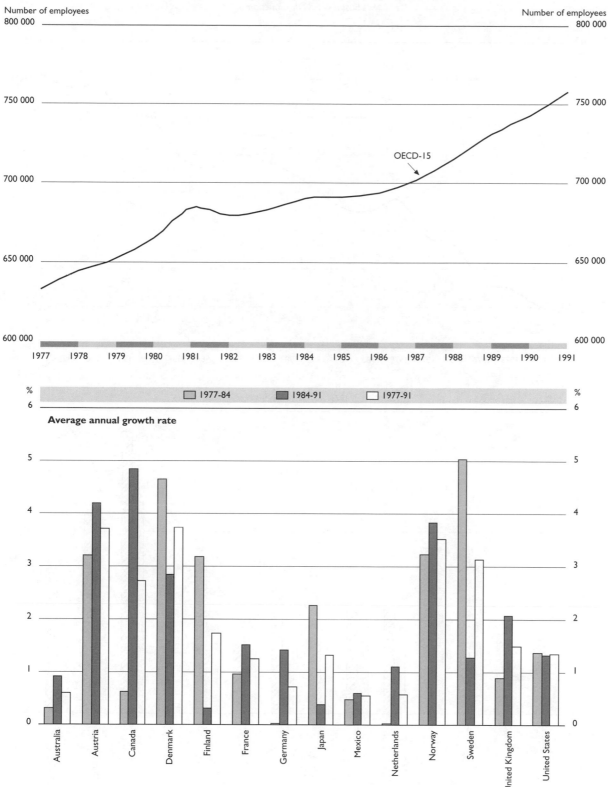

◆ Figure 2.5. **R&D intensity – Pharmaceuticals**
Business R&D/production

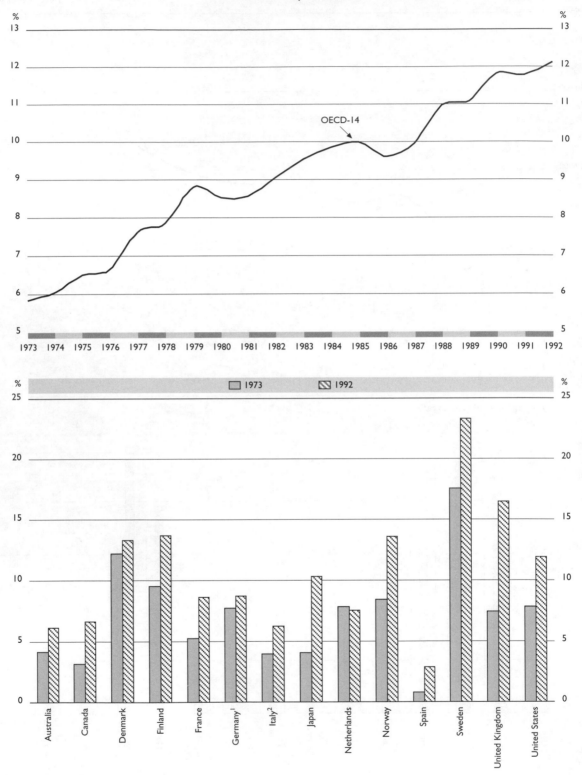

1. 1977. 2. 1987.
Source: OECD, DSTI, STAN, ANBERD Databases.

Table 2.4. **Contribution of country of origin to sales, human resources and R&D**

Percentages

	Year	Sales	Human resources	R&D	*
Akzo	1991	9	31	45	b
Bayer	1990	42	49	63	h
Boehringer	1991	25	40	51	h
Glaxo	1991	11	35	61	h
Hoechst	1991	26	34	59	b
Novo Nordisk	1989	n.a.	76	90	b
Rhone-Poulenc	1991	23	44	62	h
Sandoz	1989	4	19	55	b

Note: * b = R&D budget; h = R&D human resources.
Source: Raugel, P.-J. (1992).

biotechnology R&D facilities in the United States, of which three-quarters were European-owned (Dalton and Serapio, 1992, Department of Commerce, 1993). By 1992 it was estimated that foreign firms in the pharmaceutical industry in the United States were the largest foreign R&D spenders by industry and their expenditures had grown most rapidly through the 1980s to US$2.8 billion in 1992 in constant 1987 dollars (OTA, 1994). In current terms, US affiliates of foreign firms funded over US$3.8 billion of R&D in the United States in 1993, one-third of all foreign affiliate manufacturing R&D in the United States. In comparison, US firms spent over US$2 billion for affiliate R&D outside the United States.

Few Japanese companies have R&D centres outside Japan. But as a consequence of mounting cost-containment concerns, large Japanese companies are restructuring their R&D operations and increasingly turning to small specialist research companies, some foreign, for early-phase projects.

The pattern of R&D activities carried out abroad by drug companies has been re-shaped by the advent of new biotechnology, a generic technology whose potential is being tested mainly in pharmaceutical research. Much of this research is carried out by dedicated biotechnology companies (DBCs). These are mostly small US-based firms which first appeared in the mid-1970s, and proliferated in the first half of the 1980s. Established pharmaceutical companies soon saw the potential impact of this novel technology, but often lacked the broad-based skills to foster it. Accordingly, a web of collaboration agreements linking the large drug companies with small DBCs was set up, to trade financial and marketing support against research resources of DBCs. A 1994 survey identified more than 1 500 DBCs in the United States and around 400 in Europe (*Financial Times*, 1994), and it was estimated that drugs produced from biotechnological processes took around 4 per cent of world pharmaceutical sales (Panorama of EU Industry 94). Pharmaceuticals-related biotechnology (mostly R&D, in all sectors, including government) employed around 100 000 people in the United States in 1995, equivalent to over 40 per cent of pharmaceuticals manufacturing employment (OECD data).

Some DBCs have recently been taken over by their pharmaceutical partners, only a few DBCs have become fully-fledged operating companies, but most of the agreements still exist. The new biotechnology has driven the globalisation of the R&D function of non-US firms, which were lagging in this important area. It also suggests a new trend in the industry, with greater importance attached to external sources of research, and to the national research infrastructure, as firms have been seeking new ways (*e.g.* through alliances and external contracting) to maintain their product portfolios.

D. Capital investment

Investment in plant and equipment is relatively less important than in R&D and market development. Investment averages 4-6 per cent of production. No major changes emerged through the 1980s and early 1990s, but there are wide variations among countries. Capital investment was about one-half of national R&D expenditures in the home countries of major pharmaceutical firms (Germany, Japan, the United

Kingdom, the United States). Nordic countries invested above the OECD average, but their R&D outstripped capital expenditures at the end of the 1980s and early 1990s. In Italy and the United Kingdom capital intensity is around average, and these two countries have lower than average capital intensities across all of manufacturing, suggesting that they are relatively specialised in pharmaceutical production. Australia, Canada and Italy were the only countries with capital expenditures greater than R&D expenditures. They have large internal markets and extensive production, but are the home base for few research-based global companies, so domestic R&D is relatively low.

E. Concentration and competition

There are two different ways of measuring concentration in the industry. The first is based on the share of total production held by the largest firms in the industry ("firm concentration"). The second is based on measuring the share of competing products in narrow therapeutic specialisations.

a) Firm concentration

The industry is led by about 20 large research-based firms, none with a dominant share. The leading positions have changed frequently, but the group of large firms has remained largely the same. All firms in the top-15 in 1992 were already in the top-20 in 1981 (see Table 2.5). The major round of mergers and acquisitions in 1993-95 changed the order of the top-10 large firms; but only one, Phamacia & Upjohn, was not in the top-12 in 1992 and all of the 1995 top-10 were in the top-20 in 1981. In 1989 the 10 largest of the world's top 184 firms had a little less than one-third of their combined sales, the 20 largest more than half, and the 60 largest firms had over 85 per cent of the combined sales (data from SCRIP, Table 2.6). These shares have subsequently consolidated, with the ten largest firms in 1995 having close to 36 per cent of the world market (Secretariat estimates). The following section examines trends in the 1980s and 1990s.

Trends in global concentration (based on SCRIP) show that the industry consolidated at world level during the 1980s, but to a lesser extent than might be expected from rising trends in R&D costs and the wave of large mergers and acquisitions at the end of the 1980s. The situation in 1989 was very similar to that in 1981. The world top-8, top-16, and top-50 companies slightly increased their shares of total production, while the four-firm concentration ratio showed a decline (from 12 to 11 per cent). Europe

Table 2.5.   **The 15 largest pharmaceutical companies, 1981, 1989 and 1992**

	Nationality	1992 Rank	1992 Sales (m US$)	1992 Pharmaceutical sales as % of total sales	1989 Rank	1981 Rank
Merck	United States	1	8 214.5	85.0	1	3
Glaxo	United Kingdom	2	7 986.4	100.0	2	20
Bristol-Myers Squibb	United States	3	6 313.0	56.6	3	10/14
Hoechst	Germany	4	6 042.1	20.6	5	1
Ciba-Geigy	Switzerland	5	5 192.0	32.9	7	4
SmithKline Beecham	United Kingdom/United States	6	5 100.5	55.4	8	13/22
Hoffmann La Roche	Switzerland	7	4 896.9	53.2	16	7
Sandoz	Switzerland	8	4 885.5	47.7	9	8
Bayer	Germany	9	4 669.9	17.7	4	2
American Home Products	United States	10	4 589.3	58.3	10	6
Pfizer	United States	11	4 557.9	63.0	15	5
Eli Lilly	United States	12	4 536.5	73.6	12	9
Johnson and Johnson	United States	13	4 340.0	31.6	17	19
Rhône-Poulenc Rorer	France/United States	14	4 095.9	100.0	20	16
Abbott	United States	15	4 025.0	51.3	13	17

Source: OECD, adapted from SCRIP. Sales are pharmaceuticals only.

Table 2.6. **Firm concentration by turnover, around 1990**

Sales category (Million US$)	Number of companies	Sales	Sales (%) of total
4 000+	6	26 974.3	20.9
3 000-4 000	5	17 422.5	13.5
2 000-3 000	10	25 635.9	19.9
1 500-2 000	7	12 645.1	9.8
1 000-1 500	12	14 465.2	11.2
500-1 000	19	13 520.5	10.5
500 or less	125	18 185.8	14.1
Total	**184**	**128 849.3**	**100.0**

Source: SCRIP.

virtually kept the same concentration, Japan starting from a lower level saw a small increase, and the United States, starting from a higher level saw a decrease.

Data for 1992 suggested that at global level, the wave of mergers and acquisitions were bearing fruit and that the global market share of the top-4, top-8 and top-16 had risen since 1989. 1992 estimates: top-4 over 15 per cent, top-8 almost 26 per cent, both higher than in 1989. The second wave of mergers and acquisitions in 1993-95 continued consolidation. 1995 estimates: top-4, 18 per cent of the global market, top-8, 30 per cent, both rising from 1992. Despite consolidation, in 1992 only two firms had over 4 per cent of the world market, and no single firm had over 20 per cent of any major national market; in 1995 three firms had over 4 per cent of the world market, but only the one leading firm had over 5 per cent.

At national level, stable or downward trends in concentration were seen over the long period through to the end of the 1980s. In the United States, top-4 (around 25 per cent), top-8 and top-50 shipment concentration all trended slightly down over the period 1947-87, in Germany the top-6 (around 33 per cent), top-10 and top-50 turnover concentrations were down a little over the 1976-88 period. In Japan top-4 (down from 30 to 17 per cent) and top-10 production concentrations declined from 1965-88. (Differences in product coverage probably explain differences between SCRIP and Japanese national sources.) Similar downward trends are seen in the broader chemical industries in Italy and there has been little change in Canada's chemical industries. Thus the drug industry did not undergo marked consolidation in major national markets before the end of the 1980s. The recent round of consolidation is global more than national, with firms acquiring rivals to gain global market share, rather than national shares. More firms with specialised portfolios of globally sold drugs are operating in all national markets.

b) Major firms and markets

European-owned firms had first/second world position (Glaxo) and, overall, seven of the top-10 world positions in the industry in 1992-93 (including one joint European/US firm), accounting for almost 21 per cent of world ethical pharmaceutical sales (US$38.8 out of US$188 billion) (Table 2.5). After the 1993-95 round of acquisitions, the top-10 distribution distribution was five European including two joint Europe-US firms, and five US firms excluding joint Europe-US firms; the three major European firms (Ciba-Geigy, Sandoz, Bayer) which had been less active in acquisitions up until then dropping just out of the top-10. The Sandoz/Ciba-Geigy merger to form Novartis in early 1996 again re-ordered the ranking of large firms and increased concentration. The five European firms in the top-10 in 1995 (including joint European-US firms) accounted for almost 19 per cent of world ethical pharmaceutical sales (US$38.7 out of US$205 billion 1994 sales), the top-5 US firms accounting for 17 per cent (US$34.8 of US$205 billion 1994 sales).

The largest US pharmaceutical companies have significant positions in all major European markets, and larger US biotechnology firms have European operations, particularly in the United Kingdom. In the US market there were two European firms in the top 10 in 1990-91, three in 1995-96. There were no foreign firms in the top-10 in Japan in 1990-91. However, foreign firms had over 20 per cent of the domestic

Table 2.7. **Average effective patent life of 100 main drugs**

	1980 Drugs sold before July 1970	1980 Total	1988 Drugs sold after June 1980	1988 Total
France	16.5	13.6	12.2	10.2
Germany	14.8	11.8	11.0	10.5
United Kingdom	15.6	13.1	13.0	11.9
United States	17.9	15.1	12.3	10.7
Japan	n.a.	n.a.	11.2	11.1

Source: De Wolf (1993).

market. Most major European and American pharmaceutical firms have Japanese subsidiary operations and about two-thirds have R&D facilities there. There has been a major shift by US and European firms to set up their own operations in Japan to replace licensing of their products.

c) Product concentration and competition

Most pharmaceuticals treat a limited range of medical conditions. Within narrow therapeutic sub-markets, there is much higher concentration, particularly as patent protection and clear therapeutic advantages allow quasi-monopoly for the duration of the patent. The top three products commonly account for 45-60 per cent of total sales in a sub-market and 80-90 per cent in some sub-markets, with for example individual leading products holding 20-25 per cent of the market in Europe (UNIDO).

Competition is based on different strategies for in-patent drugs and generic drugs. Competitive advantage for in-patent drugs lies in innovation, and success depends on extensive marketing to doctors. R&D costs are high, and are mainly recovered over the short duration of the exclusive patent by means of world-wide marketing. Patent rights are effective for 10-11 years from the time of introduction of the drug, as the patent is generally obtained long before the product reaches the market (Table 2.7). The faster that patent holders enter all major markets, the faster they can recoup R&D investments.

Once the patent expires, competition is based on price, and production may shift to small and medium-sized enterprises. Profit margins are lower. Generics-only producers tend to limit activities to their home countries and regions. However most inventors will continue to compete against generic producers after their patents expire, benefiting from "brand-loyalty" and name recognition, and higher sales prices, as well as product differentiation, *e.g.* by marketing specialised dosage forms, etc.

The unique market structure in pharmaceuticals explains the relatively stable distribution and concentration of drugs firms, with a small group of research-based firms developing highly profitable, but numerically limited, portfolios of drugs over a long period, and a larger number of often smaller firms serving generic and OTC markets. Recently there has been consolidation in the generics market as research-based firms have sought acquisitions and joint ventures with generic and OTC firms to extend dominant positions after patents expire, expand markets and cut unit marketing costs. In the United States about 80 per cent of generic drugs are manufactured by research-based firms and these firms have renewed efforts in the generics field. There have been similar strategies of research-based firms to buy into independent distributors (pharmacy benefit managers in the United States) to lower distribution costs and gain market share.

F. Pricing

Product pricing depends on costs of R&D, production, marketing, and profits (to apply to further R&D), and on perceived therapeutic value. Pricing policies have a significant impact on R&D expenditures, as R&D is a high and rising share of total company expenditures. Most OECD countries control prices, but

Table 2.8. **Drug price comparison in the European Community, 1989**

	Production price	Wholesale price	Pharmacy price
Netherlands	100	120	169
Germany	83	97	137
United Kingdom	80	92	122
Belgium	59	67	97
Italy	60	67	90
Portugal	48	53	66
Spain	39	45	64
France	39	43	62
Greece	32	34	47

Note: Highest production price = 100. Values for 1989.
Source: De Wolf (1993).

there are major differences among countries in prices and widespread attempts to reduce them [see Section 5.A.*b*) on price regulation].

The United States has a limited price influencing system (*e.g.* Medicaid) on pharmaceuticals, and much recent attention has focused on prices and profits. In contrast there are pricing controls in almost all European Union member States but with wide variations in resulting prices (see Table 2.8). Denmark, Germany and the Netherlands are usually in the group of highest price European countries. Countries with lower price levels are considered to have tighter price controls, leading to parallel imports of pharmaceuticals from them. A two-tiered system of price influencing exists in Canada. Japan has a mixed system, with fixed prices on pharmaceuticals prescribed by doctors, but free-pricing (often lower) to hospitals. There has been considerable downward pressure on prices by Japanese health authorities, which has led to extensive restructuring of pharmaceuticals distribution.

3. INTERNATIONAL TRADE

A. General trends

Between 1980 and 1994, total world exports of pharmaceutical products grew rapidly, to US$57 billion, up from US$14 billion in 1980. This compares with total ethical pharmaceutical production of around US$205 billion in 1994, up from around US$75 billion in 1980 (SCRIP and Secretariat estimates).[3] Trade in pharmaceuticals has outpaced growth in production of pharmaceuticals, in line with the trend for all manufactures. However, pharmaceuticals are not as trade-intensive as many other manufactures due to the structure and global organisation of the industry. If the exports/production index for all OECD countries' manufacturing is 1, the index for pharmaceuticals is around 0.66.

The importance of foreign markets for national production varies considerably among countries, as can be seen from the relative share of exports to production (Table 2.3). Switzerland has by far the highest ratio of all major producers, exporting over 80 per cent of production, and there are high levels of exports from other smaller European countries (Denmark, the Netherlands, Sweden and Austria). These countries are followed by the United Kingdom, Germany and France, all around 30 per cent. For other large producing countries (the United States, Japan, Italy, Spain and Canada), exports are less than 12 per cent of production. For Switzerland, although imports are also significant, net trade is highly positive and the ratio of production to consumption is very high. Production also significantly exceeds consumption (exports are greater than imports) for the large European producing countries such as the United Kingdom, Germany and France as well as for Denmark (approaching Switzerland) and Sweden. The United States and Japan have low relative levels of both exports and imports compared with production, although they have high absolute values of trade.

Trade and production are strongly concentrated geographically, with exports more concentrated than imports. In 1994 OECD countries had 92 per cent of world pharmaceutical exports and 78 per cent of imports. The five largest exporting countries (Germany, Switzerland, the United States, the United

Table 2.9. **Trade in pharmaceuticals**[1]

Billions US$ and percentages

Major exporters	1980		1994		Major importers	1980		1994	
	Value	Share	Value	Share		Value	Share	Value	Share
Germany	2.43	17.3	8.72	15.4	Germany	1.32	10.8	5.25	9.5
Switzerland	1.62	11.5	6.32	11.2	United States	0.80	6.6	4.76	8.6
United States	2.02	14.4	6.09	10.8	Japan	1.07	8.8	4.22	7.7
United Kingdom	1.73	12.4	6.01	10.6	France	0.70	5.7	4.20	7.6
France	1.50	10.7	5.41	9.6	United Kingdom	0.52	4.2	3.43	6.2
Belgium-Luxembourg	0.67	4.8	3.34	5.9	Italy	0.65	5.4	3.26	5.9
Netherlands	0.62	4.4	2.78	4.9	Netherlands	0.57	4.7	2.80	5.1
Italy	0.69	4.9	2.76	4.9	Belgium-Luxembourg	0.65	5.4	2.57	4.7
Japan	0.29	2.1	1.55	2.7	Switzerland	0.41	3.4	2.32	4.2
Rest of world	2.44	17.5	13.66	24.1	Rest of world	5.49	45.0	22.28	40.4
Total	**14.01**	**100.0**	**56.64**	**100.0**	**Total**	**12.20**	**100.0**	**55.10**	**100.0**

1. SITC Rev. 2: 54.
Source: Secretariat calculations from UN Comtrade database.

Kingdom, France) represented close to 60 per cent of world pharmaceutical exports, although this share had declined, while the five largest importing countries (Germany, the United States, Japan, France, the United Kingdom) accounted for 40 per cent of world pharmaceutical imports (Table 2.9). In 1994 developing countries (excluding ex-USSR and Eastern Europe) took 17 per cent of total world imports, but contributed only 6 per cent of exports.

There is considerable overlap between leading producing, exporting and importing countries. The two extremes are Japan and Switzerland. Japan has the second largest world market, is the the largest net importer, but imports are a relatively low share of consumption. Switzerland shows the opposite structure, with a small domestic market, is the largest net exporter, and has very high exports compared with consumption and production.

Intra- and inter-regional trade

Europe is by far the most important trading region. In 1994 it accounted for over 80 per cent of world exports of finished products, and close to 65 per cent of intermediates, and imported over 60 per cent of finished products and over 50 per cent of intermediates. This largely reflects the substantial and increasing share of intra-European trade in finished products (from about 45 per cent of world exports and imports combined in 1980 to 55 per cent in 1994), and the stable 35 per cent of intra-European combined exports and imports in total world intermediates trade. North American exports of intermediates, although declining, account for 20 per cent of the world total. Overall, North America is more involved in intermediates than finished products trade, and more on the export than the import side.

Intra-regional imports of finished products grew to over 23 per cent in North American finished products imports, are remarkably high and stable (close to 95 per cent) in Europe, and low in East Asia (less than 15 per cent in 1994). Intra-regional exports of finished products more than doubled their share to over 30 per cent in North America in 1980-94, surpassed 60 per cent in Europe, and decreased to below 50 per cent in East Asia. The picture is more stable for intra-regional trade in intermediates, with the main change being in North America, notably the decrease from almost 25 per cent in 1980 to less than 19 per cent in 1994 of North American imports originating within the region. This decline and the parallel increase of North American intermediate imports from Europe, suggests that trade has been re-shaped by European companies investing in the North American market following the multinational mode of expansion previously followed by US companies. Intermediates are imported by European firms from Europe and finished products exported by them throughout the North American region. (See Figure 2.6 and Table 2.10.)

◆ Figure 2.6. ***Intra-regional trade of finished products – Pharmaceuticals***
As percentage of exports of each region

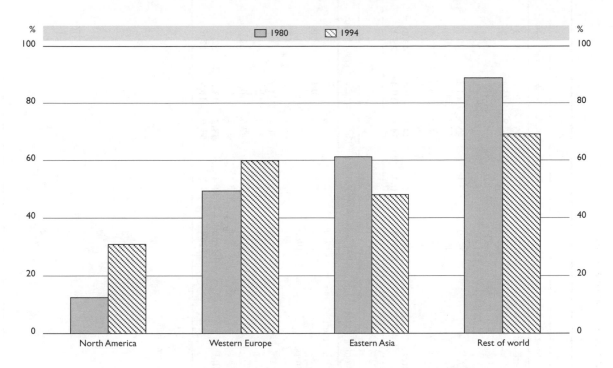

Inter-regional trade of intermediate products – Pharmaceuticals
As percentage of exports of each region

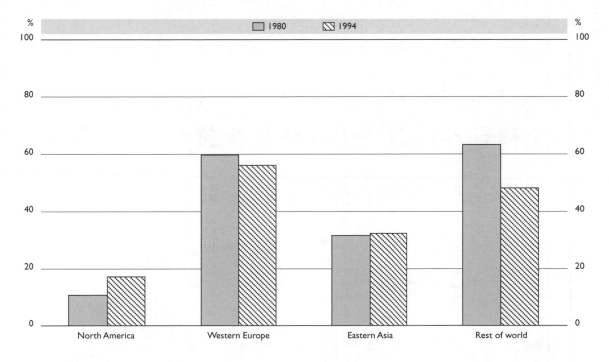

Notes: Western Europe: EC + EFTA.
North America: Canada, Mexico, United States.
East Asia: Brunei, China, Chinese Taipei, Hong Kong, Indonesia, Japan, Malaysia, Philippines, Republic of Korea, Singapore, Thailand.
Source: UN Comtrade Database.

Table 2.10.   **Inter- and intra-regional trade – Pharmaceuticals**

Percentage of reporting region's total

Imports of finished products

Reporting region		North America	Europe	SEA	Rest of world	Total
North America	1980	16.8	68.1	6.2	8.9	100.0
	1994	23.4	66.5	4.8	5.3	100.0
Europe	1980	4.3	94.6	0.4	0.7	100.0
	1994	4.8	93.1	1.1	1.0	100.0
SEA	1980	19.6	59.3	17.8	3.2	100.0
	1994	11.4	70.5	13.7	4.5	100.0
Rest of world	1980	5.7	78.4	2.6	13.2	100.0
	1994	7.4	72.0	0.4	20.1	100.0
Total	**1980**	**7.6**	**83.9**	**3.8**	**4.7**	**100.0**
	1994	**8.0**	**84.1**	**2.9**	**4.9**	**100.0**

Exports of finished products

Reporting region		North America	Europe	SEA	Rest of world	Total
North America	1980	12.3	35.0	20.0	32.8	100.0
	1994	31.0	36.9	14.4	17.8	100.0
Europe	1980	1.7	49.1	7.1	42.1	100.0
	1994	8.4	60.1	8.7	22.7	100.0
SEA	1980	3.1	5.5	61.3	30.1	100.0
	1994	13.7	17.7	48.0	20.6	100.0
Rest of world	1980	1.0	6.9	3.4	88.8	100.0
	1994	9.2	14.9	6.5	69.3	100.0
Total	**1980**	**2.7**	**44.1**	**9.4**	**43.8**	**100.0**
	1994	**10.4**	**54.1**	**10.4**	**25.2**	**100.0**

Imports of intermediate products

Reporting region		North America	Europe	SEA	Rest of world	Total
North America	1980	24.5	54.7	13.0	7.8	100.0
	1994	18.7	60.7	16.5	4.2	100.0
Europe	1980	20.1	69.6	5.5	4.9	100.0
	1994	22.7	65.9	6.9	4.6	100.0
SEA	1980	29.6	46.4	20.2	3.9	100.0
	1994	22.9	54.7	18.3	4.1	100.0
Rest of world	1980	17.8	62.8	6.8	12.7	100.0
	1994	14.9	68.2	6.7	10.1	100.0
Total	**1980**	**22.0**	**62.6**	**9.2**	**6.2**	**100.0**
	1994	**21.0**	**63.2**	**10.5**	**5.2**	**100.0**

Exports of intermediate products

Reporting region		North America	Europe	SEA	Rest of world	Total
North America	1980	10.7	49.6	21.7	18.0	100.0
	1994	17.2	49.6	20.1	13.1	100.0
Europe	1980	10.8	59.9	9.1	20.1	100.0
	1994	12.6	56.2	13.4	17.8	100.0
SEA	1980	24.1	30.2	31.7	14.1	100.0
	1994	21.6	32.2	32.7	13.5	100.0
Rest of world	1980	7.9	22.6	6.3	63.2	100.0
	1994	8.4	34.2	9.5	47.9	100.0
Total	**1980**	**11.4**	**53.3**	**13.2**	**22.1**	**100.0**
	1994	**14.5**	**51.0**	**16.9**	**17.6**	**100.0**

Notes: North America = Canada, Mexico, United States.
Europe = EU + EFTA.
SEA = Brunei, China, Hong Kong, Indonesia, Japan, Malaysia, Philippines, Singapore, Korea, Chinese Taipei, Thailand.
Source: Secretariat calculations from UN Comtrade database.

B. International sourcing and trade in intermediate products

Imports and exports of intermediates represent about 40 per cent of total pharmaceuticals imports and exports for OECD countries (Table 2.11). The relative importance of intermediates in total trade shows the global structure of the industry, with final conversion, mixing, packaging and presentation in final markets a continuing part of strategy. Declines in the share of intermediates in OECD imports probably

Table 2.11. **Exports and imports of intermediate pharmaceutical products, 1970-93**

As a percentage of total pharmaceutical products

	1970	1980	1990	1993
	Exports			
Canada	58	54	52	44
United States	58	65	70	65
Japan	53	79	76	71
Australia	25	45	35	31
New Zealand	90	47	54	57
Austria	63	41	65	59
Belgium-Luxembourg	17	18	24	32
Denmark	37	23	23	23
Finland	75	51	28	40
France	29	23	27	31
Germany	32	39	42	40
Ireland	89	59	21	25
Italy	64	56	53	45
Netherlands	44	38	37	32
Norway	66	67	70	70
Portugal	39	51	66	50
Spain	46	56	67	55
Switzerland	39	37	34	36
Turkey	10	54	24	8
United Kingdom	25	30	27	24
OECD	**41**	**42**	**40**	**38**
	Imports			
Canada	77	69	40	33
United States	88	62	56	54
Japan	39	51	56	53
Australia	41	46	31	30
New Zealand	20	21	16	19
Austria	18	31	36	36
Belgium-Luxembourg	31	32	33	39
Denmark	51	39	36	39
Finland	23	28	18	18
France	96	80	47	45
Germany	59	42	43	41
Greece	19	39	35	25
Iceland	11	13	17	16
Ireland	40	22	29	36
Italy	54	61	53	50
Netherlands	24	28	26	24
Norway	15	17	15	18
Portugal	23	37	44	30
Spain	94	88	64	42
Sweden	22	19	21	26
Switzerland	47	45	32	39
Turkey	94	97	71	66
United Kingdom	61	38	30	34
OECD	**51**	**47**	**42**	**41**

Source: OECD, NEXT database.

shows the impact of wider acceptance of common testing and inspection procedures on a regional basis, fostering greater intra-regional trade in finished products and relatively reducing trade in intermediates.

European manufacturers mainly export finished pharmaceutical products, in contrast with American and Japanese manufacturers, which have high intermediate export shares as a share of total pharmaceuticals trade (65 per cent for the United States and 71 per cent for Japan in 1993). The share of intermediate exports for many European countries has been declining. Germany and France show increasing exports of intermediates, probably linked with the expansion of international operations of their enterprises, which include intermediate exports to affiliates. In 1993 the lowest levels of exports of intermediates by large producers were for the United Kingdom, France and Switzerland. For Germany the figure is 40 per cent, for Italy 45 per cent.

On the import side, there are less marked differences between countries. Nevertheless, countries having high export levels of intermediates have relatively higher levels of imports of intermediates. Overall, countries with a strong domestic manufacturing base tend to have surpluses in both intermediate and finished products (United States, Switzerland, Germany and the United Kingdom). Japan has a large trade deficit in both intermediates and final products, and Italy a lesser deficit in both, whereas of the major producers, France has surpluses in finished products and deficits in intermediates.

The role of international purchase of intermediates (foreign sourcing) relative to domestic purchase can be analysed with the aid of input-output techniques. For the five major countries for which data on pharmaceuticals is available, foreign sourcing has grown in importance relative to domestic purchasing of inputs (see Figure 2.7). The ratio is highest for Canada and the United Kingdom, lowest for Japan. These data show that the industry is becoming increasingly globalised as it sources more inputs from abroad. However pharmaceuticals is not the most highly dependent on foreign inputs. Aerospace, computers, semiconductors, motor vehicles, and textiles and clothing all have higher foreign to domestic sourcing. Only in Japan was it among the top-10 industries to source internationally; eighth in relative importance of

◆ Figure 2.7. *Ratio of imported to domestic sourcing of inputs – Pharmaceuticals*

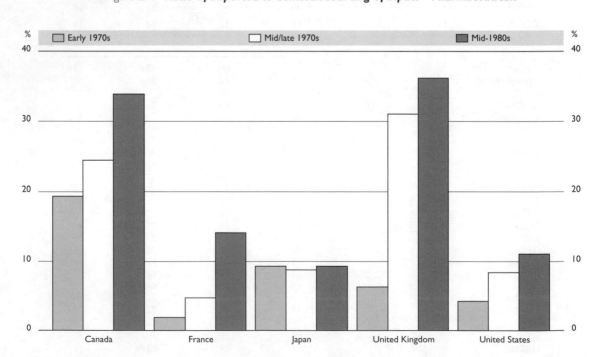

Source: OECD, DSTI, EAS Division.

international intermediate inputs compared with domestic supply. These data confirm the low trade intensity of pharmaceuticals.

C.   Intra-firm trade

Intra-firm trade (IFT) is defined as the international exchange of goods and services within a multi-national enterprise (MNE).[4] Although intra-firm trade is of increasing interest in elucidating the role of international investment in trade, detailed data are only available for the United States. Intra-firm trade represents a very large share of US foreign trade in pharmaceuticals, both on the export and on the import side. While IFT accounts for a little over a third of total US merchandise trade, US trade in pharmaceuticals is overwhelmingly composed of IFT.[5]

The relative importance of IFT for the pharmaceutical industry is clearly shown by data on the international trade with the US of foreign affiliates of US pharmaceutical firms. In 1989, 97 per cent of those firms' exports to the United States and 92 per cent of their imports from the United States went to or came from their parents. The same is true for US affiliates of foreign pharmaceutical firms, which in 1987, exported 83 per cent to and imported 93 per cent of their products from their parents or other affiliated firms. IFT as a share of affiliate trade for other manufacturing industries seldom exceeds 80 per cent. Although transfer pricing is likely to play some role in the relative importance of intra-firm trade, it is the strategies of pharmaceuticals firms to have multi-country patterns of affiliate operations which dictate the very high levels of intra-firm trade in the industry.

In terms of the geographical distribution of US IFT in pharmaceuticals, the overwhelming majority of US intra-firm imports comes from Europe. This share has increased and can be estimated at approximately 90 per cent of the total. Europe is also the most important destination of US intra-firm pharmaceutical exports, with a share of between 50 and 60 per cent of the total. Canada, Japan and Latin America are the other destinations of US intra-firm pharmaceutical exports.

Although very important overall, the relative share of IFT in US pharmaceutical trade does not appear to have increased substantially, which is also the case of the share of IFT on total US merchandise trade. Overall, foreign investment and very high levels of intra-firm trade compared with total trade are enduring features of the pharmaceuticals industry.[6]

D.   Intra-industry trade

Intra-industry trade (IIT) is defined as the exchange by two countries of goods and services within the same product category. IIT is generally a function of product differentiation and international investment, which allows countries to both import and export extensively in the same broad product categories. IIT indices provide another tool for analysing trade patterns as they show the extent of international linkages for a given industry.[7] The closer the index is to 100, the more symmetrical are exports and imports.

IIT indices in pharmaceuticals are comparable to those for other industries for most OECD countries. Table 2.12 shows IIT indices calculated for intermediate and finished pharmaceutical products for the largest producing countries in 1991. For the United States, IIT is higher for finished pharmaceutical products than for intermediate products, while the opposite is true for Japan. For most European countries, IIT in intermediate and finished products are similar, showing that trading patterns are similar. France is the exception, where similar indices are for surpluses in finished products, deficits in intermediates. Both Switzerland and Japan have low IIT indices, but for opposite reasons. Switzerland has a large trade surplus, Japan has a large trade deficit.

By partner country, US pharmaceutical IIT indices compared with those for other industries are relatively high with European countries, showing relatively balanced trade, and low with Canada. European countries on the other hand have high pharmaceutical IIT indices with each other, similar to those in other industries, showing balanced two-way trade and close integration. Japan's pharmaceutical IIT indices with the Republic of Korea are relatively high.

Table 2.12. **Intra-industry trade indices, 1991 – Pharmaceuticals**

Percentages

	Intermediates[1]	Finished[2]
France	82	70
Germany	77	79
Italy	67	73
Japan	64	32
Switzerland	45	40
United Kingdom	72	69
United States	70	98

1. Intermediate products are SITC Rev. 2 54 excluding 5417.
2. Finished products are SITC Rev. 2 5417.
Source: Calculations based on UN Comtrade data.

4. FOREIGN DIRECT INVESTMENT AND INTER-FIRM NETWORKS

Foreign operations are very important in the pharmaceutical industry. R&D costs must be recouped across as many markets as possible, a minimum presence is necessary to meet government health and safety standards and regulations, and local marketing is essential. Globalisation to establish foreign operations takes many forms:

- mergers and acquisitions are the most common form of market entry in countries with equity-based financial systems, particularly the United States, the United Kingdom and Canada, and they became more common in Europe in anticipation of the Single Market, and to accelerate the formation of globally competitive firms;

- green-field investment in new production facilities and marketing networks is common in many European countries and Japan due in part to *de facto* limits on foreign equity purchases;

- joint ventures based on agreement between two partners to pool resources in a new venture, usually with equal equity holdings;

- minority shareholdings, which may be "strategic" involving management participation, or more passive portfolio holdings;

- collaboration agreements, which may be joint ventures or minority shareholdings, but whose main features are that substantial resources are provided by participants to develop, produce or market goods and services;

- licensing of patents or other intellectual property rights.

There is relatively little data available from official sources which separately identifies international operations of pharmaceuticals within the broader chemical industry. The following text in some places describes developments for the chemical industry including pharmaceuticals.

A. Foreign direct investment

Stocks of foreign direct investment (FDI) have grown more rapidly than trade in finished and intermediate pharmaceuticals. Between the three major markets of Western Europe, Japan and the United States average annual growth in FDI was 17.5 per cent compared to 12.9 and 11.2 per cent for finished and intermediates trade through the 1980s. The main sources of new foreign direct investment were the United States and Europe and the main destinations were the United States, Western Europe and Japan (Table 2.13). Little new investment went to developing countries and their share declined overall. Major research-based companies expanded their investments in the three major world regions, with pharmaceuticals one of the few manufacturing industries with a considerable stock of inward investment in Japan.

Table 2.13. **Stocks of inter-regional direct investment in pharmaceuticals, 1980s**

US$ million

Origin (ultimate beneficial owner)	Destination				Total
	United States	Europe	Japan	Rest of the world	
End 1980					
United States	–	5 080	604	3 366	9 050
Europe	2 558	–	268	n.a.	2 826
Japan	9	4	–	47	60
Rest of world	377	n.a.	n.a.	–	377
Total	**2 944**	**5 084**	**872**	**3 413**	**12 313**
End 1988					
United States	–	13 830	3 047	5 210	22 087
Europe	10 818	–	2 660	n.a.	13 478
Japan	436	150	–	407	993
Rest of world	829	n.a.	n.a.	–	829
Total	**12 083**	**13 980**	**5 707**	**5 617**	**37 387**

Note: Intra-regional investment is not shown, *e.g.* European investment in Europe.
Source: Secretariat calculations from: US Bureau of Economic Analysis; Japan, Ministry of Finance; partly estimated.

Recent data confirm the importance of the United States as a destination and source of foreign investment, and the strengths of European firms. By 1993 the assets of foreign-controlled pharmaceutical manufacturing affiliates (by industry of affiliate) in the United States were US$37.4 billion, up from US$5.9 billion in 1985. 88 per cent of assets were European, up from 85 per cent in 1985, and Swiss firms held close to one-half of European assets. In 1993 Japanese firms had 5 per cent of total foreign-owned assets in the United States, 7 per cent of employment but, in 1992, 17 out of 74 foreign-owned biotechnology-related R&D facilities. In 1993 employment in foreign-owned affiliates was over 137 000, equivalent to over 60 per cent of US pharmaceuticals manufacturing employment. 85 per cent of employment was in European affiliates in the United States.

Assets of the US pharmaceutical industry abroad were US$36.5 billion in 1993 (by industry of affiliate), and 90 per cent of this total was in developed countries. The majority of investment was in Europe (71 per cent of total assets) and lesser amounts in Japan (12.5 per cent). In 1993 employment was 175 000, 53 per cent in Europe.

Flows of FDI for the broader combined chemicals and pharmaceuticals industries show similar trends.[8, 9] Inward investment experienced an upsurge in the late 1980s, a fall from 1990 before rising again through 1993. The United States is by far the biggest inward investment recipient in chemicals (pharmaceuticals made up 22 per cent of foreign-owned assets in the US chemical industry in 1993 and 27 per cent of employment). The United States was followed by Europe (the Netherlands, Germany, France, the United Kingdom). Trends in outward investment are similar to those for inward investment. The United States, the Netherlands, Germany and the United Kingdom have the highest outward investment stocks in chemicals and pharmaceuticals, with Japan and France increasing their activity. The net investment position for chemicals and pharmaceuticals in 1993 shows Germany, the United Kingdom, the Netherlands and Japan each with a large surplus of outward investment, whereas the United States is a net recipient.

B. International mergers, acquisitions, minority participations

International mergers and acquisitions, joint ventures, and other equity and non-equity links proliferated in the 1980s and early 1990s, increasing the activities of foreign-controlled firms in most markets.

Pharmaceutical firms were active in acquisitions and alliances to acquire strengths in biotechnology R&D, and to expand market positions in generic and OTC markets to exploit market-leading drugs after patents expire.

Mergers and acquisitions. The pattern of M&A operations in the period 1988-92 resembles that of FDI. Cross-border M&As are an important route to enter foreign markets through purchase of existing firms.[8, 9, 10] Firms from the major producing countries in particular expanded their international positions in the United States and Europe (see Table 2.14 for firm-level activity). During the period 1988-92 there were 226 cross-border mergers and acquisitions totalling US$13.1 billion in the pharmaceuticals industry.

Table 2.14. **Selected large mergers and acquisitions in the pharmaceutical industry, 1988-95**

	Purchaser	Target	Cost (mill. of US$)
1988	Eastman Kodak (US)	Sterling and Winthrop (US)	5 300.0
1988	American Home Products (US)	A.H. Robins (US)	n.a.
1988	SmithKline Beckman (US)	Bio-Science Labs (US)	7 800.0
1988	Boehringer-Ingelheim (Germany)	Bio-Mega (US)	n.a.
1989	Novo (Denmark)	Nordisk (Denmark)	n.a.
1989	Merrell Dow (US)	Marion (US)	7 700.0
1989	SmithKline Beckman (US)	Beecham (UK) (merger)	7 800.0
1989	Bristol-Myers (US)	Squibb (US)	12 700.0
1989	Fujisawa (Japan)	Lyphomed (US)	n.a.
1989	Institut Mérieux (France)	Connaught (Canada)	n.a.
1989	Johnson and Johnson-Merck Co. (US)	ICI Americas-Over-the-Counter (US)	450.0
1989	Procordia AB (Sweden)	Pharmacia AB (Pharmacia SpA) (Sweden)	2 440.4
1990	Rhône-Poulenc SA (France)	Rorer Group Inc. (US)	3 476.0
1990	Roche Holding AG (Switzerland)	Genentech Inc. (US)	2 021.5
1990	Merck and Co-European Prescript. (Switzerland)	EI du Pont de Nemours-Pharm. (US)	2 500.0
1991	Sterling Drug-N. Amer. Operations (US)	Sanofi-N. Amer. Ops., Latin Amer. (US)	2 400.0
1991	Sanofi-European Operations (France)	Sterling Drug-European Ops. (France)	4 499.7
1991	Roche Holding AG (Switzerland)	Nicholas (Nicholas Kiwi AU) (Netherlands)	820.9
1991	American Home Products Corp. (US)	Genetics Institute Inc. (US)	667.0
1992	American Cyanamid Co. (US)	Immunex Corp. (US)	736.3
1993	Kabi Pharmacia AB (Procordia) (Sweden)	Erbamont Inc., Farmitalia Carlo (Italy)	1 617.5
1993	Warner-Lamber Co.-OTC Products (US)	Wellcome PLC-OTC Products (UK)	4 397.2
1993	Hoechst Celanese Corp. (Hoechst) (US)	Copley Pharmaceutical Inc. (US)	546.0
1993	Merck and Co. (US)	Medco Containment Services (US)	6 600.0
1994	Ivax Corp. (US)	McGraw Inc. (US)	428.5
1994	Rhône-Poulenc SA (France)	Cooper (France)	484.8
1994	SmithKline Beecham PLC (UK)	Diversified Pharmac. Services (Utd. Healthcare) (US)	2 300.0
1994	Roche Holding AG (Switzerland	Syntex Corp. (US)	5 307.2
1994	American Home Products Corp. (US)	American Cyanamid Co. (US)	9 560.9
1994	Sanofi SA (France)	Sterling Withrop Inc. (prescr. drugs) (Kodak) (US)	1 680.0
1994	SmithKline Beecham PLC (UK)	Sterling Withrop Inc. OTC (Kodak) (US)	2 925.0
1994	Johnson and Johnson (US)	Eastman Kodak-Clinical (US)	1 008.0
1994	Bain Capital (US)	Baxter Intl.-Diagnostics Mfg. (US)	415.0
1994	BASF AG (Germany)	Boots Co. PLC-Pharmaceutical Ops. (UK)	1 583.6
1994	Ciba-Corning Diag., Biocine (US)	Chiron Corp. (US) (49%)	616.5
1994	Eli Lilly and Co. (US)	PCS Health Systems Inc. (McKeeson) (US)	4 000.0
1995	Glaxo Holdings PLC (UK)	Wellcome PLC (UK)	14 284.8
1995	Glaxo Venture Limited (Glaxo) (UK)	Affymax MV (Netherlands)	592.7
1995	Hoechst AG (Germany)	Marion Merrell Dow Inc. (US)	7 121.0
1995	Watson Pharmaceuticals Inc. (US)	Circa Pharmaceuticals Inc. (US)	608.7
1995	Pharmacia AB (Sweden)	Upjohn Co. (US) (merger)	6 316.4
1995	Rhône-Poulenc Rorer Inc. (US)	Fisons PLC (UK)	2 888.4

Note: Transactions over US$400 million only.
Source: IFR Securities Data and OECD compilation from other published sources.

Compared with the total for all industry and service sectors, the number of operations represents 1.9 per cent of the total, and 2.8 per cent of the total amount covered by the database. The respective shares in the motor vehicle sector were numbers, 1.8 per cent and amount, 1.9 per cent, and in the computer industry numbers, 1.3 per cent, and amount, 1.6 per cent, showing pharmaceuticals firms to be very active in mergers and acquisitions.

For the period for which details were available, the countries most active in purchases (in descending order of the amounts involved) were: France, Switzerland, Japan, the United States and the United Kingdom. The countries which were top sellers (in descending order of the amounts involved) were: the United States, the Netherlands, Canada, France, the United Kingdom.

Joint ventures and minority participations. Joint ventures are set up to complement or extend the strengths of firms. Countries with leading firms have the greatest number of cross-border joint ventures. In 1990-92, there were 125 cross-border operations totalling US$670 million in pharmaceuticals. For this period, compared with the total for all industry and service sectors, the number of operations represents 1.8 per cent of the total, and in amount 0.5 per cent of the total covered by the database. The respective shares in the motor vehicles sector were numbers, 3.8 per cent and amount, 8.8 per cent, and in the computer industry numbers, 1.7 per cent and amount, 1.1 per cent, showing pharmaceuticals to be only moderately active in joint ventures and minority participations. There were fewer operations with the economic slow-down in 1992.[8, 10] Top purchasers in 1990-92 (descending order of number of operations) were Japan, France, the United States. Top selling countries (descending order of number of operations) were the United States, Japan, France.

There have been parallels between the objectives of M&A and earlier joint venture and strategic alliance formation to achieve common aims such as sharing R&D results (alliance between Sterling Drug and Sanofi, before Sterling was acquired by Sanofi and SmithKline Beecham), broad alliances to improve product and sales development and R&D management, and moves into the OTC market (Marion Merrell Dow with SmithKline Beecham before Marion was acquired by Hoechst). The motivations for M&A and joint ventures is repeated in the use of minority shareholdings to access foreign resources. New entry into global corporate competition is reflected in high levels of minority purchases by French firms. The building of positions in the major Triad regions can be seen in high levels of minority sales in the United States and Japan, as foreign firms increased their activities in both markets.

Overall, international mergers and acquisitions, joint ventures and minority holdings are complementary approaches to global expansion. They parallel and are part of broad flows of foreign direct investment. They show the importance of M&A, the very active role of European firms, and high level of activity in North America as foreign firms, particularly European ones, have strengthened their positions, and increasing foreign firm activity in Japan, although foreign take-overs remain rare in Japan.

C. Market shares of foreign-controlled firms

A large share of most countries' pharmaceutical supply is taken by foreign-controlled firms because of the strategic necessity for firms to have a strong presence in foreign markets – at the least in final packaging and marketing, and manufacturing in larger markets. This has been accentuated by the wave of international mergers and acquisitions. The shares of foreign-controlled firms in national production, sales or turnover are estimated to range from a low of just over 20 per cent in Japan to highs of 72 per cent in Australia and 97 per cent in Ireland around 1990. All major producing countries had foreign-controlled shares between 20 and 60 per cent (Figure 2.8). UNIDO estimated that foreign-owned companies account for about two-thirds of all pharmaceuticals produced in the developing world.

By source of ownership, European firms were the most important investors in most countries, except in Ireland and the United Kingdom where US pharmaceutical firms were the most important. If production from European investment in Europe is deducted from total foreign-controlled production, the foreign-controlled share is similar in all major producing countries. The shares are in the range of 20-30 per cent, with Germany and Japan lowest, around 20 per cent, and the United States and the United Kingdom highest, around 30 per cent (see details in Figure 2.9). In contrast the share of US production in Ireland is about three-quarters of total output.

◆ Figure 2.8. **Market penetration around 1990 – Pharmaceuticals**
Share of foreign supply in total, in percentage

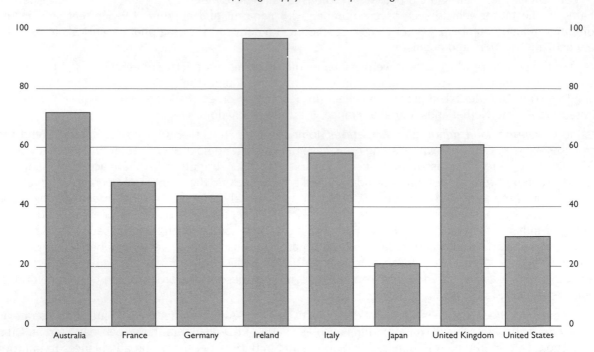

Source: P. de Wolf, based on IMS; Ministère de l'Industrie, France; OECD calculations.

Foreign-controlled production or sales are substantially more important than imports. For countries for which data are available, local production is at least twice as large as total imports and ranges up to five times larger. Imports comprise both intermediates and finished products, so that the value of local production compared with imports of finished products is approximately twice as large as the values shown in Table 2.15. The high values of foreign-firm production illustrate the highly developed local presence of foreign-controlled firms in all major markets. Sourcing of foreign intermediates also parallels the importance of foreign firms in national markets. Countries with high shares of foreign-controlled sales (*e.g.* the United Kingdom) have high shares of foreign sourcing (compare Figures 2.7 and 2.8).

D. International collaboration agreements

Collaboration agreements require substantial resource commitments by participants, with or without equity participation. They may overlap with joint ventures and minority investment, but do not necessarily take these forms. At the end of the 1980s they were a particularly important feature of globalisation to achieve objectives such as complementarities in R&D and scale economies in the regulatory process, expand marketing resources and broaden geographical reach, and make better use of the science and research base (*e.g.* in universities and research institutions). The United States is the pivot nation, particularly because of its biotechnology strengths. Product development and marketing are driving forces, and this has become more accentuated. Established companies are leading the phenomenon, but small dedicated biotechnology companies are widely involved.

To obtain a clearer understanding of the role of collaboration agreements in the industry, the structure of a sample of international agreements in pharmaceuticals/biotechnology have been surveyed by the OECD Secretariat.[11]

◆ Figure 2.9. **Market penetration, 1989 – Pharmaceuticals**
Share of foreign supply in total

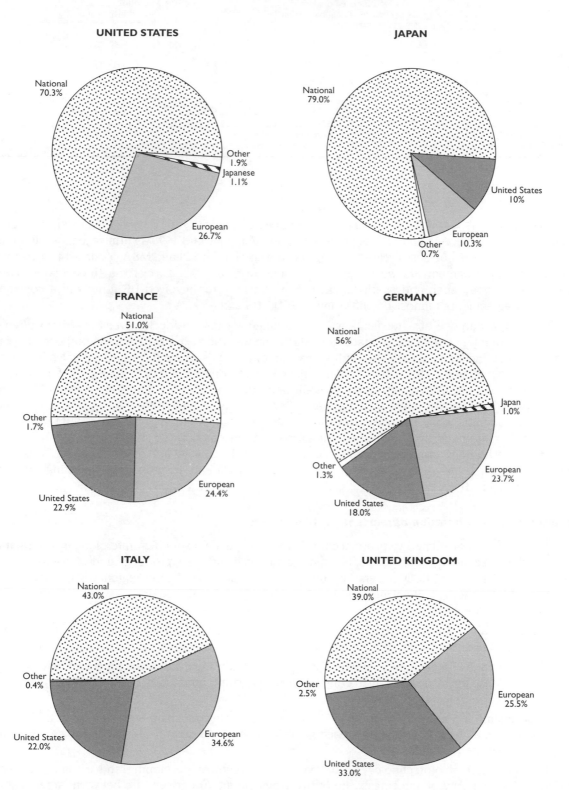

Source: P. de Wolf, based on IMS; Ministère de l'Industrie, France; OECD calculations.

97

Table 2.15.   **Production by foreign-controlled firms and imports of pharmaceuticals, around 1990**

	Foreign-controlled production as percentage of total production	Foreign-controlled production divided by imports
Australia	72 (1986/87)	2.2
France	49	3.4
Germany	34	2.0
Italy	57	4.8
Japan	21	3.4
United Kingdom	61	4.2
United States	30	4.6

Note: "Production" is sales, turnover, output or shipments, depending on source.
Source: Calculated from national sources, De Wolf and OECD, DSTI, EAS Division.

The industry is very active in using collaboration agreements, clearly outweighing its share in employment or value added. Agreements were clustered particularly around 1990 as firms expanded internationally at the end of the business cycle – this was also a peak year for FDI and M&A (Table 2.14). Two-thirds of the international agreements were between partners from at least two of the three major economic regions in Europe, Japan and North America. Almost two-thirds involved US firms and a considerable number of agreements (almost one-fifth) involved US-US agreements.

The major purpose of agreements was development of new products (over two-thirds) often combined with other purposes such as marketing. Marketing was the next most common purpose (40 per cent of agreements, including agreements with more than one purpose). Production was involved in less than one-third of agreements. This pattern is somewhat different from the purposes across all of industry where development and production were almost equally important (in 54 per cent and 50 per cent of agreements respectively), marketing less so (in 30 per cent of agreements). Clearly these agreements reflect the two primary considerations in pharmaceuticals firm strategies – to develop new products, and to market them efficiently. A clear majority of agreements involved large research-based firms, or these large firms and smaller biotechnology firms. Agreements between small firms were not common. A few large US and European research-based firms were particularly active (8 US and 4 Europeans), reflecting their importance in the industry.

International collaboration agreements in biotechnology

In biotechnology related to pharmaceuticals there has been a very high rate of alliance formation as dedicated biotechnology companies begin to commercialise new products and processes. Using a different database, an OECD Secretariat survey of a sample of 134 inter-regional collaboration agreements in biotechnology (involving Europe, Japan, the United States) in the period January 1991 to February 1993 showed:[12]

- Almost all involved at least one US partner, two-thirds involved European partners, one-fifth Japanese partners, and 10 per cent partners from other countries.

- 60 per cent of agreements for which details are known involved development of new products or processes, and one-third marketing, with a few combining both development and marketing. Production agreements were rare.

- Licensing and equity participation (joint ventures, minority share-holdings) were both relatively common as part of agreements, each involving about one-quarter of firms in the sample, particularly between smaller firms.

Consolidation of biotechnology is driven by high costs of developing and commercialising new products. The majority of agreements are of two types: about 70 per cent are between large established pharmaceuticals companies and DBCs, where the large company finances research; there is a new trend for agreements between smaller DBCs as they rationalise and merge operations.

E. Licensing agreements

Licensing has been a traditional feature of the industry, often to exploit patented products in smaller markets, where firms lack detailed experience with regulation and health requirements, or where the licenser did not have an adequate sales force. It may also represent a transition phase prior to direct investment. For smaller innovative firms, licensing or co-development is a viable alternative to in-house final development and extensive testing of new products. Many small to medium-sized companies (particularly in Japan) have relied on licensing as an entry strategy.

A comprehensive survey of international licensing in the mid-1980s (OECD, *STI Review*, No. 4) showed that pharmaceutical firms were among the most active in licensing their patented products (over 10 per cent of total international licensing activities in the sample of manufacturing firms), and their revenues from licensing were growing faster than the average. Joint ventures and other non-licensing forms of technology transfer were growing rapidly but not as rapidly as in many other industries. Licensing tended to be tightly controlled by the parent enterprise, and, compared with the average, licensing often involved mature products. Drug companies were also the most likely to supply raw materials and intermediates to their licensees.

Cross-licensing between large companies has become more important. As R&D costs and regulatory burdens increase, many firms rely on a very limited range of internally produced in-patent products for their profit streams. Cross-licensing is a means of expanding the product portfolio or entering different types of markets.

Finally, the growing importance of *biotechnology* has added a new dimension to traditional licensing arrangements. Large firms have been either buying significant equity stakes in promising biotechnology ventures (for example Hoffmann La Roche buying into Genentech) or they have been contracting R&D projects to them. This has shifted arrangements away from licensing based on patented single molecules towards long-term sharing of research results between large funding firms and the science-based R&D contractor.

5. GOVERNMENT POLICIES

Important areas of policy shaping the industry are health and safety regulations, support for the science and technology base, intellectual property rights, trade policies, and competition policies.

Probably the most important set of policies which have shaped the industry globally have been health and safety regulations and price controls administered by government or government-related health authorities. This has meant that the industry has adopted a multi-country form of organisation with major firms operating through local subsidiaries, which formulate and package drugs for final sale. It has also shaped trade flows, with intermediate products taking up a significant share of total trade and intra-firm trade of major importance. This multi-country form of organisation is underlined by the necessity of having large local sales forces to maintain customer contact.

A. Regulation

a) Health and safety

The industry is the object of considerable government regulation and supervision, even in countries where government regulation of industry is otherwise weak. For health and safety reasons all national administrations control the admission of new drugs to domestic markets through complex regulatory approval procedures. The introduction of new pharmaceutical products requires a number of administrative procedures including testing and inspection on such aspects as safety, quality and effectiveness, packaging and labelling, before being admitted to the national market. Optimal regulatory policy for the pharmaceuticals industry requires a balance between the time necessary to prove a product safe and efficacious, the time needed to launch new products on the market for patients who need them, and the time needed by companies to recoup their R&D expenditures and other associated administration and introduction costs. Delays in regulatory procedures can delay market entry, thus making product development relatively more expensive by lengthening the period before profit can be expected; they can also shorten a product's effective patent life.

An important issue has been the technology-specific regulatory treatment of genetic research, and of the resulting products. The trend in the United States has been towards easing of rules and speeding approval and registration procedures, since in the pharmaceuticals industry the products of modern biotechnology are not seen to raise radically new safety issues. In Europe the growth of biotechnology applications and firms have been restricted compared with the United States, by regulations that reflect higher concerns about perceived risks of the technology, and by patent uncertainties linked to ethical aspects. However, as regards specific regulation of pharmaceutical products, in Europe, the United States and Japan there has been continuing progress towards mutual harmonization and streamlining of procedures.[13]

Significant local presence is important during the regulatory and testing procedures. A company's global strategies may also be affected by differences between countries in the time taken for testing to be completed or in the application of regulations. For example, in the past there have been restrictions on exports of drugs which have been accepted and certified as safe in export markets, but which are still passing through regulatory procedures in the home country. This encouraged firms to establish production subsidiaries in foreign markets while they are waiting for completion of home-market testing (see Trade, Section C below).

b) Price

Most governments try to control pharmaceutical expenditures either by regulating prices of individual prescription drugs, by limiting total spending, or by encouraging competition from cheaper sources, notably generics. Pharmaceutical price controls and cost reduction are part of wider health-care cost-containment policies in place in most OECD countries. Even though pharmaceuticals are only a small part of total health-care costs they are often seen as an area where significant economies can be made. Pricing and consumption are inter-connected issues, with consumption often high in relatively low-cost countries, particularly when costs are covered by government-funded schemes. There are however exceptions, for example in Australia with low prices due to government purchasing power, combined with low consumption. Pharmaceutical costs as a share of total health expenditures in OECD countries vary from less than 10 to well over 20 per cent:

– pharmaceuticals are a low share of national health expenditures (less than 10 per cent): Australia, Denmark, Finland, the Netherlands, New Zealand, Sweden and the United States;

– moderate share (10-15 per cent): Austria, Canada, Ireland, Norway, Switzerland and the United Kingdom;

– high share (15-25 per cent): Belgium, France, Germany, Greece, Italy, Luxemburg, Portugal, Spain and Japan.

Pressures to reduce costs are seen across this whole spectrum of countries. In Europe, the United Kingdom (low overall expenditures via national health controls) and Italy (low growth since 1994, due to strict price controls) are countries which have had relatively low, or slow-growing total drug expenditures, although all countries have been trying to hold down expenditures.

Pricing policies can create distortions in the pattern of trade in the absence of any world market price for drugs and through possible discrimination between domestic and foreign manufacturers. The enactment of cost-containment programmes, price controls, or both, may also reduce revenues that can be reinvested in R&D programmes. In turn, the implementation of policies that significantly restrict R&D efforts in a country could result in a decrease in the international competitiveness of that country's pharmaceuticals industry. On the other hand, the existence of publicly funded drug benefit programmes in many countries provide pharmaceuticals companies with a substantial and virtually guaranteed market and assured cash-flow.

In many countries the product goes through a registration process, which sets the price at which the product is to be marketed, and registration on the list of drugs benefiting from government-supported or regulated third-party payments. From a trade standpoint, national registration for admission and marketing of drugs represents a form of regulatory *non-tariff barrier* which may affect trade either through differences in the standards applied by the regulatory bodies of different countries, or differences in the treatment given to indigenous and imported drugs. The area of new drug approval is one where international harmonization of standards and procedures between countries which possess, as is the case for OECD countries, very similar aims and criteria appears in principle both desirable and feasible (see Section C below). Such harmonization would reduce the effects of regulatory barriers to trade.

The high overall degree of government regulation is often seen as a major factor explaining the segmentation of the world market for pharmaceuticals into individual national markets. This has encouraged extensive globalisation of a particular kind, through the establishment of local subsidiaries and it also has prevented pharmaceutical companies from taking the world market as a single homogeneous market for each unique product. To the extent that national regulations are non-tariff measures to trade, they undermine the efficient allocation of economic resources and thus add to overall production costs.

B. Industry and technology policies

The main focus of government policies for technology, investment, regional location, and small firms has been to:

– *support the science base,* which has fostered new chemical and biotechnology advances; and

– encourage *venture capital investment* through tax breaks and promotion of venture capital funds.

The pharmaceutical industry receives very little direct R&D support from governments. The share of government funding in business enterprise pharmaceutical R&D is considerably less than 2 per cent in most OECD countries. Only in Italy and Australia is it greater than 2 per cent and only in Australia is it greater than the average of government support to all manufacturing R&D. This is in sharp contrast with the other R&D-intensive industries – aerospace, computers and electronics. Due to their importance for defence, these other industries receive very high levels of government R&D funding. However, because of its high R&D intensity the pharmaceutical industry benefits from all kinds of general support such as deductions of R&D expenditures from taxable income, tax credits and other R&D tax relief.

There has also been extensive direct support for the science base and biotechnology research, particularly in the United States. Industrial R&D spending in new biotechnology was estimated to be $1.4 billion in 1987, while various federal agencies dedicated US$2.7 billion in the same year. By 1993, US industrial expenditures were estimated to be US$3 billion and government expenditures US$4 billion, with the major share spent on therapeutic products and health care. In the mid-1980s most other OECD governments also set up extensive biotechnology research programmes, often involving industrial consortia. By 1991, national government support for biotechnology R&D in the European Community amounted to around US$600 million annually (particularly important in Germany, with *e.g.* a 5-year 1990-95 programme to industry, universities and research institutes, budgeted at US$950 million, and the United Kingdom).[14] The major impact has been in the research community, and the growth, particularly in the United States and the United Kingdom, of dedicated biotechnology companies spun off from these major programmes.

The participation by foreign-controlled firms in government-supported R&D programmes or the purchase by foreign firms of small biotechnology research firms do not seem to raise major political problems. This is in contrast to the situation in semiconductors, computers or electronics. However, there continue to be unresolved issues as to who participates and who gains from government-funded research, which require continued work in order to minimise international tensions.

C. Trade policies

Trade policies or changes in trade policies have had a limited effect on the organisation of the industry with regard to international dispersal of activities, trade patterns and foreign direct investment. *Tariffs* on pharmaceutical products are generally very low (between 6 and 8 per cent), despite tariff peaks in certain drugs. They cannot be considered a major factor in the internationalisation process of pharmaceuticals companies. The industry and governments nevertheless have attached great importance in bringing tariffs down further multilaterally, in the Uruguay Round, or bilaterally. Efforts have also been undertaken in suspending tariffs temporarily, as the United States and the European Community had done under certain circumstances.

There has been little use of quantitative restrictions in this sector. However, *other non-tariff barriers*, including specifications with regard to manufacture, labelling, packaging, standards, certification and other regulatory aspects, are important and affect overall competition. Efforts are being pursued to reduce the economic effects of these non-tariff barriers. In November 1991, the first International Conference on Harmonization took place in Brussels. The European Community, the United States and Japan agreed on a five-year harmonization programme of their technical requirements for new drug market authorisation. Three areas were considered: quality, safety and efficacy of medical products for human use. The second conference took place in Orlando (United States) in 1993 with the final conference in Japan in 1995. The agreement, by setting international standards on the data which firms must produce to get their new pharmaceuticals approved, represents a major effort in the process of harmonization of drug regulations via mutual acceptance of test data, and contributes to efficiency and cost saving in the pharmaceutical industry.

In 1992 the EC legislative framework for approval of medicinal products was changed. Starting 1 January 1995 there are three differentiated marketing authorisation procedures for pharmaceutical companies to submit new products for approval. They may apply:

– To a single national authority to obtain access to a single national market (national procedure).

– To their own national authorities in order to obtain mutual recognition by other EU Member States. This covers the majority of medicinal products and becomes mandatory from 1998 when authorisation is sought in more than one Member State. The procedure allowed for binding arbitration by the Commission if other Member States refuse recognition (decentralised procedure).

– To the newly established European Agency for the Evaluation of Medicinal Products (EMEA, London), with authorisation valid for the entire Single Market. This is mandatory for biotechnological products (including such veterinary medicinal products), and is optional for other innovative medicinal products and new chemical entities (centralised procedure).

These procedures allow more rapid access of new products to the whole of the EU.

In the past, pharmaceutical companies in the United States have been affected by *export restrictions* if drugs were approved overseas before approval in the United States. This gave companies an incentive to establish manufacturing facilities abroad for drugs not yet approved in the United States. These overseas manufacturing facilities could service other foreign markets in which the drug was approved and eventually be used to supply the US market, since other countries generally had not imposed export bans. The US provisions were amended in 1986 in the Drug Export Amendment Act, which expressly authorises exports of unapproved pharmaceuticals to countries that are deemed to have effective drug approval regimes when certain conditions are satisfied.

Pharmaceuticals have not been the object of any particular trade remedy measure. There has never been a recourse to an official safeguard measure under Article XIX of GATT with regard to these products nor are there cases of governmental grey-area measures. Pharmaceuticals also have not participated in the spate of *antidumping actions* which have characterised trade policy in some major countries (although the chemicals industry in general has been a major object of such actions). The absence of such measures and actions may be attributed, at least in part, to the multi-country structure of firms in the industry, to the low level of trade relative to production, and to the stable oligopoly of established global firms which dominate the industry and absence of new rapidly growing competitors.

However, some trade-policy actions have been taken or threatened in the context of protecting *intellectual property rights*, particularly patent rights. Pharmaceutical firms incur high costs due to patent infringement, estimated at about 5 per cent of the value of world-wide revenues. The US Trade and Tariff Act of 1984 amended section 301 of the Trade Act of 1974 to allow the imposition of import restrictions against countries that inadequately protect US intellectual property. Subsequently there have been US actions, for example, against Brazil and Thailand for lack of patent protection for American pharmaceuticals. China has been the focus of recent actions due to ineffective enforcement of IPRs in general.

D. Foreign investment policies

The concept of *national treatment* is directly relevant for pharmaceuticals, particularly whether and to what extent foreign companies can enjoy the same economic and non-economic advantages as domestic companies. Are government policies and regulations non-discriminatory once a foreign company is established on the domestic market and do these companies benefit from the same conditions under which domestic companies operate?

With respect to FDI policies, the pharmaceuticals industry is subject to the general regulatory framework of member states *vis-à-vis* foreign direct investment. In terms of *foreign access* to OECD markets, industry-specific governmental restrictions affecting the access and treatment of foreign investors are not an issue. However, this does not exclude the existence of, for example, private business practices that could be regarded as obstacles to the free flow of investment in the industry. In terms of *promotion of inward investment*, a number of countries have encouraged it as part of industrial strategies to increase high value-added activities. For example the Australian "Factor (f)" scheme allows for higher prices to be paid to a company in return for approved programmes of development and a significant commitment to local R&D and production. The objective is to restore activity constrained by low prices under the pharmaceutical benefit scheme, where average prices are below world prices. Ireland has promoted export-oriented inward investment in health-care products as part of its industrial development strategy.

Transfer pricing issues are likely to continue. About 40 per cent of total trade is intermediates, the share of total intermediates sourced internationally is increasing, and large multi-country research-based companies have a high share of most national markets and a relatively high share of their trade is intra-firm transactions. Internal pricing policies of firms are an important part of price formation, and cost containment policies in most OECD countries are demanding greater scrutiny of pharmaceutical prices.

E. Protection of intellectual property

Patents play a particularly important role in the pharmaceutical industry. New molecules or biological material are unique and can be clearly identified. Patents grant their owners exclusive property rights over the subsequent exploitation of the new product. The exclusive right creates a barrier to entry and the exploiting firm will continue to receive monopoly rents until expiry of the patent. The trade-off is between welfare losses (and higher profits) due to patent protection and monopoly during the lifetime of the patent, and benefits arising from the stimulation of innovation. Licenses are granted to licensees to allow them to exploit patent rights in return for royalty and fee payments. Licensing in pharmaceuticals is "horizontal" between firms operating at the same level in the production process.

There has been much debate over the optimum length of time to grant patent rights for new pharmaceutical products and the effects of licensing. Research-intensive firms have been affected by a creeping extension of the time taken for compulsory testing and registration, which shortens the effective length of patent life and reduces profits to plough back into further innovation of long-term benefit. On the other hand, cost-containment policies have emphasized the advantages of limiting patent life and encouraging lower-cost generic production. Similarly the advantages of wider diffusion of new drugs through licensing have to be set against the monopoly rights granted to the licensee to exploit them.

The historical situation with respect to patents has been different in different countries. Japan gave process protection, but did not introduce product patents until 1976. Italy gave no patent protection until 1978, and Spain only provided full new-product protection in line with other European Union countries in 1992. A number of non-OECD countries (*e.g.* Brazil and India) have provided scanty patent protection to pharmaceuticals, and have excluded biotechnology from patentability. Free trade arrangements between the EC/EU, EFTA and countries in Central and Eastern Europe have all paid considerable attention to IPRs.

To provide a better balance between the problem for inventors of shortening effective patent lives and the consumer welfare requirement that products be inexpensive and available from more sources, the United States introduced the Drug Price Competition and Patent Term Restoration Act in 1984. On manufacturers' application for special consideration, the Act allowed extension of effective patent lives, but reduced requirements for extensive testing of generic products. This was designed to provide stronger protection towards the end of patent lives, but stimulate competition on patent expiry. With the same objective, the European Community adopted in 1992 a regulation for the creation of a Supplementary Protection Certificate for medicinal products (in force 1 January 1993). The SPC may not exceed five years and introduces an effective protection over a period of 15 years after first marketing authorisation in Europe. One probable effect has been to increase cross-border mergers and alliances between research-intensive firms and generic producers to enable the inventing firm to maintain a healthy profit stream after patent expiry.

There have been similar attempts in *licensing policy* to provide a better balance between returns to innovation and consumer welfare. Competition regulations have tended to exempt license agreements provided that they do not include restrictive obligations and clauses (prices, quantities, territories). The "block exemptions" of the EC on patent and know-how licensing introduced in 1984, clarified those elements which are acceptable in licenses which would be exempt from competition policy scrutiny. In Canada compulsory licensing, which was aimed at expanding lower-price generics production and import, was abolished effective from February 1993, and the current patent regime provides for 20-year protection.

One of the aims of the Uruguay Round of multilateral trade negotiations completed in December 1993 was to strengthen both the level and enforcement of intellectual property protection. With respect to patents, the Final Act goes a considerable way in this regard. The agreement requires 20-year patent protection from filing of application, whether of products or processes with a general obligation to comply with the substantive provisions of the Paris Convention, and sets out obligations of member governments to ensure that intellectual property rights can be effectively enforced. Developing countries will be allowed to delay implementation (5 years, and 11 years for least-developed countries), but in the cases of pharmaceuticals (and agricultural chemicals) developing countries must accept the filing of patent applications from the beginning of the transition period ("pipeline" protection). The WTO Agreement on Trade-Related Aspects of Intellectual Property Rights entered into force on 1 January 1995, with *all* WTO members obliged to implement "pipeline" protection for pharmaceuticals (and MFN and national treatment obligations) by 1 January 1996. Among other things, the new provisions and disciplines for patents will effectively strengthen protection for new drugs, and may decrease the relative importance of generics.

F.   Competition policy

Competition policy has focused on four areas relevant to globalisation in the pharmaceuticals industry.

Patents and licenses, where the balance between rewarding inventors and increasing competition has been examined extensively (see above).

Inter-firm collaboration agreements. There has been growing acceptance of such agreements in competition policy, *e.g.* the US Justice Department's acceptance of R&D joint ventures, and the European Commission giving block exemptions to co-operative R&D joint ventures which have all the functions of an autonomous economic entity, including sales. Expansion of such agreements to allow joint exploitation of the results of R&D to be extended to joint development and exploitation of a drug for the treatment of AIDS has recently been allowed by the CEC (XXth Report on Competition Policy); and to a joint venture between the world's two largest vaccine producers to speed development and distribution of new broad-spectrum vaccines (1994).

Pricing practices such as monopoly pricing and price discrimination on domestic markets. For example, cost-containment programmes have encouraged parallel trade in pharmaceuticals within the European Union to take advantage of low-cost producers, but this has generally been limited due to firm practices in varying trademarks, presentation, packaging and labelling in different countries, and further hindered by remaining slow and complex government licensing procedures.

There have been various moves to increase competition and expand supply of products in retailing, which could help to change the way that the industry markets its products by reducing exclusivity of supply at retail level. Examples include closer examination of:

- Distribution practices involving the sale of particular products exclusively through pharmacies. A number of manufacturers have sought to restrict distribution of products such as beauty preparations to high-price outlets such as pharmacies.
- The scope of restrictive government regulations on the sale of pharmaceutical products has also been questioned in some OECD countries, with the aim of allowing greater retail level competition in pharmaceuticals.

NOTES AND REFERENCES

1. Production and consumption data for the industry come from a variety of sources: OECD, DSTI/EAS Structural Analysis Database and OECD Industrial Structure Statistics (production, trade, value added, employment, R&D), OECD Health Care data file for national consumption of pharmaceuticals and health expenditures, OECD Trade tapes for global trade data. Data on market size and activities of major firms are drawn from SCRIP. All data are in current prices and have been converted at current exchange rates. The UNIDO report (Ballance *et al.*) provides data deflated to 1980 dollar values which are not comparable with other sources.

2. Values sensitive to exchange rates. Recent estimates from the same source have varied widely year-on-year.

3. The available data do not distinguish between in-patent, generic or OTC products, although production and trade patterns are likely to differ in each category.

4. There are few sources of data on IFT, and information on the subject is not generally available in traditional trade statistics. Data on IFT are mostly available through firm surveys based on questionnaires by national authorities. This section is based on information provided by the US Department of Commerce, which conducts surveys of foreign affiliates of US companies and US affiliates of foreign companies. Similar data is not available for other countries. The US Department of Commerce uses the International Surveys Industry (ISI) classification in its surveys. There is a category for "drugs" (ISI 283), which includes the manufacturing, fabricating, or processing of medicinal chemicals and pharmaceutical products. The level of aggregation in these surveys does not allow distinction between intermediates and finished pharmaceutical products. For an explanation of availability and problems with data see OECD (1993).

5. Rough estimates put this share at over two-thirds, but classification problems prevent more precise calculation of the share of IFT in US pharmaceutical trade.

6. See OECD (1993).

7. Intra-industry trade can be readily calculated for any given product category, as only bilateral trade statistics are needed. The interpretation of IIT data depends however, on how the category is defined, as the choice of the classification system and of the level of aggregation may strongly influence the results. For this analysis, the Standard International Trade Classification Revision 2, at four digit level, was used. In the calculation of an IIT index, if exports are equal to imports, IIT is 100; if either imports or exports are equal to zero, IIT is zero. For discussion of the theory and measurement of IIT, see Grubel and Lloyd (1975).

8. Data for chemical and pharmaceutical industry FDI from OECD/DAFFE.

9. Data are not complete and vary among sources.

10. Discussion in some parts is based on the number of operations, since value data were incomplete. Data are from KPMG Peat Marwick from OECD/DAFFE.

11. The sample of 76 agreements is drawn from the INSEAD Collaborative Agreements Database. This database, covers all regions of the world, and all industries (with a focus on manufacturing), and was compiled through late-1992. It covers development, production and marketing, and currently comprises 2 565 separate agreements. The information in this section was drawn from a short report on "Collaboration agreements in pharmaceuticals" prepared by Judith Jaffe under the direction of Professor Deigan Morris, INSEAD, who designed and developed the data base and who holds the rights to it.

12. The sample was drawn from the US monthly, *Genetic Technology News,* "Strategic Partners Report", which provides comprehensive information on developments in biotechnology. For the period January 1991-February 1993, 392 biotechnology agreements were listed. Of these, 134 had one partner from the United States, Europe or Japan and one other international partner, focused on pharmaceutical products. Details discussed are for these 134 agreements. The remainder were mostly intra-US agreements in pharmaceuticals with eleven intra-European pharmaceutical-biotechnology agreements.

13. Ongoing OECD work is assessing the economic aspects of biotechnology in health care, including policy and organisational aspects.

14. Biotechnology R&D expenditures for the United States from FCCSET Committee (1992), *Biotechnology for the 21st Century,* and estimates. For the EC, estimates from Bernhard Zechendorf, DGXII.

BIBLIOGRAPHY

BALLANCE, R., J. POGÁNY, and H. FORSTNER, (1992), *The World's Pharmaceutical Industries*, UNIDO, Edward Elgar, Aldershot.

CASADIO TARABUSI, C. (1993), "Globalisation in the Pharmaceutical Industry: Technological Change and Competition in a Triad Perspective", *STI Review*, No. 13, OECD, Paris.

CHEMICAL AND ENGINEERING NEWS (1993), "Chemical industry R&D spending to rise modestly", 25 January; "Japanese chemical companies still mired in slump", 8 February.

COMMISSION OF THE EUROPEAN COMMUNITIES, *Panorama of EC Industries 1991-92*; *Panorama of EC Industries 93*.

COMMISSION OF THE EUROPEAN COMMUNITIES, *Panorama of EU Industry 94*, Brussels.

COMMISSION OF THE EUROPEAN COMMUNITIES, *Report on Competition Policy*, various issues.

CONGRESS OF THE UNITED STATES, OFFICE OF TECHNOLOGY ASSESSMENT (OTA) (1994), *Multinationals and the U.S. Technology Base*, US Government Printing Office, Washington, DC.

DALTON, D.H. and M.G. SERAPIO (1992), "U.S. Research Facilities of Foreign Companies", US Department of Commerce.

EAG (1989), *Generic Pharmaceuticals: The Threat*, EAG, London.

FINANCIAL TIMES (1994), quoting Ernst and Young, 9 May.

GRUBEL, H.G. and P.J. LLOYD (1975), Intra-industry Trade: The Theory and Measurement of International Trade in Differentiated Products, MacMillan, London.

OECD, *Competition Policy in OECD Countries*, Paris, various issues.

OECD (1985), *The Pharmaceutical Industry: Trade Related Issues*, Paris.

OECD (1992), *Globalisation of Industrial Activities: Four Case Studies*, Paris.

OECD (1992), "The International Sourcing of Manufactured Intermediate Inputs: By Canada, France, Germany, Japan, the United Kingdom and the United States", Paris.

OECD (1993), *Intra-firm Trade*, Paris.

OECD (1994), Health Care Data File, Paris.

RAUGEL, P-J. (1992), "European Biotechnology Investments in North America and Japan", *BFE*, Vol. 9, November/December.

SCHREYER, P. (1992) "Competition Policy and Industrial Adjustment", *STI Review*, No. 10, OECD, Paris.

SCRIP, *Pharmaceutical Company League Tables*, 1981, 1982, 1990, 1991, 1992, 1993 editions, PJB Publications, Surrey, United Kingdom; other SCRIP publications.

US DEPARTMENT OF COMMERCE (1991), *Foreign Direct Investment in the United States*, Washington, DC.

US DEPARTMENT OF COMMERCE (1993), *Foreign Direct Investment in the United States: An Update*, Washington, DC.

US DEPARTMENT OF COMMERCE, U.S. Industrial Outlook 1992, 1993 and 1994.

US INTERNATIONAL TRADE COMMISSION (1991), *Global Competitiveness of U.S. Advanced-Technology Manufacturing Industries: Pharmaceuticals*, USITC Publication 2437, September, Washington, DC.

VICKERY, G. (1988), "A Survey of International Technology Licensing", *STI Review*, No. 4, OECD, Paris.

DE WOLF, P. in F. Sachwald (ed.) (1993), *L'Europe et la globalisation: Acquisitions et accords dans l'industrie*, Masson, Paris.

Chapter 3

GLOBALISATION IN THE COMPUTER INDUSTRY

by

Graham Vickery

Directorate for Science, Technology and Industry, OECD

Table of contents

LIST OF TABLES

LIST OF FIGURES

SUMMARY AND CONCLUSIONS

The computer industry is highly globalised. It has relatively high levels of international investment in production, international sourcing of parts and components and peripheral equipment, intra-firm trade, and international collaboration agreements. The industry is very trade-intensive. The computer industry is among the most active of all high-technology industries in these areas.

Firms in the computer industry have tended to grow organically, through exploitation of their technological advantages, rather than through mergers and acquisitions. This has been due to the nature of the industry, dominated for a very long period by one large US firm (IBM), and more recently due to the increasing importance of established Japanese computer firms. This has been the pattern since the 1950s, when large electrical engineering firms in Europe and Japan, and to a certain extent the United States, moved into the computer industry. The pattern of globalisation has changed recently as the structure of the industry has moved from being dominated by the established firms supplying large systems and competing on technical grounds with proprietary systems, towards new entrants supplying small systems and computers for individual use competing on the basis of efficient manufacturing and marketing and using open or common systems.

The industry has also seen the advent of many new entrants into specialised areas of computing (technical work stations, super-computers, services), and the industry is increasingly using external sources of parts and components and software from specialised suppliers. Dominant firms in the industry now supply microprocessors (Intel) and software (Microsoft) for use in hardware from many different suppliers, rather than the traditional hardware suppliers. The early and rapid development of new companies to exploit successive waves of technological change, from main-frame computers to mini-computers, to personal computers, to smaller portable machines, has occurred particularly in the United States. With declining component costs and the increasing emphasis on dispersed networks of standard units, computers are becoming more user-friendly and accessible products, marketed to individual customers. In this new environment, marketing and competition with consumer-oriented electronics firms will become increasingly important if historical distinctions between the computing, telecommunications and broadcasting industries continue to disappear.

The industry is very R&D-intensive (the second or third highest among major industries after aerospace), with 60 per cent of the world's R&D carried out in the United States, one-quarter of the total in Japan, and a smaller share in Europe. R&D remains highly centralised in the home country of parent firms (predominantly US and Japanese), but large firms in the industry have been very active in establishing collaboration agreements for development. These have been centred around US firms, and the industry continued setting up new agreements through the early 1990s, in contrast to many other industries.

The industry is highly concentrated in OECD countries, with close to 80 per cent of production and 90 per cent of world consumption in OECD countries. The top five OECD producing countries produce two-thirds of the world total and consume close to three-quarters of the total, and account for close to 60 per cent of exports and 55 per cent of imports. The Dynamic Asian Economies (DAEs: Korea, Chinese Taipei, Hong Kong, Singapore, Thailand, Malaysia) have rapidly become important suppliers, particularly of peripherals and parts and components which are exported to OECD countries. Singapore is the third largest world producer and exporter, and the DAEs together produce 20 per cent of the world total, and export one-quarter. The industry is also concentrated at firm level. The top firm has close to one-fifth of the world market, although this share has declined from a quarter in five years, and the top five firms have almost 40 per cent.

Trade is inter-regional rather than intra-regional in this industry, with the exception of European trade. Both East Asia and North America trade much more outside their region than within it, with exports from East Asia (including Japan) being particularly oriented to markets outside the region. The share of intra-regional computer exports for all three major regions did not change significantly in the 1980s through to 1993. On the other hand, the share of intra-regional imports in total imports decreased greatly for North America and slightly for Europe. Intra-regional imports increased greatly for East Asia, due to the emergence of East Asian countries as major exporters and the growth of sourcing networks around East Asia.

Two-thirds of US trade in computers and other office equipment was intra-firm trade (IFT) – considerably higher than the average share of IFT for manufacturing industries; which was a little over a third. This share increased sharply in the 1980s, due to the establishment of US firms in East Asia and of East Asian firms in the United States. Intra-industry trade (IIT) indices have also increased sharply for US trade in computers, as US trade in that sector became more balanced. IIT indices for Europe are generally high due to the importance of intra-European trade. They are however, quite low for Japan and other East Asian countries, due to their large trade surplus.

An important area for government policy has been in the area of R&D support. The importance of computers for defence and their key role in the information infrastructure has meant that governments have provided extensive support to computer development and the information technology industry. Intellectual property rights play an important role in providing protection to innovators while ensuring rapid diffusion. New approaches have been developed to extend copyright protection to software, but protection and enforcement is still not uniform or certain, and there still is widespread copying and counterfeiting.

The computer industry has a high level of trade intensity. Even though the industry is perceived to have strategic importance, governments have been reluctant to apply trade-restrictive measures due to the strong linkages with other industries. Tariffs are relatively low and there are few quantitative restrictions. Trade friction exists, however, as there are perceived problems of market access, some of them addressed by bilateral initiatives. Trade friction has arisen from the introduction of a series of antidumping duties, generally focused on peripherals and parts and components from Japan and other East Asian suppliers. The computer industry was until recently the object of extensive export restrictions, mainly for security reasons.

Three current trends will re-shape the global operations of the industry. First, the shift towards "commoditisation" of computers, due to very rapid declines in hardware prices is likely to continue, and domestic and individual uses to expand. This will favour efficient international production and sourcing of parts and components and peripherals in the DAEs and induce production and exports from other industrialising countries such as China, India, and Brazil.

Second, the software and computer-related services industry is likely to remain the competitive advantage of OECD countries and of a few rapidly developing Asian countries which have highly skilled engineers and a technically trained workforce, geographically close to final consumers and users of these services.

Finally, the high research intensity of the industry suggests that international alliances and consortia are likely to become more important, particularly between computer firms, component producers and software firms, particularly if new markets develop due to the convergence of computing, telecommunications and broadcasting.

I. INTRODUCTION: CHARACTERISTICS OF THE INDUSTRY

The computer industry has been one of the most dynamic industries, with among the highest growth rates of all manufacturing industry. However, many firms in the industry faced problems in the 1990s due to the slow-down in demand with the recession and continuing technological change leading to shifts in consumer preferences. The industry has evolved:

– away from multi-user main-frame systems towards single-user systems (particularly towards personal computers, portable PCs, and work-stations, all of which are now capable of networking);

Table 3.1. **Worldwide IT market composition**

Percentages

	1987	1988	1989	1990	1991	1992	1993	1994	1995
Systems	49.7	49.5	49.3	47.9	45.1	43.5	42.9	43.2	43.5
Multi-user	27.9	26.7	25.3	22.9	20.7	18.8	16.3	14.3	12.9
Single user	21.8	22.8	24.1	25.0	24.4	24.8	26.6	28.9	30.6
Data communications	2.9	2.9	3.0	3.1	3.3	3.6	4.1	4.3	4.4
Packaged software	13.8	14.1	14.2	15.4	16.5	17.5	17.7	18.0	18.5
Services	33.6	33.5	33.4	33.6	35.1	35.4	35.3	34.6	33.7
Total	**100.0**	**100.0**	**100.0**	**100.0**	**100.0**	**100.0**	**100.0**	**100.0**	**100.0**

Source: International Data Corporation.

– towards software and services which have become more important parts of the information technology (IT) industry.

Established firms with entrenched positions in a particular technology have had difficulty in moving to the next generation of products, *e.g.* from main-frames to mini-computers, to personal computers and to new products (notebook PCs, small user-friendly products, and multimedia products).

The distribution of world-wide information technology revenues clearly illustrates these two trends (see Table 3.1). Hardware-dominated systems represented 43 per cent of the world IT market in 1995 and this share was forecast to continue to decline, whereas it was almost 50 per cent at the end of the 1980s. Large multi-user systems have been shrinking rapidly as a share of total revenues. Single-user systems are growing, and with software, data communications and services, have steadily increased their share of the total IT market. Although product specialisations vary among the world's major firms, the trend towards services and software has been notable for firms that previously specialised in systems. Most large firms have operations and sales in both hardware and software, and they may be difficult to disentangle. Wherever data for the IT industry as a whole are presented in this paper, they are identified.

The hardware industry has shifted towards standardised products with rapidly evolving networking and storage capabilities, competing largely on price and rapid introduction of new or expanded features, including modems and inter-connectability, high-capacity hard memory disks, multimedia capabilities including audio and audio-visual CD-ROM, local and wide-area interactive video and data communications based on a move towards client-server networked systems. Products are increasingly:

– made up of standard parts and components supplied by specialised component manufacturers (microprocessors, storage units, memories, screens, printers);

– run standard operating systems (an estimated 85 per cent of all PCs run MS/DOS software, and mid-sized and mini-computer systems are shifting towards adopting UNIX-based standards);

– use standard externally supplied applications programs (word-processing, business and graphics programs); and

– can be inter-linked to larger systems, communications networks, or large external databases and information systems.

There have been sharp declines in prices, for example US average price indices dropped by close to 16 per cent per year from 1989 through 1993, and by another 10 per cent in 1994. These have been due to technological change, the supply of standard products on an original equipment manufacturer basis by assemblers in the DAEs (o.e.m. – where equipment is supplied by one manufacturer to be sold under another's brand), and fierce competition between suppliers battling for market share, particularly in the personal computer segment.

Furthermore demand for computers has become more cyclical, as is the case for other investment goods. This is due to the pervasiveness of computer and IT use, the increasing share of computers and IT

Table 3.2. **Geographical distribution of IT sales for top firms, 1993**

Percentages

	North America	Europe	Asia	Other
IBM	41	33	16	10
Fujitsu	6	26	65	2
Hewlett-Packard	51	34	9	6
NEC	6	4	88	3
Digital	37	47	10	6
Hitachi	8	5	85	2
EDS	77	17	1	5
Apple	55	25	14	6
Unisys	53	22	16	9
Compaq	45	38	5	12
Siemens-Nixdorf	3	94	3	1
AT & T	55	24	10	11
Canon	30	29	37	4
Groupe Bull	19	73	6	2
Olivetti	6	80	9	5
Sun Microsystems	51	24	23	2
Toshiba	11	9	76	3
NTT	0	0	100	0
Microsoft	56	30	9	4
Matsushita	14	8	75	3

Source: Gartner Group.

products in investment, as well as a shift towards standardisation in the industry, all of which bring IT investment decision making into the mainstream of investment.

Firms in the industry have usually grown organically on the basis of new products and, increasingly, on new ways of organising production and marketing to gain manufacturing efficiencies and to compete on price. US firms have been operating internationally for the longest period and on average generate one-half of their revenues outside the United States. The share of US firm revenues coming from outside the US has been high and increasing over a long period, in part due to the relative decline of the US dollar. In the 1990s the trend reversed somewhat as the US market expanded more rapidly than European and Japanese markets. Large Japanese firms generate over 75 per cent of their revenues in Japan. The exceptions are Fujitsu, because of its ICL subsidiary, and firms such as Canon and Matsushita, which are suppliers of small business machines and peripherals (monitors, printers) and were not producers of main-frame computers. European firms generate around 80 per cent of their revenues in Europe, and with the exception of Bull which expanded in the United States through acquisition, they have have not been increasing revenues significantly outside their home base (see Table 3.2).

The challenges of adaptation for established firms and opportunities for new entrants are increasing with the convergence of computing, telecommunications, broadcasting, and entertainment towards an interactive multimedia industry. In this new environment, low cost production, efficient marketing and competition with consumer-oriented electronics firms will probably become increasingly important. New competition is currently shaping up in the home environment. It is not clear to what extent new interactive, information and entertainment services will be delivered by personal computers and to what extent by more sophisticated interactive video equipment building for example on cable and satellite TV. These developments will transform the industry and are likely to split it between technical computing functions (the traditional area of main-frame computers and large systems) and domestic consumer-oriented functions with different kinds of firms servicing the two distinct areas.

Despite these projected shifts this chapter focuses on the established conventional hardware industry, and describes the recent evolution of globalisation in that industry.

2. TRENDS IN GROWTH AND STRUCTURE

A. Production and consumption

The computer industry was the fastest growing industry in the United States, Japan, Germany, the United Kingdom and France through the 1970s and 1980s, based on constant price gross output growth. In 1994 world production of computer equipment was US$225 billion, estimated to rise to US$260 billion in 1996 (Elsevier, electronic data processing equipment only, not including developing Africa, Eastern Europe and China, constant US dollar estimates). The whole information technology market was US$464 billion in 1994, and around US$514 billion in 1995 (International Data Corporation, including hardware, software and services).

The industry is showing geographical shifts in production location, with rapid growth in hardware production in the DAEs, following earlier rapid growth in Japan. In 1994 Japan and the United States each had over one-quarter of world computer production, Europe one-fifth, and the DAEs one-fifth (see Table 3.3). The five largest producers were (1994 current values and exchange rates): Japan, the United States, Singapore, Chinese Taipei and the United Kingdom, followed by Germany and France, with the top-5 OECD producers having 67 per cent of the total. In 1996 it was estimated that the United States was the largest producer, followed by Japan, Singapore, Chinese Taipei, the United Kingdom and Germany. The US industry re-affirmed leadership in high-growth new products, and at the same time production continued to shift to Asian countries where the DAEs had 20.7 per cent of world production. Most Asian production comes from foreign affiliates of OECD-based computer firms, or is purchased (sourced) by them.

The five largest markets for equipment in 1994 were the United States, Japan, Germany, the United Kingdom and France, with a combined share of 72.5 per cent, and 6.0 per cent for the DAEs. This order was unchanged in 1996 with the DAE markets still only 6.5 per cent of the total. During the late 1980s and early 1990s, Europe was the largest market for computer equipment with one-third of the total, but the largest market has once more shifted back to the United States. Markets in the DAEs and the rest of the world are growing fastest, although they are small. A similar picture is seen in the whole IT market, with the United States leading, followed by Europe, and Japan smaller (see Figure 3.1).

Over the long term, the equipment industry doubled its share of manufacturing value added from the mid-1970s through to the late-1980s (11 OECD countries), peaking at 3 per cent and then declining in the 1990s with increasing competition and pressure on prices.[1] The share of computers in total manufacturing value added is similar to that of pharmaceuticals and considerably lower than motor vehicles. The share of the computer industry has declined since the late-1980s while the pharmaceutical industry has been increasing. This shows the inability of the computer hardware industry to maintain prices with increasing

Table 3.3. **World distribution of computer hardware production and markets, 1994**

Billion US$ and percentages

	Production	% of world production	Markets	% of world production
OECD[1]	174.1	77.4	194.7	89.5
Europe	42.7	18.9	64.1	29.5
America	69.3	30.8	86.0	39.5
of which: United States	60.8	27.0	74.1	34.0
Asia, Oceania	112.3	49.9	65.4	30.1
of which: Japan	66.7	29.6	47.7	21.9
Other[2]	0.9	0.4	2.0	0.9
Total[2]	**225.1**	**100.0**	**217.5**	**100.0**

1. OECD does not include Greece, Iceland, Luxembourg, Mexico, New Zealand, Portugal and Turkey for which detailed data are not available.
2. Not including developing Africa, Eastern Europe, China, some of Latin America and Middle East.
Source: Elsevier Advanced Technology (1996).

◆ Figure 3.1. **Worldwide IT market by region and for some countries, 1987-94**

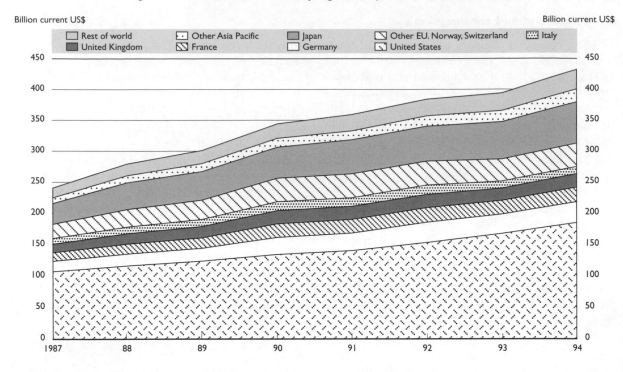

Source: OECD (1996), *Information Technology Outlook 1995.*

competition and the shift towards standardisation, particularly in the growing PC and small system markets.

Two different long-term patterns are observed for the major countries in the industry. There were increasing value-added shares in most countries, particularly notable for Japan, the United Kingdom and Australia, and falling shares in a few countries where increased competition led to severe pressures on domestic producers (Canada, Italy, Germany, Sweden) (see Figure 3.2).

Most OECD countries are net consumers of computers. Only Japan, the United States and Ireland consistently produced more than they consume. Japan has improved its position over a long period, with rising exports as a share of production and falling imports as a share of consumption, while for the United States consumption surpassed production by 1990 as imports passed exports. France, Germany, Italy and the United Kingdom covered most but not all of their consumption. Germany and Italy had production to consumption ratios above one in the 1970s, as did Sweden, but imports subsequently outstripped exports. All countries except Japan and the United States had imports equivalent to at least one-half of consumption, and the United States joined this group in the 1990s. Canada, Denmark, Norway, Spain, Sweden and the Netherlands are large net consumers. All have high levels of exports compared with production, due to re-exports and highly export-oriented domestic producers (Table 3.4).

B. Employment and productivity[2, 3]

Employment in the computer industry showed steady growth through to the mid-1980s, but has subsequently declined. Employment grew from around 750 000 in 1978 to reach almost 1.1 million in 1985, with a subsequent gradual decrease (15 OECD countries) (see Figure 3.3). More recent firm-level data shows that employment losses accelerated in the early 1990s due to restructuring and job cutting in many large established firms in the industry. Employment in the top-20 IT firms world-wide in 1993 was more

◆ Figure 3.2. **Value-added shares – Computers**

Share of computers in total manufacturing value added

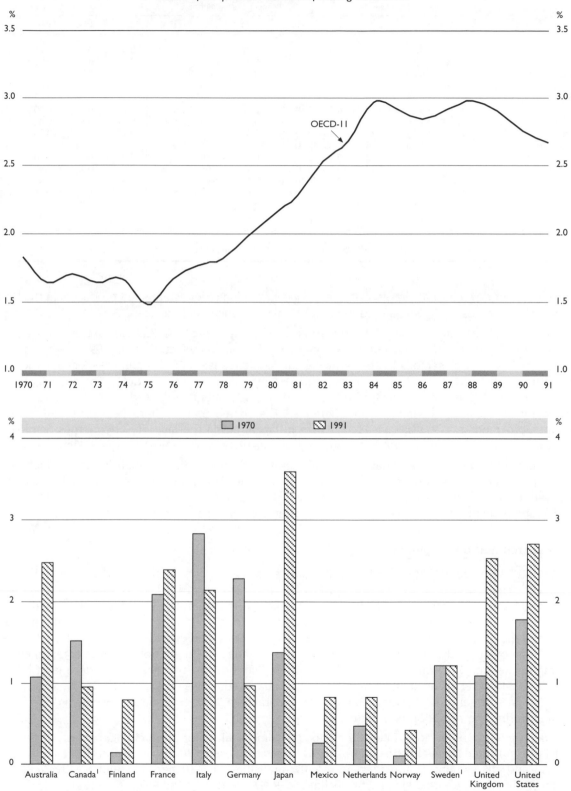

Table 3.4. **Indicators of production and consumption – Computers**

	Production/consumption				Imports/consumption				Exports/production			
	1970	1980	1990	1993	1970	1980	1990	1993	1970	1980	1990	1993
Australia	0.36	0.71	0.46	0.50	0.65	0.32	0.59	0.60	0.03	0.04	0.11	0.20
Canada	0.71	0.52	0.53	0.46	0.53	0.93	0.87	0.96	0.31	0.86	0.76	0.91
Denmark	0.33	0.29	n.a.	n.a.	0.90	0.94	n.a.	n.a.	0.68	0.78	n.a.	n.a.
Finland	0.15	0.37	0.55	0.86	0.89	0.78	0.69	0.73	0.23	0.39	0.43	0.69
France	0.90	0.89	0.80	0.84	0.31	0.43	0.50	0.56	0.23	0.36	0.37	0.42
Germany	1.10	0.99	0.75	0.71	0.44	0.72	0.79	0.66	0.49	0.72	0.70	0.51
Italy	1.15	1.10	0.89	0.95	0.20	0.89	0.49	0.76	0.31	0.90	0.45	0.69
Japan	1.00	1.09	1.24	1.26	0.14	0.07	0.08	0.08	0.14	0.15	0.26	0.27
Netherlands	0.90	0.73	0.46	0.60	0.44	0.78	1.96	2.70	0.37	0.69	3.09	3.81
New Zealand	0.16	0.08	0.12	0.12	0.84	0.93	0.89	0.91	0.00	0.12	0.10	0.25
Norway	0.18[1]	0.37	0.38	n.a.	0.95	0.91	0.96	n.a.	0.73	0.75	0.90	n.a.
Spain	0.22	0.45	0.31	0.39	0.99	0.83	0.99	0.99	0.94	0.61	0.97	0.96
Sweden	1.15	0.94	0.64	0.48	0.67	0.83	0.84	0.90	0.71	0.82	0.75	0.72
United Kingdom	0.83	0.91	0.88	0.80	0.53	0.73	0.77	0.82	0.44	0.71	0.73	0.77
United States	1.16	1.23	0.98	0.80	0.08	0.10	0.43	0.55	0.21	0.27	0.42	0.44

1. 1973.
Source: OECD DSTI STAN database. "Computers" is ISIC 3825, manufacture of office, computing and accounting machinery.

than 10 per cent down on 1988 levels. Cuts were concentrated in older established producers in the United States and Europe as they struggled to compete in new products and services.

The share of computer employment in manufacturing employment (OECD-15) rose by 0.4 percentage points from the mid-1970s to around 1.4 per cent of total manufacturing in 1991, with a peak of 1.6 per cent in 1985. The sector's low but growing employment share in most countries, despite the recent downturn, is similar to other research-intensive industries such as pharmaceuticals. The highest shares in 1991-92 were in Japan (2.5 per cent of manufacturing employment), followed by Australia, the United States, France, the United Kingdom and Germany. The United States' share peaked in 1983. Average annual employment growth was consistently high in Japan, but in the majority of countries employment growth was lower from the mid-1980s than from the mid-1970s to the mid-1980s (see Figure 3.3).

Productivity. The computer industry, like all high-growth industries, has high levels and high growth in labour productivity (Verdoorn-Kaldor Law). From the mid-1970s to the late 1980s value added per employee in the industry was well above the manufacturing average, as were pharmaceuticals and motor vehicles; it was higher than motor vehicles, but lower than pharmaceuticals.

C. Research and development[4]

The R&D intensity (business R&D expenditures as a share of production) of the computer industry has slowly increased from around 10 per cent in 1973 to 11 per cent in 1992. The industry was consistently the second most R&D-intensive industrial sector after aerospace, and is well above the manufacturing average. This position dropped to third, behind pharmaceuticals, in 1992. Traditional computer producers cut R&D as their revenues and profits declined in the early 1990s, and considerable computer-related R&D is now being carried out in the software and services industries which are not surveyed comprehensively; so computer-related R&D may well be under-reported. The industry also shared the decline in business enterprise R&D experienced in 1992 and 1993 in all major countries. The peak in R&D-intensity in the mid-1970s was largely due to the US industry maintaining R&D expenditures when production was declining during the recession (see Figure 3.4).

Since the early 1970s, R&D intensity climbed in almost all major producing countries. Of the major countries, the United States has the highest R&D intensity (close to 20 per cent) and the German, Italian, Japanese and UK computer industries have R&D intensities of 5-10 per cent along with Canada and Sweden. Only France showed significant declines in R&D-intensity in the 1973-92 period.

By far the major share of computer R&D is performed in the United States. In 1992 the shares were (Secretariat estimates calculated in purchasing power parities): United States US$11.5 billion

◆ Figure 3.3. **Employment growth – Computers**

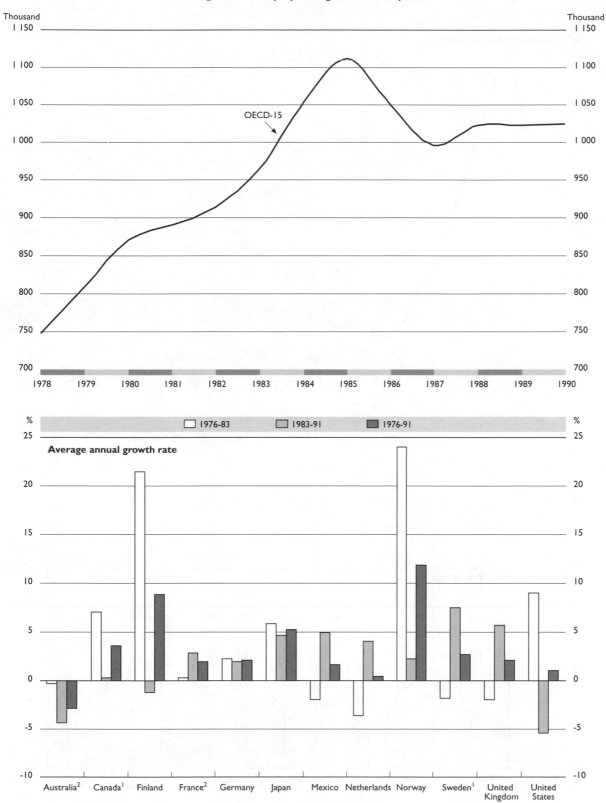

◆ Figure 3.4. **R&D intensity – Computers**

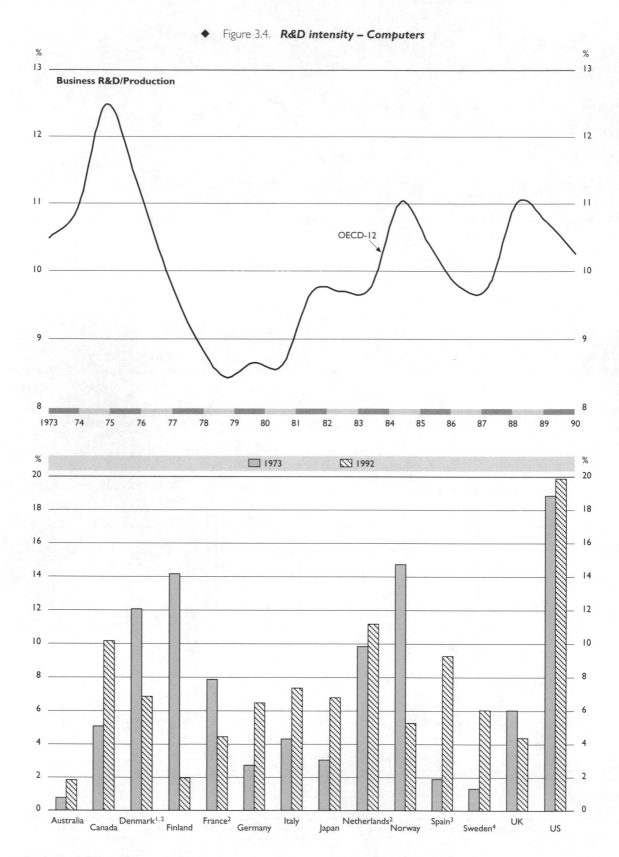

1. 1980. 2. 1991. 3. 1978. 4. 1990.
Source: OECD, DSTI, STAN, ANBERD Databases.

(60.6 per cent), Japan US$4.3 billion (22.9 per cent), EU-12 US$2.9 billion (15.3 per cent), other OECD countries US$0.2 billion, with total OECD expenditures around US$18.9 billion (compared with US$20.1 billion in 1990).

R&D employment and R&D output. A large and increasing share of employees are research scientists and engineers. The share was particularly high in the United States and the United Kingdom (15-20 per cent), lower in Germany and Italy (5-10 per cent), and low but increasing rapidly in Japan as the R&D intensity of the Japanese industry more than doubled in the 20 years between 1973-92. The output from R&D effort can be measured in patenting activity. Analysis of patenting activity in the United States shows that the Japanese industry was the only OECD country industry with a good and improving performance. The DAEs, particularly Singapore, Hong Kong and Chinese Taipei, also showed increasing but sporadic activity in the sector.

International distribution of R&D. Computer R&D is slowly spreading from home countries to host countries. A considerable share of R&D performed by foreign firms is in the computer industry, due to its R&D intensity. In France in 1989 over 12 per cent of *all* R&D performed by foreign firms was in computers, in 1990 in Canada over 11 per cent and in the United States 6 per cent.

In most cases the share of R&D performed by foreign firms is lower than their share of production. Around 1990 in France, foreign firms were only one-quarter as R&D-intensive (R&D expenditures/sales) as domestic firms, and in the United States foreign-owned computer affiliates performed 6 per cent of business R&D compared with having over 13 per cent of computer production. In the broader electronics industry in the United Kingdom, foreign firms have only one-half the share of R&D that they have of output, and in Ireland almost all computer production is in foreign-controlled firms whereas there is some R&D by Irish firms in related areas of electronics and software. Canada is an exception, where over 70 per cent of R&D is performed by foreign firms, compared with a sales share of less than 50 per cent.

Finally, detailed data on the operations of US parent firms and their majority-owned foreign affiliates show that 1993 computer sales of manufacturing affiliates are considerably larger than those of US parents (US$134 billion against US$101 billion), but that affiliate R&D expenditures were less than one-seventh of US parents (US$1.5 against US$11.3 billion).

Overall, computer R&D is probably more highly centralised in the home country than for most other industries, a tendency strengthened by government support programmes, often defence-related, that have favoured domestic firms.

D. Capital investment[5]

Capital investment is moderately high in the industry. Annual investment has been about 4-6 per cent of production in the United States and Japan. R&D is the most important investment in the industry and capital investment is considerably less than one-half of R&D in the United States, and about one-half of R&D in Japan. At the end of the 1980s, capital investment was highest in Japan and Germany and in Italy and Canada, and higher than the national average for manufacturing in the United States, Japan, Italy, Germany, Denmark and Norway, and the same level in Canada and the United Kingdom. Investment has been highly cyclical with an approximate five-year cycle: rising in the mid-1970s, falling in the late 1970s, increasing again in the early 1980s and falling again in the mid-1980s, with a general downward trend in investment intensity in most major OECD producing countries towards the end of the 1980s.

E. Concentration and competition

Firm concentration. The industry is led by a group of ten large firms with around 50 per cent of the world's IT revenues. However, between 1985 and 1992-93 the share of leading firms in the top-100 firms' world-wide IT revenues has fallen. This was due to the sharp decline in the world-wide share of revenues of the market leader, IBM, which fell from 30 to 20 per cent and has continued to fall. This decreasing share carried through the top-20, decreasing world-wide concentration. However, excluding IBM, the largest firms are gaining a larger share of the revenues of the top-99 IT firms with an increase of 2-3 per cent (see Figure 3.5).

◆ Figure 3.5a. **Global concentration[1] – Computers**

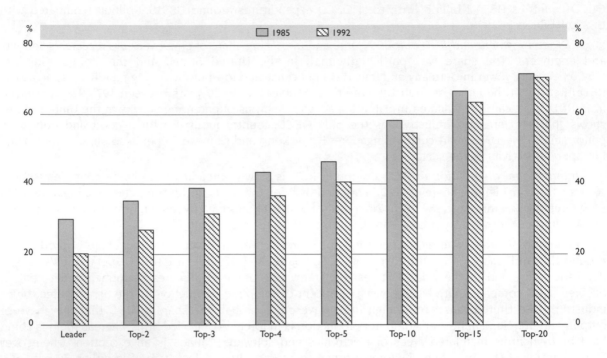

1. Based on top 100 total IT revenues.
Source: Datamation.

◆ Figure 3.5b. **Global concentration[1] – Computers**
Excluding IBM

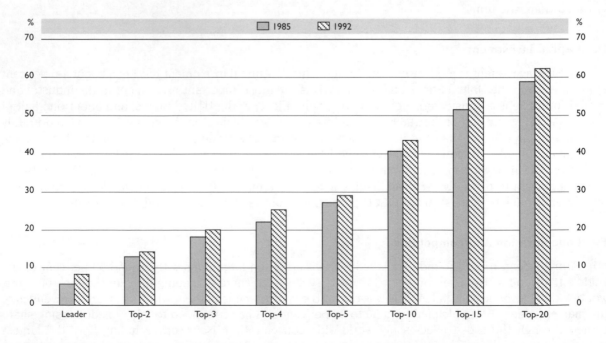

1. Based on top 99 total IT revenues.
Source: Datamation.

◆ Figure 3.5c. **Regional concentration – Computers**

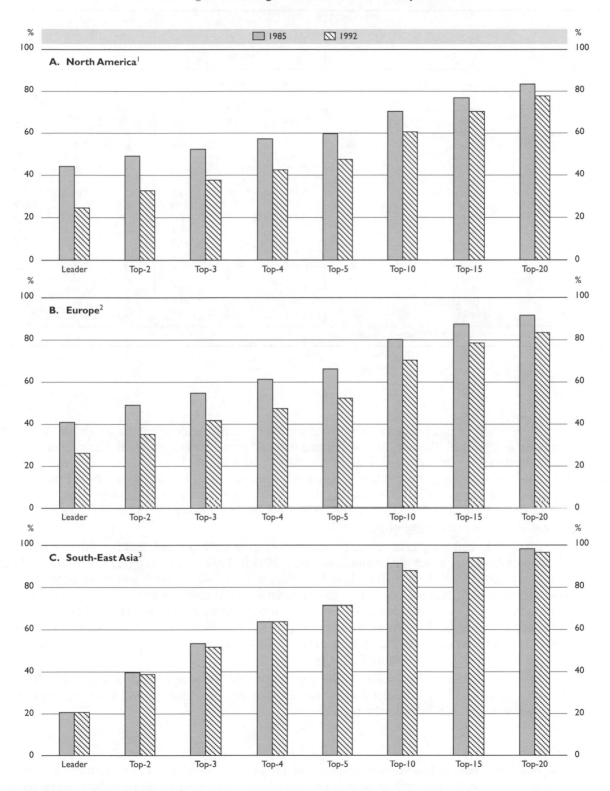

A. North America[1]

B. Europe[2]

C. South-East Asia[3]

1. Based on total IT revenues of top 60 firms.
2. Based on total IT revenues of top 50 firms.
3. Based on total IT revenues of top 30 firms.
Source: Datamation.

Table 3.5. **Top-20 firms ranked by 1993 worldwide IT revenues**

	Headquarters	1993	1993 performance			1992	1991	1985
		Rank	IT revenue (Million US$)	% total revenue	IT employment (thousands)	Rank		
IBM	United States	1	59 154	94.3	263.5	1	1	1
Fujitsu	Japan	2	18 933	69.3	97.3	2	2	2
Hewlett-Packard	United States	3	16 297	76.1	69.5	5	5	7
NEC	Japan	4	15 128	50.0	69.5	3	3	4
Digital	United States	5	13 637	100.0	92.3	4	4	3
Hitachi	Japan	6	12 755	20.2	61.1	6	6	6
EDS	United States	7	8 562	100.0	70.0	15	16	36
Apple	United States	8	8 446	100.0	14.9	11	10	19
Unisys	United States	9	7 742	100.0	49.0	9	8	5
Compaq	United States	10	7 191	100.0	10.5	18	19	54
Siemens-Nixdorf	Germany	11	7 071	14.4	42.0	8	9	10/24
AT & T	United States	12	6 111	9.1	50.9	7	7	15
Canon	Japan	13	5 017	32.2	20.1	16	15	33
Groupe Bull	France	14	4 963	100.0	31.8	13	12	18
Olivetti	Italy	15	4 848	89.0	31.8	12	11	12
Sun Microsystems	United States	16	4 493	100.0	12.8	19	17	126
Toshiba	Japan	17	4 426	11.3	19.2	10	13	11
NTT	Japan	18	4 165	7.4	9.7	–		
Microsoft	United States	19	4 021	97.9	14.9	20	24	118
Matsushita	Japan	20	3 526	6.3	15.3	14	14	14

Source: Derived from Gartner Group (for 1993) and Datamation (for other years).

The decline in IBM's top position was most dramatic in North America, where the leader has lost 20 per cent of the IT market. Without IBM, other firms retained market share overall. In Europe, the loss of market share by IBM was somewhat less than in the United States (around 13 per cent from 1985 to 1992), but other large firms also lost their share of remaining revenues, with the top-4 to top-20 firms losing 5-7 per cent of total European revenues. In Asia, the leader's share remained unchanged, the top-2 and top-3 firms losing a little, and the top-10 to top-20 firms shares decreasing by 2-4 per cent. Without IBM, the picture in Asia was little different.

Major firms. Although the global concentration of the top firms decreased, IBM remained the largest firm in IT revenues in Europe and the United States from 1985 to 1992, and moved up from fourth to third in Asia. By IT revenues, 15 of the top-20 firms in 1993 were in the top-20 in 1985, and seven of the top-10 were in the top-10 in 1985. However, only the top-2 firms preserved their ranking throughout. Furthermore, there was considerable change at the bottom end of the top-20 ranking, with new firms climbing rapidly, particularly highly innovative US firms such as Compaq in PCs, Sun in technical work-stations running on new types of microprocessors, and Microsoft in software, and new Japanese suppliers of peripherals and small systems such as Canon (see Table 3.5 for ranking).

In 1993 the distribution by nationality in the top-20 was: ten US, seven Japanese and one firm each from Germany, France and Italy. This distribution had not changed greatly since 1985, when Japan had five and the United States eleven firms in the top-20.

F. Pricing

There has been continuous downward pressure on prices due to fierce competition and rapid technological change in the industry. There has been much effort to construct price indices which reflect the continual improvement in quality and performance of computer equipment, and which deal with the continuing change in equipment, and the problem of resulting non-comparability between consecutive generations of equipment and software capabilities. Table 3.6 displays the application of these indices in

Table 3.6. **US fixed investment expenditures by type**

	1988	1989	1990	1991	1992	1993	1994
Computers and peripheral equipment:							
Current US$ (bn)	42.0	44.0	34.8	34.2	36.5	47.0	54.1
Constant 1987 US$ (bn)	44.1	49.8	45.3	51.4	68.3	105.4	134.8
Implied price deflator (1987 = 100)	105.0	113.2	130.2	150.3	187.1	224.3	249.2
Implied price index (1987 = 100)	95.2	88.4	76.8	66.5	53.4	44.6	40.1

Source: Calculated from US Department of Commerce, Survey of Current Business.

the United States ("hedonic" price indices), showing that current prices of new computers and peripheral equipment adjusted for quality more than halved from 1987 to 1994.

3. INTERNATIONAL TRADE

A. General trends

The industry is very trade-intensive. If the exports/production ratio for all manufacturing is 1 then computers is 2.2, compared with automobiles around 1.6. Between 1980 and 1993 total world exports of computers (SITC Rev.2 752, including peripherals) grew from US$12.5 to US$85.6 billion, outstripping growth in production. Parts and components trade (intermediates, SITC Rev.2 7599) was similarly dynamic, with exports growing from US$7.5 billion to US$53 billion over the same period. The ratio of trade in parts and components to computer trade remained stable over the period. Computer exports from the OECD area grew at a slower pace, from US$12.3 billion in 1980 to US$63 billion in 1993.

In 1993, OECD countries accounted for 74 per cent of world exports and 85 per cent of world imports of computers (down from 98 per cent of exports and 90 per cent of world imports in 1980). The decline in OECD export share has been due to the emergence of new producers in East Asia, particularly Singapore, Chinese Taipei and the Republic of Korea, and a corresponding decrease in the world export share from major OECD producing countries, except Japan (Figure 3.6).

The US share in world computer exports fell from 36.4 per cent in 1980 to 18.1 per cent in 1993, while the share of the top-6 European exporters (United Kingdom, Germany, the Netherlands, France, Ireland, Italy) fell from 42.3 per cent to 28.9 per cent in the same period. Of those six, only the Netherlands and Ireland increased their share of computer exports (Table 3.7).

The main source of growth in world computer exports came from East Asia. Japan increased its share of world exports from 4.3 per cent to 19.7 per cent. The DAEs plus China were exporting almost 23 per cent of the world total in 1993, whereas as a group they had less than 1 per cent of world exports in 1980. Singapore's share increased from 0.1 per cent in 1980 to 14 per cent in 1993, Chinese Taipei's share from 0 to 5.8 per cent and Korea's share from 0.05 to 3 per cent (see Figure 3.6 and Table 3.7).

The order of major computer exporting and importing countries changed dramatically between 1980 and 1993. Changes were most marked in the ranking of major exporting countries, with Singapore, Chinese Taipei and the Republic of Korea joining the top-10 league (respectively third, sixth and tenth). Although it lost a significant share of total world exports, the United States remained the second most important exporting country in 1993, surpassed by Japan which was the seventh largest in 1980. All the top-6 European countries went down in the ranking except the Netherlands.

US computer imports have increased significantly. By 1993, the United States had become by far the largest importer, whereas it was in fourth position in 1980. Germany was the second biggest importing country, followed by the United Kingdom, the Netherlands and France with the United Kingdom and France's import shares and ranking both falling (see Table 3.7).

These changes have had corresponding impacts on trade balances. The United States has become the major net importer of computers, ahead of Germany in 1993. All other European countries and most other

◆ Figure 3.6a. **World export market shares – Computers**

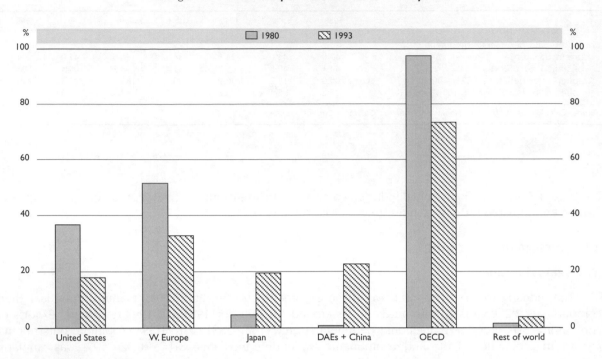

Note: Western Europe: EU + EFTA.
Source: UN Comtrade Database.

◆ Figure 3.6b. **World import market shares – Computers**

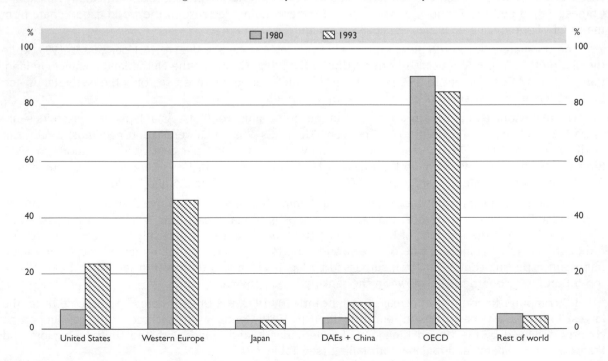

Note: Computers are SITC Rev. 2 752, including peripherals.
Source: UN Comtrade Database.

Table 3.7. **Trade in computers**

Thousand US$

Exports	1980		1993	
	Value	Share (%)	Value	Share (%)
Japan	542 052	4.3	16 860 334	19.7
United States	4 563 370	36.4	15 488 157	18.1
Singapore	7 240	0.1	11 951 310	14.0
United Kingdom	1 415 435	11.3	7 267 973	8.5
Germany[1]	1 300 000	10.4	5 196 381	6.1
Chinese Taipei	17	0.0	4 987 379	5.8
Netherlands	149 212	1.2	4 267 436	5.0
France	918 010	7.3	3 335 460	3.9
Ireland	350 118	2.8	2 615 042	3.1
Republic of Korea	5 740	0.0	2 584 738	3.0
Italy	1 157 574	9.2	2 087 385	2.4
Canada	663 584	5.3	1 408 193	1.6
Rest of world	1 447 202	11.6	7 579 980	8.9
WORLD	**12 519 553**	**100.0**	**85 629 767**	**100.0**

Imports	1980		1993	
	Value	Share (%)	Value	Share (%)
United States	880 550	7.0	22 739 081	23.5
Germany[1]	1 600 000	12.7	80 762	9.8
United Kingdom	1 413 290	11.2	7 420 560	7.7
Netherlands	657 090	5.2	7 049 776	7.3
France	1 406 837	11.2	5 234 093	5.4
Japan	445 067	3.5	3 405 555	3.5
Canada	502 680	4.0	3 356 735	3.5
Singapore	42 539	0.3	2 426 928	2.5
Italy	752 329	6.0	2 407 609	2.5
Spain	336 167	2.7	1 416 977	1.5
Switzerland	362 280	2.9	1 328 778	1.4
Rest of world	4 210 618	33.4	30 543 771	31.6
WORLD	**2 609 446**	**100.0**	**96 810 623**	**100.0**

1. Germany estimated for 1980.
Source: UN Comtrade database. Computers are SITC Rev 2 - 752, including peripherals.

OECD countries (with the exception of Ireland which has a substantial trade surplus) have had continuing trade deficits, although both the United Kingdom and Italy have been approximately in trade balance for a considerable period. Japan's computer trade surplus widened very significantly, while those of the new East Asian exporters in most cases turned from deficit to large surpluses.

Intra-regional trade. Intra-regional trade in computers (including peripheral units) is low within North America and Asia, and high in Europe. In 1993, 27 per cent of North American (United States, Canada, Mexico) computer exports were intra-regional, 21 per cent of exports went to East Asia (Japan, Korea, Chinese Taipei, Hong Kong, ASEAN countries and China), 36 per cent to Europe (EU and EFTA) and 16 per cent to the rest of the world. Intra-regional imports in total imports were even lower, having declined very sharply. For East Asia (the largest exporter) only 15 per cent of exports were intra-regional, 51 per cent went to North America, 29 per cent to Europe and 5 per cent to the rest of the world. In contrast to North America, the share of intra-regional imports for East Asia have climbed from a low base to over 55 per cent of the total, as regional sourcing networks have built up. European intra-regional exports of computers are by far the largest share of exports (82 per cent). Of the remaining European computer exports, 7 per cent went to North America, 3 per cent to East Asia. The share of intra-regional imports in total European imports is considerably lower (46 per cent) and declining, reflecting the rise of East Asia as a world computer supplier (Figure 3.7, Table 3.8).

Major differences among regions in the importance of intra-regional trade have been accompanied by stability on the export side. The share of intra-regional trade in total computer exports for North America remained below 30 per cent despite the introduction of NAFTA, East Asia's share remained below 20 per cent, and Europe's remained around 80 per cent.

Inter-regional computer trade has been most marked by the shift towards East Asia as the most important exporter, and North America as an increasingly important importer. US imports were largely sourced from Japan and East Asian countries, and Japanese imports from the United States and increasingly from East Asian countries. The United States has tended to be the most important single source of imports for the four largest European importers, while the principal destinations for all European countries' exports were other European countries.

The pattern of intra-regional trade in computer parts and components (intermediates, SITC Rev.2 7599) has paralleled that of computers. The major difference is that a higher share of total world imports and exports of intermediates is traded within East Asia (around 15 per cent of total world intermediates trade compared with only around 7 per cent of total computer trade). This trade has grown rapidly as sourcing networks have built up in the region.

B.   Trade in peripherals and international sourcing

The patterns of trade in peripheral units compared with finished computers show the relative specialisation of different regions in different segments of the production chain. With the exception of Japan, most OECD countries which are large exporters have relatively low shares of peripherals and related units (peripherals are SITC Rev.2 7525) in total exports – around 20 per cent. France has a high share of peripherals in total exports, probably due to extensive investment by IBM in France, and its use as a major supply point for peripherals for the rest of Europe. In contrast, Ireland has a very low share of peripherals in total exports, with US inward investors using Ireland for final assembly and export of complete systems to Europe.

For Japan almost one-half of exports are peripherals, due to its rapid build-up as a successful innovator and reliable producer of printers, drive units, storage units, etc. The rapidly growing Asian exporters have the highest levels of peripherals exports. Singapore has three-quarters of total exports in these products. This is due to the re-location to Singapore of many of the peripherals and parts-producing operations of leading manufacturers, and the growth of indigenous specialised producers. Chinese Taipei and Korea have 50-60 per cent of these products in total exports.

International sourcing. A further measure of globalisation is the extent and growth in international sourcing of manufactured intermediate inputs. The computer industry has the highest levels of international sourcing. All major OECD countries have been expanding their use of foreign intermediates. The ratio of imported to domestic sourcing in the computer industry increased in all major OECD countries from the early-1970s to the mid-1980s. It did however remain low in the United States and Japan, with Japan remaining below 0.2, the lowest of all. France and Germany had higher ratios, with Germany rising rapidly to 1.6. Canada had the highest ratio of imported to domestic sourcing, around 2 in the 1970s and 3 in the mid-1980s. The only exception is the United Kingdom, where the ratio of imported to domestic sourcing of inputs was well over 1 in the late 1970s, but fell back subsequently (see Figure 3.8).

Another way of looking at a country's foreign sourcing of intermediate inputs consists of tracing the effects of all intermediate inputs, *i.e.* also recording indirect imported inputs (International Linkage Index in Figure 3.8). This measure of total international inputs into the computer industry is somewhat lower than direct inputs. Overall Canada has the highest levels of foreign inputs, Japan the lowest, other countries distributed between, and the US index was growing most rapidly, reflecting the rapidly increasing international sourcing of parts and components by US firms (see Figure 3.8).

◆ Figure 3.7. **Intra-regional trade – Computers**
As percentage of exports for each region

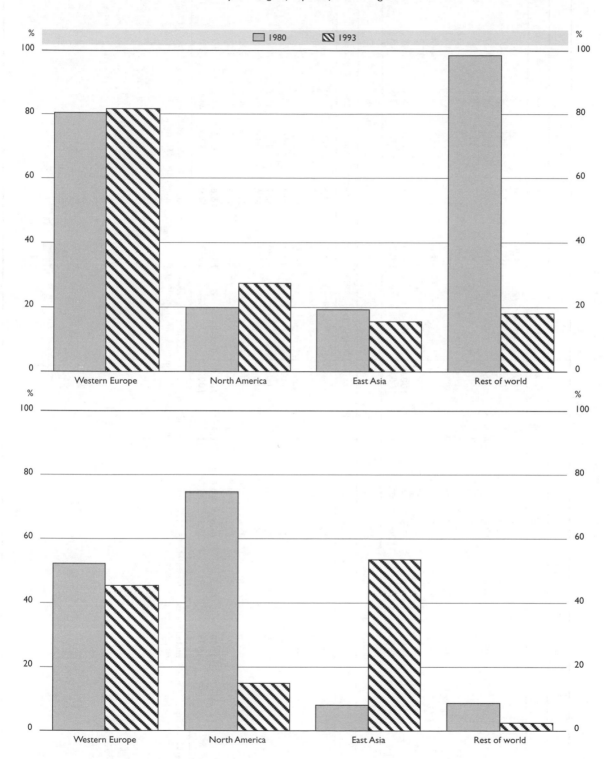

Note: Western Europe: EU + EFTA.
North America: US + Canada + Mexico.
East Asia: Republic of Korea, Chinese Taipei, Hong Kong, ASEAN countries and China.
Computers are SITC Rev. 2 752, including peripherals.
Source: UN Comtrade Database.

Table 3.8. **Inter- and intra-regional trade – Computers**

As a percentage of total imports or exports

Imports of finished products

To↓ from→		North America	Europe	EAs	Rest of world	Total
North America	1980	74.5	15.9	9.1	0.5	100.0
	1993	15.1	7.0	77.2	0.7	100.0
Europe	1980	44.8	52.0	2.3	0.9	100.0
	1993	22.3	45.6	30.8	1.3	100.0
EAs	1980	67.3	13.6	7.9	11.2	100.0
	1993	34.9	9.2	53.3	2.7	100.0
Rest of world	1980	54.6	27.7	9.0	8.7	100.0
	1993	45.5	25.1	26.6	2.7	100.0
Total	**1980**	**51.0**	**42.5**	**4.2**	**2.3**	**100.0**
	1993	**23.3**	**26.4**	**49.0**	**1.4**	**100.0**

Exports of finished products

From↓ to→		North America	Europe	EAs	Rest of world	Total
North America	1980	20.0	55.1	10.9	14.1	100.0
	1993	27.3	36.1	21.0	15.6	100.0
Europe	1980	4.7	80.7	1.9	12.7	100.0
	1993	6.9	81.7	3.1	8.2	100.0
EAs	1980	36.7	27.3	19.3	16.6	100.0
	1993	51.0	29.0	15.4	4.7	100.0
Rest of world	1980	-10.0	3.5	8.0	98.6	100.0
	1993	31.9	22.2	28.0	17.8	100.0
Total	**1980**	**12.2**	**66.1**	**6.5**	**15.2**	**100.0**
	1993	**31.3**	**47.8**	**12.6**	**8.3**	**100.0**

Imports of intermediate products

To↓ from→		North America	Europe	EAs	Rest of world	Total
North America	1980	49.7	18.5	29.2	2.6	100.0
	1993	23.9	9.0	64.4	2.6	100.0
Europe	1980	35.7	60.3	2.9	1.1	100.0
	1993	28.4	44.9	25.2	1.6	100.0
EAs	1980	68.3	9.8	20.4	1.5	100.0
	1993	27.4	4.5	66.9	1.3	100.0
Rest of world	1980	64.8	23.8	7.0	4.5	100.0
	1993	43.7	19.1	34.4	2.8	100.0
Total	**1980**	**43.5**	**44.6**	**10.3**	**1.5**	**100.0**
	1993	**27.7**	**23.1**	**47.3**	**1.9**	**100.0**

Exports of intermediate products

From↓ to→		North America	Europe	EAs	Rest of world	Total
North America	1980	14.6	56.1	17.9	11.5	100.0
	1993	29.1	37.2	21.2	12.6	100.0
Europe	1980	11.2	78.4	3.0	7.4	100.0
	1993	16.4	69.6	6.1	7.8	100.0
EAs	1980	62.7	11.9	18.3	7.1	100.0
	1993	42.6	23.0	30.7	3.7	100.0
Rest of world	1980	33.9	16.3	20.6	29.2	100.0
	1993	39.1	19.2	28.0	13.6	100.0
Total	**1980**	**18.8**	**60.7**	**11.3**	**9.2**	**100.0**
	1993	**32.0**	**39.5**	**21.5**	**7.1**	**100.0**

Note: North America = Canada, Mexico, United States; Eur = EU+EFTA, SEA = Brunei, China, Hong Kong, Indonesia, Japan, Malaysia, Philippines, Singapore, Republic of Korea, Chinese Taipei, Thailand. Finished products (computers) are SITC Rev.2 – 752, including peripherals. Intermediate products (parts and components) are SITC Rev.2 – 7599.
Source: UN Comtrade database.

◆　Figure 3.8*a*.　***Ratio of imported to domestic sourcing of inputs – Computers***

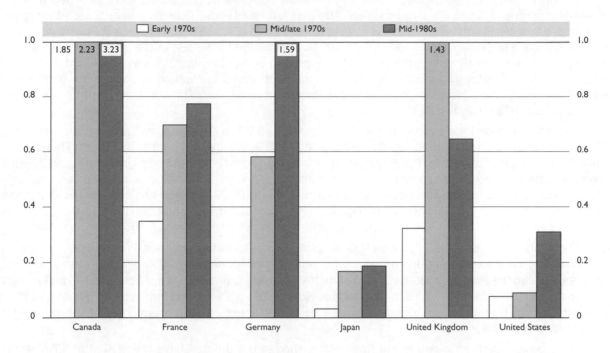

Source :　OECD, DSTI, EAS Division.

◆　Figure 3.8*b*.　***International linkage index – Computers***
Ratio of foreign to domestic interindustry linkage

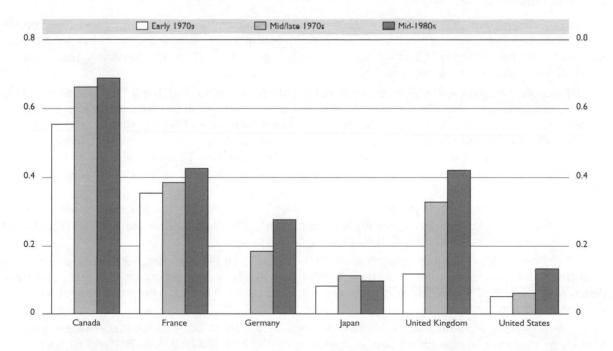

Source :　OECD, DSTI, EAS Division.

C. Intra-firm trade

Intra-firm trade (IFT) is defined as the international exchange of goods and services within a transnational enterprise.[6] While IFT accounts for a little over a third of total US merchandise trade, US trade in computers and other office equipment is largely composed of IFT. The IFT portion of US computer/office equipment trade increased dramatically in the 1980s, as opposed to the rest of the manufacturing sector.[7] This increase was mainly concentrated on US-East Asian trade. In 1982, IFT was estimated at around 30 per cent of both total US exports and total US imports of computers and office equipment. In 1990, IFT was estimated to have risen to 70-80 per cent for exports and 50-60 per cent for imports, excluding wholesale and related activities.[8]

US-based transnationals accounted for 75 per cent of US IFT in the computer/office equipment sector in 1990. Of these, US firms established in Europe and East Asia are by far the most important. There is one important difference, however: European affiliates are net importers from their US parents, while East Asian affiliates are large net exporters to their parents, increasing the US trade deficit in these products. IFT by US affiliates of foreign firms increased rapidly in the late 1980s, with recently established East Asian firms (very largely Japanese firms) clearly outstripping European firms established in the United States since an earlier date.

The relative importance of IFT for the US computer/office equipment industry is confirmed by data on the international trade of majority-owned foreign affiliates of US firms. In 1990, 95 per cent of both US imports and exports from/to majority-owned affiliates was intra-firm trade with US parents. A similar story can be told for US affiliates of foreign firms, which exported 81 per cent and imported 96 per cent of their products to/from their parents or other affiliated firms. These figures are significantly above the average for all manufacturing industries.

Foreign computer/office equipment firms established in the United States follow similar IFT patterns compared to US computer/office equipment firms established abroad, which had also been observed for the automobile sector. As opposed to the automobile sector, however, computer/office equipment firms concentrate both purchases and sales from/to their parents. In the automobile sector, foreign sales are more diversified.

D. Intra-industry trade

Intra-industry trade (IIT) is defined as the exchange by two countries of goods and services within the same product category. IIT is generally a function of product differentiation and may or may not be intra-firm trade. IIT indices provide another tool for analysing trade patterns as they show the extent of international linkages for a given industry.[9]

IIT indices for US trade in computers confirm the patterns observed with the IFT figures, as there was a significant increase in US IIT in computers, which went from about 30 per cent in 1981 to more than 70 per cent in 1991.[10] This was mainly due to the dramatic increase in US computer imports from East Asia. In 1981, the United States was the leading exporter of computers and imported relatively little. By 1991, the United States was still the largest exporter, but had also become the leading importer of computers, and had a trade deficit in that product group. More balanced trade led to higher overall IIT indices.

Data for US bilateral trade in computers reveal high IIT indices with Canada and Europe, which is common for most industries, but extremely low indices with East Asia, much lower than average. This is due to the large US trade deficit with the latter region.

IIT indices for EU trade in computers are high, between 70 and 90 per cent, but lower than for other industries such as automobiles. Even though intra-European trade is important, the European trade deficit with the rest of the world tends to lower the indices. The indices have been relatively stable, with only small decreases observed.

Intra-European bilateral indices are usually high, as for most other industries. The exception is Ireland, which has a large trade surplus in computers with the rest of Europe. Bilateral IIT indices for European computer trade with the United States and Canada are significantly lower than intra-European indices, but still higher than IIT indices for European trade with East Asia. Europe as a whole has a trade deficit with both North America and East Asia.

IIT indices for Japanese trade in computers are relatively low compared to other OECD countries, as is the case for most other industries. IIT indices for Japanese trade in computers are, however, comparable to indices for other East Asian countries. Those ranged from 30 to 50 per cent in 1991. Most of East Asia actually observed a slight increase in IIT indices as intra-regional trade increased.

Data for East Asian bilateral trade in computers reveal higher IIT indices for intra-regional trade, especially Japan-Singapore (respectively the first and third largest exporters in 1993) bilateral trade. Bilateral indices for East Asian computer trade are lower for trade with the United States and significantly lower for trade with Canada and Europe, reflecting the East Asian trade surplus in computers with those regions.

4. FOREIGN DIRECT INVESTMENT AND INTER-FIRM NETWORKS

Foreign operations are important in the computer industry. The US industry, particularly its major firm, IBM, was the first to expand extensively through international investment. Most large US IT firms now have around one-half of their revenues outside the United States. Recently, the large Japanese firms (particularly Fujitsu, Toshiba) have been expanding into Europe and North America, joining the second-tier Japanese computer and component firms (Canon, Matsushita) which rapidly increased international sales through supply of peripherals and parts and components. This international expansion is reflected in relatively high levels of Japanese activity in international mergers and acquisitions, joint ventures and minority participations. However, with the exception of parts and components suppliers and Fujitsu, the large Japanese firms still have well over three-quarters of their sales in Asia. European firms are focused on Europe, with some North American operations (Table 3.2).

A. Foreign direct investment

Disaggregated data were only available for the United States for foreign direct investment (FDI) in computers. However, the importance of the US industry, the size of the US market, and the US position as the world's major international investor and computer exporter and importer, make these patterns particularly important.

The strong outward investment position of US firms is illustrated by comparing total *assets* of US foreign affiliates (outward FDI) with assets of foreign-owned affiliates in the United States (inward FDI). For the 1985-93 period outward investment assets were usually well over ten times greater than inward investment assets. The situation of Asian computer firms is somewhat better than for Europeans, but US outward investment in Asia in 1993 was still more than eight times as important as inward investment. Total outward assets were US$52 billion in 1985 and US$121 billion in 1993, while total inward assets were US$2.8 billion in 1985 and US$8 billion in 1993 (see Table 3.9).

By geographical area, US foreign affiliates total assets in 1993 were mostly in Europe with US$75 billion, US$33 billion in Asia and the Pacific, and US$13 billion in the rest of the world, with the share in Asia increasing steadily. Foreign companies' US affiliates total assets in 1993 were US$4.3 billion of European and US$3.8 billion of Asian origin. Inward investment assets from the rest of the world were low.

The outward direct investment position (*cumulated flows*, including equity, reinvested earnings, inter-company debt, and valuation adjustments on an historical cost basis) of US firms is also much higher than the inward position. In 1993 the overseas investment position of US computer firms was US$20.6 billion, a decline from the peak in 1991, due to capital flows back to the United States and low income and reinvested earnings by US firms in foreign countries. In 1993 the inward investment position of foreign firms in the United States had dropped to below US$1 billion from the peak in 1989, due particularly to large losses on income.

Table 3.9. **Total assets of foreign affiliates of US companies and US affiliates of foreign companies – Computer and office equipment**

Million US$

	Outward	Inward	Net	Outward	Inward	Net
	1985			1987		
Europe	30 977	n.a.	n.a.	46 372	2 269	44 103
Asia	12 147	n.a.	n.a.	15 597	1 924	13 673
Rest of world	8 558	n.a.	n.a.	10 446	0	10 446
Total	**51 683**	**2 848**	**48 835**	**72 415**	**4 193**	**68 222**
	1990			1993		
Europe	68 542	4 795	63 747	74 729	4 280	70 449
Asia	26 031	6 262	19 769	32 996	3 803	29 193
Rest of world	13 127	309	12 818	13 076	254	12 822
Total	**107 700**	**11 366**	**96 334**	**120 801**	**8 337**	**112 464**

Source: Secretariat calculations from US Department of Commerce data. Outward investment data classified by industry of US parent (this includes sales and distribution service and financial activities of computer firms in foreign countries) and inward investment by industry of affiliate in the United States.

B. International mergers, acquisitions, minority participations

Mergers and acquisitions.[11] Detailed data for the period 1988-92 were analysed to explore the structure, origin and destination of merger and acquisition activity. During this period there were 149 cross-border mergers and acquisitions totalling US$7.7 billion in the computer industry (excluding software and services). Compared with the total of all industry and service sectors, the number of operations represents 1.3 per cent of the total, and the value 1.6 per cent of the total covered by the database. This compares with the motor vehicle sector where shares were: number of operations, 1.8 per cent and value, 1.9 per cent, and in pharmaceuticals number of operations, 1.9 per cent and value, 2.8 per cent, suggesting that the computer industry was moderately active in mergers and acquisitions, but not remarkably so. The most active year was 1990 with 43 operations totalling US$2.5 billion. Cross-border M&As declined sharply in the early 1990s following declines in FDI.

For the period, the countries most active in purchases (in descending order of the amounts involved) were: Japan with 27 operations (US$4 billion), the United Kingdom 22 (US$1.28 billion), France 11 (US$728 million), the United States 36 (US$477 million) and Chinese Taipei 7 (US$365 million). The countries which were the top sellers (in descending order of the amounts involved) were: the United States with 61 operations (US$4.3 billion), the United Kingdom 18 (US$1.6 billion), Sweden 8 (US$422 million), Finland 3 (US$386 million) and Spain 1 (US$300 million). A typical operation was the majority purchase of ICL by Fujitsu, and subsequent complex absorption of Nokia Data by ICL, to indirectly expand sales operations of ICL (Fujitsu) in Europe.

Joint ventures and minority participations.[11] Detailed data for the period 1990-92 were analysed to explore the structure, origin and destination of joint-venture and minority participation activity. During this period there were 117 cross-border operations totalling US$1.4 billion in computers (excluding software and services). Compared with the total of all industry and service sectors the number of operations represents 1.7 per cent of the total, and in value 1.1 per cent of the total covered by the database. The respective shares in the motor vehicles sector were number of operations, 3.8 per cent and value, 8.8 per cent, and in pharmaceuticals number of operations, 1.8 per cent and value, 0.5 per cent, suggesting that the computer industry is only moderately active in joint ventures and minority participations. There were 59 operations totalling US$356 million in 1990, and 21 operations totalling US$941 million in 1992.

Table 3.10. **Selected mergers and acquisitions – Computer industry**

Date	Acquirer	Target	Value (million US$)
1989	Bull SA (France)	Zenith Computer Group (US)	496.4
1990	Cap Gemini Sogeti SA (France)	Hoskyns Group PLC (UK)	591.6
1990	ALLTELL Corp. (US)	Systematics Inc. (US)	545.1
1990	Northern Telecom Ltd. (BCE Inc.) (Canada)	STC PLC (UK)	2 635.8[1]
1990	AT&T (US)	NCR Corp. (US)	7 893.4
1991	ICL PLC (Fujitsu Ltd.) (UK)	Nokia Data (Nokia Corp.) (Finland)	402.5
1991	Borland International Inc. (US)	Ashton-Tate Corp. (US)	547.6
1991	NCR Corp. (AT&T Co.) (US)	Teradata Corp. (US)	520.0
1992	Legent Corp. (US)	Goal Systems International Inc. (US)	407.2
1993	IBM France SA (IBM Corp.) (France)	Cie. Générale d'Informatique (France)	457.9
1993	Loral Corp. (US)	IBM Federal Systems Co. (IBM) (US)	1 575.0
1994	Adobe Systems Inc. (US)	Aldus Corp. (US)	437.7
1994	Novell Inc. (US)	WordPerfect Corp. (US)	1 416.0
1994	Pearson PLC (UK)	Software Toolworks Inc. (US)	435.4
1994	Wellfleet Communications (US)	Synoptics Communications Inc. (US)	1 174.3[2]
1994	ZEOS International Ltd. (US)	Micron Computer, Micron Custom. (US)	405.0
1994	Thomson Corp. (Canada)	Information Access Co. (US)	465.0
1994	Sybase Inc. (US)	Powersoft Corp. (US)	817.3
1994	Shareholders	Tele-Communications-Liberty (US)	3 757.5
1995	Raytheon Co. (US)	E-Systems Inc. (US)	2 255.4
1995	IBM Corp. (US)	Lotus Development Corp.(US)	3 365.6
Pending	Compaq Computer (US)	NetWorth (US)	372.0

1. Wholesale computer, telecom. equipt.
2. Design and wholesale LANs.
Source: OECD Secretariat compilation based on published sources.

Top purchasers in 1990-92 were the United States, 42 operations (US$888 million), Japan 39 (US$471 million) and the United Kingdom 9 (US$57 million). Top selling countries were the United States, 42 operations (US$467 million), Japan 9 (US$358 million) and France 15 operations (US$165 million). A typical operation was the 1992 minority purchase in Bull by IBM, to provide technology to Bull and market outlets for IBM.

Overall, the computer industry has expanded internationally through new foreign direct investment rather than through extensive mergers and acquisitions or joint ventures. This is probably due to the structure of the industry. Large firms which dominated it in the past only look to outside resources in new areas such as communications, networking and software. New entrants have grown very rapidly from internal resources as they built on their advantages in efficient low-price manufacturing and mass-marketing for PCs, rather than on supplying large-scale technical solutions to business and government customers as had the previous generation of established suppliers.

This is also suggested by examining a sample of recent mergers and acquisitions in the industry. Most of the operations involved the software and service industry (and increasingly communications) in North America and Europe, which has been subject to extensive rationalisation and purchases by existing firms. A lesser area of activity has been the purchase of hardware and product firms by Japanese producers (Fujitsu majority purchase of ICL), to expand their international operations and make them less reliant on domestic sales. Finally there have been some mergers amongst the existing established European and US firms (Siemens-Nixdorf, AT&T-NCR, IBM-Lotus, and the Bull-NEC-Motorola re-grouping) as part of the restructuring of their operations (see Table 3.10).

C. **Market shares of foreign-controlled firms**

The industry has high levels of foreign-owned production in almost all European countries. These levels are among the highest of all manufacturing. Although similar detailed data are not available, the share is high in some of the rapidly growing Asian exporters (Singapore, Malaysia, Thailand – probably around 90 per cent), low in Korea, and between the two in Chinese Taipei and Hong Kong. In the United States it is low, but growing, and foreign-controlled production is low in Japan. US firms are the dominant investors in Europe. In the United States, Japanese firms increased their share rapidly from a low base. For all countries for which data is available, the share of employment is lower than the share of output, suggesting that affiliates have lower levels of labour-intensive "headquarters" activities (R&D, planning, marketing, etc.) in their foreign affiliates, as well as having higher levels of manufacturing productivity than domestic firms, due to larger size and superior manufacturing technology.

Around 1990, in the United Kingdom the share of foreign affiliate output in total output was 79 per cent, increasing sharply from 48 per cent in 1987. It was 80 per cent in Germany and 74 per cent in France, with 63 per cent coming from US firms and 5 per cent from Japanese firms and these shares were unchanged in 1992. Data on the foreign share of output is not available for Italy, but 63 per cent of employment was in foreign affiliates in the computer industry in 1988. The foreign share in 1989 was 99 per cent in Ireland (which has a computer trade surplus due to strong foreign investment) and 93 per cent in Norway. Finland is the only European country which had a low share of foreign output. In 1988 only 9 per cent came from foreign affiliates (see Figure 3.9), but this was before the major indigenous manufacturer was acquired by ICL/Fujitsu, and the share has undoubtedly increased subsequently.

In the United States in 1990, foreign manufacturing affiliate sales were equivalent to close to 14 per cent of production of computers; 7 per cent came from Japanese affiliates and 5 per cent from European affiliates. In 1993 the shares were around 12 per cent of production, with 6 per cent from Japanese manufacturing affiliates, 4 per cent from European affiliates.[12] In Canada over 47 per cent of sales came from foreign-controlled firms in 1988, with 34 per cent from US firms, 8 per cent European, and 4 per cent Japanese firms.

◆ Figure 3.9. **Share of foreign firms in production – Computers**

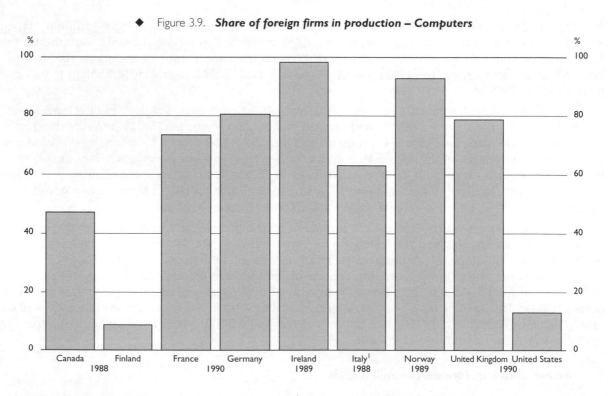

1. Based on employment figures.
Source: OECD from national sources.

Table 3.11. **Production by foreign-controlled firms and imports of computers, around 1990**

	Foreign-controlled production as percentage of total production	Foreign-controlled production divided by imports
Canada	47	0.28
France	70	0.64
Germany	78	0.74
Italy[1]	63	1.09
United Kingdom	65	0.68
United States	11	0.36
Finland	9	0.06
Norway	93	0.49

1. Estimated
Source: OECD calculated from national sources and STAN database, DSTI/EAS Division.

Despite high levels of foreign-controlled production, it is generally not as important as foreign trade, because of the trade intensity of the computer industry. Imports were more important at the end of the 1980s in the major European markets (France, Germany, Italy, the United Kingdom), but imports and foreign production were of the same order of magnitude due to the long implantation of US firms. Large inflows of parts and components from US parent firms were boosted by rapidly increasing imports into Europe from Japan and the DAEs. In North America, imports were approximately three times more important than foreign-controlled production in domestic markets, showing the generally low levels of foreign production compared with total consumption in both Canada and the United States (see Table 3.11).

D. International collaboration agreements[13]

The computer industry is very active in setting up collaboration agreements. Over the period 1964-92, 13 per cent of the total number of agreements recorded in the industry-wide database were in computers. The cumulative total number of international collaboration agreements for the whole period was 334, more than for automobiles, and much more active than pharmaceuticals. The industry had a double-peak in collaboration agreement activity, with one peak in the mid-1980s and another peak in activity in the 1990s (44 in 1990, 40 in 1991, 43 in 1992), when new collaboration agreements were generally declining (see Figure 3.10). The recent peak in collaboration parallels the development of minority participations and joint ventures in 1992, but is in contrast with the slow-down in mergers and acquisitions and broad flows of international investment (Section 4.A and B).

Firms are relatively active in collaborating within their own region: 53 per cent of agreements were between major economic regions, but 47 per cent were within. The most frequent agreements were between Europe and North America (over one-quarter) followed by those within North America (23 per cent, mostly within the United States), and within Europe (21 per cent). This was followed by agreements between North America and the Far East (18 per cent). At country level, US firms were the most active, with one-third of inter-country agreements, followed by Japan, France and the United Kingdom. The large number of US-based agreements is an indicator of the long-term leading position of US firms in both established areas of computing and in the new multimedia oriented developments. Five US firms, two French firms and one firm from each of Germany, Italy, Japan and the Netherlands had more than 15 collaboration agreements each between 1964 and 1992.

Development was by far the most important aim. It was the sole aim of one-half of agreements, and one of two or more aims of another 20 per cent of agreements, i.e. it was the aim of 70 per cent of all

◆ Figure 3.10. *International collaboration agreements – Computers*

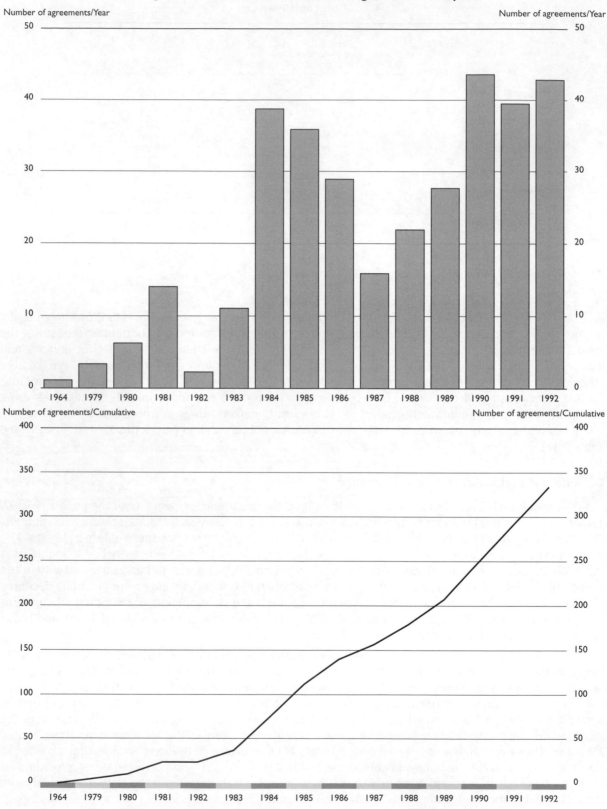

Source: INSEAD.

agreements. This was followed by marketing (the sole aim of 17 per cent of agreements) and production (sole aim in 15 per cent). (For comparison, for all industries combined, development was the sole aim of one-third of agreements, production the sole aim of one-quarter and marketing one-seventh; development was one of one, two or multiple aims of just over one-half of agreements, production one-half, and marketing one-third of agreements.) Large firms were the principal collaborators (41 per cent of agreements), followed by large and small firms (28 per cent) and large and medium-sized firms (20 per cent).

Typical collaboration agreements involve large firms, increasingly from the three major computer-producing regions (Japan, the United States, Europe) to develop new products outside of their main-line areas, e.g. in memories between IBM-Toshiba-Siemens. A typical example of a new development and production joint venture is Display Technologies Inc. (DTI), an IBM-Toshiba joint venture in Japan to design, develop and produce liquid crystal displays for portable computers. DTI produced 400 000 screens in 1993 for the joint owners' portable PCs, and it is the second largest producer of flat screens after Sharp. Collaboration agreements are also expanding in software and new-product development to achieve compatible interfacing and other standards and to ensure networking capabilities.

The major motivations of technology agreements in computers and IT have usually been to improve market access or modify market structure particularly in new areas, to make use of technological complementarities among partners, and to reduce the innovation time taken to develop new products in rapidly changing markets. With the shifts away from established computer systems and the potential for new products coming from the convergence of computers, telecommunications, broadcasting and entertainment industries, the market-oriented motive and search for complementarities have taken on new significance. In this rapidly changing environment the potential impact of complementary, market-oriented development collaboration is very high, particularly in setting market standards as well as in developing new goods and services. This has been underlined by the large numbers of collaboration arrangements set up by large US firms, often within the United States, to explore and exploit new areas.

5. GOVERNMENT POLICIES

A. Strategic industry policies and infrastructure

Historically, computers have been the focus of a large amount of R&D support and special development programmes because of the importance of computing for defence applications. These programmes initially contributed to many of the technological advances that under-pinned growth in the industry. But divergences between civilian and defence products, particularly as civilian market suppliers have proved dynamic and innovative, coupled with the administration, structure and operations of defence R&D and procurement have made defence research less relevant to civilian products and less important in the development of the computer industry. One response has been to develop new programmes aimed exclusively at civilian R&D (see below), while there has been an ongoing debate, particularly in the United States, on how to make more effective use of defence research programmes and agencies, and the "dual-use" technologies with military and civilian applications developed from defence research.

A more recent general approach has been to support the development of advanced high-speed information networks which provide a goal for civilian R&D and applications, and contribute to developing the broad global communications and computing infrastructure for business. Ambitious information networks were singled out for policy attention in the United States, Japan and the EU, and the initial scale of proposals and widespread enthusiasm in the United States led to similar schemes and proposals in other countries.

In 1994-95 most OECD governments announced plans or were studying ways to improve national information infrastructures ("highways", "societies", etc.) and link them more broadly into global networks. These infrastructures are based on broad-band digital communications and broadcasting, allowing transmission of large quantities of information at low cost, including integrated data, video, text and voice traffic. The pattern of development of these infrastructures will have far-reaching impacts on how computers will be used as tools for wider networking and information exchange, on the development of the computer industry and the way in which it will structure its global operations. The main principles underlying the development of these infrastructures include: open access (including interconnection and interoperability standards – see below), competition, universal service, an effective regulatory framework, and the major role of private investment.

B. Industry and technology policies

a) R&D support

All countries support computer R&D, either directly in government programmes focused on the industry, or through general programmes to support R&D expenditures through grants, loans and other direct assistance, and general R&D tax incentives (tax credits in Canada, France, Japan, Spain, the United States, special allowances in Australia, etc.). Because computers, software development and related engineering activities are R&D-intensive they receive a large amount of government support through general R&D tax incentives.

The direct government share of business expenditures on computer R&D is relatively high in a few large countries with large military commitments. Governments provided 10-20 per cent of R&D funding in the United States, France and the United Kingdom. These data include government contracts, as well as grants and other direct subsidies, but do not include tax expenditures, soft loans, guarantees, etc. The share is lower in most other countries, and very low in Japan (around 1 per cent) and Germany. In most countries the industry does not receive as much government support as aerospace, electronics, semiconductors or electrical engineering (including electronics, components and communications), although these industries are linked with computers.

Support programmes for IT, including computers, were launched in all major countries in the 1970s and 1980s, particularly where there were important military applications, where support was established earlier. Some of these specifically focused on computer technology (Super Computer Project, 5th Generation Computers in Japan, Strategic Computing in the United States), many others included computing as an important part (Alvey in the United Kingdom, National Information Technology Programme in Sweden, ESPRIT in the EC). In most cases civilian support promoted collaboration in pre-competitive R&D, often involving research institutions and universities as well as firms, and increasingly had elements of practical applications and widespread diffusion.

Recent examples of large industrially oriented R&D programmes include:

European Commission programmes: These sought to strengthen R&D in information technology from the early 1980s through subsidising one-half of costs of pre-competitive collaborative research. Efforts include the ESPRIT programme in electronics since 1983, RACE in telecommunications since 1986, and JESSI in semiconductor components which is part of the broader, commercially oriented EUREKA programme. ESPRIT II ran from end-1987 to end-1992 and was funded with ECU 1.6 billion; ESPRIT III with ECU 1.35 billion for IT ran as part of the third "Framework" programme 1990-94, with major projects on information processing and IT applications. The Fourth Framework Programme running 1994-98 has over one-third of funds going to information technology and telecommunications. Although the overall "Framework" expenditures only added about 3 per cent to EU R&D expenditures, they co-ordinate about 30 per cent of early-stage IT R&D. Participation has been mainly by large European electronics firms, with more limited participation by SMEs. Benefits have been diffuse, but it is generally acknowledged that cross-border collaboration and rationalisation have been accelerated and wider strategic orientations adopted by participating firms.

Plans to set up a "European Information Highway", including telecommunications and information technology inter-linkages have been announced and elaborated by the European Commission, in parallel with similar announcements in Japan, the United States, Canada and other countries. These are examples of the shift towards improving the IT environment in which business operates rather than supporting IT development or applications directly.

Japanese programmes. The 5th Generation Computer Project started in FY 1982 for ten years, and aimed mainly at improving hardware performance despite wider, more general, aims. The Institute for New Generation Computer Technology implemented R&D in conjunction with teams from the Electrotechnical Laboratory, NTT (Nippon Telegraph and Telephone) and eight computer manufacturing companies. Total funding was around Y 45 billion (US$330 million at Y 140/US$). Results included production of prototype parallel processing and inference computers and a case study using an electric power generating system to test the technology. Although this project was initially widely studied and emulated, the technology produced was surpassed by commercial developments, and the focus on hardware and parallel processing superseded by developments in software and networking.

A more modest "Interoperable Database Systems" project, to explore distributed database systems for computer interconnection and interoperation, was funded at Y 15 billion for the period 1985-91. It was a Large-scale Industrial Technology R&D Project (there were 31 Large-scale projects since 1966), with 100 per cent of R&D financed by the MITI Agency of Industrial Science and Technology, and R&D contracted out to consortia of firms. Foreign firms were not excluded as participants. A large ten-year US$450 million, "Real World Computing Project" was announced in 1992 as a follow-on to the 5th Generation project, focusing on parallel processing, optical computing and "fuzzy" logic, with plans for foreign participation. This was financed by MITI at around FY 1993 US$32 million, FY 1994 US$49 million. Despite numerous initiatives, overall government expenditures have been modest with reported government R&D expenditure on information processing averaging less than 1 per cent of total expenditures (0.81 per cent in FY 1993 (around US$80 million), 0.73 per cent in FY 1992).

In May 1994, the Japanese government announced an ambitious "Program for the Establishment of High-Performance Info-Communications Infrastructures". This has subsequently been scaled back.

US programmes. Federal funding for computer science and engineering R&D for military and civilian purposes come principally from the Department of Defense (DOD), National Science Foundation (NSF), NASA, and Department of Energy (DOE), which account for over 90 per cent of federal expenditures. Although DOD-funded projects have been directed at military objectives, they contributed to important civilian advances in the past, and were instrumental in establishing the US computer industry. But there has been continuing concern as to whether these funds can contribute effectively to the development of dual-use technologies, and what mechanisms can be developed to replace projected declines in DOD funding, with an aim in the 1992-96 period to shift towards a 50:50 civilian-defence ratio in federal support.

The High Performance Computing and Communications Program (High Performance Computing Act, 1991) is the main US civilian computer research effort, designed to develop generic computer systems and software and the research and information network and information infrastructure. It received the following funding: FY 1992 US$657 million in federal funds, FY 1993 US$772 million, FY 1994 (budget) US$938 million, FY 1995 (forecast) US$1 154 million (1995 Budget documents). Main funders over 1993-95 were DOD (36 per cent), NSF (29 per cent), DOE (12 per cent). There were some limited funds to expand computer networks and build the National Information Infrastructure (NII) or "Information Superhighway" (the common name for the whole computer R&D and infrastructure concept). A multi-agency taskforce has co-ordinated federal NII activities from January 1994, and some US$26 million was available for co-ordinating, pilot and demonstration activities in FY 1994, budgeted to be around US$100 million in FY 1995.

A new DOD initiative in 1994 aimed at fostering domestic US manufacturing and research capabilities in flat display panels, including a projected US$587 million of government funds for R&D with matching funds from firms.

b) Technology diffusion

Investment has become increasingly computer-intensive. For example, in the United States, computers and peripheral equipment make up over 10 per cent of total private equipment and transport investment (expressed in current terms). The rate and pattern of diffusion will be affected by the business cycle and the investment behaviour of leading service sectors (finance, communications, business services) in applying computer equipment to office and related functions, and utilities and industrial sectors (machinery, electrical machinery, transport equipment, the computer industry itself) which are leaders in purchasing and applying automation and computer-controlled equipment. However, there are continuing problems ensuring effective diffusion of technologies and their efficient use, and achieving expected contributions to productivity growth.

A considerable number of recent government programmes have recognised that there are market failures (in information, consulting, applied research, financing) which inhibit diffusion and application of new technologies, particular computer-related ones. Almost all countries have attempted to improve applications, particularly in small firms, with specific programmes designed to assist them obtain information and advice and improve the environment for applications. These measures increase demand for computers and computer-controlled products. The industry is also indirectly supported through general investment incentives and depreciation schedules, which affect the timing and volume of investment in computers and related equipment.

c) Industrial location/regional policy

Although the industry is not as large as automobiles, there have been considerable incentives to the computer and related electronics industry to locate in particular countries or regions. These involved the usual investment incentives and subsidies (see Section 5.D below). There has also been policy interest in ensuring linkages to the local economy and achieving reasonably high levels of local content. However, foreign-owned affiliates are highly internationally oriented, with very high levels of international sourcing and supply of parts and components and peripherals, and are unlikely to develop many local linkages unless the local supply network and infrastructure already exists.

C. Trade policies

The computer industry is perceived to be of strategic importance, and has, therefore, received considerable attention from governments, especially in the past decade. Governments have, however, been somewhat reluctant to apply restrictive trade measures in the industry, given the importance of the linkages between computers and other sectors of economic activity.

Tariffs on computers, peripherals, parts and components are relatively low in most countries. In the mid-1980s they were 4-5 per cent for OECD countries. In 1994 they were 0 per cent for Japan. In the United States, they were 3.9 per cent on almost all kinds of digital computers, and 0 per cent on most peripherals (displays, keyboards, storage units, disk drives, except printers 3.7 per cent and cathode ray tubes 3.9 per cent). In the EU, tariffs were 4.9 per cent for computers and peripherals. In other OECD countries, they were also low. In industrialising and developing countries they are somewhat higher, *e.g.* around 10 per cent for Korea, 5-7.5 per cent in Chinese Taipei but 0 per cent for Singapore.

Perverse effects of differential tariff rates due to the interlinkages between the computer and component industries have been noted in the EU. Higher tariffs on semiconductors (14 per cent) compared with computers have been seen as a disincentive to local assembly of parts and components imported from outside the EU, although they have no doubt helped encourage semiconductor component manufacturers to set up within the EU. Customs duties were suspended in the EU in 1994 reflecting production shortages in computer-related inputs in memories and CRTs.

Relatively little use has been made of quantitative restrictions in the sector. For instance, there are no quotas or VERs presently applied to computer trade in OECD countries, and most trade issues arise in other areas of electronics (consumer electronics, some peripherals such as printers, and antidumping duties applied to computer microdiscs from East Asian exporters).

Market access barriers are still perceived to exist, however. Some of these barriers have been addressed by bilateral initiatives, especially involving the United States and Japan. For instance, the 1990 Japan-US Supercomputer Agreement (revised from 1987) states that public supercomputer purchases will be open to foreign as well as domestic suppliers. Japan was working to introduce transparent, open and non-discriminatory procedures for supercomputers in accordance with bilateral and GATT agreements. Similarly in January 1992, the United States and Japan signed an agreement to open Japanese public-sector computer equipment and services purchases (including packaged software and systems integration and data processing) to foreign suppliers. The agreement covers over 100 government and quasi-government agencies and was phased in by April 1993. However there have been continuing questions and complaints by US firms regarding procurement practices.

In one instance, disputes over market access barriers in a related sector led to punitive tariffs being imposed in the computer sector. In 1987 the US imposed punitive 100 per cent import tariffs on certain Japanese goods, including lap-top computers and desktop computers, because of the US view that major provisions of the 1986 US-Japanese Semiconductor Agreement had not been enforced. These were lifted in 1991. These restrictions also led the EC to monitor imports of personal computers from Japan between 1987 and 1992.

Another source of trade friction in the sector has been the use of antidumping duties. Recent cases often involve Japanese companies, and they mostly involve parts and components or accessories for PCs, with the exception of a 1991 case where Japanese companies were found to be dumping word-processors on the US market. Examples of the use of antidumping measures include a 1988 case when the EC imposed antidumping duties on Japanese dot matrix computer printers, and daisy-wheel computer print-ers. There have also been cases of imposition of dumping duties on 3.5-inch computer microdiscs for PCs from Japan (by the United States and the EU), Chinese Taipei and China (by the EU), and subsequently on imports from Korea and Hong Kong (by the EU).

Illustrating the interlinkages present in the industry was a case where the imposition of antidumping duties on a key component caused problems for downstream producers. In September 1991, the United States imposed antidumping duties on large-area, high-resolution, active-matrix, liquid crystal displays (62.27 per cent *ad valorem*) and on electroluminescent displays (7.02 per cent) imported from Japan. Two months later, a US importer (Apple Computers) filed an appeal with the Court of International Trade, questioning the dumping duties, claiming that injury to US producers could not be substantiated, as allegedly no US producer could supply displays of the quality and quantity necessary. Even one company which had originally sought the duties asked, in December 1992, that they be revoked.

The duties have now been lifted on liquid crystal displays, but in the meantime led to some US companies moving assembly off-shore to gain access to lower-priced supplies (only one US firm produces panels in large volume). These firms export back to the United States, where complete computers are subject to the usual tariff of 3.9 per cent.

Export controls were a feature in computers, for defence (*e.g.* Central and Eastern Europe) and/or political reasons (*e.g.* with South Africa). In 1991, a US computer manufacturer (DEC) was fined for alleged violations of controls, involving unauthorised export of microcomputers and other products controlled for national security reasons, to countries in Europe, Latin America, the Far East and Middle East. These restrictions have been substantially eased in the past few years, due to political and technological changes (particularly the availability of cheap high-powered PCs). The US in September 1993 announced a National Export Strategy which in part liberalised controls on computer and supercomputer products, raised licensing thresholds, and proposed changes in the supercomputer definition, and has reviewed proce-dures for software classification for defence requirements.

In March 1994 the 17-member Co-ordinating Committee for Multilateral Export Controls (COCOM) was officially disbanded. US licensing requirements were eliminated in April 1994 on the export of nearly all civilian computers to civil end-users in most countries, although some restrictions under foreign policy controls continue to apply. Controls on software with encryption capabilities (data scrambling to ensure security and integrity of electronic communications and files) remain in place, but exports may be shipped to customers in approved countries under a single license.

D. Foreign investment policies

The computer industry is generally not subject to a specific regulatory framework for foreign direct investment in OECD countries. Industry-specific government restrictions on access to markets or treat-ment of foreign investors are not an issue, except to the extent that strategic foreign policy and defence interests are involved. In the past, due to the same considerations as those involved in the now disbanded COCOM export restrictions, there have potentially been restrictions on foreign purchase of computer and related component firms. For example, the Exon-Florio amendment to the 1988 Omnibus Trade and Competitiveness Act in the United States aimed at reviewing and if necessary blocking foreign take-overs of US companies which may threaten the "national security". However, computer-related investigations have been in the broader electronics sector in semiconductors, equipment and defence-related software, rather than in computers. Other countries have reviewed take-overs by foreign firms in defence-related areas through more general policies (e.g. the Monopolies and Mergers Commission in the United Kingdom).

In non-OECD countries such as Brazil and India there have been a wide range of obstacles to FDI. Brazil for example had a comprehensive policy to support its domestic computer industry, including promotion of joint ventures with leading foreign firms to the extent that they wished to participate. These policies in general deterred foreign investment, or at best encouraged minority holdings and joint-venture formation. They have now generally been replaced by a more liberal approach to foreign investment in the industry, and investment liberalisation has been proceeding in India.

Because of the importance of the industry, it has been the object of policies designed to attract foreign investment and measures to encourage local inputs to production once investment has occurred. The major share of the computer industry in Europe is foreign-owned, with the United States the single most important investor country (see Section 4.C). The rise of Singapore and Chinese Taipei, and to a lesser extent other Asian countries, as major exporters of computers and peripherals has largely been based on direct investment and sourcing by major computer firms from local suppliers.

A recurring issue in R&D-intensive industries is related to national treatment (equal treatment of foreign and domestic firms) with respect to participation in government-supported R&D programmes and consortia. This has been a particularly contentious issue in advanced electronics and computers. Continuing problems for example between the United States and Europe have been resolved in part by exchanging research results, and making access conditional on having substantial research facilities in foreign subsidiaries operating in the country or region. Firms have also taken initiatives, not involving government support, to set up joint ventures and alliances for development in similar technological areas. However there are examples of continuing preference for nationally-owned firms in government programmes and consortia, and agreements of the kind cited above may exclude firms which are not European or US (the treatment of ICL as a Japanese firm in European programmes is an example).

E. Protection of intellectual property and development of standards

Intellectual property rights (IPRs) are very important in the computer industry. They ensure rapid diffusion of inventions and adequate returns to inventors, and under-pin expanded investment and trade. They are applied to hardware as for other physical inventions. However, new approaches have had to be developed to extend copyright protection to software, and to protect integrated circuit layout design.

There have been continuing high levels of uncertainty regarding protection and enforcement in these areas, because multilateral agreement was lacking. Problems with copyright and IPR protection are most widespread in developing countries, but progress is being made in acceptance of IPR regimes, and elimination of copying and counterfeiting of protected goods.

The General Agreement on Tariffs and Trade (GATT) Uruguay Round was the first GATT Round to deal with IPRs, and they clarified some areas of protection. They extended application of IPRs, with the aim of decreasing illegal copying and expropriation of intellectual property without adequate compensation.

Layout designs of integrated circuits. The GATT agreement requires parties to provide protection on the basis of the Washington Treaty on Intellectual Property in Respect of Integrated Circuits, opened for signature in May 1989. In addition, minimum protection is for ten years, rights extend to articles incorporating infringing layout designs, and compulsory licensing and government use is only allowed under a number of strict conditions.

Extension of copyright protection. The GATT agreement extended copyright protection to computer programs as literary works under the Berne Convention (version Paris 1971); laid down the basis for copyright protection of original compilations of data and databases; and added new provisions on author's rights to authorise or prohibit commercial rental. Developed countries had one year to implement the IPR provisions and bring their legislation and practices into conformity; developing countries and former centrally-planned economies five years; and least developed countries 11 years.

The process of updating and adopting copyright protection of software was already under way in many countries. After a 1988 consultative Green Paper, in 1991 the European Communities approved computer software copyright protection, with the aim of ensuring that legislation in member States provides adequate software protection, and to eliminate disparities. By April 1995 all EU member States except Luxembourg had strong protection measures. In 1988 the UK Parliament introduced comprehensive copyright legislation, bringing UK law into line with the 1971 Paris text of the Berne Convention, and including protection of computer-generated works. Also in 1988, Canada approved copyright legislation to increase protection of computer software. Programs were defined as literary works and provided full copyright protection for the life of the creator plus 50 years. In 1987, Korea began enforcing laws governing computer programs. Japan amended its copyright act in 1985 to explicitly protect computer programs.

Enforcement of IPR protection. IPR protection is being more vigorously pursued. Persistent piracy problems have been reported throughout Asia. In the United States, international IPR protection is pursued in the annual Special 301 reviews of IPR regimes and related market access practices of trading partners, authorised by the 1988 Omnibus Trade and Competitiveness Act. In February 1995, the United States and China reached an agreement for improved IPR protection following extensive negotiations and the threat of US sanctions. This followed Special 301 investigations when China was identified as a "priority foreign country" in 1994. In 1992 China had committed to join the Berne Convention, protect computer programs as literary works for 50 years, provide copyright protection to both existing and new works, and grant copyright holders rental rights. In 1993 Thailand was removed from the "priority foreign country" list after agreeing to bring IPR protection up to GATT Uruguay Round standards. In 1992 Chinese Taipei was revoked as a "priority foreign country", when it passed a new copyright law that extends protection to life of the creator plus 50 years, stiffens penalties for infringement, and prohibits unauthorised translation of computer software and other literary works. Brazil was also revoked as a priority foreign country in 1994 after agreeing to implement stronger IPR measures, and India placed on the "priority watch list" along with Argentina in 1994. Practices in Indonesia, Korea and the Philippines have come under international scrutiny. In 1992, the US Congress passed legislation setting higher uniform penalties for copyright infringement of all types of copyrighted works, including computer software.

In earlier cases, in 1989 the United States withdrew import duty concessions (import duties imposed averaged 6.2 per cent, import value US$165 million) from eight Thai products in retaliation against Thailand's refusal to satisfy American demands that computer software be given adequate IPR protection. In October 1991, two Korean companies were fined by their authorities for unauthorised copy and use of software produced by US software companies. Although other companies had been fined for selling pirated software, this was the first time that the Republic of Korea enforced its Computer Program Protection Law against users of illegally-copied software.

The extent and application of IPR protection at national level is still actively being defined in parallel with more vigorous attempts to enforce property rights. For example, collaboration between competitors early in new product development to ensure efficient networking and product interfacing requires careful protection of rights. The extent of allowed decompilation (taking apart software made by another manufacturer, also known as reverse engineering) has also been under active scrutiny and debate. In 1992, US courts ruled that a program's operation and appearance can be protected if the elements are original, and decompilation is permitted for the purpose of designing interoperable or complementary products. Similarly, in EU copyright protection, the question of decompiling a program without the copyright holder's authorisation was resolved as follows: decompiling is permitted if it is necessary for interoperability and compatibility of an independently created computer program. In 1994 Japan withdrew proposals to permit decompiling after receiving wide criticism of the extent of decompiling being considered, and decompilation was not permitted.

Standards

De facto standards. Many standards have been set *de facto* by the leading firm. Competing firms adopt similar standards to allow minimum levels of compatibility between different systems. In some cases the leading firm's standards have been adopted, to supply peripherals to directly attach to the leading firm's equipment (*i.e.* plug-compatible peripherals). A pervasive example of *de facto* standard-setting has been in PC operating systems, where most machines operate on MS/DOS, the standard operating system for all major international PC producers with the exception of Apple. Widespread use of the same standards encourages rapid development of a wide range of compatible hardware and software, accelerates adoption of new systems and probably accelerates international investment and international sourcing as suppliers compete to supply standardised products at competitive prices.

On the other hand, the severe problems faced by the established main-frame and mini-computer manufacturers have been in part related to their unique, proprietary, non-standardised operating systems and software and the lack of industry communication and interoperability standards. In the past, proprietary standards provided competitive advantages. They locked-in customers to one supplier by making it costly to switch to new suppliers because of high sunk costs in installed equipment and systems. More recently, these same proprietary standards have been disadvantageous, as customers demanded flexibility and efficient interfacing between different systems and standardised equipment at low prices. Firm-specific proprietary software and systems require constant up-grading and development to keep the installed customer base abreast of technological change, but do not allow manufacturers to easily gain economies of scale and market share by developing and producing equipment and systems compatible with those of other manufacturers.

The industry is now moving towards "open" systems and standards. The aim is to enable equipment and software from different firms to interconnect and inter-operate by using standard application programming interfaces. In the middle ground between IBM large systems and Microsoft-based PC and network-based operating systems, there has been a general move by producers to adopt UNIX-based operating systems (UNIX was originally developed by AT&T's Bell Laboratories), as the basic open system with high levels of interoperability and common communication standards. Differentiation between different manufacturers is then developed in particular applications or systems characteristics, not on the basis of individual operating systems.

Official standard-setting. Standards for many electronics and telecommunications products are being updated and co-ordinated in the EU. This work is conducted by the European Electrotechnical Standards Committee (CENELEC) and European Telecommunications Standards Institute. The EU has the European Organisation for Testing and Certification (EOTC) which will eventually permit European manufacturers to have single-country certification. Other countries are adapting to this faster track, and the International Organization for Standardization (ISO) is attempting to ensure integration of European and world-level efforts.

Despite considerable advantages, concerns have been raised including: other standards organisations (*e.g.* American National Standards Institute) get standards after they have been drafted; there is potential conflict if a new standard is based on a patented product where the patent-holder will lose patent investment, or where the patent-holder gains undue advantages; firms not based in Europe cannot be members of the EOTC, and may have to go through multi-country testing.

Continuing issues. The current interest in the information infrastructure has heightened awareness of the importance of open access and open standards, particularly interconnection and interoperability standards. The acceleration of standardisation is essential to ensure compatibility, interconnectability and interoperability of the equipment of different manufacturers to enable it to communicate efficiently. This standardisation process inevitably leads to the use of IPRs owned by at least one or a few individuals or firms as the basis of standards, and to potential conflict between the interests of IPR holders in maximising their returns and the goal of promoting widespread interoperability and open access. Procedures and safeguards are required for the fair and equitable use of IPRs for both IPR holders and users, where IPRs form the basis of standards and/or are required to gain market access.

F.   Competition policy

Competition policy has focused on three areas relevant to globalisation in the computer industry.

Monopoly position. The first issue is related to whether the dominant position of the leading computer company (and more recently of the leading software company) leads to anti-competitive behaviour and abuse of dominant position which may slow the development of the industry both nationally and internationally. The US case against IBM from 1969 to 1982 was eventually terminated by the US government as being difficult to sustain. Rapid technological change had continued in the industry which had given rise to problems of market definition in the case. Products had improved and prices had fallen, from which computer users had benefited. Technological change in the industry also promoted foreign expansion to exploit technological leadership.

At the same time there were also concerns about monopoly behaviour in foreign markets. Following proceedings initiated in Europe in 1980, in 1984 IBM undertook to provide competitors, at their request, with interface information on large system hardware and software. In a joint statement published end-1988 neither side saw any changes to cause IBM to terminate the agreement with the Commission, and it has continued. As at end-1993 seven competitors had received information under technical information disclosure agreements. With the shift away from main-frame computers towards smaller systems and PCs, the increasingly dominant position of Microsoft in software and of Intel in microprocessors has raised continuing concerns regarding the extent to which they should be obliged to provide potential competitors with information on development to allow competition in applications, and the potential for them to exploit dominant positions.

Intellectual property rights. IPRs give holders a monopoly on exploiting particular inventions. Because particular operating systems or network software have very large shares of world markets, there has been increasing scrutiny of leading companies and the monopoly influence exerted through ownership of widely used software. For example, Microsoft has been under anti-trust investigation in the United States and has had complaints filed against it with EU competition policy authorities. Similarly in Finland in 1992, Digital Equipment's operating system and network software property rights were considered to give it a dominant position and it was required to separate updating rights from maintenance services, to allow competition in maintenance markets. In another example, in Borland International's 1991 acquisition of Ashton-Tate, to prevent reduced competition in the concentrated market for relational database management systems, Borland was prohibited from certain activities. This was the first time that a firm was required to waive IPRs as a condition of merger.

Impacts of mergers and collaboration. Joint-venture and co-operation activities are being expanded to gain economics of scale and to exploit joint technological development which may potentially run counter to competition rules. In the United States, computer and semiconductor companies have invested in SEMATECH, a large-scale semiconductor materials and equipment development venture in partnership with government, organised as a centralised entity operating in one location. Although collaboration in R&D is generally permitted, the original plan could have required significant changes in US anti-trust legislation to allow collaboration in manufacturing. But the consortium focused on improving links between semiconductor manufacturers and equipment suppliers, rather than providing a central joint process development and improvement facility which may have raised new competition issues. The US Department of Justice has supported legislative initiatives to extend the National Co-operative Research Act of 1984 to joint production ventures, removing legitimate ventures from the threat of anti-trust liability.

The European Commission has accepted that in some segments, joint ventures may be the only way to form viable operations. The Commission has generally endeavoured to facilitate co-operative arrangements that make economic sense, that take account of consumer interests, and that do not restrict undertakings concerned or the maintenance or development of effective competition. In 1993, a regulation entered into force which exempted joint R&D agreements where the parties exploit jointly the results of their research by setting up a joint subsidiary to market the products.

For example in 1993 the Commission cleared a joint venture between Philips, Thomson and Sagem to develop, design, manufacture and sell flat screen displays (partly for computer use), on the grounds that foreign competition is strong, rapid production and marketing essential, and there are technical and industrial uncertainties. Prior to this, in 1991 the Commission examined a specialised data management system joint venture (IBM was one partner), and concluded that the companies involved were not actual or potential competitors outside of the joint venture, as any re-entry was highly unlikely given the costs and risks compared to the size of the market.

There has also been increasing scrutiny of the impacts of mergers between firms headquartered in other countries. In 1991 the European Commission examined the AT&T/NCR combination, and found that despite synergies generated by the merger, the new entity faced important competition, and would not distort competition in other markets.

Finally, in the application of computer network systems there have been increasing concerns that, although networks promote rationalisation and increase efficiencies in production, distribution and sales, they can be used to restrict entry, strengthen existing arrangements and decrease competition by increasing entry barriers. This concern has been expressed at international level due to, for example, increasingly tight sourcing and supply arrangements, and distribution networks.

NOTES AND REFERENCES

1. OECD-11 is Australia, Finland, France, Italy, Germany, Japan, Mexico, Netherlands, Norway, the United Kingdom, the United States. Computers is ISIC 3825. Data from the OECD STAN database, DSTI, EAS Division.

2. OECD-15 is OECD-11 plus Canada, New Zealand, Spain and Sweden.

3. Datamation and Gartner Group data for employment figures of top-20 firms are adjusted for IT employees where possible, otherwise total employment is used.

4. OECD-12 is OECD-11 minus Norway, plus Canada and Sweden. Patent data can be used to measure Revealed Technological Advantage, defined as a country's share of all US patents granted in a field (computers), divided by its share of all US patents. An RTA above 1 shows relative strength in a field. It is a measure of the output and concentration of R&D.

5. No investment data (gross fixed capital formation) were available for France and Sweden.

6. There are few sources of data on IFT, as information on the subject is not generally available in traditional trade statistics. Data on IFT are mostly available through firm surveys which involve the preparation of questionnaires by national authorities. This section is based on information provided by the US Department of Commerce, which conducts surveys of foreign affiliates of US companies and US affiliates of foreign companies. Relevant data is not available for other countries. The US Department of Commerce uses the International Surveys Industry (ISI) classification in its surveys. There is a category for "computers and office equipment" (ISI 357), which includes the manufacturing or assembling of electronic computers, computer storage devices, terminals, and peripheral equipment, such as printers, plotters, and graphic displays; calculating and accounting machines, including cash registers, and other office machines and devices such as duplicating machines, typewriters, word processors, addressing machines and time clocks. For an explanation of the availability and problems with data on IFT, see OECD (1993), *Intra-firm Trade*.

7. There has been a large increase in investment in wholesale activities in the United States. This trade is technically IFT, but different in character from the case where investment takes place in assembly operations. The figures above exclude IFT due to wholesale activities.

8. See OECD (1993), *Intra-firm Trade*.

9. Intra-industry trade can be readily calculated for any given product category, as only the traditional bilateral trade statistics for that product category are needed. The interpretation of IIT data depends however, on how one defines that category, as the choice of the classification system and of the level of aggregation may strongly influence the results. For this analysis, the Standard International Trade Classification Revision 2, at the four digit level, was used. In the calculation of an IIT index, if exports are equal to imports, IIT is 100; on the other hand, if either imports or exports are equal to zero, IIT is zero. For a discussion of the theory and measurement of IIT, see Grubel and Lloyd (1975).

10. Computers are SITC Rev. 2 752 automatic data processing machines and units thereof; magnetic or optical readers, machines for transcribing data onto data media in coded form and machines for processing such data, not elsewhere specified. In Section 3.B where trade in "peripherals" is mentioned it refers to SITC Rev. 2 7525; peripheral units including control and adapting units.

11. Data on international mergers and acquisitions and joint ventures and minority participations were kindly provided by KPMG Peat Marwick to OECD/DAFFE. For joint ventures and minority participations "purchase" means that a particular firm of that country's nationality has an operation abroad; sale means that an operation takes place in that country with a firm of foreign nationality involved.

12. Values calculated from US Department of Commerce, *Foreign Direct Investment in the United States*, Washington, DC, various issues, Table E.8, "sales by affiliates industry of sales by country of UBO" for "computers and office equipment", expressed as a share of total manufacturing production for ISIC 3825 from OECD DSTI/EAS STAN database and partly estimated.

13. The sample of 334 agreements for computers is drawn from the INSEAD Collaborative Agreements Database covering some 2 565 agreements in all regions of the world and all industries, but with a focus on manufacturing, compiled through late 1992. The information in this section was drawn from a short report on "Collaboration Agreements in the Computer Sector" prepared by Judith Jaffe under the direction of Professor Deigan Morris, INSEAD, who designed and developed the database, and who holds the rights to it.

BIBLIOGRAPHY

COMMISSION OF THE EUROPEAN COMMUNITIES/EUROPEAN COMMISSION, *Panorama of EC/EU Industries*, various issues.

COMMISSION OF THE EUROPEAN COMMUNITIES/EUROPEAN COMMISSION, *Report on Competition Policy*, various issues.

DATAMATION, *The Datamation 100*, 15 June 1993.

ELECTRONICS MAGAZINE, Penton Publishers, various issues.

ELECTRONIC INDUSTRIES ASSOCIATION, *Electronic Market Data Book*, various issues.

ELSEVIER ADVANCED TECHNOLOGY, *Yearbook of World Electronics Data*, various issues.

ERNST, D. and D. O'CONNOR (1992), Competing in the Electronics Industry. The Experience of Newly Industrialising Economies, OECD Development Centre Studies, OECD, Paris.

FISHER, F.M., J.J. McGOWAN and J.E. GREENWOOD (1983), *Folded, Spindled and Mutilated. Economic Analysis and U.S. v. IBM*, MIT Press, Cambridge, MA.

FLAMM, K. (1987), Targeting the Computer. Government Support and International Competition, The Brookings Institution, Washington, DC.

FLAMM, K. (1988), Creating the Computer. Government, Industry, and High Technology, The Brookings Institution, Washington, DC.

FORTUNE, "How Toshiba Makes Alliances Work", 4 October 1993.

GARTNER GROUP, *Yardstick's Top 100*, 1994 Edition.

GRAHAM, E.M. and M.E. EBERT (1991), *Foreign Direct Investment and National Security. Fixing the Exon-Florio Process*, Institute for International Economics, Washington, DC.

GRUBEL, H.G. and P.J. LLOYD (1975), *Intra-industry Trade: The Theory and Measurement of International Trade in Differentiated Products*, Macmillan, London.

INTERNATIONAL DATA CORPORATION, *Worldwide Black Book*, 1992; other IDC sources.

OECD (1990), papers prepared for seminar on *Globalisation in the Computer Industry*, December.

OECD (1991), *Information Technology Standards: The Economic Dimension*, ICCP Report No. 25, Paris.

OECD (1992), *Information Technology Outlook 1992*, Paris.

OECD, *Industrial Policy in OECD Countries, Annual Review*, various years; (1990), Part 4, "Government assistance to industrial R&D", Paris.

OECD (1993), *Intra-firm Trade. Trade Policy Issues*, Paris.

OECD (1994), *The Performance of Foreign Affiliates in OECD Countries*, Paris.

OECD (1995), *Main Developments in Trade*, Paris.

OECD (1995), *Information Technology Outlook 1995*, Paris.

US DEPARTMENT OF COMMERCE, *US Industrial Outlook '92, '93, '94*.

US INTERNATIONAL TRADE COMMISSION (1993), *Global Competitiveness of US Advanced-technology Industries: Computers*, Washington, DC.

US INTERNATIONAL TRADE COMMISSION (1994), *Industry and Trade Summary: Computers, Peripherals, and Computer Components*, Washington, DC.

US INTERNATIONAL TRADE COMMISSION (1995), *Global Competitiveness of the US Computer Software and Service Industries*, Washington, DC.

Chapter 4

GLOBALISATION IN THE AUTOMOBILE INDUSTRY

by

Graham Vickery
Directorate for Science, Technology and Industry, OECD

Table of contents

LIST OF TABLES

LIST OF FIGURES

SUMMARY AND CONCLUSIONS

Globalisation in the automobile industry is characterised by:

- Concentration of production, consumption and trade within the major OECD regions (inter-regional trade has largely been Japanese exports to these regions).
- The increasingly important role of foreign subsidiaries and FDI, linking firms both within regions and between regions, reinforced by a very high level of intra-firm trade (available data show this particularly between the United States and Canada).
- Industrial organisation which relies on increased networking and alliances – within nations and regions but also between regions. This is related to growing external and international sourcing of components, as well as of R&D and design.

Although the automobile can be considered a "global" product, the regionalisation of production and trade in this industry corresponds to the competitive need to respond to consumer tastes, to conform with different government regulations, and to provide high quality marketing and after sales service. While not all countries or manufacturers participate to the same extent in this regionalisation, the three main OECD markets (Western Europe, North America and Japan) together account for over 80 per cent of world sales of passenger vehicles and 90 per cent of world automobile trade.

Recent developments in technology and production techniques have contributed significantly to the pattern of globalisation. New production and organisational methods have been introduced, such as "lean production" and "just-in-time" delivery, so that competitiveness is increasingly based on rapid adaptation and flexibility. To achieve this, interrelated strategies have been adopted involving "doing everything in one place", coupled with increasing externalisation of component and service inputs.

Such strategies suggest that the trend toward international sourcing could be limited by the proximity requirements of just-in-time, and inputs requiring development and customisation will be locally or regionally sourced. Many major parts and components producers are relocating activities closer to final assemblers, as shown in relative increases in intra-regional exports of components, encouraged by government policies to increase total value added and local content in the host country. However there are limits to externalisation, partly because it may be more efficient to maintain control of key components inside assembly firms, and also because the "Toyotist" model of lean and efficient production is based on very tight links (quasi-integration) between component supply and assembly.

During the last decade, new green-field investment, acquisitions of smaller, specialist automobile firms, formation of minority shareholdings and joint ventures have all been part of global strategies which have improved the relative position of major assemblers. There has also been extensive restructuring of the fragmented component industry as firms reorganised to have greater presence in each of the three major producing areas. However, the strategic directions of firms from each part of the Triad vary considerably. Japanese producers have entered US, European and Asian markets through new international investment, while US and European producers have built on established positions in Europe and Latin America and selectively entered new markets in Eastern Europe and Asia. Direct green-field investment plays a very important role in the industry, but globalisation strategies have favoured formation of complex networks of equity holdings, rather than extensive acquisitions by major assemblers.

Most large automobile companies manufacture or are planning to manufacture in major foreign markets, and this trend is increasing. International expansion is promoted by government policies, but policies to promote the national interest are increasingly complex due to globalisation. While such policies traditionally sought to help "national" firms strengthen their international competitiveness and ensure that foreign firms did not have unimpeded access to domestic markets, policies are increasingly aiming at improving linkages between foreign-owned and domestic firms and increasing local inputs into foreign-owned production.

Trade policies have been a significant instrument of government policy in the automobile industry. Voluntary restrictions and other non-tariff measures have been particularly prominent. This is partly explained by increased international competition, over-supply and tensions in domestic markets. In addition to economic and technological factors which are the main forces driving globalisation, relocation of final assembly and production of parts and components to the market of final sales may be encouraged by trade-related government policies, for example informal or formal understandings or agreements on local content (minimum levels of local value added for local production).

Government policies to attract foreign direct investment also have an impact on the location of assembly. Many countries have been examining ways of improving the linkages between small local component suppliers and large assemblers and enhancing the international competitiveness of suppliers. Other government policies, including environmental regulations and standards to achieve environmental objectives are also becoming more prominent. In response to such regulations, numerous consortia, some involving government support, have been formed to carry out R&D to achieve these objectives. These regulations may affect business decisions regarding the site of production.

Finally, despite the concentration of automobile production and trade within the OECD area, production of automobiles and parts has grown rapidly in some non-OECD countries (some DAEs and China). Exports from some of them have grown rapidly, suggesting that these countries have developed comparative advantage, making use of foreign capital, modern technology and communications. Through specialisation, investment and trade, they are playing a greater role in globalisation of the industry. Other countries may emerge as competitive producers, driven by domestic demand, geographical proximity to major markets, and economic factors including skilled labour, appropriate infrastructure and the ability to absorb foreign investment.

1. INTRODUCTION: CHARACTERISTICS OF THE INDUSTRY

The focus in this study is on passenger cars. However, the distinction between passenger cars and commercial and other vehicles is not clear-cut. Changing tastes coupled in some cases with lower import duties and final consumption taxes have shifted patterns of consumption between different vehicles. A considerable share of utility vehicles, multipurpose vehicles (MPVs), vans, light trucks and other commercial vehicles, along with four-wheel drive and off-road vehicles, are now purchased as passenger cars rather than for commercial or work-related uses. Parts and components are covered separately in this study in some instances, particularly in the trade chapter, but their in-depth analysis would require a separate study.

The automobile sector has been very dynamic, with strong consumer demand for motor vehicles world-wide. Production, trade and investment have increased steadily, but patterns differ widely between regions and the automobile sector is not homogeneous world-wide. After craft beginnings, automobiles were subsequently produced to one design for all markets with minor local adaptations, mainly using assembly-line methods associated with "Fordism". This pattern was first applied by American companies, which expanded internationally through direct exports of cars, and later through foreign direct investment mainly in Europe, followed by Latin America. This export strategy was also adopted by Japanese firms in their initial stage of international expansion, later complemented by foreign direct investment.

Some of the main forces that are currently shaping patterns of production, trade and sourcing in the automobile industry are related to technological evolution and new approaches to organisation, including "lean" production, or "Toyotism". Technological and organisational innovations facilitate flexibility in production and enable a wider range of products to be produced efficiently and rapidly to meet new consumer, energy and environmental demands. The new production methods are based on low inventories (just-in-time), exacting quality control, flexibility and rapid response to changing consumer preferences. These have fostered rapid model introduction and product differentiation and are largely responsible for changes that are now occurring in the geographical distribution of operations as producers are able to locate production in major markets, and respond more effectively to changing consumer tastes.

As a result of new production techniques and changing market conditions, international activities of the main producers have expanded considerably with a strong focus on regional production. This process has been underpinned by the need to establish top to bottom integrated assembly operations covering design, development, engineering and component sourcing, in each region (North America, Europe and East Asia) rather than satisfying consumer demand in markets abroad through exports from the home base. In addition, this process is driven by economic factors such as realising efficiency gains and economies of scale, and being closer to final markets to increase the effectiveness of marketing and market feedback and to spread exchange rate risk. Government policies relating to inward investment, trade and other policies have also hastened relocation. However, patterns of expansion also depend on the characteristics of the producer (craft or large scale), and the size and segment of the market aimed at ("niche" products are likely to be produced in the home market for example).

Another related development is externalisation of former internal production of goods and services by assemblers (vertical disintegration), driving further changes in industry structure and new patterns of investment and production. The industry is characterised by extensive foreign investment and international alliances, with high levels of intra-firm and intra-industry trade and international sourcing. High levels of trade in components and parts, to supply foreign affiliates and final assembly plants, are a notable feature of the industry. These patterns may change however as producers of parts and components establish extensive production facilities abroad to supply more locally with just-in-time delivery. This process is currently under way.

Automobile firms were among the first to set up foreign manufacturing facilities, and many automobile firms are multinational with extensive foreign development, production and marketing activities. The process under way is not new, but final assembly operations have begun in many new locations, including government-supported enterprises in some developing countries. A relatively new development in the automobile industry however is the formation of strategic alliances and external production networks and the specific forms these have taken. In addition, firms are often linked through transnational equity holdings and other arrangements to develop and produce cars and components, including new products to meet environmental standards.

This internationalisation process is becoming more complex, with increased foreign investment by component suppliers, possibly leading to declining intra-firm component trade between parents and subsidiaries. Rising costs of product development and increasing competition have also resulted in strategies to spread costs of developing new products and producing them. These strategies have ranged from minority investment and transfer of product technology to minority-owned firms, joint development by major firms (e.g. engines, new materials), production joint ventures and "re-badging" (selling other makes of cars under one's own brand) and other forms of co-operation.

Data for major passenger car manufacturers show the importance of foreign production operations (i.e. production in countries other than the country of headquarters). This is an indication of how large firms are globalising their operations (see Table 4.1). Most of the top-10 firms have considerably more than 15 per cent of production in foreign countries, with Japanese producers having the lowest shares (Toyota, Mitsubishi). Foreign production as a share of total production is highest for General Motors and Ford, the two largest car producers; it is around 60 per cent for Ford, 50 per cent for General Motors. Foreign production is over 30 per cent for Volkswagen, Nissan, Chrysler and Honda. Major firms with no foreign passenger car production operations are either planning or starting them (e.g. Mercedes-Benz and BMW in the United States, Daihatsu in China and India), or are indirectly involved in foreign production through their equity holders (Daihatsu through Toyota, Isuzu through GM, Rover initially through Honda and from end-1993 through BMW). Furthermore, the share of foreign production compared with domestic production continued to rise during the sales recession of 1990-92, and was higher for most producers in 1993.

Exports from the home country are high for most manufacturers. The exceptions are US producers, for which no comparable data are available, although aggregate data show US car exports gaining world

Table 4.1. **Domestic and foreign production of passenger cars by the world's leading international producers, 1993**

As a percentage of worldwide production in number of passenger cars

	Domestic production			Foreign production										
	Total	Domestic new registrations	Export	Total	Australia	South America	Canada	Mexico	United States	Germany	Spain	United Kingdom	Other Europe	Chinese Taipei
General Motors	52.40	58.77[1]		47.60	1.69	4.88	9.43	2.91		16.66	7.23	4.80		
Ford	41.15	50.73[1]		58.85	2.80	4.59	9.31	4.69		12.07	5.85	7.51	9.60	2.43
Toyota	85.23	41.39[2]	33.28	14.77	2.08		2.16		10.53					
Volkswagen	57.17	31.75	21.80	42.83		16.21		8.63			17.98			
Nissan	68.81	37.07	30.83	31.19	0.67			6.21	13.19			11.12		
Chrysler	54.32	84.15[1]		45.68			28.20	17.48						
Fiat	74.87	57.20[1]	36.44	25.13		25.13								
PSA	81.14	26.35	55.88	18.86							15.10	3.76		
Renault	76.98	32.08	44.64	23.02		5.11					17.91			
Mitsubishi	83.26	31.53	37.31	16.74	4.74				12.00					
Honda	66.95	27.56	34.25	33.05			6.60		26.45					
Mazda	79.78	25.06	53.67	20.22					20.22					
Hyundai	98.15	56.31[3]	42.73	1.85			1.85							
BMW	100.00	39.73	61.20	0.00										
Suzuki	99.36	48.66	43.27	0.64			0.64							
Mercedes-Benz	100.00	46.54	56.39	0.00										

Notes: Ranked in 1994 order of worldwide production of passenger cars and commercial vehicles combined. BMW (14), Daimler-Benz (16), and Kia (17) are not shown as they had no significant foreign passenger car production.

1. Retail sales including imports and rebadging.
2. Estimated using top-15 models.
3. Estimated using sales.

Source: OECD, calculated from AAMA (1995), World Motor Vehicle Data.

market shares. Between 20 and 60 per cent of home-country production is exported by non-US producers, with this share tending to fall recently for all Japanese and some European producers, as they relocate production to final regional markets. For US firms, apparent domestic car sales are higher than domestic production, due to imports from foreign subsidiaries for sale in the United States, and "re-badging" of imports and US production of other producers, mostly Japanese. Re-badging is likely to be a continuing feature in the industry for producers to extend their product ranges and markets by selling cars produced by other assemblers under their own model names.

2. TRENDS IN GROWTH AND STRUCTURE

A. Production and consumption

The industry has shown steady growth overall, but has experienced marked cyclical downturns following the two oil shocks and during recession. Recent growth has been in new markets such as East Asia and China where rising incomes and improved road infrastructure have encouraged automobile use.

Over 80 per cent of the world market for passenger cars is in OECD countries (1994 data), about 20 per cent in other countries, with over 10 per cent in Asia, mostly in rapidly growing Asian economies. The major world markets are in Europe (the EU is the largest market with one-third of world sales), followed by the United States and Japan. There has been a long-term shift towards production and markets in Asia and Europe, but North America has recovered relatively strongly from its major production and sales trough in 1990 (Figure 4.1 and Table 4.2).

World production of automobiles in 1994 was 35.25 million passenger cars (24.96 million in 1975) and 14.42 million commercial vehicles, a total of 49.67 million, up only 3 per cent from 1990. Total production (passenger plus commercial vehicle numbers) grew sharply across the OECD area in 1994, by some 5.7 per cent, compared with the 1980-90 average annual growth of 3.2 per cent. However, expansion slowed in 1995 in many OECD countries, recovering slowly in some larger European countries (Germany, Italy, United Kingdom) and in some smaller ones, and in Japan (IIA and ACEA data).

Historically the industry has tended to expand somewhat faster than manufacturing as a whole. From 1970 to the 1990s the share of motor vehicles in manufacturing value added increased by about 0.5 per cent to over 7 per cent. The cyclical nature of the sector is shown in its sharp decline in value-added share in 1974, 1980, and the early 1990s (Figure 4.2).

Motor vehicles value added was highest and increasing in Germany (11 per cent of the manufacturing total in the early 1990s), Canada (over 9 per cent), Japan, Spain, Sweden, and France of major producers, as well as Mexico. Countries with low value-added shares (Netherlands, Finland, Denmark, Norway) also showed an increase. The UK, US and Italian industries were declining from the average and Australia from above average levels.

A few OECD countries produce more motor vehicles than they consume, a few are in balance, but the majority consume more motor vehicles than they produce. Japan, Germany, France and Sweden have consistently been large surplus producers in the motor vehicle industry. The positions of these national industries have tended to decline due to a combination of decreasing competitiveness (strong currencies in Germany, Japan and France) and increasing overseas production (see Table 4.3).

Of large producing countries where production and consumption are approximately equal, Canada has very high imports and exports because of its tight integration into the North American production system. French imports are slowly overtaking exports but a considerable production surplus has been maintained, and Spain has built its surplus due to foreign investment in assembly and parts production for domestic and export markets. The United States and Italy have become large net importers, with declining production relative to consumption.

The United Kingdom showed the most dramatic shift from net producer to net consumer from 1970, although exports have risen recently as foreign producers, particularly Japanese, expand production and exports. Australia increased its net consumption. Smaller European countries had low but increasing production to consumption ratios (Austria, Denmark, Finland, the Netherlands and Norway) due to their

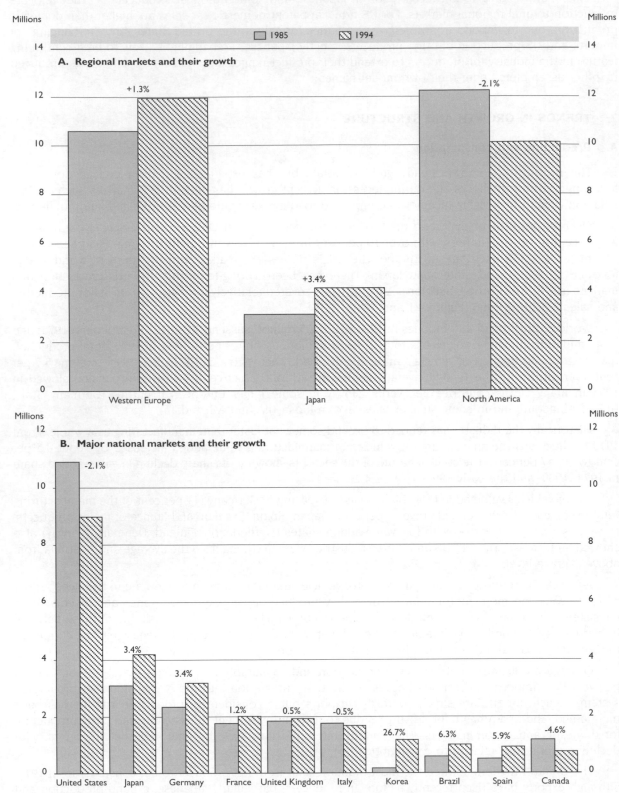

◆ Figure 4.1. **Motor vehicles**
Number of new passenger car registrations and average annualised growth rate

Millions

☐ 1985   ▨ 1994

A. Regional markets and their growth

Western Europe: +1.3%
Japan: +3.4%
North America: -2.1%

B. Major national markets and their growth

United States: -2.1%
Japan: 3.4%
Germany: 3.4%
France: 1.2%
United Kingdom: 0.5%
Italy: -0.5%
Korea: 26.7%
Brazil: 6.3%
Spain: 5.9%
Canada: -4.6%

Source: CCFA.

Table 4.2. **World distribution of passenger car production and sales, 1994**

Thousands of vehicles and percentages

	Production	Share (%)		Sales	Share (%)	
		1994	1993		1994	1993
Europe	13 893	39.4	37.8	13 513	40.2	41.0
of which: EU	11 859	33.6	31.4	11 062	32.9	32.5
America	10 052	28.5	27.8	11 930	35.5	34.6
of which:						
NAFTA	8 672	24.6	24.2	10 154	30.2	29.9
South and Central America	1 380	3.9	3.6	1 776	5.3	4.7
Asia Oceania	11 101	31.5	33.8	7 911	23.5	23.5
of which: Japan	7 801	22.1	25.2	4 210	12.5	13.0
Africa	199	0.6	0.6	275	0.8	0.9
Total	**35 245**	**100.0**	**100.0**	**33 630**	**100.0**	**100.0**

Source: CCFA.

increasing supplies of parts and components to the European automobile industry, and in the Dutch case, expansion of foreign investment in assembly.

B. Employment[1]

Motor vehicle producers are major employers, but employment grew only slowly or declined in most OECD countries from the 1970s through the 1990s, although the share of motor vehicle employment in total manufacturing has grown overall. Sluggish employment performance has been due to increased import competition and subsequent new green-field investment by Japanese and Korean producers in the United States and Europe, leading to the adoption of new labour-saving "lean" production methods by European and US automakers.

From the 1970s to the early 1990s, employment in motor vehicles for 17 OECD countries for which data are available remained flat, around 4.3 million, with a peak of 4.5 million in 1979 and a trough of 4 million during the recession of the early 1980s (see Figure 4.3). Employment declined in the 1990s in all major producing countries due to retrenchments by all large automakers. Automobile employment turned down initially in North America and the United Kingdom, and then fell sharply in continental Europe and declined, unusually, in Japan in 1993-95. Japan had been, until then, the only major producer where employment consistently increased. As the industry has pulled out of recession, employment growth has lagged production, due to restructuring, rationalisation and cost-cutting, particularly in Europe. This is the case even in the United States and Canada: although output in 1995 was considerably above 1990 levels, employment was lagging output due to labour-saving firm reorganisation and the impacts of new Japanese investment.

In detail, between 1977 and 1992 employment dropped by 4 per cent per year in the United Kingdom and Italy, and by 1 to 2 per cent in the United States, France and Australia. Most of the remaining larger producers had positive employment growth, with higher growth in Germany, Japan, Spain and Mexico. Then, through to 1995 employment in the motor vehicle industry fell in most countries, with the exception of North America. There were marked declines in Sweden (down 30 per cent from 1990 employment), the United Kingdom (down 25 per cent), Germany (down 17 per cent), France (down 8 per cent). Japan grew through to 1991, but has shown an overall decline in employment since. On the other hand the United States (up 20 per cent over 1990) and Canada (up 5 per cent), and a few countries with smaller component supply or assembly industries (e.g. Turkey) expanded employment.

◆ Figure 4.2. **Value-added shares – Motor vehicles**

Share of motor vehicles in total manufacturing value added

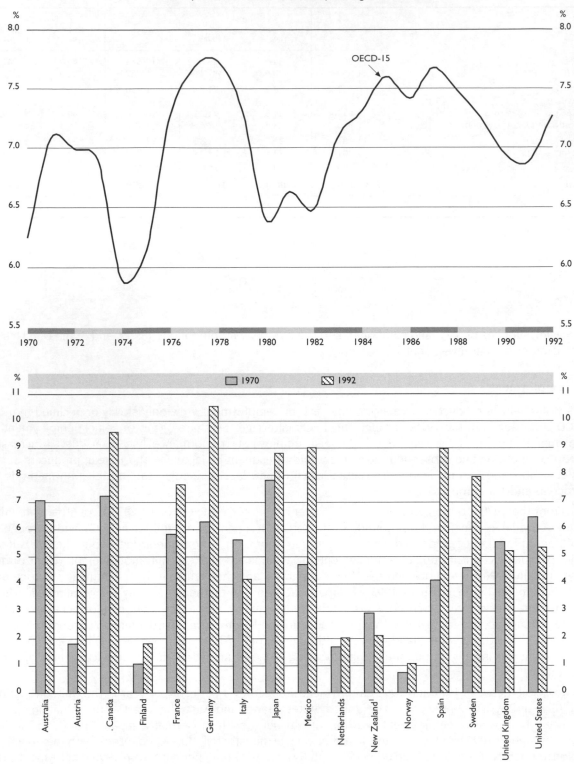

1. 1987.
Source: OECD, DSTI, STAN Database.

Table 4.3. **Indicators for production and consumption – Motor vehicles**

	Production/consumption				Imports/consumption				Exports/production			
	1970	1980	1990	1993	1970	1980	1990	1993	1970	1980	1990	1993
Australia	0.84	0.78	0.74	0.68	0.21	0.25	0.32	0.39	0.06	0.04	0.07	0.10
Austria	0.45	0.59	0.69	0.78	0.69	0.61	0.93	0.84	0.31	0.34	0.88	0.76
Canada	1.07	0.86	1.09	1.16	0.68	0.74	0.72	0.82	0.67	0.70	0.75	0.84
Denmark [1]	0.26	0.41	0.20	. .	0.88	0.96	0.97	. .	0.56	0.91	0.86	. .
Finland	0.27	0.44	0.46	. .	0.80	0.74	0.84	. .	0.25	0.42	0.64	. .
France	1.19	1.21	1.08	1.17	0.18	0.28	0.39	0.40	0.30	0.41	0.43	0.44
Germany	1.36	1.43	1.37	1.27	0.13	0.18	0.26	0.27	0.36	0.42	0.44	0.43
Italy	1.14	0.94	0.90	0.98	0.21	0.30	0.33	0.49	0.31	0.26	0.27	0.42
Japan	1.09	1.36	1.28	1.26	0.01	0.01	0.03	0.02	0.09	0.27	0.24	0.23
Netherlands	0.41	0.51	0.58	. .	0.80	0.89	0.98	. .	0.52	0.78	0.97	0.90
New Zealand	0.51	0.61	0.48	0.46	0.50	0.42	0.54	0.55	0.01	0.05	0.04	0.05
Norway	0.19	0.26	0.29	0.26	0.91	0.89	0.94	0.95	0.50	0.57	0.80	0.82
Portugal [1]	0.51	0.58	0.44	0.41	0.51	0.52	0.84	0.82	0.03	0.17	0.64	0.55
Spain	0.98	1.09	1.05	1.11	0.04	0.09	0.36	0.58	0.03	0.16	0.39	0.62
Sweden	1.14	1.35	1.30	1.89	0.36	0.45	0.48	0.64	0.44	0.60	0.59	0.73
United Kingdom	1.27	1.02	0.84	0.80	0.07	0.33	0.46	0.50	0.26	0.34	0.35	0.38
United States	0.96	0.90	0.82	0.86	0.13	0.24	0.30	0.27	0.10	0.16	0.15	0.15

1. 1986 figures instead of 1990.
Source: OECD, STAN database (DSTI, EAS Division).

Labour productivity: motor vehicle output per employee

One widely used indicator of the relative efficiency of production of automobiles is output per employee. Values depend on the structure of the industry, and the extent of vertical integration and internal component production within firms. However country-level and firm-level data show the same broad trends. Using unadjusted gross national output in numbers of motor vehicles divided by the number of employees in the whole motor vehicle industry (including parts production), Canada, Japan, the United States and France produce the most motor vehicles per employee. Values declined in the early 1990s, particularly in Japan, due to declining output and initial labour-hoarding. The European producers of more expensive automobiles (Germany and Sweden) had considerably lower car output per employee. The United Kingdom had low output per employee among major producers, although output per employee increased rapidly from the early 1980s, as did both French and Italian output per employee (Table 4.4).

Firm-level data for individual assemblers show broadly the same trends. Overall, Japanese firms have the highest output per employee, followed by the United States and Europe, depending on the time period and method of calculation used (see de Banville and Chanaron, 1991; Womack *et al.*, 1990; IMVP). These data reflect vertical integration, relative efficiency and the complexity of automobiles produced. Firms which are less vertically integrated will produce the most cars per employee and have lower value added, particularly if they are only final assemblers. This has been the case for Japanese automobile firms. On the other hand, for the same degree of vertical integration, more efficient firms will produce more cars of the same type per employee, or alternatively, fewer, more expensive and complex cars.[2]

C. Research and development

The industry is increasingly R&D-intensive. Business R&D expenditures as a share of production increased from 2.4 to 3.3 per cent over 1973-92.[3] Compared with total manufacturing the sector is above average R&D intensity, and moved up to sixth place in overall R&D intensity ranking in the 1990s, from seventh in the 1970s. Manufacturing R&D intensity increased from 1.6 to 2.5 per cent over the same

◆ Figure 4.3. **Employment growth – Motor vehicles**

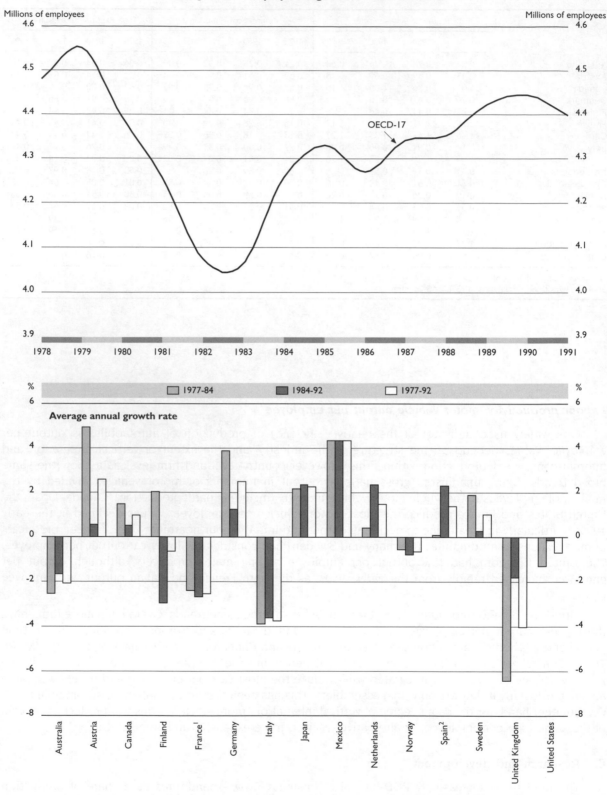

1. 1991.
2. 1978.
Source: OECD, DSTI, STAN Database.

Table 4.4.   **Productivity for the whole industry – Motor vehicles per employee per year**

	1976	1980	1985	1990	1992
Canada	12.4	11.4	12.7	12.5	13.3
France	7.0	6.9	7.7	10.0	9.7[1]
Germany	7.6	5.6	6.4	6.4	6.4
Italy	4.8	4.8	6.4	9.7	8.9
Japan	9.8	12.1	12.1	12.6	10.8
Sweden	6.4	4.8	6.3	4.9	5.1
United Kingdom	4.1	3.2	5.0	5.8	6.5
United States	11.9	9.0	11.9	10.6	10.6

1.   1991.
Source: OECD, calculated from AAMA and STAN database (DSTI, EAS Division).

period. R&D is sensitive to cyclical declines in output and R&D intensity fell in the recessions of the mid-1970s and remained flat during the early 1980s and early 1990s (see Figure 4.4).

The United States and Sweden had the highest and increasing R&D intensities throughout the period. Germany, France and Italy also had R&D-intensive industries, along with Japan which increased rapidly from a low base. The United Kingdom was also increasing from below average, while Canada remained very low. All countries had increasing R&D intensities.

Revealed technological advantage

Revealed technological advantage is a measure of the output, efficiency and concentration of R&D. Here it is defined as a country's share of all US patents granted in a field (motor vehicles), divided by its share of all US patents. An RTA above 1 shows the relative strength of a country's industry in that field. In the period 1976-90 Japan and Germany had high and increasing RTAs – 1.64 and 1.46 respectively in 1990 indicating relative industrial competitiveness. Italy with a constant increase, and Sweden in spite of a drop during the early 1980s had RTAs above 1. Canada and France had increasing RTAs but were still below 1 in 1990. The UK RTA fell constantly throughout the period to below 1, and the United States dropped from below 1 to 0.73.

D.   Capital investment

The motor vehicle industry is relatively investment-intensive, and has been particularly important in adopting advanced manufacturing technology (computer-aided design, production, handling and storage) and associated management techniques (just-in-time, materials resource planning, total quality management). The industry tends to be more investment-intensive than total manufacturing in the United States, Japan, Germany, and the United Kingdom, all of which have large automobile industries, as well as in the Netherlands.

Investment intensities (annual gross fixed capital formation as a share of production) for the motor vehicle sector have fluctuated widely in most countries.[4] Overall investment intensity tended to decrease during the mid-1970s and increase in the mid-1980s. Over the long period from the early 1970s, investment intensities increased in the United States, Canada and the Netherlands and decreased elsewhere.

Advanced manufacturing technology and new manufacturing techniques

Japan and Sweden have been particularly important pioneers of new manufacturing techniques. Both had low unemployment, and sought to modify the traditional Taylorist organisation of work to overcome labour shortages and improve efficiency and quality. Japanese firms developed new approaches to manufacturing based on design for production, rapid model change, flexible production, low stocks (just-in-time methods), high quality and continuous improvement, and a mix of automation and decentralised management. This is often characterised as "lean" production or the "Toyota" model of production.

◆ Figure 4.4. **R&D intensity – Motor vehicles**

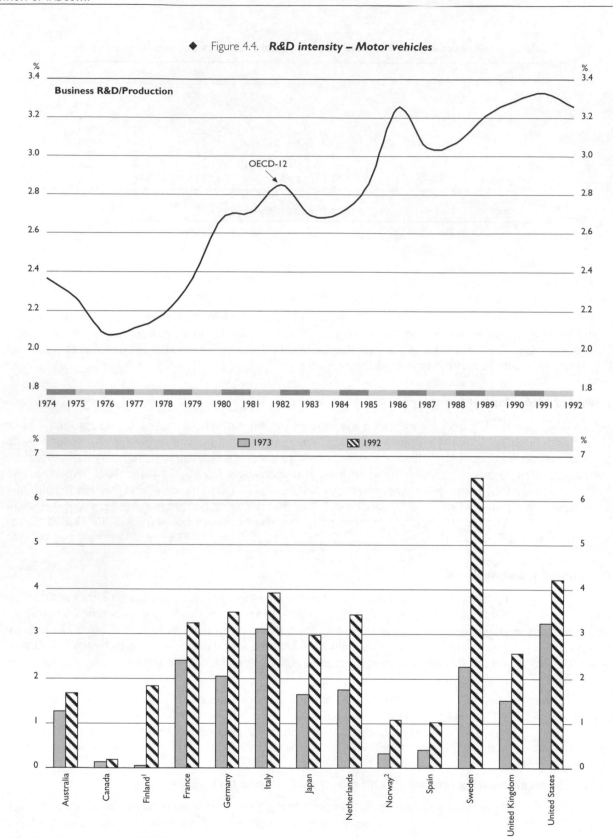

1. 1974. 2. 1978.
Source: OECD, DSTI, STAN, ANBERD Databases.

These flexible, high-quality production methods shaped global reorganisation of the industry. They provided competitive advantages to Japanese firms and others adopting their methods, and drove overseas investment in new clusters of component manufacturing and assembly. Swedish firms meanwhile experimented extensively with team assembly and more varied assembly tasks to provide variety and responsibility in production work. Besides these well-known new models of production and their application in Japan and Sweden, almost all automobile firms adopted various modified versions of lean production, extensively using production automation and computer-integrated design and control. There are relatively high overall levels of use of advanced manufacturing technology for example in Germany, Italy and France, but most firms use mixes of new and traditional techniques.

E.   Concentration and competition

a)   *Firm concentration*

The industry is dominated by a small number of large firms which have increasing global spread. This oligopoly has remained relatively stable, with General Motors retaining top position world-wide for a very long period and Ford and Toyota vying for the position of the second producer.

Trends in global concentration in automobiles (CCFA and AAMA data, passenger cars and commercial vehicles) show that the industry has consolidated somewhat at world level over the last ten years. The top-20 firms now take over 95 per cent of world-wide production (Figure 4.5). Furthermore, equity crossholdings and alliances between many of these firms suggest that effective world shares of major interconnected groups are more concentrated (see Sections 4.A, B and D below). However there has been relatively little change in the share of world production of the top firms in the period 1981-94, and a decline in the share of the top firm (General Motors), as Japanese and Korean firms, and to a lesser extent some European firms, increased in importance relative to the leading firm.

At national level there has been a decline in the production share of the top-2 producers in most large countries, as new foreign entrants and established foreign firms expanded their share of national production (AAMA data, Figure 4.5). However where there are only one or two large domestic producers (France, Italy, Sweden), they retained almost total control of final production. Sales data also show that the share of sales of the top firms in most major national markets is declining due to greater production and import competition. There are more large producers competing in most national markets, lowering national production and market concentration, despite exit or acquisition of many smaller producers and the group of large producers becoming more dominant at world level. Japan is an exception. The data reflect shifting production and market shares of Japanese producers, not competition from foreign investment or from the relatively little import competition.

b)   *Major firms and world markets*

Although global concentration of the top group of firms has increased, there have been relatively few changes in the composition of this group. The top-12 auto firms in 1994 were all in the top-12 in 1981 and intervening years although their ranking changed. Changes in the top-20 were due to the relative decline of the indigenous UK industry (Leyland, now Rover with majority ownership by BMW), collapse of the ex-USSR (Vaz and Moskvitch) and Eastern European industries, and fierce competition amongst Japanese producers which eroded market shares of the smallest producers (*e.g.* Daihatsu). BMW moved into the top-20 notably after acquisition of Rover, and the only new producers to join the upper ranks are the Koreans Hyundai and Kia, and to a lesser extent Daewoo. The Koreans had significant shares of equity held respectively by Mitsubishi, Ford/Mazda and GM (dissolved in 1992) and all received design, model production and technical assistance from their Japanese and US partners. Table 4.5 shows ranking of major firms.

Overall, Japanese and North American firms each have close to one-third of world auto production, and Western European firms under 25 per cent. Since the early 1990s, the North American share has grown while the Japanese and European producers declined. In 1994, the Big-3 US firms held almost 35 per cent of world automobile production (totalling 49.7 million passenger cars and commercial vehicles) and held

◆ Figure 4.5a. **Global production concentration – Motor vehicles**

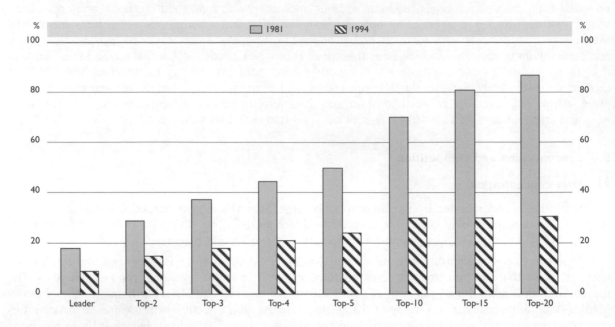

Source: CCFA.

◆ Figure 4.5b. **Production concentration by country – Motor vehicles**
Passenger cars

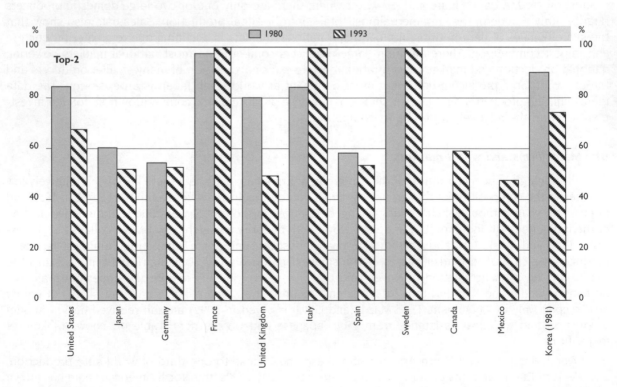

Source: AAMA.

Table 4.5. **Top-20 manufacturers ranked by 1994 worldwide production**

Ranks in 1994, 1993, 1992, 1981

| | Headquarters | 1994 | | 1993 | | 1992 | 1981 |
		Rank	Production[1]	Rank	Production[1]	Rank	Rank
General Motors	United States	1	8 035 000	1	7 113 000	1	1
Ford	United States	2	6 518 000	2	5 852 000	2	2
Toyota	Japan	3	5 164 000	3	5 072 000	3	3
Volkswagen	Germany	4	3 153 888	4	3 013 548	4	5
Nissan	Japan	5	2 784 000	5	3 001 000	5	4
Chrysler	United States	6	2 774 718	6	2 392 000	8	12
Fiat	Italy	7	2 410 000	7	2 143 545	6	7
PSA Peugeot Citroën	France	8	1 989 810	11	1 751 600	9	8
Renault	France	9	1 914 682	9	1 761 306	7	6
Mitsubishi	Japan	10	1 797 000	10	1 754 000	11	10
Honda	Japan	11	1 744 000	8	1 772 000	10	11
Mazda	Japan	12	1 227 000	12	1 237 000	12	9
Hyundai	Korea	13	1 174 041	13	996 140	14	–
BMW Rover[2]	Germany	14	1 051 185	18	532 960	18	21
Suzuki	Japan	15	970 300	14	992 344	13	15
Mercedes-Benz	Germany	16	886 533	15	725 718	15	14
Kia	Korea	17	675 461	17	655 396	20	–
Isuzu	Japan	18	544 303	20	425 000	17	19
Autovaz	Russia	19	535 000	16	665 000	16	13
Fuji Heavy	Japan	20	488 093	19	484 801	19	17

1. Passenger cars and commercial vehicles.
2. BMW only before 1994.
Source: OECD, calculated from CCFA.

the top-3 shares of US sales of automobiles (passenger cars and commercial vehicles combined), although by 1990-91 Toyota was challenging the position of Chrysler in US sales of passenger cars. The top-3 Japanese producers (Toyota, Nissan, Honda) held 19.5 per cent of world automobile production, with sales steadily increasing over a long period in the United States and Europe despite recent downturns, and the top-3 shares of passenger car sales in Japan. The top-4 Europeans (Volkswagen, Fiat, Renault, PSA in 1994) held 19 per cent of world auto production, and held top sales positions in their home markets. However, large shares of Western European new car sales are held by GM and Ford (second and fourth positions in 1994-95) and Japanese producers (combined they held sixth position, close to Fiat and Renault in 1994-95).

Re-badging. The increase in re-badging (selling other manufacturers cars under your own name or trade-mark) illustrates the increasingly complex links between firms. Data for some makes of cars for production and new registrations can diverge markedly, and affect measures of concentration. The Big-3 firms in the United States (General Motors, Ford, Chrysler) sell Japanese cars under their own badges, both direct imports from Japan and cars assembled locally in Japanese plants, as well as co-manufacturing, co-designing and integrating parts sourcing for some models (*e.g.* GM and Toyota). It was estimated that the three firms sold almost 500 000 Japanese-derived cars in the United States in 1991, accounting for 16 per cent of all Japanese-related sales in that year, and the volume has probably remained around that level.

c) New factors in competition: the shift towards external sourcing

Assemblers have generally shifted towards external sources of components, to decrease use of internally produced components and become less "vertically integrated". Japan's automobile industry has been characterised by extensive external sourcing, with a small group of first-tier suppliers linked very closely with major automobile assemblers. Component supply relations have been more varied in North America and Europe, but there has been a trend towards an external sourcing system more akin to the Japanese one, as this has been seen as a major factor in Japanese competitiveness.

Table 4.6. **Vertical integration – Motor vehicles**

Value added/production

	1970	1975	1980	1985	1992
Australia	0.36	0.38	0.36	0.34	0.34
Austria	0.42	0.38	0.27	0.41	0.37[1]
Canada	0.26	0.24	0.19	0.24	0.22[1]
Finland	0.36	0.35	0.33	0.32	0.39
France	0.40	0.40	0.35	0.29	0.32
Germany	0.32	0.31	0.33	0.34	0.30[2]
Italy	0.42	0.37	0.28	0.25	0.25[2]
Japan	0.34	0.32	0.29	0.28	0.27[2]
Mexico	0.34	0.30	0.36	0.40	0.32
Netherlands	0.33	0.29	0.29	0.25	0.21[2]
Norway	0.42	0.43	0.35	0.32	0.34[2]
Spain	0.13	0.19	0.28	0.27	0.32[1]
Sweden	0.27	0.31	0.27	0.33	0.28[1]
United Kingdom	0.27	0.25	0.27	0.28	0.23
United States	0.38	0.30	0.26	0.30	0.20

1. 1990.
2. 1991.
Source: OECD, calculated from STAN database (DSTI, EAS Division), 1994.

There are few general economic measures of this aspect of structural change, despite broad recognition and detailed case studies of this new type of organisation in the industry. One measure of the relative importance of externally supplied components is the ratio of value added to production or sales, although this measure is affected by the business cycle, increasing as margins increase, decreasing as margins decrease. Firms and industries which have lower value added use external sources of components to a greater extent and are less vertically integrated, as other firms and industries are major sources of inputs into final production. By this measure, over the period 1970-92 the industry swung towards greater external sourcing and lower vertical integration. Of major producers, Japan has low vertical integration measured by value added to production, and Canada, the United Kingdom, and the United States also have low levels of vertical integration. By this measure, the industries in France and Italy were becoming less vertically integrated and increasing external sourcing. Germany and Sweden had shown little change. Company level data show rather similar patterns. Firms in Japan and the United Kingdom have lower levels of vertical integration, France and the United States moderate levels, while German and Italian firms have had the highest levels (see Table 4.6).

The restructuring process is however slow, and differs among countries. The number of major external suppliers has remained higher outside of Japan and price competition and short-term contracts among multiple suppliers have been a durable feature of the external supply system.

Around 1990 the average number of suppliers was:

Japan	(Toyota, Nissan, Honda, Mazda):	220	"First-tier" suppliers
United States	(GM, Ford):	2 000	GM largely single source
	(Chrysler):	750	
Germany	(Mercedes, VW):	2 500	750 single source
	(US subsidiaries, Ford, Opel):	1 200	900 single source
	(Audi, BMW):	1 000	850 single source
France	(Renault, PSA):	1 050	850 (1992)

Source : OECD Secretariat, adapted from various sources.

But the switch towards longer-term contracts with single suppliers is expected to continue. For example the German industry estimated a shift from less than 5 per cent of contracts being of more than 3 years duration in 1987 to over 60 per cent of contracts in 1995. This enables component suppliers to develop tightly integrated delivery (just-in-time) with assemblers, meet their quality standards, and most importantly over the long term, to develop new products in conjunction with assemblers. Most of the supply of components remains local. Only 5-20 per cent of components were imported by German assemblers around 1990, and 90 per cent of European sourcing overall was with national suppliers until recently. Subsidiaries of foreign-owned firms are more likely to source internationally – up to 45 per cent by Ford and GM subsidiaries in Germany.

Components increasingly sourced externally are in many cases more specialised kinds such as seats and associated mountings which are likely to be customised, and electronic and electrical assemblies requiring specialised technological skills. The need for tighter links between electronics firms and auto assemblers are likely to continue as the electronic content of automobiles increases. Automobiles are a growing end-use of semiconductors, consuming 6.5 per cent of world semiconductor production in 1992. Market research suggests a sharp increase in the use of electronics in all automobile systems and components by the year 2000 (growing by 75 per cent 1993-2000 according to Dataquest), with power train and safety and convenience applications expected to retain over one-half of total applications.

F. Pricing

Prices of new cars have generally fallen relative to total consumer prices even after allowing for improved safety and emission standards. However three pricing issues of a general nature in the automobile industry are as follows:

Variable pricing strategies adopted by producers in different markets. They have been partly due to producers attempting to overcome exchange rate fluctuations in export markets by quoting fixed prices for as long as possible in currencies of final markets, partly as a result of producers changing their range, quality and options on automobiles as they attempt to move to higher value-added more expensive cars in markets which are becoming saturated, and partly due to firm strategies to capture market share.

Unit values of car trade with the United States reflect all of these influences on prices. Unit values (in US$) of Japanese cars exported to the United States have been consistently higher than unit values of Japanese exports of cars to the EC/EU as a whole, and to the United Kingdom, France and Germany.[5] The higher unit values for Japanese cars sold on the American market reflect market factors and models sold, as well as VER limitations (see Section 5). An increase in unit values from 1985 reflected depreciation of the dollar passing through into foreign unit dollar values. The unit values for exports of EU cars to the United States are considerably higher, consisting mainly of luxury cars, while unit values of US cars sold into the EU are also higher, partly related to the type of American cars sold abroad.

The impacts of the distribution system on final prices. Producers usually have exclusive dealing arrangements with distributors, whereby one or at most several brands are sold by a distributor. There has been a continuing debate on benefits (reliability of supply, brand image-building, financing, guarantees, after-sales service) and costs (price inflation, anti-competitive behaviour, limits to choice) of these distribution systems. There have been recent attempts to overcome some of these costs, widen consumer choice, and for example facilitate individual purchases in foreign countries and parallel imports from lower price sources (see Section 5E, Competition policy).

The costs of environmental and safety standards. Most governments have had a two-pronged strategy to pass the costs of improved standards to final users. First, all OECD countries have increased the initial costs of automobiles by increasing the requirements for cars to meet environmental standards, reduce noise and improve safety and quality. The AAMA estimated that in the United States the average retail price increase per new car due to federal emission control regulations cumulated over 1968-95 was US$1 791 per new car (1994 US$) and for safety standards was US$1 563, totalling US$3 355 per car, or about 17 per cent of average new car expenditure in 1995. Total quality improvement costs were estimated to average US$5 411 per new car. Estimates in other countries confirm that marginal costs increase rapidly to achieve very low emission levels (*i.e.* it is increasingly expensive to reduce remaining emissions).

Furthermore, improved infrastructures and reduced traffic congestion are necessary to achieve effective low emission levels. Second, many governments have used differential fuel taxes or purchase taxes to direct consumers towards less polluting (lead-free) and more efficient (diesel) fuels as well as encouraging fuel efficiency in general. In the United States where fuel costs are very low, high fuel consumption new cars are taxed through "gas-guzzler" purchase taxes (maximum of US$7 700 for high consumption cars from 1991) and the "CAFE" taxes aimed at achieving lower average fuel consumption for new cars (see below, Section 5). Re-cycling costs of used cars may also be added to the initial purchase price.

3. INTERNATIONAL TRADE

A. General trends

Trade in automobiles has become significant only in recent decades. Prior to World War II, there was little trade, but from the early 1960s trade grew rapidly, facilitated by successive rounds of multilateral trade negotiations in GATT resulting in a general reduction in tariffs and the gradual opening of markets. The value of both world exports and imports of finished automobiles and parts and components has increased rapidly since then and more than tripled between 1980 and 1993 (Tables 4.7-4.9). World imports and exports of finished cars each amounted to US$180 billion and to US$115 billion for parts. Trade has outpaced production, and the industry is highly trade intensive compared with the average. If the exports/production index for all manufacturing is 1, then the index for automobiles is around 1.6. It is noteworthy that trade increased rapidly in parallel with higher flows of foreign direct investment.

Trade remains predominantly concentrated within the OECD area. OECD trade slowly declined by 1994 to 94 per cent of world exports and 88 per cent of world imports of finished cars, and 95 per cent of world exports and 85 per cent of world imports of parts.

a) Intra-regional and inter-regional trade

A major characteristic of trade in automobile products, both for finished cars, and parts and components is its marked regional concentration in North America and Europe (Table 4.9 and Figure 4.6). Intra-regional automobile trade in Europe, North America and East Asia combined is a steady 60 per cent of total world trade. In particular intra-European and intra-North American exports (United States, Canada and Mexico) have grown faster than total automobile trade for these regions.

Table 4.7. **Trade in automobiles (finished and parts)**

SITC Rev. 2: 7132 + 7783 + 781 + 7841 + 7842 + 7849

Major exporters	1980		1993		Major importers	1980		1993	
	Value (bil. US$)	Share (%)	Value (bil. US$)	Share (%)		Value (bil. US$)	Share (%)	Value (bil. US$)	Share (%)
Japan	19.10	19.7	68.96	23.1	United States	24.61	27.0	78.75	27.2
Germany	22.78	23.5	55.20	18.5	Germany	7.58	8.3	28.13	9.7
United States	12.80	13.2	38.26	12.8	Canada	10.44	11.5	25.68	8.9
Canada	6.71	6.9	27.39	9.2	United Kingdom	6.70	7.4	21.49	7.4
France	11.36	11.7	22.46	7.5	France	5.74	6.3	16.64	5.7
Belgium-Luxembourg	5.56	5.7	16.20	5.4	Italy	6.16	6.8	12.26	4.2
Spain	2.10	2.2	12.94	4.3	Spain	1.05	1.2	11.10	3.8
United Kingdom	6.20	6.4	11.91	4.0	Belgium-Luxembourg	6.46	7.1	10.34	3.6
Italy	4.78	4.9	9.44	3.2	Japan	0.58	0.6	6.60	2.3
Mexico	0.00	0.0	7.57	2.5					
Sweden	2.42	2.5	5.28	1.8					
Republic of Korea	0.07	0.1	4.37	1.5					
Rest of world	3.17	3.3	18.76	6.3	Rest of world	21.84	24.0	78.94	27.2
World	**97.04**	**100.0**	**298.74**	**100.0**	**World**	**91.15**	**100.0**	**289.93**	**100.0**

Source: Secretariat estimates from UN Comtrade database.

Table 4.8a. **Trade in finished automobiles**

SITC Rev. 2: 781

Major exporters	1980		1993		Major importers	1980		1993	
	Value (bil. US$)	Share (%)	Value (bil. US$)	Share (%)		Value (bil. US$)	Share (%)	Value (bil. US$)	Share (%)
Japan	16.11	27.5	47.13	25.9	United States	18.02	32.8	53.45	30.3
United States	14.62	24.9	35.46	19.5	Germany	4.83	8.8	17.30	9.8
Germany	3.97	6.8	19.04	10.5	Canada	4.90	8.9	13.04	7.4
Canada	4.60	7.8	14.21	7.8	United Kingdom	3.24	5.9	11.60	6.6
France	4.03	6.9	14.04	7.7	France	4.60	8.4	9.98	5.7
Belgium-Luxembourg	6.75	11.5	12.30	6.8	Italy	3.83	7.0	9.36	5.3
Spain	1.50	2.6	9.88	5.4	Spain	2.25	4.1	5.84	3.3
United Kingdom	1.95	3.3	6.53	3.6	Belgium-Luxembourg	0.36	0.7	5.31	3.0
Italy	2.45	4.2	4.63	2.5	Japan	0.39	0.7	4.95	2.8
Mexico	0.00	0.0	4.04	2.2					
Republic of Korea	0.05	0.1	3.88	2.1					
Sweden	1.20	2.0	2.99	1.6					
Rest of world	1.40	2.4	7.52	4.1	Rest of world	12.56	22.8	45.36	25.7
World	**58.62**	**100.0**	**181.65**	**100.0**	**World**	**54.98**	**100.0**	**176.20**	**100.0**

Source: Secretariat estimates from UN Comtrade database.

Table 4.8b. **Trade in automobile parts**

SITC Rev. 2: 7132 + 7783 + 7841 + 7842 + 7849

Major exporters	1980		1993		Major importers	1980		1993	
	Value (bil. US$)	Share (%)	Value (bil. US$)	Share (%)		Value (bil. US$)	Share (%)	Value (bil. US$)	Share (%)
United States	8.77	22.8	24.22	20.7	United States	6.59	18.2	25.30	22.2
Japan	2.99	7.8	21.83	18.6	Canada	6.61	18.3	16.32	14.3
Germany	8.16	21.2	19.74	16.9	Germany	2.75	7.6	10.83	9.5
France	4.61	12.0	10.17	8.7	United Kingdom	1.80	5.0	8.45	7.4
Canada	2.74	7.1	8.35	7.1	Mexico	0.00	0.0	7.86	6.9
United Kingdom	4.25	11.1	5.38	4.6	Spain	0.69	1.9	5.78	5.1
Italy	2.33	6.1	4.81	4.1	France	2.49	6.9	5.04	4.4
Mexico	0.00	0.0	3.53	3.0	Belgium-Luxembourg	4.21	11.6	4.50	4.0
Spain	0.60	1.6	3.06	2.6	Italy	1.56	4.3	2.28	2.0
Sweden	1.22	3.2	2.29	2.0	Japan	0.19	0.5	1.65	1.5
Belgium-Luxembourg	0.96	2.5	1.98	1.7	Chinese Taipei	0.26	0.7	1.54	1.4
Chinese Taipei	0.12	0.3	1.18	1.0					
Republic of Korea	0.02	0.1	0.48	0.4					
Rest of world	1.64	4.3	10.07	8.6	Rest of world	9.02	24.9	24.17	21.3
World	**38.42**	**100.0**	**117.09**	**100.0**	**World**	**36.18**	**100.0**	**113.73**	**100.0**

Source: Secretariat estimates from UN Comtrade database.

Table 4.9. **Inter- and intra-regional trade – Motor vehicles**

In percentage of reporting region's total

Imports of finished products

Reporting region		North America	Europe	SEA	Rest of world	Total
North America	1980	31.1	24.4	44.4	0.1	100
	1993	46.0	13.9	39.8	0.3	100
Europe	1980	1.2	81.8	14.9	2.2	100
	1993	2.2	79.9	15.9	2.0	100
SEA	1980	9.3	37.5	52.8	0.4	100
	1993	21.9	45.3	28.9	4.0	100
Rest of world	1980	15.4	33.7	45.1	5.9	100
	1993	10.7	26.1	50.5	12.7	100
Total	**1980**	**14.4**	**54.1**	**30.0**	**1.6**	**100**
	1993	**20.4**	**48.5**	**28.6**	**2.5**	**100**

Exports of finished products

Reporting region		North America	Europe	SEA	Rest of world	Total
North America	1980	83.9	2.8	1.2	12.1	100
	1993	78.3	4.8	9.5	7.4	100
Europe	1980	15.5	72.3	2.0	10.2	100
	1993	8.8	74.0	7.8	9.3	100
SEA	1980	55.8	20.3	5.5	18.3	100
	1993	47.8	23.2	9.3	19.7	100
Rest of world	1980	0.3	41.0	1.7	57.0	100
	1993	4.8	34.7	10.3	50.2	100
Total	**1980**	**35.9**	**48.1**	**2.8**	**13.1**	**100**
	1993	**34.0**	**44.6**	**8.6**	**12.7**	**100**

Imports of intermediate products

Reporting region		North America	Europe	SEA	Rest of world	Total
North America	1980	67.7	14.8	15.3	2.2	100
	1993	62.9	9.7	24.9	2.5	100
Europe	1980	4.1	91.3	2.0	2.6	100
	1993	4.5	84.4	8.7	2.5	100
SEA	1980	14.1	30.3	51.3	4.2	100
	1993	10.3	19.0	67.2	3.5	100
Rest of world	1980	22.8	55.9	14.5	6.8	100
	1993	13.2	46.5	21.9	18.4	100
Total	**1980**	**29.7**	**56.9**	**10.5**	**3.0**	**100**
	1993	**31.1**	**43.0**	**22.0**	**3.9**	**100**

Exports of intermediate products

Reporting region		North America	Europe	SEA	Rest of world	Total
North America	1980	72.1	9.0	2.7	16.2	100
	1993	83.2	7.1	4.2	5.4	100
Europe	1980	10.1	64.6	2.1	23.1	100
	1993	9.2	73.0	4.9	12.9	100
SEA	1980	29.3	9.9	26.3	34.5	100
	1993	48.8	12.5	26.9	11.8	100
Rest of world	1980	5.5	7.7	9.0	77.8	100
	1993	21.9	21.3	6.3	50.5	100
Total	**1980**	**30.3**	**42.6**	**4.5**	**22.7**	**100**
	1993	**40.8**	**38.2**	**9.4**	**11.6**	**100**

1. North America = Canada, Mexico, United States.
2. Europe = European Union + EFTA (European Free Trade Agreement).
3. SEA = Brunei, China, Hong Kong, Indonesia, Japan, Malaysia, Philippines, Singapore, Republic of Korea, Chinese Taipei, Thailand.
Source: Secretariat estimates from UN Comtrade database.

◆ Figure 4.6a. **Intra-regional trade of finished automobiles**
As percentage of exports for each region

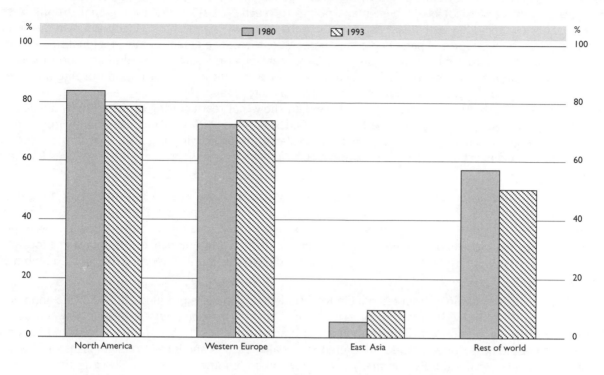

◆ Figure 4.6b. **Intra-regional trade of automobile parts**
As percentage of exports for each region

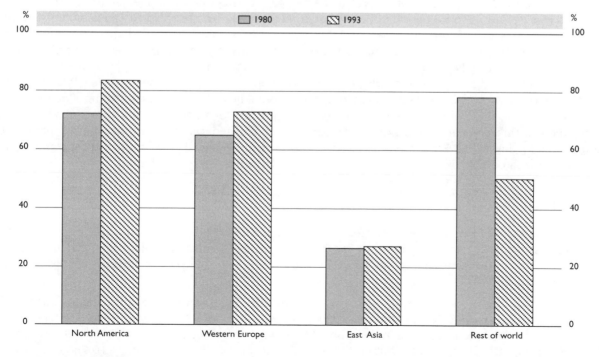

Notes: Western Europe: EU + EFTA.
North America: Canada, Mexico, United States.
East Asia: Brunei, China, Chinese Taipei, Hong Kong, Indonesia, Japan, Malaysia, Philippines, Republic of Korea, Singapore, Thailand.
Source: UN Comtrade Database.

For parts and components, between 1980 and 1993, European intra-regional exports as a share of total European parts exports increased by 8 percentage points, reaching over 73 per cent, and in North America (including Mexico) by 11 percentage points to reach 83 per cent. Intra-regional exports were considerably lower and flat in the East Asian region (Japan, the DAEs and China) (Figure 4.6). On the other hand, intra-regional imports of parts and components were the only element of intra-regional trade (both parts and finished automobiles) which declined as a share of world auto trade, although intra-regional imports still retained over two-thirds of world imports of parts. Intra-regional imports of intermediates declined by around 5 percentage points of imports for Europe and North America. In contrast, intra-regional imports grew strongly in East Asia. These data show that restructuring of the industry has led to somewhat greater supply of imported parts from outside Europe and North America – mainly from Japan into new green-field subsidiaries. This is also the explanation for growing intra-regional imports within Asia. Parts producers established in Europe and North America have an increasing regional focus for their exports.

Intra-regional trade is lower in finished cars than in parts. There was an increase of intra-regional exports of finished cars of almost 2 percentage points in Western Europe, but a decrease of 5 per cent in North America, to below 80 per cent. Intra-regional exports in East Asia remained very low, below 10 per cent. Intra-regional imports of finished cars have risen rapidly in North America, due to increasing location of Japanese assemblers in North America and a slow relative decline in imports from Japan, combined with a slump in imports from Europe.

While the overall share of intra-regional in total trade in automobile products (finished cars and parts and components combined) is very impressive, it is based on particularly strong ties between some trading partners. Canada exports almost all of its automobile products to the United States, and imports three-quarters from the United States. The United States also exports and imports a significant share of its total with Canada. Within the EU, Germany is a major source of imports by other EU countries, but it is also a main destination for other European exports of automobiles and parts.

Inter-regional trade between Europe and North America has never been high (see Table 4.9). From Europe to North America the export share has decreased for parts and components, and particularly for finished cars (from 15.5 to 8.8 per cent of European total exports). Exports of North American finished cars to Europe increased (from 2.8 to 4.8 per cent), but parts and components dropped. Inter-regional exports from Japan and other East Asian countries expanded considerably in the past decade, particularly in components, offsetting flat export shares in automobiles. This was mainly one way trade from Japan and Korea to Europe and North America, with relatively low import values by those countries. Within OECD, North America represents the main market for Asian automobiles, with a declining share of automobiles and an increasing share of components to just below 50 per cent of all exported Asian cars and parts and components. This compares with around 25 per cent of finished cars and 13 per cent of parts and components going to the EU. Despite increased exports of mainly finished cars from Europe and North America to Japan, these exports are still far below exports to other trading partners.

b) Finished cars

Trade in finished cars is strongly concentrated within the OECD area, with over 90 per cent of imports and exports combined. Trade in this sector has in some cases been subdued, reflecting import regulations (see Section 5, Government policy) and investment flows and the establishment of car assembly plants in major markets, as well as cyclical factors.

The overall share of the OECD area in world imports has remained roughly stable, with some increases for example into Japan, albeit at a low level. An exception to this trend is the United States, which showed a 3 per cent decrease in the share of total imports between 1980 and 1993 (to 30 per cent of total world imports, although the United States remained the largest single importer). The decrease in imports has been paralleled by an increase in foreign production, with a steady increase in the stock of inward foreign direct investment. At the same time, the United States increased exports to the EU and to Japan, but overall levels remain low and the US share of world exports has not grown significantly.

Imports by EU countries from all sources (including intra-EU trade) has remained approximately flat, at somewhat less than 50 per cent of total trade. Within the EU, the evolution of trade patterns has differed, the most notable change being the decrease in the German world export share to below 20 per cent in 1993, and the increase in imports of finished cars, to 10 per cent; developments that can be related to exchange rate changes, and increased competition in more expensive cars. France, too, lost considerable export market shares, while Spain emerged as a strong importer and exporter.

Japan's world export share remained steady at around 26-27 per cent, while imports grew to 3 per cent, up from less than 1 per cent a decade before. This shows the gradual opening of the Japanese market, but the import level remains well below all other major OECD car producers. Around half Japanese exports had North America as a final destination, but with a decrease in this share. Exports to the EU increased to around one-quarter of total Japanese exports, up from 20 per cent a decade before. Mexico's exports also grew very rapidly from a low base, with increasing foreign investment.

The non-OECD area increased their exports of finished cars, doubling their share. The most impressive has been the Republic of Korea's exports which grew from 0.1 to 2.1 per cent between 1980 and 1993, and they have continued to expand rapidly, taking a larger share of world exports of cars than many OECD countries. Imports into the non-OECD area as a percentage of world imports have increased more slowly, which indicates that some of these countries are satisfying local demand with local production while building export capacity. Korea's imports of cars remained very low due to extensive import restrictions. However, total imports by non-OECD countries still clearly outweigh their exports.

The CEECs and NIS are almost absent in trade in both finished cars and parts and components. The picture will probably change in the future, given the moves by various car manufacturers to relocate part of production to these countries to supply local markets and the EU market, with which many of these countries have preferential arrangements. There have been strong inflows of FDI into some countries (Poland, Hungary, Czech Republic).

c)   *Parts and components*

Due to the restructuring and re-location of automobile production, changes in patterns of trade are more strongly marked for parts and components than in finished cars. Trade in parts and components remains predominantly concentrated within OECD. Western Europe is the largest exporter (45 per cent in 1993) and a major importer (40 per cent), and North America (the United States, Canada and Mexico) accounted for over 30 per cent of world exports and over 40 per cent of world imports in 1993. Some non-OECD countries emerged as newly dynamic exporters of parts, but their shares remain low.

Western Europe's world export and import shares of parts and components declined, largely due to the lingering recession in the early 1990s in Europe. Overall, within the EU there are marked differences between countries, with Germany accounting for the bulk of exports of parts and components – around 40 per cent of total EU, or 17 per cent of world exports in 1993. With increasing inward investment, the United Kingdom has become a large net importer of parts and components, after having been a large net exporter, and Spain notably increased its import shares of parts for the same reason.

Japan rapidly increased in its share of world exports of parts and components, which more than doubled from 1980 to 1993 (over 18 per cent in 1993), while imports increased only moderately. The United States has taken much of this increase in Japanese exports. This is due to increased Japanese production and assembly in the United States, initially based on supplies of parts and components shipped from the home country, as well as the import of parts for replacement and repair of large numbers of Japanese cars in circulation. Trade in parts and components could decline as Japanese firms in the United States increase local sourcing in response to pressures to increase local purchasing. Mexico also experienced marked growth in trade, particularly in imports due to NAFTA and location of foreign-owned plants in Mexico.

The DAEs saw an increase in their world market shares although from low levels, and China emerged as an importer of parts and components.

B. International sourcing

With the exception of Japan all major motor vehicle producing countries have been increasingly using foreign intermediate inputs. The industry has relatively high levels of international sourcing of intermediates, being respectively first and fourth in the ranking of the relative importance of imported intermediates (across 33 industries) in Canada and the United States and in the top-10 in the United Kingdom and Germany.

In the mid-1980s the ratio of imported to domestic inputs was highest in Canada and lowest in Japan – close to five times as large and increasing in Canada and consistently close to zero in Japan. UK foreign sourcing, after rapid increases in the 1970s, was the highest of other major countries. The French and German levels were similar by the mid-1980s with around one-quarter of all intermediate components being imported and the United States had increased to a level similar to those of France and Germany (see Figure 4.7).

The foreign to domestic inter-industry linkage ratio (the ratio of foreign intermediate inputs from all sources including upstream intermediate inputs into automobile components compared with all upstream domestic intermediate inputs) is generally increasing although lower than the direct foreign/domestic ratio for all countries except Japan. In Japan, by this measure foreign intermediate inputs are higher, but they still made up only about 5 per cent of all intermediate inputs.

C. Intra-firm trade

Intra-firm trade (IFT) is defined as the international exchange of goods and services within a multinational enterprise (MNE).[6] While IFT accounts for a little over a third of total US merchandise trade, US trade in autos and auto parts is largely composed of IFT. Intra-firm trade in the United States auto manufacturing sector was over US$50 billion in 1989, with intra-firm imports higher than intra-firm exports. Although classification problems prevent the calculation of the exact share of IFT in US automobile trade, estimates put it at over 80 per cent of US auto exports and between 40-50 per cent of US auto imports in 1989, excluding wholesale and related activities.[7] These values have been confirmed in other recent studies (OTA, 1994).

US firms established abroad accounted for 90 per cent of US IFT in the auto sector in 1989. Of these, US firms established in Canada are by far the most important. IFT by foreign firms established in the United States was relatively small. This share has however, increased in the 1980s, especially due to Japanese firm imports from their parents in Japan (over 80 per cent of the total).

The relative importance of IFT for the US automobile industry is highlighted by data on the international trade of majority owned foreign affiliates of US automobile firms. In 1989, 96 per cent of US imports from those affiliates and 86 per cent of US exports to majority-owned affiliates were intra-firm. The same is true for US affiliates of foreign automobile firms, which in 1989, exported 52 per cent to and imported 97 per cent of their merchandise from their parents or other affiliated firms. Those figures are significantly above the average for all manufacturing industries.

More strikingly, the figures for the direction of trade between parents and affiliates are similarly high. This indicates that foreign automobile firms established in the US follow similar IFT patterns compared to US automobile firms established abroad. In both cases, affiliates tend to concentrate their international purchases within the firm, and mostly from their parents, while their foreign sales are more diversified.

Although important overall, the relative share of IFT on US automobile trade does not appear to have increased substantially between 1977 and 1990. This is also the case of the share of IFT on total US merchandise trade.[8] The exception to this rule is the increase of US intra-firm imports related to the establishment of assembly plants by Japanese auto firms. In three years, intra-firm imports by US manufacturing affiliates of Japanese auto firms quadrupled, reaching US$4.5 billion in 1990, and it has continued growing. In that year, Japanese firms accounted for 95 per cent of US automobile intra-firm imports associated with foreign MNEs, as opposed to 75 per cent in 1987.

◆ Figure 4.7*a*. **Ratio of imported to domestic sourcing of inputs – Motor vehicles**

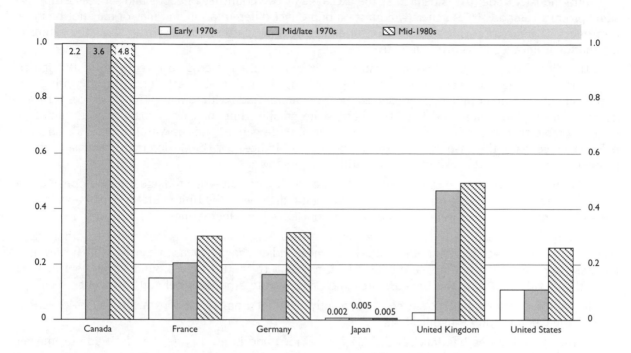

◆ Figure 4.7*b*. **International linkage index – Motor vehicles**
Ratio of foreign to domestic interindustry linkage

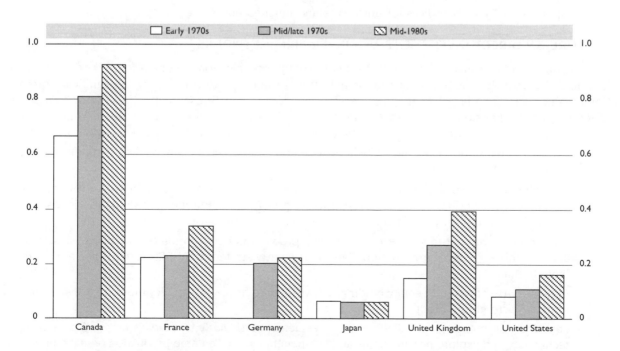

Source : OECD, DSTI, EAS Division.

D. Intra-industry trade

Intra-industry trade (IIT) is defined as the exchange by two countries of goods and services within the same product category. IIT is generally a function of product differentiation and may or may not be intra-firm trade. IIT indices provide another tool for analysing trade patterns as they may show the extent of international linkages for a given industry.[9]

IIT indices for US trade in passenger motor cars[10] confirm the patterns observed with the IFT figures. US IIT indices have not seen a large increase, hovering around 30-40 per cent, although with some improvement. The larger indices are observed on the bilateral trade with Canada. The IIT indices for trade between the United States and the EU countries are smaller, but increased as US exports increased relatively more than imports, partly closing the bilateral trade gap. IIT indices with Japan are significantly below average, as is the case with most other sectors. IIT indices for US-Mexico trade increased significantly due to increased US exports, but are still relatively low.

IIT indices for EU trade in cars are very high – around 90 per cent – due to large intra-European trade. This is also the case for most other industries. Bilateral indices with the United States, Japan and Canada are significantly lower than intra-European indices but have been increasing.

IIT indices for Japanese trade in passenger motor cars are relatively low compared to other OECD countries, as is the case for most other industries. These indices have increased considerably however, as Japanese imports increased. Japanese bilateral IIT indices with the EU were around 50 per cent in 1993, while those with the DAEs, the United States and Canada were around or below 10 per cent.

IIT indices for auto parts[11] are not significantly different from those for finished autos described above. A few points can be highlighted:

- The United States has much higher IIT indices for trade in auto parts than for trade in finished autos, reflecting more balanced US trade in parts, although this is changing somewhat with FDI growth.

- IIT indices for intra-European trade in parts also hovered around 90 per cent. Indices for European bilateral trade with Japan, the United States and Canada are significantly lower. IIT indices for trade in parts between Europe and those three countries have not changed greatly, compared with the changes for finished autos.

- Japan has similar IIT indices for auto parts and finished autos.

4. FOREIGN DIRECT INVESTMENT AND INTER-FIRM NETWORKS

The automobile industry was one of the first to set up extensive foreign operations. Shortly after Ford had mastered its new model of industrial organisation for mass production, it set up significant production operations in Canada (1916) and in the United Kingdom (1920). Subsequently there followed a period of international expansion by US manufacturers (GM and Chrysler) mainly into Canada and Europe, but also into Australia and Latin America. The main features of the current round of expansion are:

- Extensive green-field investments by large assemblers and increasingly by their component suppliers – particularly Japanese.

- Consolidation of the industry through acquisitions of smaller producers in Western Europe and uncompetitive producers in need of restructuring in Eastern Europe. Consolidation is also more generally occurring in components.

- Creation of joint ventures in development and production between major established assemblers, and assemblers and component suppliers, and as entry strategies into Eastern Europe and increasingly in Asia.

- Extensive use of minority equity holdings between large firms and smaller more specialised ones to form *de facto* global groups.

- Formation of international collaboration agreements, particularly to develop new products, acquire technology and explore new materials and components and to enlarge production of niche products.

- Licensing has been limited to some markets and component production.

Overall, US firms have maintained their presence in Europe and have been building on and reorganising equity relations and alliances in East Asian markets and exploring new ones in China and India. Japanese firms have taken an increasing share of North American production, and after initial entry in Europe are now also directing efforts to establishing an Asian production network. European firms, despite established presences in Latin America and some operations in Asia, have mainly focused on Europe through investment, joint ventures and alliances, with recent focus on Central and Eastern Europe, and renewed interest in the United States. All major firms are exploring Asian markets and potential for direct production operations, often in partnership with local producers.

A. Foreign direct investment

International investment has grown rapidly in the automobile industry, as Japanese producers entered the US, European and Asian markets, and as both US and European producers consolidated their positions, particularly in Europe, but began to enter, or re-enter, other markets.

Stocks of foreign investment have grown rapidly, with some modifications to previous trends due to rapid expansion of Japanese investment, as Japanese firms switched strategies from relying entirely on exports to increasingly produce cars in the regions of final sales, first in North America, then Europe and now in Asia. However, outward investment and net investment stocks for 1993 showed that the United States remained the largest outward investor, even though Japan outpaced the United States through much of the 1980s and early 1990s in annual outflows of *new* investment. Japan and Germany are large net outward investors, and France is a net investor at lower levels. Canada, the United Kingdom and Australia are large net recipients (Figure 4.8, data is unavailable for Spain, some data are for all transport equipment).[12]

◆ Figure 4.8. **FDI net balance, 1993 – Motor vehicles**
Outward stock/Inward stock in million US$

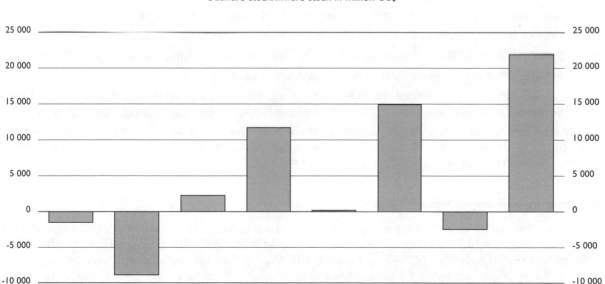

1. Other transport equipment.
2. Other transport equipment including motor vehicles.
3. 1992 data.
4. Outward stocks only.
Source: OECD, *International Direct Investment Statistics Yearbook.*

The United States was the largest investor with US$25 billion outward stock in 1993, up from US$11 billion in 1985. Germany and Japan followed with US$15.9 and 15.0 billion respectively, with the stock of Japanese investment tripling in current terms from the 1985 level. France, the United Kingdom (marginally) and Italy also had increasing stocks of outward investment over the period. Stocks of outward investment in 1993 represented 8 per cent of all outward investments from Germany, 5 per cent from the United States, 4 per cent from France, 3.6 per cent from Japan, 2.8 per cent from Italy and less than 1 per cent from the United Kingdom.

Of major OECD countries, Canada had the highest stock of inward investment in 1993, US$11.3 billion, followed by the United Kingdom, US$4.1 billion, Germany, France, and the United States follow with US$4.1, 3.4 and 2.7 billion, respectively. Italy and Australia had stocks of inward investment below US$2 billion. Stocks of inward investment in motor vehicles represented over 10 per cent of all investment in Canada, 3.5 per cent in France 3.4 per cent in Germany and Italy, 2.3 per cent in the United Kingdom, 2 per cent in Australia, and less than 1 per cent in the United States.

One feature of the recent expansion of Japanese automobile assemblers has been parallel overseas investment by parts and components makers. By 1992-93 there was extensive Japanese auto parts investment in the United States where there were 295 subsidiaries, of which 170 were wholly owned and 125 joint ventures. This was some 60 per cent of the total of around 475 foreign parts ventures operating in the United States. In the EU, growth of Japanese parts investment has been slower due to the later entry of Japanese assemblers, and EU value-added requirements [see Section 5.C.d]. By 1991 there were already 64 Japanese suppliers, largely in the United Kingdom and Spain to supply Japanese auto producers there, with a considerable number of joint ventures (one-third), or European firms taken over by Japanese firms. However they are competing against a large number of European component suppliers which have also rationalised to cover a larger part of the European market.

B. International mergers, acquisitions, minority participations

International mergers and acquisitions, joint ventures and other equity operations proliferated at the end of the 1980s and again in the mid-1990s as part of the high level of international investment in the industry. Heightened activity was due to:

- International expansion of Japanese assemblers and component suppliers.
- Take-overs and joint ventures with uncompetitive auto operations in Eastern Europe.
- Reorganisation of the assembly industry in Europe, mainly involving European and US firms.
- Prospects for market expansion in South-East and East Asia.
- Consolidation in the component industry to meet the changing supply structure in the industry. Suppliers require economies of scale and wider international scope to meet new demands.

In comparison with many other industries there have been relatively *low* levels of mergers and acquisitions and *higher* levels of joint venture and minority investment activity in automobiles. This is probably due to the highly oligopolistic structure of the industry.

a) Mergers and acquisitions[12]

During the period 1988-92 there were 216 cross-border mergers and acquisitions totalling US$9.2 billion in the motor vehicle industry. The most active year was 1989 with 61 operations totalling over US$4 billion. For the period 1988-92, compared with the total of all industry and service sectors the number of operations represent 1.8 per cent of the total, and in amount 1.9 per cent of the total covered by the database. The respective shares in the pharmaceuticals sector were numbers, 1.9 per cent and amount, 2.8 per cent, and in computer industry numbers, 1.3 per cent and amount, 1.6 per cent, suggesting that the motor vehicle sector is only moderately active in mergers and acquisitions.

Purchasers mainly come from the largest auto-producing countries, where major firms have their headquarters. US firms were by far the most active with 49 purchase operations (US$3.8 billion), followed by Italy 15 (US$2.2 billion), the UK 34 (US$1.2 billion), Canada 11 (US$810 million), France 19

(US$380 million), Germany 35 (US$268 million), Japan 16 (US$231 million) and Sweden 13 purchase operations (US$72 million). Acquisitions were largely in the United Kingdom with 26 sales (US$3.1 billion), followed by the US 27 (US$1.7 billion), Sweden 7 (US$557 million), Italy 13 (US$396 million), Germany 28 (US$298 million), France 22 (US$266 million), Canada 22 (US$263 million) and Spain 17 (US$190 million) operations. Part of expansion into Eastern Europe through 1992 was through acquisitions, with two major operations in Poland worth US$2 billion (notably Fiat's purchase of FSM), and in Czechoslovakia.

b) Joint ventures and minority participations[12]

During 1990-92 there were 263 cross-border operations totalling US$11.5 billion in the motor vehicle industry. 1990 was the most active year with 121 operations totalling US$9.6 billion. For the period 1990-92, compared with the total of all industry and service sectors the number of operations represents 3.8 per cent of the total, and in amount 8.8 per cent of the total covered by the database. The respective shares in the pharmaceuticals industry were numbers, 1.8 per cent and amount, 0.5 per cent, and in the computer industry numbers, 1.7 per cent and amount, 1.1 per cent, suggesting that the motor vehicle industry is considerably more active in joint ventures and minority participations than in M&A.

Firms most actively setting up joint ventures or buying stakes came from major auto-producing countries. Firms from Japan with 79 operations (US$920 million), Germany 45 (US$7.3 billion) and the United States 38 operations (US$2 billion) were most active, next were France with 30 (US$526 million), Italy 23 (US$141 million), and the Netherlands 8 operations (US$399 million).

Joint ventures have been set up and minority holdings purchased in a wide range of countries, mostly in Eastern Europe, Asia, or in OECD countries which are developing automobile industries. The most common target countries were Czechoslovakia with 13 operations worth US$5 billion (including VW with Skoda and BAZ), Portugal 4 operations worth US$3 billion (notably the VW-Ford joint venture), China 12 (US$975 million, including operations by PSA and Chrysler), Hungary 15 (US$554 million, including GM and Suzuki operations), the United Kingdom 20 (US$394 million), Indonesia 7 operations (US$381 million). The remainder were also mainly in Eastern Europe and Asia, where major firms are expanding operations.

Overall, the motor vehicle industry has developed a dense network of equity cross-holdings, joint ventures and minority investments. There have also been recent re-alignments, particularly involving US firms as they restructured following their crises of the early 1990s, reducing equity in some Asian firms (progressive reductions to zero by Chrysler in Mitsubishi, GM severing ties with Daewoo), or increasing it (Ford with Mazda, and also Toyota with Daihatsu, VW with Skoda) and in other cases setting up new joint ventures (Ford with VW in Portugal, GM with Toyota in Australia). Figure 4.9 shows equity cross-holdings in 1992.

C. Market shares of foreign-controlled firms

a) Output of foreign-controlled firms

US firms have a major share of foreign-controlled production world-wide, with large shares in Australia, Canada, Europe and Latin America. In the United States and in some European countries the share of foreign affiliates in output or sales of the motor vehicle industry is increasing rapidly largely due to recent investment by Japanese automakers.

In the United States the share of new car sales from transplants in the United States rose to 16 per cent in model year 1994 and 18.4 per cent in model year 1995 (October 1994 to September 1995), up from 7.2 per cent in 1989, which was double the share of 1985. At the same time, sales of imported cars decreased to below 2 million units in 1994 and 1995 (20 per cent of sales in 1995), the lowest since 1978. Japanese affiliates had the major share of these sales. Sales of light trucks − which have rapidly substituted for car sales in the United States and were equivalent to around 65 per cent of car sales in 1995 − are less affected by transplants (less than 8 per cent of light truck sales in 1995) or imports (less than 3 per cent) (US Department of Commerce, *Survey of Current Business*).

◆ Figure 4.9. **Cross equity holdings in the automobile industry, June 1992**

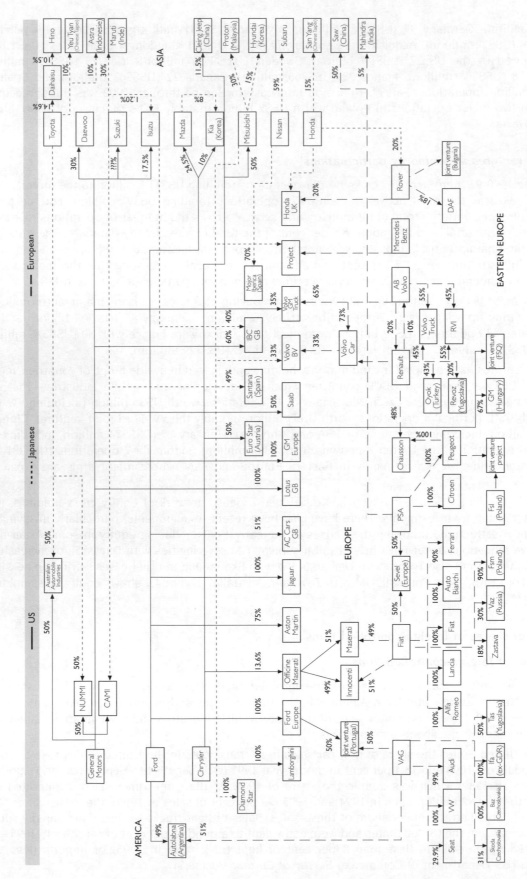

Source: OECD Secretariat.

◆ Figure 4.10. **Market penetration, around 1990 – Motor vehicles**
Share of foreign supply in total, in percentage

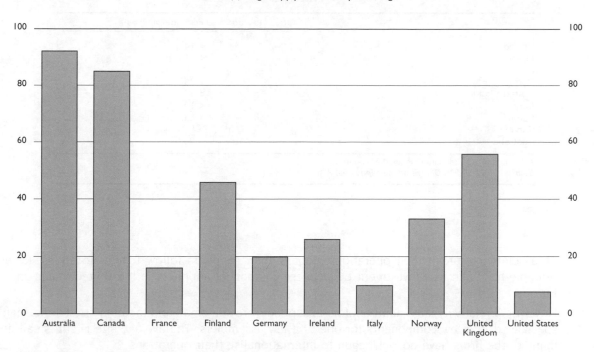

Note: Australia: 1987; Canada and Finland: 1988; Italy: based on foreign employment data.
Source: OECD Secretariat from national sources.

In the United Kingdom the share of foreign affiliate gross output in the motor vehicle industry (including parts) increased from 50 per cent in 1987 to reach 62 per cent in 1992. This trend has continued, with the United Kingdom becoming a centre for European production by foreign-owned producers. In early-1993, passenger car production by US firms was close to 45 per cent of total UK car production, Japanese production 22 per cent, French production close to 6 per cent, while the UK-owned share was 28 per cent of the total. The share of UK-owned production has dropped further with the purchase of Rover by BMW in 1993 (finalised in 1994). In France the total foreign share in motor vehicle manufacturing turnover was 15 per cent in 1980, 19 per cent in 1990, 17 per cent in 1993. The breakdown of this total in 1993 was 7.6 per cent US, 9.2 per cent European and 0.3 per cent Japanese. In Germany the foreign share of production remained around 20 per cent from 1980 to 1990. The importance of foreign affiliates is higher in European countries with smaller industries based on more limited assembly and component production (32 per cent in Norway and 27 per cent in Ireland) (see Figure 4.10.)

In Canada and Australia the foreign-owned share of total production is very high. The Canadian share was 86 per cent in 1988, with 83 per cent US-owned. The share of foreign-owned production was over 94 per cent in Australia in 1987 (it was less than 40 per cent in non-electrical parts production); the Australian industry has been dominated by large multinationals initially from the United States, subsequently joined by Japanese producers.

The share of foreign-controlled production in automotive parts production is lower than for the motor vehicle industry as a whole. However, the industry in most countries is internationalised, with a relatively high share of production from foreign-controlled firms (see Table 4.10). There are three main factors explaining the extent of internationalisation:

– There are a number of highly globalised large firms (automotive electronics, tyres, hydraulics) which supply many assemblers, and these are particularly dominant in markets where assembly is by foreign-controlled firms.

Table 4.10. **Foreign investment in automotive parts production, around 1990**

Percentages

	Production share of foreign firms[1]
United States	> 10
Japan	< 1
France	> 50
Germany	< 20
United Kingdom	> 30
Italy	< 10
Spain	> 85
Canada	> 80
Australia	> 70

1. Firms with headquarters in another country.
Source: OECD (1992), *Globalisation of Industrial Activities,* Paris.

– As assemblers spread their operations globally their suppliers follow to new locations. Recent example has been new investment by Japanese component suppliers in the United States and in Europe.

– However, a relatively large number of parts suppliers are still small and medium-sized firms, highly specialised in a few components for one or a few assemblers. The average size is still small and many of the firms have not yet begun to internationalise their operations.

b)   *Market penetration measured by new registrations*

The share of foreign passenger cars in new registrations is considerably higher than the share of output from foreign-owned production in most countries, because of the continued importance of imports of foreign-made cars.

Combining imports with production by ultimate foreign owner of production, there were high levels of foreign car registrations in European auto-producing countries in 1993, ranging from 40 per cent in France to almost 100 per cent in the United Kingdom following BMW's acquisition of Rover. There were high foreign market shares in Germany and Sweden (60 and 75 per cent, respectively), two countries with strong indigenous automakers. Foreign market shares were more moderate in the United States (around one-third), and there were very low levels in Japan (4 per cent, although this share grew to 6 per cent in 1995, excluding imports into Japan from Japanese transplants in the United States which were another 2 per cent of sales (see Table 4.11.) These data are calculated on the basis that greater than 50 per cent foreign ownership attributes the brand to the owner's country. For example, SEAT is German, OPEL is US, Rover is German, Japanese transplant production is Japanese, etc.

In all major auto-producing countries except Sweden and the United Kingdom, indigenous producers take the largest share of the domestic market. In both of these markets US producers had the largest share, but Japanese producers had significant and growing shares (third in Sweden, fourth in the United Kingdom in 1993). European firms penetrated most European markets fairly evenly, with German and French cars at higher levels and Italian and Swedish at lower levels. Japanese cars, with high penetrations elsewhere, had only 4.4 and 4.2 per cent of French and Italian markets respectively in 1993.

Japanese cars had dominant shares in the United States with close to 30 per cent of the total market, followed by German cars with less than 3 per cent. German cars had the highest foreign share of Japanese new registrations, with 2.3 per cent in 1993 and growing (Europe had 5 per cent in 1995). Although US cars have high shares in other countries, they had only 1 per cent of total new registrations in Japan.

Foreign-controlled production of automobiles and components is still not as important as imports in many markets, but the picture is changing rapidly as assemblers from Japan, Germany and France shift towards more extensive foreign production. Foreign-controlled production tends to outweigh imports in

Table 4.11. **Passenger car new registrations by country of ultimate ownership of producing unit, 1993**

Percentage of total new registrations

	French	German	Italian	Japanese	Swedish	United States	Other European	Other Asian	Other	Total Foreign
France	60.3	13.8	5.5	4.4	0.5	14.5	0.3	0.2	0.5	39.7
Germany	10.0	42.0	3.6	13.7	0.4	25.6	0.0	0.0	4.3	57.6
Italy[1]	13.3	18.5	44.9	4.2	0.8	16.8	0.2	0.4	0.7	55.0
Japan	0.1	2.3	0.1	96.0	0.3	1.1			0.0	4.0
Sweden	7.5	16.4	0.8	20.3	26.6	27.5	0.0	0.7	0.3	73.4
United Kingdom	17.8	22.1	3.1	12.7	2.5	39.4	0.5	1.6	0.3	100.0
United States[2]	0.0	2.3	0.0	29.3	0.9	66.4	0.0	1.1	0.0	33.6

Note: Country of ultimate ownership of producing unit is defined by ultimate ownership of the production plant which produced the passenger car. 50 per cent or above ownership attributes the brand to the owner's country. For example, SEAT is German by country of ultimate ownership. OPEL is US, etc. The total comprises total domestic production (domestic owned producers plus foreign-controlled producers) plus imports.

1. Retail sales including imports.
2. Retail sales including imports and re-badging.

Source: OECD, calculated from AAMA (1995).

countries with a long history of foreign investment (Australia, Canada, Germany and the United Kingdom) (see Table 4.12.) In smaller countries without the industrial base for large-scale auto production, the balance is strongly in favour of imports. In major auto-producing countries where inward foreign investment was not important in the past (France, Italy, the United States until recently) imports were two to four times greater than foreign-controlled production around 1990, but with a falling trend. For example, in the United States the ratio of imports over transplant production fell from 4 in 1989 to 1.1 in 1995 with increasing transplant operations substituting for declining US imports. Overall, however, the market share of car imports plus transplant production has remained stable at around 35-40 per cent of US new car registrations.

Table 4.12. **Production by foreign-controlled firms and imports of motor vehicles, around 1990**

	Foreign-controlled production as percentage of total production	Foreign-controlled production divided by total imports
Australia	74	2.0
Canada	86	1.2
France	16	0.51
Germany	20	1.3
Italy	11	0.41
United Kingdom	52	0.91
Finland	47	0.28
Norway	32	0.10
United States	9	0.26

Source: Calculated from national sources and OECD, DSTI/EAS. Data are for motor vehicle industry, including components and parts. "Production" is sales, turnover, output or shipments of domestic manufacturing operations, depending on the source. Australia is 1986/87.

c) *Linkages and R&D location*

Much policy interest in foreign investment has revolved around the links between green-field plants and the local sub-national economy and suppliers. On the one hand if new plants are set up in regions where the existing infrastructure of component and service suppliers is weak, then there will be few links with the local economy, relatively low levels of local content and continuing imports of parts and components. On the other hand, if there is an existing network of suppliers, local linkages will be stronger, particularly given the current organisation of the industry, where regional clusters of suppliers and assemblers are becoming the predominant organisational form.

A further interest has focused on the extent of R&D re-location in new markets, following assembly operations. In general, R&D follows production with a lag, being generally maintained as a headquarters function because of its strategic significance. The main Japanese assemblers (Toyota, Nissan, Honda) are slowly establishing development operations along with their assembly facilities. Each has at least two development centres in both the United States and Europe. A detailed survey in 1993 suggested that there may have been as many as 40 separate foreign-owned development facilities in the United States in 1992, with around three-quarters of them Japanese (US Department of Commerce (1993), *Foreign Direct Investment in the United States: An Update*). Much of the activity of these centres is however in component testing, procurement and process development, but more substantial product development is slowly gathering pace. The Honda Accord in the United States and Nissan Primera in the United Kingdom had substantial local design inputs. This follows the pattern of Ford and GM, which have had top to bottom operations in Europe for a long time, including comprehensive local development operations. (See also OECD, 1994, *Trade and Investment: Transplants.*)

D. International collaboration agreements[13]

International collaboration is a particular feature in producing and developing motor vehicles and components. Over the period 1970-92, 12 per cent of a large cross-industry sample of new collaboration was in motor vehicles. From low numbers in the 1970s, inter-firm agreements became more common at the turn of the decade and were particularly common during the second half of the 1980s. There were 25 to 40 important new agreements per year from 1985 to 1990, but they became less common in the early 1990s (see Figure 4.11).

Almost two-thirds (62.5 per cent) of agreements were between major economic blocs, with the remainder within blocs. The majority of the inter-bloc agreements were between Europe and the Far East (mainly Japan) and the majority of the intra-economic bloc agreements were within Europe. Agreements with the Far East (Japan) were much more common than in most other sectors for both European and North American firms. Japan has been the most active country, and seven Japanese auto and component firms had more than ten major agreements each. The United States is second in inter-country agreements.

Agreements focused first on production and then on development, with 39 per cent for production (out of a sample of 292 agreements for which details were known), 24 per cent for development and 18 per cent for both production and development. Marketing alone accounted for less than 9 per cent of agreements. Production featured as the main purpose or as an important purpose combined with others in two-thirds of all agreements, development almost one-half, whereas less than one-fifth of agreements were for marketing, usually combined with other purposes. This is quite different from the distribution of purposes for agreements across all of industry, where production and development are almost equally important (in 50 per cent and 54 per cent of agreements respectively, either alone or with other purposes), and marketing is relatively important (in 30 per cent of agreements). As far as the size of the firms involved, over-one half of all agreements are between large firms, over one-third between large and smaller firms, and less than one-tenth were between small firms.

Typical collaboration agreements are of three kinds:

– private agreements between assemblers to jointly develop new components or jointly explore new technological areas, often with some support from government;

– production collaboration, often involving "re-badging" of cars and commercial vehicles, usually Japanese, for US or European markets;

– component development and supply agreements between assemblers and component suppliers.

E. Licensing agreements

Licensing has mainly been concentrated on two areas of the industry: assembly of vehicles in smaller markets or in countries where there have been constraints on foreign ownership; and manufacture of parts and components.

There has been a long development of building completely-knocked-down vehicles (CKDVs) under licence for small production in developing country markets. However, with the liberalisation of foreign investment and more encouragement of inward investment, much of this production is now being absorbed into more extensive foreign investment networks and joint ventures. This is particularly the case in China and India and in other large developing countries with prospects for market expansion.

Parts and components have also been manufactured under license based on patent and know-how licensing. However, although leading manufacturers of cars and components have patented extensively (particularly German, Japanese and Swedish firms), they have been increasingly using their technological advantages as the basis for more extensive collaboration agreements to supply parts or design and technical services, rather than for product licensing.

◆ Figure 4.11. *International collaboration agreements – Motor vehicles*

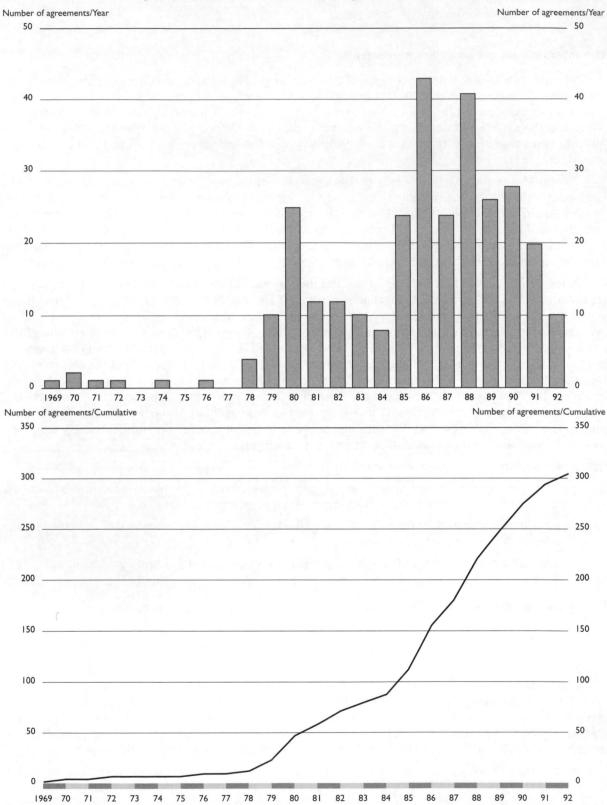

Source: INSEAD.

5. GOVERNMENT POLICIES

A wide range of government policies have important impacts on the automobile industry. It has long been seen as a key industry because of its direct and indirect impacts and multiplier effects on the rest of manufacturing and services, and there is extensive policy interest in the smooth operation of production, investment and trade mechanisms, and in encouraging technological advance and competition in the industry.

A. General policies: Transport and infrastructure, environment and safety

a) Transport and infrastructure

Major factors influencing the expansion of automobile use are the provision of infrastructure (roads, parking), the impacts of congestion and the general government policy stance towards the transport infrastructure. Governments are the major suppliers of infrastructure, and private individuals or private operators the major users. However, demand has continually outpaced supply, leading to inefficiency and congestion with attendant high economic costs. To address this problem most governments are now shifting towards the principle that users pay a larger share of the direct and indirect costs of their use of a particular transport mode, in this case either through vehicle purchase and fuel taxes or road use and allocation taxes (e.g. peak-hour tolls), or both. The lack of developed road networks and urban infrastructure is also a particularly noticeable feature accompanying the rapid expansion of modern passenger vehicle ownership in developing countries and in Eastern Europe. Limits on automobile use, re-design of traffic management and flow systems as well as new approaches to the supply of infrastructure will all influence automobile ownership and have important impacts on the structure and distribution of long-term demand.

b) Environment and safety

Stricter environmental controls are being introduced to limit or reduce pollutants (CO, nitrogen oxides, hydrocarbons) and greenhouse gases (CO_2, chlorofluorocarbons). These are inducing a range of industrial responses aimed at improving environmental quality: emission control equipment to remove exhaust pollutants, improving fuel efficiency and developing electric vehicles, increasing transport system efficiency, and developing non-fossil energy sources (renewable electricity sources and hydrogen). At the same time there have been extensive improvements in automobile design (e.g. air bags, better brakes) and road design to improve safety. Stricter environmental controls (of the kind originally mandated in California, and subsequently in some 13 other US states and suspended early 1996, required 2 per cent of all vehicles sold from the 1998 model year to be zero-emission vehicles, rising to 10 per cent by 2003) have a major influence on world-wide patterns of supply, and provide strategic advantages to producers which can meet the new standards in markets where they are first required.

B. Industry and technology policies

Government policies to support the industry cover a wide field: support for generic R&D programmes, subsidies encouraging location of new plants and improving component supply, and in a few cases financial infusions to state-owned firms.

a) Government R&D funding

The share of government funding in motor vehicle R&D is relatively low, but there are wide differences among countries in its importance. OECD data for 1973-93 show that it was highest in the United States and Sweden (15-20 per cent of the total), probably due to diversification of automobile firms into defence and space-related areas. Italy and Norway also had relatively high government R&D funding, around 10-20 per cent of the total, relatively high compared with their government funding for all industry. The share was around 1-2 per cent in France and Germany and 2-3 per cent in the United Kingdom, Australia and Canada, lower than government R&D funding for all industry. Japan had very low government funding of business enterprise R&D in the motor vehicle sector, as in all manufacturing.

b) Major R&D programmes

There have been a wide range of government programmes to fund basic and pre-competitive R&D, usually through consortia of firms and institutions. These have covered research aimed at improving propulsion systems, better conformance with environmental standards, and enhancing competitiveness, for example:

- new materials (CARMAT and MOSAIC, part of the European Eureka programme);

- cleaner, more efficient engines and automobiles (AGATA/Eureka, ceramic engines and new fuels in Japan's Moonlight and Sunshine Projects, new generation of vehicles in the US Council for Automotive Research consortium programme, France's clean engines project);

- new sources of propulsion (US Advanced Battery Consortium, Big-3 with the Department of Energy, Japan's work on batteries begun in the Moonlight Project);

- new manufacturing methods (Japan's proposed international development of an Intelligent Manufacturing System, and domestic Large-Scale Projects on Ultra-Advanced Manufacturing Systems, and Advanced Robots, and AMT support in the United States); and

- guidance and traffic control systems (PROMETHEUS/Eureka, DRIVE/European Commission, Intelligent Transportation Society America, and Vehicle, Road and Traffic Intelligence Society Japan).

Human resources and organisation. A special focus of a number of recent government initiatives has been to promote organisational innovations and organisational change, and expand vocational training. Organisational change involves flattening of hierarchies and increasing horizontal communication to enhance flexibility, responsibility and decision making at the work-place, all requiring new and greater skills and training. Projections suggest that in Europe by 2010, unskilled workers in the industry will decline to about one-tenth of the total workforce, vocationally trained will increase to almost three-quarters, and technical university graduates increase to approximately one-sixth. The European Commission's 1994 *Communication on the Automobile Industry* emphasized the need for retraining and vocational training in the industry and a number of initiatives are being taken under the new, general LEONARDO and ADAPT training programmes.

Industrial location/regional policy. Considerable funds have gone to attract new plants (usually foreign assemblers) to particular regions, with the aim of improving employment prospects and the industrial balance. These were particularly noteworthy at the end of the 1980s when the industry was in its last expansion, and numerous new plants were being planned. Overall the effect was to engage in bidding exercises which provided large subsidies to new capacity. Plants have often had high subsidy costs per new job, due to escalating subsidy races between countries or sub-national levels of government competing for new investment, as some data for the United States suggest:

Start-up subsidies
State subsidy per person employed in US$

Honda	Marysville, Ohio	1982	2 500
Nissan	Smyrna, Tennessee	1983	6 470
Mazda	Flat Rock, Michigan	1987	14 263
Diamond Star	Normal, Illinois	1988	28 724
Toyota	Georgetown, Kentucky	1988	42 771
Subaru-Isuzu	Lafayette, Indiana	1989	98 059

Source : Kenney and Florida (1991), quoted in Ruigrok *et al.* (1991).

Location subsidies have also accompanied much new investment in Europe. Within the EC/EU, transparency and stricter discipline in granting aid has been encouraged through the "Community framework on state aid to the motor vehicle industry" introduced with effect from 1 January 1989 on the basis of Article 93(1) EEC. Investments considered by the Commission include, for foreign firms: Ford-Volkswagen in Portugal (MPV assembly, eligible investment ECU 1.66 billion, aid ECU 547 million); GM R&D centre in Luxemburg; GM parts subsidiary in Portugal; aid in land purchase for a Toyota plant in the north of the United Kingdom; aid for innovation and environment protection for Volvo in the Netherlands; in Spain, Ford braking system investment, and VW plant rationalisation. For domestic firms: VW (car assembly), Opel (car assembly and engine production) and Mercedes-Benz (trucks) in the new *Länder* of Eastern Germany with support from regional and new *Länder* investment allowances, aid for land purchase by Daimler-Benz in Berlin; Fiat investments in the *Mezzogiorno* (car assembly, engines, eligible investment ECU 4.75 billion, aid ECU 1.57 billion from different schemes, plus R&D assistance); Renault and PSA, R&D for car and road safety. Allowed aid for investments in peripheral and disadvantaged areas has been of the order of one-third of total eligible investment, with lower levels in more central disadvantaged regions.

c) Local content and local linkages

Most countries which are host to foreign assembly operations have attempted either formally or informally to encourage local value added and improve the linkages between local component suppliers and assemblers. The issue has attracted most attention with respect to the level of local content in assembly operations of Japanese firms in North America and Europe. New investors begin assembly operations at relatively low levels of local content and progressively increase them as local supplier networks are built up and as Japanese component suppliers have joined local producers. The progressive build-up in local content over time is shown in the following data (percentages of total content):

United States

Honda	start-up 1982	North American content:	1988	60	1990	75
Subaru-Isuzu	start-up 1989	North American content.			1990	50

Canada

Honda	start-up 1986	North American content:	1988	40	1990	50
Hyundai	start-up 1989	North American content:			1990	50

United Kingdom

Nissan	start-up 1986	European content:	1986	40	1989	70
Toyota	start-up 1992	European content (plan):	1993	60	1995	80

Source : OECD (1992), *Globalisation of Industrial Activities*; OECD (1994), *Trade and Investment: Transplants*.

Assembly firms are moving to relatively higher levels of local content, including significant levels of locally-supplied components. In many cases this has been encouraged by host government programmes to improve the capabilities of small supplier firms (for example, Australia, Canada, the Netherlands, Norway and some US federal states all have programmes of this kind). These focus on improving management capabilities, diffusing manufacturing technology, networking with assembly firms, improving quality and setting standards, and encouraging technical assistance from the large assembly firms. These kinds of policies for SMEs are receiving greater attention and greater budgetary allocations despite current budget constraints.

Other support

Finally there has been an ongoing issue regarding the role of infusions of equity, loans and other advantages to restructure (partly) state-owned firms. Renault and British Aerospace/Rover received particular attention as to whether they received financial assistance which was, respectively, unfair to competition, or was not reflected fully in the privatisation price.

C.   Trade policies

Trade measures have often been an important instrument of government policy in the automobile industry. Despite the reduction of tariffs in various rounds of multilateral trade negotiations, they remain significant in certain countries. In addition, since the beginning of the last decade, resort to non-tariff measures has become particularly prominent, partly due to increased international competition in automobiles, over-supply and tensions in domestic markets. The importance and timing of trade-policy instruments and related measures is clearly demonstrated in arrangements worked out to complete the European Single Market, with abolition of national quantitative restrictions and liberalisation of the automobile market over a transition period. It is also apparent in bilateral relations between the United States and Japan. One further aspect of trade-policy intervention is the establishment of mostly informal understandings or agreements on value added for local production as well as for production and supply of parts and components.

a)   Tariffs

Overall, tariffs on automobiles and parts and components in the main car-producing countries and the EU are in line with average tariffs for manufactures and following the Uruguay Round will in many cases be further reduced when average industrial tariffs of 6.3 per cent in developed countries will be reduced to less than 4 per cent. Tariff protection has been significant in some Member countries and particularly in developing countries, and reductions are likely to increase sales and trade. Japan applies no tariffs, either on passenger cars or on parts and components; the United States applies a tariff of 2.5 per cent on passenger cars and 2-4 per cent on most parts and components, but 25 per cent on trucks; the EU has a 10 per cent import duty on automobiles and 4.9-6.9 per cent on parts and components (parts tariffs to be reduced along with tariffs on commercial vehicles); in Australia tariffs on passenger motor vehicles are planned to be progressively lowered from 32.5 per cent in 1993 to 15 per cent in 2000; a similar tariff duty is applied in New Zealand; in the EFTA countries before joining the EU, duties ranged from 0 per cent in Sweden to 17.9 per cent in Austria, the applied rate being lower under certain conditions. These tariff duties do not take into account the preferential treatment provided under regional or free trade arrangements.

In some major non-member car-producing countries, tariffs are well above the OECD average tariff rates, but overall they have been and continue to be lowered. The Republic of Korea reduced its tariffs on automobiles from 100-150 per cent in 1982, to 15 per cent in 1992, 10 per cent in 1994, and 8 per cent in 1995, with elimination of some other taxes and improvements in market access arrangements for US and EU cars announced in 1994. In September 1995, following US-Korea negotiations, it was agreed that *inter alia* vehicle taxes would be lowered further, certification procedures streamlined and foreign advertising in Korea liberalised, all on a MFN basis. Car imports into Korea were prohibited until 1988, imports from Japan are still prohibited and overall import penetration is less than 1 per cent. In Mexico, the import tariffs applied on motor vehicles are 14.5 per cent. Brazil is gradually reducing its import tariffs on finished cars, which were cut from 85 per cent to 60 per cent by the end of 1991 and further reduced to 35 per cent by 1994.[14] In many developing countries tariffs are highest on passenger cars (with very high rates), lower on commercial vehicles, lower again on kits for assembly, and lowest on parts and components to encourage domestic assembly.

Tariff reclassification, although not practised frequently, is an issue of concern, as it creates uncertainty for exporters. In January 1989, the US Customs Service issued a classification ruling that reclassified two types of vehicles – mini-vans and sports utility vehicles – as trucks, thereby subjecting them to the

25 per cent *ad valorem* tariff associated with light trucks, compared to the previously applied 2.5 per cent passenger car duty. The proposed duty was later reversed by the Department of Treasury, which decided nevertheless that two-door sports utility vehicles would be classified as "other vehicles for the transport of goods", and would therefore be dutiable at 25 per cent.

The economic effect of tariffs is determined by a number of factors specific to this sector and its level of globalisation. The use of unofficial import restrictions and voluntary export restraints (grey area measures) for automobiles since the early 1980s may have reduced the economic effect of tariffs, as the quota generally is the more restricting factor. In addition, to the extent that production in the protected market may replace trade, the economic effect of trade restrictions is reduced. Tariffs could theoretically be more important for parts and components than for finished cars, as parts are overall less affected by quantitative restrictions and they appear to be subject to higher effective tariffs in some countries (*e.g.* the United States), despite relatively low levels on components overall.[15] Finally, different tariff rates between components and finished cars leads to inconsistent effective rates of protection overall, which may affect the location of production activities.

b) *Official and unofficial arrangements*

It appears that the major automobile producing countries are in one way or another involved in managed trade, *i.e.* official or unofficial arrangements that affect patterns of trade in automobiles, parts and components.[16]

United States – Japan

Beginning in the mid-1970s, Japan rapidly increased its shares of the US automobile market, initially through exports, later by local production. The surge in exports since the mid-1970s led to tensions on the market. In order to ease these tensions, Japan undertook voluntary export restraints from 1981 until March 1994. The upper limit varied over time, starting from an initial level of 1.68 million units in 1981, gradually increasing to 1.85 million units in 1984 and 2.3 million in 1985 for a period of two years. In March 1992, given the declining trend of Japanese exports of cars to the United States and the fact that the upper limit of the VER had not been reached for some time, Japan unilaterally lowered the ceiling for its export restraints to 1.65 million cars. This new ceiling was reconfirmed unilaterally in March 1993 until Japan abolished its VER in 1994. The relative decline in trade from Japan to the United States has been paralleled by increased production of Japanese affiliates in the United States (see Section 4.C).

Since the mid-1980s, the US Government has become increasingly concerned with the opening of the Japanese market for automotive products. In May 1986 the United States and Japan added transportation machinery to the Market Oriented Sector Selective (MOSS) talks, which provided a forum for discussing ways to expand access to the Japanese auto parts market. The talks resulted in the initiation of a data collection system to monitor US auto parts sales to Japanese automakers, the establishment of a US auto parts industry office in Japan and other steps for facilitating contracts between US auto parts suppliers and potential Japanese customers. In January 1992, the United States and Japan concluded the "Tokyo Declaration on the US-Japan Global Partnership", with implications for the two governments and their automobile manufacturers. The agreement related to imports and local procurement of parts and components and expanding local R&D and promoting design, measures designed to contribute to redressing an important imbalance between the two countries. This was followed in July 1993 by broader agreement to a "Framework for a New Economic Partnership", serving as a mechanism of consultation for two years. No conclusions were reached with respect to the auto and auto parts sector, and in September 1994 the US launched a Section 301 investigation in the aftermarket for auto parts in Japan, following extensive bilateral talks on distribution of foreign vehicles and sales of original equipment parts and aftermarket parts in Japan and to Japanese transplants in the United States. Subsequently, in May 1995, the United States announced the intention of applying Section 301 sanctions (in this case 100 per cent duties) on selected Japanese luxury cars if further progress was not achieved. A bilateral agreement was reached end-June 1995 covering automobiles and automobile parts which refers to private business plans to increase access and accelerate deregulation of the Japanese auto parts market and stimulate competition in

Japanese car-dealerships, as well as expanding Japanese overseas production and purchase of competitive foreign parts. Final documents on "US-Japan Autos and Auto Parts Consultations" were signed on 23 August 1995.

European Union – Japan

EU governments have often been under pressure from their industry to directly or indirectly intervene, particularly following the rapidly increasing market shares of Japanese producers on some European markets. To control imports of Japanese cars, official and unofficial import restrictions have been in place in several EU countries particularly France, Italy, Portugal, Spain and the United Kingdom. As a result of the abolition of all barriers to trade following the conclusion of the European Single Market, the European Commission reviewed its external policy for automobile trade, with the aim of achieving a fully open European market for cars.

Bilateral discussions between the EC and Japan were initially held in the summer of 1991, and have been held intermittently since on forecasts of import levels. Consistent with the objectives of completing the Single Market, the results of the talks included the elimination of all national restrictions on Japanese motor vehicles entering the EU by the start of 1993, although specific national monitoring of allocations continues. In addition, it was agreed that Japan would monitor exports to the EU as a whole in accordance with forecast level of exports of 1.23 million in 1999, based on the assumption of demand in the EU of 15.1 million in that year. Japan will similarly monitor exports to the EU countries mentioned above. Given uncertainties with demand developments, since the fall of 1992 the two parties have continued their discussions on the evolution of the market, including forecasts for motor vehicle demand in EU markets and the implications for the management of the new arrangement for exports of Japanese motor vehicles to the EU.

In April 1993, Japan agreed to a reduction in the level of car exports to the EU. In September 1993 the Commission and Japan agreed on new forecasts for Japanese exports which were reduced to 980 000 vehicles (down 18.5 per cent compared with 1992), with forecasts for exports to France, Spain, Portugal, Italy and the United Kingdom adjusted accordingly. The situation was reviewed in March 1994 and mid-1994, forecasts of export levels were raised to 993 000 for 1994 (up 1.3 per cent over 1993). The situation was reviewed again in March 1995 and October 1995 with export levels adjusted to 1 071 000 for 1995 for the EU-15. Imports in 1994 and 1995 stayed well below forecast. The arrangement must expire end-1999 according to an EU commitment to the WTO.

Deregulation of automobile standards in some fields was agreed in 1995, which should facilitate market access to Japan.

c) Regional arrangements

North America

Trade in automotive products between the United States and Canada has been governed by the United States-Canada Automotive Products Trade Agreement of 1965 (Auto Pact). The Auto Pact was left intact under the Free Trade Agreement (FTA) between the United States and Canada and continues to prevail under the NAFTA rules. Under the agreement, each party is obliged to accord duty-free treatment to imports from the other party of specified motor vehicles and parts for use as original equipment in the manufacture of these motor vehicles. The United States obtained in 1965 a waiver under GATT Article XXV for according such preferential treatment to Canada. Canada, however, implements the Pact on a Most Favoured Nation basis. Under the Auto Pact, Canada will continue to offer duty-free entry to qualified automotive products irrespective of the country of origin to certain importing automotive manufacturers as long as they meet specified performance requirements.

According to the terms of the North American Free Trade Agreement (NAFTA), the agreement will eliminate barriers to trade in North American automobiles, trucks, buses and parts ("automotive goods") within the free trade area, and eliminate investment restrictions over a ten-year transition period. The NAFTA rules are largely based on the same principles as the US-Canada FTA, and form an extension of those provisions to include trade with Mexico. Modifications such as the calculation method of origin rules and new provisions, are included, *e.g.* for environmental standards. Under the NAFTA, the United States modifies the fleet content definition found in the Corporate Average Fuel Economy (CAFE) rules (see section (e) below), so that vehicle manufacturers may choose to have Mexican-produced parts and vehicles they export to the United States classified as domestic.

European Single Market

As is referred to in the previous section, the completion of the European Single Market included free trade in automobiles within the Union. The implementation has been phased in, taking into account the level of national restrictions that were in place.

d) Rules of origin and local content

Rules of origin are intended to confer origin to a product in order to determine the treatment it should receive while crossing a border. They are not designed as a trade policy instrument. But as the criteria in the Kyoto Convention for establishing origin vary, in practice rules of origin sometimes seem to be used as trade-policy instruments. Negotiations in the Uruguay Round arrived at an agreement aimed at harmonization of rules of origin, setting up a harmonization programme with a three year-time-span to make rules objective, understandable and predictable, enhance transparency and non-discrimination, and prevent the arbitrary use of these rules. Problems nevertheless have arisen in the past and may continue to arise with respect to preferential (including regional integration) arrangements.

Similarly, rules relating to "local content" requirements imposed on foreign investors have been controversial. Local content is variously defined but is a measure of local value added, *i.e.* the sum of the value of parts and materials procured from domestic sources plus the value of domestic assembly, labour, overhead and mark-ups. Most OECD countries do not have mandatory local content requirements, but negotiate commitments from foreign assemblers in return for location and other assistance. They are much more explicitly extensive in Latin America and Asia, and policies setting levels of local content or local sourcing have become more widespread as foreign investment in automobile assembly has increased. They are intended to ensure that inward investment is not merely to circumvent trade measures and that high-value, high-technology operations be transferred to or fostered in the host country.

One example of changes in local content and rules of origin with regional integration relates to the treatment of automobile operations under NAFTA rules, as the requirement under the Canada US FTA of 50 per cent local content was raised to 62.5 per cent, which carmakers will have to meet to qualify for duty-free access to the North American market. In addition, the NAFTA rules foresee a different method of calculating the value of certain automobile components and inputs when measuring the regional value of finished automobiles. This will reduce home-country sourcing by European and Asian car manufacturers, placing them at a disadvantage compared with North American firms. At the same time the restrictive automotive trade regime in Mexico is being dismantled. Another example relates to the treatment of cars manufactured in the EU by foreign producers and the amount of value added required to qualify as European. Australia until very recently had a local content plan of 85 per cent for automobile manufacturers. Local content measures, encouraging the use of local parts and components in the production and assembly of cars, are widespread in some Asian countries, including Korea, Malaysia, Thailand and China.

e) Standards and environment-related measures

As automobile production becomes increasingly internationalised, interactions between trade and the environment become more important. One example relates to differing emission standards. Manufacturers must adapt cars to these standards, with implications for production, trade and investment. For example it may be more efficient to shift production capacity to a specific market to meet national standards, rather than differentiate production in the home country. Even within single markets, standards can vary considerably. In the United States, because of high pollution levels, Californian environmental laws are generally stricter. In the EU, environmental standard regulations are now harmonized, and car manufacturers can obtain a type approval allowing their cars to be marketed in all EU countries. A separate example relating to trade/environment concerns are European Commission proposals for vehicle "waste management", which could lead to legislation to recycle all cars sold within the EU. This is likely to add to the direct cost of cars on the basis of the "polluter pays" principle and may pose particular problems for small-scale producers or manufacturers with low sales if their material content differs from higher-volume cars, and could also pose problems for foreign high-volume manufacturers exporting to Europe.

Strict standards may be justified from an environment point of view, but may give rise to trade frictions, for example the concerns expressed by the EU with regard to the Corporate Average Fuel Economy (CAFE) rules. In May 1993, a GATT panel was established under Article XXIII:2 to review a European Commission complaint against various taxes levied by the United States on automobiles, including the CAFE standards payments, along with the "gas-guzzler" tax and the luxury automobiles tax. The Commission maintained that European producers were being discriminated against as a result of CAFE, which is a penalty payment paid by a car manufacturer or importer if the sales-weighted average fuel economies of all model types produced by that manufacturer fall below a certain level (federal standard 27.5 miles per gallon, 1990 through 1995 for passenger car fleets, 20.6 m.p.g. in 1995 for light truck fleets). The panel found that the separate fleet accounting requirement and fleet averaging methodology of the CAFE regulation were inconsistent with GATT Article III, but that the gas-guzzler tax and luxury tax were not GATT-inconsistent and did not discriminate against European automobiles.

D. Foreign investment policies

With respect to general policies for foreign direct investment, the automobile industry is subject to the same regulatory framework of OECD countries as is foreign direct investment in general. Industry-specific government restrictions on access to markets or treatment of foreign investors are not an issue. However there may be business practices or particular national circumstances which create effective obstacles to foreign investment (in non-OECD countries such as Korea, India and China there have been a wide range of obstacles to FDI in automobiles), and which have deterred foreign investment or encouraged minority holdings and joint-venture formation.

However, because of the size of the industry, its backward and forward linkages, importance in fostering small and medium-sized supplying firms, employment opportunities and impacts on the trade balance, it has been the object of policies designed to attract foreign investment and informal measures to localise inputs to production once investment has occurred. The two most common are location subsidies and local content requirements, some of the impacts of which are described in Sections B and C above. Both have had considerable impacts on the final location of production within particular regions, and have helped to speed the regional development of the industry, with important clusters of green-field investment and local supply networks being set up in North America and Europe.

International taxation issues

With the wider spread of international investment in the industry, high levels of intra-firm trade and the shift towards greater out-sourcing of components from fewer, quasi-integrated, firms, transfer pricing is likely to be a continuing issue. Although out-sourcing to independent firms reduces the role of intra-firm transactions, the increasing reliance on external suppliers to develop components and operate on a single-source basis is likely to make new kinds of transfer pricing an important aspect of price formation.

E. Competition policy

Four areas of competition relevant to globalisation in the industry which have received competition policy attention are:

- treatment of R&D co-operation and its extension to joint production;
- investment subsidies and distortion of competition;

- impacts of voluntary export restraints;
- regulation of selective and exclusive distribution.

Because of the increasing costs of long-term research, many firms, often as part of government-sponsored schemes, are carrying out joint long-term research on new materials, new propulsion systems, traffic guidance and navigation systems, but also on new components and assemblies which are of more immediate application. In principle automobile R&D co-operation is excluded from competition policy scrutiny in the EU ("pre-competitive" R&D), the United States and Japan, in the same way that most co-operative research is now excluded, provided that it is not a cover for price fixing, market sharing or investment co-ordination. However, reduced competition in sources of component supply may well come into conflict with competition policy rules as joint component development moves downstream to joint production, or as component development is out-sourced to component manufacturers on a single-source basis.

Investment subsidies to attract foreign investment have been widespread. They potentially lead to artificially lower start-up costs and operating costs, and hence prices, distorting competition. To overcome this problem for example in the EU market, new investments have been subjected to scrutiny and moderation within the "Community framework on state aid to the motor vehicle industry" outlined in Section B above.

A number of studies, including a 1992 UK Monopolies and Mergers Commission report on exclusive distribution, identified voluntary export restraints as a source of restriction of competition, artificially increasing prices and restricting consumer choice in the protected market. Furthermore, benefits to labour under such arrangements have at best been limited [see OECD, 1988, and Section 5.C.b.) above].

Selective and exclusive distribution arrangements are widespread in the automobile industry in all major countries, and have generally been viewed as pro-competitive, because for example they can promote efficiencies in manufacturer responsiveness to customer demands and in repairs and maintenance. For example in the European Union, unless they lead to the partitioning of national markets or to excessive price differentials, such arrangements are exempted from competition rules by a block exemption. After considerable examination the exemption is to be maintained for a further seven years from October 1995. The new exemption will allow dealers greater freedom to sell and service more than one make of car, to advertise more widely, to contribute to the setting of sales targets, prices, conditions of sale, and to have greater flexibility in the sourcing of spare parts. There have also been continuing attempts to reduce price differentials in different markets and help consumers shop for cars across the EU, for example by publication of comparative prices of top-selling new vehicles, but exchange rate movements can change relative prices (and producers' margins) dramatically, and car taxation levels in the EU range from 15 per cent in Luxembourg to 213 per cent in Denmark, having very large impacts on final prices of cars.

NOTES AND REFERENCES

1. Coverage of employment data is not as extensive as for production.

2. See De Banville and Chanaron, *op. cit.*

3. Because of problems allocating disaggregated R&D expenditures, some data are partly estimated.

4. Data for motor vehicle investment is not available for all OECD countries.

5. Unit values are defined as the value of trade divided by the volume of trade. This excludes distribution costs, taxes etc., thus making the figures comparable FOB.

6. There are few sources of data on IFT. Information on the subject is not generally available in traditional trade statistics. Data on IFT are mostly available through firm surveys by national authorities. This section is based on information provided by the US Department of Commerce, which conducts surveys of foreign affiliates of US companies and US affiliates of foreign companies. Similar data is not available for other countries. The US Department of Commerce uses the International Surveys Industry (ISI) classification in its surveys. The category for "motor vehicles and equipment" (ISI 371) includes manufacturing or assembling of complete passenger automobiles, commercial automobiles, buses and trucks, as well as truck and bus bodies, self-contained motor homes on purchased chassis, and motor vehicle parts and accessories, including engines, except diesel. The level of aggregation in these surveys does not distinguish between finished automobiles and auto parts. For an explanation of availability and problems with data, see OECD (1993).

7. There has been a large increase in investment by Japanese auto producers in wholesale activities in the United States. Trade involving these wholesale activities is technically IFT, but is different in character from that taking place in assembly operations. The figures above exclude IFT due to wholesale activities.

8. See OECD (1993).

9. Intra-industry trade can be readily calculated for any given product category, as only the traditional bilateral trade statistics for that product category are needed. The interpretation of IIT data depends however, on how the category is defined, as the choice of classification system and level of aggregation may strongly influence the results. For the analysis below, the Standard International Trade Classification Revision 2, at four digit level, was used. In the calculation of an IIT index, if exports are equal to imports, IIT is 100; if either imports or exports are equal to zero, IIT is zero. For a discussion of theory and measurement of IIT, see Grubel and Lloyd (1975).

10. SITC Rev2 7810: passenger motor cars (other than public-service type vehicles), including vehicles for the transport of passengers and goods.

11. SITC Rev2 7841, 7842 and 7849: parts and accessories of several motor vehicles, including passenger motor cars, vehicles for the transport of goods, other road vehicles and tractors.

12. Data on FDI from OECD/DAFFE. Data on international mergers and acquisitions, and minority participations were kindly provided by KPMG Peat Marwick to OECD/DAFFE. For joint ventures and minority participations, "purchase" means that a firm of the specified country has a joint venture operation or minority participation in a foreign country and "sale" means that an operation takes place in that country where a firm of foreign nationality is involved.

13. The sample of 301 agreements for motor vehicles and components is drawn from the INSEAD Collaborative Agreements Database covering some 2 565 agreements in all regions of the world and all industries, but with a focus on manufacturing, compiled through late 1992. The information in this section was drawn from a report on "Collaboration Agreements in the Motor Vehicles Sector" prepared by Judith Jaffe under the direction of Professor Deigan Morris, INSEAD, who designed and developed the data base, and who holds the rights to it.

14. Source: *International Customs Bulletin* and OECD sources.

15. Another way of measuring the incidence of tariffs is to consider the tariff escalation that would occur if there is a major difference in tariff rates applied for the inputs (parts and components), compared to the tariffs on the final

product (finished cars). As the nominal tariff rate applied to imports of parts and components and the duty on finished vehicles are quite similar, there may be little tariff escalation, except for the EU, which applies higher duties on finished cars than on parts. Closely related to this is the concept of effective rate of protection. The effective rate of protection measures the percentage increase in value added resulting from protection in an activity, taking full account of the tariff and non-tariff measures affecting inputs and outputs. The effective rate of protection in a particular activity is a function of the tariff on finished goods, the average rate on material inputs and components and the value added under free trade in an activity (see GATT TPRM report Korea for details).

16. Import quotas and voluntary export restraints are economically more costly than tariffs, as they not only raise prices in the importing country, but also lead to greater trade diversion, economic rents, welfare losses and global and national resource misallocation in the exporting and especially the importing country.

BIBLIOGRAPHY

AMERICAN AUTOMOBILE MANUFACTURERS ASSOCIATION (AAMA, formerly MMVA), various publications and documents.

ASSOCIATION OF EUROPEAN AUTOMOBILE MANUFACTURERS (ACEA), monthly *Newsletter* and various documents.

DE BANVILLE, E. and J.J. CHANARON (1991), *Vers un système automobile européen,* Economica.

COMITÉ DES CONSTRUCTEURS FRANÇAIS D'AUTOMOBILES (CCFA), *Analyse et Statistiques,* various issues.

CONGRESS OF THE UNITED STATES, OFFICE OF TECHNOLOGY ASSESSMENT (OTA) (1994), *Multinationals and the US Technology Base,* Washington DC: US Government Printing Office.

DATAQUEST, "Emerging Automotive Electronics Applications", reported in the *Financial Times,* 25 May 1995.

EUROPEAN COMMISSION, *Panorama of EU Industries,* various years.

EUROPEAN COMMISSION, *Report on Competition Policy,* various issues.

GRUBEL, H.G. and P.J. LLOYD (1975), *Intra-industry Trade: The Theory and Measurement of International Trade in Differentiated Products,* MacMillan, London.

INTERNATIONAL MOTOR VEHICLE PROJECT (IMVP), surveys various years.

JAPAN AUTOMOBILE MANUFACTURERS ASSOCIATION (JAMA), various documents.

MOTOR VEHICLE MANUFACTURERS ASSOCIATION OF THE UNITED STATES (MVMA), various publications and documents.

NISHIYAMA, H. (1992), "Japan's Auto Industry: Under Pressure to Improve Profit Structure, *Nomura Research Institute Quarterly,* Vol. 1, No. 2, Autumn.

OECD, *Indicators of Industrial Activity* (IIA), various issues, Paris.

OECD, *Competition Policy in OECD Countries,* various issues, Paris.

OECD (1983), *Long-term Outlook for the World Automobile Industry,* Paris.

OECD (1988), *The Costs of Restricting Imports: The Automobile Industry,* Paris.

OECD (1991), *Managing Manpower for Advanced Manufacturing Technology,* Paris.

OECD (1992), *Globalisation of Industrial Activities: Four Case Studies,* Paris.

OECD (1992), The International Sourcing of Manufactured Intermediate Inputs: Canada, France, Germany, Japan, the United Kingdom and the United States, Paris.

OECD (1993), *Intra-firm trade,* Paris.

OECD (1994), *Trade and Investment: Transplants,* Paris.

OECD (1994), *The Performance of Foreign Affiliates in OECD Countries,* Paris.

RUIGROK, W., R. VAN TULDER and G. BAVEN (1991), *Cars and Complexes: Globalisation versus Global Localisation Strategies in the World Car Industry,* FAST, Vol. 13, Prospective Dossier No. 2, CEC.

SACHWALD, F. (1993), *L'Europe et la globalisation: Acquisitions et accords dans l'industrie,* Masson, Paris.

SACHWALD, F. (ed.) (1993), *Les entreprises japonaises en Europe : Motivations et stratégies,* Masson, Paris.

SACHWALD, F. (ed.) (1994), *Les défis de la mondialisation : Innovation et concurrence,* Masson, Paris.

SOCIETY OF MOTOR VEHICLE MANUFACTURERS (UK) (1993), various reports, *e.g.* as quoted in *Financial Times,* 29-30 May.

US DEPARTMENT OF COMMERCE, *US Industrial Outlook '92, 1993, 1994,* Washington, DC.

US DEPARTMENT OF COMMERCE, *Survey of Current Business,* various issues, Washington, DC.

US DEPARTMENT OF COMMERCE (1993), *Foreign Direct Investment in the United States: An Update,* Washington, DC.

VAN LIEMT, G. (ed.) (1992), *Industry on the Move: Causes and Consequences of International Relocation in the Manufacturing Industry*, ILO/World Employment Programme.

WOMACK, J., D. JONES and D. ROOS (1990), *The Machine that Changed the World,* Rawson, New York.

Chapter 5

GLOBALISATION IN THE CONSUMER ELECTRONICS INDUSTRY

by

Americo Beviglia Zampetti
Trade Directorate, OECD

Table of contents

LIST OF TABLES

LIST OF FIGURES

SUMMARY AND CONCLUSIONS

The consumer electronics industry mainly produces mass consumption audio and video products which require a relatively low degree of customisation. The industry is dominated by a few companies which produce and market globally, and engage in world-wide rivalry. The patterns of globalisation can be well traced by observing the strategies of the global leaders. With the exception of Philips, which has pursued an international strategy very early on in its history, all the major competitors have done so only more recently. Two principal driving forces seem to have characterised the process of global siting of production, although in opposing geographical directions. On the one hand, the economics of production has encouraged the dispersal of manufacturing activities in search of efficiency maximisation. On the other hand, growing trade competition has engendered some strong protectionist pressures which have induced the relocation of some manufacturing operations, above all from Asia to Europe and North America.

The industry is highly scale-intensive, with rapidly decreasing unit production costs. Sales are in general very price-sensitive and global companies are constantly vying for market shares in order to minimise costs and ensure profitability. This implies that they are fiercely competing in all the three major markets – Europe, North America and Asia. Barriers to market access, including structural ones, may have a significant impact on companies strategies and performances.

The consumer electronics industry is of vital importance as a technology driver for the electronics industry as well as for the economy as a whole, contributing both to innovation and the development of commercial applications. In this light the dominant world position acquired by Japanese companies has led other countries to make significant use of trade-policy measures. The latter have generally proved ineffective at a time when competition between leading companies was shifting from being mainly international-trade-based to being global in production and marketing strategies.

International trade has continued to grow, but it has become more concentrated within the three main regions noted above, as a result of foreign investments. And it has been partly replaced by local production-cum-international sourcing, with the effect of substituting some trade in end-products for trade in components, which is showing a rising trend. In particular the relative decline of inter-regional trade in consumer electronics products, especially from East Asia and Japan toward both Europe and North America, is in large measure attributable to the parallel increase in investment flows and the establishment of regional production operations.

Consumer electronics products tend to incorporate an increasing number of high-tech components, such as microprocessors, memory devices and other forms of digital circuitry. Consumer electronics companies are often vertically-integrated manufacturers, which design, produce and sell a number of electronic components. Consumer electronics may thus be considered a quite R&D-and capital-intensive industry, above all at the high end of the market. Automation has been spreading and has led to substantial productivity gains.

The rising costs of product development and of capacity building have increased the barriers to entry in the industry. These trends have contributed to growth in the number and importance of international collaboration agreements, adding a new dimension to the leading firms' global strategies. They allow companies to share the costs and the risks of pursuing expensive research and development (R&D) programmes and reduce product lines, thus ensuring a high degree of competitiveness by concentrating on their core competencies.

In the consumer electronics industry the main players consider the world as their reference market and have developed very sophisticated global strategies aimed at taking advantage of the best production and technological opportunities available globally in terms of locations and of inter-firm collaboration. But, on the other hand, their strategies remain quite constrained and strongly influenced by factors such as the macroeconomic environment, including in particular relative exchange rates, and public policies, especially trade and technology policies.

1. INTRODUCTION: SCOPE OF THE INDUSTRY

The emergence of the consumer electronics industry can be traced back to the second quarter of the century with the development and widespread sale of radio sets and gramophones. A fundamental technological breakthrough came about with the discovery of the transistor by a group of scientists at the AT&T Bell laboratories in New Jersey. This discovery made possible substantial reductions in product dimensions, improved quality and decreased prices. The transistor technology has also paved the way for an endless stream of innovations and of new products, from televisions to computers, from compact discs to cellular telephones which have had a profound impact on economic and social systems.

Consumer electronics is one of the three main segments of the electronic industry, the other two being industrial electronic equipment, which includes computers and communications systems, and electronic components and devices. The consumer segment is generally considered to encompass audio products, such as hi-fi systems, compact disk players (CDs), portable audio equipment, in-car entertainment systems and video products, such as television receivers (TVs), video cassette recorders (VCRs), CD video and video camera recorders (camcorders). The bulk of the industry's production value is represented by colour TVs and VCRs.

Some professional items, including telephone and facsimile sets, CD-based information systems as well as personal computers, are becoming increasingly "consumerised", and are considered in some

◆ Figure 5.1. ***World electronics production***
Billion US$

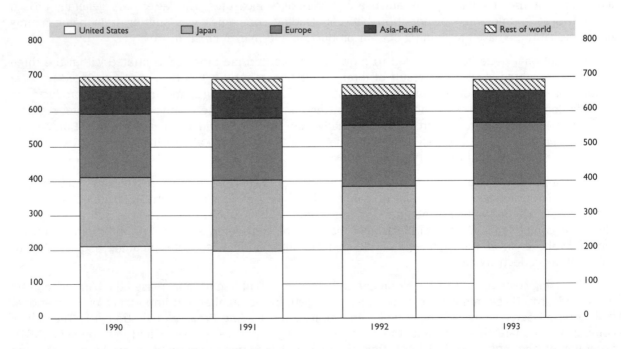

Source: *Yearbook of World Electronics Data 1993,* Volume 2, Elsevier Science Publisher, Ltd., United Kingdom.

statistical sources already as part of the consumer electronics segment.[1] On the other hand, it is noteworthy that innovations, such as high-definition TV (HDTV) and flat-panel displays, which were initially conceived for the consumer segment, have subsequently found widespread industrial and even military applications. These trends underscore a very important characteristic of the industry, above all in a forward-looking perspective, namely the blurring and cross-fertilisation between the segments of personal and business products, which builds upon the increasing convergence between the technologies and applications of the computer, telecommunications, consumer electronics, entertainment and publishing industries in what are now called "multimedia" and "interactive" systems.

2. TRENDS IN GROWTH AND STRUCTURE

A. Production

World-wide electronics production is estimated to represent around US$700 billion (Figure 5.1) and it represents one of the largest sectors of industrial activity on its way to overtaking other large sectors such as transport equipment, chemicals and food products. In terms of its share in gross domestic product (GDP) it represents around 5 per cent in Europe, 5.5 per cent in Japan and over 6 per cent in the United States. Consumer electronics production accounts for around US$80 billion, or 11 per cent of the whole industry (Table 5.1a and b). Japan, accounting for over 40 per cent of total output, is by far the largest

Table 5.1a. **Production, 1991**[1]

Millions of US dollars

	Consumer electronics products		Total electronics
Austria	1 174		3 385
Belgium	698		5 457
Denmark	146		1 739
Finland	181		2 503
France	1 960		29 650
Germany	4 163		50 810
Ireland	15		5 113
Italy	1 040		22 610
Netherlands	95		8 449
Norway	7		1 432
Spain	1 222		7 395
Sweden	109		6 136
Switzerland	2 304		6 987
United Kingdom	2 511		28 418
Western Europe total	15 624	(19.2%)	180 084
United States	6 162	(7.6%)	199 398
Canada	339		9 016
Japan	37 141	(45.7%)	207 489
Republic of Korea	6 657	(8.2%)	25 484
Hong Kong	2 824		8 292
Malaysia	2 925		9 105
Singapore	2 045		16 850
Chinese Taipei	1 712		15 594
Thailand	1 149		5 404
DAEs total	17 312	(21.2%)	80 729
Australia	135		2 752
Brazil	2 263		12 663
India	1 165		3 737
Indonesia	647		1 646
Philippines	156		2 222
Israel	170		2 358
South Africa	203		1 303
Total	**81 317**		**696 395**

1. In brackets are the shares of total consumer electronics production
Source: Yearbook of World Economic Data 1993, Elsevier Science Publisher, Ltd., UK, Vol. 1 and 2.

Table 5.1b. **Production, 1992**[1]

Millions of US dollars

	Consumer electronics products		Total electronics products
Austria	1 078		3 453
Belgium	701		5 347
Denmark	152		1 857
Finland	136		2 567
France	1 837		31 302
Germany	3 288		48 480
Ireland	15		5 683
Italy	954		22 490
Netherlands	128		8 781
Norway	7		1 373
Spain	1 169		6 431
Sweden	57		6 399
Switzerland	2 489		7 262
United Kingdom	1 847		27 700
Western Europe total	13 859	(20.1%)	179 125
United States	6 254	(8.1%)	
Canada	350		8 420
Japan	31 638	(41.3%)	195 969
Republic of Korea	6 363	(8.3%)	26 417
Hong Kong	2 613		8 320
Malaysia	3 451		12 128
Singapore	2 484		20 252
Chinese Taipei	1 542		18 001
Thailand	1 456		6 705
DAEs total	17 909	(23.3%)	91 823
Australia	142		2 778
Brazil	2 331		12 709
India	1 098		3 830
Indonesia	904		2 163
Philippines	159		2 105
Israel	122		2 728
South Africa	216		1 308
Total	**76 553**		**712 725**

1.   In brackets are the shares of total consumer electronics production.
Source: *Yearbook of World Electronics Data 1994*, Elsevier Science Publisher, Ltd., UK, Vol. 1 and 2.

producer, followed by the Republic of Korea, the United States, Germany, Malaysia, Singapore and the United Kingdom. The overall share of the European Community (EC) is around 15 per cent. The annual growth of the industry although still recording double-digit rates during the 1980s, has shown a decreasing trend (Figure 5.2).

The economics of production and the competitive conditions of individual product markets may differ substantially. In general the production process for consumer electronics products is subject to significant scale economies. Very high volumes of production, often exceeding the domestic market potential, are needed to achieve international competitiveness. For instance, in the production of colour TVs, scale economies derive from the fixed investment in tooling, automated assembly equipment, testing equipment and specialised equipment for coil winding and other operations required for sub-assemblies of the television set. Production process efficiency is thus a key factor of success in this high-volume industry.

From one perspective, the consumer electronics industry could be viewed as an assembly business, adding a relatively small value to the parts and components incorporated into the end-product. Components[2] in fact make up a large part of the production costs[3] and if purchased separately in small lots, would typically cost more than the final product. Part and component manufacturing and final assembly are often carried out in different locations or countries by different companies. But in light of the

◆ Figure 5.2. **Consumer electronics industry annual growth rate**
In percentage

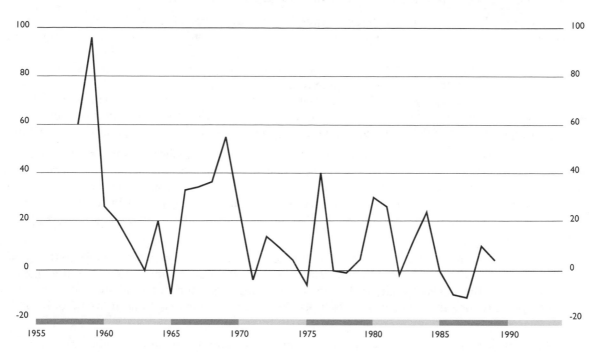

Source: *The Economist,* 13 April 1991.

◆ Figure 5.3. **Semiconductor demand by end use, 1991**

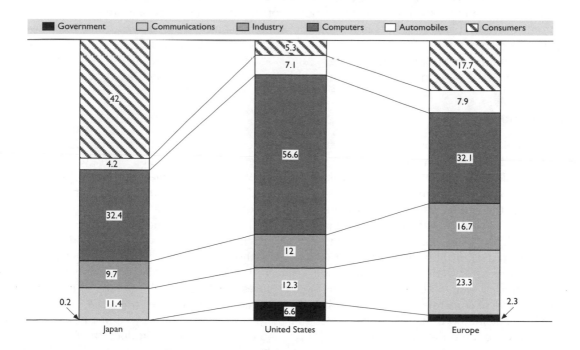

Note: Figures are rounded, so that the total does not necessarily equal 100%.
Source: Electronic Industries Association of Japan (1993).

strong production and technological interlinkages and integration between components and end-products manufacturers, it is often useful to consider them in a more comprehensive fashion.

To a varying degree all manufacturers, depending on the level of vertical integration, need to purchase some components on the open market. The possibility of sourcing components in a timely way and with the required specifications and characteristics of quality and price is thus a key factor of competitiveness. The production of components also benefits from substantial economies of scale. The consumer electronics manufacturers are very large volume purchasers of components (Figure 5.3) creating interdependencies in the supply chain. The minimum efficient scale of component production is often so high that vertically integrated consumer electronic manufacturers still have to sell part of their components on the open market. This has proven to be a very successful strategy for Japanese manufacturers.

Anyway the increasing spread of digital technology in consumer applications makes it increasingly possible to use the same components for both professional and consumer equipment, thus increasing the economies of scale and scope. This development also tends to reduce the cost of producing professional products, which may sometimes migrate to the consumer market. There are an increasing number of products which are becoming "consumerised", such as personal computers, camcorders, mobile phones, home fax and home copiers.

Noteworthy is the trend towards reducing the number of parts and components, thanks to the greater integration of functions into single components (integrated circuits) and to miniaturisation, thus increasing productivity in the assembly phase. For instance, since 1984, technological improvements have allowed Philips to reduce the number of parts in its CD player by 75 per cent and in its VCRs by 55 per cent.

Labour cost is still quite important at the low end of the market in the assembly stage but it is becoming increasingly less so due to automation.[4] In Japan, for instance, labour accounts for only around 5-10 per cent of overall direct cost of production of consumer electronics products. But depending on the production method or in specific stages of the production process, labour can still represent a larger share of costs.

The "lean" production system, more common among automobile manufacturers, is also making some inroads in the consumer electronics industry. Sony, for instance, has been adopting it in its domestic video production with positive results in terms of flexibility, assembly time savings, quality improvements and reduction of production costs. In order to be a successful strategy, lean production requires a high degree of integration in the production process, and of co-ordination with components suppliers, which may prove somewhat more difficult in an industry characterised by short product cycles.

B. Consumption

Consumer electronics products are in general mass-consumption products which need a relatively low degree of customisation. The size of the consumer electronics market has been growing in parallel with the diffusion of "boom" products: black and white TVs and stereo hi-fis in the 1960s; colour TVs, cassette decks and video games in the 1970s; and VCRs, CD players, Walkmans, and camcorders in the 1980s. The EC, the United States and Japan are the three most important markets, accounting respectively for around 33, 25 and 20 per cent of consumption in 1991 (Table 5.2a and Figure 5.4). However, their markets for TVs and VCRs appear to be saturated or approaching that stage, with sales falling off in recent years. TV penetration of households in the United States and Japan is over 99 per cent, while it exceeds 90 per cent in most of the EC. More than 50 per cent of American homes already own two or more TVs. VCR penetration is over 75 per cent in both the United States and Japan, while still somewhat lower in the EC. The life-cycle of consumer products usually shows a rapid increase of sales when the item is launched, followed by a decline until manufacturers target a larger group of consumers by adding new features and/ or offering lower price variations. Once the majority of households own the product, the market becomes dependent on replacement sales, a stage now reached by TVs and rapidly approaching for VCRs and CD players. On the other hand, in some markets, such as the United States, sales of TVs and VCRs remain at a high level, driven by demand for upgrades and, in many households, for a second or third set.

Table 5.2a. **Markets, 1991**[1]

Millions of US dollars

	Consumer electronics products		Total electronics products
Austria	669		4 378
Belgium	611		7 076
Denmark	343		2 516
Finland	293		3 133
France	3 460		34 581
Germany	8 009		58 303
Ireland	150		3 176
Italy	3 638		30 248
Netherlands	1 422		13 230
Norway	240		2 747
Spain	2 526		13 695
Sweden	747		7 157
Switzerland	777		7 062
United Kingdom	3 442		32 847
Western Europe total	26 327	(35.1%)	220 150
United States	19 508	(26.0%)	216 669
Canada	1 880		15 710
Japan	16 407	(21.9%)	140 778
Republic of Korea	2 287	(3.0%)	15 785
Hong Kong	703		5 866
Malaysia	370		4 529
Chinese Taipei	859		9 111
Thailand	457		3 686
Singapore	690		8 913
DAEs total	5 366	(7.1%)	47 890
Australia	821		6 913
Brazil	2 203		14 786
India	1 161		4 019
Indonesia	577		2 605
Israel	188		2 486
Philippines	122		979
South Africa	324		3 027
Total	**74 885**		**676 011**

1. In brackets are the shares of total consumer electronics market.
Source: See Table 5.1a.

Thus, notwithstanding brand loyalty that manufacturers pursue at great cost, and a continuous research of product differentiation and innovation, price competition is becoming increasingly more important. In addition, consumption is quite income-elastic, which partly explains the problems that many manufacturers are facing in the current recessionary phase. In general consumer demand can be divided into two main segments. High-end-users interested in quality products and service, and low-end-users wanting cheaper and easier to use products. In order to get the right mix of features for the different segments, producers have to balance price, service and distribution quality and product user friendliness. In Japan consumers tend to be more sophisticated, seeking products of high quality and performance. This has meant that new product and market development are taking place primarily in Japan.

The medium-term outlook for the consumer electronics market seems to be one of moderate growth, waiting for technological improvements to make available new "hit" products, which will probably be based on digital technology. Various new products, such as personal digital assistants, digital audio tape recorders, digital compact cassettes, mini-discs and compact disc interactive systems have been already launched, but it is still unclear what their market potential is. The Electronics Association of Japan estimates that the global market for such "multimedia" products could eventually be worth Y 325 000 billion a year.

Table 5.2b. **Markets, 1992**[1]

Millions of US dollars

	Consumer electronics products		Total electronics products
Austria	649		4 633
Belgium	757		7 610
Denmark	345		2 647
Finland	233		2 863
France	3 356		36 083
Germany	6 803		57 132
Ireland	146		3 236
Italy	3 184		30 359
Netherlands	1 383		13 926
Norway	268		2 893
Spain	2 478		12 160
Sweden	633		7 520
Switzerland	682		6 965
United Kingdom	3 219		34 551
Western Europe total	24 133	(33.9%)	222 578
United States	20 539	(28.9%)	231 268
Canada	1 871		15 279
Japan	13 433	(18.9%)	125 496
Republic of Korea	2 175	(3.0%)	15 206
Hong Kong	743		6 503
Malaysia	427		5 702
Chinese Taipei	1 032		10 331
Thailand	564		4 571
Singapore	721		10 077
DAEs total	5 662	(7.9%)	52 390
Australia	871		7 101
Brazil	2 147		14 115
India	1 047		4 285
Indonesia	617		2 982
Israel	219		2 870
Philippines	141		1 076
South Africa	375		3 075
Total	**71 056**		**682 515**

1. In brackets are the shares of total consumer electronics market.
Source: See Table 5.1b.

C. Employment

As mentioned, automation and the ensuing productivity growth has brought about a decline in employment levels in the consumer electronics industry of most OECD countries. In addition manufacturers have tried to take advantage of low-wage off-shore labour[5] through both procuring labour-intensive products and sub-assemblies from developing countries and moving labour-intensive operations there (Table 5.3).

For instance in the EC, employment in production dropped from 250 000 in 1978 to 119 000 in 1990, while the United States, which in 1966 had 100 000 production workers in the TV segment, was left in 1990 with 22 500 production workers (and a total employment of 30 800) in the whole consumer electronics industry. In Japan, the consumer electronics segment employed in 1990 over 290 000 workers (down from 316 000 in 1987) or 14.6 per cent of total employment in the electric and electronic appliances industry and 2.5 per cent of total manufacturing employment.

D. Research and development

Despite its high-volume, low-profit character, consumer electronics is now a source of critical innovations and is strongly driving high-tech electronics, also thanks to the technological convergence with the

◆ Figure 5.4. **World electronics market**
Billion US$

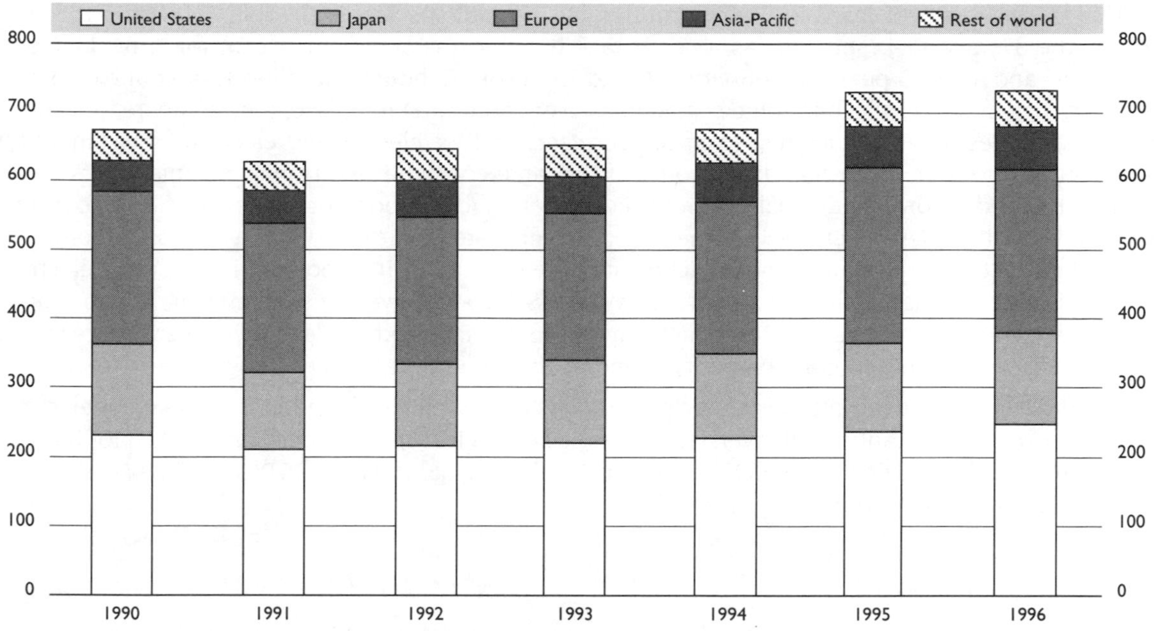

Source: Yearbook of World Electronics Data 1993, Volume 2, Elsevier Science Publisher, Ltd., United Kingdom.

Table 5.3. **Thomson Consumer Electronics**

Locations	Hourly labour cost	Production	Workforce	Share of workforce	Share of sales
France	100	Headquarter, research, large-screen TVs, components	5 400	10%	10%
Western Europe	60-120	Large-screen TVs, components	7 200	13%	29%
America			19 200	36%	56%
United States	45-90	US market			
Mexico	6-12	US market			
Asia			18 200	34%	3%
China	2	Radios, radio alarm-clocks			
Malaysia	5	Radios, radio alarm-clocks			
Singapore	22	Small TVs, VCRs			
Other			4 000	7%	2%
Poland	11	Small TVs			
Total			**54 000**	**100%**	**100%**

Source: J. Arthuis (1993), Les délocalisations et l'emploi, Paris, Les Éditions d'Organisation, p. 68.

computer and telecommunications sectors. It is thus becoming one of the dominant forces exercising control over the underlying technological base.[6] But given the pervasiveness of the electronics technology, its role as a driver is increasingly felt in the whole economy.[7]

This is the result of large R&D expenditures by the industry leaders (Table 5.4). Over the period 1986-90, the average R&D spending as a percentage of sales was above 7 per cent for Sony, Matsushita and Philips, and above 5 per cent for Sharp, JVC and Thomson. Although these levels are quite common in the electronics industry, which in some segments is even more R&D-intensive, they compare well with the Japanese averages for manufacturing (over 3.3 per cent) and for electric and electronic machinery (over 5.8 per cent). However, given that the majority of the large consumer electronics manufacturers are also active in the production of industrial electronic equipment and components, the evaluation of consumer-electronics-specific R&D intensity becomes more complicated. The production of components often requires larger R&D expenditures, and in fact most of the technology incorporated in consumer electronics products is due to high-tech components. Anyway R&D costs have become extremely important for leading-edge firms. The substantial and risky investments[8] involved in developing new processes and products are unavoidable to stay competitive, and at the same time create strong barriers to entry.

The driving and critical value of the technology which is being developed in the consumer electronics industry allows for substantial spill-overs and synergies of the R&D programmes undertaken for individual product groups. The ensuing economies of scope partially mitigate the high R&D costs. They may induce a strategy of vertical integration.

E. Capital investment

Consumer electronics is a high-volume industry which, at the high end of the market is also technology- and capital-intensive, with a high rate of equipment renewal. Manufacturers need to make heavy investments to reach large volumes, which, thanks to production efficiencies (steep learning curve) involved, can decrease costs and achieve higher yields. In turn the cost reduction allows for the setting of lower prices and the expansion of sales. In this way manufacturers may be able to recoup the large development costs and to gain profits, albeit on smaller margins. First-comer advantages may be particularly important given the short consumer electronics products life-cycles and the often higher profitability of the initial period of a new product's life-cycle. The time between the introduction and the maturity of products has decreased from three to four years to something in the order of 18-24 months.

As is the case for high R&D costs, the high investment costs incurred in setting up production facilities constitute a substantial barrier to entry and to exit, given the large amount of sunk costs involved. Pricing strategies are in turn largely influenced by this industry characteristic.

The heavy capital and R&D investments[9] have brought about large improvements in productivity.[10] But there appear to be large differences between companies and countries. For instance in 1990 sales per employee at Philips were less than half those at Sony and Matsushita. In a recent study[11] Japan emerged to be 15 and 28 per cent more productive in consumer electronics than the United States and Germany, respectively.

F. Concentration and competition

The industry is characterised by a high degree of concentration. Japanese corporations dominate the market world-wide, with Philips and Thomson as the only global challengers. Taking into account also the ownership of foreign production facilities, Japanese companies control around 55 per cent of world production, accounting for over 99 per cent of domestic production, and respectively 27 and 20 per cent of production in Europe and the United States. The EC industry represents around 15 per cent of world production. After Thomson's acquisition of RCA, there are no US-owned companies among the industry leaders (Tables 5.4 and 5.5). The Finnish multinational Nokia, through a series of acquisitions in France and Germany, has become a third European company of major size. As for developing country firms, Korea's Samsung and Goldstar can be considered global players. They are particularly strong in the most mature and low end-products.

Table 5.4. **Major manufactures, 1991 – Consumer electronics**

Company	Location	Total electronic sales[1]	Total sales[2]	Net income[3]	Return on equity[4]	R&D[5]	Foreign sales[6]	Fiscal year ended
Matsushita	Japan	36 638	56 014	999	3.8	5.6	48.0	3/1992
Toshiba	Japan	26 602	35 507	297	3.3	6.7	29.0	3/1992
Hitachi	Japan	25 169	58 388	959	4.4	6.7	24.0	3/1992
Philips	Netherlands	23 784	30 487	525	7.4	6.8	94.4	12/1992
Sony	Japan	22 959	28 734	903	7.8	6.3	75.0	3/1992
Thomson	France	12 640	12 640	124	3.5	6.1	69.0	12/1991
Mitsubishi	Japan	12 510	25 137	271	4.4	5.0	21.0	3/1992
Sharp	Japan	9 704	11 691	294	5.2	6.5	50.0	3/1992
Samsung	Republic of Korea	7 131	7 131	94	6.9	8.5	58.0	12/1991
Sanyo	Japan	6 360	11 933	127	2.3	5.2	41.0	11/1991
Goldstar	Republic of Korea	5 025	5 025	25	0.5	3.2	51.0	12/1991
Pioneer	Japan	4 609	4 609	214	8.6	4.3	59.0	3/1992
Nokia	Finland	3 010	3 813	149	7.6	6.0	62.3	12/1991

1. US$ million; either a published figure or an *Electronic Business* estimate of revenue earned by each company from sales of electronics products and services.
2. US$ million.
3. US$ million: income from continuing operations after taxes and before extraordinary items or charges; includes minority interest.
4. Net Income after taxes as a percentage of shareholders equity (preferred stock, capital stock surpluses, and retained earnings at the company's year end).
5. Company-sponsored research and development expenses.
6. Includes the country of origin's sales to other regions as a percentage of total sales.

Source: "The Electronic Business International 100", *Electronic Business*, December 1992, p. 84-85.

Table 5.5. **Turnover of major companies, 1989 – Consumer electronics**

ECU billion

Matsushita	19.5
Sony	10.7
Philips	10.1
Toshiba	7.1
Hitachi	6.1
Thomson	5.0
JVC	4.9
Mitsubishi	4.1
Samsung	3.4
Goldstar	3.1
Sharp	2.7
Pioneer	2.6 (1988)
Sanyo	2.3
Grundig	1.4
Nokia	1.2 (1988)
Zenith	1.2

Source: BIS-Mackintosh, reproduced in European Communities (1991*b*), p. 7.

In Japan, five companies control three quarters of the TV and VCR markets. High degrees of market concentration are also evident in other product markets (Table 5.6). Five companies make up for almost 60 per cent of the US TV market (Table 5.7). In order to improve productivity and respond to fierce competition from Asian manufacturers, the European industry has undertaken a wide-ranging process of industrial restructuring. The result has been an extremely high level of concentration. For instance in France six groups currently account for 92 per cent of the radio and TV industry's total turnover and employ 91 per cent of its workforce, while in 1963 25 enterprises accounted for 83 and 81 per cent of turnover and employment, respectively.[12] The Korean market also appears very concentrated, with the three major groups sharing the total VCR and over 80 per cent of the TV markets (Table 5.8).

Another outstanding characteristic of the sector is the high degree of vertical integration of all the major companies, and particularly the Japanese ones. They are in fact important players in the components markets as well as in the industrial equipment and telecommunications sector. The technology

Table 5.6. **Market share of the five leading producers of audio and video products in Japan**

Percentages, 1987-88

Colour TV sets 1988		VCRs 1988		Camcorders 1987	
Matsushita	24.0	Matsushita	24.0	Matsushita	23.0
Sharp	15.5	Victor JVC	15.5	JVC	20.0
Toshiba	15.0	Hitachi	13.0	Sony	20.0
Hitachi	10.5	Toshiba	11.0	Sharp	10.0
Sony	10.5	Sharp	11.0	Toshiba	9.0
Total	75.5	Total	74.5	Total	82.0

CD players 1987		Car stereos 1987	
Sony	30.0	Clarion	18.2
Columbia	12.0	Matsushita	17.3
Pioneer	10.0	Fujitsu	12.0
Matsushita	10.0	Pioneer	11.0
JVC	8.0	Sanyo	6.5
Total	70.0	**Total**	65.0

Source: Keizai Koho Centre, *Japan 1990: An International Comparison,* quoting *Nikkei Sangyo Shimbun,* June 5, 1989, for 1988 data and *Tokyo Keizai* for 1987 data, reproduced in *The Economist Intelligence Unit* (1990), p. 69.

Table 5.7. **US market shares**[1]

Percentages

Producer	Brands	1986	1990
Thomson	GE, RCA	24	22
Philips	Magnavox, Philips, Sylvania	10	12
Zenith	Zenith	16	12
Sony	Sony	6	7
Matsushita	Panasonic, Quasar	8	5

1. Shares are of sales to US dealers.
Source: Television Digest, August 6, 1990, p. 10, reproduced in USITC (1992), p. 2.

Table 5.8. **Production share of major electronic companies in the Republic of Korea, 1988**[1]

Rank and share in percentages

	1st	2nd	3rd	Total
Colour-TV	SS (33.0)	GS (31.7)	DW (17.5)	82.2
Black & white TV	GS (32.2)	SS (23.9)	DW (8.7)	64.8
VCR	SS (46.9)	GS (38.3)	DW (14.8)	100.0

1. SS: Samsung; GS: Gold-Star; DW: Daewoo.
Source: KIET, *The Competitiveness and the Structural Change of Korea's Electronic Industries*, 1990.3, reproduced in Bark (1991) p. 32.

spin-offs which arise from R&D programmes in the telecommunications, computer and semiconductor fields have proven quite important. In addition to being vertically integrated, Japanese companies are able to take advantage domestically of a network of thousands of high-quality components makers, which greatly contribute to their innovative capacity and productivity. Recently, with a view of achieving new synergies, both Sony and Matsushita have acquired a strong position in the "software"[13] side of the business through the acquisition of major US entertainment companies. Philips also owns the British company Polygram, one of the world's largest record firms.

Fierce competition characterises the industry. The once prosperous US industry was largely displaced in the audio segment during the 1950s, and in the TV segment during the 1960s and 1970s by Japanese and later South-East Asian manufacturers. The European industry, which managed to remain sheltered from foreign competition somewhat longer, at least since the 1970s has been subjected to stiff competition as well. It is now experiencing strong pressures both at the low end of the market from South-East Asian manufacturers, which still enjoy substantial labour cost advantages, and at the high end of the market from Japanese companies, thanks to their mastering of product and production technologies.

G. Pricing

Price competition is intense in the consumer electronic market, with retailing prices showing a declining trend (Figure 5.5) in the face of overall consumer prices increases and both the improvements in quality and the incorporation of more advanced features into products (Tables 5.9 and 5.10). This has meant that, in general, much of the productivity gain has been passed on to consumers. In particular for more "mature" products, such as TVs and increasingly VCRs, profit margins tend to be fairly small.

Pricing strategies are quite complex in the high-volume consumer electronics industry. In order to recover high development costs, manufacturers may want to command premium prices at least in the initial period after introducing a new product, but without limiting sales volume which allows for economies of scale, scope and learning. On the other hand, to realise these economies, manufacturers may be

◆ Figure 5.5. **VCR unit factory prices and output**

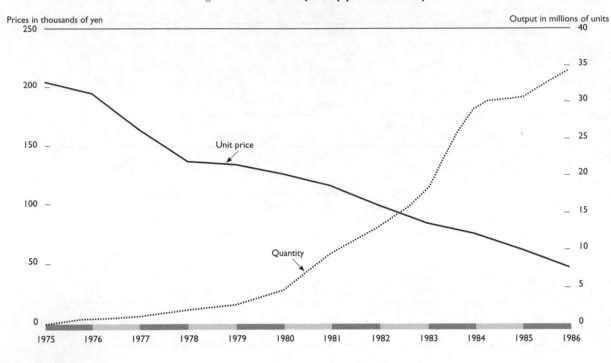

Note: Average unit prices are not necessarily comparable because models improved significantly from year to year.
Source: *Japan Electronics Almanac 1987*, as reproduced in Yoffie (1990).

Table 5.9. **US Consumer and producer price indices, 1986-90**

1986 = 100

	US consumer price index		US producer price index
	All items	TV receivers	
1986	100.0	100.0	100.0
1987	103.6	95.8	99.0
1988	107.9	93.3	95.3
1989	113.1	91.4	95.8
1990	119.3	89.7	94.6

Source: USITC (1992), p. 5.

Table 5.10. **Evolution of retail price indices in France, 1990-91**

1980 = 100

	Annual average 1990	Annual average 1991	% change 1991/1990
Total (index of 296 items)	184.0	189.9	3.2
Bread	186.0	192.7	3.6
Cars	178.3	182.2	2.3
Television sets	92.9	89.8	−3.3
Radios	83.5	80.5	−3.6
Recording and playing apparatus	76.3	72.2	−5.4

Source: INSEE, reproduced in EIU, *Marketing in Europe*, March 1993, p. 72.

even induced to practice "forward pricing", namely pricing at less than marginal cost, in the expectation that such low prices will generate enough volume to eventually cut production costs and generate profits.

Non-price competition also plays an important role. Product differentiation strategies through product innovation, design, quality and service are actively pursued. The Japanese manufacturers in particular are renowned for their extraordinary rate of new product development. Brand loyalty and strategic control of distribution allow a broader range of pricing options, including price discrimination, which may lead to larger profit margins.[14] Besides, through their own network of retailers, some manufacturers have the advantage of maintaining close contact with their customers and of being able to provide pre- and after-sale services.[15] Recently the manufacturers' control over distribution has been somewhat weakened by the growing role of mass merchandisers and buying groups.

Access to distribution channels has proved very important to penetrate foreign markets. Stencil brands (standardised products labelled with the buyer's brand) were largely used in the United States. For instance, the possibility of marketing monochrome TVs through Sears Roebuck proved for several Japanese manufacturers very effective in gaining a large share of the US market.

3.   INTERNATIONAL TRADE

A.   General trends

International trade in consumer electronics has been growing fast, with above-average rates during the 1980s (Table 5.18). Total exports now stand at around US$45 billion.[16] With a share of over 30 per cent in 1992 (Table 5.11), Japan is definitely the prominent source of exports globally, but it is fiercely contested by both European and Far-East Asian manufacturers (Tables 5.12a, 5.12b, 5.13a and 5.13b). Although new digital technology applications may provide a window of opportunity for a come-back, the US industry has been relegated to a secondary role.

An important component of Japan's post-war industrial development policy has been the strategy of export expansion in the consumer electronic industry. The ratio of exports to production in fact steadily grew, reaching 77.5 per cent in 1985. But after this spectacular expansion up to the mid-1980s a declining trend has set in (Table 5.14), which has been more than compensated by the growth of other segments of the electronics industry. The export composition has thus substantially shifted. The consumer segment, which accounted for 39.1 per cent of total electronics exports in 1985, decreased in 1992 to only 20 per cent, while both the industrial equipment and the component segments have shown an increase (quite large for the latter rising from 30.6 in 1985 to 47.4 in 1992). This change may be attributable to macroeconomic factors such as the rise of the yen which, *inter alia*, has induced a substantial migration off-shore of production facilities, as well as to the increasing international competition in the segment, especially from South-East Asian countries.

Import penetration,[17] although rising in recent years, remains at very low levels in Japan as compared to those registered in other OECD countries. From 2.1 per cent in 1985, it reached 5.8 per cent in 1990 and 9.4 per cent in 1992. Some of this increase is the result of shipments from Japanese foreign subsidiaries, which may also partly explain the increase in components trade.

The geographical distribution of Japanese consumer electronics exports is very balanced, with Europe accounting for 33.3 per cent of the total, North America 32.2 per cent and Asia 28.2 per cent (Table 5.15). On the contrary imports, while steadily rising, still remain in absolute terms at a quite low level, and are very concentrated in Asia, which accounts for 84 per cent of total imports (Table 5.16). Also quite concentrated in Asia appears to be the export of components, with a share of 43 per cent. Again, both these trends seem to be explainable, at least in part, by extensive Japanese investments in this area.

Both the United States and the EC have large structural trade deficits. Import penetration is also high, well over 50 per cent and 60 per cent respectively in the EC and the United States. Japan is the first exporter to both markets, followed by South-East Asian countries, such as the Republic of Korea in particular and, recently, also China (Tables 5.12a, 5.12b, 5.13a and 5.13b). As for the United States, Mexico is the second largest supplier, but much of the export flows originate from *maquiladora* plants of US, Japanese and Korean ownership. The countries of the European Free Trade Agreement (EFTA), and in

Tableau 5.11. **Trade in consumer electronics products**

SITC Rev. 2 761, 762, 763

	1982		1992		
	Value in billions of US$	Share in percentage	Value in billions of US$	Share in percentage	
Major importers					Principal origin of imports (1992)
United States	4.90	26.71	13.21	27.48	Japan (32.61%); Mexico (17.79%); Malaysia (13.37%); Korea (10.40%).
Hong Kong	0.40	2.20	5.54	11.52	China (49.84%); Japan (36.06%); Singapore (8.30%); Chinese Taipei (1.96%).
Germany	1.61	8.78	5.08	10.57	Japan (24.87%); United Kingdom (9.04%); France (8.22%); China (7.93%).
France	1.04	5.66	2.55	5.30	Japan (18.69%); Germany (11.87%); United Kingdom (11.12%); China (8.67%).
United Kingdom	1.82	9.90	2.46	5.12	Japan (21.14%); Germany (11.40%); France (8.19%); Hong Kong (7.90%).
Singapore	0.54	2.94	2.40	5.00	Malaysia (51.90%); Japan (36.34%); Thailand (2.46%); Hong Kong (2.44%).
Italy	0.70	3.81	2.09	4.36	Germany (16.66%); Netherlands (12.06%); Belgium-Luxembourg (11.62%); United Kingdom (11.55%).
Netherlands	0.58	3.17	1.60	3.32	Japan (24.16%); Belgium-Luxembourg (14.58%); Germany (13.63%); United Kingdom (9.31%).
Spain	0.35	1.93	1.50	3.12	Japan (20.62%); United Kingdom (10.65%); Germany (10.52%); France (7.46%).
Canada	0.61	3.34	1.42	2.95	United States (31.03%); Japan (26%); Korea (10.14%); Malaysia (8.78%).
Rest of world	5.79	31.56	10.23	21.27	
World	18.36	100.00	48.08	100.00	
Major exporters					Principal destination of exports (1992)
Japan	9.79	58.02	13.17	32.99	United States (30.55%); Hong Kong (11.36%); China (7.60%); Germany (6.89%).
Singapore	0.87	5.14	4.42	11.08	United States (22.54%); Germany (9.75%); Hong Kong (8.13%); United Kingdom (4.12%).
Korea	0.82	4.87	4.20	10.52	United States (30.74%); Argentina (5.56%); Japan (5.48%); Panama (5.03%).
Germany	1.32	7.84	2.56	6.42	France (17.73%); Italy (13.98%); United Kingdom (10.94%); Spain (8.67%).
China	n.a.[1]	n.a.[1]	2.53	6.34	Hong Kong (81.24%); United States (3.86%); Japan (2.94%); Germany (1.66%).
United Kingdom	0.26	1.51	1.69	4.23	Germany (25.45%); France (15.49%); Italy (11.57%); Spain (9.81%).
France	0.15	0.90	1.53	3.85	Germany (29.68%); United Kingdom (13.44%); Italy (12.04%); Netherlands (10.10%).
United States	0.60	3.55	1.49	3.73	Canada (29.90%); Mexico (23.10%); Chinese Taipei (8.06%); Japan (4.18%).
Austria	0.43	2.56	0.96	2.41	Germany (31.63%); Italy (14.94%); France (13.17%); Netherlands (8.08%).
Belgium-Luxembourg	0.40	2.35	0.90	2.25	France (23.40%); Netherlands (19.91%); Germany (14.47%); Italy (10.67%).
Rest of world	2.24	13.25	6.46	16.19	
World	16.87	100.00	39.91	100.00	

1.   China is included in the rest of world.
Source: UN Comtrade database.

Table 5.12a. **EC structure of imports and exports, 1991 – Consumer electronics**

ECU million

	Exports from EC	Imports to EC	Ratio exports/imports (%)
Japan	40	5 960	0.7
Republic of Korea	16	1 046	1.5
China	2	870	0.2
Austria	319	867	36.8
Singapore	48	853	5.6
Malaysia	9	707	1.3
United States	287	690	41.6
Chinese Taipei	27	422	6.4
Hong Kong	38	307	12.4
Thailand	7	251	2.8
Turkey	40	202	19.8
Brazil	13	98	13.3
Total extra-EC	**2 200**	**12 743**	**17.3**
of which: from EFTA	995	1 111	89.6

Source: European Commission, *Panorama of EC Industry,* 1993.

Table 5.12b. **EC structure of imports and exports, 1992 – Consumer electronics**

Million ECUs

	Exports from EC	Imports to EC	Ratio exports/imports (%)
Japan	54	5 255	1.0
China	5	955	0.5
Republic of Korea	12	800	1.5
Austria	317	761	41.7
Singapore	67	745	9.0
United States	282	735	38.4
Malaysia	14	727	1.9
Chinese Taipei	32	354	9.0
Thailand	7	338	2.1
Hong Kong	50	227	22.0
Turkey	38	186	20.4
Indonesia	3	88	3.4
Brazil	15	72	20.8
Total extra-EC	**2 167**	**11 643**	**18.6**
of which: from EFTA	960	941	102.0

Source: European Commission, *Panorama of EU Industry,* 1994.

particular Austria, represent an important trade partner for the EC. As is the case in Asia, international trade has grown more concentrated regionally also within Europe and North America (Tables 5.17a and b). Foreign investments seem to have played an important role by substituting inter-regional trade, mainly from Asia towards Europe and North America, with regional production and trade.

The consumer electronics industry has proved very important also for the economic development of developing countries, which have substantially increased their share in world consumer electronics trade (Table 5.18). The DAEs have been particularly successful. They have recorded very positive trade performances thanks, above all, to their competitiveness as low-cost manufacturers of standard products, but also thanks to the economic policies pursued by their governments. Both these factors have contributed to induce numerous export-oriented investments from OECD countries.

Table 5.13a. **US trade patterns – Household audio and video equipment, 1991**

SIC 3651, millions US$, percentages

	Exports			Imports	
	Value	Share		Value	Share
Canada and Mexico	1 163	51.0	Canada and Mexico	1 633	12.4
European Community	351	15.4	European Community	170	1.3
Japan	159	7.0	Japan	6 161	46.8
East Asian NICs	267	11.7	East Asian NICs	5 051	38.4
South America	153	6.7	South America	66	0.5
Other	186	8.2	Other	73	0.6
World total	**2 279**	**100.0**	**World total**	**13 154**	**100.0**

Top five countries

	Value	Share		Value	Share
Mexico	589	25.9	Japan	6 161	46.8
Canada	574	25.2	Mexico	1 558	11.8
Japan	159	7.0	Republic of Korea	1 265	9.6
Chinese Taipei	111	4.9	Malaysia	1 118	8.5
Germany	99	4.3	China	904	6.9

Source: US Department of Commerce (1993), p. 36-13.

5.13b. **US trade patterns – Household audio and video equipment, 1992**

SIC 3651, millions US$, percentages

	Exports			Imports	
	Value	Share		Value	Share
Canada and Mexico	1 255	51.7	Canada and Mexico	1 816	12.7
European Community	353	14.5	European Community	224	1.6
Japan	146	6.0	Japan	5 685	39.9
East Asian NICs	301	12.4	East Asian NICs	6 350	44.6
South America	180	7.4	South America	89	0.6
Other	195	8.0	Other	80	0.6
World total	**2 430**	**100.0**	**World total**	**14 243**	**100.0**

Top five countries

	Value	Share		Value	Share
Mexico	700	28.8	Japan	5 685	39.9
Canada	556	22.9	Mexico	1 743	12.2
Chinese Taipei	152	6.3	Malaysia	1 684	11.8
Japan	146	6.0	Republic of Korea	1 439	10.1
Germany	86	3.6	China	1 114	7.8

Source: US Department of Commerce (1994), p. 36-17.

B. Trade in intermediate products and international sourcing

Components are essential for the production of consumer electronics items. But since electronic components find their way into consumer products as well as industrial electronic equipment, automobiles and numerous other products ranging from photographic to medical equipment, it is not easy to estimate where the component's industry output is used. Similarly it is hard to evaluate the international

Table 5.14. **Production and trade of the Japanese electronics industry, 1960-92**

Billion yen

	1960	1970	1980	1985	1990	1992
Consumer electronics						
Production	241.3	1 473.3	2 932.1	4 911.6	4 436.2	3 758.4
Exports	57.2	587.0	2 047.1	3 805.5	2 617.8	2 257.5
Imports	0.2	4.9	38.2	23.7	113.0	156.0
Industrial electronics						
Production	107.5	1 030.1	3 396.0	7 614.1	11 341.6	10 531.0
Exports	3.2	137.3	1 049.1	2 918.9	3 442.7	3 691.6
Imports	6.1	121.5	297.5	397.6	692.4	633.3
Electronic components						
Production	142.5	893.3	2 677.1	6 027.0	8 373.3	7 985.3
Exports	13.1	138.2	1 461.8	2 970.8	4 933.3	5 360.6
Imports	2.9	68.9	367.5	613.3	1 195.0	1 256.2
Total electronics						
Production	491.3	3 396.7	9 005.3	18 552.7	24 151.0	22 274.6
Exports	73.5	862.5	4 558.0	9 695.1	10 993.9	11 309.8
Imports	9.2	195.3	703.1	1 034.6	2 000.5	2 045.6

Source: Electronics Industries Association of Japan (1992) and Urata (1991).

Table 5.15. **Japan's electronics exports by destination**

1992, million yen, percentage change 1992/91

	Consumer electronics equipment	Colour televisions	Video tape recorders	Industrial electronics equipment	Electronics components and devices	Electronics Industry total
Asia	636 485	190 105	48 729	702 215	2 304 413	3 643 113
(percentage change 1992/91)	−3.2	13.8	−17.3	3.4	11.2	6.8
Europe	752 916	12 213	285 138	1 157 477	1 118 961	3 029 354
	−24.0	−60.6	−20.0	0.6	−3.5	−8.2
EC	658 061	5 932	263 605	1 064 504	1 043 953	2 766 520
	−20.2	−51.5	−19.2	2.0	−2.7	−5.9
North America	727 756	5 020	194 503	1 647 245	1 721 581	4 096 581
	−17.9	16.2	−36.7	10.1	6.0	2.3
United States	672 759	4 826	178 384	1 582 129	1 675 391	3 930 279
	−17.6	−14.5	−36.9	11.5	5.4	2.8
Latin America	65 570	4 693	10 633	78 782	147 262	291 614
	−8.2	37.5	−25.5	17.4	6.0	5.1
Africa	18 999	3 032	4 622	31 411	12 079	62 489
	−35.2	−40.1	−30.7	−2.5	−21.2	−18.7
Oceania	55 787	5 093	12 069	74 501	56 366	186 654
	−8.8	21.3	−24.7	−10.3	1.5	−6.6
Total	**2 257 514**	**220 156**	**555 694**	**3 691 630**	**5 360 663**	**11 309 806**
	−16.3	**1.6**	**−26.9**	**5.2**	**5.8**	**0.3**

Source: Electronics Industries Association of Japan (1993).

trade flows of electronic components related to the production of consumer electronics items. One estimate assigns to consumer electronics around 18 per cent of total component demand.[18] Total world exports of parts and components mainly incorporated in audio and video products,[19] which anyway do not include all those used, accounted in 1992 for over US$23 billion. Japan represented 20 per cent of the total (Tables 5.17C and D).

The availability of quality components is extremely important for the competitiveness of consumer electronics producers. Large manufacturers, in particular Japanese, are typically vertically integrated in the

Table 5.16. **Japan's electronics imports by origin**

1992, million yen, percentage change 1992/91

	Consumer electronics equipment	Industrial electronics equipment	Electronics components and devices	Electronics industry total
Asia	130 838	124 045	559 459	814 342
(percentage change 1992/91)	12.6	−3.8	4.6	4.4
Europe	7 603	89 599	83 738	180 939
	7.8	17.9	2.3	9.7
EC	5 480	79 847	77 755	163 082
	4.5	21.5	4.2	12.0
North America	17 546	395 551	597 756	1 010 853
	42.1	−12.6	−8.3	−9.5
United States	16 624	390 413	581 577	988 613
	46.6	−12.9	−8.7	−9.8
Latin America	37	12 449	12 532	25 019
	−12.4	−36.2	−24.6	−30.8
Africa	1	1	13	15
	−98.3	−99.4	50.7	−90.7
Oceania	15	11 688	2 731	14 434
	−50.1	14.7	147.0	27.4
Total	**156 041**	**633 332**	**1 256 228**	**2 045 601**
	15.0	**−7.9**	**−2.3**	**−3.0**

Source: See Table 5.15.

design and production of various components, thus enjoying substantial technological spin-offs. Their vertical integration is considered a quite important competitive advantage. On the contrary the excessive reliance of both US and European manufacturers on external sourcing has been sometimes blamed as a source of "hollowing out". Furthermore, dominating the supply of a key component gives an important leverage in downstream product markets. These considerations have provided some of the rationales for the introduction of *de jure* or *de facto* local content rules.

An extensive network of procurement relations links the major consumer electronics companies. Some of them have established a series of component production facilities and/or international purchasing offices, above all in the Asia-Pacific region. Again Japanese companies have spearheaded the process. For example, through co-operating firms, a Japanese company can procure resistors made in Korea, condensers made in Chinese Taipei, transformers made in Hong Kong, magnetic heads and integrated circuits made in Malaysia and TV cathode-ray tubes made in Singapore, and assemble them in Singapore or Malaysia for markets in Asia, the United States or Europe.[20] These relations are by no means only restricted to the Asia-Pacific region. For instance Korea's Goldstar TV plant in Italy uses picture tubes made by Finland's Nokia.

A particularly intense form of collaboration between companies, which gives rise to large flows of trade in components, is represented by the "Original Equipment Manufacturer" (OEM) arrangements. OEMs build products to their customers' specifications for sale under their customers' label. OEMs located in developing countries usually import a large share of the components. For instance over 99 per cent of the components used in Mexico's electronics *maquiladoras* are imported.[21] OEMs in turn sometimes subcontract part of the manufacturing process. As a result, the origin of consumer electronics products becomes increasingly more difficult to ascertain.

Subcontracting, also known as contract electronics manufacturing (CEM), has grown very intensely and is projected as a US$22 billion global business by the mid-1990s. It is quite important also for the consumer segment. Industry leaders, such as Sony and Matsushita, are making use of CEM as part of their global strategies to foster international competitiveness. CEM is considered to provide fast response time, flexibility, quality and cost-effectiveness. CEM clearly entails flows of both components and intermediate products.

Table 5.17a. **Intra-regional trade – Consumer electronics, 1982**
SITC Rev. 2 761, 762, 763
In billion US dollars

Reporting country	United States, Canada, Mexico[1]		East Asia[2]		EC + EFTA		Rest of world		World	
	Imports	Exports	Imports	Exports	Imports	Exports	Imports	Exports	Imports	Exports
United States, Canada, Mexico[1]	0.51	0.44	5.03	0.05	0.08	0.12	0.08	0.15	5.71	0.77
East Asia[2]	0.03	4.29	1.33	1.21	0.05	4.18	0.01	2.67	1.43	12.36
EC + EFTA	0.15	0.09	4.60	0.04	2.86	2.81	0.06	0.50	7.68	3.44
Rest of world	0.22	0.08	2.74	0.01	0.33	0.04	0.26	0.18	3.54	0.31
World	**0.92**	**4.90**	**13.71**	**1.31**	**3.33**	**7.16**	**0.41**	**3.50**	**18.36**	**16.87**

In percentage of the world total

Reporting country	United States, Canada, Mexico[1]		East Asia[2]		EC + EFTA		Rest of world		World	
	Imports	Exports	Imports	Exports	Imports	Exports	Imports	Exports	Imports	Exports
United States, Canada, Mexico[1]	2.79	2.64	27.41	0.30	0.46	0.71	0.44	0.91	31.10	4.55
East Asia[2]	0.19	25.44	7.27	7.19	0.28	24.80	0.04	15.80	7.78	73.22
EC + EFTA	0.83	0.54	25.06	0.25	15.60	16.65	0.35	2.96	41.84	20.41
Rest of world	1.18	0.45	14.94	0.04	1.77	0.25	1.40	1.08	19.29	1.82
World	**4.98**	**29.06**	**74.67**	**7.78**	**18.11**	**42.41**	**2.23**	**20.75**	**100.00**	**100.00**

In percentage of the region total

Reporting country	United States, Canada, Mexico[1]		East Asia[2]		EC + EFTA		Rest of world		World	
	Imports	Exports	Imports	Exports	Imports	Exports	Imports	Exports	Imports	Exports
United States, Canada, Mexico[1]	8.97	57.89	88.12	6.55	1.48	15.62	1.43	19.94	100.00	100.00
East Asia[2]	2.42	34.74	93.44	9.81	3.63	33.87	0.50	21.58	100.00	100.00
EC + EFTA	1.97	2.67	59.90	1.23	37.28	81.59	0.84	14.51	100.00	100.00
Rest of world	6.12	24.63	77.45	2.18	9.20	13.73	7.24	59.45	100.00	100.00
World	**4.98**	**29.06**	**74.67**	**7.78**	**18.11**	**42.41**	**2.23**	**20.75**	**100.00**	**100.00**

1. Aside from the usual disrepancies between import and export flows between countries, Mexico does not record in its national statistics trade which takes place from its export processing zones (Maquilladoras).
2. East Asia includes the ASEAN countries (Brunei, Indonesia, Malaysia, Philippines, Singapore and Thailand), China, Hong Kong, Japan, Republic of Korea and Chinese Taipei.
Source: UN Comtrade database.

Table 5.17b. **Intra-regional trade – Consumer electronics, 1992**

SITC Rev. 2 761, 762, 763
In billion US dollars

Reporting country	United States, Canada, Mexico[1]		East Asia[2]		EC + EFTA		Rest of world		World	
	Imports	Exports	Imports	Exports	Imports	Exports	Imports	Exports	Imports	Exports
United States, Canada, Mexico[1]	3.23	0.86	11.79	0.28	0.16	0.18	0.29	0.27	15.48	1.58
East Asia[2]	0.33	8.51	10.03	7.95	0.12	6.51	0.03	4.19	10.51	27.16
EC + EFTA	0.16	0.18	9.23	0.12	9.32	9.36	0.45	0.74	19.17	10.40
Rest of world	0.34	0.29	2.04	0.01	0.26	0.33	0.40	0.15	3.04	0.78
World	**4.07**	**9.84**	**33.10**	**8.36**	**9.86**	**16.37**	**1.17**	**5.36**	**48.19**	**39.92**

In percentage of the world total

Reporting country	United States, Canada, Mexico[1]		East Asia[2]		EC + EFTA		Rest of world		World	
	Imports	Exports	Imports	Exports	Imports	Exports	Imports	Exports	Imports	Exports
United States, Canada, Mexico[1]	6.71	2.15	24.47	0.69	0.33	0.44	0.60	0.68	32.11	3.97
East Asia[2]	0.69	21.32	20.82	19.91	0.25	16.30	0.06	10.50	21.82	68.03
EC + EFTA	0.34	0.44	19.16	0.31	19.34	23.44	0.93	1.86	39.77	26.05
Rest of world	0.70	0.73	4.24	0.03	0.54	0.81	0.83	0.37	6.30	1.95
World	**8.44**	**24.64**	**68.69**	**20.94**	**20.45**	**41.00**	**2.42**	**13.42**	**100.00**	**100.00**

In percentage of the region total

Reporting country	United States, Canada, Mexico[1]		East Asia[2]		EC + EFTA		Rest of world		World	
	Imports	Exports	Imports	Exports	Imports	Exports	Imports	Exports	Imports	Exports
United States, Canada, Mexico[1]	20.88	54.17	76.21	17.46	1.03	11.14	1.88	17.22	100.00	100.00
East Asia[2]	3.17	31.34	95.43	29.27	1.14	23.96	0.26	15.43	100.00	100.00
EC + EFTA	0.86	1.70	48.17	1.18	48.62	89.97	2.35	7.15	100.00	100.00
Rest of world	11.11	37.48	67.28	1.72	8.49	41.66	13.12	19.14	100.00	100.00
World	**8.44**	**24.64**	**68.69**	**20.94**	**20.45**	**41.00**	**2.42**	**13.42**	**100.00**	**100.00**

1. Aside from the usual disrepancies between import and export flows between countries, Mexico does not record in its national statistics trade which takes place from its export processing zones (Maquilladoras).
2. East Asia includes the ASEAN countries (Brunei, Indonesia, Malaysia, Philippines, Singapore and Thailand), China, Hong Kong, Japan, Republic of Korea and Chinese Taipei.
Source: UN Comtrade database.

Table 5.17c. **Intra-regional trade – Intermediate consumer electronics products[1], 1982**

SITC Rev. 2 76492, 76493, 76499, 7761

In billion US dollars

Reporting country	United States, Canada, Mexico[1]		East Asia[2]		EC + EFTA		Rest of world		World	
	Imports	Exports	Imports	Exports	Imports	Exports	Imports	Exports	Imports	Exports
United States, Canada, Mexico[1]	1.11	0.50	1.71	0.25	0.16	0.38	0.17	0.97	3.15	2.10
East Asia[3]	0.22	0.70	0.76	0.92	0.09	0.48	0.00	0.41	1.07	2.51
EC + EFTA	0.32	0.11	0.56	0.14	1.76	1.97	0.17	0.84	2.81	3.06
Rest of world	0.08	0.00	0.32	0.01	0.13	0.01	0.47	0.06	1.00	0.08
World	**1.74**	**1.30**	**3.35**	**1.32**	**2.13**	**2.85**	**0.81**	**2.28**	**8.03**	**7.75**

In percentage of the world total

Reporting country	United States, Canada, Mexico[1]		East Asia[2]		EC + EFTA		Rest of world		World	
	Imports	Exports	Imports	Exports	Imports	Exports	Imports	Exports	Imports	Exports
United States, Canada, Mexico[1]	13.87	6.40	21.31	3.22	1.96	4.90	2.12	12.58	39.25	27.09
East Asia[3]	2.74	8.97	9.45	11.83	1.07	6.23	0.04	5.35	13.29	32.38
EC + EFTA	4.02	1.40	6.99	1.83	21.88	25.48	2.06	10.80	34.95	39.50
Rest of world	1.02	0.06	4.00	0.12	1.65	0.14	5.83	0.71	12.50	1.03
World	**21.64**	**16.28**	**41.75**	**17.01**	**26.56**	**36.74**	**10.05**	**29.43**	**100.00**	**100.00**

In percentage of the region total

Reporting country	United States, Canada, Mexico[1]		East Asia[2]		EC + EFTA		Rest of world		World	
	Imports	Exports	Imports	Exports	Imports	Exports	Imports	Exports	Imports	Exports
United States, Canada, Mexico[1]	35.33	23.62	54.29	11.88	4.99	18.08	5.39	46.42	100.00	100.00
East Asia[3]	20.58	27.70	71.11	36.55	8.04	19.23	0.27	16.52	100.00	100.00
EC + EFTA	11.50	3.53	20.00	4.63	62.60	64.50	5.90	27.34	100.00	100.00
Rest of world	8.12	5.38	32.00	11.93	13.22	13.75	46.66	68.94	100.00	100.00
World	**21.64**	**16.82**	**41.75**	**17.01**	**26.56**	**36.74**	**10.05**	**29.43**	**100.00**	**100.00**

1. Some of these items are also used in various other end products.
2. Aside from the usual disrepancies between import and export flows between countries, Mexico does not record in its national statistics trade which takes place from its export processing zones (Maquilladoras).
3. East Asia includes the ASEAN countries (Brunei, Indonesia, Malaysia, Philippines, Singapore and Thailand), China, Hong Kong, Japan, Republic of Korea and Chinese Taipei.
Source: UN Comtrade database.

Table 5.17d. **Intra-regional trade – Intermediate consumer electronics products[1], 1992**
SITC Rev. 2 76492, 76493, 76499, 7761
In billion US dollars

Reporting country	United States, Canada, Mexico[1]		East Asia[2]		EC + EFTA		Rest of world		World	
	Imports	Exports	Imports	Exports	Imports	Exports	Imports	Exports	Imports	Exports
United States, Canada, Mexico[2]	1.40	1.60	1.87	0.75	0.37	0.53	0.08	0.77	3.72	3.65
East Asia[3]	0.81	2.37	9.57	7.43	0.39	1.70	0.07	0.88	10.82	12.38
EC + EFTA	0.69	0.39	2.30	0.59	4.41	4.55	0.38	1.33	7.79	6.85
Rest of world	0.28	0.08	1.01	0.03	0.51	0.06	0.07	0.10	1.88	0.28
World	**3.18**	**4.44**	**14.75**	**8.80**	**5.68**	**6.84**	**0.61**	**3.09**	**24.21**	**23.17**

In percentage of the world total

Reporting country	United States, Canada, Mexico[1]		East Asia[2]		EC + EFTA		Rest of world		World	
	Imports	Exports	Imports	Exports	Imports	Exports	Imports	Exports	Imports	Exports
United States, Canada, Mexico[1]	5.77	6.90	7.71	3.23	1.55	2.31	0.34	3.33	15.37	15.77
East Asia[3]	3.33	10.25	39.52	32.07	1.59	7.32	0.27	3.79	44.71	53.43
EC + EFTA	2.86	1.67	9.51	2.53	18.22	19.62	1.59	5.76	32.17	29.58
Rest of world	1.16	0.36	4.18	0.14	2.11	0.27	0.30	0.45	7.75	1.22
World	**13.12**	**19.18**	**60.91**	**37.98**	**23.47**	**29.51**	**2.50**	**13.33**	**100.00**	**100.00**

In percentage of the region total

Reporting country	United States, Canada, Mexico[1]		East Asia[2]		EC + EFTA		Rest of world		World	
	Imports	Exports	Imports	Exports	Imports	Exports	Imports	Exports	Imports	Exports
United States, Canada, Mexico[1]	37.55	43.77	50.16	20.46	10.07	14.63	2.22	21.14	100.00	100.00
East Asia[3]	7.45	19.18	88.38	60.03	3.56	13.70	0.61	7.08	100.00	100.00
EC + EFTA	8.88	5.64	29.55	8.57	56.63	66.33	4.94	19.46	100.00	100.00
Rest of world	14.93	29.46	53.90	11.71	27.26	21.88	3.92	36.95	100.00	100.00
World	**13.12**	**19.18**	**60.91**	**37.98**	**23.47**	**29.51**	**2.50**	**13.33**	**100.00**	**100.00**

1. Some of these items are also used in various other end products.
2. Aside from the usual disrepancies between import and export flows between countries, Mexico does not record in its national statistics trade which takes place from its export processing zones (Maquilladoras).
3. East Asia includes the ASEAN countries (Brunei, Indonesia, Malaysia, Philippines, Singapore and Thailand), China, Hong Kong, Japan, Republic of Korea and Chinese Taipei.

Source: UN Comtrade database.

Table 5.18. **Export structure**[1]

SITC Rev. 2, 3-digit group level, ranked by average 1989-90 values

	1980-81			1989-90			Growth rates (% 1980-90)	
	Value (thousand US$)	% of the grouping total	% of world	Value (thousand US$)	% of the grouping total	% of world	Value	Difference from world
World								
761 Television receivers	5 456 338	0.27	100.00	14 460 571	0.45	100.00	11.8	0
762 Radio broadcast receivers	5 975 891	0.30	100.00	10 828 156	0.34	100.00	6.6	0
763 Sound recorders, phonograph	6 765 895	0.34	100.00	15 155 896	0.48	100.00	10.5	0
Developed market economy countries								
761 Television receivers	4 541 235	0.36	83.22	8 749 838	0.38	60.48	8.1	3.7
762 Radio broadcast receivers	4 108 214	0.33	68.75	4 344 266	0.19	40.06	1.4	5.1
763 Sound recorders, phonograph	6 115 147	0.49	90.17	11 290 353	0.50	74.49	8.6	1.9
Developing countries								
761 Television receivers	902 201	0.16	16.54	4 972 158	0.77	34.67	21.1	9.3
762 Radio broadcast receivers	1 843 557	0.33	30.85	5 134 540	0.80	47.52	10.4	3.8
763 Sound recorders, phonograph	576 991	0.10	8.71	3 721 990	0.58	24.56	21.0	10.5

1. Total growth rate 1980-90: 5.2%
Source: UNCTAD (1993), Handbook of International Trade and Development Statistics 1992, New York.

C. Intra-firm trade

Intra-firm trade (IFT) is defined as the international exchange of goods and services within a multinational enterprise (MNE).[22] IFT accounts for a little over a third of total US merchandise trade.[23] It is particularly difficult to calculate the share of IFT in US trade in consumer electronics due to classification problems.

In the category which includes radio, TV and communication (RTC) equipment,[24] IFT accounts for less than 10 per cent of total US trade. It is impossible, unfortunately, to separate trade in communication equipment, such as transmitters, receivers and antennas, where IFT is probably less important, from trade in consumer electronics, where IFT could be higher.

In the category which includes electrical household appliances,[25] data are available for US firms abroad, but not for foreign firms in the United States. It is possible to estimate, however, that at least a third – and perhaps as much as half – of US trade in appliances is IFT.

IFT in either sector does not appear to have increased in the 1980s. These figures exclude wholesale and related activities, in which the United States has seen a large increase in inward foreign direct investment in the 1980s.[26]

Most of the intra-firm trade in the RTC sector consists of US affiliates of Japanese and European firms importing into the United States. Intra-firm trade by US affiliates of foreign firms is twice as large as IFT by US-based multinationals in the sector. US-based multinationals in the RTC sector export as much as they import intra-firm. While their intra-firm exports are highly concentrated – 85 per cent go to Canada, with most of the rest going to Latin America – their intra-firm imports are more diversified – coming from East Asia, Latin America, Canada and Europe.

US-based multinationals in the household appliance sector export more than they import intra-firm. Both intra-firm exports and imports are highly diversified geographically.

D. Intra-industry trade

Intra-industry trade (IIT) is defined as the exchange by two countries of goods and services within the same product category. IIT is generally a function of product differentiation and may or may not be intra-firm trade. IIT indices provide another tool for analysing trade patterns as they may show the extent of international linkages for a given industry.[27]

IIT indices for US trade in consumer electronics[28] are considerably below the average for all manufacturing, due to the large US trade deficit in that sector. US IIT indices for trade in consumer electronics decreased from about 30 per cent in the early 1980s, to about 20 per cent in the early 1990s.

Bilateral IIT indices are highest with Europe, but there is relatively little transatlantic trade. US bilateral indices with Mexico and Canada are close to the average for the sector. IIT indices with Canada decreased sharply in the 1980s, as US imports went down, increasing the US trade surplus with Canada in that sector. IIT indices with Mexico were relatively stable in the 1980s. The United States went from a net exporter to a net importer from Mexico, as US imports increased substantially. Bilateral indices with Japan, Korea and other East Asian countries are extremely small, due to the large US sectoral trade deficit with those countries.

IIT indices for Japanese trade in consumer electronics have increased in the 1980s, but are still below the Japanese average for all manufacturing – which, in turn, is quite low for OECD standards. Japanese sectoral IIT went from less than 5 per cent in the early 1980s to more than 10 per cent in the early 1990s. This was mostly due to the increase in Japanese imports from the rest of East Asia, which reduced the overall Japanese trade surplus in that sector.

Japan's bilateral IIT indices are extremely low with North America and Europe, due to the large Japanese trade surplus. They are higher with the Republic of Korea – between 50 and 60 per cent – where

Japan has a sectoral trade deficit and where trade is more balanced. Bilateral IIT indices for consumer electronic trade with other DAEs – excluding Korea – have seen the largest increase in the 1980s, going from less than 15 to more than 30 per cent. This was due to the increase in Japanese imports from those countries, which considerably reduced the Japanese trade surplus with that region.

IIT indices for European trade are large – between 60 and 70 per cent – but somewhat below the average for all manufacturing sector. Although intra-European trade has high IIT indices, the overall European trade deficit in the sector – mostly with East Asia – reduces the indices.

4. FOREIGN DIRECT INVESTMENT AND INTER-FIRM NETWORKS

A. Foreign direct investment

Foreign direct investment (FDI) has been actively pursued by all the major players in the consumer electronics industry. Unfortunately no aggregate FDI data on the industry seem to be available, hence the following review focuses on firm experiences. Philips, a company over one hundred years old, has probably the longest history as a foreign investor in the sector. Already in the 1930s, it was present in the United States and now the company manufactures in around 60 countries. Philips has also various participations in Japan, including the subsidiary Marantz Japan Inc. Confronted with stiff competition initially mainly from Japan, many of the large European manufacturers have started to invest in the low-wage countries of South-East Asia, but also in Mexico and very recently in Eastern Europe. For instance, Thomson has now 39 industrial operations in 17 countries in addition to seven research centres.

More recently the innovation in production methods, through the use of labour-cost-reducing and labour-quality-augmenting automation equipment, are even inducing some manufacturers to relocate the production of low end-products in developed countries. Nokia, for instance, in order to cut costs and improve quality has recently shifted production of its small-screen TVs from Singapore to Germany.

The Japanese companies began investing abroad much later than Philips. In general, they have done so also less intensively. The industry leader, Matsushita, albeit admittedly a quite "conservative firm", has been particularly slow to shift production abroad, at least until the mid-1980s. Still in 1985, its overseas production accounted for only about 12 per cent of its world-wide sales and has now reached 18 per cent.

After a gradual increase in the 1960s, the 1970s saw an expansion of Japanese investments, above all in the neighbouring Asian countries, in order to take advantage of low-wage labour; and still today, more than half of the overseas production facilities of Japanese companies are in Asia (Table 5.19). The successful export performance in the United States and Europe, which elicited protectionist responses in both markets, is at the basis of a second vintage of "defensive" investments in Europe and the United States during the 1970s and afterward.

In the EC, as a result, by 1987, there were 32 Japanese plants making or assembling colour TVs and other items, 18 of which were in the United Kingdom. After being the target of various trade-policy measures, Korea's "big three"– Goldstar, Samsung and Daewoo – followed suit during the second half of the 1980s. In 1991, there were 68 Japanese and Korean plants in the EC, as opposed to 108 European, employing around one-sixth of the total workforce. The United Kingdom remains the preferred location, followed by Germany, Spain and France.

A quite similar pattern can be detected in the United States. In 1972, Sony was the first Japanese company to manufacture TVs in the United States. It was subsequently followed by all other major companies. Then, starting with Goldstar in 1981, the three Korean companies set up shop in the United States. Since 1976, the Chinese Taipei electronics company Tatung has also been manufacturing colour TVs in the United States. Practically all the FDI in Mexico is related to the US market, so that all the major TV manufacturers that sell in the United States have Mexican assembly facilities. Philips has based half of its North American production in Mexico.

It may be argued that most of the Japanese "defensive" investments in Europe and the United States were probably regarded as second-best solutions, mainly motivated by market-access considerations; but after the initial start-up difficulties were overcome, production cost differentials between overseas and Japanese operations seem to have levelled off.[29] It is noteworthy that one Japanese-owned US manufac-

Table 5.19. **Number of overseas electronics production facilities of Japanese corporations, 1992**

	Consumer electronics equipment	Industrial electronics equipment	Electronics components and devices	Total
United Kingdom	14	18	23	50
Germany	11	7	20	37
France	11	10	4	24
Spain	5	1	3	8
Ireland	–	2	5	6
Belgium	1	–	2	3
Netherlands	–	2	2	4
Italy	3	2	1	6
Others	1	–	2	4
Europe	46	42	62	142
United States	34	45	78	141
Canada	3	–	5	7
Puerto Rico	1	–	2	2
North America	38	45	85	150
Chinese Taipei	21	12	67	93
Malaysia	37	13	83	121
Republic of Korea	7	9	52	62
Singapore	20	9	47	71
Thailand	21	11	36	63
China	8	13	26	42
Hong Kong	3	4	16	22
Philippines	5	3	9	16
India	4	1	1	6
Indonesia	8	1	6	14
Others	1	–	3	4
Asia	135	76	348	514
Brazil	7	6	13	24
Mexico	7	3	15	23
Others	10	1	2	11
Latin America	24	10	30	58
Oceania	3	3	1	6
Africa	4	1	–	4
Total	**250**	**177**	**524**	**874**

Source: See Table 5.15.

turer has recently begun exporting large-screen TVs to Japan, incorporating picture tubes also made in the United States.

Japanese companies have recently been confronted with various developments, including the appreciation of the yen in the mid-1980s, increased competition of DAEs manufacturers and the near saturation of some markets. These factors, together with the rapid innovation in both product and production methods, have contributed to the emergence of a more coherent strategy of "global specialisation" based on an intra-firm division of labour along two main lines.

First, the production process may be divided into sub-processes to be located where they can be carried out most efficiently. For instance, the yen appreciation led less productive, small to medium-sized part and component manufacturers to shift production to other Asian countries. Second, geographical specialisation by product lines is pursued. "Commoditised" items including radios, tape recorders and small and medium TVs,[30] which require a standardised technology and a large amount of labour, are produced in Asian developing countries, such as Malaysia, Thailand and recently China, as well as Mexico, mainly to serve the US market,[31] while more high-technology and high-value-added products, such as some VCRs and large-screen TVs, are manufactured either in Japan or in other developed countries. In this respect a strategic choice is made whether to retain the production in Japan. For CD players,[32] laser discs or camcorders, which have not quite reached the peak of the product cycle, there is still some reluctance to transfer production overseas. Thus this global specialisation strategy has also the beneficial effect of allowing Japanese firms to concentrate domestically on higher-value-added, more-knowledge-intensive and higher-income upscale products. A similar pattern applies in general to the manufacture of components.

Transportation costs and physical qualities of products are also an element in the firms' production location decisions. TV's fragility in fact increases with the monitor size as do transportation costs. On the contrary, these factors are much less important for audio products or for the majority of components such as printed circuit boards, which are cheap and easy to transport.

Thus it appears clear that in the consumer electronics industry exchange rates, trade policies, production and product characteristics, and technological developments have a momentous impact on companies' strategies and, specifically, on the ratio of exports to overseas production as well as of imports – from foreign affiliates – to domestic production.

Some new developments in the business are again somewhat modifying the global strategies of the industry leaders. The importance of keeping product developers and manufacturers in contact with consumers, the mounting pressure to "localise" by increasing local content, which also entails some local component development, and the growing difficulty of managing world-wide operations from a centralised home base have given rise to a tendency towards a "regionalisation" of overseas operations. More management decisions, product development and manufacturing operations are undertaken in each of the main regions, increasingly seen as self-contained.

To this end, for instance, both Thomson and Matsushita have adopted a tripolar system of headquarters (Europe, North America and Asia), while Sony has separated the management of the domestic operation from that of its three main markets, giving responsibility for Asia to the regional headquarters in Singapore. But quite clearly, at the management level, the "regionalisation" trend is countered by the necessity to take strategic decisions centrally, in part because some of the most important consumer electronics products are essentially "global" ones, such as Walkman personal stereos, CD players or video cameras.

Finally, the importance for manufacturers of keeping in touch with leading-edge research and innovation centres needs to be underscored. This is one of the motivations which has led practically all the major Japanese manufacturers to establish significant wholly owned R&D facilities in the United States[33] and often in Europe as well. This development represents an important element in the global strategies of "network" multinationals which aim to take advantage of the "best" elements of each of their many locations, in terms of technological, production and marketing capabilities. At the same time, it seems still possible to argue that, unlike European companies, the bulk of Japanese R&D is done at home. Overseas R&D centres concentrate on adapting technology to local requirements, such as different voltages or broadcasting systems, while development of new technologies and products is still rare. One example is the digital video recorder which was developed by Sony in the United Kingdom.

B. International acquisitions and minority participations

International acquisitions are an important weapon in the consumer electronics companies' globalisation strategy arsenal. Both US and European market structures have been largely affected by international acquisitions. Virtually all US manufacturers, with the exception of Zenith, have been taken over by either Japanese or European competitors; and even Zenith has recently sold a 5 per cent participation to Korea's Goldstar. In 1974, Matsushita acquired the TV division of Motorola and its brand Quasar; in the same year, Philips purchased Magnavox and in 1980, it bought the Sylvania and Philco brands; in 1977, Sanyo acquired Worwick; in 1987, Thomson acquired the consumer electronic division of General Electric, which had absorbed RCA a year earlier. Already by 1980 of the 27 US TV producers existing in 1960, only three remained – RCA, GE and Zenith.

Recently, both Sony and Matsushita have invested heavily in the US entertainment industry, which is considered to be strategically complementary to consumer electronics. The former bought CBS record company in 1988 and Columbia Pictures in 1989, while the latter purchased MCA the following year. Toshiba has acquired a 6.25 per cent stake in Time Warner, the media conglomerate. The role of the entertainment "software" seems to be particularly important in view of the new digital technology which removes the differences between the various information media – video, text, sound –, merging them into the framework of "multimedia". This means the introduction of "multimedia" systems, based on the combination of consumer electronics, telecommunications, computers and entertainment products and services. To face this new challenge, various Japanese companies have been investing in small but leading-edge US companies which are already developing these new systems and the related multimedia software. The only European firm active in the entertainment business is Philips which owns the record company Polygram.

Over the past 15 years, European manufacturers have engaged in extensive restructuring to face the stiff competition of Japanese and South-East Asian companies and, more recently, in preparation for the completion of the Single Market programme. After taking over GE's consumer electronics activities in Spain in 1974, Thomson acquired, between 1978 and 1983, Nordmende, Saba, Dual and Telefunken in Germany and in 1987 the consumer electronics division of Thorn EMI, the leading TV maker in the United Kingdom, under the brand name of Ferguson. In 1979, Philips purchased a minority stake in Grundig, which it increased to a controlling interest in 1984. In 1990 it also bought a minority stake in the Danish company Bang and Olufsen. Since 1987, Finland's Nokia has become the third European consumer electronics company through its acquisitions of the Electrolux group's shareholding in Oceanic in France and of the ITT subsidiary in Germany.

According to one source[34] in the aggregate, between 1988 and 1992, there were 73 acquisitions totaling over US$1.1 billion. The countries most active in purchases were the United Kingdom (with 12 operations involving US$284 million), Hong Kong (5 and US$274 million), Japan (6 and US$236 million), Korea (1 and US$140 million) and the United States (8 and US$104 million). The top seller countries were the United States (17 operations involving US$531 million), Japan (3 and US$236 million), the United Kingdom (11 and US$216 million), Germany (10 and US$148 million) and France (7 and US$20 million). If compared to other sectors, the total amount recorded in the database does not seem to indicate a strong acquisition activity in the period of observation, which is consistent with the high degree of concentration already reached by the industry.

Again in relative terms, and for the period 1988-92, minority participations and joint ventures totalling US$388 million appear to have been even less important. Countries with companies more frequently involved in international operations of this kind were Japan, the Netherlands, Germany, the United States and France. Countries most frequently hosting these transactions were the United States, Japan, Germany, the United Kingdom and Malaysia.

Although the aggregate outlays involved may not be particularly large, some ventures certainly have a strategic value when, for instance, they are geared towards developing key technologies, or technology-intensive components. An example could be the recent joint venture between Philips and Thomson in the field of active-matrix liquid crystal displays, a very important component for HDTV systems. Japanese manufacturers appear to have formed several joint ventures in Europe as a way, *inter alia*, to ease trade frictions. Agreements, such as the joint venture between Thomson and JVC, have allowed EC companies to reduce the technological gap,[35] while making available their marketing strengths to their Japanese partners. Joint ventures may also still be a very important vehicle to invest in developing countries.

C. Market shares of foreign-controlled firms

In 1990, the European market was supplied for over 50 per cent by imports, and for another 17 per cent by local production carried out by manufacturers under foreign control, which represented almost one-third of total European production (Table 5.20). But in Europe substantial differences in market shares exist depending on the specific product market and country. The TV market is dominated by the three major European manufacturers, which share around 45 per cent of sales. In some countries, local producers, such as Finlux in Finland (until Nokia's acquisition in 1992) and Seleco in Italy, still keep a substantial share in the national market, while in others, for instance the United Kingdom, virtually all domestically produced colour TVs and VCRs are made by foreign-owned firms. As for VCRs in general, Philips and Thomson share less than 20 per cent of the market, while the rest is dominated by Japanese manufacturers (Table 5.21).

Table 5.20. **Structure of the European consumer electronics market, 1990**

Sales in ECU billion

European market	23
European production	13
Under European control	9
Under foreign control	4
Of which: under Japanese control	3.3
Imports	12
From Japan	5
From Republic of Korea	1
Exports	2

Source: Bloom (1993), p. 223.

Table 5.21. **Market shares – Videocassette recorders, 1988**

By country, percentages

Source of product	United States	European Community	Japan	Other	World
Japanese firms:					
Japanese operations	73.8	23.7	98.1	72.1	66.3
Offshore operations	6.0	0.4	0.0	10.2	16.3
US operations	1.9	0.0	0.0	0.0	0.0
EC operations	0.0	49.5	0.0	0.0	0.0
Non-Japanese suppliers in:					
Republic of Korea	17.5	9.1	1.9	13.4	12.2
Chinese Taipei	0.8	0.0	0.0	2.5	0.8
United States	0.0	0.0	0.0	0.0	0.0
European Community	0.0	17.3	0.0	1.8	4.3
Total	**100.0**	**100.0**	**100.0**	**100.0**	**100.0**

Source: *Japan Electronics Almanac 1989*, reproduced in Tyson (1992), p. 235.

In the United States, Zenith is the only remaining US-owned TV manufacturer. In 1990, it held a 12-13 per cent share of the domestic market. The rest of the US production of TVs is shared by foreign-controlled companies. In the same year, EC- and Japanese-owned companies each held 35 per cent of the US market, with Korean and Chinese Taipei manufacturers sharing the remaining 17 per cent. In 1992, Zenith closed its US plants and relied entirely on its factories in Mexico, thus practically leaving no domestic TV production made by US-owned firms. With virtually no domestic sources of the main components, almost no VCRs, camcorders, tape players, recorders, radios, phonographs, or CD players are produced in the United States.

In Japan, the market share of foreign-controlled firms in the consumer electronics sector is negligible.

D. International collaboration agreements

As mentioned above, OEM and subcontracting arrangements are quite common among consumer electronics manufacturers. They are often used to take advantage of developing countries' comparative advantage in terms of labour costs; but they are also increasingly employed for the fabrication of technology-intensive items. For instance, all the camcorders marketed by Philips are actually produced by other manufacturers on an OEM basis and Matsushita's new high-definition laser-disc player is procured from Sony through an OEM agreement. This reliance on collaboration between firms, possibly emphasized in a recessionary period, may be due, *inter alia*, to the increasing costs needed to develop new technologies and products.

The same rationale could motivate the use of other forms of collaboration between corporations, generally referred to as "international alliances". In the aggregate over the period 1964-92, consumer electronics manufacturers seem to have made recourse to alliances less frequently than firms in other sectors. In general, large manufacturers from France, Germany, the Netherlands, the United Kingdom, the United States and Japan have been the most active. The most important aims have been production and development followed by marketing.[36] Recently, prompted by strong global competition, technological and commercial alliances as well as partnerships seem to have become more frequent.

Moreover, the digital technology which is merging computing, communication and video functions into consumer (and professional) products has been spurring a number of alliances. They involve consumer electronics manufacturers and computer, software and telecommunication companies such as AT&T, Texas Instruments and Apple. Cable TV and pay-TV is another sector in which media, telecommunications and consumer electronics companies are likely to set up more alliances.

A related motivation is the desire to avoid costly "standard wars" similar to that which pitted Philips, Sony and JVC/Matsushita against each other over the VCR standard. So great are the economic stakes involved that manufacturers are increasingly entering into risk-hedging arrangements. For instance, Matsushita, Pioneer, Sanyo, Sony and Toshiba have all agreed on the standard for high-definition laser-disc players. Eight Japanese and two European manufacturers are also developing a single world standard for digital VCRs. Sony and Philips, which are strongly pushing respectively their Mini Disc and Digital Compact Cassette (DCC) systems, have at the same time signed an agreement to share the Mini Disc know-how in exchange for a DCC licence. Philips' DCCs are also produced by Matsushita.

In an industry characterised by innovation, high R&D spending and proprietary technology, licensing agreements are strategically important. For instance the possibility of widely licensing from the technological leaders – RCA and Philips – clearly facilitated the Japanese successes in TV manufacturing. The general, but not universal willingness to license, may in part be explained by the technological inter-linkages existing in complex products which incorporate many components covered by patents belonging to different companies. In addition, to gain industry acceptance for its standard, a company may be induced to let other companies produce through licensing. This was Matsushita and JVC's decision which secured the victory of their VHS format for VCRs in the battle against Sony's Betamax format.

Together with sharing technological and manufacturing capabilities, collaboration agreements may allow a company to profit from another's local marketing expertise and distribution strength. In a database of strategic alliances for the period 1980-89, more than half of those recorded gave market access and market restructuring as the main motives.[37]

5. GOVERNMENT POLICIES

A. Standards and regulation

Standards can open up new market opportunities or can stifle product sales, can remove trade barriers or create them, can promote or inhibit innovation, all with great economic consequences. Standards may emerge from market-place rivalry, when one competing standard manages to muster enough support in the market to become the industry standard. The current confrontation between the Mini Disc and the DCC systems is a case in point.

In other areas, such as TV broadcasting, the standard-setting process is reserved for public authorities, both national and international. The fact that in Europe, two standards, different from that adopted in the United States and Japan, were chosen, together with the refusal of the patent-holders to grant licenses to non-European companies, significantly restricted access to the European market until the early 1970s. It is thus clear that the selection of a common or multiple standard for HDTV will have a very large impact on the consumer electronics industry. HDTV sales are now projected to reach 5 million units by 2001 and more than double that level by 2003.

HDTV is a major technical improvement over the existing system based on the PAL and SECAM standards in Europe and the NTSC standard in the United States and Japan. It will allow visual images to be transmitted with much greater clarity, especially if used with large, flat-screen panel displays. When integrated into a "multimedia" system, it also holds the promise of making available to the consumers a wide range of video and data services through their TVs. HDTV makes use of a large variety of technologies with related standard issues. The HDTV signal contains much more information than the signals used today, which means that the transmission system and equipment and the programming format as well as the TV sets need to be able to convey and receive it.

Consumer electronics manufacturers are heavily involved in HDTV research in Japan as well as in Europe and the United States. In Europe and Japan, the two respective systems, HD-MAC and MUSE, developed with the substantial assistance of public funds, are both based on basically analogue technology and are thus becoming obsolete, as digital technology is rapidly advancing. This has prompted the recent EC move toward supporting digital technology. Japan is also reviewing its policy. In the United States, there are presently four digital systems under consideration by the Federal Communications Commission (FCC), which has already indicated its preference for the digital technology. The four systems have been developed by three consortia which involve US- and European-controlled companies. Recently they have agreed to form one alliance to co-operate technologically and to share the future licensing fees.

The importance of using environment-friendly products and production methods has started to be felt also in the consumer electronics industry. Aside from the growing consumer preference for "green products", manufacturers have also to comply with new legislation in the field. For instance, Germany has recently introduced a law requiring equipment manufacturers to take back used TVs and other electronic items for recycling. Five European companies, supported by the German Ministry for Research and Technology, are currently pursuing a project for the design of a "green TV" which could be easily disassembled and recycled.

B. Industry and technology policies

In general, the consumer electronics sector has enjoyed little direct support in OECD countries. Government assistance and guidance have played an important role in the development of the Japanese electronics industry. Already in 1955 the Ministry for International Trade and Industry (Japan) (MITI) had formed a Computer Research Committee, specifically entrusted with promoting transistor research, which has proved to be a winning strategy for the development of the whole electronics industry. In the following years other initiatives were taken to foster the growth of the sector. In particular, government support focused on research and development activities and was carried out under "The Law on Extraordinary Measures for Promotion of the Electronics Industry" of May 1957. Since 1968, under the guidance of MITI and the Ministry of Posts and Telecommunications, the Japanese broadcasting Corporation (NHK) has been researching and developing its HDTV system, MUSE. This early start has meant that Japanese manufacturers are already supplying some niche markets in industrial TV systems, film-making, electronic publishing, medical training and super-computer graphics.

Some EC member States have tried to support the consumer electronics industry mainly with the view of preserving employment, with mixed results. Much more important appears to be the EC technology policy organised around various co-operative research programmes, such as JESSI, EUREKA, ESPRIT and RACE. They cover various areas, from semiconductors to telecommunications, which all have a potential beneficial effect on the consumer electronics sector. In particular since 1986, the EC and the leading European companies have devoted great efforts to the development of an analogue HDTV system under the framework of the EUREKA 95 project. The much smaller EUREKA 256 project is engaged in the definition of a digital HDTV transmission standard. In July 1993, the EC Council also approved a ECU 228 million action plan to aid the European broadcasting industry to produce and transmit wide-screen programmes which are an important element towards the introduction of HDTV. The new generation HDTV sets will require large flat-screens. Substantial research work is being pursued on this technology through the EUREKA, RACE and ESPRIT programmes.

The strategic importance of HDTV technology was clearly felt also in the United States, both because of the interlinkages with the semiconductor and computer industries and because of its military applications, such as military aircraft displays in cockpits.[38] The approach chosen has been to make available a limited amount of public funds for precompetitive research on generic technologies. The Department of

Defense, and in particular the Defense Advanced Research Projects Agency, has provided some funding to industry to finance the development of HDTV flat-panel displays. The National Institute of Standards and Technology has also allocated some resources to HDTV projects. A plan to provide larger funds for the development and manufacturing of flat-panel displays is currently under consideration.

Government support policies have been instrumental to the success of the consumer electronics industries in some South-East Asian countries, and notably in Korea and Chinese Taipei. Trying to upgrade its electronics industry, Korea has recently set up a HDTV development plan which provides for a jointly funded partnership between electronics corporations and public research institutes.

Eligibility requirements for participation in publicly sponsored programmes seem to be quite restrictive everywhere, raising the question of how to treat foreign-controlled subsidiaries which engage in substantial local production and R&D activities.

Finally it should be noted that some of the large consumer electronics manufacturers are also very active in the telecommunication and data processing sectors where public regulation and procurement may have provided some protection and economic advantages beneficial to the overall performance of the companies.

C. Foreign investment policies

Europe, the South-East Asian countries and the United States have been the major recipients of foreign investment flows. Until the early 1970s, some EC member States[39] maintained a negative posture towards Japanese inward investments. Thereafter, instead, with some exceptions, they have been actively competing to attract inward investments. The United Kingdom has been particularly successful, making ample use of EC regional aid funds.

Japan does not seem to have specific foreign investment policies in the sector. The very low presence of foreign investors parallels low activity in other sectors and might be viewed as an indication that some structural impediments exist in the market.

After a period of import substitution policies, which somewhat constrained foreign investments in the form of joint ventures, some South-East Asian countries have adopted more liberal policies toward FDI. This has clearly facilitated the flow of investments. Some restrictions still remain. For instance in Korea, while foreign companies are allowed to manufacture parts and components, they cannot fabricate final electronics products. Starting in the second half of the 1980s, Malaysia and Thailand have been particularly successful in attracting foreign investments, thanks both to their good economic performances and to their more consistent FDI promotion policies. Export-processing zones have been an effective instrument of investment promotion in Malaysia but also in Mexico, the only non-Asian developing country to have achieved a substantial development in the consumer electronics sector.

In the United States, inward investments in consumer electronics do not appear to have ever encountered any restriction. But the "national security" implications of the production of many electronics components and of HDTV systems might require that foreign companies wanting to make an acquisition in these sectors file an Exon-Florio notice and possibly undergo an investigation by the Committee on Foreign Investment in the United States (CFIUS). As for investment promotion, mainly state governments have provided incentives for foreign investors, such as low-interest financing.

D. Trade policies

In both the United States and the EC, trade-policy instruments have been actively used to try to protect domestic producers mainly from Japanese and later Korean competition. Starting in the 1950s in the audio market, and in the 1960s and 1970s in the video market, US manufacturers rapidly lost market shares to the Japanese companies. Although a series of management miscalculations led to a substantial loss of competitiveness, US manufacturers also alleged unfair trade practices on the part of the Japanese competitors.

From the 1960s onward, a number of antidumping actions were pursued, albeit with little success, also due to protracted litigation. Meanwhile in 1977, an Orderly Market Agreement (OMA) was negotiated with Japan. Both the OMA and the AD actions proved ineffective in affording relief to local producers partly because the Japanese manufacturers moved some production and assembly operations to the United States, through green-field investments and acquisitions,[40] and increased their exports of components.[41] Furthermore exports from countries not covered by the OMA went up, prompting the negotiation of similar agreements with Korea and Chinese Taipei. They all lapsed in 1982. Ultimately, OMAs may have had the effect of allowing the foreign manufacturers involved to command higher prices and to enjoy larger profits. In 1984, stiff antidumping duties were imposed against Korean and Chinese Taipei colour TVs. Together with an antidumping order against colour TVs from Japan, they are still in place to date. In 1989, Zenith charged Asian manufacturers with circumventing the antidumping measures by shifting production away from headquarters countries. After one year monitoring, the US Department of Commerce decided not to open an antidumping investigation. In September 1991, steep antidumping duties were imposed on Japanese producers of active-matrix liquid crystal displays, accused of engaging in predatory pricing. The duties were strongly criticised by both Japanese manufacturers and US downstream users, especially portable computers producers. In November 1991, Apple Computer filed an appeal with the US Court of International Trade, questioning the antidumping duties, claiming that injury to US producers could not be substantiated, as allegedly no US producer could supply displays of the quantity and quality necessary. The duties were lifted in June 1993, but in the meantime had induced some US companies to move assembly operations off-shore to gain access to lower-priced supplies.

An important trade policy instrument, which may also constitute an incentive for foreign investments, is the provision of subheading 9802.00.80 which sets forth tariff treatment for eligible imported goods that contain US-made components. Under this provision the duty is applied to the full value of the imported article, less the value of the US components. As for TV receivers, the share of total imports accounted for by imports under subheading 9802.00.80 almost tripled during 1985-88, from 14 to 41 per cent. In 1988, the share of total imports entered under this subheading was also a substantial 10 per cent for other commodity groups such as tape recorders (including VCRs), radio receivers and related parts. The main source of imports was Mexico, followed by Canada, Chinese Taipei and Malaysia.[42] On the other hand, the somewhat similar EC "outward processing arrangements" play a negligible role in the consumer electronics sector. EC imports after outward processing are more significant for some components and in particular semiconductors.

The EC and its member States have also made ample use of trade-policy instruments, such as quotas, voluntary export restraints (VERs), antidumping duties and high tariffs on particular products to protect European consumer electronics manufacturers from the competition of Japanese and Far Eastern producers. Aside from causing the European consumers a substantial loss,[43] these measures have clearly induced Japanese, Korean and Chinese Taipeiese companies to invest in Europe and to increasingly "localise" their operations in terms of components procurement[44] and later, partly, also of R&D. But they do not seem to have allowed any substantial improvement in the competitiveness of European manufacturers.[45] For instance in the case of CDs, Philips, notwithstanding its initial technological lead and the subsequent tariff hike and imposition of antidumping duties, has not been able to prevail in the EC market.

In Japan tariff protection is generally low, for instance, 4 per cent *ad valorem* for TVs as compared to 5 per cent in the United States and 14 per cent in the EC. But market access problems of a structural nature have often been alleged. The largely captive and regulated distribution system is considered as creating an effective barrier against import penetration. Foreign manufacturers view this impediment as particularly damaging because it denies them access to one of the three major world markets with ensuing losses in terms of economies of scale and learning, which are particularly important in a high-volume sector such as consumer electronics.

E. Protection of intellectual property

Consumer electronics is a technology-intensive sector where intellectual property rights (IPRs) represent an important source of income for many companies. For instance RCA, one of the most successful innovators, has been receiving roughly US$100 million annually since the 1970s in consumer electronics licence fees.

The strengthening of IPR protection both unilaterally and through bilateral or multilateral negotiations, including those undertaken in the framework of the World Intellectual Property Organisation (WIPO) and GATT/WTO, should be considered beneficial for global companies with dispersed operations. Better IPR protection can in fact lessen the concerns that companies may have when engaging in technology transfers.

Rising R&D costs and technological interlinkages have been inducing companies to increase their recourse to technological tie-ups, but they have also spurred an increase in patent litigation which in turn may contribute to pushing corporations into collaborative agreements. The stake in high-technology patent litigation may be very high, as in the ongoing dispute between Eastman Kodak and Sony over the Sony's alleged infringement of Kodak's patent on the recording technology used in high-end VCRs and camcorders.

Consumer electronics products may be a vehicle of copyright infringement when they allow pirate recording of video or audio proprietary materials. The issue came up with the introduction of the dual-deck VCR, and again recently when the advancement in digital recording technology was embodied in a new product jointly developed by Philips and Sony – the Digital Audio Tape (DAT) – which could both play and record digitally. The strong opposition of music publishers, which refused to make available DAT versions of their music titles, substantially contributed to the commercial failure of the product. In 1989 the industry representatives agreed on a device, called the Serial Copy Management System, which only allows the recording of digital copies from which no further digital copies can be made, through the encoding of a special signal. In the United States, the agreement was subsequently codified in the Digital Audio Tape Recorder Act. A similar problem will arise when digital VCRs become available.

F. Competition policy

The development of the consumer electronics industry has posed a series of very important competition policy issues. Although US plaintiffs have not been able to prove any anti-trust violations, protracted litigation has focused the attention on the alleged collusive practices prevailing in the Japanese market. Indeed, in its investigations in the late 1950s and 1960s, the Japanese Fair Trade Commission found evidence that companies had engaged in horizontal and vertical price fixing.[46]

The relation between alleged collusion in one market and international trade was clearly put forward by the US producers, when they charged that Japanese dumping practices were all part of a larger attempt to monopolise the US market. In 1970, National Union Electric Corporation, and in 1974, Zenith, alleged that seven Japanese manufacturers and their subsidiaries had engaged in a predatory pricing conspiracy including the use of a cartel arrangement in Japan to charge supra-competitive prices there and to cross-subsidise, with the ensuing profits, below-cost predatory prices in the United States. After lengthy litigation, in 1986, the US Supreme Court ruled that the Court of Appeals, which had in general supported the plaintiffs, had not applied the proper legal standards in evaluating the supporting evidence for anti-trust conspiracy.[47] More recently, a small US company, Go-Video, alleged that a number of Japanese companies had conspired against its attempt to bring the dual-deck VCR to the market, for which it holds a patent. The US company claimed that the Japanese competitors had pooled their numerous patents, which Go-Video needed to licence in order to manufacture the end-product, and they had refused to deal.[48] The case foundered on procedural grounds.

The general argument of collusion in the Japanese domestic market, while strongly disputed by the Japanese companies, is also often mentioned in trade-policy discussions and in antidumping litigation. The low import penetration, allegedly partly due to the vertical integration into distribution, and the ensuing lack of import competition, is also considered an important factor in allowing collusion in the domestic market, which, in turn, may foster dumping. In addition, the importance of import competition seems to be clear in the European context, where impediments to parallel imports may be considered responsible for the still widely diverging prices in various national markets.

The strong entry barriers and the high degree of concentration in the industry, both in national markets and world-wide, may also be a cause of some concern. At least on one occasion, the merger of two companies was blocked on competition grounds. The German cartel office considered unacceptable the proposed merger of Thomson and Grundig because it would have represented a 55 per cent share of the domestic market. Finally, strategic alliances and other co-operation arrangements have been regarded by competition authorities as being generally pro-competitive, particularly when they allow synergies in the innovation efforts of different companies. On the other hand, monitoring remains important as they could become a vehicle for collusion.

NOTES AND REFERENCES

1. This classification problem may create some difficulty when comparing different statistical sources.

2. The key components may be classified according to their main functions. They are: capture: optics, electro-optics, charge-couple device, microphones, sensors; processing: magnetic tapes and discs, optical discs, CDs, printers, semiconductor memories; transmission cables, satellites, optical fibres, microwaves; display: cathode ray tubes, flat-panels [LCDs, electroluminescent flat-panels (ELs), plasma based screens].

3. One estimate puts the cost breakdown of TV assembly in the United States at US$90 for labour, 70 for overhead and US$225 for components. A typical cost breakdown of manufacturing a colour TV in the EC is 22 per cent overhead, interest etc., 10 per cent labour, 40 per cent colour picture tube, and 28 per cent other materials and components

4. "In a factory where Matsushita Electric makes Panasonic VCRs, a robot winds wire a little thinner than a human hair 16 times through a pinhole in the video head, and then solders it. There are 530 of these robots in the factory and they wind, and they wind some more 24 hours a day. They do it five times faster and more reliably than the 3,000 housewives who, until recently, did the same job with microscopes on a subcontract base in Japan's countryside. The robots even inspect their own work. ... Matsushita invented and custom-made all the 530 wire-winders to gain a competitive edge." A. Tanzer and R. Simon, "Why Japan Loves Robots and We Don't", *Forbes*, 16 April 1990, p.148.

5. The US hourly wage in consumer electronics in 1991 was US$10.97 as compared for instance with US$1.09 in a Mexican electronics maquiladora. See Office of Technology Assessment (1992), *US-Mexico Trade: Pulling Together or Pulling Apart?*, US Government Printing Office, Washington, DC, p. 164.

6. Several examples are: "Miniature TV has been a driving force in display technology. Digital audio tape is a leader in storage technology. Compact discs are driving laser technology, digital signal processor design, and optical storage techniques. Camcorders are at the frontier in making demands on silicon chip processing power, and in miniaturisation technologies", see statement of Dr. Ian M. Ross, President Emeritus, AT&T Bell Laboratories before the Committee on Science, Space and Technology, Subcommittee on Technology and Competitiveness, US House of Representatives, 3 October 1991.

7. "Today's technology is not being driven by the Strategic Defence Initiative. It is being driven by Sony Camcorders." Statement by Mr. W. Spencer, head of the US Sematech Consortium, quoted in *Fortune*, 6 May 1991, p. 32.

8. For instance, RCA spent US$300 million to develop its commercially unsuccessful Selecta Vision system (videodisc).

9. In the US consumer electronic industry the capital stock per labour hour has increased from US$2.75 to US$14.50 (1972 US$) between 1960 and 1985.

10. "If a Rolls-Royce had achieved the same productivity gains as the TV industry, a Rolls would cost today as a bicycle." Statement by the head of business development at a European electronics group quoted in "How to Stand Out in a Crowd", *Financial Times*, 10 September 1993, p. 17.

11. See McKinsey Global Institute (1993), *Manufacturing Productivity*, Washington, DC.

12. See *EIU Marketing in Europe*, March 1993, p. 62.

13. In this context the term "software" refers to entertainment which runs on consumer products, such as films, TV programme, recorded music, etc.

14. See *Financial Times*, "Price flows undermining EC's single market hopes", 3 August 1992. In Europe for instance most of the major consumer electronics companies have wholly- or majority-owned distributors in each of the large markets to handle the distribution up to the point of wholesaler or retailer.

15. In Japan, the major consumer electronics companies maintain large networks of "keiretsu" retail stores. Matsushita owns around 25,000 retailers; Toshiba 12,500; Hitachi 10,000; Sanyo 6,000. But the number of stores is steadily declining. See *Tokyo Business Today*, September 1990, p. 35.

16. There may be some differences in trade data depending on the differing aggregations used in the various statistical sources.

17. Import penetration is calculated as import over apparent consumption in value terms.

18. Quoted in The Economist Intelligence Unit (1990), *The International Electronic Industry*, London, p. 18.

19. SITC Rev. 2 subgroup 776.1 and items 764.92, 764.93 and 764.99.

20. See UNIDO (1990), *Industry and Development Global Report 1990/91*, Vienna, p. 81.

21. Products such as complete TV receivers or sub-assemblies manufactured in maquiladoras may enter the United States under special classification provisions, subheading 9802.00.60 or 9802.00.80, of the HTS. Under these subheadings, US duty is applied only on the value of the imported product minus the value of the US content. See infra 5.d.

22. There are few sources of data on IFT, as information on the subject is not generally available in traditional trade statistics. Data on IFT are mostly available through firm surveys which involve the preparation of questionnaires by national authorities. This section is based on information provided by the US Department of Commerce, which conducts surveys of foreign affiliates of US companies and US affiliates of foreign companies. Relevant data is not available for other countries. For an explanation of the availability and problems with data on IFT, see OECD (1993).

23. See OECD (1993).

24. The US Department of Commerce uses the International Surveys Industry (ISI) classification in its surveys. There is a category for "household audio and video, and communications, equipment" (ISI 366), which includes electronic equipment for home entertainment, such as radio and television sets, video recorders, and compact disc players; auto radios, tape players, public address systems, and music distribution apparatus; phonograph records, pre-recorded magnetic tapes, and compact discs; radio and television broadcasting and communication equipment, such as cable television equipment, studio equipment, transmitters, transreceivers, receiver and communication antennas; telephone and telegraph apparatus; and other communication equipment such as burglar and fire alarm apparatus, highway and railroad signals, etc.

25. Category ISI 363, which includes household cooking equipment, electric and nonelectric; household refrigerators and home and farm freezers; household laundry equipment, electric and nonelectric; electric housewares and fans, including household humidifiers; household vacuum cleaners; sewing machines; and other appliances such as dishwashers, water heaters, food waste disposal units, air space heaters and household floor washers.

26. There has been a large increase in investment in wholesale activities in the United States. This trade is technically IFT, but different in character from the case where investment takes place in assembly operations.

27. Intra-industry trade can be readily calculated for any given product category, as only the traditional bilateral trade statistics for that product category are needed. The interpretation of IIT data depends, however, on how one defines that category, as the choice of the classification system and of the level of aggregation may strongly influence the results. For the analysis below, the Standard International Trade Classification Revision 2, at the four digit level, was used. In the calculation of an IIT index, if exports are equal to imports, IIT is 100; on the other hand, if either imports or exports are equal to zero, IIT is zero. For a discussion of the theory and measurement of IIT, see Grubel and Lloyd (1975).

28. SITC Rev2 761, 762 and 763; television receivers, radio-broadcast receivers, gramophones, dictating machines, and other sound recorders and reproducers.

29. See Cawson and Holmes (1979, p. 174) and National Research Council (1992, p. 41)

30. Overall offshore production of colour TVs by Japanese manufacturers has exceeded domestic production since 1988.

31. Electronics maquiladoras usually produce finished items with high labour content and low profit margins, such as small and medium-sized TVs and telephones, and labour intensive components or subassemblies, such as circuit boards and subassemblies for large-screen TVs, to be shipped to the United States to be incorporated into final products.

32. In 1992, the domestic production was well over 11 million units, which compared with a overseas production of less than 5 000.

33. See D. Eleanor Westney (1993), "Cross-Pacific internationalisation of R&D by US and Japanese firms", *R&D Management* 23, 2, p. 171 et seq.

34. Data on international acquisitions, joint ventures and minority participations were kindly provided by KPMG Peat Marwick.

35. See J. McCormick and N. Stone (1990), "From National Champion to Global Competitor: An Interview with Thomson's Alain Gomez", *Harvard Business Review* (May-June), p. 130.

36. The INSEAD Collaborative Agreement Database, covering some 2565 agreements in all regions of the world and all industries, but with a focus on manufacturing, contains 108 agreements in the consumer electronics sector. Professor Deigan Morris, INSEAD, designed and developed the data base and holds the rights to it.

37. Quoted in *The Economist*, "Survey of Multinationals", 27 March 1993, p. 20.

38. HD imaging and displays has been included in the list of "National Critical Technologies" established by the National Critical Technologies Panel.

39. For instance, British manufacturers persuaded the Government not to offer regional assistance to Hitachi in 1973. See W. Eltis and D. Fraser (1992), "The Contribution of Japanese Industrial Success to Britain and to Europe", *National Westminster Bank Quarterly Review* (November), p. 2 et seq.

40. A 50 per cent local content requirement was imposed on these transplant operations.

41. The anticircumvention provisions of the 1988 Omnibus Trade and Competitiveness Act represent an attempt to eliminate this problem.

42. See US International Trade Commission (USITC) (1989), *Production Sharing: US Imports under Harmonized Tariff Schedule Subheadings 9802.00.60 and 9802.00.80, 1985-1988*, Washington, DC.

43. See National Consumer Council (1993), *International Trade – The Consumer Agenda*, London, pp. 95-100.

44. Although there are no statutory local content rules, in order to skirt frictions, some Japanese investors have aimed at reaching a 50 per cent local content ratio which is similar to EC-owned companies' ratio. Because particular components may not be available in Europe, some Japanese companies have encouraged their main Japanese components suppliers to establish operations in Europe. As for radios, TVs and audio tape recorders specifically, Commission Regulations 2632/70 (OJ 1970 L279/35) and 861/71 (OJ 1971 L95/11) provide that these items acquire in general the origin of the country where the assembly or the incorporation of components attains at least 45 per cent of their ex-works invoice price. This rule of origin has been regarded as a useful local content guideline for various consumer electronics products. The EC also mantains a 14 per cent tariff rate against critical semiconductor components, such as D-Rams, used in many consumer electronics products. With almost no production capacity in Europe, many downstream manufacturers consider this barrier damaging.

45. "In Europe, trade regulation may protect short-term profitability, but in the long run, productivity gap with the world leading-edge companies will increase. Protection designed to sustain a so-called "domestic" industry or protect existing jobs is done at the cost of high consumer prices, often much more expensive than the cost associated with the loss of jobs." See McKinsey Global Institute (1993), *Manufacturing Productivity*, Washington, DC., p.15.

46. See Matsushita Electric Industrial Co. v. Zenith Radio Corp., 475 US 574 (1986).

47. See K. Yamamura and J. Vandemberg (1986), "Japan's Rapid-Growth Policy on Trial: The Television Case", in G. Saxonhouse and K. Yamamura (eds.), *Law and Trade Issues of the Japanese Economy*, University of Washington, Seattle.

48. See In re Dual-Deck Video Cassette Recorder, 1990-2 Trade Cas. (CCH) par. 69,141 (D. Ariz. 25 July 1990).

BIBLIOGRAPHY

BARK, T. (1991), *Antidumping Restrictions Against Korean Exports: Major Focus on Consumer Electronic Products*, KIEP, Seoul.

BLOOM, M. (1993), "L'industrie européenne de l'électronique grand public", in F. Sachwald (ed.), *L'Europe et la globalisation – Aquisitions et accords dans l'industrie*, Masson, Paris.

BOWEN, H. (1991), "Consumer Electronics", in D. Mayes (ed.), *The European Challenge – Industry's Responses to the 1992 Programme*, Harvester Wheatsheaf, London.

CAWSON, A., and P. HOLMES (1991), "The New Consumer Electronics", in C. Freeman, M. Sharp and P. Holmes (eds.), *Technology and the Future of Europe: Competition and the Global Environment in the 1990s*, Pinter, London.

ELECTRONIC INDUSTRIES ASSOCIATION OF JAPAN (1992 and 1993), *Facts and Figures on the Japanese Electronics Industries*, Tokyo.

ERNST, D. and D. O'CONNOR (1992*), Competing in the Electronics Industry – The Experience of Newly Industrialising Economies*, OECD, Paris.

EUROPEAN COMMUNITIES (1984), *The European Consumer Electronics Industry*, report by Mackintosh International Ltd., Brussels.

EUROPEAN COMMUNITIES - COMMISION (1991*a*), "The European Electronics and Information Technology Industry – State of Play, Issues at Stake and Proposals for Action", *Bulletin of the European Communities*, Supplement 3/91, p. 25 *et seq.*

EUROPEAN COMMUNITIES – Report of the Directors General for Industry (1991*b), *"Improving the Functioning of the Consumer Electronics Markets", mimeo.

EUROPEAN COMMUNITIES – COMMISSION, *Panorama of EC Industry*, various issues.

FORESTER, T. (1993), *Silicon Samurai – How Japan Conquered the World's I.T. Industry*, Blackwell, Cambridge, MA.

GRUBEL, H.G. and P.J. LLOYD (1975), *Intra-industry trade: The theory and measurement of International Trade in Differentiated Products*, Macmillan, London.

HART, J. (1993), "Consumer Electronics", in B. Wellenius, A. Miller and C. Dahlman (eds.), *Developing the Electronics Industry*, The World Bank, Washington, DC.

JACKSON, T. (1992), *Turning Japanese – The Fight for Industrial Control in the New Europe*, Harper Collins, London.

MCKINSEY GLOBAL INSTITUTE (1993), *Manufacturing Productivity*, Washington, DC.

NATIONAL RESEARCH COUNCIL (1992), *Dispelling the Manufacturing Myth – American Factories Can Compete in the Global Market-place*, National Academy Press, Washington, DC.

OECD (1993), *Intra-firm Trade*, Trade Policy Issues, No. 1, Paris.

SCHERER, F.M. (1992), *International High-Technology Competition*, Harvard University Press, Cambridge, MA.

STAELIN, D. *et al.* (1989), "The Decline of US Consumer Electronics Manufacturing: History, Hypotheses, and Remedies", in *The Working Papers of the MIT Commission on Industrial Productivity*, MIT Press, Cambridge, MA.

STRANGE, R. (1993), *Japanese Manufacturing Investment in Europe – Its Impact on the UK Economy*, Routledge, London.

THE ECONOMIST (1991), "A Survey of Consumer Electronics", 13 April.

THE ECONOMIST INTELLIGENCE UNIT (1990), *The International Electronic Industry*, London.

TYSON, L. (1992), *Who's Bashing Whom? Trade Conflict in High-Technology Industries*, Institute for International Economics, Washington, DC.

URATA, S. and H. KOHAMA (1991), "Electronics Industry", in I. Yamazawa and A. Hirata (eds.), *Industrial Adjustment in Developed Countries and Its Implication for Developing Countries*, Institute of Developing Economies, Tokyo.

US DEPARTMENT OF COMMERCE, *US Industrial Outlook*, various issues.

US INTERNATIONAL TRADE COMMISSION (1992), *Industry and Trade Summary Television Receivers and Video Monitors*, Washington, DC.

WALSH SANDERSON, S. (1989), *The Consumer Electronics Industry and the Future Of American Manufacturing*, Economic Policy Institute, Washington, DC.

VAN MARION, M. (1993), *Liberal Trade and Japan – The Incompatibility Issue*, Physica-Verlag, Heidelberg.

VICKERY, G. (1989), "Recent Developments in the Consumer Electronics Industry", *STI Review*, No. 5, Paris, pp. 113-128.

YOFFIE, D. (1990), *International Trade and Competition – Cases and Notes in Strategy and Management*, McGraw-Hill, New York.

Chapter 6

GLOBALISATION IN THE NON-FERROUS METALS INDUSTRY

by
Dale Andrew
Trade Directorate, OECD

Table of contents

LIST OF TABLES

LIST OF FIGURES

SUMMARY AND CONCLUSIONS

The non-ferrous metals industry has long been an industry with characteristics which could justify it being termed "globalised". These included:

- the wide geographical distribution of ore deposits;

- a large part of output entering international trade;

- recourse to foreign investment to develop both mining and metals activities, through transfer of capital and technology.

The large metals firms' strategies generally consisted of ensuring sources of ores and concentrates for their smelters/refineries through integration of operations upstream.

The 1970s and 1980s represented a watershed in the industrial organisation of this sector. Today, if the above three factors remain important, the nature of the industry's globalisation has shifted:

- the integrated nature of the major companies has loosened in the upstream direction, with the rise of developing country producers and other independents in mining;

- smelting and refining operations have shifted to a number of choice sites known for the low costs of essential inputs, such as electricity;

- global siting at the production of the metals stage has led to rising trade intensity, particularly in unwrought metal, but also in worked metal or semi-manufactures and recycled metal;

- foreign direct investment (FDI) has shifted towards various forms of risk sharing, *e.g.* involving several partners in consortia and joint ventures, or new structures with interlocking ownerships straddling economic activity, continent and metal;

- joint venture and collaboration agreements have been established in certain downstream operations.

This chapter examines more specifically the aluminium industry, particularly the production of aluminium metal and aluminium semi-manufactures. After World War II, the aluminium oligopoly consisted entirely of integrated producers, with captive bauxite mines and alumina plants. The oil shocks in the 1970s, followed by a serious downturn in consumption, led to the withdrawal of a number of firms in the United States and the dismantling of the Japanese primary aluminium industry. At the firm level, the Big-6 concentration weakened as they abandoned their leadership strategy, thereby further lowering barriers to entry and hastening the entrance of new independent operators. By the late 1980s, most major firms had reduced their dependency on primary metal. Either they had strengthened their downstream operations where they enjoyed higher margins or they had diversified horizontally into related, but non-aluminium businesses, such as ceramics, plastics or other advanced materials. Many new firms had appeared in the smelting business with new production sited to take advantage of lower-cost inputs and based on mixed ownership.

The nature of the global orientation of the aluminium industry has changed during the period from the crisis of the early 1970s up to the late 1980s. The "disintegration" and "deverticalisation" strategies adopted by the former members of the oligopoly have included going "short" on aluminium metal. This probably has led to a lesser role, relatively, for shipments of metal between affiliates, including a weakening of intra-firm trade for many majors, as affiliates have bought primary metal from independent sources. On the other hand, certain medium-sized firms have been among the joint-venture partners in new, or expanding, smelter capacity in a move to increase their coverage of metal needs, which may be leading to greater intra-firm trade from these firms. Overall there has been greater cross-border movement in trade. The ratio of world exports to world production of metal has doubled in 20 years; since 1991, nearly 500 kilos per tonne of aluminium produced have been exported.

With respect to the new primary smelting capacity, cheaper energy sources not only represent a move away from earlier centres of production, but have had a certain dispersal effect in terms of the number of countries where capacity has been installed. Foreign investment is attracting greater numbers of partners in order to share risks in US$1-2 billion dollar projects.

In the case of aluminium semis, production appears to have become more concentrated at the firm level, although geographical dispersal of production sites has continued as several North American firms acquired holdings in Europe, and several European companies invested in semi-fabricating activities in the United States. The share of semis output which is exported has doubled over the past two decades. Intra-industry trade indices for several OECD countries show a rising trend for worked aluminium, indicating a specialisation in various aluminium semis. More recently cross-boundary strategic alliances have appeared to exploit strengths of the car and aluminium companies in the forthcoming "aluminised" car. These alliances involve Japanese steel and aluminium firms (with links to the car industry); US aluminium and Japanese aluminium/steel firms; and a few European aluminium firms and carmakers.

Overall, aluminium metal production is and has been a globalised industry in terms of trade and foreign investment, but shows few signs of increases in external sourcing or new alliances, such as collaboration arrangements, e.g. to share research and development (R&D). Customisation is not relevant to aluminium metal production, since the ingot is produced to just a few standard sizes and alloys. On the other hand, FDI appears to be increasingly involving joint ventures in which the smaller and medium-sized companies are participating. For aluminium semis, on the other hand, globalisation appears to be on a rising trend in the sense that external sourcing (i.e. ingot) is increasing, as is the density of networks among firms, and firms are working directly with the customer to customise products. Cross-border alliances in technology, production and marketing arrangements have begun to appear.

Recent and future buoyant growth in the aluminium sector is centring on secondary aluminium and recycling of scrap, favouring the appearance of secondary smelters whose feedstock is generally dependent on a network of local collection centres, i.e. locally sourced.

Even if governments do not generally have laws and regulations today which specifically target non-ferrous metals, policies of a horizontal nature affect this sector pervasively. Previous controls on foreign investment in natural resource ventures have tended to be liberalised and today, as foreign investment in the low-cost energy countries are eagerly courted, they entail few delays. Technology policies, including support to R&D, are aimed at promoting research in targeted areas or at rationalising private and public efforts by ensuring a co-ordination role. As non-ferrous metals and aluminium in particular are large electricity users, the government power monopolies' conditions for large customers entail policy issues affecting national competitive advantage. The current widespread usage of variable power tariffs linked to the price of aluminium is a case in point.

Competition policies have been a major issue for aluminium and other non-ferrous metals in the past. With a tendency in mergers and acquisitions over the past decade towards concentration in the aluminium semis plants, there are signs that competition laws may be posing barriers to industry plans for further rationalisation.

Trade disputes in the non-ferrous metals area have been less frequent than for other metals. Reducing tariff peaks and tariff escalation are issues which the Uruguay Round addressed. Only limited progress was made in reducing tariffs on higher stages of processed metal, and the proposal to eliminate tariffs on primary metal was not successfully adopted. In the case of aluminium metal, ingot continues to be protected by a 6 per cent tariff in the European Union. Australia, Canada and Japan dropped their peak tariffs on aluminium semi-manufactures, and the EU reduced tariffs on certain semis. In view of the growing importance of trade in scrap, export controls which have been in place in the past could again become an area for concern.

Effects of environmental policies constitute without a doubt industry's greatest preoccupation today. Besides first generation environmental issues of competitiveness and substitution issues arising from emission regulations, and liabilities for clean-up of hazardous wastes, new issues concern the shipments of secondary raw materials, which in some national laws and international environmental conventions could be subject to strict controls.

1. INTRODUCTION: CHARACTERISTICS OF THE INDUSTRY

This chapter focuses on aluminium, the most widely produced of the six non-ferrous metals and the most modern. First exploited at the end of the nineteenth century when simultaneously in France and the United States the process for using electrolysis to reduce alumina was discovered, aluminium in the post-war period knew growth rates of some 9 per cent per annum through the first oil shock. Since then, growth rates have been less than 2 per cent per year. Over the last two decades the industry has gone through profound changes, driven largely by the change in relative prices of inputs. Reactions by aluminium firms have not all been the same. For this reason alone it is a sector of interest to examine within the *problématique* of globalisation.

As illustrated in Figure 6.1, manufacturing products from aluminium entails several distinct processes. These are briefly explained below.

Aluminium is the second most widely found metalliferous element in the world's crust. Its technical properties of malleability, lightness, conductivity, corrosion resistance and recyclability have given it a place in all sectors of the economy. It is derived from bauxite, which today is mined principally in Australia, Jamaica, Guinea and Brazil. After being crushed, and washed, it is transported to a refinery where it is mixed with liquid caustic soda and calcinated in rotary kilns to produce alumina, a fine white powder. Large alumina refineries exist today both near bauxite mines (*e.g.* Australia and Jamaica) and in smelting countries, *e.g.* the United States, Germany, France and Canada. The trend has been away from the latter towards the former category of alumina producers. No further place is given in this chapter to the mining of bauxite and production of alumina.

Alumina is reduced into aluminium metal by electrolysis (a process called smelting) in cells or pots, through which electric current, up to 300 000 amperes, is run involving a series of cathodes and anodes. In a continuous process, the molten metal is siphoned out of the cells and transported to a casthouse where it is cast into ingots in standard sizes for trading. These may be small 50 lb. ingots or 10 metre long, 20 tonne rolling ingots destined for large rolling mills to produce sheet for beverage cans or foil. Other forms traded include extrusion billets, for use on extrusion presses to make window frames, or rod for drawing wire products, or ingots for casting diverse shapes (*e.g.* cylinder heads). Because pure aluminium is soft, it is often alloyed with any number of other metals, the most common being copper, manganese, magnesium, zinc or silicon.

Before reaching the final end-user or manufacturer, aluminium ingots or billets from the smelter's casthouse are fabricated into "semi-manufactures" (hereinafter called "semis") or cast by pouring a molten metal mixture into a sand or permanent mould or die. In mills or foundries, the pure or alloyed metal is rolled, extruded, drawn, forged or cast in order to make sheet and plate; foil; rod and bar; wire and conductor; cable (bare and insulated); drawn tube and pipe; welded tube; forgings and impacts; castings; extrusions; and power and paste. Over one-half of fabricated aluminium falls into the category of sheet and plate. Another 40 per cent is rod, bar and wire and extrusions and castings.

All of the large aluminium companies are also involved in fabricating semis. Whereas the extent of their involvement has taken on new proportions, the phenomenon is not new. Alcoa, which began producing aluminium ingot in 1888, was not immediately successful in selling ingot directly to manufacturers and got involved itself in the fabricating stage. Fabricators are classified into integrated producers – those which also produce bauxite, alumina and aluminium – and independent fabricators who buy primary aluminium or scrap from the arm's length market.

Following a significant restructuring and a prolonged period of below average growth rates in consumption, the industry appears to be driven today by:

– continuing search to keep costs down, most notably for electricity, which is its most expensive input;

◆ Figure 6.1. ***Overview of the integrated aluminium business***

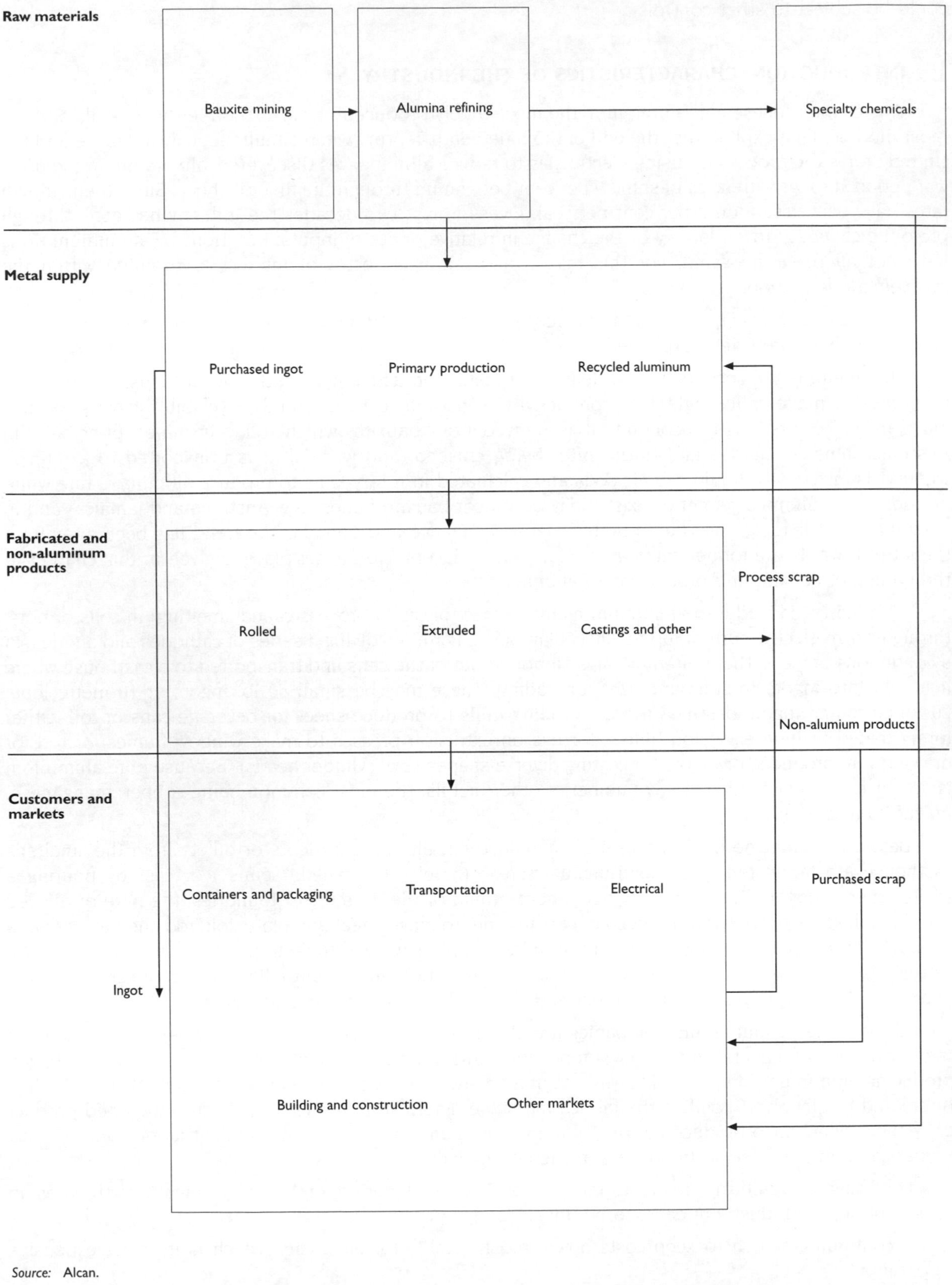

Raw materials

Bauxite mining → Alumina refining → Specialty chemicals

Metal supply

Purchased ingot   Primary production   Recycled aluminum

Fabricated and non-aluminum products

Rolled   Extruded   Castings and other

Process scrap

Non-alumium products

Customers and markets

Containers and packaging   Transportation   Electrical

Purchased scrap

Ingot

Building and construction   Other markets

Source: Alcan.

- intensifying R&D on new end-uses in the developed markets;
- developing traditional uses of the light metal in areas with low per capita consumption;
- widening the market in low income, developing regions where increase in metals use, *e.g.* in basic infrastructure and consumer goods, can be expected relatively soon;
- integrating downstream raw material sourcing through recycling initiatives.

2. TRENDS IN GROWTH AND STRUCTURE

A. Production and consumption

Production of the six main non-ferrous metals over the post-war era at five year intervals is illustrated in Figure 6.2. An estimate of the total value of production in 1993 of the 44 million tonnes of the six principal non-ferrous metals, based on market values, is US$55 billion. Due to the strong fluctuations in metal prices, this value figure also fluctuates widely; thus already in 1988, at a level of 42 million tonnes, the value for production of the six was nearly US$100 billion. Aluminium is today the most important of the six non-ferrous metals in terms of quantity produced.[1] Figure 6.3 shows the evolution in production and primary and secondary consumption of aluminium from 1971 to 1992.

The geographical distribution of production varies by metal. However, unlike the mining of ores and first stage dressing and concentration, which are located where rich deposits make their exploitation economical, metal refining has tended to be closer to larger consuming markets. In the case of aluminium, the capital role of input costs and particularly energy has driven a re-location towards low-cost energy sources, mainly hydro-power and natural gas which otherwise might have been flared. Important new smelter capacity has grown up in Canada, Brazil, Venezuela and the Persian Gulf area, based on low energy costs. Figure 6.4, illustrating the geographical shifts in production of bauxite, alumina and aluminium, shows the disappearance of Japanese metal output where electricity for smelters was oil-based and the drop by nearly half since 1960 in shares for the United States. With the exception of Canada and Australia, OECD Member countries have at best stayed constant (*e.g.* Norway) or more generally lost world production shares. As a result, the world's aluminimum industry, as a whole, has improved its overall economics by making use of more competitive inputs. This can be seen by the flattening of the cost curve over time.

The pattern of consumption of aluminium varies considerably among regions. Table 6.1 sets out the shares taken by the various end-uses in US, European and Japanese markets. The United States stands out by its difference; the overwhelming area of demand in the United States is for containers and packaging, some three times higher than in other countries. Most of this demand is for can stock, used in manufacturing the beverage can.

The transportation sector uses aluminium alloys in the construction of all types of equipment. Not only air planes, but railway rolling stock and marine vessels are consuming increasing quantities of aluminium. But it is the passenger car which many aluminium companies are banking on to become "aluminised" in the relatively near future. Up until now, certain discrete pieces have been substituted: radiators, wheels and cylinder heads. Or luxury or race cars have been specially designed with aluminium parts. Attention is focused on where and how the motor car can make further significant improvements in fuel efficiency and to improve recyclability. One major aluminium company is predicting that the current average of 87 kg of aluminium in a US automobile could rise to 225 kg by 2005; this is up from 25 kg in 1960 (see Table 6.2.)

The cyclical nature of the metals industry is reflected in the sharp fluctuations of the sector's contribution to total manufacturing value added, with high price years (1973-74 and 1980) corresponding to peaks in Figure 6.5. The sector as a whole contributed about 2.1 per cent on average over the 1970-87 period for a group of 13 OECD countries. Industries with above-average contribution to value added can be found in Australia, Canada and Norway. For this latter country, the large aluminium industry (largest primary metal output in Europe) combined with very strong prices in 1988, resulted in some 9 per cent of total manufacturing value added originating in the non-ferrous metals sector.

Indicators using volume data provide a clearer picture of the sector's changes over the last two decades. Thus in Table 6.3, the significant shifts in the production to consumption ratios for primary

◆ Figure 6.2. **World production and consumption of six main non-ferrous metals**
1946-92

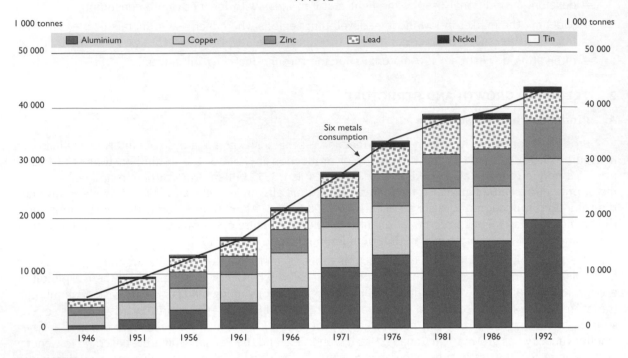

Source: *Statistical Yearbook*, 1993 Edition, MINEMET (Metaleurop).

◆ Figure 6.3. **Production and consumption – Aluminium**
1971-92

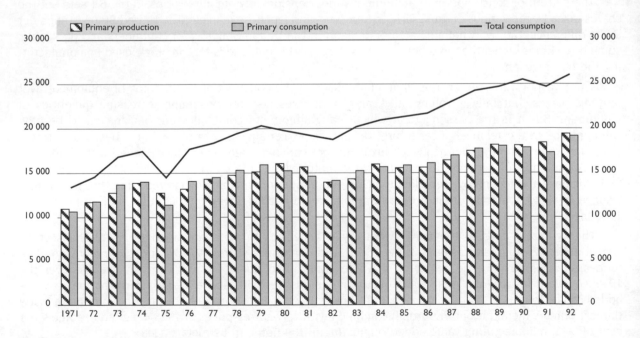

Note: Total consumption is the sum of primary consumption plus secondary consumption.
Source: Metallgesellschaft, Metallatistik.

◆ Figure 6.4. **Production of bauxite, alumina and aluminium, 1960, 1975 and 1992**

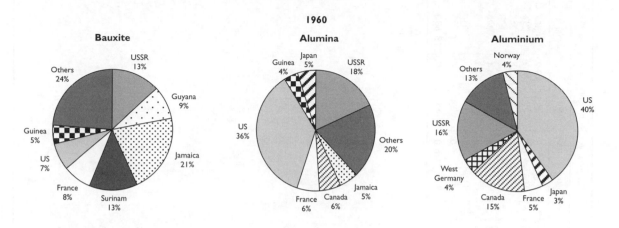

1960

Bauxite — Alumina — Aluminium

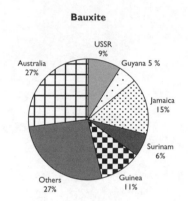
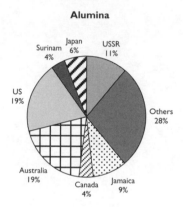
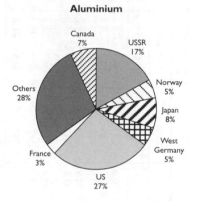

1975

Bauxite — Alumina — Aluminium

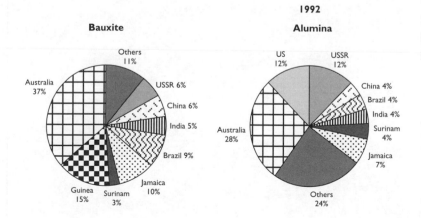
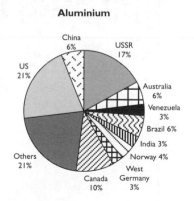

1992

Bauxite — Alumina — Aluminium

Source: NAPPI, C., "Aluminium", in Tilton *et al.*; 1992 from MG, Metallstatistk.

Table 6.1. **Consumption of aluminium by end use, 1992**

	Building and construction		Transport		Electrical		Packaging		Household articles		Machinery		Other		Total	
	000 t	(%)	000 t	(%)	000 t	(%)	000 t	(%)	000 t	(%)	000 t	(%)	000 t	(%)	000 t	(%)
Europe-5																
Germany[1]	709	21.4	991	30.0	293	8.9	404	12.2	216	6.5	259	7.8	435	13.2	3 307	100
France	231	19.0	411	33.8	83	6.8	99	8.1	66	5.4	105	8.6	222	18.3	1 216	100
Italy	88	15.0	234	39.8	77	13.1	57	9.7	25	4.3	33	5.6	75	12.8	588	100
Spain	314	32.1	244	24.9	75	7.7	97	9.9	100	10.2	88	8.8	61	6.2	978	100
United Kingdom	21	9.3	85	37.8	33	14.7	56	24.9	12	5.3	8	3.6	10	4.4	225	100
Japan	55	18.3	17	5.7	25	8.3	95	31.7	13	4.3	27	9.0	67	22.3	300	100
United States	901	25.4	1 150	32.4	253	7.1	363	10.2	–[2]	–[2]	113	3.2	768	21.6	3 548	100
	1 144	16.9	1 558	23.0	587	8.7	2 259	33.3	523	7.7	448	6.6	256	3.8	6 775	100
Total 7	**2 754**	**20.2**	**3 699**	**27.1**	**1 133**	**8.3**	**3 026**	**22.2**	**739**	**5.4**	**820**	**6.0**	**1 459**	**10.7**	**13 630**	**100**

1. 1991.
2. Included in "Other".
Source: Metallgesellschaft, *Metallstatistik, 1982-92*

Table 6.2. **Use of aluminium in the automobile, 1960-2005**

	Kilogrammes/car
1960	25
1971	35
1981	59
1991	87
2000 [1]	159
2005 [1]	225

1. Projection.
Source: Based on US Aluminum Association research and estimates, trade press and Reynolds, *Annual Report, 1992.*

Table 6.3. **Indicators for production and consumption – Aluminium**

	Primary metal					
	Production to consumption			Exports to production		
	1971	1981	1993	1971	1981	1993
Australia	1.6	1.5	3.7	0.4	0.3	0.78
Austria	1.2	0.9	0.0	0.3	0.3	n.a.
Canada	3.9	3.6	5.5	0.8	0.7	0.79
France	1.0	0.8	0.6	0.4	0.4	0.56
Germany	0.6	0.7	0.5	0.1	0.2	0.44
Italy	0.5	0.7	0.3	0.1	0.2	0.22
Japan	0.9	0.5	0.01	0.0	0.0	0.47
Netherlands	2.0	3.6	1.9	1.2	1.3	1.73
New Zealand	1.5	5.3	13.0	0.1	0.8	0.82
Norway	6.4	5.7	6.4	0.8	0.8	0.89
Spain	0.8	2.0	1.2	0.0	0.4	0.55
Sweden	1.0	1.0	0.9	0.3	0.5	0.64
Switzerland	1.1	0.8	0.3	0.2	0.5	0.16
United Kingdom	0.4	1.0	0.4	0.4	0.5	0.54
United States	0.9	1.1	0.8	0.0	0.1	0.12

	Semi-manufactures: exports to production		
	1971	1981	1992
Australia	0.0	0.1	0.3
Austria	0.5	0.8	0.7
Belgium	0.8	1.0	1.0
Canada	0.1	0.1	0.8
France	0.3	0.5	0.5
Germany	0.3	0.5	0.5
Italy	0.2	0.2	0.3
Japan	0.1	0.1	0.07
Netherlands	0.4	0.9	1.1
Norway	0.6	0.6	0.9
Spain	0.3	0.2	0.4
Sweden	0.4	0.6	0.3
Switzerland	0.4	0.6	0.6
United Kingdom	0.1	0.3	0.6
United States	0.0	0.1	0.1

Source: OECD based on WBMS, *World Metal Statistics*, and Metallgesellschaft, *Metallstatistik.*

◆ Figure 6.5a. **Value-added shares – Non-ferrous metals**

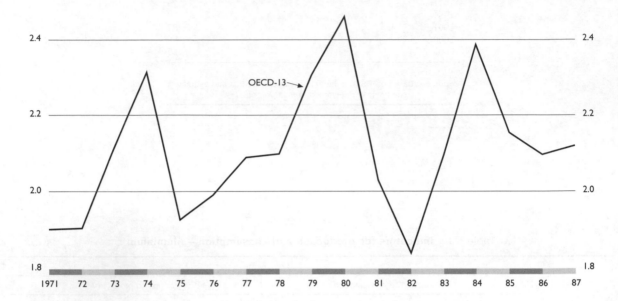

OECD-13 →

Source: OECD, DSTI, STAN Database.

◆ Figure 6.5b. **Value-added shares – Non-ferrous metals**

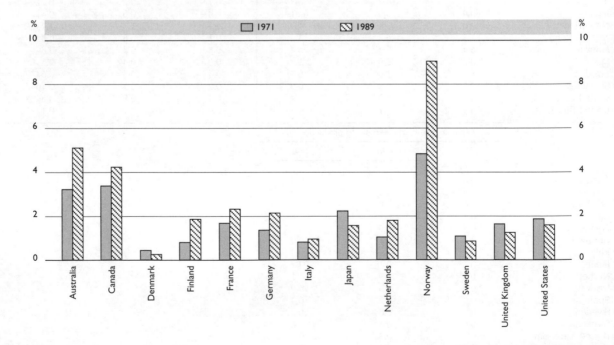

□ 1971   ▨ 1989

Note: Netherlands: 1987 data; Australia and United Kingdom: 1988 data.
Source: OECD, DSTI, STAN database.

aluminium correspond to the increasing importance of *e.g.* Canada and Australia as world producers, and the concomitant drop reflects relative loss in smelter capacity in the United States and Japan. With regard to semi-manufactures, shifts in Table 6.3 reveal that it is not necessarily the metal exporters which have become important suppliers of aluminium fabricated goods. In general, the European countries have high export to production ratios for semis.

B.   Employment

The non-ferrous metals sector has consistently lost jobs over the last two decades, as has employment in manufacturing generally (see Figure 6.6). In larger countries, such as the United States and Japan, the loss in the sector's share in overall manufacturing employment has been minimal. Even in countries like Canada and Australia where the non-ferrous metals sector is important, employment since 1980 has fallen, both in absolute levels and as a share of total manufacturing employment.

◆   Figure 6.6.   *Employment growth – Non-ferrous metals*

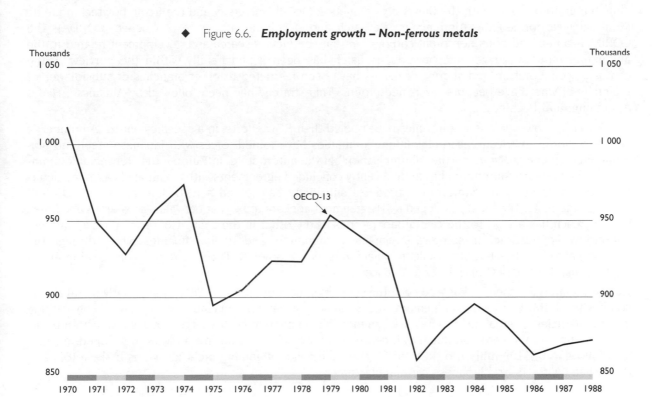

Source: OECD, DSTI, STAN database.

C.   Research and development

The non-ferrous metals industries have over the last years intensified their efforts to develop new processes and end-uses for their metal. Unlike the chemical industry companies which can change a formula to produce a new product, non-ferrous metals must basically work with the qualities of their metal. Continued growth in markets depend both on remaining cost competitive and finding new outlets. Four basic directions of R&D can be discerned in the case of the aluminium companies: *i)* improvements in the basic, century-old Hall-Héroult electrolytic process to reduce alumina into aluminium, *e.g.* in the area of energy efficiency; *ii)* techniques to increase throughput in processing of aluminium into semi-fabricated goods; *iii)* development of new end-uses for aluminium; and *iv)* development of new composite materials, *i.e.* through aluminium powder metallurgy.

R&D intensity for the non-ferrous metals industry as a whole has risen, as shown in Figure 6.7. Nonetheless, the OECD-13 average at just over 1 per cent of production, is half of that for total manufacturing and significantly below certain R&D-intensive sectors such as pharmaceuticals which were near 9 per cent of production at the end of the 1980s. R&D expenditures by the large aluminium companies would tend to confirm the modern, dynamic image of the industry, situating it above other non-ferrous metals. R&D expenditures of a few large aluminium companies range from US$40 million to US$250 million, or an intensity ratio of between 1 and 2.5 per cent of sales.

Research is carried out in a variety of locations and types of arrangements. Unlike other sectors, it is not solely headquarter-located. When associated with a particular stage of processing, labs are established next to the plants for that stage. In fact, in keeping with the downstreaming of activities, many large companies have trumpeted the decentralised nature of their R&D activities. A few, such as Pechiney and Comalco, are working closely with universities and the public R&D infrastructure. In Canada, the primary aluminimum producers, with the University of Quebec, McGill University and the École polytechnique de Montréal have formed the Aluminimum Research and Development Centre of Quebec (CQRDA). The CQRDA is an autonomous non-profit corporation that conducts research and development related to the aluminium industry. In general, however, research has been kept carefully within the purview of the company; collaboration and sharing of results have been restricted to other branches or subsidiaries or members of what have become diversified groups. This strategy has been followed by Alusuisse, Hydro Aluminium and Pechiney.

Recently, however, a few companies have pooled their R&D efforts, in a specific context. A number of generally North-American-based aluminium companies have joined forces with Japanese steel and aluminium companies to work on the "aluminisation" of the automobile. In Europe, the Norwegian aluminium company Hydro Aluminium has more recently concluded agreements with a couple of car manufacturers and the Pechiney aluminium mill products subsidiary has joined a R&D agreement with US and Japanese interests. The most developed R&D agreement appears to be that between Alcoa and Kobe Steel, whereby each has access to the central laboratories of the other in the context of developing aluminium automotive applications. In some cases, Japanese aluminium and steel companies, which through the *kereitsu* have close ties to automobile manufacturers, have pooled R&D efforts to work on the aluminised car [see also Section 4.C.*b*) below on Alliances].

New materials research has also been the subject of the aluminium industry, particularly metal matrix composites (MMC), utilising aluminium and ceramic powder reinforcements, such as silicon carbide ceramic particles. Honda and Toyota have commercially implemented MMCs on a mass production basis, including fibre-reinforced aluminium cylinder liners and blocks. "Duralcan", an MMC developed in Alcan labs following US$100 million of R&D effort, is on the verge of gaining broad usage as brake rotors and drive shafts with US and Japanese car manufacturers.

D. Capital investment

Smelting and refining of metals is capital-intensive. Due to the sector's relatively small share in total manufacturing production, investment shares nonetheless appear low. From the late 1970s through the 1980s, investment in the non-ferrous metals sector has taken from a little less than 3 to as much as 3.5 per cent of all investment going to manufacturing for the group of OECD-13. This compares to higher ratios of 6-7 per cent for the steel sector and 8-9 per cent for paper and print. However, as a share of the value of non-ferrous metals production, investment to this sector has run between 4 and 5.5 per cent, high relative to other sectors.

Aluminium smelters completed in recent years have cost around US$1 billion; feasibility studies under way for those in the 1990s are expected to run as high as US$1.5 billion. Occasionally in the case of an aluminium smelter, a hydroelectricity project may be associated, increasing costs even further. For this reason, a preferred solution in many cases has consisted of expanding existing plant rather than embarking on building green-field smelters. Nonetheless, the attraction of cheap electricity has been so great to

◆ Figure 6.7a. **R&D intensity – Non-ferrous metals**

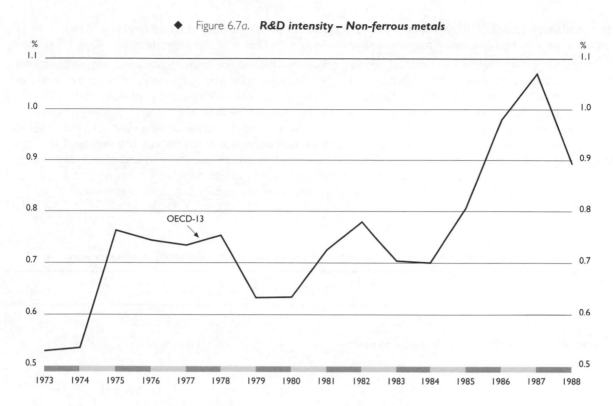

Source: OECD, DSTI, STAN database.

◆ Figure 6.7b. **R&D intensity – Non-ferrous metals**

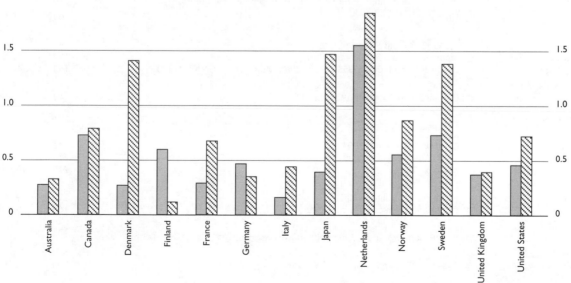

Note: Australia and Netherlands: 1988 data.
Source: OECD, DSTI, STAN database.

the smelting business, where power is almost 30 per cent of operating costs, that over the planned life of a smelter, guaranteed low rates may nonetheless win out in favour of the new smelter.

The huge amounts of fixed capital needed, together with the importance of significant variable costs, have constituted an important "globalising" factor. Already under way in the late 1970s, a trend towards relocation of the primary aluminium industry was maturing in the 1980s, and continues today. The cost factor – both fixed capital costs and variable electricity costs – has had several consequences. First, smelters have been increasingly located further away from the ingot-consuming industries. This "dislocation", while not universal, is widespread. Smelters in Venezuela, Iceland, Canada, the Persian Gulf states and Australia are highly, or even quasi-exclusively, export-oriented. Secondly in order to share the risk, consortia are formed to pool capital in joint ventures. A glance at Table 6.4 reveals that recent and planned smelters are almost all being financed as joint ventures, involving several partners.[2]

Table 6.4. **Major capacity increases (recent, planned or under consideration) in primary aluminium**

Region/country Location or company	Major partners	Amount (000 t)	Date
Europe			
Iceland			
Atlantal	Austria, Granges, Hoogovens	200	98
Norway			
Hydro Aluminium			
Sore-Norge	Alusuisse (50%)	93	97-98
France			
Dunkirk	Pechiney (100%)	215	92-93
Africa			
Nigeria	German Gov't. Reynolds	90-180	98
South Africa	Alusuisse (22%)	466	95-97
Egypt	Nag Nammadi/Egyptalum	60	
Australasia			
Bahrain	Bahrain Govt., Saudi Arabia and Breton Investments (Germany)	247	92-94
Iran	Iran Govt. and Dubai International Development Co-operation	110	92-93
India	Hindalco	60	96-97
Australia			
Portland	Alcoa (23%) and Victoria State	40	97
Boyne	Japanese (Kobe, Sumitomo, et al.)	230/150	95
Tomago	Pechiney (35%); Gove (35%), Australian Mutual (15%); VAW (12%)	140	93
New Zealand			
Tiwai	Comalco and Sumitomo Chemical	43	96
Americas			
Canada			
Baie Corneau	Canadian Reynolds (100%)	41	92
Sept-Iles	VAW; Austria; Kobe Steel; Hoogovens; SGF	215	92-94
Deschambault	Alumax (100%)	215	92-94
Brazil			
Alumar	Alcoa (61%); Billiton (40%)	190	97-98
Albras	CVRD and Japanese led by Mitsui	166	97-98
Trinidad			
Point Lisas	JV with Jamaica and German-Nigerian consortium		
Chile			
Alumysa	Aysen (Chile) and Noranda (Canada)	230	98
Venezuela			
Venalum	Venez. govt. and 6 Japanese partners	19	94-95
Aluyana	Italimpianti (Italy –40%) and CVG (15%) + Venezuelan private	215	98

Source: UNCTAD Secretariat, based on company annual reports; trade journals.

Thirdly, the major companies which are participating in the new joint ventures have generally been rationalising their existing capacity or wishing to replace high-cost capacity – rather than trying to keep up with the growth in primary metal demand by maintaining their share of world smelting capacity. Fourthly, high capital and energy costs have contributed to the growth in secondary smelters which are both less capital- and energy-intensive (using about 5 per cent of the energy required to produce primary aluminium from bauxite.) Secondary plants are thus being built closer to the sources of supply of their raw material, for example the used beverage can (UBC). This trend is acting in another direction from the "dislocation" seen in the installation of primary smelters. A force to spread such secondary activities more globally can be seen in the recent promotion of such plants, e.g. in Europe by certain North American firms which have accumulated experience with remelt and other recycling facilities.

E. Integration, concentration, dispersal and product substitution

a) Integrated metal firms and independents

Non-ferrous metals firms generally can be classified either as: i) producers which have been integrated upstream from metals processing and (depending on the metal) downstream into semi-fabricating; or ii) those non-integrated companies involved in one phase of the industry, such as smelting or refining of ores and concentrates, which are bought from a mining company or on a metal exchange at arm's length prices. Early strategies of the larger mining houses were to develop captive mines to ensure sources of raw materials for metal refining. However, in the course of depleting mine deposits close to home, not all companies integrated upstream by investing abroad. These "custom smelters" enter into tolling arrangements through which they process dressed ores or concentrates for a commission or treatment charge. Several of the European refineries fall into this category, that is they toll smelt and refine zinc or copper concentrates. The Japanese copper refining industry is also a case in point. Originally built up on the basis of locally mined concentrates, it was kept in place after local ore deposits were exhausted and now thrives almost exclusively on imported concentrates. A similar situation prevails for zinc. In addition, custom smelters are relying more and more heavily upon secondary raw materials sourced from recycling activities to supplement their traditional feedstock.

b) Firm concentration

The case is somewhat different in the aluminium industry. The group known as the Big-6 – made up of Alcoa and its three spin-offs in the 1940s (Kaiser and Reynolds in the United States and Alcan in Canada) and the two largest European producers (Alusuisse and Pechiney) – have all been integrated with upstream operations in bauxite mining and alumina refining. The oligopoly was dealt a serious blow by the 1970s oil shocks and increased price volatility, together with the decision of certain to abandon the leadership strategy. These various factors facilitated the expansion of some small independents and the entry of new ones. As illustrated in Table 6.5, the result was a drop in Big-6 shares of Western World

Table 6.5. **Concentration of primary aluminium production: the Big Six, 1955-98**

Percentage of Western world production

	1955	1965	1970	1972	1981	1986	1992	1998
Alcoa	23.2	17.1	16.3	15.4	13.8	11.6	10.8	10.4
Alcan	24.5	15.6	16.3	15.3	11.9	12.5	10.7	10.0
Reynolds	13.5	13.2	12.8	11.0	9.8	6.0	6.5	6.2
Kaiser	13.3	11.5	9.4	8.8	8.4	6.8	3.4	3.1
Pechiney	6.1	8.4	9.3	8.1	8.0	5.1	4.9	4.4
Alusuisse	4.0	6.8	6.6	5.6	5.7	3.4	2.2	1.7
Big six	**84.5**	**72.3**	**70.7**	**64.2**	**57.7**	**45.4**	**38.6**	**35.9**

Source: J.L. Mardonese et al., "The Copper and Aluminium Industries: A Review of Structural Changes", *Resources Policy*, March 1985, updated in de SA, "From Oligopoly to Competition" and from UNCTAD Secretariat, company annual reports and the *Spector Report*.

production from pre-oil shock levels in 1972 of 64 per cent to 45 in 1986 and down to 38.5 in 1992. In fact two of the original Big-6 – Kaiser and Alusuisse – have dropped to ranks 8 and 12. Hydro Aluminium, owned by the Norwegian government, holds place number 5 and Alumax, a newcomer to the North American aluminium market since the oil shocks, is number 6; each holds 4.4 per cent of Western World Production. But even this new line-up of the top six holds only some 45 per cent of Western World Production.

Current plans – although in limbo due to the current depressed market – point to a continued weakening of the supply leadership of the Big-6. Their combined production has been projected at 36 per cent of world capacity in 1998, with Alcoa and Alcan each dropping to around 10 per cent.

Together with the loss of oligopoly power to control prices and decide on capacity expansions, the majors' concentration in downstream fabricating operations, led to what has been termed "disintegration", as certain majors are turning to the independents and exchanges for part of their metal needs. The sourcing of inputs from outside the parent company represents a change in industrial organisation which continues to affect the pattern of investments upstream.[3]

Table 6.6. **The 15 largest primary aluminium companies, 1975, 1984 and 1990**

Controlling company/ state producer	Country of incorporation	Controlled production (000 t)	Share of western world production (%)	1984 rank	1975 rank
Aluminium Co. of America	United States	1 862e	12.8	2	2
Alcan Aluminium Ltd	Canada	1 762	12.1	1	1
State of France (Pechiney)	France	927e	6.4	5	4
Reynolds Metals Co.	United States	809e	5.6	3	3
State of Norway (Hydro Aluminium)	Norway	638	4.4	7	7
Amax Inc. (Alumax)	United States	637e	4.4	11	–
State of Venezuela (CVG and FIV)	Venezuela	595e	4.1	10	–
Maxxam group Inc (Kaiser)	United States	514	3.5	8	5
RTZ Corporation plc (Comalco)	United Kingdom	460	3.2	6	22
Marc Rich & Co.	Switzerland	451e	3.1	–	–
Viag AG (VAW)	Germany	429e	2.9	9	8
Alusuisse-Lonza Holding Ltd	Switzerland	413e	2.8	4	6
State of Spain (Inespal)	Spain	355	2.4	17	24
State of Yugoslavia	Yugoslavia	349	2.4	14	14
State of India (Federal and regional)	India	268	1.8	–	17
Total 15		10 469	71.8		
Total Western world		14 575	100.0		
Total world		**18 200**			

e = estimate.
Source: Unctad and Raw Material Group, *Who owns Who in Mining 1992.*

c) *Geographical dispersal*

As aluminium is a commodity – that is a product made to a few standard specifications and which is traded independently of a brand name or customer allegiance – the advantages for firms involved in smelting to position themselves globally cannot be for reasons of seeking out specialised demand or niche markets. Indeed, as has been seen, the primary reason for "dislocation" has been the attraction of cheap energy sources. Alcoa, Alcan, Pechiney and Reynolds – the current top four producers – have full control or own shares in smelters in Australia, Brazil or Canada, *i.e.* in countries charging low energy costs outside their home country. Only Hydro Aluminium, fully owned by Norsk Hydro, has no aluminium reduction plants elsewhere than in Norway.[4] Conversely, practically no non-North-American companies have equity shares in primary smelting capacity in the United States.[5]

At the stage of semi-fabricating, the aluminium industry is showing increased signs of globalisation in terms of firms investing in other markets. European firms have taken up positions in the US fabricating market. Hydro Aluminium, Alusuisse and Pechiney have a significant presence in the US market, although the latter two European companies have moved there in line with their general group strategies of diversification, including into the aluminium manufacturing or packaging and containers sector. Alcan, has, for many years, had major investments in semi-manufacturing in Europe; it has owned and operated semi-fabricating facilities in Germany since 1924, France since 1956, Italy since 1927, and the United Kingdom since 1930. More recently, it has expanded its holdings in rolling mills in Germany. Other North American firms have also been investing in European semi-manufacturing capacity, in order to get a foothold in the EU Single Market.

d) Product substitution

Just as aluminium grew by leaps and bounds (ca. 9 per cent annually) in the period up until the 1970s by carving out new end-uses and taking over other materials and metals, aluminium has been facing steep competition and has lost certain markets in recent years. Despite many technical qualities, its relatively high price means that markets are constantly threatened. For example, siding for housing, originally seen as an important future home for aluminium growth, has almost disappeared now in favour of vinyl siding; aluminium bottle closures have been losing out to plastic closures. Table 6.1 also indicated how end-uses vary considerably among national markets. Part of firms' globalising strategies currently is to develop product uses in national markets where aluminium has not yet spread.

The much higher growth rate of secondary aluminimum relative to primary ingot since 1980 suggests too a certain degree of substitution, at least for a limited number of end-uses. Thus over the decade 1982 to 1992, consumption of primary aluminium grew at a compound rate of 2.7 per cent per annum, whereas secondary consumption grew 5.3 per cent per year. The growth in scrap collection and recycling, particularly of the used beverage can (UBC), has contributed to the slowing of demand of primary aluminimum. The inroads into the automotive industry, particularly for castings, e.g. of engine blocks, are largely attributable to availability of cheaper secondary aluminium, and as such complementary secondary aluminimum to primary sources.

It is interesting to note firms' reactions to the growth in demand for secondary aluminium. A few of the big firms – traditionally specialised in the primary aluminium business – showed reticence, leaving much of the growth to small independent firms. Partly due to the weak primary market since 1991 and also in view of public environmental concerns, interest seems to be increasing by the majors.

F. Pricing

Like most primary commodities, prices of aluminium fluctuate strongly in reaction to changes in supply and demand. Figure 6.8 shows movements over the last ten years. Recent weak prices are due to the combined effects of weak demand due to recession in many OECD countries and the exceptionally large volume of exports from Russia leading to the build-up of stocks, particularly in London Metal Exchange warehouses in Europe (see below). Strong prices in 1988 have been explained as the result of a strong boost in demand from an upswing in business activity coming after the lengthy structural over-capacity had been worked out and stocks run down to historic lows. Cut-backs in production at several smelters around the world in 1993 and 1994 have had only a limited effect, since at the same time new, low-cost smelters have come on-stream.

Today's volatile aluminium prices, however, are relatively new. Part of the Big-6 strategy was to promote demand of aluminium by ensuring price stability, which could be done by meeting demand surges with adjustments to stocks and increased operating rates. Over the longer run, they could, by setting "cost-plus" prices, ensure "planned excess capacity" in order to be in a position to meet increases in demand (and which also acted as additional barriers to entry for independents).

◆ Figure 6.8. **Aluminium prices**
Monthly averages from 1986 to 1995

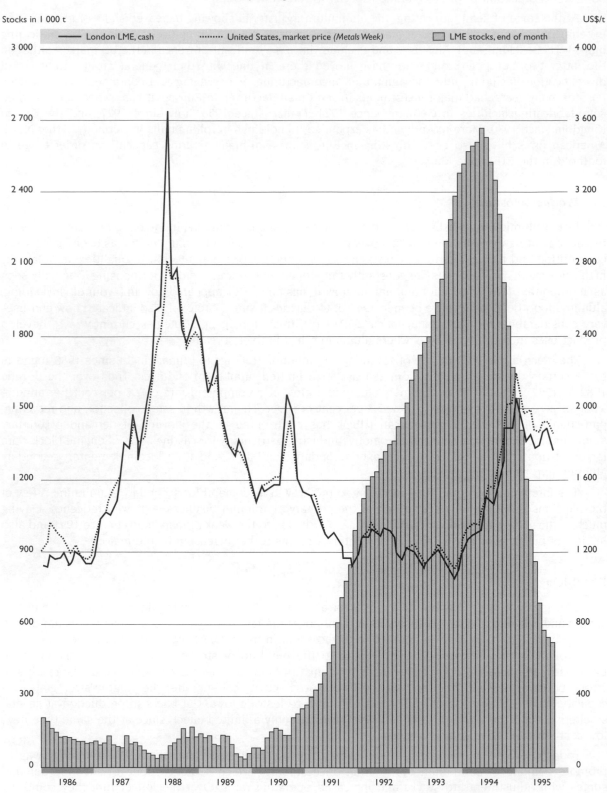

Stocks in 1 000 t

—— London LME, cash .... United States, market price *(Metals Week)* ☐ LME stocks, end of month

US$/t

Source: Metallgesellschaft.

In the wake of the disintegrating oligopoly and the increase in numbers of producers, prices became more volatile and demand from consumers for a hedging mechanism led to the introduction of ingot trading on the LME in October 1978. In the course of the 1980s the various systems of producer prices all collapsed. The Alcan World Price, which had been used in price transactions between buyers in Japan and producers in developing countries, was discontinued in late 1984. A "major US producer" price had also been used as a reference point for transactions. After not having budged from 1983 to 1986, it was discontinued in November 1986. As for the US majors', the European producer price was suspended in early 1988 after having sat immutable for over four years. Considerable controversy has reigned over the appropriateness and efficiency of the two systems, with producers charging that the LME system, together with instantaneous information on the level of stocks, has contributed to the volatility of prices. But after 15 years, the LME contract does not today appear to be seriously in danger. The rapid growth and importance of secondary aluminium products prompted the LME to establish a separate trading contract for secondary aluminimum ingot in 1992.

Prices for semis, on the other hand, show much less volatility. Unlike for other commodities, and notably copper, most aluminium semi production is controlled by the integrated aluminium companies. As seen above, the majors in the 1970s and 1980s all tended to concentrate downstream on fabricating. Thus fairly concentrated market power has allowed recourse to list, or administered, prices. The majors can ride out periods of high ingot prices, (which represent 70 per cent of the semi prices), and squeeze margins, if they can realise large margins on semis in periods of low ingot prices. In addition, firms have for many products made their production correspond to particular consumer demands, *i.e.* market niches. Also aware of the inherent limit on prices due to the danger of substitution, integrated fabricators are willing to exercise moderation, even when their margins are low in periods of high ingot prices.

3. INTERNATIONAL TRADE

A. Patterns of trade

a) *Growth in OECD and world trade*

Between 1971 and 1992, total imports by OECD countries of non-ferrous metals grew from US$7.2 billion to US$44.3 billion, with exports growing from US$5.5 billion to US$40.4 billion. Average growth was thus just under 10 per cent, in current value terms, per year. Aluminium, both unwrought and worked, accounted for 25 (33) per cent of OECD non-ferrous metals imports (exports) in 1971 and 50 (53) per cent in 1991, indicating faster growth in aluminium trade than for the other non-ferrous metals.

World exports (imports) of unwrought aluminium in 1992 were US$ 11.7 billion (US$12.8 billion); for aluminium semis, another US$14.8 billion (US$14.7 billion). Thus trade totalled some US$26.5-27.5 billion for both unwrought and worked aluminium. In real (volume) terms, world exports of aluminium metal grew some 6 per cent per year since 1971. This compares with growth in output of primary metal of only 2.6 per cent over the same period. Thus, as for manufacturing exports in general, trade in aluminium grew faster than output. As can be seen in Table 6.7, on average, for one tonne of metal produced, almost 500 kilos has entered world trade since 1991. This was nearly twice the 1971 figure of 260 kilos exported per tonne produced.

B. Directions of trade

a) *Aluminium metal*

The OECD region has been, and remains, the dominant aluminium producing and exporting area. Nonetheless, the developing region has been gaining market shares, moving from 7 per cent of world exports in the early 1970s to one-quarter in 1990. These market shares have been taken about equally from the OECD region and from the eastern European countries. The OECD region as a whole still exports some 64 per cent of primary aluminium, down from 73 per cent in 1971. Among OECD members, Canadian and Australian exports progressed the most. The EC dropped from an 18 per cent share to 13.5 per cent in 1990.

Table 6.7. **Exports relative to production, 1971-92 – Aluminium**

	World exports (000 t)	World production (000 t)	Exports to production (%)
1971	2 813	10 944	25.7
1972	3 252	11 649	27.9
1973	3 704	12 742	29.1
1974	3 696	13 818	26.7
1975	3 291	12 714	25.9
1976	3 631	13 209	27.5
1977	3 856	14 339	26.9
1978	4 337	14 764	29.4
1979	4 116	15 168	27.1
1980	4 875	16 031	30.4
1981	4 796	15 701	30.5
1982	5 328	13 972	38.1
1984	5 892	15 989	36.9
1986	6 616	15 673	42.2
1987	7 313	16 492	44.3
1988	7 470	17 496	42.7
1989	8 016	19 172	41.8
1990	8 717	19 346	45.1
1991	9 644	19 685	49.0
1992	9 583	19 453	49.3

Source: Based on UNCTAD, *Commodity Yearbook* and Minemmet, *Annuaire Statistique*, 1992

The United States has been, and still remains, the world's largest primary aluminium producer, with output at slightly more than 4 million tonnes. US production entering trade has fluctuated a great deal. Traditionally most output has been directed towards domestic consumption. Thus through the 1970s exports were only 100-200 Kt. After dropping from higher levels in the early 1980s, US exports of primary aluminium doubled between 1986 and 1988 and more than doubled again between 1988 and 1991, only to drop back by half, almost to the 1988 level, in 1993. This sharp surge in exports during the late 1980s was not due to new additions in capacity (the last US smelter was built in 1980), but is to be explained in part by a drop in domestic demand, and by structural factors. During the restructuring of the US industry in the 1980s, the large US companies divested, closed or reduced capacity in nearly 20 smelters, ten of which were closed permanently. Several of the smelters which were sold off by the US majors were bought by independents. These "abandoned for dead" or Lazarus smelters, being non-integrated, increased the share of production exported. For example one independent smelter toll converts alumina for the Norwegian state producer, Hydro Aluminium and BHP, an Australian company.

Canada's share of world exports fell between the early 1970s and the late 1980s. Following its impressive increase in new smelter capacity in recent years, Canada's share of world exports rose in 1992 and again in 1993 to over the one-sixth mark. Preliminary indications are that in 1994 its share dropped slightly, due to the surge in exports from the New Independent States (NIS).

The developing country producers which contributed most to this group's increased share of world exports are found above all in Latin America – particularly Brazil and Venezuela.

Imports of aluminium are even more concentrated than exports in the OECD region, which takes four-fifths of world imports. Since the dismantling of its domestic industry in the 1980s,[6] Japan is by far the world's largest importer, taking about 30 per cent of total world exports. Most of these imports come from Japanese firms' equity participations in smelters around the world, via long-term contracts or as "spot" metal from the commodity exchanges (where origin may be unknown or of little interest). In 1991, in decreasing order of importance, Japanese imports originated in the United States, Australia, Brazil and Venezuela. The United States and Germany have been almost equally sharing second and third places over the last several years, each taking about 12 per cent of world imports. The quasi-totality of US imports has traditionally come from Canada. While the United States still imports the bulk of its aluminium from Canada, imports from non-Canadian sources, particularly the Commonwealth of Independent States (CIS),

Table 6.8. **Production/consumption and exports of primary aluminium from the NIS, 1988-94**

Million tonnes

	1988	1989	1990	1991	1992	1993	1994[1]
Smelter capacity	3.4	3.5	3.5	3.6	3.6	3.6	3.6
Production	3.2-3.5	3.3-3.5	3.2-3.5	3.1-3.3	3.1-3.2	3.1	2.8
(Russia)			(2.92)	(2.73)	(2.73)	(2.72)	
Consumption	2.6-2.9	2.5-2.7	2.4-2.7	1.8-2.3	1.6-2.1	1.2	0.9
(Russia)			(2.39)	(2.06)	(1.43)	(1.12)	
Exports	0.6-0.7	0.6-0.7	0.6-0.7	0.8-0.9	0.95-1.4	1.6-2.0	1.9
(Russia)			(0.53)	(0.67)	(1.29)	(1.6)	(1.4)

1. Forecast.
Source: US Bureau of Mines; Natural Resources Canada; CRU; WBMS; Russian Goskomstat.

rose significantly in 1994. Germany's first source of imports in 1991 was Norway, and then rather evenly spread among its European neighbours (Netherlands, the United Kingdom, France) and from Ghana, Brazil and Venezuela. These top-3 OECD importing countries account for over one-half of aluminium ingot shipments. Growth in imports by certain DAEs has been impressive. In 1992 imports from Chinese Taipei and the Republic of Korea were on a par or even slightly higher than certain European countries with large consuming industries, such as Belgium and the United Kingdom.

The collapse of internal demand in the republics of the former Soviet Union, including that for base metals deriving from military hardware, has translated since 1991 in large surpluses available for export. Of the 14 smelters in the NIS with a total capacity of 3.6 million tonnes, 11 are in Russia (with 80 per cent of total NIS capacity) and one each in Ukraine, Azerbaijan and Tadjikistan. As shown in Table 6.8, estimates for production of primary metal range from 3.2 to 3.5 million tonnes from 1988-90, with consumption between 2.6 to 2.9 million tonnes. Accompanying these levels of production and consumption in the final years of the Soviet Union were exports at somewhere around 600 Kt in 1988, rising 100 Kt in the following two years. In 1991-92 exports rose to a level estimated at 900 Kt for the NIS.[7] It was however in 1993 that exports were really unleashed; estimates for that year range from 1.6 million tonnes to 2 million tonnes. Thus in the space of five years, NIS exports of primary aluminium tripled. Most were sent in the beginning to LME warehouses in Western Europe, where accumulating inventories led to continued downward pressure on prices (see Figure 6.8). In late 1993, following imposition of quotas by the EC (see Section 5.D. below), NIS exports of aluminium were re-directed to the United States, and a lesser extent Asia. Thus from levels in the late 1980s and 1990 of under 100 Kt, EC imports rose sharply in 1991 and again in 1992 to some half a million tonnes and then again in the first part of 1993, until the Community imposed import quotas later in the year. Due to the relatively low quota (60 Kt per quarter) in place until end of February 1994, imports were much lower for the first four months of 1994. US aluminium imports from the NIS passed from nearly nothing in 1991 and a very low level in 1992 (16 Kt) to just under half a million tonnes; annualising on the basis of four months data in 1994, imports could reach 700 Kt in 1994.

b) Aluminium semis

The picture is somewhat different for trade in semis, as presented in Table 6.8 (data presented here are in value terms). Production is concentrated in the OECD countries. Germany is far and away the most important trader in semis, taking one-fifth of world exports and one-sixth of world imports of aluminium semis. The bulk of its trade is with its EC partners. Similarly the United States and Canada are each other's most important trading partners, with almost half of US semis going to Canada and 90 per cent of Canada's imports coming from the United States. The three most important destinations for Japan's exports of semis are about equally the Korea, Chinese Taipei and the United States. It would appear therefore that, notwithstanding the impressive growth rates in semis trade over 20 years of some 14 per cent per annum, such trade has had a dominantly regional character.

Unlike the difficult situation for primary metal, the EC semis industry continues to thrive. Some two-thirds of world exports of aluminium semis originated in six EC countries in 1992. Canada has also been developing its aluminium semis export industry. In the last decade it has progressed several places to rank number ten. The US market, growing at an average rate of almost 15 per cent over the last 20 years, has been the target of exporters of aluminium semis. Recent trade data for the United States shows however that imports of semis have been stagnating since 1990, as US producers have increasingly met domestic demand as well as increased their exports by nearly 50 per cent between 1990 and 1993. Above all, sheet has been exported to supply can stock for increased use of aluminium beverage cans, in areas of the OECD region, notably Europe and Japan, where can consumption is still low relative to the United States.

C.   Intra-firm trade

Intra-firm trade (IFT) is defined as the international exchange of goods and services within a multinational enterprise. Survey results for US firms operating abroad and foreign firms operating in the United States are published only for the entire non-ferrous metals sector; separate data on aluminium is not available (and a fortiori distinguished between metal and semis).[8] Such US data shows that IFT accounted towards the end of the 1980s for less than a third of total US trade in non-ferrous metals. This is close to the average for the share of IFT in US manufacturing trade;[9] whilst higher than for the US steel industry, this share is considerably lower than is seen in other sectors such as pharmaceuticals and automobiles. Intra-firm imports by the US are considerably more important than its intra-firm exports in US non-ferrous metals trade. This is true for both US affiliates of foreign companies and foreign affiliates of US companies. IFT for the United States in the non-ferrous metals sector is approximately equally divided between IFT due to the operation of US firms abroad and IFT arising from the operation of foreign firms in the United States.

The relative importance of intra-firm trade for the whole of the non-ferrous metals sector associated with foreign affiliates of US firms posted a rather substantial increase between 1982 and 1989, to a level of about 15 per cent.[10] Most of this increase was due to the enhanced operations of US firms in Canada, which accounted for approximately two-thirds of total IFT associated with US firms abroad in 1989. The share of IFT due to the operation of US firms in developing countries decreased sharply in the 1980s. This co-incides with the growing importance of Canada as a source of US imports of primary aluminium metal. As data on IFT does not separate out metal from semis, it is not possible to distinguish the relative contribution of each to these trade flows.

Intra-firm trade associated with the operation of foreign firms in the United States has not changed substantially as a share of total US trade in non-ferrous metals. Most of the data on the national origin of those firms has been suppressed to avoid disclosure of firm-specific data. It is possible, however, to estimate that firms from Europe, Canada and the Asia/Pacific region (not necessarily Japan) are all active in this regard.

D.   Intra-industry trade

Intra-industry trade (IIT) is defined as the exchange by two countries of goods and services within the same product category. IIT is generally a function of product differentiation and may or may not be intra-firm trade. IIT indices provide another tool for analysing trade patterns as they may show the extent of international linkages for a given industry.[11]

In this section, IIT indices were calculated for trade in aluminium, unworked and wrought. Data at such a level of disaggregation are hard to interpret as they vary considerably from year to year, reflecting large swings in trade flows. A few general points can still be made, however.

a)   Aluminium metal

IIT indices for unwrought aluminium reflect the significant changes in trade patterns over the past two decades. From a very high level (i.e. imports were almost equal to exports), IIT for Japan has dropped to nearly zero, reflecting the dismantling of the domestic industry and fabricators' almost total dependency on imports of metal. The US index moved in the opposite direction, towards an equilibrium in exports and imports of unwrought metal, from a position 20 years ago of a net importer. European countries have differing IIT indices, based on their situation as aluminium producers. France, for example, whose aluminium production stagnated in the 1980s, saw a drop by over one-half in its IIT, due to a large increase in imports. Germany has shown the same trend. Holding a relatively low IIT index, Norway, on the other hand, has increased exports over the last decade, to a level about ten times its imports.

b) Aluminium semis and other wrought forms

Between 1971 and 1991, IIT indices for Australia, Japan and Korea showed substantial increases. Chinese Taipei's index fell, reflecting a large surge in imports. Bilateral IIT indices for Japanese trade in aluminium semis tend to be higher for trade with Canada and the United States and much smaller for trade with other Pacific-Asian countries. Japan has a large trade surplus in aluminium products with the latter. IIT indices for the United States and Canada are relatively high. Although it is difficult to discern a trend due to the high volatility of the indices, they seem to have increased between 1971 and 1991. Bilateral indices for US trade in aluminium are high for US trade with Canada, Japan and EC + European Free Trade Agreement (EFTA). European IIT indices are high, especially for intra-European trade, as is also the case for other industries. These indices have been increasing even further since 1971.

4. FOREIGN DIRECT INVESTMENT AND INTER-FIRM NETWORKS

Foreign investment has traditionally played and is still playing a vital role in the non-ferrous mining and metals industry. Whereas in the earlier half of the century this typically concerned exploration and development of ore deposits and mills to dress mined ores, investments were later made overseas in smelters and refineries. In the case of aluminium smelting, the situation of foreign involvement is probably more recent, since the Big-6 tended to build their own smelters in their home country through the 1960s and 1970s. As discussed above, the energy crises of the 1970s very largely changed that. Some of the highlights of the numerous changes occurring in the 1980s in the OECD-based industries are examined, before looking at ownership changes in the aluminium industry in the last five years.

A. 1980s: a globalising restructuring

a) The non-ferrous sector as a whole

Essential objectives behind the widespread restructurings in the non-ferrous metals sector were varied, but many of them correspond to a move towards strengthening the firms' place in a global industry, by forming cross-border networks. Among the announced goals are:

- ensured access to mines and/or ores for the concentrate-poor companies;
- cementing closer relationship between mines and smelters, with an eye to ensuring adequate smelter and refining capacity;
- concentrate operations to benefit from economies of scale;
- becoming a metal producer in a mix of currency areas to reduce exposure to currency volatility;
- gaining footholds in new markets, particularly the dynamic Asian markets;
- exploiting the trading expertise of certain firms;
- pooling R&D in the development of new smelter technologies to reduce emissions in view of strong environmental standards;
- developing expertise, including supply circuits, in recycling.

Highlights of changes in the industry are set out below.

United States

The copper industry is perhaps the most striking example of this radical restructuring. Five smelters and three refineries closed and more than half a dozen large producers left the industry. Of a dozen well known companies, only four major players remain today. Two European firms moved into the primary copper industry and two Japanese firms have partial holdings. RTZ, today the world's largest non-ferrous mining house, bought out British Petroleum's metals mining division. Metal Mining, a Canadian subsidiary of Metallgesellschaft, bought a mine, smelter and refinery. Several US mining firms, which no longer have holdings in the domestic copper industry, still have important operations in Latin America and the Asia/Pacific region. In the zinc industry, St. Joe and the New Jersey Zinc group merged to form the Zinc Corporation of America. In lead, Doe Run, which today with one other company dominates the US lead industry, was formed in 1986 through the merger of Fluor and Homestake.

Australia

From the merger of CRA and North Broken Hill, Pasminco of Australia was born, with smelter facilities in Europe and mines and smelters in Australia. MIM was formed from Mount Isa Mines with holdings by Asarco (United States), Preussag (Germany) and Metal Mining (Canada).

Canada

Cominco was formed with a minority interest of Teck (Canada), MIM (Australia) and Metallgesellschaft (Germany). Together, in what this company refers to as a global networking structure, they hold interests in lead and zinc in Canada, the United States, Australia, Spain and Japan. In 1989, Noranda (Canada) and Trelleborg (Sweden) acquired Falconbridge (number two nickel producer) in equal partnership, resulting in a large copper/nickel combine. Alcan divested much of its downstream business, including its North American building activities, in order to refocus itself on primary aluminimum production and on its rolling business. Many Canadian firms continued to invest in foreign projects in an effort to diversify their operations geographically, while continuing to maintain a strong Canadian base.

Europe

The zinc interest of Preussag merged with the French-based Peñarroya to form Metaleurop, today a strong Franco-German presence on the non-ferrous scene. Acec-Union Minière consists of Vieille Montagne, MHO, Asturienne and Jersey Minière, with interests in lead, zinc and copper refining and recovery of precious metals. Also in zinc, Spain's Asturiana de Zinc and the Canadian Curragh Resources have formed an alliance. In the copper-fabricating industry, France's Tréfimétaux merged with the Italian La Metalli to form Europa Metalli-LMI, which has now incorporated two important German and Spanish producers. Outokumpu (Finland) has acquired Germany's Metallwerken and Spain's Iberia de Cobre. Hydro Aluminium was formed from the merger of Norsk Hydro and ASV.

Japan

While domestic mines have been closing, Japanese firms have been acquiring minority interests in a number of mines and processing facilities around the world. For copper, this includes US mines and the recently opened Chilean copper mine, La Escondida.

b) Aluminium

In aluminium, some of these factors have also been at play. But the overriding factor for most of the Big-6 involved the decision to strengthen holdings downstream in the fabricating sector. Other firms decided to diversify horizontally, that is branch out into related activities, such as non-aluminium uses of alumina or ceramics and plastics, or move into aluminium end-use manufacturing, such as beverage cans and even non-aluminium packaging, including plastics,[12] although this is no longer true for Alcan.

Either by "disintegrating" (*i.e.* moving away) their operations from an upstream emphasis on bauxite and alumina holdings to concentrate downstream in semi-fabricating or by "deverticalising" and moving into related, but non-aluminium, activities, the aluminium companies adopted varied strategies to deal with the crisis of the 1980s.

B. Recent trends in joint ventures, minority participations and acquisitions (1988-92)

If the examples above are perhaps the most dramatic emerging from a decade of crisis in the industry, foreign investment is ongoing, as evidenced by the acquisitions and joint ventures in Figures 6.9*a* and 6.9*b* and accompanying tables. This data,[13] undoubtedly partial, reflects continuing changes in the sector since 1988.

Of the 155 entries from the database, about one-third each are copper and aluminium businesses (primary metal or fabricating activities), and the final third concern other metals. According to this survey, a minimum of US$3.5 billion in ownership changes occurred in the last five years. This figure is a minimum since many of the catalogued deals do not have a dollar amount associated with them. The most important purchasing countries were the United States, the United Kingdom and Italy in the case of acquisitions, and Japan, the United States and Canada for minority holdings and joint ventures. Firms selling were, in the case of acquisitions, primarily located in Canada, Germany and the United States and for minority holdings and joint ventures, in Indonesia, Australia and the United States.

C. Future

a) Planned investment in smelters

As for the more recently built smelters, plans currently under way or under consideration are being made on the basis of consortia in joint ventures. A glance at the major plans on the boards (*cf.* Table 6.4), shows that the "new" producers – Canada, Australia, Venezuela and Brazil – still predominate the scene, although other new players may emerge as well (*e.g.* Chile and Nigeria).

b) Alliances in downstream activities

Table 6.9 sets out a series of alliances involving major aluminium companies. Most of these concern collaboration in the technology and marketing areas, or are joint ventures in downstream activities. The following general themes emerge:

– Alliances between North American aluminium companies and Japanese aluminium and steel companies aimed at promoting the "aluminised" automobile. As can be seen by comparing Tables 6.9 and 6.10, each of the seven main Japanese producers of aluminium semis are involved in such alliances. Several companies are banking on this area as an important source of increased demand in the relatively near term and are devoting considerable resources to R&D and direct co-operation with the car industries. The Alcoa/Kobe Steel joint ventures are harbingers in this regard, involving reciprocal access to the other partner's main technology centre.

– The relative absence of European aluminium firms on the list. The exceptions involve Norsk Hydro (Hydro Aluminium) with a couple of car manufacturers, the involvement of Pechiney's mill products division with US and Japanese interests and the expansion of the Norf (Germany) can stock cold rolling mill, a joint venture between Alcan and VAW. Most European firms appear to continue to work alone – although often within the context of a R&D infrastructure involving the vast resources in a horizontally diversified Group, such as Alusuisse-Lonza or Pechiney.

5. GOVERNMENT POLICIES

Today there are relatively few government policies explicitly directed at the non-ferrous metals sector. Nonetheless, numerous policies of a horizontal nature affect the economic activities undertaken to smelt and refine minerals and fabricate metals.

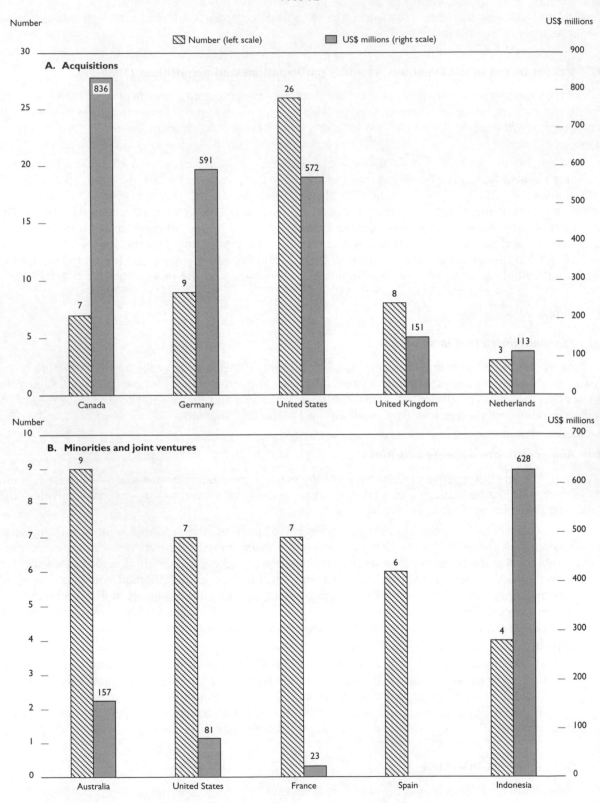

◆ Figure 6.9a. **Selling countries – Non-ferrous metals**
1988-92

Source: KPGM.

◆ Figure 6.9b. **Purchasing countries – Non-ferrous metals**
1988-92

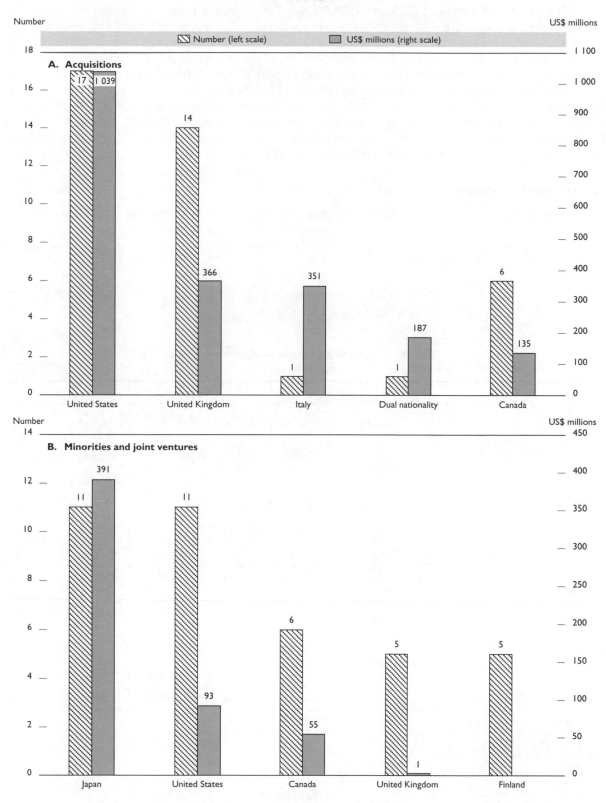

A.   Government assistance

Following the oil shocks of 1973 and 1979-80, direct aid to ailing firms was widespread in the non-ferrous metals sector. In some cases, outright nationalisation occurred, as in France with Pechiney or in Portugal. More frequently, the state intervened with a variety of instruments to shore up firms through national holdings, as in Italy and Spain, or through financial intermediaries as in Greece. In recent years, a certain tendency for the government to withdraw can be noted, as in Germany's privatisation of the state aluminium firm, VAW, or Italy's offering for privatisation of its non-ferrous leader Nuova SAMIM, the Irish Government's selling off of its share of the Aughinish alumina refinery and the French Government's decision to place Pechiney on the list of privatisable companies. Substantial state presence remains in Finland with Outokumpu Oy; in Norway via Hydro Aluminium; Aluvic, in which the Government of Victoria (Australia) holds a large share; the Spanish aluminium firm INESPAL.

a)   Financial assistance

Issues concerning support of state firms generally coalesce around the terms and conditions of financial assistance and budgetary support made available. Injections of capital through the budget, non-market-related interest rates on loans, buy-up of debt and state guarantees on loans are all instruments which have been used in the sector.

Table 6.9.   **Direction of trade in aluminium semis**

SITC Rev. 2: 6842

Major exporters[1]	1972		1982		1992	
	Value (bn US$)	Share %	Value (bn US$)	Share %	Value (bn US$)	Share %
Germany[2]	0.21	19.1	1.03	20.3	2.86	19.7
United States[3]	0.14	13.4	0.53	10.5	1.76	12.1
France[4]	0.12	11.0	0.57	11.1	1.41	9.7
Belgium-Luxembourg[5]	0.13	12.5	0.43	8.5	0.98	6.7
United Kingdom[6]	0.04	3.9	0.25	4.9	0.83	5.7
Italy[7]	0.06	5.7	0.25	4.9	0.76	5.2
Netherlands[8]	0.08	7.3	0.23	4.6	0.72	4.9
Japan[9]	0.04	3.3	0.38	7.5	0.68	4.7
Switzerland[10]	0.05	4.9	0.23	4.5	0.60	4.1
Canada	0.01	1.3	0.06	1.3	0.50	3.5
Austria	0.02	1.9	0.16	3.2	0.50	3.5
Norway	0.04	3.4	0.12	2.4	0.35	2.4
Sweden	0.03	2.9	0.12	2.3	0.27	1.9
Spain	0.01	0.5	0.03	0.7	0.23	1.6
Greece	0.00	0.4	0.06	1.1	0.20	1.4
Australia	0.00	0.4	0.07	1.4	0.20	1.4
Egypt	0.00	0.0	0.05	1.0	0.19	1.3
Croatia	n.a.		n.a.		n.a.	
Korea, Republic of	0.00	0.0	0.03	0.6	0.12	0.8
Rest of the World	0.09	8.1	0.48	9.4	1.18	8.2
World	**1.08**	**100.0**	**5.08**	**100.0**	**14.52**	**100.0**

1.   Principal destinations of exports (1992).
2.   United Kingdom (17.7%), France (14.7%), Netherlands (9.7%), Italy (8.9%), Belgium-Luxembourg (7.9%).
3.   Canada (41.7%), Mexico (16.%), Japan (5.1%).
4.   Germany (26.5%), United Kingdom (16.2%), Italy (8.9%), Belgium-Luxembourg (7.7%).
5.   Germany (25.2%), France (25.0%), Netherlands (18.2%), United Kingdom (7.6%).
6.   Germany (18.6%), Italy (16.7%), France (12.5%), Ireland (10.6%), Netherlands (6.4%).
7.   Germany (26.7%), France (16.4%), Spain (8.5%).
8.   Germany (42.8%), Belgium-Luxembourg (18.5%), France (11.2%), Special Category (7.1%), United Kingdom (7.1%).
9.   Korea, Republic of (20.4%), Chinese Taipei (18.6%), USA (16.6%), Singapore (7.4%).
10.   Germany (34.7%), France (16.4%), United Kingdom (7.3%), Italy (6.6%), Netherlands (6.4%).

Table 6.9.   **Direction of trade in aluminium semis** *(cont.)*

SITC Rev. 2: 6842

Major importers[1]	1972		1982		1992	
	Value (bn US$)	Share %	Value (bn US$)	Share %	Value (bn US$)	Share %
Germany[2]	0.14	13.1	0.56	11.3	2.30	16.0
France[3]	0.11	10.9	0.46	9.4	1.35	9.4
United Kingdom[4]	0.09	8.6	0.49	10.0	1.15	8.0
United States[5]	0.07	6.7	0.50	10.2	1.05	7.3
Italy[6]	0.04	3.9	0.20	4.1	0.82	5.7
Canada[7]	0.08	7.6	0.21	4.3	0.78	5.4
Netherlands[8]	0.07	6.4	0.24	5.0	0.76	5.3
Belgium-Luxembourg[9]	0.05	4.6	0.19	3.8	0.60	4.2
Korea, Republic of	0.00	0.4	0.05	1.0	0.39	2.7
Austria	0.02	2.0	0.10	2.0	0.35	2.4
Switzerland	0.02	1.5	0.11	2.3	0.34	2.4
China	n.a.		n.a.		n.a.	
Sweden	0.04	3.4	0.15	3.1	0.32	2.2
Spain	0.01	1.1	0.06	1.2	0.32	2.2
Chinese Taipei	0.00	0.4	0.05	1.0	0.30	2.1
Mexico	0.01	0.9	0.10	2.1	0.28	1.9
Hong Kong	0.01	0.8	0.05	1.1	0.26	1.8
Japan	0.01	1.0	0.08	1.6	0.24	1.7
Singapore	0.01	0.9	0.07	1.4	0.22	1.5
Denmark	0.04	3.7	0.12	2.4	0.20	1.4
Rest of the World	0.24	22.4	1.12	22.7	2.05	14.2
World	**1.06**	**100.0**	**4.92**	**100.0**	**14.41**	**100.0**

n.a.: not available.
1. Principal sources of imports (1992).
2. France (18.4%), Netherlands (14.5%), Austria (11.0%), Belgium-Luxembourg (10.7%).
3. Germany (29.6%), Belgium-Luxembourg (17.7%), Italy (9.4%), Switzerland (7.2%).
4. Germany (34.7%), France (19.4%), Belgium-Luxembourg (7.3%), Netherlands (6.4%).
5. Canada (44.2%), Germany (12.8%), Japan (9.6%), France (6.0%).
6. Germany (30.1%), United Kingdom (17.5%), France (15.1%).
7. United States (89.5%), France (4.0%).
8. Germany (35.4%), Belgium-Luxembourg (23.7%), United Kingdom (6.5%), France (6.5%).
9. Germany (35.4%), Netherlands (22.8%), France (18.8%).
Source: United Nations, COMTRADE database.

b)   Taxation

Depletion and other taxation allowances, that is special taxation benefits in recognition of the "depletable" nature of a mining company's assets, are offered in the United States, France and other OECD Member countries.[14]

c)   Energy pricing

Electricity costs are a substantial part of costs of smelting of non-ferrous ores, particularly for zinc and aluminium. For the latter it is estimated that close to 30 per cent of costs are accounted for by electricity. Since electricity production is often a state monopoly, energy policy is a powerful means for governments to affect competitive advantage of their non-ferrous metals industry.

B.   Foreign investment

The minerals sector has tended to attract controls on foreign investment in developing countries but also in developed countries. A recent survey by the OECD[15] found that, whereas many laws are still on the books, the current period of liberalisation has also extended to the minerals and metals sector. Review of foreign direct investment is still carried out in many OECD Member countries to ensure that the

Table 6.10. **Alliances involving major aluminium companies**

Company	Date	Nature/comments
ALCAN/Nippon Light Metal Co.	Mid-1992	In exchange for Alcan's shareholdings in Alcom, Alcan Siam and Nonfemet, Alcan increased its shareholding in NLM to 48%. In 1993 Alcan strengthened the working relationship between Alcan and NLM building on advanced technology, including the development of an aluminium space frame for cars, and long-term customer relationships in Asia.
ALCAN/Toyota Aluminium	1987	Alcan-Toyo America (effective 60% Alcan ownership), JV commissioned an atomised Al powder plant to maintain leadership in aerospace propulsion.
ALCAN/Sumitomo Electric Industries		JV in North Carolina to manufacture composite fiber optic overhead ground wire.
ALCAN/Thrall Car Manuf.		JV to produce Al coal cars, according to ALCAN process.
ALCAN/VAW		JV at Norf (Germany). Expansion of largest rolling mill in Europe, principally for canstock.
ALCAN/Nippon Steel & Nippon Light Metal		Collaboration for joint development being studied.
ALCAN/Ford Motor Co.	Late 1992	Joint research to develop light-alloy fenders for Taurus line and Al sheet for car body applications; May 1994 delivery of limited series of test Al Intensive Vehicles (AIV).
ALCAN/General Motors	1992	Research on weldable and bondable sheet for GM's electric car programme.
ALCAN/Teksid (Fiat)	1993	JV for engineered Al castings for cars.
ALCAN/ALUAR		Merged to form C&K Aluminio to jointly market Al products in Southern Cone nations.
ALCOA/KOBE Steel Ltd.	July 1992	50:50 JVs.
a) Kobe Alcoa Transportation		Production and marketing of Al sheet at Moka plant (Japan); 3 labs in Kobe Steel plants to study sheet, extrusions and castings and forgings and work with market development teams.
b) Alcoa Kobe Transportation Products		Production under a tolling arrangement at Alcoa's Davenport works plant of Al sheet for US auto manufacturers, Japanese transplants and other customers. AKTP to carry out R&D in Alcoa technical center; market development, marketing and sales of Al sheet.
c) KSL Alcoa Alun Co. (Kaal)	September 1990	Produce and market Al canstock; 180 ktpy cold strip plant adjacent to Kobe's plant at Moka came on stream in mid-1993; ouput marketed to China and South East Asia via Kaal Asia; a marketing company formed in 1993.
d) Alcoa Kobe Tube Specialists	December 1991	Originally to supply North American market with photoreceptor tubes used in fax machines, computers. JV dissolved in July 1994; absorbed by Alcoa.
Alcoa/Kobe Steel and China National Non-ferrous metals	March 1994	Joint study to explore co-operation opportunities from mining to fabrication.
ALCOA/Sam Sun Co. (South Korea)		Under discussion; to produce Al extrusions for aerospace application in Korean market.
Alcoa Automotive Structures		US$70 million plant to serve auto industry in Soest, Germany. Onstream in 1993. Audi agreement to supply Al spaceframe components for new Audi avus quattro.
ALCO/Akzo	1991	JV with Dutch chemical company to produce fiber metal laminates for aerospace applications.
ALCOA Fujikura		Acquired majority interest in Stribel GMBH electro-mechanical and electronic components for European automotive market.
ALCOA-Kofem (HUNGALU)	December 1992	JV with Hungarian company making flat rolled products and extrusions. European subsidiaries of mother companies have joint marketing responsibility. Expanded output in 1994, targeting France and UK as export markets.

Table 6.10. **Alliances involving major aluminium companies** (cont.)

Company	Date	Nature/comments
ALCOA/VAW	November 1993	JV (60:40) formed to produce and market Al extrusions, tube and rod for European aircraft, auto and defense industries; aim to move service and technology closer to European customers.
ALCOA ALUMINIO (Brazil)		Manufacture closures for beverage containers.
ALUSUD Embalajes (Chile and Argentina)		ditto
ALCOA/ALZAYANI Investments (Bahrain)		Set up Gulf Closures, a JV.
Alcoa, Reynolds and Alcan/Ford		Commitments to help in the development of body panel applications for Al in the next generation of the midsize Taurus cars scheduled for 1995.
Alumax/Mitsui	March 1992	With Mitsui (lead in Japanese consortium with 25% of Alumax's US smelters) management, new unit based in Tokyo to handle sales and seek partnership ventures in Japan and other Asian markets. Alumax Japan is forming test samples for SSF Japan's first licensee, Nippon Light Metal, which are going to three major Japanese car builders.
Alusuisse-Lonza/ALCOA	July 1992	Discussions under way for 9 months broke off, reportedly due to lack of agreement on control; preliminary understanding was for Alcoa's 60% interest in rolling facilities involving SF 300 million modernisation and capacity expansion programme.
ALUVIC [Alcoa, Govt of Victoria, Marubeni/Golden Aluminium (Adolph Coors)]		JV agreement to build 105 Kt/yr Al can sheet rolling mill at Bendigo, Victoria.
COMALCO	1991	Following restructuring of debt and equity, Southern Aluminium (casting aluminium wheels) became 100% owned subsidiary of Comalco. Former shareholders Mitsubishi and Enkei, the large Japanese wheel producer, and CITIC (China) continue collaboration via marketing agreements and technical assistance.
COMALCO/Internet		JV:ICA Castings Foundry for production of automotive aluminium castings to produce prototype Al heads and blocks.
Doehler-Jarvic/KS Aluminium Technologie	1992	JV of 2 German companies to produce Al auto parts, including transmissions for sale to Ford Motor.
Hydro Aluminium/Chrysler		Develop structural applications for vehicles, including cross-members and suspension supports into minivans and luxury cars.
Hydro Aluminium/BMW		Joint research on automotive applications for extruded Al structures.
Hydro Aluminium/Sumitomo Light		JV to jointly develop Al extruded products for auto sector, including heat exchanges, bumpers and space frames; followed up by marketing and technology sharing agreement in 1994.
KAISER/Furukawa Electric and Furukawa Aluminium Co.		Companies study feasibility of joint research product development, marketing and production for ground transportation and other markets.
KAISER/Kawasaki Steel, Furukawa Electric and Furukawa Aluminium		JV formed after viability study on producing Al body and sheet, extrusions (space frames), castings and forgings for auto applications. Kawasaki Steel's close connections with Nissan, Mazda and Toyota expected to help sales of Al sheet.
KAISER/Furukawa Electric Co./Kawasaki Steel/Pechiney Rhenalu	1993	Joint work on developing superior Al auto body sheet to make Al body panels more competitive. Multi-year RandD agreement covers alloy metallurgy, formability, surface preparation and joining methods.
Kawasaki Steel/Furukawa Aluminium	1991	JV between steelmaker and flat rolled Al sector.
NKK/Mitsubishi Aluminium		ditto
Sumitomo Metal Industries/ Sumitomo Light Metal Industries		ditto
Nippon Steel/Sky Aluminium	May 1991	R&D agreement. Increased investment by Nippon in developing markets for automotive Al sheet which, in 1993, it was agreed, would be marketed exclusively by Nippon.
Nippon Steel/Nippon Light Metal Nippon Steel/Showa aluminium	February 1993	R&D agreements for new technology, manufacturing and marketing of cast, forged and extruded Al products for automobiles, ships and rolling stock, i.a. to catch up with the Kobe Steel/Alcoa JVs.

Table 6.10. **Alliances involving major aluminium companies** *(cont.)*

Company	Date	Nature/comments
Reynolds/Ford		R&D programme to develop a space frame. 5-year contract for Al driveshaft tubes.
Reynolds/Mitsubishi	1992	JV formed for joint development of automotive extrusions. In 1994, followed up by JV to market extruded Al auto products.
Reynolds/Fata Group (Italy)	1989	JV at Sayansk, Russia for producing and exporting foil.
Reynolds/Russian Co.		JV in St. Petersburg with castings producer to produce Al alloy wheels.
Reynolds/Samara Metallurgical Co.	1994	Technology transfer agreement with Russian aerospace/defense company to make Al beverage cans.
Reynolds/Sumitomo Light Metal Indust.		Agreement on technical collaboration for joint R&D of new Al sheet products such as body and brasing sheet and processes for the worldwide automotive market. Initially for 3 years.
Sumitomo Metal Industries (steel)/Sumitomo Light Metal		Agreement on technical support to backstop the Reynolds/Sumitomo project.

Source: OECD Secretariat, based on company annual reports and trade press.

investment will be in accordance with national goals and policies, but very rarely leads to curtailment of such investment. In some countries, recent reforms have lifted these restrictions. In other cases, thresholds expressed in monetary terms exist or review can be triggered by invoking a national interest clause.

In any vertically integrated business, such as the bauxite/alumina/aluminium/metal fabricating integration of several of the large multinationals, the issue of transfer pricing arises. This was an issue of some acrimony between bauxite-producing governments and the multinationals who, according to the producing governments, were under-invoicing the value of the bauxite to their producing unit downstream, *e.g.* the alumina refinery. In principle, most multinationals now subscribe to the principle of arm's length transaction pricing among their subsidiary and affiliate firms. In practice, it may be difficult to assess the value of an input if there is no independent market. In periods when the price of one or the other input under the control of the parent company moves against the interests of one of the parties, the issue of the correct transfer price may still arise.

C. Research and development and technology support

All large non-ferrous metals firms have R&D departments; some of them expend considerable amounts. Emphasis today is on the development of new end-uses or of a material using the non-ferrous metal. Environmentally clean processes and recycling technologies have been an increasing focus of public research in recent years. In several cases, the public R&D infrastructure, including national laboratories and university and technology centres, collaborates closely with the non-ferrous metals companies. In Australia, the United States and Canada, the government has specialised research bodies active in metals and materials research and in co-ordinating research. The EC has R&D framework programmes involving not only the EC-12 but also EFTA countries. By setting priorities and allocating research funds, government can affect competitiveness of private firms with access to research results.

D. Trade policy

In general, tariffs are low on imports of non-ferrous metals. But tariffs in all main OECD countries escalate with the degree of processing (see Table 6.11). Whereas ores and concentrates are admitted free to all OECD Member countries (except to the United States on copper, lead and zinc), unwrought metal imports face duties in the range of 0-6 per cent (with a few peaks, *e.g.* of 19 per cent on zinc alloys in the United States and 10+ per cent on certain refined copper products entering Canada). In addition, the 6 per cent import tariff on unwrought aluminium into the Community (and the recent harmonization of Swedish

Table 6.11. **Japanese production of aluminium rolled products by producer, 1993**

Thousand tonnes

	Sheeting	Extruded products	Total
Sumitomo Light Metal Industries Nagoya (R, E, F) Chiba (E, F)	224.1	54.1	278.1
Kobe Steel Moka (R) Chofu (E, F)	252.0	38.5	290.5
Furukawa Electric Nikko (R) Oyama (E, F) Shiga (E, F) Fukui (R)	176.7	44.4	221.1
Nippon Light Metal Co. Ltd Nagoya(R) Osaka (E, F) Funabashi (E, F) Niigata (E, F) Kanbara (E)	103.5	78.9	182.3
Mitsubishi Aluminium Fuji (R, E, F)	114.7	25.0	139.1
Sky Aluminium Fukaya (R)	136.1		136.1
Showa Aluminium Sakai (R, E) Oyama (E, F) Hikone (E, F)	29.7	70.2	99.9
Total (companies listed)	**1 036.8**	**311.0**	**1 347.8**

R = Flat rolled products; E = Extruded products; F = Fabricated products.
Source: Japanese Aluminium Federation.

aluminium tariffs with the EU 6 per cent rate) continues to be an irritant for Canadian and Australian suppliers particularly in periods of low prices when, without the import duty, adjustments to output could be expected to be made more quickly by higher cost producers. Import tariffs do become consequential in several, albeit not all, OECD Member countries on wrought metal, such as semis and manufactures.

During the Uruguay Round of trade negotiations tariff peaks and tariff escalation in non-ferrous metals were addressed. A proposal to eliminate duties on unwrought metal (known as "zero for zero") however did not in the event find widespread approval. Some peaks did come down and a few residual tariffs were eliminated. However, in general some of the earlier offers for greater cuts in import tariffs, particularly on semis, were not accepted in the bargaining process. In aluminium, the Japanese eliminated its 1 per cent tariff on ingot, and Japan, Canada and Australia dropped tariffs on semis and manufacturers and the EU on certain tubes and pipes; the EU did not lower the above-mentioned import tariff on unwrought aluminium metal.

Export controls on non-ferrous scrap had been in place in the Community through the 1970s and 1980s. Quotas were established each year for copper and copper alloy scrap through 1989, when the system was not renewed. The authority to extend them still exists. In view of the strong and growing importance of scrap and the environmental concern to promote recycling, allowing free movement for scrap, as a significant source of secondary raw material, underscores the other side of the trade-policy equation for this sector.

While not in the forefront of recent trade disputes like other metals such as steel and ferroalloys, non-ferrous metals have been subject to filing of dumping and subsidy charges, leading to investigations. Imports of aluminium rod from Venezuela faced investigations by the US International Trade Commission into alleged dumping and subsidisation in 1987. Countervailing duty orders on brass sheet and strip were imposed on imports from a number of countries. In 1992 the US authorities imposed countervailing and antidumping duties on Norsk Hydro's Canadian magnesium production. At the same time, the US International Trade Commission confirmed that the terms of Norsk's variable rate electricity contract were not countervailable. In 1988, the United States and Japan concluded a bilateral trade agreement on reductions in the Japanese tariff on aluminium sheet, plate and strip.

The sudden surges in imports of aluminium from Russia and other NIS in 1991, 1992 and above all in early 1993, led to European attempts to work out voluntary restraint agreements with NIS. Having been unsuccessful in negotiating such, the European Commission used generally applicable powers to take unilateral safeguard action against aluminium imports from the NIS effective August 1993. Initially for a period of four months, the quantitative restrictions, equivalent to 15 000 tonnes per month, were renewed through the end of February 1994. Following diversion of NIS exports to North America, antidumping suits were being threatened by major aluminium companies there. In October 1993, Russia took the initiative to invite the government of the countries with the largest production of primary aluminium, including the European Community, to a multilateral conference in Moscow. Similar meetings were held in quick succession in Washington, Brussels and Ottawa where a Memorandum of Understanding (MOU) was finalised covering three major points: size of market imbalance; transparency arrangements to improve available information on output; and need for technical assistance to restructure and modernise the Russian aluminium plants. Industry estimated that market imbalance was in the order of 1.5 to 2.0 million tonnes. Russian authorities committed to police production cuts of 500 Kt in Russian smelters. The MOU provided for an undertaking by Russia to reduce its aluminium production by 500 000 tonnes per year and recognised that Western production decisions must be market driven with producers making such decisions on the basis of the usual commercial considerations. In the depressed market conditions of early 1994, individual producers announced production cuts which, along with the cuts made by Russia, totalled approximately 1 million tonnes.[16] The parties to the MOU also took steps to increase statistical transparency for world markets by establishing a working group of experts to exchange and publish data on production and trade in primary aluminium, as well as encouraging the participation of Russian producers in the statistical reporting system of the International Primary Aluminium Institute (IPAI). The parties last met in Canberra in July 1994 and there are no plans for further meetings at this time. In the event, pure trade-policy measures were rejected. Indeed the parties stated that unilateral trade actions would be

Table 6.12. **OECD Member country tariff treatment of aluminium according to stage of processing: pre- and post-Uruguay Round**

Stage of processing	Tariff Heading No. HS[1]	Australia		Canada		European Union	
		Pre-UR[2]	Post-UR	Pre-UR	Post-UR	Pre-UR	Post-UR
Ores and concentrates	26.08	0	0	0	0	0	0
Unwrought	76.01	0	0	0-10.3 1.98 ¢/kg	0-6.8 1.23-1.31 ¢/kg	6	6
Waste and scrap	76.02	0	0	0	0	0; 3.2	0
Powders and flakes	76.03	0	0	9.2-10.3	6.1-6.8	5.3; 6.3	5
Wrought							
Semis	76.04-07	10;15	5	0-12.2	0-8	7.5-10	7.5; 10
Tubes, pipes and fittings	76.08-09	10; 15	5	0; 8.1-10.3	0-6.8	0-10	0; 7.0; 7.5
Chemicals	28.18-41	10	10	0-12.5	0; 5.5	3-12	4.0-5.5
Finished manufactures	76.10-16	15	5	0-11.4	0-7.5	6	6; 7

Note: Pre-UR: MFN applied rates; per cent unless otherwise indicated. Post-UR: Bound rate of (MFN) duty, at end of staged reductions.
1. Harmonised system.
2. Unbound.
Source: Pre-UR: OECD (1994), *Mining and Non-ferrous Metals Policies of OECD Countries*. Post-UR: Tariff schedules submitted at end of Uruguay Round.

Table 6.12. **OECD Member country tariff treatment of aluminium according to stage of processing: pre- and post-Uruguay Round** (cont.)

Stage of processing	Tariff Heading No. HS[1]	Japan		Norway		Sweden	
		Pre-UR[2]	Post-UR	Pre-UR	Post-UR	Pre-UR	Post-UR
Ores and concentrates	26.08	0	0	0	0	0	
Unwrought	76.01	1	0	0	0	0	0
Waste and scrap	76.02	0	0	0	0	0	0
Powders and flakes	76.03	4.6	3	0	0	0; 3.8	0; 2.5
Wrought							
Semis	76.04-07	0-10.2	0; 2; 7.5	0-5.8 NKrl.0/kg	0-7.5 NKr0.77/kg	2.5	1.7
Tubes, pipes and fittings	76.08-09	0.12.2	3; 7.5	5.8-6.2	5	2.5-3.2	0; 1.7; 2.1
Chemicals	28.18-4.1	3.0-4.6	0; 3.3; 3.9	0; 7.7	0	0-5.8	0-5.5
Finished manufactures	76.10-16	4.1-6.3	0; 3	3.8-13 NKr0.16-1.12/kg	0; 3; 8	2.5-3.8	1.7; 2.1; 2.5

Note: Pre-UR: MFN applied rates; per cent unless otherwise indicated. Post-UR: Bound rate of (MFN) duty, at end of staged reductions.
Source: Pre-UR: OECD (1994), *Mining and Non-ferrous Metals Policies of OECD Countries*. Post-UR: Tariff schedules submitted at end of Uruguay Round.

inconsistent with the MOU, although the existing (EU) quotas were allowed to expire under the existing terms. All five participants pledged co-operation and technical assistance to the Russian Federation for modernisation and restructuring of the aluminium industry, including training, policy development, investment guarantees, etc., as well as the use of their best offices with the European Bank for Reconstruction and Development (EBRD) and World Bank concerning viable investment projects. The MOU contains a sunset clause, whereby it expires after 24 months.

E. Environmental policies

Laws and regulations controlling emissions, waste disposal and recycling are the main areas of environmental policy affecting the non-ferrous metals sector. Smelting and refining of metals are potentially heavily polluting activities. Emissions into the air in the case of aluminium include particulates, toxic gases such as fluorine gases and PAH (polycyclic aromatic hydrocarbons) and greenhouse gases. Environmental-impact assessments are required in most OECD countries for large industrial projects, such as smelters and refineries; such permitting has added significant delays and has at times been taken to the courts. Electricity being the single most costly input to the production of aluminium, increased costs passed on to the large power consumers to meet higher standards on sulphur dioxide emissions (*e.g.* US Clean Air Act of 1990) could affect competitiveness. Greenhouse gases, emissions of which are heavy from coal burning power plants, are also being targeted for serious curbing. A significant share of aluminium smelters in the United States and Australia use electricity generated from coal.

Waste management is an issue high on the environmental policy agenda which has considerable implications for the non-ferrous metals industry. The general policy consensus on the necessity to control toxic wastes has in most OECD countries led to the drawing up of lists by environmental regulators which have included certain base metals in scrap form. In view of the now considerable importance of the secondary industry, the industry considers scrap as a "raw material input" and not a waste. International trade in scrap could have been affected by the stringent controls imposed by the Basle Convention concerning the control of transfrontier movements of hazardous waste. This Convention, which has now entered into force, provoked a flurry of activity in the OECD to negotiate a "green" list of wastes, including non-ferrous scrap, which could move among OECD countries with a bare minimum of controls. The ambiguous situation on movements of scrap between OECD Members and non-members could still hamper trade in non-ferrous scrap. In the aluminium industry, spent pot-liners have been declared a toxic waste in some countries and hence not to be disposed of in normal landfills. Different methods of treating spent pot-liners have been developed by Alcan, Reynolds Metals, Elkem, Comalco and Pechiney. Processing the residues from secondary aluminium smelters which must be disposed of in hazardous landfills is currently also the subject of R&D work.

These trends towards the tightening of environmental regulations raise a series of problems for the industry affecting decisions on level and location of production and therefore investment and trade. Many of the problems are finding solutions, but at added costs. In some cases, improved environmental performances can lead to improved techniques and the use of more efficient technologies that can translate into significant cost savings in the long run. This is more the case when building green-field projects or expansion of existing facilities. Since metals face vigorous competition, both from each other as well as from plastics, ceramics and advanced materials, such added costs can lead to substitution away from the metal affected. Differing levels of environmental standards and hence costs among countries affect industry competitiveness. Suggestions have already been heard to compensate for the implicit subsidy in lower environmental standards by imposing countervailing or other compensatory trade measures. Liability provisions in hazardous waste clean-up, such as the US Superfund, have already affected financial statements of the US aluminium firms, some of which have been declared Potentially Responsible Parties, in terms of Superfund legislation. Charges against earnings are being set aside to build up financial reserves for clean-up. Uncertainty as to costs and liability becomes another risk to be managed. In globalisation terms, reducing the uncertainty becomes a factor in the determination of investment decisions as to locating activities most likely to be subject to control.

Recyclability being one of the major trumps in the hands of the aluminium industry and one factor for its continued relative health, the debate around environmental levies on packaging, and particularly aluminium beverage cans, has mobilised the industry to lobby against what they see as discriminatory taxes.

F. Competition policy

OECD Member countries have competition policies, including anti-trust laws and regulations, which have affected the non-ferrous metals sector. In fact, the US aluminium industry could be said to have been born from anti-trust action taken by the government. From the end of the nineteenth century through the Second World War, Alcoa was the sole aluminium company in the United States. Following an anti-trust suit brought by the government in 1944, Alcoa had to divest itself of certain smelters, built by the US Government to meet military needs, and sell them to Reynolds and Kaiser. Similarly in 1950, Alcoa was ordered to sell its Canadian affiliate, which became Alcan. In Europe, Pechiney and Alusuisse enjoyed oligopolistic positions.

Inco was also on several occasions the target of US anti-trust laws. Some analysts have argued that US threatened or implied action even had the reverse policy results of that promoted, *viz.* the weakening of the monopoly by promoting interests of other nickel firms. According to this interpretation, the constant US watchdogging of Inco's behaviour appears to have been a factor leading to a "costs-plus" pricing policy, which coupled with a strong technological drive by Inco, had the effect of keeping nickel prices low and barriers to entry for potential competitors high.

Competition policy is also a concern today for the aluminium industry. In the United States, concerns include the frustrated desire of Alcan to buy out the share in an aluminium can stock plant from its (willing) joint venture partner. This acquisition has on more than one occasion been blocked by the courts for announced reasons of concentration. In Germany, two companies wishing to merge their secondary aluminium activities, were awaiting approval of the merger by the German Federal Cartel Office in 1991.

The European Commission has considerable powers in the field of competition policy and has exercised them in recent years to determine the nature and extent of mergers, including in the non-ferrous metals sector. State aids provided by member States to their industries are watched over and in some cases rejected when they are found not to meet guidelines for their usage. Following scrutiny and negotiations between the Commission and Pechiney, the reportedly preferential terms of the power contract it had negotiated with Électricité de France, were increased above operating costs and aligned more closely with marginal costing.

G. Security of supply policies

Strategic stockpiling has long been a government policy instrument used to shield countries against supply disruptions. Government interventions in markets for non-consumption related uses may distort market signals. Furthermore, stockpile objectives have been subject to relatively frequent changes, leading to changes in purchases and releases. Despite consultation procedures in place for some stockpiles, releases – particularly in depressed markets – tend to raise the ire of producers. In addition to the large US strategic stockpile, Japan and France also currently operate stockpiles, although the former's has been cut back and the latter's, it is understood, is being sold off.

Large consuming and resource-poor countries have introduced a series of polices in the past to foster development of mineral supplies and metal production overseas. Japan has undoubtedly been the most active in this area with its develop-for-import projects. Whilst many of these are today considered to be more in the nature of development aid programmes, government support to the development of mineral-producing countries competing with OECD-based firms still elicits criticism in some quarters.

NOTES

1. With today's aluminium prices at just over half of copper prices, a market-based value of world copper production places value of copper output above that of aluminium. In 1988, the nearly equal prices prevailing for the two metals placed value of aluminium output at 50 per cent higher than copper's.

2. 1991 and 1992 saw the opening or expansion of smelters in Canada and France, all owned by a single aluminium company; but this may be seen as part of the respective company strategy to replace existing capacity, already closed or expected to be so, and were financed largely by cash flows from the high price years of 1988-89.

3. Alcan, Alcoa, Reynolds and Kaiser still hold significant investments in bauxite and alumina. But in the case of Kaiser, these holdings still remain an explicit part of company strategy. Another company, *e.g.* Comalco in Australia, has purposely reversed an earlier decision on downstreaming in order to concentrate on bauxite and alumina operations, in which they see their comparative advantage.

4. But Norsk Hydro owns a magnesium plant in Canada.

5. The exception is Marc Rich, a Swiss metals trader, who took over two smelters in the 1980s and a share of an Alumax-controlled smelter in 1988. A consortium of Japanese companies has a one-quarter stake in two smelters controlled by Alumax.

6. The dismantling of Japanese smelter capacity was a deliberate policy choice in response to the 1970 oil shocks. Japanese tariffs on ingots were reduced (progressively through the use of tariff quotas), with the unpaid duties put into a special restructuring fund. This surge in ingot imports, made at world prices, also served to improve the competitiveness of the Japanese semis industry by lowering input costs.

7. This latter figure may be low, as Russia has submitted statistics to the other parties having signed the Memorandum of Understanding of March 1994, which show that official statistics were 670 Kt in 1991 and 1992, but that in 1992 in addition, some 623 Kt were toll smelted (alumina specifically shipped for smelting and returned to original owner, without changing hands), *i.e.* exports were 1.29 million tonnes in 1992 alone for Russia.

8. There are few sources of data on IFT, as information on the subject is not generally available in traditional trade statistics. Data on IFT are mostly available through firm surveys which involve the preparation of questionnaires by national authorities. This section is based on information provided by the US Department of Commerce, which conducts surveys of foreign affiliates of US companies and US affiliates of foreign companies. Relevant data is not available for other countries. The US Department of Commerce uses the International Surveys Industry (ISI) classification in its surveys. There is a category for "non-ferrous primary metal industries" (ISI 335), which includes the primary and secondary smelting and refining of non-ferrous metals, such as copper, lead, zinc, and aluminium; the rolling drawing and extruding of those metals; as well as the products of non-ferrous foundries. The level of aggregation in these surveys does not allow the distinction between different non-ferrous metals.

9. *cf. Intra-firm trade*, Trade Policy Issues No. 1 (OECD, 1993).

10. For the relatively less important intra-firm exports, the increase in the 1980s merely offsets a fall experienced between 1977 and 1982. The share of intra-firm imports in US total non-ferrous metals imports on the other hand, doubled between 1977 and 1990.

11. Intra-industry trade (IIT) can be readily calculated for any given product category, as only the traditional bilateral trade statistics for that product category are needed. The interpretation of IIT data depends however, on how one defines that category, as the choice of the classification system and of the level of aggregation may strongly influence the results. For the analysis below, the Standard International Trade Classification, Revision 2, at the four digit level, was used. In the calculation of an IIT index, if exports are equal to imports, IIT is 100; on the other hand, if either imports or exports are equal to zero, IIT is zero.

12. The Japanese firms developed their equity participations in overseas smelters, spread among several Japanese firms, whose combined total was generally 50 per cent or less.

13. Figures 9*a* and 9*b* are taken from the KPMG Peat Marwick (Amsterdam) data collection of acquisitions, joint ventures and minority participations.

14. See Tables 1.1 and 1.2 in OECD (1994), *Mining and Non-ferrous Metals Policies of OECD Countries*; OECD Documents, Paris 1994.

15. See Overview chapter in OECD (1994) *ibid.*

16. In its statement of 29 January 1994, Russia made its commitment conditional on total reductions outside Russia of not less than 1.5 million tonnes, compared with the November 1993 level. As of mid-1994, the announced cuts, outside Russia, were shy of this level.

BIBLIOGRAPHY

ADAMS, R.G. (1990) "Restructuring of the Aluminium Industry: Real or Imaginary?", *Resources Policy,* May.

ALUMINIUM ASSOCIATION (1992), *Aluminium Statistical Review, 1991,* Washington, DC.

ANNUAL REPORT, Alcan, Alcoa, Alumax, Alusuisse-Lonza, Comalco, Kaiser, Noranda, Pechiney, Reynolds, Norsk Hydro, various years.

ANONYMOUS, "Fabricator Operations", *Aluminium: Profile of an Industry.*

ANYADIKE, N. (1991), "Boliden gives Trelleborg a New Outlook", *Metal Bulletin Monthly,* August.

CERNA (1990), *Rapport sur l'Aluminium,* Paris.

CHOKSI, S (1991), "Aluminium Price Behaviour: A Decade on the LME", *Resources Policy,* March, pp. 13-21.

ENERGY MINES AND RESOURCES, "Aluminimum", *Canadian Minerals Yearbook,* various years, Ottawa.

GATT (1987), *Problems of Trade in Certain Natural Resource Products, Background Study on Aluminium and Aluminium Products,* Geneva.

HATEM, F. (1989), "Aluminium: la délocalisation n'est pas une fatalité", *Revue d'Économie industrielle,* No. 50, pp. 32-56.

LEGRAND, B, (1992), "L'industrie de l'aluminium dans la compétition mondiale : armes technologiques et choix géographiques", *Colloque sur les matières premières du ministère de l'Économie,* Paris.

METAL BULLETIN MONTHLY (1993), "Aluminium", March.

METAL BULLETIN MONTHLY (1991), "Aluminium joint venture has experienced mentor", September.

METALEUROP, *Annuaire statistique,* Minemet, 1992, Fontenay-sous-Bois.

METALLGESELLSCHART, *Metallstatistik,* various years. Frankfurt am Main.

MORTENSEN, A. and M.J. KOCZAK, "The Status of Metal-Matrix Composite Research and Development in Japan", *Journal of Metals.*

NAPPI, C. (1992), "Aluminium", in Tilton, J. *et al., Public Policy and Competitiveness: The Non-Ferrous Metals Industry,* Metal Bulletin Books, London.

OECD (1992), *Globalisation of Industrial Activities: Four Case Studies,* Paris.

OECD (1993), *Intra-firm trade,* Trade Policy Issues No. 1, Paris.

OECD (1994), *Mining and Non-ferrous Metals Policies of OECD Countries;* OECD Documents, Paris.

ORGANISATION OF EUROPEAN ALUMINIUM SMELTERS (1992), *Secondary Aluminium. Europe, Japan, USA,* June, Düsseldorf.

RAW MATERIALS GROUP (1992), *Who Owns Who in Mining, 1992 Ownership and Control in the World Mining and Refining Industry,* London.

SA, P., de (1992), "Industrie minière mondiale : leçons d'une crise", *Observatoire des matières premières du ministère de l'Industrie et du Commerce extérieur,* Paris.

SA, P., de (1991), "From Oligopoly to Competition: The Changing Aluminium Industry", *Materials and Society,* Vol. 15, No. 2, pp. 149-175.

SA, P., de (1991), "The European non-ferrous metals industry, 1993 and beyond", *Resources Policy,* September, pp. 211-225.

SCHEYE, K. (1990), "Mergers and Acquisitions in the Mining Industry", *Mining Magazine,* March.

UNCTAD, *Commodity Yearbook,* various years, Geneva.

UNCTAD (1992), *Structural Changes in the World Minerals Industry During the 1980s,* Geneva.

US BUREAU OF MINES, "Aluminium, Bauxite and Alumina", *Minerals Yearbook,* various years, Washington.

US BUREAU OF MINES (1993), *Recycling – Non-ferrous Metals 1991,* Washington.

US DEPARTMENT OF COMMERCE, "Metals", *Industrial Outlook*, various years, Washington.

US OFFICE OF TECHNOLOGY ASSESSMENT (1988), *Non-ferrous Metals: Industry Structure Background Paper*, Washington.

WOJCIECHOWSKI, M.J. (1990), "Effects of Public Policy on Competitive Position in Nonferrous Metals: Nickel", Centre for Resources Studies, Kingston, Ontario, mimeo.

WORLD BUREAU OF METAL STATISTICS, *World Metal Statistics*, monthly and yearly, various issues, London.

ZEITLER, K.M. (1991), "Mineral Resources Development: Global Partnership Towards the 21st Century", paper for the Metal Mining Agency of Japan Forum, London.

Chapter 7

GLOBALISATION IN THE STEEL INDUSTRY

by

Joseph B. Kaesshaefer
Trade Directorate, OECD

Table of contents

LIST OF TABLES

SUMMARY AND CONCLUSIONS

Globalisation in the steel industry is seen in primarily three areas: international sourcing of raw materials; international trade; and inter-firm alliances and foreign investment. Since World War II, steel plants have been constructed in both resource-poor and resource-rich countries, so many steelmakers are obliged to source principal raw materials from outside the host country's borders. From an international trade perspective, over one-quarter of the world's production of finished steel crosses international boundaries. More recently globalisation in the steel industry is seen in a number of joint ventures, mergers and acquisitions and strategic alliances, particularly among US and Japanese firms, and European firms.

The steel industry has experienced major turmoil and change since the 1970s, and major developments or changes in a number of areas, including adjustments in growth and production, technology, raw materials, international trade, and foreign investment, will most likely continue.

Reduced consumption, over-capacity, imports from the central and eastern European countries (CEECs), price declines and reduction in workforces are some of the specific problems facing steelmakers in the OECD area. Many steelmakers throughout the world are using national trade laws to deal with these problems in order to protect their domestic markets from low-priced or subsidised steel.

On a global basis, the steel industry should experience growth in developing countries as the industrialised countries continue to maintain or reduce their capacities. In general, growth should be tempered by technological improvements throughout the steel industry, which have reduced the tonnage of crude steel used in making finished steel products. Whatever growth occurs in industrialised countries will probably not come from the large integrated producers, but from the smaller, more efficient minimills. The availability and price of scrap metal (or scrap substitutes), however, will affect the extent to which these smaller mills can successfully expand production.

The principal raw materials (*i.e.* iron ore, coal and scrap) for steel production vary in their availability. The steelmakers of the Far East continue to import all of their requirements, and Western Europe is tending in that direction. Brazil and Australia will continue to predominate the 400 million tonnes exported annually. Trade will continue to be a necessity as well for coal and scrap.

Despite the existence of numerous measures to restrict steel trade, the proportion of production traded internationally tended to rise, albeit slowly, during the 1970s and 1980s. The outlook for the 1990s and beyond, however, is unclear. On the one hand, steelmakers in industrialised countries are moving towards obtaining part of their steel requirements in semi-finished form, thus reducing their iron ore imports and the accompanying pollution problems associated with coke oven and blast furnace operations. Trade in semi-finished steel is therefore likely to grow during the next decade. The outlook for trade in finished products, however, seems less predictable as some factors suggest growth while others would tend to reduce the importance of trade. What seems clear is that increased steel production in developing countries will reduce the amount of steel imported from industrialised countries.

Substantial foreign investments in steelmakers located in industrialised countries are directed to modernising steel plants to reduce costs, increase productivity and improve quality. In the developing countries, investment is being directed toward increasing capacity.

In light of the structural problems affecting the steel industry, government involvement has been widespread, taking such forms as quantitative import restrictions, antidumping and countervailing duties, subsidies, price controls, export promotion, etc. Other policies have also affected competitiveness, *e.g.* environmental policies.

The pattern of government policies has affected the ways in which this industry has been globalising. For example, low or zero tariff levels on inputs have fostered international sourcing; similarly, investment and competition policies have been conducive to foreign direct investment (FDI) and inter-firm alliances.

With respect to trade policies, restrictive measures affecting steel imports, however, have been common, and given the long-term adjustment problems in the steel industry, there could be continued pressures for trade actions. Successfully concluding a Multilateral Steel Agreement (MSA) could, over the longer term, diminish pressures for trade actions concerning subsidisation. Trade actions concerning dumping could also diminish as steelmakers form strategic alliances or joint ventures thereby making steelmakers more reticent to accuse their foreign partners of unfair trading (pricing) practices. More open access to markets (which will occur under the agreements reached in the Uruguay Round) should reduce the extent to which producers can price discriminate in different national markets; this too should tend to diminish the possibilities for dumping actions.

The decisions that globalised steel companies make on production, trade and capital investment (including investment in new facilities as well as the closure of operations) will have a direct effect on the countries in which they operate. Governments may feel a need to balance the interests of such companies (which might seek to maximise efficiency through foreign investment) with national interests (which focus on promoting domestic economic activity).

The growth in the importance of minimills and the rise in steel production in the non-OECD countries have tended to decrease global concentration in the industry. The recent growth in transnational inter-firm alliances and investment, however, represents a tendency towards increased concentration. Governments may be concerned about the competitive implications of such growth in investment activity, and the effects of such activity on overall industry efficiency.

The analysis of globalisation in the steel industry suggests that environmental regulation could have significant effects on international trade and investment patterns in steel. The greater the differences in national environmental regulations, the greater it seems the potential effect on production, trade and investment patterns (*i.e.* through increased incentives to promote production and investment in less restrictive areas).

1. TRENDS IN GROWTH AND STRUCTURE

A. Steelmaking

The steel industry consists of integrated mills, minimills, specialty mills and service centres.[1] The final result of both casting methods is steel in one of three semi-finished shapes: slabs, blooms or billets. Slabs are wide semi-finished products from which flat-rolled sheets, strips and plates are made. After passing through a hot strip mill, a slab takes the form of either plate or a coil of thin sheet. Coils may be shipped to customers directly or may undergo further processing, including cold rolling, to form cold rolled sheet; slitting, to form steel strip; and welding, to form welded pipe. Some applications of sheets and strips include construction, appliances, auto bodies and electrical machinery. For applications where corrosion resistance is important, sheet is generally coated. These sheets with "galvanised" coatings are used in many automotive and appliance industry applications. Blooms and billets are frequently used to manufacture structural shapes, rails, bars and rods, and are principally used in the construction industry. Other major consumers of steel include the shipbuilding, container and oil and gas sectors. Specialty steel companies make stainless and alloy steels by adding a variety of alloys, such as chromium, nickel and molybdenum, to the liquid steel to impart specific properties to finished steel products. Specialty products are used in a variety of applications, including automobiles, food-processing equipment, medical instruments and household flatware. Integrated mills are relatively large capital-intensive facilities that produce mainly carbon steels from basic, naturally occurring raw materials. Integrated mills vary significantly in size, and nearly three-quarters of the world's steel is produced by these integrated facilities. Non-integrated facilities produce steel by melting recycled scrap in electric arc furnaces. This method generally involves less up-front investment and lower operating costs. Non-integrated producers include minimills, which produce mainly carbon steels, and specialty steel mills which generally focus production on higher value stainless products. Service centres do not produce molten steel but instead purchase steel for further processing and distribution.

B. Production

Developed countries continue to dominate the steel industry in terms of production and trade. In 1970, the world's 20 largest steelmakers were located in only four developed regions or countries: the European Community, the United States, Japan and Australia. However, since 1970, steelmakers located in developing countries have come to rival firms in developed countries, and by 1994, five of the 20 largest steelmakers were located in either China, the Republic of Korea or India. Many firms in developing countries benefited from government-sponsored industrialisation programmes which were designed to promote the formation of heavy industries and the substitution of domestically produced steel for imports.

Significant market entrants to the global steel industry since 1970 have been minimills. Four of the smaller, more efficient minimill groups were among the world's 50 largest steelmakers in 1994.

The global steel industry has undergone explosive growth since the end of World War II. In 1950, 192 million tonnes of raw steel were produced, and in 1993, about 730 million tonnes. In 1947, about 57 per cent of the world's raw steel was produced in the United States, as compared to 12 per cent in 1993. During the 1950s, as the war-torn nations of Europe and Japan began to rebuild their steel industries, their share of the world's steel production rapidly increased. In 1950, Western Europe's output was about 53 million tonnes, and for the period 1989-93, average annual production was over 161 million tonnes. Japan produced only 5 million tonnes in 1950, while the average annual production for the period 1989-93 was over 105 million tonnes.

Output from the principal steel-producing developing countries grew as well. For example, for the period 1957-61, average annual production in these countries (i.e. Brazil, China, India, the Republic of Korea, Mexico and Chinese Taipei) was 17 million tonnes. For the 1989-93 period, average annual production was 159 million tonnes.

Another aspect of the global steel industry that has changed dramatically in the post-World War II period is international trade in steel. In 1950, about 10 per cent of the world's steel products were traded; in 1970, about 23 per cent was traded; and in 1992 close to 29 per cent was traded.

C. Consumption

The level of economic activity in steel-consuming industries and the extent to which such industries use steel are the main factors on which steel consumption is based. From the end of World War II until 1970, consumption increased as demand increased from the principal consumers in the construction, machinery and equipment, and automotive industries. Overall slower economic growth since 1970 has meant relatively diminished steel demand. Consumption in industrialised countries has steadily fallen as economies approach an advanced industrialised age, while consumption has increased in developing countries as industrial and commercial infrastructures are constructed. The shift of major steel-consuming industries – such as shipbuilding, mining and heavy engineering – from industrialised countries to developing areas has also influenced changes in consumption, as has the growing efficiency of steel users. With respect to the intensity of steel use, competition from substitute materials, such as wood, cement and glass, is always keen, and newer materials, especially aluminium and plastics, are continuously replacing steel in many applications. A further reduction in steel use is caused by new technologies that have reduced the volume of steel required as heavier steels are being replaced with lighter steels. In addition, yield rates have improved as the steelmaking process has become more efficient.

D. Capacity

Increased production potential, coupled with a decrease in demand, has meant excess capacity for the global steel industry. The period before 1974 was generally one of optimism and steady capacity growth for the global steel industry, and steel was thought to be an industry with steady, long-term growth potential. This optimism resulted in increases in both industrialised and developing country steel making capacity through much of the 1970s. Between 1975 and 1986, steelmakers suffered through economic downturns and, contrary to previously optimistic forecasts, faced contraction or relatively slow growth in steel consumption. During the 1970s and 1980s, even with demand falling, developing countries continued to establish considerable steelmaking facilities. As a result of this additional capacity and depressed economies, industrialised countries abandoned or decommissioned an extensive number of facilities, and today, major steelmakers continue to plan the restructuring of their industries in order to cut excess capacity.

E. Employment

The International Metalworkers' Federation estimates that in 1974, employment in the steel industry was approximately 4.1 million, and fell in 1987 to about 3.4 million (if China is included in the 1987 figure, steel industry employment is estimated at 5.7 million).

In the OECD area from 1974 to 1993, the number of jobs in the steel industry has fallen by about 56 per cent. In 1993 alone, the iron and steel industry in the OECD area shed around 52 300 jobs, representing a 5 per cent decrease from 1992 levels.

The geographical shifts in production and consumption caused a decline in the number of workers employed in the steel industries of industrialised countries. This decline can be attributed to the reduction in steel consumption, the increase in steel imports from developing countries (which forced producers to cut back production) and the modernisation of facilities which installed labour-saving technologies. Employment in the steel industry in developing countries, contrary to trends in the industrialised world, has risen – an increase of about 6 per cent for the period 1970-87 (including China). Manpower increases have been needed to keep pace with the increased demand for steel, and steel plants in developing countries tend to be more labour-intensive than those in industrialised countries.

2. INTERNATIONAL SOURCING OF INPUTS

A. Background

International sourcing of the principal raw materials used in steelmaking – iron ore, coal and scrap – is common (Table 7.1). For the period 1983-92, 41 per cent of the world's iron ore production was exported, and 10 per cent of the world's ferrous scrap consumption was from exports (historical coking coal data are not readily available). In the case of iron ore and coal, such sourcing reflects the fact that steelmaking facilities are often located in countries with limited economically viable reserves, or with

Table 7.1. **International trade and production of iron ore, coking coal and ferrous scrap, 1992**

Material	World production	World exports	Exports/production
	Million tonnes		%
Iron ore	934	368	39
Coking coal [1]	217	146	67
Ferrous scrap	300 [2]	33	11

1. Production and exports for the OECD area only.
2. World consumption used as a proxy for production.
Source: IISI, *Steel Statistical Yearbook 1993*; OECD, *Coal Information 1993*.

reserves that have diminished in quantity and quality over time. On the other hand, scrap, which is recovered from manufacturing operations and discarded steel-bearing items, is generated in significant quantities in all industrialised countries. Trade, however, plays an important role in balancing the needs of specific countries.

B. International trade of inputs

Import dependence on iron ore varies among countries, with Japan and the Republic of Korea relying on foreign sources for virtually all of their needs. In Europe, though iron ore is mined, steelmakers are heavily dependent on imports. Major importing countries of the European Community (EC) include Germany, Belgium, Luxembourg, France and Italy. In North America, the United States is a significant importer of Canadian iron ore. On the supply side, the major iron ore exporters are Brazil and Australia, which together account for close to 60 per cent of the world's iron ore exports, followed by India, Canada, South Africa and Sweden, which each account for less than 10 per cent.

Coking coal, unlike iron ore, is not as abundant throughout the world and is mined in fewer countries. Like iron ore, it still must be shipped from country to country since many steelmakers are often located in resource-poor areas. Principal exporting countries include the United States, Canada, Australia, Poland and, to a lesser degree, Germany, China, South Africa and the Newly Independent States of the former USSR (NIS). The world's major coking coal importers include Japan, Korea, Chinese Taipei, Belgium and France.

Scrap, unlike iron ore and coking coal, is generated from manufacturing operations, so every steel-producing country generates significant quantities. Scrap exports are dominated by the mature industrial economies. The United States, Germany, France, the Netherlands and the United Kingdom collectively accounted for approximately 69 per cent of the world total in 1992. The principal importing countries were Italy, Turkey and Spain, followed by the Republic of Korea, India and China.

C. Outlook

International sourcing of the principal raw materials used in steelmaking is likely to change, though in different ways, during the 1990s. In the case of iron ore, increased reliance on Brazil and Australia could result in further increases in the share of production that is traded internationally. One factor that is difficult to assess at this point, however, is the effect that the political and economic changes occurring in the economies in transition will have on world production and trade patterns.

Coal trade patterns are likely to change as a result of the development of new technologies and processes that permit the use of alternative coals. Moreover, in some areas, the cost of compliance with environmental regulations and constraints on capital spending could result in the phasing out of coke ovens (which process coal into coke), leading to an increase in finished coke imports. And finally, scrap consumption and trade patterns could be significantly affected by the continued rise in the importance of steel minimills in countries like the United States and Japan. The growth of minimills, which use scrap intensively, could diminish the quantities available for export, resulting in a decline in the share traded.

3. INTERNATIONAL TRADE OF STEEL PRODUCTS

A. Background

While a high percentage of steel is consumed in the geographical area in which it is produced, substantial quantities are traded internationally between fairly distant countries. Such trade is driven by a number of factors, including:

- differences in steelmaking costs among countries;
- differences in national capacity and consumption levels (which create demand for imports or export potential); and

– product specialisation (*i.e.*, the need for steel-consuming industries to purchase products not available domestically from foreign suppliers).

It may seem surprising that steel, which has a low unit value (*i.e.* averaging US$0.30-0.80 per kilogramme) and is therefore relatively costly to transport, is as important as it is in world trade. During 1983-87, iron and steel accounted for about 3.5 per cent of the total world value of exports (or 5.5 per cent of total manufactured exports). Such trade has been facilitated, in part, by the advantageous positioning of major steel mills at deepwater ports. Relatively low ocean freight rates often enable such mills to serve many foreign markets on a cost-effective basis.

The importance of steel trade has tended to increase over time, though not as rapidly as trade in general (Table 7.2). It reached its peak in 1992, when exports accounted for 28.6 per cent of production; it has been even more important for the OECD countries, accounting for about 34 per cent of production during the 1980s.

Table 7.2. **World steel exports and production, 1975-92**

Period or year	Exports	Production	Exports/Production
	Million tonnes [1]		%
1975-79	651.7	2 747.4	23.7
1980-84	721.8	2 816.6	25.6
1985-89	828.6	3 134.3	26.4
1985	170.4	598.2	28.5
1986	161.0	595.9	27.0
1987	161.1	617.6	26.1
1988	167.3	657.6	25.4
1989	168.8	665.0	25.4
1990	168.3	654.4	25.7
1991	174.7	630.0	27.7
1992	177.6	620.8	28.6

1. In finished steel equivalent.
Source: IISI, *Steel Statistical Yearbook 1993.*

B. Trade patterns

The 12 countries comprising the EC (before its recent enlargement) have collectively accounted for the largest share of world steel exports for many years, although over one-half of those exports represent intra-EC trade (see Annex Table B). If intra-EC trade is excluded, the EC share of world exports has been steadily falling since the 1970s, and in recent years has represented 20 to 25 per cent of the world total.

Japan is the second largest exporter, though its role diminished during the 1980s. In terms of tonnage, Japan's exports have been sharply lower in recent years than during the first half of the 1980s. The unit value of Japanese exports, however, has been increasing, reflecting the industry's growing focus on higher-valued finished products.

Developing countries in Latin America and Asia became increasingly important exporters during the 1980s. The principal steel-producing countries' share of world exports rose from 2 per cent during the early 1970s to 14 per cent during the period 1988-92.

EC countries collectively account for the largest share of total world imports, but if intra-EC trade is excluded, imports have generally been less than those of the United States, the single largest national market for imports. Japan's share of world imports has substantially increased since 1980, rising from 1.2 million tonnes to a peak of 9.0 million tonnes in 1991. Japan's share of world imports rose from 1.6 per cent in 1980 to 5.3 per cent in 1991. Japan's import growth has been particularly strong in lower-value plate and sheet products.

C.   Intra-firm trade

Intra-firm trade (IFT) is defined as the international exchange of goods and services within a multinational enterprise (MNE).[2] While IFT accounts for over a third of total US merchandise trade, IFT in the US steel sector is relatively unimportant. Although classification problems prevent the calculation of the exact share of IFT on US steel trade, estimates put it at less than 10 per cent – and perhaps even less than 5 per cent – of both US steel exports and imports in 1989.

Two-thirds of IFT in the US steel sector are sales by European and Japanese firms to their US affiliates. There is also some IFT due to the establishment of US firms in Canada and to a lesser extent, in Europe.

The relative unimportance of IFT in the US steel industry is highlighted by data on the international trade of foreign affiliates of US steelmakers. In 1990, less than 15 per cent of those firm's exports to the United States and less than 10 per cent of their imports from the United States went to or came from their parents. Figures are somewhat higher for US affiliates of foreign steel firms, which in 1990, exported 24 per cent and imported 50 per cent of their products from their parents or other affiliated firms. These figures are significantly below the average for all manufacturing industries.

The relative share of IFT in US steel trade does not appear to have changed substantially between 1977 and 1989. This is also the case of the share of IFT on total US merchandise.[3]

D.   Intra-industry trade

Intra-industry trade (IIT) is defined as the exchange by two countries of goods and services within the same product category. IIT is generally a function of product differentiation and may or may not be intra-firm trade. IIT indices provide another tool for analysing trade patterns as they may show the extent of international linkages for a given industry.[4]

IIT indices for trade in steel products are hard to interpret as they vary considerably from year to year, reflecting large shifts in trade flows. A few general points can still be made, however.

First, IIT indices for US trade in iron and steel products[5] confirm the patterns observed with IFT figures. US IIT indices for steel trade are below the average for all manufacturing, reflecting the US trade deficit in most steel products. There does not seem to be a general trend in the 1980s towards an increase in US steel sector IIT. Of bilateral IIT indices, those for trade with Canada tend to be higher than average, as is the case for most other industries.

Second, IIT indices for Japanese steel trade are comparable to those of the United States, but about average for Japanese manufacturing industries. Japanese IIT indices generally tend to be lower than those for other OECD countries. The low indices for Japanese steel trade reflect the Japanese trade surplus in most steel products. There has been, however, a strong increase in Japanese steel IIT indices in the 1980s due to the large surge in Japanese imports in the period. Japan has higher than average IIT indices in its bilateral steel trade with the Republic of Korea, which is by far the largest source of its imports.

Third, steel sector IIT indices for individual EC countries are high, as is the case for most other industries. This is mostly due to the importance of intra-EC trade. There have not been any significant changes in EC IIT indices in the 1980s. EC countries have low IIT indices on their bilateral steel trade with the United States, as the EC has had a trade surplus for the majority of steel products. EC IIT indices for bilateral steel trade with Japan are somewhat higher, but there is relatively little trade between the two.

E.   Outlook

The outlook for steel trade is unclear as there are factors supporting trade expansion and other factors that would diminish trade.

On the one hand, implementation of the agreements reached in the Uruguay Round will create an environment supportive of increased trade in steel. Many countries, for example, will be phasing out their steel tariffs and, under the agreement on safeguards, countries agreed that they would not seek to take or maintain any voluntary export restraints, orderly marketing arrangements or any other similar measures on exports or imports. Further liberalisation could occur in the event separate negotiations that have been underway on steel for a number of years succeed. Certain structural changes in the industry could also act to increase trade. For example, in the United States, the closure of non-competitive facilities that process iron ore into pig iron and molten steel has already resulted in the industry's import of significant quantities of partially advanced steel for further rolling or processing. The reliance on imported semi-finished steel could increase and expand to other industrialised countries faced with the costly renovation of coke ovens and blast furnaces, and growing concern with environmental issues. The increasing role of steel service centres in the industry is also likely to affect trade, particularly to the extent that these centres are foreign-owned.

Increased reliance on semi-finished steel would also have an implication for inter-firm alliances. As has often been the case, joint ventures would probably be formed to help assure stable supplies of the semi-finished material.

Finally, over time steel appears to have become a more differentiated product, reflecting the fact that not all producers are capable of producing the same products to the same standards (particularly for the more sophisticated products). The increase in the degree to which producers can differentiate their products could result in more specialisation, which in turn, could translate into higher levels of trade.

On the other hand, increases in foreign investment could result in declines in trade, especially to the extent that a country's exports are replaced by shipments from the foreign facility. For example, Japanese exports of galvanised sheets to the US market are being replaced to a large extent by production from the US-Japanese joint ventures. Trade may also decline due to the rising importance of minimills, whose efficiency in labour use has tended to minimise the effect of wage rate differences on relative costs. In addition to narrowing cost differences, the relatively low entry costs could result in more localised production of steel products. Finally, uncertainty over measures that might yet be taken on trade could affect the extent to which producers choose to develop foreign markets.

4. FOREIGN DIRECT INVESTMENT AND INTER-FIRM ALLIANCES

A. Background

International exchanges of technology (through licensing or sales) between steelmakers have been relatively free for decades. Until recent years, however, cross-border ownership of steelmaking assets was relatively limited. As shown in Annex Tables A-1 through A-4, this changed during the 1970s and 1980s, with a great deal of the change occurring during the past several years. The changes were driven by a number of interrelated factors, including significant structural changes in the industry and the recent globalisation of the automobile industry, which is one of the largest markets for steel products.

The structural changes in the industry include an important reorientation of many of the leading integrated steel producers in the OECD area. In the early 1970s, these companies tended to produce a broad range of steel products. Over-capacity and the rising importance of production from steel minimills and non-OECD countries, however, resulted in a consolidation of activities in many of these companies. In general, they are now focusing on the production of the more sophisticated steel products. This has required investment in costly advanced technologies to improve the consistency, finish and properties of the steel they produce. The high cost of the equipment is one of the factors that has made joint ventures attractive.

The interest in investing in foreign facilities has also been driven by the need to produce in reasonably close proximity to many types of end-users. This is particularly important in the case of industries like the automobile industry, which works closely with its steel suppliers in the development of materials to produce parts for various models. Servicing the needs of such industries, which frequently requires flexible delivery, is often impractical from distant supplying points.

There are, of course, many other reasons that could underlie foreign investment. A summary of the principal factors follows:

- potential cost savings, or improved profitability, in materials, labour, and land;
- avoidance of tariff and non-tariff barriers (actual or potential);
- avoidance of exchange rate variability;
- avoidance of regulation, *e.g.* taxation, competition, environmental standards and rules, national procurement;
- improved distribution capabilities;
- improved servicing capabilities (technical assistance and just-in-time deliveries); and
- acquisition of technical or marketing expertise.

Following are comments on the form that inter-firm alliances and foreign investment have taken in various geographical regions.

B. North America

a) *Integrated mills*

Much of the investment and alliance activity that has occurred in North America has involved Japanese alliances with US integrated steelmakers. By 1981 most major US steelmakers had entered into agreements to receive technical assistance from Japanese steelmakers. For example, US Steel (now USX) had an agreement for "comprehensive co-operation" with Nippon Steel and one for assistance with its cold strip mill and continuous casting facilities with Sumitomo. Sumitomo was able to help US Steel improve its management of technology, especially with regard to scheduled maintenance programmes, energy conservation, and quality control. Bethlehem worked with Kawasaki to help improve yields and approached NKK for continuous annealing technology and Nippon for coke oven technology. Armco had a comprehensive co-operation agreement with Nippon and asked Nippon to do a "plant diagnosis" of one of its mills. Inland used NKK as a consultant in planning a new blast furnace. Many Japanese steelmakers also offered advice to US steel executives on management-related matters, such as inventory control, production controls and scheduling.

As the examples above show, much of the technology that the American steelmakers acquired from the Japanese at the beginning of the 1980s involved the transfer of "tacit knowledge" which is substantially unpatentable and difficult to quantify in dollar terms. By the mid-1980s, these collaborative agreements concerning technology transfer began to evolve into agreements for equity participation. The agreements enabled US producers to acquire technology at a reduced cost, while providing Japanese producers with a vehicle for increasing their activities in the US market.

An example of how the relationships evolved is found in NKK's acquisition of 50 per cent of National Steel in 1984; by April 1993, its interest had risen to 72 per cent. Prior to 1984, the two firms had been associated in research projects for over 15 years. Its interest in buying a portion of National appears to have reflected a desire to enter the US market for steel sheet to serve the auto transplants. Following the purchase, National built a modern electrogalvanising line at its Great Lakes Works near Detroit using NKK's technology. The new line was the first of its type in the United States, and it represented the first export order NKK received for the technology. Total investment in the facility came to US$120 million, and Marubeni, a Japanese trading company, helped to arrange financing. As part of the agreement to build the plant, NKK sent three of its top managers with backgrounds in sales, technology and international trade, to National. These executives worked towards upgrading National's technology in many areas of production, often acquiring a market for NKK's own technologies in the process.

NKK later received an order from National for the construction of a ladle furnace and supporting facilities for National's Granite City Works, and then another contract to supply a molten steel surface level control system for continuous casting moulds at Granite City. In an effort to promote this joint venture, National and NKK formed a new technical co-ordinating and planning department, staffed by both National and NKK employees.

As the NKK-National venture shows, the globalisation of another sector in the 1980s, the automotive sector, is one of the important factors driving Japanese investment in the United States. Two other joint ventures with Japanese steelmakers (Inland-Nippon and LTV-Sumitomo) were formed primarily because the auto industry desired to improve its anti-corrosion programme by using galvanised sheets in exposed parts of car bodies.

b) Minimills

Globalisation has not been limited to integrated mills. The profitability, success and prospects of US minimills have attracted foreign interest from steelmakers in Japan and Europe. In 1989 Nucor, the largest US minimill and one of the world's top 50 steelmakers, and Yamato Kogyo of Japan, opened a green-field wide-flange beam facility. The Korf group of Germany designed, built and operated a plant now run by North Star, the second largest minimill in the United States and one of the world's top-50 steelmakers as well. Canadian, French, Austrian, Swiss, British and Brazilian firms have, since the late 1970s, either built, owned, financed or provided technology to US-based minimills.

c) Service centres

In addition to integrated mills and minimills, globalisation has touched downstream activities, such as finishing and customisation, of steel products. This has taken the form of investment in service centres, which purchase steel from mills for processing and sales to final users. A service centre may, for example, have extensive equipment for the bending, cutting, sawing, slotting, punching, deburring, levelling and surface preparation of steel. Investment in service centres has enabled steelmakers to provide more effective support to traditional customers who demand more customised service.

European interests have long been involved in this segment of the US steel industry. Uddeholm of Sweden started service centres to market tool steels in 1927. Krupp and Klockner of Germany have also had service centres in the United States. Most recently, it is Japanese trading companies, such as Mitsui, C. Itoh, Nissho Iwai and Marubeni, that have been most active in acquiring total or partial ownership of US service centres. Japanese and European investors alike appear to have been motivated to form inter-firm alliances in part for the same reasons as their integrated counterparts, particularly auto transplants in the case of the Japanese. In 1990, approximately 20 per cent of US service centres had some foreign ownership.

C. Europe

While North America's globalised activities mainly concern investments from Japan, European activities have generally been regional. They have not been as extensive in nature, rather they have been confined to joint ventures to produce specific steel products. Steelmakers in the European Community have a long history of owning distribution and steelmaking facilities in neighbouring European countries. More recently, with an eye towards a fully integrated EC, European steelmakers have actively pursued EC and globally-focused corporate strategies in production, marketing and research and development (R&D). As Annex Table A-2 shows, almost every major steelmaker in Europe, with Usinor-Sacilor of France taking the lead, has entered into a joint venture, either with another steel company or with service centres in Europe.

D. Economies in transition

Foreign investment in the steel industries of the central and eastern European countries (CEECs) and the NIS, which was virtually non-existent prior to the political changes of the past several years, is beginning to increase. Lucchini (Italy) has invested in a Polish steelmaker, while Voest Alpine (Austria) has invested in Hungary and Rautaruukki of Finland has entered into a joint venture with a producer in Estonia. While it is limited, and could remain so, most CEECs are linking up with European and Japanese steelmakers in order to acquire technical assistance. Over time, these relationships could deepen.

In the NIS, as in the CEECs, foreign investment has been limited. Agreements exist at the present with foreign engineering and construction companies to modernise existing plants.

E. Asia/Africa/Oceania

As Annex Table A-3 shows, investment in the Asian steel industry has been primarily from other Asian countries, and is increasingly in production and distribution facilities, with Japan, Malaysia and Chinese Taipei experiencing the most activity. The DAEs' expanding need for steel represents a growing export market for Japan, and Japanese trading companies have invested in service centres in DAEs in order to process and distribute the growing volume of steel imported by these countries. Japanese producers and trading companies have been active in production facilities as well, investing heavily in Malaysia and Thailand. As Japanese investment activity in the United States slows, Japan is looking increasingly towards the markets of the DAEs.

POSCO of the Republic of Korea has recently invested in several Chinese steel concerns, and is exploring the newly-opened market of Vietnam.

The Chinese Taipei steel industry has engaged in activities with Malaysia and the People's Republic of China in order to address the production problems associated with steel facilities. It has also entered into agreements with German and Korean producers to assist with its efforts to focus more on high-quality specialty steels. In the past, India's state-owned steel industry has been offered substantial funds and concessionary financing by mainly German, Japanese and USSR firms for the establishment or modernisation of Indian steel facilities. More recently, India's only private integrated steelmaker has entered into a joint venture with a US firm.

F. Latin America

In Latin America, foreign investment in the steel industry is relatively low (see Annex Table A-4). Chile has sold an interest in its sole integrated steel mill, CAP, to Japanese and Swiss investors. Germany is heavily involved in steel distribution, selling Brazilian and other Latin American steel products on the world market. Gerdau of Brazil has been active in acquiring smaller producers in neighbouring Chile and Uruguay. CST of Brazil is partially owned by Kawasaki of Japan and ILVA of Italy.

G. Foreign investment in principal raw materials

Foreign investment in the production of the principal raw materials used in steelmaking is most prevalent in the iron ore industry, less so in the coal industry and is believed to be rare in the scrap industry. Such investment has helped assure companies stable, or preferential, access to inputs.

In North America, Canada's largest steelmakers, Stelco and Dofasco, partially own three US iron ore mines, and most iron ore pellet plants are joint ventures between the largest Canadian and US steelmakers. British Steel also has large iron ore interests in Canadian mines. In Asia, Japanese companies have a vested interest in a number of Australian mines. Of the five major producing locations in Australia, four of them are joint ventures with Japanese steelmakers. Moreover, capital from Japanese steelmakers has assisted India in developing some of its iron ore deposits.

H. Outlook

As indicated earlier, technical co-operation among the world's steelmakers is long-standing and appears likely to continue to be strong during the 1990s. Concerning foreign investment in principal raw materials, there do not appear to be any developments that would significantly alter foreign investment in mining operations. However, the outlook for foreign investment in steelmakers is somewhat more complicated. The burst of foreign investment that occurred during the 1980s followed a period of substantial structural adjustment, in which firms consolidated activities and redefined their corporate strategies. A further round of significant restructuring now appears to be under way involving companies in Europe and the economies in transition.

This could prompt further transnational mergers or acquisitions. In the case of North America, foreign investment may continue, but, if so, it is difficult to see it doing so on anywhere near the scale of the last several years. In Latin America, the privatisation of companies has helped create conditions that are conducive to foreign alliances, while in Asia, the high growth in steel consumption in many countries is likely to attract increased foreign investment.

The future level and form of foreign investment will also depend on production patterns in key consuming industries, of which the automobile industry is one of the most important. Establishment or significant expansion of auto production facilities, particularly in new geographical areas, could well result in increased foreign investment in those areas by steelmakers.

5.   GOVERNMENT POLICIES

A.   Background

There has been significant government involvement in the world's steel industries in the form of ownership, financial assistance, regulation and trade measures. Government policies have affected the industry's performance and structure, world steel production and trade patterns and investment flows. From 1970 to 1975, governments generally supported steel-industry expansion through ownership (particularly in developing countries), financial assistance, trade policies that discouraged imports through tariff and non-tariff barriers, and export promotion. From 1976 to the mid-1980s, continued support to expand capacity in certain countries was joined by massive governmental intervention to support financially troubled steelmakers. From the mid-1980s, many governments began to reduce involvement in the industry by either cutting back or withdrawing assistance.

Government involvement in the industry appears to have negatively affected the competitive environment of the steel industry. Financial assistance programmes were instrumental in constructing new facilities, thereby increasing access to investment capital and leading to the preservation of certain steelmakers. Further, the creation and maintenance of capacity has likely contributed to imbalances between steel capacity and consumption. Excess capacity tended to reduce prices, and therefore profitability, which diminished the incentive of steelmakers to invest in their industry. Government efforts to enhance the poor financial performance of these firms through trade measures affected production and trade patterns for high and low performers alike in all steel-producing countries.

B.   Government assistance

Among industrialised countries, between 1968 and 1986, governments assumed ownership of failing steelmakers; the United Kingdom, Belgium and France nationalised companies. Only a few countries – such as the United States, Japan, Switzerland and Australia – held no ownership during this period. In developing countries, state-owned companies dominated steel production in Mexico, Brazil, Venezuela, Argentina, Korea, Chinese Taipei, India, Indonesia, Malaysia and Thailand. Government ownership began declining around 1986 as full or partial divestiture occurred in the United Kingdom, Belgium, Germany, South Africa, the Republic of Korea, Chinese Taipei, Mexico, Brazil, Malaysia and Thailand, and privatisation of more facilities is being contemplated. In 1993 governments of the CEECs and the NIS have begun to sell off state-owned steel enterprises, or have pledged to do so.

Financial assistance to both government and privately owned steelmakers has been provided to the industry since the 1970s in many forms, including loans, grants and preferential access to capital markets. Access to low-cost investment capital and operating subsidies has enabled steelmakers to undertake significant investment programmes despite serious financial losses. Other forms of assistance depend on the government, but in general, have included liberal depreciation allowances, local tax concessions, numerous tax credits, research funds, development grants, government repayment or guarantee of loans, preferential financial treatment for export enterprises, technical assistance funds and loans from extra-governmental agencies, such as the World Bank, to developing country steel industries. Since the mid-1980s, this assistance has in general been reduced or eliminated. Where assistance is continuing, it is often being used to facilitate workforce adjustment or plant closures.

C. Regulation

a) Price controls

Price controls by governments have been more extensive in developing countries than in industrialised ones, though in the 1970s the United States and the EC attempted to regulate prices. India still controls both the prices of inputs, such as scrap, and domestic prices for most products manufactured by both government and privately owned steelmakers. Other developing-country governments maintain tiered pricing systems, one price for the domestic market and a lower price for steel exports.

b) Competition

In the United States, anti-trust policies place conditions on acquisitions if they result in reduced competition. The 1984 merger of two large steelmakers resulted in the divestiture of two mills, and in another case, a steelmaker turned to a Japanese firm for a joint venture after being prevented from merging with another US steelmaker. Some observers of US anti-trust policy believe that it has forced US steelmakers to seek foreign rather than domestic merger partners. In the EC many steelmakers have entered into producer alliances that resulted in informal market sharing arrangements, such as the formation of German "Rationalisation Groups" in 1971 which reportedly provided an institutional framework for self-regulated competition and price co-ordination among 31 German producers. In Japan the Ministry of International Trade and Industry reportedly provides production guidance and provides a forum for producers to meet to discuss appropriate production levels and exchange market data. In less developed countries, governments have limited the size of private companies permitted to compete with state-owned companies. In addition, governments frequently veto expansion or modernisation plans by private companies, and often grant state-owned companies exclusive rights to manufacture, import or export certain types of steel products.

c) Environment

The production of steel generates significant amounts of waste, and because of the potential environmental impact, laws and regulations, mainly in the OECD area, have been directed at reducing the pollution associated with such waste. As a result, government policies have affected the industry in areas such as costs, investment and operations.

Costs have been affected both by the administrative cost of complying with regulations and the cost of operating and maintaining equipment associated with environmental control. Investment has been affected because compliance with regulations often requires the purchase and installation of equipment, without which steelmaking facilities might not be able to comply with standards resulting in fines or closure. Plant site selection and development may be affected because proposed facilities are often subject to a process in which their environmental impact is closely examined. National environmental regulations that require modifications of steelmaking practices may affect operation levels and practices. The inefficient steelmakers in the CEECs and the NIS could experience particular difficulties in transforming facilities to meet world environmental standards.

In general, OECD countries and many newly industrialised countries appear to have comparable air and water pollution standards. Significant disparities in the stringency of environmental enforcement and in the financing of explicit costs associated with environmental controls, however, may put some steel industries at a comparative disadvantage in meeting regulatory requirements.

d) Export promotion

Many governments in steel-producing countries have adopted polices that are designed to support and expand steel exports, including export tax credits and preferential export financing. In some countries the policies have also included assistance for infrastructure development, such as ports, as well as tax benefits on equipment purchased in support of export production.

D. Trade

Since 1970 many steel-producing countries adopted policies (*i.e.* tariffs, taxes, quantitative restrictions and foreign exchange restrictions) to protect their steel industries from foreign competition. These policies may have affected the competitive environment by altering production and trade flows that otherwise could have resulted from inter-firm competition.

Tariffs on steel imports were relatively high during the 1970s, but have generally been reduced since then as a result of unilateral and multilateral actions. Though *ad valorem* tariff rates vary greatly among products, the approximate rates in developed countries range from 4-8 per cent while approximate rates in developing countries range from 15 to 20 per cent.

As tariffs have declined, the use of non-tariff measures affecting imports, including various market arrangements, became widespread. Since 1970 non-tariff measures used by governments have encompassed import quotas, licensing requirements, foreign exchange restrictions, indirect and direct taxes, preferential procurement regulations, price controls and other regulations.

The United States concluded "voluntary" restraint arrangements on imports from the EC and Japan from 1969-74. In 1978 and until 1982 the United States implemented a programme to monitor prices of imported steel to facilitate detection of sales at less than fair value. In 1982 the United States and the EC entered into another market arrangement, and in 1984 and 1989, the United States concluded bilateral "voluntary restraint agreements" (VRA) with the EC, Japan and numerous large and small steel-producing countries. Bilateral Consensus Agreements were concluded between the United States and the EC, Japan and other signatories of the 1989 VRAs whereby countries agreed to restrict trade-distorting practices and committed themselves to prohibiting subsidies for steel production. The voluntary restraint agreements expired on 31 March 1992. Since that time, US steel producers have filed a large number of unfair trade cases against foreign producers, with mixed results.

In the EC, imports from Japan were limited by agreement after 1971, and imports from the CEECs were restricted after 1973. In 1978 the EC concluded 15 bilateral restraint arrangements that placed limits on signatory countries' exports. Since 1986, most trade measures have been phased out. In 1994 only imports from the states comprising the former USSR were subject to quantitative restrictions. Certain sensitive steel imports from the Czech and Slovak Republics are subject to additional tariffs, once tonnages exceed certain levels.

In the 1970s and most of the 1980s, Mexico, Brazil and other developing countries placed several restrictions on steel imports. Mexico liberalised restrictions on steel imports following Mexico's accession to the GATT in 1986, and Brazil only recently started to dismantle its import licensing schemes. Until 1987 the Republic of Korea applied high tariffs and quotas. Many developing countries however continue restrictive trade practices, including high import tariffs, import or export bans and discriminatory duty waivers.

The assessment of antidumping and countervailing duties on steel products under national unfair trade laws appears to have grown in recent years. In addition to the United States, Canada, the EC and Mexico have also recently used their unfair trade laws to initiate antidumping investigations of foreign steelmakers.

As indicated earlier, implementation of the agreements reached in the Uruguay Round will strengthen the multilateral system and will help create a more open competitive environment. The conclusion of a separate multilateral steel agreement would go even further, as many forms of government assistance would be prohibited. To the extent that the underlying causes of trade problems are addressed effectively through multilateral agreements, the need for trade remedies should diminish.

NOTES AND REFERENCES

1. Integrated producers smelt processed iron ore and coke in a blast furnace to produce molten iron, which is subsequently poured into a steelmaking furnace together with scrap. The hot metal is processed into steel when oxygen is blown into the metal bath. Once molten steel with the correct properties has been produced, it is cast into a form that can enter the rolling process. Currently the industry uses two principal methods of casting: ingot teeming and continuous casting. Ingot teeming is the traditional process in which steel is poured into individual moulds, allowed to solidify and then separated from the moulds. Continuous casting, the newer process, by-passes several steps of the conventional ingot casting process by casting steel directly into semi-finished shapes. Benefits derived from the quicker casting method include increased yield, improved product quality, decreased energy consumption and less pollution.

2. There are few sources of date on IFT, as information on the subject is not generally available in traditional trade statistics. Data on IFT are mostly available through firm surveys which involve the preparation of questionnaires by national authorities. This section is based on information provided by the US Department of Commerce, which conducts surveys of foreign affiliates of US companies and US affiliates of foreign companies. Relevant data is not available for other countries. The US Department of Commerce uses the International Surveys Industry (ISI) classification in its surveys. There is a category for "ferrous primary metal industries" (ISI 31), which includes the manufacturing of hot metal, pig iron, ferroalloys, cold and hot rolled steel, electrometallurgical products, steel wire, nails and spikes, steel pipes and tubes, etc. The level of aggregation in these surveys does not allow the distinction between different steel products. For an explanation of the availability and problems with date on IFT, please consult OECD (1993), *Intra-firm Trade*, Trade Policy Issues, Paris.

3. See OECD (1993) *Intra-firm Trade*, Trade Policy Issues, Paris.

4. Intra-industry trade can be readily calculated for any given product category, as only the traditional bilateral trade statistics for that product category are needed. The interpretation of IIT data depends, however, on how one defines that category, as the choice of the classification system and of the level of aggregation may strongly influence the results. For the analysis below, the Standard International Trade Classification (SITC) Revision 2, at the four digit level, was used. In the calculation of an IIT index, if exports are equal to imports, IIT is 100; on the other hand, if either imports or exports are equal to zero, IIT is zero. For a discussion of the theory and measurement of IIT, see Grubel and Lloyd (1975).

5. SITC Rev2 67; Iron and steel. This can be further disaggregated into nine sub-categories: pig iron, spiegeleisen, sponge iron, iron/steel powders and ferroalloys (671); ingots (672); bars, rods, angles, shapes and sections (673); universals, plates and sheets (674); hoops and strips (675); rails and railway track construction material (676); wire (677); tubes, pipes and fittings (678); castings, forgings and stampings (679).

BIBLIOGRAPHY

CARSON, I. (1992), "Steel's Second Smeltdown", *International Management*, May.

"Globalisation of Steel Conference", Atlanta, Georgia, 25-27 February 1990, from texts of speeches given by various participants.

GRUBEL, H.G. and P.J. LLOYD (1975), *Intra-industry Trade: The Theory and Measurement of International Trade in Differentiated Products*, Macmillan and Company, London.

HOGAN, W.T. (1991), *Global Steel in the 1990s: Growth or Decline*, Lexington Books, Lexington, MA.

INTERNATIONAL IRON AND STEEL INSTITUTE (1993), *Steel Statistical Yearbook 1993*, Brussels.

INTERNATIONAL METALWORKERS' FEDERATION (1991), *Europe 1992 and the Steel Industry Worldwide*, Geneva.

LICHTENSTEIN, J. (1990), "Globalisation of Steel", 33 *Metal Producing*, April.

LYNN, L.H. (1988), "Multinational Joint Ventures in the Steel Industry", *International Collaborative Ventures in US Manufacturing*, Ballinger Publishing Company, Cambridge, MA.

METAL BULLETIN BOOKS (1991), *Iron and Steel Works of the World*, 10th edition, Surrey, England.

NATIONAL ACADEMY OF ENGINEERING (1991), *Prospering in a Global Economy: National Interests in an Age of Global Technology*, National Academy Press, Washington, DC.

OECD (1992), *Globalisation, Corporate Citizenship and Industrial Policy*, Paris.

OECD (1994), *The Steel Market in 1993 and the Outlook for 1994 and 1995*, Paris.

OECD (1994), *The Iron and Steel Industry in 1992*, Paris.

SCHEUERMAN, W.E. (1990), "Joint Ventures in the US Steel Industry", *American Journal of Economics and Sociology*, Vol. 49, No. 4, October.

UNCTAD (1992), *Iron Ore Statistics*, October, Geneva.

US INTERNATIONAL TRADE COMMISSION (1991), *Steel Industry Annual Report*, USITC Publication 2436, September, Washington, DC.

US INTERNATIONAL TRADE COMMISSION (1994), *Steel Semiannual Monitoring Report*, USITC Publication 2807, September, Washington, DC.

US TRADE REPRESENTATIVE (1992), *1992 National Trade Estimate Report on Foreign Trade Barriers*, March.

Statistical Annex

1. NOTES TO ANNEX TABLES A-1 THROUGH A-4

Four tables concerning the globalisation of the steel industry are attached. The investment activity of the world's 50 largest steelmakers is presented according to the region in which the investment occurs:

- Annex Table A-1. North America (Canada, Mexico, United States).
- Annex Table A-2. Europe (Western, CEECs, NIS).
- Annex Table A-3. Asia, Africa, Oceania.
- Annex Table A-4. Latin America.

The data contained in the tables do not include the most comprehensive view of the degree to which steelmakers of the world have entered into alliances. Only the world's top-50 largest steelmakers are presented. Thus, the international investment activity of many small and medium-sized enterprises, such as specialty steel producers and minimills located throughout the world, though extensive, is not represented here.

Data is presented in the following manner:

Column 1: Country-company. Following each host country heading is the alphabetical listing of a country's major (*i.e.* top-50) steelmakers that have been involved with foreign investors in the host country. This is followed by an alphabetical listing of other companies which are aligned with a major foreign steelmaker.

Column 2: Total employment. Total corporate employment figures.

Column 3: Foreign partner/affiliate/subsidiary. The foreign company making the investment.

Column 4: Country. The country of origin of the partner, affiliate or subsidiary.

Column 5: Description. Information that provides details on the globalised activity, such as its name, location, product line, etc.

Column 6: Investment type. This information is coded: AC = Acquisition; JV = Joint Venture; GF = Green-field (or new facility).

Column 7: Product activity. This information is coded and indicates the major product or service supplied as a result of the investment: CR = Carbon steel; SP = Speciality steel; DS = Distribution or service centre.

Column 8: Share of ownership (percentage). The percentage share the foreign partner owns in the globalised activity.

Column 9: Total investment (approx.) (US$ mn). The approximate US$ amount (in millions of US$) of foreign investment in the globalised activity.

Column 10: Start up year. The year the investment occurred.

Column 11: Capacity or annual turnover ('000 mt). The approximate annual turnover, or the approximate capacity of the facility, in thousands of metric tonnes.

Column 12: Employment (estim.). The estimated number of employees working in the globalised activity.

Table A-1. **Globalisation of the steel industry: selected investment activity in North America by the world's 50 largest steelmakers**

Country: Company	Total employment	Foreign partner /affiliate/subsidiary	Country	Description	Investment type[1]	Product activity[2]	Share of ownership (%)	Total investment (approx.) (US$ mn)	Start up year	Capacity or annual turnover ('000 mt)	Employment (estim.)
Canada											
Dofasco	7 000	NKK/National	Japan/US	DNN Galvanising	GF	CR	40/10	120	1993	360	100
Stelco	12 000	Mitsubishi Corp.	Japan	Galv.-Hilton	IV	CR	40	172	1991	350	n.a.
Courtice	275	Gerdau	Brazil	Long products	AC	CR	100	52	n.a.	500	300
Mexico				Globalised activity							
Mexinox	921	Acerinox/Thyssen	Spain/Germany		IV	SP	33/33	n.a.	1990	n.a.	921
United States											
Armco	n.a.	Kawasaki	Japan	All facilities	IV	CR	50	700	1989	n.a.	n.a.
		Acerinox	Spain	N. AM. Stainless	GF	SP	50	222	1992	150	n.a.
Bethlehem	30 500	Usinor-Sacilor	France	Bethforge	AC	CR	50	n.a.	1990	n.a.	n.a.
		Saw Pipe	India	Baytown	AC	CR	100	n.a.	1992	n.a.	n.a.
Inland	18 600	Nippon	Japan	Equity share	AC	CR	13	185	1989	4 243	n.a.
		Nippon	Japan	I/N tek	GF	CR	40	78	1987	1 000	290
		Nippon	Japan	I/N Kote	GF	CR	50	60	1991	900	260
LTV	n.a.	Mitsui	Japan	2 slit/cut fac;	IV	DS	33	40	1991	n.a.	n.a.
		Sumitomo	Japan	LS	GF	CR	40	100	1987	400	n.a.
		Sumitomo	Japan	LS II	GF	CR	50	205	1991	360	n.a.
National	n.a.	Marubeni/Mits./NKK	Japan	Procoil	IV	DS	56	9	1986	300	n.a.
		NKK	Japan	All facilities	IV	CR	70	469	1984	5 900	10 300
Nucor	5 500	Yamato Kogyo	Japan	Nucor-Yamato	GF	CR	49	190	1987	1 900	435
USX	n.a.	Kobe	Japan	USS-Kobe	IV	CR	50	300	1989	2 400	2 800
		Kobe	Japan	Pro-Tec coating	IV	CR	50	100	1990	600	100
		POSCO	Korea	USS-POSCO	IV	CR	50	400	1986	1 350	1 150
Wheeling	6 600	Nisshin	Japan	All facilities	AC	CR	10	18	1984	2 656	6 000
Pittsburgh		Nisshin	Japan	Wheeling-Nisshin	IV	CR	80	45	1986	463	156
Alloy and Stainless	n.a.	Usinor-Salicor	France	All facilities	AC	SP	100	n.a.	1990	n.a.	n.a.
Auburn	n.a.	Sumitomo	Japan	All facilities	AC	CR	100	n.a.	1977	325	310
Berg	258	Usinor-Salicor	France	Pipe products	AC	CR	65	n.a.	n.a.	250	258
Blake Steel Service	n.a.	Klockner	Germany		AC	DS	100	n.a.	1989	n.a.	335
Bliss and Laughlin	n.a.	Stelco	Canada		AC	CR	40	19	1990	n.a.	n.a.
California	n.a.	Kawasaki/CVRD	Jap./Braz.	Flat rolling plant	AC	CR	75	120	1986	n.a.	n.a.
Capitol Metals	n.a.	Hoogovens	Netherlands		n.a.	n.a.	n.a.	n.a.	1979	n.a.	n.a.
Century Tube	n.a.	Daiwa/Nippon	Japan		IV	CR	100	4	1992	n.a.	n.a.
Diversified Steel Serv.	n.a.	Krupp	Germany		AC	DS	n.a.	1	1981	n.a.	n.a.
Edgecomb Metals	n.a.	Usinor-Sacilor	France		IV	DS	100	110	1990	n.a.	n.a.
Estel	n.a.	Hoogovens	Netherlands		GF	n.a.	n.a.	28	1980	n.a.	n.a.
Georgetown	776	Usinor-Sacilor	France		IV	CR	50	n.a.	1990	2 000	776
Hoesch Tubular	n.a.	Hoogovens	Netherlands		n.a.	n.a.	n.a.	n.a.	1982	n.a.	n.a.

Table A-1. **Globalisation of the steel industry: selected investment activity in North America by the world's 50 largest steelmakers** (cont.)

Globalised activity

Country: Company	Total employment	Foreign partner /affiliate/subsidiary	Country	Description	Investment type[1]	Product activity[2]	Share of ownership (%)	Total investment (approx.) (US$ mn)	Start up year	Capacity or annual turnover ('000 mt)	Employment (estim.)
United States (cont.)											
International Crankshaft	n.a.	Sumitomo	Japan		IV	CR	80	n.a.	1992	n.a.	n.a.
Interstate	n.a.	Usinor-Sacilor	France		AC	DS	100	n.a.	1989	n.a.	n.a.
J&L Specialty	450	Usinor-Sacilor	France		AC	SP	100	n.a.	1990	n.a.	450
Klockner Namasco	n.a.	Klockner/Androsorbis	Germ./Switz.		GF	DS	100	n.a.	1989	n.a.	n.a.
Mannesmann Meer	n.a.	Mannesman	Germany		n.a.	DS	n.a.	n.a.	1973	n.a.	n.a.
Metalimphy Alloys	n.a.	Usinor-Sacilor	France		AC	SP	100	n.a.	n.a.	n.a.	n.a.
Metron	n.a.	Usinor-Sacilor	France		AC	DS	n.a.	n.a.	1989	n.a.	n.a.
Michigan	n.a.	Sumitomo	Japan		AC	DS	80	5	1988	n.a.	n.a.
Midrex Corp.	n.a.	Kobe	Japan		AC	CR	100	n.a.	n.a.	n.a.	n.a.
North American	n.a.	Rautaruukki	Finland		AC	DS	35	n.a.	1991	n.a.	n.a.
Pen Extruded Tube	n.a.	Sumitomo/Sandvik	Japan/Sweden		GF	SP	30/70	45	1993	n.a.	n.a.
Quantech	n.a.	SSAB	Sweden		AC	DS	100	n.a.	1987	n.a.	n.a.
Seymour Tube	n.a.	Sumitomo	Japan		GF	CR	n.a.	11	1990	n.a.	n.a.
Slater Specialty	750	Dofasco	Canada		AC	SP	n.a.	20	1988	60	750
Tamco	n.a.	Tokyo Steel/Mitsui	Japan		AC	CR	50	n.a.	1977	n.a.	n.a.
Techalloy	n.a.	Usinor-Sacilor	France		IV	SP	100	n.a.	1990	n.a.	n.a.
Tennesse Metal	n.a.	Usinor-Sacilor	France		AC	DS	100	n.a.	1990	n.a.	n.a.
Trefil/Arbed Arkansas	n.a.	Arbed/Belgo-Meneira	Lux./Brazil		GF	CR	100	70	1992	n.a.	n.a.
T.S. Alloys	n.a.	British Steel	UK		AC	DS	n.a.	n.a.	1990	n.a.	n.a.
Tubemeuse	n.a.	Cockerill Sambre	Belgium		n.a.	DS	n.a.	n.a.	1983	n.a.	n.a.
Tuscaloosa	500	British Steel	UK		AC	CR	100	n.a.	1990	193	500
Voest Alpine International	n.a.	Voest Alpine	Austria		n.a.	n.a.	n.a.	n.a.	1977	n.a.	n.a.
Western Tube	250	Sumitomo	Japan		AC	CR	75	n.a.	1964	150	200
Worthington	n.a.	Thyssen	Germany		IV	DS	50	n.a.	1990	n.a.	n.a.

n.a. = not available.
1. Investment types are described as follows: AC = Acquisition, IV = Joint Venture, GF = Greenfield.
2. Product activities are described as follows: CR = Carbon Steel, SP = Specialty Steel, DS = Distribution or Service Centre.
Source: US International Trade Commission (ITC), Annual Report (1991), International Advisory Group (Washington, 1992), Iron and Steel Works of the World (10th edition, 1991), various metals press, and Global Steel in the 1990s (William T. Hogan, 1990), Japanese Iron and Steel Federation.

Table A-2. **Globalisation of the steel industry: selected investment activity in Europe by the world's 50 largest steelmakers**

Country: Company	Total employment	Globalised activity									
		Foreign partner/ affiliate/subsidiary	Country	Description	Investment type[1]	Product activity[2]	Share of ownership (%)	Total investment (approx.) (US$ mn)	Start up year	Capacity or annual turnover ('000 mt)	Employment (estim.)
Belgium											
Europrofil	n.a.	Arbed/Usinor-Sac.	Lux./France		AC	CR	100	n.a.	1992	n.a.	n.a.
Fontainunion	n.a.	Usinor-Sacilor	France	Trefilunion	AC	CR	100	n.a.	1992	n.a.	n.a.
Sidmar	n.a.	Klockner	Germany		IV	CR	n.a.	n.a.	n.a.	n.a.	n.a.
	n.a.	Arbed	Luxembourg		IV	CR	67	n.a.	n.a.	3 500	n.a.
Denmark											
Nordisk Simplex	n.a.	Rautaruukki	Finland		AC	CR	100	n.a.	1990	n.a.	n.a.
Metacolour AS	n.a.	Rautaruukki	Finland		AC	CR	100	n.a.	1990	n.a.	n.a.
Estonia											
Rannila Profil	n.a.	Rautaruukki	Finland		IV	CR	n.a.	n.a.	1992	n.a.	n.a.
Germany											
Klockner	n.a.	British Steel	UK	Mannestaedt	AC	CR	100	180	1990	300	n.a.
Bregal		C. Itoh	Japan	Steel/engin. ops.	AC	CR	5	66	1990	n.a.	n.a.
		C. Itoh	Japan	Galv. sheet plant	AC	CR	25	n.a.	n.a.	400	n.a.
		C. Itoh/Rautaruukki	Japan/Finland		GF	CR/SP	25/25	n.a.	1993	n.a.	n.a.
Krupp	17 380	National Iranian	Iran		AC	CR	25	765	1974	n.a.	n.a.
Thyssen	24 814	Hoogovens	Netherlands	Duisburg galv.	IV	CR	25	n.a.	1992	n.a.	n.a.
		Beltrane	Italy	Oberhausen	IV	DS	60	n.a.	1993	n.a.	n.a.
Ancofer Feinsthal	n.a.	Usinor-Sacilor	France		AC	CR	61	n.a.	1992	n.a.	n.a.
Bauer & Schaurte	n.a.	Usinor-Sacilor	France		AC	CR	100	n.a.	n.a.	n.a.	n.a.
Bergrohr	n.a.	Usinor-Sacilor	France		AC	CR	50	n.a.	n.a.	n.a.	n.a.
Conti Systembau	n.a.	Usinor-Sacilor	France		AC	CR	100	n.a.	n.a.	n.a.	n.a.
Dillinger Huttenwerke	n.a.	Usinor-Sacilor/Arbed	France/Lux.		AC	CR	70/2.5	n.a.	1989	n.a.	n.a.
Drahtwerke St. Ingbert	n.a.	Usinor-Sacilor	France		AC	CR	100	n.a.	1989	n.a.	n.a.
Europipe	n.a.	Usinor-Sacilor	France		AC	CR	50	n.a.	1991	n.a.	n.a.
Hille & Muller	n.a.	Hoogovens	Netherlands		AC	CR	100	n.a.	n.a.	n.a.	n.a.
Hoesch Rothe Erde-Schmiedag	3 700	Usinor-Sacilor	France	Stamping forge	AC	DS	100	n.a.	1990	n.a.	3 700
Homberger	n.a.	Usinor-Sacilor	France	Welded tube	IV	CR	50	n.a.	1990	n.a.	n.a.
Ludwig Roberenwerke	n.a.	Usinor-Sacilor	France		AC	CR	100	n.a.	1990	n.a.	n.a.
Maxhutte Unterwellenborn	n.a.	Arbed	Luxembourg		AC	CR	100	175	1992	n.a.	n.a.
Zeletel Coilco	n.a.	Rautaruukki	Finland	Long products	AC	DS	26	n.a.	n.a.	n.a.	n.a.
Saarstahl	n.a.	Usinor-Sacilor	France		AC	CR	70	n.a.	1989	n.a.	n.a.

Table A-2. **Globalisation of the steel industry: selected investment activity in Europe by the world's 50 largest steelmakers** (cont.)

Globalised activity

Country: Company	Total employment	Foreign partner/ affiliate/subsidiary	Country	Description	Investment type[1]	Product activity[2]	Share of ownership (%)	Total investment (approx.) (US$ mn)	Start up year	Capacity or annual turnover ('000 mt)	Employment (estim.)
Arl Fron	n.a.	Rautaruukki	Finland		AC	CR	100	n.a.	n.a.	n.a.	n.a.
Sprint Metal	n.a.	Usinor-Sacilor	France		AC	SP	100	n.a.	n.a.	n.a.	n.a.
Trefilarbed Drahtwerke	n.a.	Usinor-Sacilor	France		AC	CR	100	n.a.	n.a.	n.a.	n.a.
Hungary											
Dunai Vasmu	n.a.	Voest Alpine	Austria		AC	CR	30	9	1992	n.a.	n.a.
Salgotarjan	n.a.	ILVA	Italy		AC	CR	51	13	1990	155	n.a.
Italy											
ILVA	n.a.	Usinor-Sacilor	France	2 stainless mills	AC	SP	51	n.a.	1989	n.a.	n.a.
Bedini	n.a.	Usinor-Sacilor	France		AC	SP	100	n.a.	1990	n.a.	n.a.
Castelli Acciai	n.a.	Usinor-Sacilor	France		AC	SP	90	n.a.	1989	n.a.	n.a.
Castelli Inox	n.a.	Usinor-Sacilor	France		AC	DS	95	n.a.	1989	n.a.	n.a.
Ilro	n.a.	Usinor-Sacilor	France		AC	CR	100	n.a.	1991	n.a.	n.a.
Inox tubi	n.a.	Usinor-Sacilor	France		AC	SP	100	n.a.	1991	n.a.	n.a.
Lutrix	n.a.	Usinor-Sacilor	France		AC	CR	24	3	1988	n.a.	n.a.
Metico	n.a.	Usinor-Sacilor	France		AC	DS	100	n.a.	1990	n.a.	n.a.
Neirotti Tubi	n.a.	Usinor-Sacilor	France		AC	CR	n.a.	n.a.	n.a.	n.a.	n.a.
Nuova Castelli	n.a.	Usinor-Sacilor	France		AC	DS	90	n.a.	n.a.	n.a.	n.a.
Nuova Sait	n.a.	Usinor-Sacilor	France		AC	DS	90	n.a.	n.a.	n.a.	n.a.
Sait	n.a.	Usinor-Sacilor	France		AC	DS	95	n.a.	n.a.	n.a.	n.a.
Tubificio di Terni	n.a.	Nisshin	Japan		AC	SP	10	n.a.	1992	n.a.	n.a.
Luxembourg											
A-bed	n.a.	Usinor-Sacilor	France		IV	CR	n.a.	n.a.	1990	n.a.	n.a.
Netherlands											
Nedstaal	1 250	Thyssen	Germany		AC	CR	100	n.a.	n.a.	775	1 250
Norway											
Blikkvalseverk	350	Hoogovens	Netherlands	Tin plate	AC	CR	100	n.a.	1992	280	350
Carl Christiansen	n.a.	Rautaruukki	Finland		AC	DS	100	n.a.	n.a.	n.a.	n.a.
Scanprofil	n.a.	Rautaruukki	Finland		AC	n.a.	100	n.a.	n.a.	n.a.	n.a.
Spain											
Ensidesa	14 767	Usinor-Sacilor	France	Sidmed facilities	AC	CR	33	n.a.	1991	n.a.	n.a.
Acerinox Armco	n.a.	Armco	US		IV	SP	50	n.a.	n.a.	n.a.	n.a.
Aceros Inoxidables	n.a.	Usinor-Sacilor	France		AC	SP	64	n.a.	1988	n.a.	n.a.
Aristrain	n.a.	British Steel	UK		AC	CR	45	n.a.	1990	n.a.	n.a.
Bercelanos de Matales	n.a.	Usinor-Sacilor	France		AC	DS	30	n.a.	1992	n.a.	n.a.

Table A-2. **Globalisation of the steel industry: selected investment activity in Europe by the world's 50 largest steelmakers** *(cont.)*

Country: Company	Total employment	Foreign partner/ affiliate/subsidiary	Country	Globalised activity							
				Description	Investment type [1]	Product activity [2]	Share of ownership (%)	Total investment (approx.) (US$ mn)	Start up year	Capacity or annual turnover ('000 mt)	Employment (estim.)
Spain *(cont.)*											
Galmed	n.a.	Thyssen/Usinor-Sacilor	Ger/France		JV	CR	25/25	n.a.	1992	n.a.	n.a.
Gonvarri	n.a.	Usinor-Sacilor	France		AC	DS	20	n.a.	1992	n.a.	n.a.
Laminacion y Derivados	n.a.	British Steel	UK		AC	CR	34	n.a.	n.a.	n.a.	n.a.
Tubos de Cebra	n.a.	Usinor-Sacilor	France		AC	CR	100	n.a.	n.a.	n.a.	n.a.
Sweden											
Avesta	n.a.	British Steel	UK		AC	SP	40	160	1992	n.a.	n.a.
European Electric	n.a.	British Steel	UK		JV	SP	75	n.a.	1992	n.a.	n.a.
Gavle Ahlsell	n.a.	Rautaruukki	Finland		AC	DS	100	n.a.	1991	n.a.	n.a.
Helens Ror	n.a.	Rautaruukki	Finland		AC	DS	25	n.a.	n.a.	n.a.	n.a.
SSAB Stainless	n.a.	British Steel	UK		AC	SP	40	n.a.	1992	n.a.	n.a.
Structo DOM Europe	n.a.	Rautaruukki	Finland		AC	SP	67	n.a.	1989	n.a.	n.a.
Uddeholm	n.a.	Voest Alpine	Austria		AC	SP	100	n.a.	1991	n.a.	n.a.
Wirsbo Stalror	n.a.	Rautaruukki	Finland		AC	CR	100	n.a.	n.a.	62	n.a.
Turkey											
Borcelik	n.a.	ILVA/Usinor-Sacilor	Ita/France		GF	CR	25/25	90	1993	300	n.a.
United Kingdom											
Albion Pressed Metal	n.a.	Thyssen	Germany	Fabricator	AC	CR	100	n.a.	1990	n.a.	n.a.
ASD	n.a.	Usinor-Sacilor	France	Large distributor	AC	DS	80	81	1991	n.a.	n.a.
Emisa Trefileria	n.a.	Spain	Spain		JV	DS	n.a.	n.a.	1992	n.a.	n.a.
Gwent Steel	n.a.	Hoesch	Germany	Fabricator	AC	CR	80	n.a.	1990	n.a.	n.a.
Howard Perry	n.a.	Usinor-Sacilor	France		AC	DS	30	n.a.	1989	n.a.	n.a.
Star Tubes	n.a.	Rautaruukki	Finland		AC	DS	99	n.a.	n.a.	n.a.	n.a.

n.a. = not available.
1. Investment types are described as follows: AC = Acquisition, JV = Joint Venture, GF = Greenfield.
2. Product activities are described as follows: CR = Carbon Steel, SP = Specialty Steel, DS = Distribution or Service Centre.
Source: ITC Annual Report (1991), International Advisory Group (Washington, 1992), *Iron & Steel Works of the World* (10th Edition, 1991), various metals press, and *Global Steel in the 1990s* (William T. Hogan, 1990).

Table A-3. **Globalisation of the steel industry: selected investment activity in Asia, Africa and Oceania by the world's 50 largest steelmakers**

Globalised activity

Country: Company	Total employment	Foreign partner/ affiliate/subsidiary	Country	Description	Investment type[1]	Product activity[2]	Share of ownership (%)	Total investment (approx.) (US$ mn)	Start up year	Capacity or annual turnover ('000 mt)	Employment (estim.)
China											
China Steel	n.a.	POSCO	South Korea		GF	CR	50	n.a.	n.a.	n.a.	n.a.
Shanghai	n.a.	POSCO	South Korea		GF	CR	n.a.	97	1995	n.a.	n.a.
TISCO/CITIC	n.a.	Krupp	Germany		GF	CR	n.a.	400	n.a.	415	n.a.
Egypt											
Alexandria	n.a.	NKK/Kobe/Tomen	Japan		GF	CR	10	700	1986	750	2 400
India											
Tata	30 442	Timken Co.	US	Roller bearings	IV	SP	50	n.a.	1991	n.a.	n.a.
Indonesia											
PT Sermani	n.a.	NKK/Marubeni	Japan		IV	CR	49	n.a.	1970	32	170
Malaysia											
n.a.	n.a.	China Steel	Chinese Taipei	Integrated mill	GF	CR	40	n.a.	1995	n.a.	n.a.
New Zealand											
New Zealand	1 700	BHP	Australia		AC	CR	69	n.a.	1992	750	n.a.
Singapore											
BRC Weldmesh	n.a.	BHP	Australia		AC	CR	100	n.a.	1991	n.a.	n.a.
Steel Tubes	n.a.	Kobe	Japan	Welded tube	IV	CR	7	n.a.	1982	50	68
Chinese Taipei											
Tung Mung	n.a.	Krupp	Germany		GF	SP	n.a.	n.a.	1993	150	n.a.
Thailand											
Sahaviriya	n.a.	NKK/Marubeni	Japan	Electro galvanizing	GF	CR	51	n.a.	1994	140	230
Siam Tinplat	n.a.	Nippon/NKK	Japan		GF	CR	40	320	1988	120	357
Thai Steel Pipe	n.a.	Sumitomo	Japan	Weld pipe and tube	IV	CR	50	12	1963	n.a.	n.a.
Thainox Steel	n.a.	Usinor-Sacilor/ILVA Nippon/Nisshin Kawasaki/Sumitomo	France/Italy Japan		GF	SP	21/14 14	240	1993	60	400
n.a.	n.a.	ILVA	Italy	(Pruchuab Province)	GF	SP	n.a.	n.a.	n.a.	50	n.a.
Vietnam											
Posvina	n.a.	POSCO	Korea		IV	CR	50	n.a.	1992	n.a.	n.a.
n.a.	n.a.	POSCO/Kangwong	Korea		IV	CR	25	50	1992	n.a.	n.a.
n.a.	n.a.	POSCO/Pusan	Korea		IV	CR	15	8	1992	n.a.	n.a.

n.a. = not available.

1. Investment types are described as follows: AC = Acquisition, IV = Joint Venture, GF = Greenfield.
2. Product activities are described as follows: CR = Carbon Steel, SP = Specialty Steel, DS = Distribution or Service Centre.

Source: ITC Annual Report (1991), International Advisory Group (Washington, 1992), *Iron and Steel Works of the World* (10th Edition, 1991), various metals press, and *Global steel in the 1990s* (William T. Hogan, 1990), Japanese Iron and Steel Federation.

Table A-4. **Globalisation of the steel industry: selected investment activity in Latin America by the world's largest steelmakers**

Country: Company	Total employment	Foreign partner/ affiliate/subsidiary	Country	Globalised activity							
				Description	Investment type[1]	Product activity[2]	Share of ownership (%)	Total investment (approx.) (US$ mn)	Start up year	Capacity or annual turnover ('000 mt)	Employment (estim.)
Argentina											
Siderca	4 961	ILVA	Italy		AC	CR	11	n.a.	n.a.	770	n.a.
SOMISA	n.a.	USIMINAS	Brazil		AC	CR	n.a.	n.a.	1992	2 500	n.a.
Brazil											
Belgo-Mineira	n.a.	Arbed	Luxembourg		AC	CR	n.a.	n.a.	n.a.	n.a.	n.a.
CST	n.a.	Kawasaki/ILVA	Japan/Italy	Slab facility	IV	CR	25/25	1 500	1983	n.a.	n.a.
USIMINAS	13 600	Nippon	Japan	Flat rolled products	AC	CR	12	n.a.	1991	n.a.	n.a.
Chile											
Industrias del Acero	n.a.	Gerdau	Brazil		AC	CR	100	3	1992	n.a.	n.a.
Siderurgica	n.a.	Gerdau	Brazil		AC	CR	100	7	1992	n.a.	n.a.
Trinidad and Tobago											
n.a.	n.a.	Nucor	US	DRI facility	GF	CR	100	60	1993	320	n.a.
Uruguay											
Inlasa	300	Gerdau	Brazil		AC	CR	100	7	1992	100	n.a.
Siderurgica Laisa	141	Gerdau	Brazil		AC	CR	100	n.a.	1980	36	n.a.
Venezuela											
Orinoco C.A.	n.a.	Kobe	Japan	DRI facility	AC	CR	100	n.a.	n.a.	n.a.	n.a.

n.a. = not available.
1. Investment types are described as follows: AC = Acquisition, IV = Joint Venture, GF = Greenfield.
2. Product activities are described as follows: CR = Carbon Steel, SP = Specialty Steel, DS = Distribution or Service Centre.
Source: ITC Annual Report (1991), International Advisory Group (Washington, 1992), Iron et Steel Works of the World (10th Edition, 1991), various metals press, and Global Steel in the 1990s (William T. Hogan, 1990), Japanese Iron and Steel Federation.

Table B. **Trade in iron and steel products**

SITC Rev 2: 671 + 672 + 673 + 674 + 676 + 677 + 678 + 679

Billion US$ and percentages

Major exporters	1980 Value (US$ billion)	Share (%)	1991 Value (US$ billion)	Share (%)	Principal destinations of exports (1991)
Japan	15.45	22.9	13.57	14.1	United States (15.3%); Rep. of Korea (11.7%); Chinese Taipei (11.2%); China (10.0%).
Germany	11.55	17.1	14.52	15.1	France (11.9%); Netherlands (11.1%); United Kingdom (9.9%); Belg.-Lux. (8.6%).
France	7.29	10.8	8.79	9.0	Germany (21.9%); Italy (14.1%); Belg.-Lux. (11.9%); United Kingdom (7.5).
Belg.-Lux.	6.41	9.5	8.53	8.9	Germany (28.7%); France (26.4%); Netherlands (9.0%).
Italy	3.77	5.6	5.74	5.9	Germany (21.3%); France (17.5%).
United States	3.12	4.6	4.68	4.8	Canada (31.5%); Mexico (19.7%); Korea (7.7%).
United Kingdom	2.29	3.4	5.49	5.7	Germany (17.4%); France (9.0%); Italy (7.1%); United States (6.8%).
Rest of world	17.66	26.1	35.51	36.6	
World	67.53	100.0	97.13	100.0	

Major importers	1980 Value (US$ billion)	Share (%)	1991 Value (US$ billion)	Share (%)	Principal destinations of imports (1991)
United States	8.15	14.4	10.23	10.5	Japan (21.9%); Canada (15.7%); Germany (8.3%).
Germany	6.73	11.9	12.20	12.5	Belg.-Lux. (20.0%); France (15.0%); Italy (10.0%); United Kingdom (8.9%).
France	5.37	9.5	7.0	7.2	Belg.-Lux. (30.0%); Germany (25.0%); Italy (14.2%).
Italy	4.10	7.2	6.11	6.3	France (20.9%); Germany (19.1%); Belg.-Lux (12.2%).
United Kingdom	3.36	5.9	4.74	4.9	Germany (28.6%); France (13.6%); Netherlands (9.9%); Belg.-Lux. (9.5%).
Netherlands	2.37	4.2	3.76	3.9	Germany (43.6%); Belg.-Lux. (21.6%); France (8.3%).
Chinese Taipei	1.13	2.0	4.12	4.2	Japan (39.2%); Brazil (12.2%).
Republic of Korea	0.99	1.7	4.62	4.7	Japan (35.9%); United States (9.3%); Brazil (7.7%).
Japan	0.89	1.6	5.54	5.7	Korea (30.0%); Brazil (10.5%); China (9.4%).
Rest of world	23.63	41.7	39.07	40.1	
World	56.73	100.0	97.39	100.0	

Source: UN Comtrade database.

Chapter 8

GLOBALISATION IN THE CLOTHING INDUSTRY

by

Denis Audet
Trade Directorate, OECD

Table of contents

LIST OF TABLES

SUMMARY AND CONCLUSIONS

Globalisation in the clothing industry is seen in the increasing level of import penetration of clothing in national markets (globalisation of supply) and an emerging trend in which the production process is separated between pre-assembly and assembly activities on a global basis [see definition in Section 1.A.*a*)]. Textiles trade, providing an input to clothing production, is substantial and it grew at about the same rate as total world exports since 1975. Trade in cut textile components for further assembly is relatively small but growing in the context of preferential market access measures. Trade in assembled clothing parts is however not significant. Separate statistical items for assembled clothing parts are not usually provided for in trade classification systems. Increasing trade in textiles and clothing took place against a managed trade environment characterised by discriminatory quantitative trade restrictions and high tariff levels applied to imports originating from low-cost countries. Textiles protection acted as a tax on domestic clothing production and may have reduced its production options and quality.

Both foreign direct investment and research and development efforts were less than proportional to the relative importance of this sector in the economy. Outward investment was found to be strongly correlated to preferential market access measures established by some OECD countries which, in practice, have benefited only a few selected low-cost countries. Intra-firm trade has remained low and concentrated in qualifying projects under preferential market access measures. Mergers, vertical integration and strategic alliances are isolated cases and cannot be associated with an emerging trend.

Barriers to entry in the industry rank among the lowest in industrial production processes, the industry is therefore characterised by a multitude of small and medium-sized enterprises which concentrate production in few product categories. As a result of structural changes in the 1980s and early 1990s, small and medium-sized enterprises have adopted more flexible production processes. Large enterprises have adopted advanced technological equipment, concentrated production in clothing lines offering economies of scale in production, and increased subcontracting to minimise direct labour costs and capital requirements. During the 1980s, despite trade protection measures, competition in the clothing industry intensified as a result of increased import competition, an increased number of small firms and reduced importance of larger firms in total production.

Technological developments have profoundly modified pre-assembly activities but have failed to modify the highly labour-intensive process of assembly activities. Developments in computer-aided design (CAD) and cutting systems have permitted an integration of pre-assembly activities and substantial productivity gains. Within the assembly process, the use of conventional sewing machines still offers adequate flexibility to most manufacturers to remain viable in a fashion-oriented business with short production runs. The application of modern telecommunication networks has facilitated a separation of pre-assembly and assembly activities without sacrificing quality and process efficiency. This process of separation has happened both within national markets and on a global basis.

Research and development efforts in complete automation processes have not yet resulted in commercial application. Inherent technical difficulties associated with the complex manipulation of limp materials are very difficult to overcome. Technological improvements were however made in dedicated applications. The automation of the clothing manufacturing process has the potential to gradually modify the structure of the industry from being labour-intensive to capital-intensive. The general view in the industry is that even if there is a technological breakthrough, the nature of the fashion business with short production runs will still leave a considerable share of production by standard technologies in the assembly stage.

During the 1980s, several factors have influenced the structure of the industry and have had implications for the location of production plants and employment. In response to just-in-time delivery requirements, the adoption of electronic point of sale systems at the retail level and rapidly changing demand, clothing manufacturers have had to adapt to short production runs, smaller orders and shorter production-delivery cycles. Clothing manufacturers have modified their production processes accordingly. These structural changes have benefited domestic manufacturers over overseas manufacturers as they were able to meet short delivery requirements. However, increasing concentration of clothing sales among larger retail groups meant that these larger groups were better placed to compare domestically-made with imported clothing. The concentration of retail sales within large groups has favoured overseas clothing manufacturers whenever delivery requirement was less of a priority.

The simple average post-Tokyo Round tariff is a poor indicator of the level of protection afforded to clothing production in OECD countries. It masks tariff peaks and the fact that several regional trading arrangements have provided for, or are in the process of establishing, free trade in clothing trade among participating OECD countries. However tariff protection was not the main instrument of protection as several OECD countries applied discriminatory quantitative restrictions to clothing imports originating from low-cost countries in the context of the Multifibre Arrangement (MFA). The average tariff-equivalent of MFA quotas were estimated to be within a range of 25 per cent for clothing and 15 per cent for textiles.

Despite trade protection afforded by OECD countries, the share of OECD clothing imports originating from non-OECD countries increased significantly from 44.3 to 61.3 per cent between 1975 and 1992. Most of the increase occurred prior to 1985 and since then the share of non-OECD countries has continued to rise albeit at a reduced rate. Since 1985, the share of OECD clothing imports originating from China increased strongly and displaced imports from other non-OECD countries and particularly from Hong Kong and the Republic of Korea.

Intra-regional trade in clothing has increased in all major regions of the world and particularly in East Asia. Intra-regional trade has remained the highest in Europe, between countries of the European Community (EC) and the European Free Trade Agreement (EFTA), and reached 83.9 per cent of total trade in 1991.

Government intervention in the clothing industry has concentrated on protection against foreign competition. Otherwise government intervention has been modulated to ease specific problems faced by small and medium-sized enterprises and implemented through horizontal programmes such as regional development assistance, research and development and training activities.

1. TRENDS IN GROWTH AND STRUCTURE

A. Production and consumption

a) Industrial characteristics

There is a wide range of clothing categories with product segmentations, among others, for men, women, children, sportswear, casual, high fashion and working apparel. Within each of these categories, there is a large number of specific product types, each with its particular set of characteristics which affect the nature of the production process.

The clothing production process may be described by the following grouping of activities: pre-assembly which involves designing, grading and marking of patterns, and cutting of textiles into individual components; assembly when components are sewn together; and finishing when garments are pressed, packaged and dispatched. Each stage in the production process uses different labour compositions and capital proportions which explain different possibilities for plant location and introduction of new technology.

Generally, the assembly stage accounts for about 80 per cent of the value added. The nature of the assembly process is highly labour-intensive since the handling of soft and limp materials, which are subject to complicated manipulation and assembly processes, to become three-dimensional products is infinitely more difficult to mechanise than other activities assembling rigid materials. The ability to switch the assembly process quickly to adapt to various designs, fashions and production runs offers another obstacle in the development of automated assembly processes.

Relative to other industrial processes, barriers to entry (and exit) in the clothing industry are low and, as a result, the industry is characterised by a large number of producers with typically a very large number of small and medium-sized firms which concentrate production on just a few product categories. The industry also includes a small number of multi-division firms producing a wide range of products. Competition within the clothing industry is perhaps the closest to the perfect competition assumption of the economic theory and most firms have no or little influence on selling prices. Under such conditions, the economic viability of firms is directly related to their ability to minimise production costs.

Technology is essentially available on a world basis at roughly similar costs, thus clothing manufacturers in developing countries are not significantly disadvantaged by a technological gap. Although certain types of capital-intensive processes are widely available, their use is more feasible in developed countries. The availability of textiles on a world basis is constrained by quantitative trade restrictions and high tariffs, as a result textile quality, selection and prices vary among major producing areas.

Because of the absence of barriers to entry and of high labour intensity, the development of a clothing industry is a natural step for developing countries to begin a process of industrialisation. This process could be both import-substituting and export-oriented and would facilitate graduation into more advanced technological processes. Notwithstanding trade barriers raised by developed countries since the 1960s to protect their domestic producers against low-cost imports, the share of OECD clothing imports originating from developing countries has increased continuously from 44.3 per cent in 1975 to 61.3 per cent in 1992 (see Table 8.13).

Table 8.1 shows that clothing production measured as a proportion of total manufacturing production declined in most OECD countries between 1980 and 1990 – the average ratio for comparable OECD countries declined from 1.78 to 1.49 per cent. However, production in Greece and Turkey increased significantly during the second half of the 1980s. In Italy and Portugal, clothing production has also

Table 8.1. **Production as a percentage of total manufacturing production, 1980-90 – Clothing**

	1980	1985	1989	1990
Austria	2.19	1.84	1.56	–
Canada	2.30	1.92	–	–
Denmark	1.37	1.41	1.01	1.01
Finland	2.42	2.20	1.39	1.21
France	2.24	2.25	1.96	1.98
Germany	1.59	1.36	1.31	1.32
Greece	3.06	2.98	3.60	4.06
Iceland	2.09	1.83	1.15	1.14
Italy	2.88	3.20	3.43	–
Japan	1.05	0.99	1.04	1.00
Netherlands	0.92	0.71	0.66	–
New Zealand	–	4.51	3.82	–
Norway	0.77	0.55	0.28	0.30
Portugal	3.11	3.23	–	–
Spain	2.24	1.71	–	–
Sweden	0.71	0.49	0.39	0.33
Switzerland	2.35	1.88	2.29	2.33
Turkey	–	1.63	4.08	4.12
United Kingdom	1.71	1.73	1.52	1.49
United States	2.03	1.93	1.70	1.66
Average	2.23	1.91	1.83	1.49
Average for comparable countries [1]	1.78	1.63	1.47	1.49

1. Includes OECD countries from which data are available in 1980, 1985, 1989 and 1990.
Source: OECD, 1991 *Industrial Structure Statistics*, Paris 1993.

increased as a proportion of total manufacturing production. Although the relative importance of clothing production declined in most OECD countries, it nevertheless remains important on a regional basis.

Because of the fashion orientation of the clothing industry, manufacturers must adapt very rapidly to emerging fashion trends, short clothing seasons and they must remain price competitive. For these reasons, the clothing industry is very dynamic. During the 1980s and early 1990s, several factors have influenced the structure of the industry and have had implications on the location of production plants and employment. The main factors were: shifts in the composition of demand; technological changes; changes in retailer-manufacturer relations; and organisational changes. Each of these factors is elaborated below.

b) Composition of demand

Demand for clothing is influenced by several factors including: demographic changes, incomes and relative prices. Several consumer trends are commonly reported in the specialised press, sometimes contradictory, about the emergence of a shift in consumer tastes towards higher style content, broader selection of clothes and strong demand for casual wear and sportswear. Another reported view is about the standardisation of style, e.g. jeans, and an increasing price consciousness of consumers for clothing. There is however a consensus about the quality of clothing which has improved as a result of consumer awareness.

Table 8.2 shows that the average expenditure on clothing and footwear in constant prices, as a percentage of total private consumption, decreased slightly in the 1980s. This suggests that the income elasticity of demand is less than one as consumers have spent relatively less on clothing and footwear whilst their income has increased. This may also suggest that clothing and footwear are considered by consumers as basic has necessity goods.

There is a significant difference between these countries on their expenditure preferences for clothing and footwear albeit the difference is narrowing as illustrated by the declining variation indicator. These results would suggest that, during the 1980s, the price consciousness of consumers has prevailed over other fashion criteria.

c) Technological changes

Developments in computer-aided design (CAD) and computer-numerically controlled (CNC) cutting systems in the late 1970s and early 1980s have permitted an integration of pre-assembly activities. The

Table 8.2. **Expenditure as a percentage
of private consumption, 1980-90 – Clothing and footwear**

Constant prices

	1980	1985	1990
Australia [1]	6.45	6.73	5.66
Denmark [2]	5.86	6.01	5.72
France [2]	7.42	7.04	6.20
Italy [3]	11.10	10.14	9.95
Japan [3]	7.24	6.70	5.89
Norway [3]	8.25	7.77	7.64
Sweden [3]	7.55	7.14	8.28
United Kingdom [3]	6.08	6.81	6.41
United States [4]	5.15	5.54	5.70
Average	7.23	7.10	6.83
Variation (high-low)	5.95	4.60	4.25

1. Constant prices 1984-85.
2. Constant prices 1980.
3. Constant prices 1985.
4. Constant prices 1987.
Source: OECD (1992), Quarterly National Accounts, "Private consumption expenditure by object", Table 7b.

CAD systems are used for grading and marking patterns as a guide for cutting. Fully automated cutting systems have replaced manual cutting techniques in several applications.

These pre-assembly systems have sustained increased productivity gains in these activities, reduced material waste, reduced training time required for grading and marker-making, and reduced lead times involved in responding to fashion changes. They have facilitated managerial decisions in production planning, sourcing, product costing and factory loading in multi-plant firms. One of the most important advantages is that manufacturers can now respond more rapidly to re-orders from retailers – increasingly retailers re-order on the basis of weekly sale records which usually leave only few weeks to manufacturers for assembly and delivery. Although pre-assembly activities have become more capital-intensive, this has not fundamentally altered the overall labour-intensive process of clothing production since the pre-assembly stage only accounts for about 10 to 15 per cent of the whole clothing manufacturing process.

In the early 1980s, the installation of CAD systems was limited because such an investment was only considered economically viable for firms with a minimum annual turnover of US$20 million. Firms large enough accounted for less than 20 per cent of output in most developed countries and it was estimated that one-half of these intended to adopt new technology within the next five years (Hoffman, 1984). In the late 1980s, it was estimated that over 50 per cent of all clothes produced in the United States came from firms using CAD systems and computer-controlled cutters (Hoffman, 1989). This would represent a rapid rate of technological diffusion.

Within the assembly process, microelectronic-related innovations (MRIs) have been developed for sewing machines with pre-programmable data input devices which can perform decorative and functional stitching in a sequential fashion. Special purpose machines are used for specific tasks such as belt-loop attachment and collar stitching. For other assembly activities, computer-controlled overhead rail systems have been developed that reduce handling time for work-in-progress. Complete automated assembly processes have been the subject of significant research and development efforts (see Section 1.C).

Notwithstanding these technological developments, the application of automated sewing machines has only proved to be cost effective in a limited range of products. The use of a conventional sewing machine costing between US$500 and US$1 500, which is associated with a highly labour-intensive process, still offers adequate flexibility to most manufacturers to remain viable in a fashion-oriented business with short production runs. The diffusion of new technology is concentrated within the larger manufacturing segment of the industry where economies of scale in production can be achieved by greater use of automated equipment.

The application of modern telecommunication networks has facilitated a separation of the more capital-intensive activities from the labour-intensive assembly activities without sacrificing quality and process efficiency. One important criterion in this case is the transportation costs incurred in moving inputs to assembly points and finished products to end-markets. With greater uses of containerisation, shipping and air freight efficiency, world-wide transportation has become an increasingly viable possibility. This is true, at least, as long as transportation costs do not offset labour-cost savings associated with global processes.

Computer-based applications have proliferated in all related fields of business operations such as computerised accounting, invoicing, payrolls and stock control. At the retail level, daily or weekly sale records are gathered up through electronic point of sale systems which allow multi-store retailers to be linked to manufacturers, thereby reducing inventory costs and improving overall work efficiency and purchase requirements. MRI developments have also occurred in pressing activities.

d) Retailer-manufacturer relationships

Competition at the retail level has forced retailers to adapt rapidly to changes in consumer demand and to minimise costs, in particular inventory costs. Several factors are reported to have had direct implications for the whole clothing chain.

First, there is a trend toward increasing concentration of clothing sales among larger retail groups. Because of their large turnover, they can afford overseas search trips for new clothing suppliers and they are well-placed to compare domestically-made clothing with imported products. It is generally believed that the share of imported clothing in total sales of large retail groups is higher than for independent retailers.

Second, to minimise inventory costs some retailers have modified their purchasing strategies by contracting only a portion of their requirements for delivery at the beginning of the corresponding fashion season and re-ordering during the season on the basis of daily or weekly sales records. Clothing manufacturers are therefore required to produce and deliver on short delays. It is generally estimated that the order-delivery cycle has been reduced from a typical 15-22 weeks period to a 2-8 weeks period for orders requiring land delivery. Overseas sourcing requires a much longer cycle, ranging from 6 months to over a year. Nevertheless, overseas sourcing remains very important and efforts are been made by overseas manufacturers to reduce this cycle.

Third, the size of purchasing orders has correspondingly diminished to meet product variety, various fashion seasons and shorter order-delivery cycles. This has meant shorter production runs which, in turn, have favoured small and flexible manufacturers located close to consumer markets.

Fourth, in a fashion-oriented business, the selection of fabrics and the colour assortment are crucial functions which can make the difference between selling at profit or at substantial discounts. Clothing manufacturers minimise this inherent risk and associated quality control costs by keeping closer contact with their textiles suppliers. Overseas sourcing of fabrics by small clothing manufacturers is associated with considerable risks in terms of the quality of delivered fabrics and delays in delivery. Quick response and improved flexibility exercised by clothing manufacturers is complemented by closer relations with textiles manufacturers. There are positive externalities for clothing manufacturers to locate pre-assembly activities and flexible assembly activities close to existing polls of fashion expertise – where there is a critical mass of related activities including textiles manufacturers, designers, and service-related consultants.

Fifth, some clothing manufacturers have diversified their operations horizontally by becoming importers of finished clothing and thus complementing their product ranges. This diversification is usually performed by large and medium-sized manufacturers which have developed closer relations with retailers and foreign clothing manufacturers.

Sixth, retailers have increased the priority attached to quality. This has been translated into various forms of closer consultation between retailers and manufacturers involving amongst others: the exchange of sales information, technical specifications and designs; the pre-selection of manufacturers who can demonstrate an ability to adapt style, colour and fabrics without sacrificing quality; and a reliability in delivery against short notices.

Factors that have influenced retail sales seem to have benefited imported clothing whenever a long order-delivery cycle is not considered as a major factor. However, efforts to minimise inventory costs at the retail level tend to have favoured geographically close clothing manufacturers as they are better placed to deliver on a just-in-time basis. Geographically close manufacturers are also better placed to respond to re-orders which may require modifications in the colour assortment and styles relative to initial orders.

e) Organisational changes

The structural determinants of the clothing market have changed significantly and the viability of manufacturers increasingly depends on their ability to minimise the time required at each stage of the work-in-progress and to deliver on a just-in-time basis. Price competitiveness is not simply a function of low production costs based on economies of scale achieved on longer production runs.

Just-in-time delivery and work organised to minimise inefficiencies are not unique to the clothing industry. Organisational changes are related to improvement in all related fields of the production process including the organisation of workers, quality controls, management-worker relations, payments and incentives, improved use of existing capital investment, adapting new technology to production processes and closer relationships between both textiles manufacturers and retailers. Technological developments, described in Section 1.A.c) above, have had significant impacts in particular on pre-assembly processes. Efficiency at the manufacturing level therefore is increasingly a function of organising production units in a more flexible way.

As noted above, the application of modern telecommunication networks has permitted the separation of the more capital-intensive activities, *e.g.* pre-assembly, from the purely labour-intensive assembly activities without sacrificing quality and process efficiency. This process of separation is possible at both the national and international levels.

At the national level, it partly took the form of actual re-location of assembly plants in peripheral regions where untapped low-wage labour was still available in the southern parts of the United States and Italy. This relocation to the periphery has often been supported by sub-regional governmental programmes towards less developed regions. In many countries, this process of separation has not necessarily involved an actual geographical re-location of plants. Work has often been re-organised on the basis of a network of subcontractors to minimise direct labour costs in particular, and also to exploit more effectively the opportunities offered by changing demand trends. Again, various national legislation has partly played a role in encouraging such a re-organisation, for example, tax exemptions for small firms and high employer's social security contributions.

At the international level, notwithstanding MFA restrictions, investment in low-labour-cost countries is attractive given the labour-intensive process of clothing manufacturing. National legislation in developed countries in terms of preferential market arrangements has stimulated production in selected developing countries and also has encouraged investment flows from developed to developing countries to exploit these preferential arrangements. The main preferential arrangements are: the 9802 provision of the Harmonized Tariff Schedule of the United States (HTSUS 9802) which provides for duty concessions for imports of products assembled abroad from US components-tariffs are applied only on the value-added abroad; the outward processing arrangements or *trafic de perfectionnement passif* of the EC, which in combination with the Lomé Convention and Mediterranean Agreements, have extended preferential market access in terms of lower tariffs and higher volumes under quantitative restriction arrangements to selected beneficiaries.

Turkey has been a major beneficiary of the EC arrangements due partly to its labour-cost advantage and partly to various incentive programmes established by the Turkish government covering investment, production and exports (Silberston, 1989). Morocco, Tunisia and the ex-Yugoslavia were also major beneficiaries of the EC arrangements. Under the US programme, factories abroad that assembled clothing from US components accounted for 9.8 per cent of US clothing imports in 1989, this figure was estimated at 14.1 per cent in 1992. The Caribbean Basin countries and Mexico are the major beneficiaries of the US programme.

In Asia, a similar process of separation has occurred in which Japanese firms have entered into contractual arrangements with clothing firms in other Asian countries, particularly China, where assembly activities are performed (see Section 4). The main justification in this case would appear to be related to the appreciation of the yen, the scarcity of Japanese labour and low labour costs in neighbouring countries.

B. Employment and productivity

The application of computer-based technologies in the pre-assembly stage has modified the organisation of work, the capital-labour ratio and the demand for skilled labour. Increasingly the industry needs computer-trained designers and operators of automated cutting systems. It is generally estimated that about 80 per cent of labour employed by the clothing industry is devoted to the assembly stage. While specific task-oriented sewing operators are required for longer production runs, multiple skills and adaptability are required from employees involved in short production runs.

Table 8.3 indicates the level of employment in the clothing industry between 1980 and 1990. It shows that the loss of employment has been particularly strong among Nordic countries, falling by more than 50 per cent within the period. Clothing employment declined in most OECD countries except in Canada, Japan, Greece, Portugal and Turkey (see Table 8.3 for respective time periods). Clothing employment fell by 20.9 per cent for comparable OECD countries between 1980 and 1989.

Table 8.4 shows that clothing employment as a percentage of total manufacturing employment declined for most OECD countries between 1980 and 1990. This ratio rose for Greece, Italy, Japan, Portugal

Table 8.3. **Employment in the clothing industry, 1980-90**

Units

	1980	1985	1988	1989	1990
Austria	35 800	31 100	27 000	25 000	–
Belgium	54 300	43 800	39 200	39 800	38 700
Canada	113 463	110 910	115 485	–	–
Denmark	11 300	12 300	9 200	8 400	13 061
Finland	33 600	29 600	20 500	18 500	14 800
France	255 400	195 700	165 500	158 300	152 900
Germany	226 737	170 249	151 124	147 555	143 234
Greece	34 980	33 828	38 231	38 450	39 713
Iceland	–	1 057	686	504	472
Italy	172 000	162 000	174 000	163 147	–
Japan	437 000	459 000	484 000	486 000	488 000
Netherlands	17 400	12 629	12 077	11 570	–
New Zealand	–	18 484	–	14 701	13 500
Norway	6 789	4 290	2 846	2 303	2 086
Portugal	41 429	46 596	–	–	–
Spain	118 000	83 830	98 441	–	–
Sweden	14 098	10 882	8 991	7 989	6 815
Switzerland	36 100	29 700	28 100	27 900	27 000
Turkey	–	29 000	62 000	72 000	74 000
United Kingdom	276 684	237 000	233 629	218 916	203 253
United States	1 150 000	887 000	872 000	832 000	807 000
Total comparable countries [1]	2 762 188	2 319 078		2 185 830	
Total above	3 035 080	2 608 956	2 543 010	2 273 035	2 024 534

1. Includes above countries where data are available in 1980, 1985 and 1989.
Source: OECD (1993), *Industrial Structure Statistics 1991.*

Table 8.4. **Employment in the clothing industry
as a share of total manufacturing workforce, 1980-90**

Percentages

	1980	1985	1988	1989	1990
Austria	5.1	4.7	4.3	3.9	–
Belgium	5.9	5.5	5.1	5.1	5.0
Canada	5.3	5.7	–	–	–
Denmark	3.0	3.0	2.3	2.1	2.4
Finland	6.3	5.9	4.5	4.1	3.4
France	4.8	4.2	3.8	3.6	3.4
Germany	3.1	2.6	2.2	2.1	2.0
Greece	9.3	9.6	10.9	11.0	11.5
Iceland	–	3.9	2.7	2.1	2.0
Italy	5.1	5.6	5.9	5.7	–
Japan	4.2	4.2	4.4	4.4	4.4
Netherlands	2.0	1.6	1.5	1.4	–
New Zealand	–	6.1	–	5.9	5.7
Norway	1.9	1.4	1.0	0.8	0.8
Portugal	6.1	7.4	–	–	–
Spain	4.7	4.3	5.0	–	–
Sweden	1.7	1.4	1.2	1.0	0.9
Switzerland	4.4	3.6	3.4	3.3	3.2
Turkey	–	3.4	6.5	7.4	7.6
United Kingdom	4.2	4.8	4.7	4.4	4.2
United States	6.0	5.1	4.9	4.7	4.6
Average comparable countries [1]	4.7	4.4		4.1	–
Average above	4.8	4.5	4.3	4.2	4.0

1. Includes above countries where data are available in 1980, 1985 and 1989.
Source: OECD (1993), *Industrial Structure Statistics 1991.*

and Turkey but remained stable for the United Kingdom. In Italy, this ratio increased while clothing employment actually declined – suggesting that total manufacturing employment fell proportionally more than employment in the clothing industry. In 1989, employment in the clothing industry accounted for 4.1 per cent of total manufacturing employment for comparable OECD countries, down from 4.7 per cent in 1980. There are however, considerable differences in the relative importance of this sector among OECD countries. For example, clothing employment accounted for 11.5 per cent of total employment in Greece but only 0.8 per cent in Norway in 1990.

Labour-productivity ratios for the clothing industry and the manufacturing sector as a whole are presented in Table 8.5 for most OECD countries. Productivity is calculated as the value of production in US dollars divided by the level of employment. The labour intensity of the clothing industry is striking when the productivity in the clothing industry is compared with the productivity of the manufacturing sector. It has remained relatively stable throughout the 1980s at about 38 to 40 per cent of the average productivity of the manufacturing sector for OECD countries as a whole.

There are large differences between the levels of productivity achieved by individual OECD countries for both clothing and manufacturing industries which may be partially explained by the relative strength or weakness of domestic currencies to the US dollar. Also, under-reporting of employment statistics would overstate the level of productivity for some countries. For these reasons, any country comparison should be done with caution.

Table 8.6a shows that the ratio of value added to production declined between 1983 and 1990 for most European countries but remained relatively stable for Greece and Turkey – two countries whose production expanded rapidly during that period. The ratios however increased for the United States, the United Kingdom and Japan. It is striking to note that Japan, Sweden and the United Kingdom have maintained low labour productivity while they sustained at the same time high value-added ratios.

C. Technology, research and development

The main changes in applied technology in the clothing industry are described in the production section (see Section 1.A. above). In terms of research and development activities, Japan has made substantial efforts in areas of complete automation processes under the Japanese Automated Sewing System project. This project was established in 1983 and approximately US$100 million of government and industry support covered the whole assembly process from design, sewing, pressing, finishing to retail. Technical difficulties are very complex to overcome.

In the United States, the Textile and Clothing Technology Corporation project in the early 1980s covered some forms of automated systems. Several projects examined dedicated applications such as the automated assembly of sleeves, coat backs and trousers.

Under the European Commission's BRITE programmes, several clothing-industry-oriented research and technological development projects were carried out and completed in 1991. These projects included the following: creating a prototype for a flexible automated garment-assembly system in which work modules can be exchanged along one main work surface or automated line; developing concepts for sequential automation of sewing cells, then creating electromechanical devices to carry out each sewing cell function; developing a prototype modular machine capable of picking up pockets, positioning them on shirt fronts and sewing them in place; developing a sewing station and ironing unit with heads coupled to achieve simultaneous manufacturing of two opposite seams of a clothing garment.

The European Commission is currently pursuing research efforts with the following projects: mathematical modelling of three-dimensional flexible material surfaces to aid design and manufacture of clothing; realisation and tests of a prototype of a basic module of computer-integrated manufacturing in the clothing industry; development and evaluation of technologies as support for flexible production groups in the clothing industry.

The general view in the industry is that even if there is a technological breakthrough in automated sewing machines, the nature of the fashion business with short production runs will still leave a considerable share of production from standard technology in the assembly stage. The other consideration is that

Table 8.5. **Labour productivity in the clothing and manufacturing industries, 1980-90**

US$

	1980 Clothing	1980 Manufactur.	1985 Clothing	1985 Manufactur.	1989 Clothing	1989 Manufactur.	1990 Clothing	1990 Manufactur.
Austria	25 409	59 123	34 391	88 118	41 879	105 438	–	–
Canada	36 576	83 305	42 629	126 725	39 611	83 824	–	–
Denmark	23 460	50 686	33 316	71 780	33 777	99 839	26 793	64 750
Finland	21 776	56 346	29 861	80 522	–	119 781	36 377	102 724
France	29 700	63 730	50 635	93 848	65 521	113 555	71 886	124 950
Germany	32 630	63 720	52 138	98 660	69 517	95 136	78 025	119 081
Greece	18 644	56 386	25 730	82 826	31 260	75 305	34 099	96 390
Iceland	–	–	26 929	57 188	41 897	141 259	44 293	79 078
Italy	43 564	77 154	65 552	113 990	84 475	137 344	–	–
Japan	19 979	80 446	26 076	110 737	32 138	158 333	34 268	149 028
Netherlands	34 708	75 491	60 497	135 061	74 557	93 603	–	–
New Zealand	–	–	64 107	86 238	61 312	113 680	–	–
Norway	20 949	52 127	32 428	80 867	38 001	–	47 125	118 587
Portugal	20 558	40 543	29 488	67 170	–	–	–	–
Spain	28 508	59 629	39 285	99 678	38 214	96 223	–	–
Sweden	22 151	51 812	28 934	83 397	71 253	103 683	37 184	98 910
Switzerland	31 840	59 497	42 028	81 121	67 441	122 945	80 123	109 938
Turkey	–	–	40 973	86 222	38 337	111 065	–	–
United Kingdom	21 084	52 363	32 250	88 689	56 740	156 994	41 267	115 951
United States	32 809	96 660	49 290	130 114	–	132 763	58 839	163 539
Average comparable countries[1]	29 373	76 969	42 447	108 823	51 276	132 763	51 389	138 702
Average above	29 459	76 076	42 975	109 640	55 114	134 298	52 435	140 911

1. Includes above countries where data are available in 1980, 1985, 1989 and 1990.
Source: OECD (1993), *Industrial Structure Statistics 1991.*

Table 8.6a. **Value added as a percentage of production in the clothing industry, 1983-90**

Percentages

	1983	1985	1987	1988	1989	1990
France	45.85	42.32	–	43.02	41.77	41.80
Germany	43.74	42.21	42.36	41.21	42.02	40.76
Greece	44.67	46.42	47.76	45.99	47.34	44.84
Italy	35.63	34.09	33.35	31.27	31.48	–
Japan	50.37	50.81	51.44	52.00	52.57	52.85
Portugal	–	35.07	34.86	–	–	–
Spain	45.25	42.24	41.43	40.91	–	–
Sweden [1]	54.74	53.94	54.59	53.97	47.52	44.16
Turkey	28.53	27.67	29.22	30.16	29.39	–
United Kingdom	49.21	48.45	49.55	50.47	50.78	51.90
United States	50.57	50.67	52.66	51.90	53.50	53.65
Switzerland	47.31	47.30	–	42.03	40.26	38.50

1. Major break in series between 1988 and 1989.
Source: OECD (1993), *Industrial Structure Statistics 1991.*

Table 8.6b. **World distribution of value added and production, 1990 – Clothing**

Constant 1980 prices, percentages

	Value added	Value added/production	Production
Western Europe	24.5	44.3	25.1
North America	18.5	52.0	22.2
Asia	15.9	39.3	14.5
of which: Japan	4.2	52.5	5.1
Eastern Europe and former Soviet Union	33.9	40.2	31.5
Others	7.2	40.0	6.7

Source: OECD Secretariat estimates based on UNIDO data.

there are few firms with sufficient size and economies of scale in production which could commercially operate automated systems as these are actually conceived. Albeit, with continuing R&D efforts, automated systems will be improved and cost will be reduced so that they may become commercially viable in the next decades.

Table 8.7 shows the business expenditure on research and development (BERD) on textiles and clothing as a percentage of total BERD by country. It also indicates the total R&D expenditure as a percentage of gross domestic product by country. In 1988, the average percentage of BERD on textiles and clothing in 17 OECD countries represented only 1.06 per cent of total BERD. These sectors together received proportionally less than the relative importance in the production of clothing in the total manufacturing production (see Table 8.1). There are considerable differences between countries in the relative importance of R&D expenditure afforded to textile and clothing; for example, Italy has much lower percentages of R&D to these sectors relative to other major EC producers.

In most countries, government R&D efforts have been carried out in co-operation with the domestic industry with a view to strengthening the competitiveness of domestic firms in developing applied technologies. There is little evidence of international collaboration among firms or countries in R&D efforts. In fact, there is competition among OECD countries, particularly between the United States, Japan and the European Community, in achieving technological leadership in the field of automated assembly systems. The potential gains from the successful development of such systems are substantial and could gradually modify the nature of the clothing industry from being labour-intensive to becoming capital-intensive.

Table 8.7. **Research and development – Clothing**

Percentages

	Business expenditure on R&D on textile and clothing as a % of total expenditure on R&D[1]				Total expenditure on R&D as a % of gross domestic product[2]	
	1985	1986	1987	1988	1988	1989
Australia	1.09	–	0.52	–	1.25	–
Belgium	1.69	1.66	1.87	1.72	1.64	1.69
Canada	0.94	0.91	0.97	0.96	1.37	1.36
Denmark	0.30	–	0.18	–	1.49	1.54
Finland	0.60	–	1.00	–	1.77	1.80
France	0.59	0.58	0.53	0.48	2.28	2.33
Germany	0.47	–	0.43	–	2.86	2.87
Ireland	5.91	2.98	2.80	2.67	0.85	0.86
Italy	0.14	0.21	0.13	0.10	1.22	1.24
Japan	1.05	1.02	1.02	1.01	2.86	2.98
Netherlands	0.28	0.30	0.28	0.30	2.26	2.16
Norway	–	0.18	–	–	1.86	–
Portugal	–	2.29	–	2.56	0.50	–
Spain	0.43	0.40	0.50	–	0.72	0.75
Sweden	–	0.22	–	–	–	2.85
United Kingdom	0.42	0.38	0.27	0.28	2.20	2.23
United States	–	–	–	–	2.84	2.80
Average	1.07			1.06		

Source: 1. OECD (1991), *Basic Science and Technology Statistics*, Table 9 of country chapters.
2. OECD (1993), *Main Science and Technology Indicators*, Table 5, 1993-1.

D. Capital investment

Table 8.8 shows that investment as a percentage of production in the clothing industry remained relatively stable between 1983-90. Exceptions were Greece, Japan and Turkey who saw their investment ratios rising during the period. The labour intensity of the clothing industry is illustrated by the lower ratio of investment relative to the manufacturing sector as a whole. The comparison of the two sets of ratios also indicates that the difference between the ratios has widened during the 1980s, suggesting that the clothing industry is not keeping up with the general tendency in the manufacturing sector of OECD countries to become more capital-intensive.

Table 8.8. **Investment in the clothing industry**

Percentages

	1983		1989			1990	
	A	B	A	B		A	B
Germany	1.54	4.15	–	–		1.45	5.34
Greece	2.54	7.31	3.75	5.41		3.82	5.36
Italy	2.26	4.26	2.18	5.26		–	–
Japan	1.09	3.53	2.15	4.51		–	–
Portugal	4.35	6.31	3.91	5.46	(1987)	–	–
Spain	1.35	2.63	1.25	3.37		–	–
Turkey	2.10	4.32	16.57	5.76	(1987)	–	–
United Kingdom	2.54	3.10	2.43	4.89		2.42	4.67
United States	0.97	3.00	1.10	3.48		0.98	3.55

Note: A: Investment as a percentage of clothing production. B: Investment in all manufacturing industries as a percentage of overall manufacturing.
Source: OECD (1993), *Industrial Structure Statistics 1991.*

E. Concentration and competition

The average number of employees per establishment in the clothing industry (see Table 8.9) differs significantly between countries and the contrast is more pronounced between North America and Japan – North American firms employing about four times more employees per establishment than Japanese firms. Significant differences are also noticeable within the EC, with much lower averages for Germany and Italy compared to Greece and the United Kingdom. There is however a common trend in that the average number of employees has declined everywhere. Correspondingly, the percentage of firms employing less than 20 employees has increased.

The trend towards smaller firms is consistent with production trends mentioned earlier as firms have become smaller in response to changes in market conditions. Within large firms with more than 500 employees, the absence of comparable data complicates any comparison. For example, there is a large difference between the composition of the industry in Italy and the United Kingdom, large firms respectively accounted for 9.6 and 40.0 per cent of clothing production in 1989, these shares were respectively 13.4 and 41.3 per cent in 1987. The latter numbers however overstate the actual importance of large firms in total production since the production of firms of less than 20 employees was omitted from total production figures.

If this declining importance of large firms within these two countries is indicative of similar trends elsewhere, it follows that the industrial concentration within the clothing industry is also declining and conversely competitive pressure is increasing. Generally, large firms have adopted new technology and specialised in clothing segments where economies of scale in production existed. It is also widely reported that large firms have increasingly subcontracted specific activities to specialised firms in order to reduce the number of direct employees while maintaining production volume and turnover.

Table 8.9.   **Establishments by employment size range – Clothing**

	Number of establishments			Number of employees	Employees per establishment
	Total	−20[1]	+20[1]		
Canada					
1977	2 067	39.6%	60.4%	112 676	54.5
1988	2 821	53.6%	46.4%	115 485	41.0
United States					
1972	24 441	50.0%	50.0%	1 368 200	56.0
1977	26 505	55.0%	45.0%	1 334 300	50.3
1982	24 391	55.3%	44.7%	1 189 000	48.7
1990	23 862	61.8%	38.2%	1 027 458	43.1
Japan					
1980	38 256	84.3%	15.7%	478 673	12.5
1991	41 208	83.0%	17.0%	449 796	10.9
EC					
1988	83 797	–	–	1 325 690	15.8
1991	89 285	–	–	1 130 016	13.4
Italy (1989)	25 779	–	–	299 376	11.6
Germany (1990)	24 210	–	–	213 648	8.8
United Kingdom (1991)	7 789	–	–	182 580	23.4
France (1991)	11 841	–	–	169 735	14.3
Spain (1989)	9 896	–	–	142 000	14.3
Portugal (1989)	6 305	–	–	135 573	21.5
Greece (1990)	1 185	–	–	38 715	32.7
Belgium (1989)	1 443	–	–	30 640	21.2
Denmark (1991)	403	–	–	8 218	20.4

1.   Employees.
Source: Canada: *Clothing Industry, Statistical Data 1991*; Industry, Science and Technology Canada. *EC: Données structurelles de base sur l'industrie des textiles et de l'habillement dans la Communauté Européenne, 1988-1992*, juillet 1993. *United States:* US Department of Commerce, various publications, Washington. *Japan:* MITI, production classification numbers 2054, 2055, 211, 212 and 215 for 1980; and 1454, 1455, 151, 152 and 155 for 1991.

F.   Pricing

Clothing prices are affected by prevailing supply and demand conditions. On the supply side, import quotas on both textiles and clothing directly restrain supplies and exert upward pressures on clothing prices in developed-country markets who apply such restrictions. Estimates of the price effect of MFA restrictions in developed countries have usually been based on levels of quota premia in Hong Kong – trade in quota is permitted in Hong Kong, thus the prices paid (quota premia) for obtaining unused quotas are used to approximate the economic rent associated with the right to export to a certain country. A good summary of tariff-equivalent estimates of MFA quotas can be found in Cline (1990). His conclusion is that the tariff-equivalent of MFA quotas on clothing is in a range of 25 per cent (beyond the tariff), and that on textiles stands at some 15 per cent.

The use of quota premia may however overstate the estimated tariff-equivalent or import price effects since quota premia are generally paid for marginal volumes and they vary greatly over time, and from product to product. Moreover, they are high when market conditions are strong and low when they are weak. Quota premia do not necessarily represent the average quota rents earned by Hong Kong exporters. Also, exchange rate movements may partially exacerbate or offset quotas and tariff effects. It has been estimated that for the United Kingdom, the elimination of MFA quotas would likely lead to a fall of 8 per cent in imported prices which, in turn, would lead to a fall of 5 per cent in retail prices (Silberston, 1989).

Tariff-equivalents of MFA restrictions have also been estimated by the United States International Trade Commission for the year 1987 for each 3-digit textiles and apparel category. It was found that on average the tariff-equivalent for apparel was 28.3 per cent. The Commission however warned that its estimates overstated the restrictiveness of MFA quotas because of the restrictive nature of underlying assumptions of its econometric model.

At the retail level, the diversified structure of retail trade including independent stores, specialised chains offering trademark items, and fashion stores are all exploiting to a various degree local monopoly conditions and market segmentation niches. One implication of this fragmentation is that some retailers are able to capture a portion of any reduction in clothing manufactured prices resulting from either cost saving at the manufactured level or lower import prices. Lack of competitive pressure at the retail level inevitably leads to higher retail prices.

The shortage of raw materials, such as cotton, wool and synthetic fibres could have, in the short run, some cost-push effects. However, in the longer run, raw materials production could be expanded without much difficulty even though some long gestation period is needed for wool production as well as long lead time for capital-intensive investment in synthetic fibre processes.

On the demand side, income, prices and demographic conditions are influencing clothing demand. The price elasticity of demand for clothing in the United Kingdom was estimated by Silberston as –0.5 – this means that a fall in price of 10 per cent would increase demand by 5 per cent.

2.   INTERNATIONAL TRADE

A.   General trends

The share of world clothing exports as a percentage of total world exports increased continuously between 1975 and 1991, rising from 1.9 to 3.4 per cent (Table 8.10). In effect, clothing exports grew at a faster rate than total world exports, respectively 13.0 and 9.0 per cent (compounded annual rate of increase). The share of world textile exports as a percentage of total world exports during the same period initially declined but increased slightly afterward to reach 3.3 per cent of world total exports. Textile exports grew at about the same rate as total world exports, respectively 9.4 and 9.0 per cent. In 1991, for the first time, clothing exports were more important than textile exports.

Table 8.10 also shows that, between 1975 and 1991, OECD clothing exports as a percentage of world clothing exports declined from 59.2 to 47.4 per cent. It indicates that the overwhelming share of OECD exports are intra-OECD, 88.5 per cent in 1991 and this portion remained relatively stable since 1975. On the import side, OECD countries were the largest end destinations for world traded clothing between 1975 and 1991. The OECD share of world imports remained relatively stable at about 88 per cent.

Table 8.10. **World clothing and textile exports as a share
of world total exports, 1975-91**

Percentages

	1975	1980	1985	1990	1991	1991/75
Clothing	1.9	2.0	2.5	3.3	3.4	13.0
Textiles	3.1	2.8	2.9	3.3	3.3	9.4
Total exports	–	–	–	–	–	9.0

OECD exports of clothing

Percentages

	1975	1980	1985	1990	1991
OECD-world	59.2	54.2	49.2	47.4	47.4
Intra-OECD	87.0	86.4	87.9	89.1	88.5

World and OECD imports of clothing

Million US$

	1975	1980	1985	1990	1991
World	15 850.5	39 566.3	46 888.1	111 970.3	123 132.6
OECD	14 230.0	34 676.5	42 151.9	100 200.1	109 217.9
OECD-world	89.8%	87.6%	89.9%	89.5%	88.7%

Source: UN Comtrade database.

Table 8.11 indicates for each OECD country the percentage of total exports accounted for by clothing exports for selected years between 1975 and 1991. For the OECD as a whole, while the share of clothing exports increased from 1.6 to 2.0 percentage points, this result masks considerable variations among OECD countries. In particular, for Turkey, Greece and Portugal, the respective share jumped to above 20 per cent. This reflects, on the one hand, the accession of Greece and Portugal to the European Community and the preferential market access granted by the EC to Turkey. On the other hand, it reflects the competitive position of these countries in labour-intensive activities within the EC region. The share of clothing in total exports nevertheless increased in the United States, Germany, Italy, Denmark, New Zealand, Australia, the Netherlands and the United Kingdom. Elsewhere, the respective shares declined more or less but more significantly for Japan.

Table 8.12 indicates for each OECD country the percentage of total imports accounted for by clothing imports for selected years between 1975 and 1991. For the OECD as a whole, the share of clothing imports increased significantly during the period, from 2.4 to 4.2 per cent. Shares increased for all countries except Australia whose share remained stable. The largest increases in percentage points occurred in Japan, the United States, Iceland and Finland. In 1991, Germany, the United States and Switzerland had the highest import shares among OECD countries.

Despite MFA restrictions and high tariff rates afforded by several OECD countries, the share of clothing imports originating from non-OECD countries increased significantly from 44.3 to 58.2 per cent between 1975 and 1985, as shown in Table 8.13. Since 1985, the share of non-OECD imports continued to increase albeit at a reduced rate. The share of imports originating from China jumped and, in 1992, China displaced Italy as the largest clothing exporter to OECD countries by a considerable margin. The increase in the Chinese share has in fact accelerated considerably since 1985, and more than offset the decline in the share of intra-OECD import. The Chinese gains, since 1985, were mostly achieved at the expense of

Table 8.11. **Clothing exports by OECD countries as a share of total exports, 1975-91**

Percentages

	1975	1980	1985	1990	1991
Australia	0.1	0.1	0.1	0.2	0.3
Austria	2.9	3.3	3.3	2.8	2.9
Belgium-Luxembourg	2.3	1.6	1.4	1.7	1.8
Canada	0.3	0.3	0.3	0.2	0.3
Denmark	2.0	2.3	2.8	2.6	2.9
Finland	6.2	5.2	3.9	1.9	1.4
France	2.6	2.1	2.0	2.2	2.2
Germany	1.3	1.5	1.6	1.8	1.9
Greece	5.4	7.7	13.8	20.9	20.2
Iceland	1.8	2.7	2.9	0.7	0.7
Ireland	3.3	2.4	1.9	1.9	2.0
Italy	5.3	5.8	6.7	7.0	6.9
Japan	0.6	0.4	0.4	0.2	0.2
Netherlands	1.5	1.2	1.1	1.7	1.8
New Zealand	0.4	0.7	0.7	0.7	0.8
Norway	0.4	0.4	0.3	0.2	0.2
Portugal	11.3	13.6	17.8	21.3	22.0
Spain	2.4	1.5	1.3	1.1	1.0
Sweden	1.1	1.0	0.8	0.7	0.7
Switzerland	1.3	1.2	1.1	1.1	1.1
Turkey	5.9	4.5	15.2	25.7	25.6
United Kingdom	1.3	1.6	1.5	1.6	1.8
United States	0.4	0.6	0.4	0.7	0.8
OECD total	1.6	1.6	1.6	2.0	2.0
OECD Europe	2.2	2.2	2.5	2.8	2.9

Source: OECD, Comex database.

Table 8.12. **Clothing imports by OECD countries as a share of total imports, 1975-91**

Percentages

	1975	1980	1985	1990	1991
Australia	2.1	1.7	1.7	1.8	2.1
Austria	3.4	3.9	4.2	4.7	4.8
Belgium-Luxembourg	2.7	2.6	2.4	3.0	3.2
Canada	1.4	1.2	1.7	2.1	1.9
Denmark	2.2	2.6	2.8	3.4	4.0
Finland	1.1	1.4	1.9	3.3	3.7
France	1.7	2.0	2.5	3.6	3.8
Germany	4.9	4.5	4.5	5.9	6.2
Greece	0.1	0.3	0.7	2.2	2.2
Iceland	2.2	3.3	4.3	4.5	4.9
Ireland	2.6	3.7	3.7	4.0	4.2
Italy	0.6	0.8	0.9	1.5	1.9
Japan	0.9	1.1	1.6	3.8	4.0
Netherlands	3.9	3.8	3.1	3.8	4.2
New-Zealand	0.2	0.3	0.5	1.6	1.9
Norway	3.3	4.2	5.0	4.5	4.9
Portugal	0.6	0.2	0.2	1.7	2.3
Spain	0.3	0.4	0.4	1.9	2.6
Sweden	3.6	4.0	3.9	4.6	4.9
Switzerland	4.5	4.0	4.8	5.0	5.3
Turkey	0.0	0.0	0.0	0.1	0.1
United Kingdom	2.1	2.4	2.5	3.1	3.5
United States	2.6	2.8	4.5	5.2	5.5
OECD total	2.4	2.5	3.1	3.9	4.2
OECD Europe	2.7	2.8	2.8	3.7	4.1

Source: OECD, Comex database.

Table 8.13. **OECD imports of clothing, main origins, 1975-92**

Percentages

	1975	1980	1985	1990	1992	1992/75	1992/85
OECD imports	100.0	100.0	100.0	100.0	100.0	0.0	0.0
Intra-OECD	55.7	50.9	41.8	42.1	38.7	−17.0	−3.1
Italy	12.5	13.1	12.1	11.4	9.5	−3.0	−2.6
Germany	7.2	7.1	5.7	5.7	5.1	−2.1	−0.6
France	8.0	5.7	3.8	3.8	3.5	−4.5	−0.3
Turkey	0.6	0.3	1.7	3.5	3.5	+2.9	+1.8
Portugal	1.7	1.9	2.5	3.7	3.4	+1.7	+1.9
United Kingdom	3.7	4.4	3.1	2.6	2.6	−1.1	−0.5
Greece	2.1	2.9	1.8	2.0	1.7	−0.4	−0.1
Netherlands	3.3	1.8	1.5	1.8	1.9	−1.4	+0.4
Belgium and Luxembourg	4.0	2.4	1.6	1.6	1.4	−2.6	−0.2
United States	1.6	2.2	0.7	1.2	1.5	−0.1	+0.8
Denmark	1.2	1.0	1.0	0.8	0.9	−0.3	−0.1
Spain	1.1	0.7	0.5	0.5	0.5	−0.6	0.0
Japan	1.5	1.1	1.5	0.4	0.3	−1.2	−1.2
Others	44.3	49.1	58.2	57.9	61.3	+17.0	+3.1
China	1.1	2.7	5.1	9.6	13.6	+12.5	+8.5
Hong Kong	14.1	13.5	14.4	9.6	8.4	−5.7	−6.0
Rep. of Korea	7.3	8.1	10.2	7.8	5.5	−1.8	−4.7
India	1.3	2.0	1.9	2.6	2.6	+1.3	+0.7
Yugoslavia	2.7	1.6	1.8	2.3	0.6	−2.1	−1.2
Thailand	0.3	0.6	1.1	1.7	2.0	+1.7	+0.9
Indonesia	0.0	0.2	0.7	1.5	2.1	+2.1	+1.4
Philippines	0.7	1.3	1.5	1.6	1.6	+0.9	+0.1
Malaysia	0.3	0.5	0.8	1.3	1.5	+1.2	+0.7
Singapore	0.7	1.0	1.0	1.0	0.9	+0.2	−0.1
Other sources	15.8	17.6	19.7	18.9	22.5	+6.7	+2.8

Note: The last two columns are expressed in percentage points.
Source: OECD, Comex database, SITC Rev. 2 code 84: Articles of apparel and clothing accessories.

other non-OECD countries and, particularly, from Hong Kong and the Republic of Korea which together have lost 10.7 percentage points of OECD clothing import share.

With the exception of Hong Kong, the Republic of Korea and Yugoslavia, all other non-OECD countries listed in Table 8.13 have recorded increases in their shares of OECD clothing imports. Among OECD countries, the share of Italy remained relatively stable between 1975 and 1990 but dropped significantly in the following two years. The shares of France and Germany dropped considerably between 1975 and 1985, remained stable between 1985 and 1990 and resumed a downward trend in the early 90s.

The above results suggest that MFA protection and high tariff rates have in practice not prevented OECD imports originating from developing countries to grow and that, since 1985, clothing imports appear not to have displaced significantly intra-OECD imports but mainly imports from other non-OECD countries, in particular from Hong Kong and the Republic of Korea.

Intra-regional trade in clothing is provided in Table 8.14. It shows that for all regions – US/Canada, EC/EFTA and East Asia -intra-regional trade increased between 1981 and 1991. The largest increase occurred in East Asia, growing from 9.7 to 30.4 per cent. Intra-regional trade remained the highest in the EC/EFTA region, increasing from 80.7 to 83.9 per cent. For the US/Canada region, more than half of total exports were to other regions (other than the three above regions). This contrasted with EC/EFTA and East Asia regions, whose shares of total exports to other regions dropped by more than half between 1981 and 1991 to respectively 6.5 and 7.0 per cent.

Table 8.15 provides the ratios of clothing exports as a percentage of clothing production for most OECD countries for selected years between 1980 and 1990. The use of average annual exchange rates causes some distortions in the ratios, thus country comparisons should be done with caution. For Canada, Japan, New Zealand and the United States, the ratios are the lowest, all below 10 per cent of production. For Denmark, the Netherlands and Sweden, exports are larger than domestic production as a significant

Table 8.14. **Intra-regional trade – Clothing, 1981 and 1991**

Percentages

Importers/exporters	US/Canada	EC/EFTA	East Asia[1]	Others	Total
1981					
US/Canada	12.4	29.7	8.5	49.4	100.0
EC/EFTA	3.4	80.7	2.4	13.5	100.0
East Asia[1]	42.7	30.7	9.7	16.9	100.0
1991					
US/Canada	16.2	16.0	14.4	53.4	100.0
EC/EFTA	4.6	83.9	4.9	6.5	100.0
East Asia[1]	36.7	25.9	30.4	7.0	100.0

1. East Asia includes Japan, Republic of Korea, Chinese Taipei, Hong Kong, ASEAN countries and China.
Source: UN Comtrade database.

Table 8.15. **Exports as a percentage of production, 1980-90 – Clothing**

Percentages

	1980	1985	1989	1990
Austria	63.8	53.7	87.8	–
Canada	5.9	5.8	5.8	5.9
Denmark	142.8	115.2	193.4	247.2
Finland	99.6	59.3	78.0	92.4
France	30.2	19.5	35.0	42.5
Germany	39.0	32.3	54.9	63.0
Greece	61.0	72.1	122.4	123.7
Iceland	105.4	82.9	73.4	53.3
Italy	61.2	49.9	68.5	–
Japan	5.6	5.9	3.6	3.4
Netherlands	144.9	98.9	182.2	–
New Zealand	–	3.5	5.4	–
Norway	50.5	36.2	67.4	65.8
Portugal	74.2	73.8	–	–
Spain	9.3	9.7	–	–
Sweden	94.3	76.5	107.6	153.7
Switzerland	31.8	23.4	25.7	32.3
Turkey	–	101.7	56.4	–
United Kingdom	32.2	19.8	28.1	36.3
United States	3.2	1.7	4.4	5.2

Source: Production data: OECD (1993), *Industrial Structure Statistics 1991*; trade data: UN Comtrade database.

portion of imports is re-exported, *e.g.* transhipment without further processing. In Greece, the ratio is also above one as a significant portion of domestic production is effectively exported and also because of re-exports.

Table 8.16 provides the ratios of clothing imports as a percentage of domestic consumption for most OECD countries for selected years between 1980 and 1990. Consistent with rising imports, the ratio has increased for all countries with the exception of Iceland and Finland whose ratios have declined slightly, and Spain and Portugal for which recent data are missing. Denmark, the Netherlands, Sweden and Greece have ratios above 100 due to re-export transactions. Turkey had a negative ratio in 1985 as exports were larger than the sum of imports and domestic production measured in US dollars – it should be noted that changes in inventory levels have not been taken into account and that some distortions are caused by the use of an average annual exchange rate. It appears that the trade intensity of clothing, measured by the ratio of imports to domestic consumption, is more intensive than for overall manufacturing products in

Table 8.16. **Imports as a percentage of domestic consumption, 1980-90 – Clothing**

Percentages

	1980	1985	1989	1990
Austria	74.1	64.2	93.1	–
Canada	17.6	24.1	30.7	34.0
Denmark	129.2	114.1	155.2	192.0
Finland	98.6	41.5	83.9	95.6
France	33.3	25.3	48.7	57.0
Germany	64.8	53.9	76.0	82.9
Greece	10.9	21.5	850.5	390.2
Iceland	104.2	88.7	92.4	88.5
Italy	21.5	12.7	31.8	–
Japan	15.7	15.2	37.3	35.1
Netherlands	110.4	99.6	123.7	–
New Zealand	–	2.3	11.5	–
Norway	91.0	89.8	97.3	97.3
Portugal	6.0	4.9	–	–
Spain	4.8	3.9	–	–
Sweden	98.7	93.8	101.1	105.7
Switzerland	65.0	60.7	65.4	70.5
Turkey	–	-9.9	0.3	–
United Kingdom	41.9	30.6	49.0	56.6
United States	16.0	27.4	36.6	37.5

Source: Production data: OECD (1993), *Industrial Structure Statistics 1991*; trade data: UN Comtrade database.

OECD countries. However, the ratio of exports to production for clothing is smaller than for overall manufacturing products in OECD countries.

Some indications of the international competitiveness of countries in the production of clothing may be revealed by the index of export specialisation represented in Table 8.17. This index compares the share of clothing in total exports of a country relative to the share of world clothing exports in world total exports. A ratio above one indicates that a country has performed better than the intrinsic importance of the product itself in world trade and that such a country is assumed to be internationally competitive in the production of clothing. However, given that OECD clothing exports are carried out predominantly on a preferential basis – intra-OECD exports are not subject to MFA restrictions, and a substantial share of intra-OECD exports is carried out under regional integration arrangements providing for duty-free access among participant countries unlike competing exports from non-OECD countries – such ratios overstate the international competitiveness of OECD countries in the production of clothing.

B. Trade in intermediary products and international sourcing

Textiles as intermediary products for clothing production are also extensively traded – until 1991 trade in textiles was more important in value terms than trade in clothing products. MFA restrictions and high tariff rates applied by several OECD countries on textiles imports act as a tax on OECD clothing manufacturers and restrain the availability of textiles needed for clothing production. As a result, the competitive position of OECD clothing manufacturers is adversely affected by these restrictions. Despite trade measures, all developed members to the MFA have increased the share of their textiles imports from developing exporting MFA members between 1978 and 1988 (GATT, 1990).

The magnitude of trade in assembled clothing parts, excluding textiles, is difficult to measure since trade classification systems do not usually provide for separate classification items for clothing parts. Trade under the US provision HTSUS 9802 involves the exports of cut textile components to be assembled abroad and then re-entered in the United States. Assuming that the components represented about 40 per cent of the final imports value, US exports of cut textiles components would be equivalent to about two-fifths of the estimated 14.1 per cent of US total clothing imports in 1992 as imported under the HTSUS 9802 provision, *e.g.* equivalent to 5.64 per cent of US total clothing imports in 1992.

Table 8.17. **Trade specialisation indices, 1975-91 – Clothing**

	1975	1980	1985	1990	1991
Turkey	3.09	2.30	5.99	7.91	–
Portugal	5.95	7.08	7.12	6.53	6.56
Greece	2.87	4.10	5.62	6.61	6.13
Italy	2.79	3.05	2.68	2.14	2.05
France	1.37	1.07	0.80	0.68	0.66
Germany	0.67	0.78	0.62	0.54	–
United Kingdom	0.71	0.84	0.59	0.50	0.54
United States	0.21	0.29	0.14	0.20	0.24
Canada	0.18	0.17	0.12	0.08	0.09
Japan	0.31	0.20	0.16	0.06	0.05
Hong Kong	22.76	17.36	13.62	9.70	9.68
China	–	–	–	4.70	4.99
India [1]	2.36	4.02	4.03	4.62	4.49
Thailand	1.31	2.14	3.20	3.73	3.83
Republic of Korea	11.94	8.64	5.80	3.75	3.08
Indonesia	0.02	0.23	0.72	1.99	2.34
Chinese Taipei	8.84	6.27	4.51	1.78	1.71
Malaysia	0.58	0.59	0.83	1.36	1.32
Singapore	1.15	1.13	0.93	0.92	0.87

1.   Year ending 30 March.
Source: UN Comtrade database.

Table 8.18. **Ratio of imported to domestic sourcing of inputs
– Textiles, apparel and footwear**

	Early 1970s	Mid/late 1970s	Mid-1980s
Canada	0.41	0.50	0.60
France	0.15	0.26	0.42
Germany	–	0.49	0.64
Japan	0.03	0.06	0.09
United Kingdom	0.19	0.33	0.48
United States	0.07	0.06	0.13

Source: OECD, DSTI, EAS Division.

While it is increasingly possible to separate capital-intensive activities, such as pre-assembly, from labour-intensive assembly activities as a whole, separating activities within the assembly stage is not a widespread practice given inherent technical difficulties involved in matching design patterns and colours and at the same time minimising work-in-progress at the assembly stage. It is the general view within the industry that international trade in assembled clothing parts is not significant.

Furthermore it is not possible to quantify the value of the pre-assembly activities that are now internationally transmitted through computer networks – design, colour and cutting specifications may all be prepared in one country and then transmitted to another country without any customs forms. Another measure of globalisation is the extent and growth in international sourcing of manufactured intermediate inputs compared with domestic sourcing (see Table 8.18). The textiles, apparel and footwear industry as a whole has remained in the top group of industries ranked by international sourcing of major OECD countries. It does not source internationally to the same extent as computers, but it was more internationally oriented than motor vehicles in France, Germany and Japan. The ratio of imported to domestic sourcing in the textiles, apparel and footwear industry increased in all major OECD countries between the early 1970s and the mid-1980s. Germany and Canada had the highest ratios and the United States and

Japan had the lowest. The highest increases in the ratios occurred in France and the United Kingdom. Data for the clothing industry alone are not available.

C.   Intra-firm trade

Intra-firm trade (IFT) is defined as the international exchange of goods and services within a multinational enterprise (MNE).[1] While IFT accounts for a little over a third of total US merchandise trade,[2] it is relatively insignificant for US trade in textiles products and apparel. Although classification problems prevent the calculation of the exact share of IFT in US clothing trade, estimates put it at about 20 per cent of US sectoral exports and less than 5 per cent of US sectoral imports in 1990, excluding wholesale and related activities.[3] Given that US clothing imports are approximately eight times larger than US clothing exports, the overall share of IFT in US clothing trade is significantly below 10 per cent.

US-based multinationals accounted for the largest share of US IFT in the clothing sector in 1989. Of these, US firms established in Canada, Europe and Latin America/Caribbean are the most important clothing exporters, while US firms established in East Asia, excluding Japan, are the most important clothing importers. Overall, there is very little IFT conducted by US-based clothing multinationals, as their foreign affiliates tend to sell locally and export to third countries rather than sell back to the United States. The US affiliates of foreign firms do not conduct a significant amount of IFT either. Of those, US affiliates of European firms are by far the most important, with UK- and German-based firms predominant.

D.   Intra-industry trade

Intra-industry trade (IIT) is defined as the exchange by two countries of goods and services within the same product category. IIT is generally a function of product differentiation and may or may not be intra-firm trade. IIT indices provide another tool for analysing trade patterns as they may show the extent of international linkages for a given industry.[4]

IIT indices for US trade in clothing[5] are considerably below the average for all manufacturing, as is also the case for intra-firm trade. Due to the large US trade deficit in clothing trade, US IIT indices in that sector ranged from 20 to 30 per cent throughout the 1980s. Bilateral IIT indices are highest with Canada, Mexico and Europe, reaching up to 70 per cent, but considerably lower with the DAEs, at is less than 1 per cent. IIT indices for US-Japanese clothing trade stand in between, ranging from 30 to 40 per cent. The United States has a trade surplus with Japan in the clothing sector.

IIT indices for Japanese trade in clothing have declined markedly in the 1980s, due to the increase in Japan's trade deficit in the sector. In the early 1990s, they stood at around 10 to 15 per cent, lower than the average for the manufacturing sector. Bilateral IIT indices are highest for trade with Europe and North America, and considerably lower for Japan-DAE trade, especially Korea, with which Japan has a large trade deficit in the clothing sector.

IIT indices for European trade are large and close to the average for all manufacturing sectors. This is due to the large importance of intra-European trade, which accounts for over 80 per cent of total European exports in the clothing sector.

3.   FOREIGN DIRECT INVESTMENT AND INTER-FIRM NETWORKS

A.   Foreign direct investment

The year-end values of inward and outward foreign direct investment (FDI) within the textiles, clothing and leather (TCL) industry for 1983, 1987 and 1991 are presented in Table 8.19. For the OECD countries listed, only Japan and the United States have maintained outward FDI larger than inward FDI in the industry. The United Kingdom was by far the largest recipient of FDI while Japan was the largest outward investor. Italy and France were both sizeable recipients and suppliers of FDI.

Outward FDI by OECD countries in the TCL industry is small relative to FDI in the manufacturing sector as a whole, representing less than 2 per cent for most countries, except for Japan and Italy. In 1983,

Table 8.19. **Foreign direct investment – Textiles, clothing and leather**

Position at year-end
Million US$

	Inward			Outward		
	1983	1987	1991	1983	1987	1991
Australia	146	329	355	13	–	–
Austria	110	192	239	9	23	35
Canada	547	738	989	–	–	–
France	–	–	997 (90)	–	510	844
Italy	203	509	1 039	93	302	823
Japan	58	96	210	2 060	2 442	4 615
Netherlands	–	–	–	–	–	–
New Zealand	–	–	–	–	–	–
Norway	–	15	15	–	–	14 (89)
United Kingdom	–	8 002 (88)	–	–	–	–
United States	421	1 169	1 632	1 293	1 453	1 954

Source: OECD (1993), *International Direct Investment Statistics Yearbook 1993*, country tables 3 and 4.

Japan had about 9.5 per cent of its outward manufacturing FDI invested in the TCL industry. This share however declined to 4.9 per cent at the end of 1991 – the nominal value of outward FDI nevertheless more than doubled during this period. The opposite trend happened in Italy: this share increased from 2.2 to 4.3 per cent during the same period.

About 65 per cent of Japanese investment projects abroad were in the Asian region. During the 1970s and first half of the 1980s, Japanese outward FDI was primarily oriented to the textiles sector. Since the mid-1980s, with the rising strength of the yen and domestic scarcity of labour, outward FDI has shifted to the clothing sector. The majority of Japanese investments is in the form of joint ventures or contractual assembly arrangements under which Japanese partners are providing the technology, pre-assembly inputs and textiles. Assembly activities are performed by Asian partners, increasingly in China. Most of the clothing produced under such arrangements is then exported to Japan. Between 1986 and 1991, the number of Chinese clothing firms under some form of contractual arrangement with Japanese firms had increased seventeen-fold (MITI).

Outward FDI by the United States in the TCL industry was at least twice as large than inward FDI in 1983, this ratio however declined as significant inward FDI was made in the United States in this industry. A substantial share of US outward FDI was made in the Caribbean, Mexican and Colombian clothing operations and was linked to projects to exploit the advantage offered by the US provision HTSUS 9802 providing for value-added customs duties for qualifying imports. American firms have also invested significantly in Asian clothing operations but these investments were not related to the 9802 provision. American firms have also made sizeable investments in Canadian textile operations given the closer integration of Canadian and American markets. In terms of inward FDI in the United States, it appears that most of these investments were made in the textile industry with significant investment originating from Chinese Taipei, Germany and the United Kingdom.

Outward FDI by EC firms were primarily in Turkish, Moroccan and Tunisian clothing operations to exploit the advantage associated with preferential market access in the Community. Under such arrangements, assembly activities are performed in these countries and the final production is exported to the EC.

In terms of inward FDI in OECD countries, the TCL industry has attracted a relatively small share of manufacturing investment with the notable exception of the United Kingdom, where 19 per cent of the manufacturing FDI in 1988 was in the TCL industry. In Italy and France, respectively 4.6 and 3.3 per cent of manufacturing investments were in the TCL industry in 1991.

Table 8.20. **Foreign subsidiaries**

Percentages

	Share of foreign subsidiaries in gross output or turnover of the textiles, clothing and leather industry		Share of foreign subsidiaries in employment of the textiles, clothing and leather industry	
	1980	1990	1980	1990
Australia[1, 3]	21.5 (82)	–	18.2 (82)	–
Canada[1, 4]	32.0	26.2 (87)	21.6	–
Denmark[2, 4]	–	5.2 (86)	–	4.3 (86)
Finland[2, 4]	5.9	3.9	7.7	3.8
France[1, 3]	12.2	15.8	–	13.5
Germany[1, 3]	3.1	3.6	2.14	2.34
Ireland[2, 4]	48.0 (83)	53.5 (88)	37.4 (83)	48.3 (88)
Italy[1, 4]	9.3 (81)	–	9.9 (81)	–
Japan[2, 4]	0.2	0.06 (89)	0.18	0.02 (89)
Norway[2, 4]	2.1	6.4 (89)	1.7	5.2 (89)
Sweden[1, 4]	7.3	6.7 (89)	5.0	5.2 (89)
Turkey[2, 4]	–	1.5	–	1.2
United Kingdom[2, 4]	5.3 (81)	–	3.5 (81)	–
United States[1, 3]	1.5	7.2 (89)	1.2	4.8 (89)

1. Turnover.
2. Gross output.
3. Majority and minority-owned subsidiaries.
4. Majority-owned subsidiaries (+50 per cent).
Source: OECD, Industrial Activity of Foreign Affiliates databank (DSTI, EAS Division).

B. Market shares of foreign-controlled firms

The shares of foreign subsidiaries in terms of employment and output for the textiles, clothing and leather industry are presented in Table 8.20. Shares vary significantly among OECD countries, from being practically zero in Japan to about half the industry in Ireland. It is in the United States and Norway that the share increased the most during the 1980s – although levels are still below 10 per cent – and it decreased significantly in Canada during the period. Elsewhere variations are small in both directions. The high level of foreign investment in Ireland is associated with favourable tax incentives to FDI.

C. Inter-firm networks

Firms increasingly subcontract work to minimise direct labour costs and capital requirements. Licensing arrangements are also used frequently by owners of brand names. Brand-name products are either manufactured in affiliated facilities or subcontracted to independent manufacturers. The latter arrangement is however the most frequent as it provides greater flexibility to brand-name owners and minimises capital requirements. There is no reliable source of data for these types of arrangements but it is generally considered that the vertical relationship between the clothing and retail industries is low.

With relatively few barriers to entry in the industry, the economic rationale for clothing manufacturers to enter into strategic alliances with other clothing manufacturers appears to be dictated more as a cost minimisation strategy (achieving economies of scale) rather than as an oligopolistic strategy (seeking to increase market concentration to influence price determination). The fashion-oriented characteristic of the industry requires frequent adjustments in production processes and calls for flexibility in the organisation of work.

In terms of vertical integration with textiles and clothing equipment manufacturers, arm's length transactions characterise the relationships between clothing firms and these industries. Differences in market composition, production processes and barriers to entry explain such an absence of vertical integration. Strategic alliances may be pursued among technology firms or large retailers.

4. GOVERNMENT POLICIES

A. Government assistance

Within OECD countries, government interventions in the clothing sector have concentrated on protection against foreign competition with significantly higher import tariffs applied to clothing relative to other manufactured products (see Section 4.C below) and discriminatory non-tariff protection applied to imports from low-cost countries. Otherwise government interventions have generally been modulated to ease the specific problems faced by small and medium-sized enterprises and implemented through horizontal government programmes such as regional development assistance, research and development, and training activities.

Recent OECD work on industrial support policies has examined the allocation of net spending among major policy objectives pursued by government support programmes (OECD, 1992). It concluded that expenditures were concentrated in four policy objectives: general investment aids; regional development programmes; support to research and development; and aid to exports and international investment. It also found that more limited expenditures were allocated to: sectoral programmes; support to small and medium-sized enterprises; support to employment/training activities; and aid to enterprises in difficulty. Among sectoral programmes, textiles was identified as one sector which has been the focus of a significant number of programmes. The clothing sector however was not identified as a large recipient.

In developing countries, with the exceptions of Hong Kong, Macao and Singapore, the infant industry argument is extensively used to shield domestic production from import competition or in pursuing an import substitution objective. Although more and more developing countries are adopting trade liberalisation as a general strategy to sustain economic growth, most developing countries are still applying extremely high nominal tariffs to clothing products and are also resorting to non-tariff barriers and import bans. Government assistance in the form of investment incentives, tax relief for expansion of modernisation and export credit is equally common.

B. Foreign investment policies

The majority of outward FDI has been made in low-labour-cost countries which benefited from some kinds of preferential market access to OECD countries. There is a strong correlation between preferential market access and outward FDI in the clothing sector. Most of these investment projects have involved a separation of pre-assembly and assembly activities among countries of a common geographical region taking into account the comparative advantages of respective parties.

Inward FDI in OECD countries was primarily directed to textile projects; the clothing sector has not received substantial investment with the exception of perhaps Greece and Portugal. This low inward investment reflects the generally poor economic rationale for investing in a labour-intensive industry in OECD countries. It cannot be related to domestic obstacles to the establishment of FDI in OECD countries. The trade protection afforded under MFA restrictions and high tariff levels are also not perceived to be immutable thus pushing potential investors to search for economically sounder environments. The viability of investment in the clothing sector is also influenced by the development of a close relationship with domestic retail distributors. The perceived difficulties to establish such relationships may also act as a disincentive for inward investment in OECD countries.

C. Trade policies

Simple average tariff levels for clothing and manufactured products, prior to and after the Tokyo Round, are presented in Table 8.21. It shows that for all listed countries, tariff levels resulting from the Tokyo Round reductions have remained significantly higher for clothing than for manufactured products. There are significant differences in the level of tariff protection among listed countries, tariffs being significantly higher in Finland and Austria than in Switzerland, the EC and the United States.

However, simple average tariffs mask tariff peaks which are revealed by examining the dispersion of tariffs (see Table 8.22) and also by the average applied tariffs – measured by dividing the duty collected on

Table 8.21. **Average tariff levels in selected OECD countries – Clothing**

Percentages

	Manufactures[1] Simple average		Clothing Simple average		Clothing Applied average[2]	
	Tokyo Round[3]		Tokyo Round[3]		1982	1992
	Pre-	Post-	Pre-	Post-		
Australia	–	–	32.5[4]	70.4[4]	40.4 (83)	40.2
Austria	12.0	8.5	32.0	30.5	22.2 (83)	15.2
Canada	13.0	7.5	23.0	20.0	–	–
EC	9.5	6.5	16.0	12.5	–	–
Finland	14.0	12.0	41.0	39.5	33.4	35.0 (91)
Japan	11.0	6.5	18.0	13.0	–	–
Mexico	–	–	–	18.1[5]	–	–
New Zealand	–	–	–	40.0[6]	21.1 (87)	24.0
Norway	–	–	–	18.0[7]	–	–
Sweden	6.5	6.0	14.5	14.0	–	5.7
Switzerland	4.0	3.0	11.5	9.0	–	–
United States	11.5	6.5	24.0	12.5	25.9	17.8

1. Manufactures excluding petroleum.
2. Applied averages were calculated by dividing the total duty collected from the total dutiable value of clothing imports classified under HS chapters 61 and 62 for 1992 and corresponding classification categories for 1982. Data supplied by respective countries.
3. Pre-Tokyo Round and Post-Tokyo Round simple average tariff levels.
   Source: GATT, *Textiles and Clothing in the World Economy, July 1984.*
4. The average duty of 32.5 per cent is based on *ad valorem* tariffs in Schedule 3 of the Australian Customs Tariff for the year 1989. The specific tariffs and tariff quota categories are not taken into account. The tariff average of 70.4 per cent is for 1985-86 and is the tariff equivalent of specific tariffs and tariff quotas.
   Source: GATT, *Trade Policy Review, Australia 1989,* Tables V.7 and V.18.
5. This is the 1991 simple average tariff for clothing.
   Source: GATT, *Trade Policy Review, Mexico 1993,* p.186.
6. In July 1989, New Zealand introduced a four stage tariff reduction programme for clothing. Under this, the standard tariff rate [to be] applied in 1992 [is] 40 per cent, with all specific duties removed.
   Source: GATT, *Trade Policy Review, New Zealand 1990,* p.226.
7. GATT, *Trade Policy Review, Norway 1991,* Table AV.15.

imported clothing by the value of clothing imports (see last two columns of Table 8.21). In the United States, the applied average rate is significantly higher than the simple average rate for clothing as large volumes of imports are affected by tariff peaks.

In New Zealand, clothing imports from Australia and SPARTECA countries enter duty free and these represent a significant share of total imports. It is for this reason that its average applied tariff, *i.e.* 24 per cent in 1992, was much lower than the 37.5 per cent tariff rate prescribed for in 92 per cent of its *ad valorem* tariff lines (see Table 8.22). It should be noted that New Zealand removed the last of its quantitative restrictions on clothing imports on 30 June 1992.

Clothing trade between EC and EFTA countries is carried out on a duty-free basis as provided for in the free trade agreement in application since 1974. The applied average tariff in the EC is not yet available but it should be very low since its tariff structure is highly concentrated in tariff levels ranging between 10 to 15 per cent and since duty-free intra-regional trade among EC and EFTA countries accounts for more than 80 per cent of total trade.

In Sweden, the tariff dispersion is highly concentrated in tariff levels ranging between 10 to 15 per cent and the average applied tariff is much smaller as Sweden imported about 60 per cent of clothing imports from countries members of the EC and EFTA free trade agreement. On 31 July 1991, Sweden ceased to apply MFA quantitative restrictions. In Finland, the tariff dispersion is concentrated in high tariff levels but its average applied tariff is slightly smaller than the simple average.

In sum, the simple average post-Tokyo Round tariff is a poor indicator of the level of protection afforded to clothing production by OECD countries. Wider dispersion of tariffs tends to mask tariff peaks, thus the simple average tariff underestimates actual degrees of protection. Preferential market access

Table 8.22. **Dispersion of tariffs, 1993 – Clothing**

Percentages

	United States	EC	New Zealand	Finland	Australia
Free	1.9	0.0	3.1	0.0	10.3
0.1-5.0	12.2	0.0	0.0	0.0	0.0
5.1-10.0	25.8	10.1	1.4	0.7	0.0
10.1 -15.0	12.2	89.9	0.0	2.4	0.4
15.1-20.0	28.6	0.0	2.1	0.0	0.0
20.1-25.0	6.8	0.0	1.4	0.0	10.0
25.1+	12.5	0.0	92.0	96.9	79.3

	Canada	Sweden (1992)	Austria	Japan	Switzerland
Free	0.0	0.0	0.0	[1]	[2]
0.1-5.0	0.0	0.0	0.0		
5.1-10.0	0.8	2.6	0.0		
10.1-15.0	1.7	93.1	0.0		
15.1-20.0	5.5	4.2	0.0		
20.1-25.0	91.6	0.1	7.6		
25.1+	0.4	0.0	92.4		

Note: For New Zealand, more than one-third of its tariff items are specifics. For the United States, 33 tariff items are compounded rates. Canada has four compounded rates. In these cases, only the *ad valorem* element was taken into account. For Australia, in 1993 it operates a tariff-only import regime and the tariff structure is composed of four tariff levels: free, 12, 21 and 47 per cent. The 12 per cent tariff rates will be phased down to 5 per cent by 1 July 1996, the 21 and 47 per cent tariff rates will be phased down to 10 and 25 per cent respectively by 1 July 2000. Tariff rates were the applied MFN rates in 1993 as specified in Chapters 61 and 62 of the Harmonised System of classification. Only *ad valorem* rates were taken into account in the above percentages – it was not possible to calculate the tariff equivalent of specific duty rates.

1. In Japan, the Post-Tokyo average tariff for clothing was 13.0 per cent, with the highest rates being 16.8 per cent. *Source:* GATT, *Trade Policy Review, Japan 1992*, p. 190. This would suggests a relatively low dispersion.

2. In Switzerland, the Post-Tokyo average tariff for clothing was 9.0 per cent, with a considerable dispersion of individual *ad valorem* equivalents: on a range of items they exceed by far 20 per cent. *Source:* GATT, *Trade Policy Review, Switzerland 1991*, p. 164.

Source: Calculated by the Secretariat, except for Finland, Sweden, Austria and Australia for which percentages were provided by the respective administrations.

programmes in the context of free trade agreements or selective sectoral programmes have the opposite effect, as the simple average tariff overstates the actual protection to domestic producers.

More importantly, tariff protection is not the main instrument of protection for several OECD countries as quantitative restrictions are applied in the context of the MFA. The tariff-equivalent of MFA quotas were estimated to be within a range of 25 per cent for clothing and 15 per cent for textiles beyond nominal tariffs (see Section 1.F. above).

Before the 1950s, the clothing industry was mostly a domestically oriented industry. In the 1950s, the emergence of Japan, Hong Kong and other developing countries as low-cost exporting countries created pressure in the clothing industry of developed countries. In 1961 and 1962, respectively the Short-term Arrangement Regarding International Trade in Textiles (STA) and the Long-Term Arrangement Regarding International Trade in Cotton Textiles (LTA) came into force as major derogations to GATT disciplines.

In 1974, a large part of the textiles and clothing imports by developed countries were subjected to a series of voluntary restraint arrangements (VRAs) negotiated bilaterally under the Multifibre Arrangements (MFA). These exceptions to GATT rules were legitimised as developed countries requested time to adjust to competition from low-cost countries. In return, exporting developing countries obtained the right to allocate export licenses in their respective country and, in this way, they captured the economic rent associated with the right to export at artificially high prices.

The initial bilateral agreements that resulted from MFA I included general provisions providing for a minimum annual growth of 6 per cent for clothing imports and a certain flexibility in the quota system was established through the provisions of "carry-over", "carry-forward" and "swing". MFA II, which entered into force in 1978, resulted in a general tightening of restrictions with lower annual growth, an expanded coverage of clothing items and countries subjected to restrictions, and reduced flexibility provisions.

MFA III, which entered into force in 1982, included an "anti-surge" provision providing for special restraint in situations where exporters attempted to fulfil previously unfilled quotas. MFA IV entering into force on 31 July 1986 for a period of five years, increased the product coverage. In 1991 and 1992, the essential of MFA IV provisions were extended pending the conclusion of the Uruguay Round.

MFA protection has created strong vested interests in developed countries, developing countries with the largest quotas and developing countries benefiting from preferential market access arrangements for maintaining the system basically unaltered while shifting the cost of protection onto clothing consumers in developed countries. It is argued by some that MFA protection has prevented stronger export competition among developing countries for clothing exports to developed countries and, in particular, contributed to delay the development of a stronger clothing industry in least developed countries. This is a moot point since trade in clothing products without the MFA may be concentrated in few developing countries with sufficient critical mass to sustain strong developments in textiles and clothing.

One related issue with MFA restrictions is the problem of circumvention of quotas by transhipment and false declarations on the origin of products. The circumvention of quotas has been a matter of concern in recent years and it was acknowledged as a growing concern by the Textiles Surveillance Body of the GATT (GATT, 1992). Quantifying the magnitude of circumvention by transhipment is a difficult and assiduous task which requires an in-depth examination of the whole chain of transactions from manufacturing to final destination – such an investigation is beyond the scope of this study and raises the difficult problem of access to confidential import documentation. The United States Trade Representative has estimated the value of textiles and clothing transhipment to amount at about US$2 billion a year (USTR).

While circumvention raises the problem of an accurate apportionment of imports from a limited number of developing countries, the overall level of OECD imports from non-OECD clothing imports does not appear to be affected. In the circumstances, the distortion in trade data implied by circumvention would not fundamentally alter the factors influencing the globalisation of economic activities in the clothing industry which are the primary scope of this study.

The MFA agreements have included provisions about the circumvention of quotas which provided for consultation among concerned parties and commitments to collaborate to avoid such circumvention. With the conclusion of the Uruguay Round, the circumvention provisions of the Textiles and Clothing Agreement are more elaborate than the previous ones. They set out more clearly the process of consultation, the nature of collaboration expected, the possible remedies that an importing Member can implement and recourses, including the possible denial of entry of goods. It is hoped that these provisions will contribute to a resorption of the incidence of circumvention.

MFA quotas being specified in physical terms, they have also encouraged upgrading of quality by exporters and, conversely, encouraged clothing manufacturers in developed countries to maintain production in lower value added items than otherwise – this is somehow validated by examining the ratios of value added to production in Table 8.6a. MFA quotas and high tariffs have however not prevented imports from developing countries to grow in importance in OECD countries; the share of OECD imports originating from non-OECD countries increased from 44.3 to 61.3 per cent between 1975 and 1992.

The cost of protecting clothing production in several OECD countries is substantial. The elimination of quotas and tariffs on developed countries' textiles and clothing imports was estimated by Trela and Whalley (1990) to generate an annual global welfare gain of around US$23 billion. These gains would be US$12.3 billion for the United States, US$0.8 billion for Canada and US$2.2 billion for the EC. In aggregate, developing countries would gain around US$8 billion. The latter result suggests that the economic rent transfers associated with the MFA would be more than offset by improved market access associated with the dismantling of the MFA.

With the exception of Japan, all OECD countries are now involved in some form or other in regional trading arrangements and providing, or in the process of establishing, duty-free market access in clothing products among participant countries. Within the EC, clothing capacity increased significantly in the Southern member countries and intra-trade flows have shifted accordingly. The eventual enlargement of the EC to include some EFTA countries and some CEECs is likely to further increase intra-regional trade flows which were already at a very high level in 1991, i.e. 83.9 per cent. Between Canada and the United

States, bilateral tariffs are gradually being reduced and the low level of intra-regional trade is likely to grow as further integration is taking place. The North American Free Trade Agreement (NAFTA) between Canada, the United States and Mexico should produce further integration of the respective clothing market.

D. Issues of intellectual property rights

Owners of well-known brand names have set up international networks of specialised or affiliated retail stores which are supplied by a network of clothing manufacturers. In several instances, brand-name clothing is manufactured by independent manufacturers operating under contract for brand-name owners. These large retail groups have adopted for sometime already an international sourcing strategy as a way to maximise profits.

Counterfeit of brand-name clothing and designs is claimed to be important in some developing countries where enforcement of domestic legislation on the protection of intellectual property rights is deficient or lacking. There is no reliable source data to quantify the magnitude of lost income owing to counterfeit in the clothing sector.

E. Competition policy

Despite MFA restrictions and high tariffs in several OECD countries, domestic competitive conditions in the clothing manufacturing industry have intensified mainly because barriers to entry in the clothing industry are among the lowest of industrial processes. The price wedge associated with trade restrictions, *e.g.* higher domestic prices over world prices, confers an economic advantage to domestic clothing manufacturers but domestic competition for this economic advantage is strong. The pursuit of domestic oligopolistic strategies to create domestic price premia would soon be eroded by new competitors seeking to earn the price premia.

Access to domestic distribution networks by small clothing manufacturers may cause some difficulties as large retailers often prefer to deal with a limited number of medium-sized manufacturers to minimise transaction costs and time. However, given the arm's length transactions that characterise the retailer-manufacturer relationships, it is in the best interest of large retailers to deal with most efficient suppliers, be they domestic or from abroad. There is little evidence to suggest that restrictive business practices in the clothing manufacturing industry are causing structural problems.

Concerns about restrictive business practices are more likely to be targeted at the retail side of the clothing chain. Competitive conditions at the retail level differ from those prevailing at the manufacturing level. It is generally agreed that retail concentration is increasing within large retail groups; these groups and other specialised retail chains are able to exploit, to a various degree, local monopoly conditions and thus have an influence on retail clothing prices.

NOTES AND REFERENCES

1. There are few sources of data on intra-firm trade (IFT), as information on the subject is not generally available in traditional trade statistics. Data on IFT are mostly available through firm surveys which involve the preparation of questionnaires by national authorities. This section is based on information provided by the US Department of Commerce, which conducts surveys of foreign affiliates of US companies and US affiliates of foreign companies. Relevant data is not available for other countries. The US Department of Commerce uses the International Surveys Industry (ISI) classification in its surveys. There is a category for "apparel and other textile products" (ISI 230), which includes the production of clothing and fabrication products by cutting and sewing purchased woven or knit textile fabrics and related materials such as leather, rubberised fabrics, plastics and furs. It includes men's, women's and children's clothing; hats, caps and millinery; fur goods; miscellaneous apparel such as gloves, robes and belts; and other miscellaneous fabricated textile goods. For an explanation of the availability and problems with data on IFT, please consult OECD (1993), *Intra-firm Trade*, Trade Policy Issues No. 1, Paris.

2. See: OECD (1993), *Intra-firm Trade*, Trade Policy Issues No. 1, Paris.

3. There has been a large increase in investment in wholesale activities in the United States. This trade is technically IFT but different in character from the case where investment takes place in assembly operations. The figures above exclude IFT due to wholesale activities.

4. Intra-industry trade (IIT) can be readily calculated for any given product category, as only the traditional bilateral trade statistics for that product category are needed. The interpretation of IIT data depends however, on how one defines that category, as the choice of the classification system and of the level of aggregation may strongly influence the results. For the analysis below, the Standard International Trade Classification (SITC) Revision 2, at the four digit level, was used. In the calculation of an IIT index, if exports are equal to zero, IIT is 100; on the other hand, if either imports or exports are equal to zero, IIT is zero. For a discussion of the theory and measurement of IIT, see Grubel and Lloyd (1975).

5. SITC REV2 84; articles of apparel and clothing accessories.

BIBLIOGRAPHY

CLINE, W.R. (1990), *The Future of World Trade in Textiles and Apparel*, revised edition, Institute for International Economics.

GATT (General Agreement on Tariffs and Trade) (1984), "Textiles and Clothing in the World Economy", background study prepared by the GATT Secretariat, Geneva.

GATT (1988, 1989, 1990), *International Trade*, Geneva.

GRUEBEL, H.G. and P.J. LLOYD (1975), *Intra-industry Trade: The Theory and Measurement of International Trade in Differentiated Products,* MacMillan, London.

HAMILTON, C.B. (1990), *Textiles Trade and the Developing Countries: Eliminating the Multi-Fibre Arrangement in the 1990s*, The World Bank, Washington, DC.

HOFFMAN, K. (1989), *Technological and Organisational Change in the Global Textile-Clothing Industry, in New Technologies and Global Industrialisation: Prospects for Developing Countries*, United Nations Industrial Development Organisation.

HOFFMAN, K. and H. RUSH (1984), *Microelectronics and the Technological Transformation of the Clothing Industry*, International Labour Organisation, Geneva.

MITI (1992), *Yearbook of Textiles Statistics*, Research and Statistics Department, Ministry of International Trade and Industry, 4, Tokyo.

OECD (1983), *Textile and Clothing Industries, Structural Problems and Policies in OECD Countries*, Paris.

OECD (1988), *Industrial Revival Through Technology*, Paris.

OECD (1989a), "The Regional Implications of Industrial Restructuring", Report of a meeting of trade union experts held under the OECD Labour/Management Programme, Paris.

OECD (1989b), *New Forms of Investment*, Development Centre, Reprint Series No. 7, Paris.

OECD (1992), *Industrial Support Policies in OECD Countries, 1986-1989,* Paris.

OECD (1993), *Intra-Firm Trade*, Trade Policy Issues, No. 1, Paris.

PARK, T.A. and D. PICK (1992), "Structural Adjustment and the Japanese Textile Industry:a A Production Theory Approach, *Applied Economics*, No. 24, pp. 437-444.

PARK, Y.I., and K. ANDERSON (1991), "The Rise and Demise of Textiles and Clothing in Economic Development: The Case of Japan", *Economic Development and Cultural Change*, April, 39(3), pp. 531-548.

PARK, Y.I., and K. ANDERSON (1989), "China and the International Relocation of World Textile and Clothing Activity", *Weltwirtschaftliches Archiv*, No. 125, pp. 124-148.

PENT, G.F. (1992), "Product Differentiation and Process Innovation in the Italian Clothing Industry", in *Industry on the Move: Causes and Consequences of International Relocation in the Manufacturing Industry*, International Labour Office, Geneva, pp. 209-230.

SILBERSTON, Z.A. (1989), *The Future of the Multi-Fibre Arrangement, Implications for the UK Economy*, Department of Trade and Industry, London.

TRELA, I. and J. WHALLEY (1990), "Global Effects of Developed Countries" Trade Restrictions on Textiles and Apparel, *Economic Journal*, Vol. 100, December, pp. 1190-1205.

UNITED STATES INTERNATIONAL TRADE COMMISSION (1989), "The Economic Effects of Significant US Import Restraints, Phase I: Manufacturing", USITC Publication 2222, October, Washington, DC.

UNITED STATES TRADE REPRESENTATIVE (USTR), Press Release, 6 January 1994.

VAN LIEMT, G. (1992), *Industry on the Move: Causes and Consequences of International Relocation in the Manufacturing Industry*, International Labour Office, Geneva.

WOLF, M. (1987), "Handmaiden under Harassment: The Multi-Fibre Arrangement as an Obstacle to Development", in H. Giersch (ed.), *Free Trade in the World Economy: Towards an Opening of Markets*, Westview Press, Boulder, pp. 252-286.

MAIN SALES OUTLETS OF OECD PUBLICATIONS
PRINCIPAUX POINTS DE VENTE DES PUBLICATIONS DE L'OCDE

AUSTRALIA – AUSTRALIE
D.A. Information Services
648 Whitehorse Road, P.O.B 163
Mitcham, Victoria 3132   Tel. (03) 9210.7777
                            Fax: (03) 9210.7788

AUSTRIA – AUTRICHE
Gerold & Co.
Graben 31
Wien I   Tel. (0222) 533.50.14
                            Fax: (0222) 512.47.31.29

BELGIUM – BELGIQUE
Jean De Lannoy
Avenue du Roi, Koningslaan 202
B-1060 Bruxelles   Tel. (02) 538.51.69/538.08.41
                            Fax: (02) 538.08.41

CANADA
Renouf Publishing Company Ltd.
1294 Algoma Road
Ottawa, ON K1B 3W8   Tel. (613) 741.4333
                            Fax: (613) 741.5439

Stores:
61 Sparks Street
Ottawa, ON K1P 5R1   Tel. (613) 238.8985

12 Adelaide Street West
Toronto, ON M5H 1L6   Tel. (416) 363.3171
                            Fax: (416)363.59.63

Les Éditions La Liberté Inc.
3020 Chemin Sainte-Foy
Sainte-Foy, PQ G1X 3V6   Tel. (418) 658.3763
                            Fax: (418) 658.3763

Federal Publications Inc.
165 University Avenue, Suite 701
Toronto, ON M5H 3B8   Tel. (416) 860.1611
                            Fax: (416) 860.1608

Les Publications Fédérales
1185 Université
Montréal, QC H3B 3A7   Tel. (514) 954.1633
                            Fax: (514) 954.1635

CHINA – CHINE
China National Publications Import
Export Corporation (CNPIEC)
16 Gongti E. Road, Chaoyang District
P.O. Box 88 or 50
Beijing 100704 PR   Tel. (01) 506.6688
                            Fax: (01) 506.3101

CHINESE TAIPEI – TAIPEI CHINOIS
Good Faith Worldwide Int'l. Co. Ltd.
9th Floor, No. 118, Sec. 2
Chung Hsiao E. Road
Taipei   Tel. (02) 391.7396/391.7397
                            Fax: (02) 394.9176

**CZECH REPUBLIC – RÉPUBLIQUE
TCHÈQUE**
National Information Centre
NIS – prodejna
Konviktská 5
Praha 1 – 113 57   Tel. (02) 24.23.09.07
                            Fax: (02) 24.22.94.33
(*Contact* Ms Jana Pospisilova, nkposp@dec.niz.cz)

DENMARK – DANEMARK
Munksgaard Book and Subscription Service
35, Nørre Søgade, P.O. Box 2148
DK-1016 København K   Tel. (33) 12.85.70
                            Fax: (33) 12.93.87

J. H. Schultz Information A/S,
Herstedvang 12,
DK – 2620 Albertslung   Tel. 43 63 23 00
                            Fax: 43 63 19 69

Internet: s-info@inet.uni-c.dk

EGYPT – ÉGYPTE
The Middle East Observer
41 Sherif Street
Cairo   Tel. 392.6919
                            Fax: 360-6804

FINLAND – FINLANDE
Akateeminen Kirjakauppa
Keskuskatu 1, P.O. Box 128
00100 Helsinki

Subscription Services/Agence d'abonnements :
P.O. Box 23
00371 Helsinki   Tel. (358 0) 121 4416
                            Fax: (358 0) 121.4450

FRANCE
OECD/OCDE
Mail Orders/Commandes par correspondance :
2, rue André-Pascal
75775 Paris Cedex 16   Tel. (33-1) 45.24.82.00
                        Fax: (33-1) 49.10.42.76
                        Telex: 640048 OCDE
Internet: Compte.PUBSINQ@oecd.org

Orders via Minitel, France only/
Commandes par Minitel, France exclusivement :
36 15 OCDE

OECD Bookshop/Librairie de l'OCDE :
33, rue Octave-Feuillet
75016 Paris   Tél. (33-1) 45.24.81.81
                             (33-1) 45.24.81.67

Dawson
B.P. 40
91121 Palaiseau Cedex   Tel. 69.10.47.00
                            Fax: 64.54.83.26

Documentation Française
29, quai Voltaire
75007 Paris   Tel. 40.15.70.00
Economica
49, rue Héricart
75015 Paris   Tel. 45.75.05.67
                            Fax: 40.58.15.70

Gibert Jeune (Droit-Économie)
6, place Saint-Michel
75006 Paris   Tel. 43.25.91.19

Librairie du Commerce International
10, avenue d'Iéna
75016 Paris   Tel. 40.73.34.60

Librairie Dunod
Université Paris-Dauphine
Place du Maréchal-de-Lattre-de-Tassigny
75016 Paris   Tel. 44.05.40.13

Librairie Lavoisier
11, rue Lavoisier
75008 Paris   Tel. 42.65.39.95

Librairie des Sciences Politiques
30, rue Saint-Guillaume
75007 Paris   Tel. 45.48.36.02

P.U.F.
49, boulevard Saint-Michel
75005 Paris   Tel. 43.25.83.40

Librairie de l'Université
12a, rue Nazareth
13100 Aix-en-Provence   Tel. (16) 42.26.18.08

Documentation Française
165, rue Garibaldi
69003 Lyon   Tel. (16) 78.63.32.23

Librairie Decitre
29, place Bellecour
69002 Lyon   Tel. (16) 72.40.54.54

Librairie Sauramps
Le Triangle
34967 Montpellier Cedex 2 Tel. (16) 67.58.85.15
                           Fax: (16) 67.58.27.36

A la Sorbonne Actual
23, rue de l'Hôtel-des-Postes
06000 Nice   Tel. (16) 93.13.77.75
                            Fax: (16) 93.80.75.69

GERMANY – ALLEMAGNE
OECD Bonn Centre
August-Bebel-Allee 6
D-53175 Bonn   Tel. (0228) 959.120
                            Fax: (0228) 959.12.17

GREECE – GRÈCE
Librairie Kauffmann
Stadiou 28
10564 Athens   Tel. (01) 32.55.321
                            Fax: (01) 32.30.320

HONG-KONG
Swindon Book Co. Ltd.
Astoria Bldg. 3F
34 Ashley Road, Tsimshatsui
Kowloon, Hong Kong   Tel. 2376.2062
                            Fax: 2376.0685

HUNGARY – HONGRIE
Euro Info Service
Margitsziget, Európa Ház
1138 Budapest   Tel. (1) 111.62.16
                            Fax: (1) 111.60.61

ICELAND – ISLANDE
Mál Mog Menning
Laugavegi 18, Pósthólf 392
121 Reykjavik   Tel. (1) 552.4240
                            Fax: (1) 562.3523

INDIA – INDE
Oxford Book and Stationery Co.
Scindia House
New Delhi 110001   Tel. (11) 331.5896/5308
                            Fax: (11) 371.8275

17 Park Street
Calcutta 700016   Tel. 240832

INDONESIA – INDONÉSIE
Pdii-Lipi
P.O. Box 4298
Jakarta 12042   Tel. (21) 573.34.67
                            Fax: (21) 573.34.67

IRELAND – IRLANDE
Government Supplies Agency
Publications Section
4/5 Harcourt Road
Dublin 2   Tel. 661.31.11
                            Fax: 475.27.60

ISRAEL – ISRAËL
Praedicta
5 Shatner Street
P.O. Box 34030
Jerusalem 91430   Tel. (2) 52.84.90/1/2
                            Fax: (2) 52.84.93

R.O.Y. International
P.O. Box 13056
Tel Aviv 61130   Tel. (3) 546 1423
                            Fax: (3) 546 1442

Palestinian Authority/Middle East:
INDEX Information Services
P.O.B. 19502
Jerusalem   Tel. (2) 27.12.19
                            Fax: (2) 27.16.34

ITALY – ITALIE
Libreria Commissionaria Sansoni
Via Duca di Calabria 1/1
50125 Firenze   Tel. (055) 64.54.15
                            Fax: (055) 64.12.57

Via Bartolini 29
20155 Milano   Tel. (02) 36.50.83

Editrice e Libreria Herder
Piazza Montecitorio 120
00186 Roma   Tel. 679.46.28
      Fax: 678.47.51

Libreria Hoepli
Via Hoepli 5
20121 Milano   Tel. (02) 86.54.46
      Fax: (02) 805.28.86

Libreria Scientifica
Dott. Lucio de Biasio 'Aeiou'
Via Coronelli, 6
20146 Milano   Tel. (02) 48.95.45.52
      Fax: (02) 48.95.45.48

JAPAN – JAPON
OECD Tokyo Centre
Landic Akasaka Building
2-3-4 Akasaka, Minato-ku
Tokyo 107   Tel. (81.3) 3586.2016
      Fax: (81.3) 3584.7929

KOREA – CORÉE
Kyobo Book Centre Co. Ltd.
P.O. Box 1658, Kwang Hwa Moon
Seoul   Tel. 730.78.91
      Fax: 735.00.30

MALAYSIA – MALAISIE
University of Malaya Bookshop
University of Malaya
P.O. Box 1127, Jalan Pantai Baru
59700 Kuala Lumpur
Malaysia   Tel. 756.5000/756.5425
      Fax: 756.3246

MEXICO – MEXIQUE
OECD Mexico Centre
Edificio INFOTEC
Av. San Fernando no. 37
Col. Toriello Guerra
Tlalpan C.P. 14050
Mexico D.F.   Tel. (525) 665 47 99
      Fax: (525) 606 13 07

NETHERLANDS – PAYS-BAS
SDU Uitgeverij Plantijnstraat
Externe Fondsen
Postbus 20014
2500 EA's-Gravenhage   Tel. (070) 37.89.880
Voor bestellingen: Fax: (070) 34.75.778

Subscription Agency/
Agence d'abonnements :
SWETS & ZEITLINGER BV
Heereweg 347B
P.O. Box 830
2160 SZ Lisse   Tel. 252.435.111
      Fax: 252.415.888

NEW ZEALAND – NOUVELLE-ZÉLANDE
GPLegislation Services
P.O. Box 12418
Thorndon, Wellington   Tel. (04) 496.5655
      Fax: (04) 496.5698

NORWAY – NORVÈGE
NIC INFO A/S
Ostensjoveien 18
P.O. Box 6512 Etterstad
0606 Oslo   Tel. (22) 97.45.00
      Fax: (22) 97.45.45

PAKISTAN
Mirza Book Agency
65 Shahrah Quaid-E-Azam
Lahore 54000   Tel. (42) 735.36.01
      Fax: (42) 576.37.14

PHILIPPINE – PHILIPPINES
International Booksource Center Inc.
Rm 179/920 Cityland 10 Condo Tower 2
HV dela Costa Ext cor Valero St.
Makati Metro Manila   Tel. (632) 817 9676
      Fax: (632) 817 1741

POLAND – POLOGNE
Ars Polona
00-950 Warszawa
Krakowskie Prezdmiescie 7   Tel. (22) 264760
      Fax: (22) 265334

PORTUGAL
Livraria Portugal
Rua do Carmo 70-74
Apart. 2681
1200 Lisboa   Tel. (01) 347.49.82/5
      Fax: (01) 347.02.64

SINGAPORE – SINGAPOUR
Ashgate Publishing
Asia Pacific Pte. Ltd
Golden Wheel Building, 04-03
41, Kallang Pudding Road
Singapore 349316   Tel. 741.5166
      Fax: 742.9356

SPAIN – ESPAGNE
Mundi-Prensa Libros S.A.
Castelló 37, Apartado 1223
Madrid 28001   Tel. (91) 431.33.99
      Fax: (91) 575.39.98

Mundi-Prensa Barcelona
Consell de Cent No. 391
08009 – Barcelona   Tel. (93) 488.34.92
      Fax: (93) 487.76.59

Llibreria de la Generalitat
Palau Moja
Rambla dels Estudis, 118
08002 – Barcelona
      (Subscripcions) Tel. (93) 318.80.12
      (Publicacions) Tel. (93) 302.67.23
      Fax: (93) 412.18.54

SRI LANKA
Centre for Policy Research
c/o Colombo Agencies Ltd.
No. 300-304, Galle Road
Colombo 3   Tel. (1) 574240, 573551-2
      Fax: (1) 575394, 510711

SWEDEN – SUÈDE
CE Fritzes AB
S–106 47 Stockholm   Tel. (08) 690.90.90
      Fax: (08) 20.50.21

For electronic publications only/
Publications électroniques seulement
STATISTICS SWEDEN
Informationsservice
S-115 81 Stockholm   Tel. 8 783 5066
      Fax: 8 783 4045

Subscription Agency/Agence d'abonnements :
Wennergren-Williams Info AB
P.O. Box 1305
171 25 Solna   Tel. (08) 705.97.50
      Fax: (08) 27.00.71

SWITZERLAND – SUISSE
Maditec S.A. (Books and Periodicals/Livres
et périodiques)
Chemin des Palettes 4
Case postale 266
1020 Renens VD 1   Tel. (021) 635.08.65
      Fax: (021) 635.07.80

Librairie Payot S.A.
4, place Pépinet
CP 3212
1002 Lausanne   Tel. (021) 320.25.11
      Fax: (021) 320.25.14

Librairie Unilivres
6, rue de Candolle
1205 Genève   Tel. (022) 320.26.23
      Fax: (022) 329.73.18

Subscription Agency/Agence d'abonnements :
Dynapresse Marketing S.A.
38, avenue Vibert
1227 Carouge   Tel. (022) 308.08.70
      Fax: (022) 308.07.99

See also – Voir aussi :
OECD Bonn Centre
August-Bebel-Allee 6
D-53175 Bonn (Germany)   Tel. (0228) 959.120
      Fax: (0228) 959.12.17

THAILAND – THAÏLANDE
Suksit Siam Co. Ltd.
113, 115 Fuang Nakhon Rd.
Opp. Wat Rajbopith
Bangkok 10200   Tel. (662) 225.9531/2
      Fax: (662) 222.5188

TRINIDAD & TOBAGO, CARIBBEAN TRINITÉ-ET-TOBAGO, CARAÏBES
SSL Systematics Studies Limited
9 Watts Street
Curepe
Trinidad & Tobago, W.I.   Tel. (1809) 645.3475
      Fax: (1809) 662.5654

TUNISIA – TUNISIE
Grande Librairie Spécialisée
Fendri Ali
Avenue Haffouz Imm El-Intilaka
Bloc B 1 Sfax 3000   Tel. (216-4) 296 855
      Fax: (216-4) 298.270

TURKEY – TURQUIE
Kültür Yayinlari Is-Türk Ltd. Sti.
Atatürk Bulvari No. 191/Kat 13
06684 Kavaklidere/Ankara
      Tél. (312) 428.11.40 Ext. 2458
      Fax : (312) 417.24.90
      et 425.07.50-51-52-53

Dolmabahce Cad. No. 29
Besiktas/Istanbul   Tel. (212) 260 7188

UNITED KINGDOM – ROYAUME-UNI
HMSO
Gen. enquiries   Tel. (0171) 873 0011

Postal orders only:
P.O. Box 276, London SW8 5DT
Personal Callers HMSO Bookshop
49 High Holborn, London WC1V 6HB
      Fax: (0171) 873 8463

Branches at: Belfast, Birmingham, Bristol,
Edinburgh, Manchester

UNITED STATES – ÉTATS-UNIS
OECD Washington Center
2001 L Street N.W., Suite 650
Washington, D.C. 20036-4922 Tel. (202) 785.6323
      Fax: (202) 785.0350
Internet: washcont@oecd.org
Subscriptions to OECD periodicals may also be
placed through main subscription agencies.

Les abonnements aux publications périodiques de
l'OCDE peuvent être souscrits auprès des
principales agences d'abonnement.

Orders and inquiries from countries where Distribu-
tors have not yet been appointed should be sent to:
OECD Publications, 2, rue André-Pascal, 75775
Paris Cedex 16, France.

Les commandes provenant de pays où l'OCDE n'a
pas encore désigné de distributeur peuvent être
adressées aux Éditions de l'OCDE, 2, rue André-
Pascal, 75775 Paris Cedex 16, France.

8-1996

OECD PUBLICATIONS, 2, rue André-Pascal, 75775 PARIS CEDEX 16
PRINTED IN FRANCE
(70 96 05 1) ISBN 92-64-14688-1 – No. 48373 1996